KV-639-140

SOCIAL PROTEST, VIOLENCE AND TERROR IN NINETEENTH- AND TWENTIETH-CENTURY EUROPE

R/LEND/001

WITHDRAWN

Social Protest, Violence and Terror in Nineteenth- and Twentieth-century Europe

Edited by

Wolfgang J. Mommsen
and
Gerhard Hirschfeld

U.W.E.L.
LEARNING RESOURCES

ACC. No.
2254947

CLASS

322,
420
94

CONTROL
0333320026

DATE
10. JUN. 2002

SITE
DY

SOC

in association with Berg Publishers Ltd
for the German Historical Institute, London

© Wolfgang J. Mommsen and Gerhard Hirschfeld 1982

All rights reserved. No reproduction, copy or transmission of
this publication may be made without written permission.

No paragraph of this publication may be reproduced, copied or
transmitted save with written permission or in accordance with
the provisions of the Copyright, Designs and Patents Act 1988,
or under the terms of any licence permitting limited copying
issued by the Copyright Licensing Agency, 90 Tottenham Court
Road, London W1P 9HE.

Any person who does any unauthorised act in relation to this
publication may be liable to criminal prosecution and civil
claims for damages.

First published 1982 by
MACMILLAN PRESS LTD
Houndmills, Basingstoke, Hampshire RG21 6XS
and London
Companies and representatives
throughout the world

ISBN 0–333–32002–6

A catalogue record for this book is available
from the British Library.

10   9   8   7   6   5   4   3   2
03   02   01   00 99 98 97 96

Printed in Great Britain by
Biddles Ltd of Guildford and King's Lynn

Contents

Notes on the Contributors and Editors

Dr Peter Alter — Fellow of the German Historical Institute, London

Dr Walther L. Bernecker — Senior Lecturer in Modern History, University of Augsburg

Dr Astrid von Borcke — Federal Institute for East European and International Studies, Cologne

Professor Gerhard Botz — Professor of Contemporary History, University of Salzburg, Austria

Professor Gerhard Brunn — Reader in Modern History, University of Cologne

Dr Andrew R. Carlson — civil servant, Michigan, USA

Professor Franklin L. Ford — Professor of History, Harvard University, Cambridge, Mass., USA

Dr Manfred Hildermeier — Lecturer, Free University of Berlin

Dr Gerhard Hirschfeld — Fellow of the German Historical Institute, London

Professor Eric J. Hobsbawm — Professor of History, Birkbeck College, University of London

Dr Hans-Gerhard Husung — Fellow of the German Historical Institute, London

Dr Michael Laffan — Lecturer in Modern History, University College, Dublin

Dr Ulrich Linse — teacher at a grammar school, Munich

Professor Adrian Lyttelton — Professor of History, Johns Hopkins Center, Bologna, Italy

Professor Peter H. Merkl — Professor of Political Science, University of California, Santa Barbara, USA

Professor Wolfgang J. Mommsen — Professor of History, University of Düsseldorf; Director of the German Historical Institute, London

Dr Maureen Perrie — Lecturer in Russian and East European Studies, University of Birmingham

Dr Jens Petersen — Fellow of the German Historical Institute, Rome

Professor F. F. Ridley	Professor of Political Theory and Institutions, University of Liverpool
Professor Wilfried Röhrich	Professor of Political Science, University of Kiel
Dr Eve Rosenhaft	Lecturer in German Studies, University of Liverpool
Dr David B. Southern	Lecturer in Social Science, University of Kent at Canterbury
Professor Malcolm I. Thomis	Professor of History, University of Queensland, Australia

Preface

The essays assembled in this volume originated from contributions to a conference on 'Social Protest, Violence, Terror: Strategies of violence resorted to by social and political fringe groups in the nineteenth and twentieth centuries' which was arranged by the German Historical Institute and took place from 15 to 17 November 1979 at the Werner-Reimers-Stiftung in Bad Homburg. The studies presented here are intended to give, as it were in a joint venture, an assessment of the many political groups and movements which in the course of the last one-and-a-half centuries – i.e. the time during which the modern constitutional state emerged and the industrial revolution changed society in an irreversible way – have resorted to means of violence and individual terror in one way or another in order to press certain political or economic demands upon reluctant governments, regardless of whether they were authoritarian, constitutional or democratic; in some cases, strategies of violence aimed even further, they were meant to pave the way for far-reaching change and revolutionary upheaval. The field of enquiry covered by these essays has been deliberately restricted to those cases where recourse to violence and terror was taken in open revolt against an effective, though not always sufficiently legitimate, governmental order. In other words, we are concerned here with forms of violence and terror which operated or were, from the vantage point of the established order, in deliberate violation of the established legal system. We also deal only with groups or movements which could or can count solely upon the support of marginal or, at best, small groups within society. Accordingly revolutionary movements which enjoyed massive popular support, e.g. the 1848 Revolution, have not been included in this analysis, though, at various times and in various ways, they also resorted to what must initially be considered as non-legal violence, and at times even terror of some sort.

The spectrum of political groupings which at one time or another, under specific historical conditions, resorted to strategies of violence and individual terror, or even guerrilla war, must be considered extraordinarily wide-ranging. Contrary to currently fashionable beliefs, recourse to violence in deliberate violation of the law, as well as of governmental authority, is a widespread phenomenon throughout history. It can be argued that during the last two centuries most European states gradually succeeded in eliminating open, violent conflicts by opening up legal channels to solve them, thanks to the development of a comprehensive legal system. In a way, the development of the modern constitutional state, which assigns to the governmental authority a monopoly of violence, can be considered a major contribution to the history of mankind. Nonetheless, it would be quite wrong to assume that the increasing challenge to governmental authority by leftist or rightist groupings alike is a new phenomenon. It is one that the historian continuously encounters in the social history of modern Europe.

In view of this fact, some sort of limitation of the subject was inevitable. Thus, for one thing, the manifold forms of non-legal violence, terror and social protest which we encounter in the countries of the Third World have, with a few exceptions, been left aside, even though in some respects this is regrettable, since the various terrorist movements operating in these countries have, in many ways, substantially influenced the course of events in the advanced industrial societies of the West. Equally, present-day terrorist movements – such as the West German RAF and its affiliations, or the *brigate rosse* in Italy, or the various neo-fascist groupings which only recently committed brutal acts of violence in Bologna and Munich for instance – have not been dealt with as such, though they are given some consideration in a comparative perspective.

The case-studies presented here cover the great majority of all known cases of non-legal violence, terror or violent social protest which occurred within Europe during the nineteenth and early twentieth centuries. They describe the typical patterns of terrorist strategies of violence as well as the social conditions within which these groups operated. At the same time the question is examined as to how far the rise of terrorist groups or movements was caused by specific historical developments. In a way they must be seen as a by-product of a fundamental distortion in the socio-economic or constitutional development of the various European societies, or as the offspring of a widespread dissatisfaction with traditional systems of rule no longer in line with societies subjected to a process of modernisation. Finally, an attempt is made to produce a sort of typology of various forms of terrorist or non-legal violence in modern European history which also includes present-day terrorist activities.*

Primarily for pragmatic reasons the enquiry concentrates on those groupings or movements which, while violently opposed to the established order, did not receive wider support from the population at large. However, we are well aware that such an approach tends to be biased from the very outset in favour of the established order rather than its opponents. It cannot be denied that such an approach runs the risk of underrating the crucial importance of 'structural' or, as it has been put more recently, of 'institutional violence', in view of which recourse to non-legal violence may be morally justified and,

---

* This contribution by W. J. Mommsen, entitled 'Non-legal Violence and Terrorism in Western Industrial Societies' was added to the volume after the conference; it is, however, largely based on the proceedings and attempts to draw some further conclusions from them.

therefore, rightly called mere 'counter-violence'. This may be all the more so in view of the fact that in very many cases the governments themselves had recourse to strategies of violence and terror in order to defend themselves against these forms of radical protest or revolutionary activity. Therefore, some endeavour has been made to counterbalance this bias in the concrete empirical analysis as much as possible. However, any other approach would not have been able to identify the issues in question in a sufficiently clear way and to describe them in operational terms.

This apart, we deliberately tried to analyse various forms of non-legal violence or terrorism without giving primary consideration to the respective ideologies. Violent movements with social, nationalist, proletarian or fascist connotations are dealt with alongside one another with a view to bringing out those features which they all have in common and also their interdependence. The editors hope that these studies suggest a useful way of approaching the problem. Thus the discussion about present-day forms of non-legal violence and terror may be brought onto a more rational and, at the same time, a more objective level.

At this point the editors should like to express their thanks to all those who have made the publication of this volume possible, in particular the Werner-Reimers-Stiftung, without whose financial support and hospitality the conference could not have taken place. We are particularly grateful to Dr v. Krosigk, the Director of the Werner-Reimers-Stiftung, and to Frau Söntgen for all their efforts and for ensuring that the conference could be held in an unusually pleasant atmosphere. Thanks are also due to the staff of the German Historical Institute for their assistance, in particular to Mrs Jane Rafferty. We should like to thank Mrs Elke Jessett and also Mr Stephen Conn who translated the German texts.

1 Reflections on Political Murder: Europe in the Nineteenth and Twentieth Centuries

Franklin L. Ford

For several years past, my research interests have centered on the place of purposeful homicide in political history. As one who shares the ancient belief that politics ought ideally to be identified with life, both of the *polis* and of its individual members, I recognise the elements of anomaly implicit in this sombre linkage. Nevertheless, the course of history does not permit us to ignore the record of political murder as an aspect of individual and group behavior affecting public affairs.

Such exploration, if it is to fulfil its purpose, must investigate settings, motives, attempts at justification, and results both intended and actual, from Biblical (indeed pre-Biblical) episodes, through classical formulations of tyrannicide theory in Greco-Roman antiquity, all the way down to the place occupied by other forms of assassination and terrorism in the annals of our own era. Signs of concern for this chronological range will be found in the present article, for instance in occasional allusions to eighteenth-century and even earlier history, where they are needed to throw light upon more recent developments. Still, the scholarly meeting which occasioned the remarks to follow was focussed upon the nineteenth and twentieth centuries. Furthermore, the topic was effectively, if not quite explicitly, confined to the European experience, inviting only the most selective references to the rest of the world, including the United States.

That being so, let me at the outset acknowledge, and in so doing attempt to minimise, the danger of historical narcissism. How special, it is only fair to ask, how nearly unique in the story of the species, have Europe's latest two centuries really been? To what extent do they constitute a segment of history easy to distinguish from the rest of the long and complex stream of recorded human experience? The late Carl Becker, a learned and sometimes quizzical American student of the Old Regime, used to remind members of his seminar that every historian has to weigh the choice between saying, when whatever

1

else he can think of has been said on a particular subject, that while the world
may change, it changes slowly, or that, while it may change slowly, it does
change. Becker would concede, of course, just in time to avoid overdrawing
the dilemma, that we generally end by saying both things; for both are true.
The matter of final emphasis, however, has always to be faced.

What about the topic now before us, when approached with this obligation
in mind? On balance, I find myself stressing the element of change, but there is
undeniably a balance to be struck. Take for example the numerical incidence
of political murder. In quantitative terms, based on the tabulation of episodes
involving lethal intent, not just public protest, the 150 years preceding the
1790s are easily distinguishable from the period which began with that decade.
This is not to minimise the importance of popular uprisings in the earlier age,
from the Cevennes under Louis XIV to Hungary and Transylvania under
Rakóczy, from Pugachev's Russia in the 1770s to the London of the Lord
Gordon riots in 1780. More to the present point, an awareness of subsequent
change does not require or even permit us to overlook scattered assaults upon
individuals, from the lynching of the brothers De Witt at The Hague in 1672 to
the attempts against the kings of France and of Portugal in 1757 and 1758,
respectively. All things considered, however, the list of political crimes under
the ancien regime seems very short. Its brevity alone points to another of those
somewhat puzzling moratoriums in political murder which in the more remote
past had characterised ancient Athens, the Roman Republic until late in its
history, and Europe's own 'high' middle ages.[1]

There can be no denying – this much, I think, must be conceded to the
skepticism of Carl Becker – that some by no means insignificant lines of
continuity run straight through into the nineteenth and twentieth centuries.
The tradition of tyrannicide had never lost its fascination even for an
eighteenth century largely spared – or denied, depending on one's
preferences – the immediacy of contemporary examples; and it lived on
thereafter. It inspired the use of 'Sic semper tyrannis!' both by Felice Orsini on
trial at Paris in 1858 and by John Wilkes Booth seven years later, as he jumped
down onto the stage of the Ford Theatre in Washington after shooting
President Abraham Lincoln. It still inspired young Friedrich Adler, the killer
of Austria-Hungary's prime minister, Count Stürgkh, in 1916. Its influence,
including soul-searching over the willingness of the slayer to sacrifice himself
and over questions of the relationship between the motivation of the act and
its success or failure, permeates the debates among at least some of the
Germans who tried in 1944 to assassinate Adolf Hitler.[2]

Mention of what is often, and altogether inadequately, referred to as the
'Beck-Goerdeler' conspiracy is a reminder of another important link connecting earlier and more recent history: the undiminished importance of elite
advantages, which is to say of official access and of social contact – 'he is
entitled to bear arms in the presence of the prince' – even in an age of
putatively democratic revolution. At the opposite pole from elaborate

conspiracies stands another familiar figure out of the past: the loner, the single assassin who often affronts, even as he confounds, determinedly rational analysts of aims and outcomes. David Hume in the eighteenth century considered, I suspect fairly briefly, the murderer of the Duke of Buckingham in the seventeenth and dismissed Captain John Felton as the possessor of 'a dull, unsociable mind'.[3] Hume's terse description fits equally well a number of later figures, ranging from Luigi Luccheni, who at Geneva in 1898 fatally stabbed the elderly Empress of Austria (because his intended victim, the French Duc d'Orléans, had failed to turn up as expected), all the way to Lee Harvey Oswald at Dallas in 1963.

These illustrations, combined with others that spring to mind, might suggest continuity as the principal feature of our modern experience with political murder. It seems to me, however, that what really confronts us here is not so much continuity as an atavistic return to tendencies with which Europe from the middle decades of the seventeenth century until the last of the eighteenth had had remarkably little to do. I have in mind in particular the call of religious faith, long muted but loud and clear once more as a part of Carl Sand's resolve to stab Kotzebue to death at Mannheim in 1819.[4] In Father Verger, who killed Archbishop Sibour of Paris in 1857 under the mistaken impression that Sibour was deeply committed to Pope Pius IX's newly enunciated dogma of the Immaculate Conception, the call was undiluted by any other motive.[5] Even the would-be assassin of Napoleon at Schönbrunn in 1809, young Friedrich Stapps, whose act might seem an attempt at tyrannicide in the classical mold, was the pious son of a Lutheran pastor in Naumburg and seems to have considered himself a kind of Protestant Ravaillac, called into action by God.[6]

Yet despite the presence of these elements, I should still insist that the recent history of lethal political gestures is dominated by novel characteristics. Take the matter of weaponry. For about three hundred years after the first assassinations employing firearms took place in the sixteenth century, there was no more than a slow and uneven increase in the variety and power of implements used for this purpose. The pistols fired at Prime Minister Perceval as he prepared to enter the House of Commons in 1812 and at President Andrew Jackson under the colonnade of the American capitol in 1835 were only marginally different from those that had killed William the Silent at Delft in 1584, and in the case of the assault on Jackson were notably inferior in performance.[7] The unevenness of technological change is, I admit, revealed by the fact that whereas high explosives begin to figure in projects as old as that of Guy Fawkes in 1605, both poison and the dagger have remained popular with their admittedly specialised clientele down to the present day.

These reminders of earlier means, however, should not obscure the degree and rapidity of change. Encouraged by the military 'advances' made in two World Wars, the high-powered rifle with its telescopic sight and the machine gun or pistol capable of firing almost unbelievably rapid bursts have altered the odds, as between attacker and victim, beyond comparison with those of an earlier past. In the matter of explosives, *pace* Master Fawkes, it is difficult to compare his barrels of black powder even with the fulminate of mercury used in the hand bombs hurled at the coach of Napoleon III and Empress Eugénie by Orsini and his accomplices outside the Paris Opera in 1858, or the nitroglycerine grenades one of which killed Tsar Alexander II beside the Catherine Canal in 1881.[8] Still more remote from earlier devices is the immensely powerful charge detonated by a delicate time mechanism or – as appears to have occurred in the case of Lord Mountbatten's death aboard his boat off the Irish coast in 1979 – set off by a radio signal from a safely hidden operator or operators.

Another comparatively new aspect of political murder in modern times, once perhaps classifiable as secondary but by now of central concern, is its heavy reliance on publicity for full effect. Even in the eighteenth century, needless to say, popular excitement surrounded if not always the trials at least the executions of Damiens in Louis XV's France and the Távoras family and their doomed collaborators in Pombal's Portugal. Not until the nineteenth century, however, did the accused make purposeful use of their day in court to glorify their own efforts and the principles for which they were prepared to face personal extinction. One recalls Felice Orsini with Jules Favre for a lawyer,[9] as well as Zhelyabov in particular among the Russians charged with Alexander II's death. In our own day, the eagerness to 'claim credit' for what on their face may seem cowardly slayings has come to be taken for granted as intrinsic to the acts themselves.

More, of course, is involved in publicity than the perpetrators' wishes. At least equally significant is the opportunity, rapidly increased by the march of popular journalism, motion pictures, radio, and, above all, television. Between the sympathetic (though still generally apologetic) treatment accorded the Jena student Sand by certain English works hastily published within months of his murder of Kotzebue in 1819[10] and the live TV coverage of the tragedy at the Munich Olympic Games in 1972, the world has seen the triumph of a new empire, that of 'media exposure'. With it has come the assurance of quick and massive public attention paid to the deeds and the claims of a new breed of political dramatist.

This suggests a connection with still another new element in political violence as it is encountered in modern times: the explicit appeal through the individual act, the *geste*, for some general demonstration of support, ideally culminating in popular revolution. Nothing, I submit, is more indicative of the special quality of nineteenth- and twentieth-century European notions of insurgency than the hope of achieving revolutionary ends by translating a specific attack on an individual target into the signal for mass action. It is a hope of astounding vitality, given the fact that it has never, to my knowledge, been fulfilled or even come very close to realisation. In a strange way, it combines both romantic and classical notions of the 'Great French

Revolution', rather like Delacroix's vision of what things are like at the barricades.

Here again, one might argue that the tactic of action is not wholly modern. Some earlier assassins, in killing Julius Caesar, for example, or King Gustaf III of Sweden in 1792, may well have hoped to trigger 'revolution' understood simply as the overturning of a regime and with it some undesired policies. However, each of these assaults was essentially an elite action, undertaken by a restricted circle of senators or titled aristocrats or some other category of highly placed dissidents. Something very different, I suggest, was implied by the 'spark-on-tinder' theory of an Orsini arguing (in devotion to Bakunin) that revolutions all across Europe hungered for ignition and that Paris was demonstrably the best place in which to ignite them. *Narodnaya Volya*'s zealots appear to have shared that vision as they discussed the killing of an admittedly rather inoffensive Tsar Alexander II and dreamt of uprisings in All the Russias.

The reader must now, I think, be asked to accept a shift of emphasis. For the most part the pages immediately preceding have concentrated on some continuities, some reversions, and most important in the present context, some new departures as seen against the background of history prior to the nineteenth century. The center of attention has been the relationship between selected features of the past (almost) two hundred years and certain older characteristics of European history. What remains is to look if only briefly at these latest centuries in particular, asking how much change has occurred within the period they constitute. Hand in hand with that question goes a related one, namely, how much internal periodisation can usefully be imposed upon that time span.

From what has already been said, it should be clear that I have difficulty with the concept of just one 'rebellious century' embodied in the book published under that title by Charles, Louise, and Richard Tilly.[11] This is not to deny the value of their effort or of the challenges they direct at certain well-known approaches to the history of collective violence – Durkheim's 'breakdown thesis' for example. Let me also concede in fairness to the Tillys that mass behaviour is indeed what particularly interests them and that their arguments have been marshaled with an eye to manifestations often quite distinct from the individual or small-group actions toward which my own inquiries have been directed. Nevertheless, to the extent that our interests do overlap, it strikes me that a time span beginning in 1830 and ending in 1930 is at once too neat, too short, and, at least inferentially, too 'flat', that is to say, too undifferentiated internally. The expanse of history prior to 1830 cannot, I think, be quite so easily dismissed – seventeenth-century uprisings come particularly to mind, as do earlier nineteenth-century demonstrations of, to take an obvious example, Luddite violence in England. By the same token, although the record of more or less liberal national societies in the 1920s does indeed differ from that of an increasing number of authoritarian states in the

1930s so far as popular rebellion is concerned, I doubt that we can justify tying everything after 1930 off from the events of late nineteenth- and earlier twentieth-century history.

Instead of one rebellious century, therefore, I envisage a rather longer period, extending from the early 1790s to the present and subdivided by important changes most clearly discernible in the fateful decade of the 1920s. Up to this point, be it repeated, my emphasis has fallen upon elements which characterise the entire stretch of nearly two hundred years since the assassinations of Gustaf III and Marat and the institutionalisation of the French revolutionary Terror. Hence there really is a change of standpoint implied by now raising the question: how different, and in what ways different, from that of the immediately preceding era has the European record of political murder been since the First World War? To what extent, in terms of political homicide, did an older Europe begin after the First World War to transform itself into something definably 'different'?

As was true of the nineteenth century, so in the case of European history covering the past sixty years, there are plenty of incidents which may recall familiar models. The striking concentration of Bulgarian assassinations in the 1920s, for example, followed closely a pattern of homicide established in that country by the 1890s at the latest. There was even a bizarre strain of generational repetition: in 1924 one of the Agrarian Party's most prominent members, Petkov, was killed in a Sofia Street almost precisely as his father had been before him in 1907.[12] Elsewhere, the murder of Matthias Erzberger in 1921 while strolling along a Black Forest path recalled nineteenth-century episodes including not only the Phoenix Park murders in Dublin but also attacks upon Kaiser William I and upon Bismarck in the Tiergarten. And certainly the shooting of King Alexander of Yugoslavia and Foreign Minister Louis Barthou as they drove in an open car through Marseille in 1934 was eerily *déjà vu* for anyone who remembered – as who did not? – the bullets of Sarajevo twenty years before.

Beginning with the 1920s, however, there were signs that a new and in this regard by no means welcome world was aborning. For one thing, the frequency of assassination attempts and of resulting 'political' trials increased so sharply, compared to their incidence during the preceding half-century, that we have little choice but to see in the figures proof of something more than just a change in degree. The chronological and geographical tables compiled in the course of my own work reveal that between 1851 and 1900 – itself quite a busy period for European assassins – there were attacks, either actually or potentially fatal, on a total of about forty prominent Europeans, including Russians and also including as a single case Vaillant's bombing of the French Chamber of Deputies in 1893. Applying the same criteria to the years 1919–28 inclusive (the same even to the counting of another bombing, Sofia's in 1924, as a single case), one arrives at a total of fifty-four assaults. However crude such measurements must remain, this increase from an average of less than one attempt per year for half a century before 1900 to an average of more than five per year throughout the decade beginning in 1919 surely deserves serious attention.

It should be pointed out that commencing the above count in 1919 and not in the shambles of 1918 excludes from the reckoning such events as the killing of the Tsar, his family, and twelve other Romanovs in Russia, the death of Germany's ambassador Count Mirbach in Moscow, and the attack upon Lenin there on 30 August 1919, a day which also saw the death by assassination of M. Uritsky, head of the *Cheka* in Petrograd. Similarly excluded are the murders of the Hungarian premier Count Tisza and Portugal's President Sidonio Pais. I have, in short, made no effort to 'pad' the post-war figures.

Before leaving the realm of statistics, it may be useful to consider another difference between Europe before and Europe after the Great War which can be shown only through recourse to quantification. Most observers, myself definitely included, have tended to accept without much argument the generalisation that the years just preceding Tsar Alexander II's assassination in 1881 were for Russia a time of massive repression, at once responding to and further inciting massive terrorist resistance. As a matter of fact, there were no more than a half-dozen serious attacks on high officials other than the Emperor throughout the five supposed peak years 1878–82. As for judicial action we find that according to the underground's own count, as shown by figures printed in the *Calendar of the People's Will (Narodnaya Volya)*,[13] those years witnessed a total of 72 trials involving 397 defendants and resulting, when they ran to completion at all, in 19 sentences of imprisonment, 159 of forced labour (generally in Siberia), 57 of exile, 52 acquittals, and 31 death penalties carried out. Of the executions, five in 1881 and one in 1882 stemmed directly from Alexander's assassination. Now these figures unquestionably bespeak a great deal of individual suffering. They are not, however, very startling, especially when set against the imagined slaughter evoked by populist folklore or against the actual records of Lenin's, Stalin's, Hitler's, and other regimes in our own century.

The increased volume of violence in twentieth-century Europe does not alone represent all dimensions of the change from older patterns. The briefest look at the rest of the world will show such patterns spreading even as they changed, especially in the aftermath of the Second World War. That extension – not just to the United States, which had already by the 1860s entered the world history of assassination with bloody emphasis – began increasingly to assume the proportions of a global epidemic. European styles of political warfare, with their accompanying rhetoric, seemed everywhere to encroach upon the once differing mores of the Middle East, the Far East, Africa, all of them, be it said, long endowed with their own traditions in this regard.

The imitation of European models might have produced at least one advantage for the historian: to wit, a reduction in the sheer variety of motives and acts encountered on the world stage. But no such simplification has in fact occurred. Instead, there has been a marked proliferation of 'causes', that is to say, of the grievances, demands, and visions cited by exponents of political violence as worth killing and, if need be dying, for. Throughout much of previous history, religion offered about the only such cause (dynastic and other forms of elite rivalry having had no claim to, and apparently little need for, transcendent justification). Even nineteenth-century assassins, when they did not still revert to religious sanctions, seldom offered any alternatives going beyond patriotic or populist slogans.

By contrast, political murder in our own era has put forward a greatly expanded shopping list of motives, some old, some new, and some amalgamated: religious, pseudo-religious, libertarian, nihilistic, anti-colonial, Marxist, anti-Marxist, meta-Marxist, *völkisch*, Maoist, and at times, one is tempted to conclude, simply purgative for the individual doing the deed. This last category is, alas, not fanciful. Only a few years ago, after a peculiar lady had fired several shots at the then President of the United States, I heard a noted psychologist say, with all professional solemnity, that 'unfortunate as her action had been, it probably constituted the first clear statement she had ever been able to make'.

It is, I think, a waste of time to argue with self-justificatory statements which seek to explain murder, even random murder, as 'the only course open' to protestors who naturally claim the right to combat 'injustice' by any and all means. There is, however, some reason to pause over this insistence on having one's own way, whatever the cost to other people, as a further indication of change in the patterns of violence grown prevalent in the twentieth century.

This is not to say that 'claiming credit' for assassination was unknown in the nineteenth century, as various publications and courtroom speeches attest. Nevertheless – and apart from the fact that killing innocent bystanders did seem to worry the Russian revolutionaries of Vera Figner's generation – explicit repudiation of many acts of lethal violence remained characteristic of numerous oppositional spokesmen. German Social Democrats, even while outlawed as a party in Bismarck's Reich, repeatedly condemned terrorism. Not surprisingly, they showed themselves still quicker, once they had recovered legal status, to condemn such murders as that of the Empress Elizabeth in 1898. The same could have been said of practically the entire political spectrum of editorial opinion to be found in European newspapers before 1918.

At this point, of course, criticism of 'legal opposition' and of its self-imposed limits is sure to be expressed. The evaluation of such complaints, however, is not central to my own position here. What is central is the evidence of change, the reflection that it would have been virtually unthinkable for a pre-war reader to have opened his morning paper to any such editorial as appeared in Germany's nationalist *Oletzkoer Zeitung* on the day following

Matthias Erzberger's murder at Bad Griesbach in 1921:

> Erzberger . . . has suffered the fate which the vast majority of patriotic Germans have long desired for him. Erzberger, the man who is alone responsible for the humiliating armistice,

and so on.[14] Though naturally more measured in expression and more ambitious (as well as confused) in its historical allusions to Charlotte Corday, William Tell, and even Brutus, the venerable *Kreuzzeitung* ended on a note not too different from that struck by other, openly jubilant editors:

> Those who now praise Erzberger and attack his enemies seem to forget completely that the entire campaign against [him] has been essentially a defensive struggle.[15]

The whole question of public sympathy, or at least apathy, toward the most extreme and random acts of political warfare must, I readily concede, be seen in terms of other terrible acts of war and of government-sponsored terror, as distinguished from the ordinary workings of police forces and of the criminal courts. All I hope to establish here is the difference between, on the one hand, recognising that relationship and, on the other, hastening to condone virtually any form or level of insurrectional violence as 'understandable'. There is, after all, no atrocity that cannot be understood, in terms of its author's specific grievances, beliefs, state of mind, and calculation of self-interest; but does our ability to comprehend automatically impose the obligation to applaud? Does not a certain *Schadenfreude* at the victim's expense sometimes masquerade as allegiance to the generous principle, *tout comprendre, tout pardonner*, applied on behalf of the perpetrator?

The last point I have to make involves two separate, albeit related, levels of analysis. It has to do with exchanges, both in tactics and sometimes in theory as well, occurring along different axes. One of these co-ordinates is that of governmental-versus-insurrectionary behaviour, the other that of social, economic and political doctrine, whether it be conceived as extending from right to left, from liberty and order to equality and distributive justice, or between some other set of comparably idealised poles. Let me suggest as briefly as possible the kinds of interaction and the sometimes rather curious sharing I have in mind.

As for the first of my proposed axes, running from official repression at one end to organised revolution at the other (with a continuum of various forms of harassment and/or protest stretching between), its significance for twentieth-century history is not hard to demonstrate. The most extreme governments of the post-1918 era – extreme, that is, in the ruthlessness and the comprehensiveness of their police measures against putative opponents – were born of previous resistance movements that had managed to seize full power in the state. Lenin's, Stalin's, and Hitler's methods of rule, however different their announced philosophies may have been, were related in that they showed clearly what the new tyrants had learned during their days in opposition – not so much from their own difficulties, which were slight compared with what their later opponents had to face, as from the contempt they appear to have conceived for the failures of will, of vigilance, and of ingenuity shown by the regimes they had themselves succeeded in overthrowing. Few if any historic revolutions, of course, whether violent or ostensibly 'legal', have brought with them any reduction in previous levels of police power. By the same token, without the schooling in conspiracy required to survive underground in rebellion against governments disposing of the Nazi *Sicherheitsdienst* or comparable agencies, World War II's 'resistance tradition' would offer present-day terrorists little beyond a lingering aura of heroic resolve. Instead, the wartime Resistance has provided a variety of organisational models and tactical lessons, as well as a number of spurious parallels. It is in this sense that the escalation of political violence in our century may be said to display a dialectical quality in which anti-liberalism has supplied perhaps the only constant, apart from techniques themselves.

The progress of a corresponding exchange of tactics and of battle cries, as between right and left, between 'forces of order' and 'forces of freedom', may be less readily acknowledged by either side; but it is scarcely less significant than that between violent regimes and violent opposition. By the end of the nineteenth century, there appeared to be a very good chance that Europe's democratic socialists, having lately demonstrated their growing electoral power, might in fact achieve what had once been viewed as revolutionary aims by legal, i.e., parliamentary means. There was already, however, some reason to fear that unabashed reactionaries would henceforth be the political actors most likely to resort to extra-legal, increasingly anti-constitutional, and ultimately violent means. That forecast was to prove remarkably accurate when tested against developments in Italy, Germany, and elsewhere after 1918. For whatever confusion may persist concerning the 'rightist' and 'leftist' features of the congeries of national movements we call fascist, all of them were explicitly counter-revolutionary, anti-Marxist, and ostentatiously, not to say lethally, violent. 'Right-wing revolution' became a familiar term in our own century's vocabulary.

What I suppose could hardly have been so shrewdly predicted was still a further development: the emergence of an increasingly authoritarian left, some of whose spokesmen claim a Marxist, others only an anarchist identity, while both borrow heavily from what older leftists would have called right-wing, ultra-nationalist, and above all fascist applications of political terrorism. That is not, I need hardly say, to deny that many, probably most, people who think of themselves as 'progressives' today still repudiate such terrorism as a betrayal of the humanitarian tradition. It is, however, to insist that the audible tribunes of Germany's *Rote Armee Fraktion*, Italy's *brigate rosse* and numerous parallel formations inside Europe and out, invoke leftist ideals while at the same time employing tactics chillingly reminiscent of the *Organisation Consul's* war against Weimar democracy.

As I have remarked in the course of my argument, reflections confined to political murder cannot claim, and should not seek, to explore all the issues, both pragmatic and ethical, which are raised by debate over political violence defined in the most general terms. Even with respect to the possible paradox identified at this paper's beginning, it is quite apparent that death, whether it results from disease or accident or malice aforethought, is an ever-present factor in politics, an uncontrollable variable to be reckoned with there as in every other activity to which mortals set their hands. The question nevertheless remains: does purposeful homicide deserve to be treated as an acceptable, because familiar, feature of political life? Or should it not be more accurately described as an obstacle to the rational conduct of human affairs, and its perpetrators labeled accordingly?

NOTES

1. F. L. Ford, 'Assassination in the Eighteenth Century: The Dog That Did Not Bark in the Night', *Proceedings of the American Philosophical Society* 120 (1976), pp. 211–15.
2. While a political intelligence officer in Germany in 1945, assigned to an investigation of 20 July, I was struck by the remarkable variety of motives which informed the conspiracy behind the bomb attempt at Rastenburg. My impressions and necessarily fragmentary findings appeared as an article, 'The Twentieth of July in the History of the German Resistance', *The American Historical Review* 51 (1946), pp. 609–26.
3. D. Hume, *The History of England* new ed., vol. v (Boston, 1849–50) p. 48.
4. C. E. Jarcke, *Carl Ludwig Sand und sein, an dem kaiserlich-russischen Staatsrath v. Kotzebue veruebter Mord. Eine psychologisch-criminalistische Eroerterung aus der Geschichte unserer Zeit* (Berlin, 1831).
5. R. L. Williams, *Manners and Murders in the World of Louis-Napoleon* (Seattle/London, 1975) pp. 44–67.
6. P. Liman, *Der politische Mord im Wandel der Geschichte* (Berlin, 1912) pp. 151–3.
7. Prime Minister Perceval was shot to death in 1812 by John Billingham just outside the chamber of the House of Commons. The two pistols used against President Andrew Jackson by Richard Lawrence in 1835 both misfired at point-blank range.
8. M. St John Packe, *The Bombs at Orsini* (London, 1957); and R. Hingley, *Nihilists. Russian Radicals and Revolutionaries in the Reign of Alexander II, 1855–81* (London, 1967).
9. G. L. Chaix-d'Est-Ange, *Discours et plaidoyers*, vol. I (Paris, 1862) pp. 403–70.
10. See for example the anonymous *Memoir of L. Sand: Including a Narrative of the Circumstances Attending the Death of Augustus von Kotzebue* [and] *A Defense of the German Universities* (London, 1819).
11. C., L., and R. Tilly, *The Rebellious Century, 1830–1930* (Cambridge, Mass., 1975).
12. *New York Times*, 16 June 1924.

13. *Kalender des Volkswillen für 1883* (Geneva, 1883) pp. 135–45. Summarised in tabular form by A. Thun, *Geschichte der revolutionären Bewegungen in Russland* (Leipzig, 1883) p. 375.
14. K. Epstein, *Matthias Erzberger and the Dilemma of German Democracy* (Princeton, 1959) p. 388.
15. Ibid.

2 Political Violence and Political Murder: Comments on Franklin Ford's Essay

Eric J. Hobsbawm

Any analysis of political violence is faced with the fundamental problem of how to delimit its subject. It is surely too narrow a view to consider political violence by marginal and fringe groups as the whole of the matter. Although this is in itself an interesting subject, I think it would probably be wrong to take such a restricted view. An even more limited approach would be to deal with this phenomenon exclusively in terms of 'political murder' as has been done by Franklin Ford. The key question is rather whether any such narrow definition of political violence will do, or whether we should approach the phenomenon along other lines of argumentation which lead us into much wider fields. Even though one may not wish to do so, the advisability or otherwise of trying to broaden our definition needs to be discussed, and this is what I should like to say a few words about.

It seems to me that Franklin Ford is essentially making three points. First, he notes a secular growth in extreme political violence and if one were to generalise, I think this is a basic and rather sad facet of the modern world. For a number of decades we have been living through a period of growing political barbarism, a reversal of the era of secular growth in civilised behaviour, political or otherwise, which I suppose we can date back from the middle or late eighteenth century on. The practical test of this is the use of torture which was abolished gradually from the end of the eighteenth century until by 1914 it was believed to be used only in the most backward and barbarous states, not as yet accessible to the influence of civilisation, whereas by today it has once again become a regular method, and I wish to underline this, a regular method used by police forces and forces of order in virtually every state that one can think. And in this sense the analysis of political murder is a marginal contribution to the study of this rather regrettable reversal of tendencies.

Second, Ford criticises the usual periodisation and tries to establish, as it were, the watershed of the *Grand Tournant* within 'the rebellious century', 1830–1930. He situates it, I think probably correctly, in the years after the First World War. Not only does he establish statistically that the 1920s were the first black era of mass political assassination, but also he suggests that there is a major difference between the time before 1914 when even the terrorists, or a lot of them, attempted to confine their violence within the moral framework of the rationalist enlightenment or perhaps just the ancient conventions society actually gives to violence, and our era when these limits are no longer accepted. I hasten to add, they are accepted as little by states and governments as by their opponents. I recall that Friedrich Engels was outraged by the Irish in the 1880s killing bystanders. Even revolutionaries, he believed, behaved like soldiers and killed only people actually fighting against them. The *Narodnaya Volya* was, as Ford suggests, worried about killing the innocent. It shows how desperate, and incidentally ineffective, the attempts of the social revolutionaries were to impose limits on terrorism or expropriation, and indeed it is extremely clear to anyone who works on topics like expropriation, how worried people were about limiting and legitimising these activities and fitting them into what was still believed to be a system of generally valid moral imperatives. Today it is the innocent who are the real and often intended victims. But this is not merely the signature of fringe groups. After all in modern mass war, certainly in the Second World War, a great deal of the strategy was deliberately aimed at the innocent, those who were not fighting rather than those who were fighting. Here we might consider the role of the two World Wars which were essentially machines for indiscriminate massacre or the massacre of people defined as groups irrespective of their attitudes and attributes. And it may be worth considering the role of these wars in the change of this moral climate.

Thirdly, Ford suggests the left learns from the experience of repression by states – and here perhaps the experience of the Paris commune of 1871 might have been mentioned – and of states tolerating terror by the right – free corps, fascists and so on – to fight in turn to the bitter end in order to survive. In turn, as Ford himself points out, the most extreme governments, the most repressive governments, whether of left or right, are those which emerge from resistance movements or direct action movements, and are thus trained in the experience of fighting to the bitter end against what they believe to be irreconcilable and relentless enemies. These I take it are the main points made here and they are in themselves interesting. It seems to me nevertheless that if we are to discuss the narrow problems thus posed we still have to situate them. I should like, not so much to situate them as briefly to consider some problems of situating them. The first is that we have to distinguish two things, the violence of marginal groups and the violence which is built into state, class struggle, or if you prefer, social relations in general. Now the violence of marginal groups is overwhelmingly symptomatic rather than effective. We can discuss under what circumstances it could achieve concrete results, of which incidentally by far the most likely historically has been to create effective counter-violence. No doubt we can also discuss under what conditions it is positively successful, insofar as its objects could be formulated in terms of achievable ends.

Nevertheless, as Ford points out, the most usual rationalisation of small-group terrorism, namely that it will set off major mass actions by its example or by its stimulus, has never been fulfilled or even come close to realisation. In short a great deal of this kind of violence makes no sense, as it were, by being analysed as a goal-oriented activity today. We could argue about this, but on the whole it is true; what Ford calls the astounding vitality of a hope for which very little empirical evidence exists, or has ever existed, shows that in fact it does not rest on rational analysis.

Now the question that we have to ask is: what it does rest on? Under what conditions do individuals or groups return time and again to this policy? Who are they? What is their social composition or their individual selection? How, if at all, has it changed? And under what conditions may they actually believe that these activities can have, except in the most exceptional circumstances, a genuine effectiveness? However, there is a much wider problem and this is, I think, separate from the distinction between fringe-group violence and structural violence, or however you choose to define it. What do we understand by violence and social protest in politics? The question is begged by concentrating on the extreme examples which in fact are the subject matter of most of the papers – assassination, terror and so on – because nobody really doubts that these are cases of violence. However, the issue is fudged if these phenomena are confused with other cases which are clearly less easily defined. And here I suggest that some conceptual discriminations are necessary. First that the very use of the term violence as a separate social category assumes a certain discrimination already, a certain selection out of acts of violence which are classified as social or political. Thus so long as husbands are assumed to be entitled to beat wives, or fathers children, or schoolmasters pupils, nobody will regard an example of a schoolmaster beating a pupil or a husband a wife as an example of violence.

Today indeed we would worry, but in those days one would take note only in quite exceptional cases and indeed in traditional societies there are mechanisms, that have been much discussed – for instance *Charivari*, and others – for public opinion to express its condemnation of excessive violence within a society which accepts a certain degree of it. Now it is true that until fairly recently the gradual decline of such socially accepted violence was accepted as a fact although today it may be increasing once again. Eighteenth century England was a notoriously riotous country, but nobody discussed political violence as such very much, or correlated the very large endemic degree of violence in that country with any specific variables. If anything it was regarded, at least by British governments, as a helpful sign of the British love of liberty. The very high degree of interpersonal violence in some backward countries, for instance the very high murder rate in some backward regions, say in the nineteenth century in Sicily as against the Veneto or in Colombia or Mexico in the twentieth century against Chile and Uruguay was not considered basically as a political problem but as a problem of historic or cultural differences, though it might have political consequences. So in a sense what we are discussing is something selected out by us from the reservoir of existing violence.

Secondly, violence as the occasional expression of social and political force again raises no problems of principle until, as in our era, its traditional rules and conventions break down or until its effectiveness changes. Ideally the balance of force can be established by the recognition of relative strength without very much open violence which is in a sense merely the margin beyond the establishment of this regular balance. Police forces are successful in proportion as they do not have to use guns or beat up people. This is actually what nineteenth-century British governments realised, very systematically rejecting other and less discriminating forces of keeping order. Conversely, the counterforce of the poor can establish limits which the rich recognise they cannot regularly overstep without a certain risk to property or possibly even to lives. This was the case for certain strongly organised Luddite groups of workers. Their real strength occurs when they do *not* have to smash machines, when it is accepted that you do not introduce new technology, because the introduction of new technology leads to trouble. So in a sense we cannot judge the phenomenon simply by the numbers of machines smashed and then count them up and put them in a computer as an index of violence, because these may merely indicate the breakdown of this balance of forces, a balance of unequal forces no doubt, but nevertheless one in which one side is not completely disarmed compared with the other. Of course, this operates only in relatively stable societies in which this classic structure does not break down into civil or indeed international wars, or where society changes in such a way that the old tug-of-war no longer produces the expected balanced results. Moreover, as in the case of food riots a certain degree of legitimacy of both pressure and counter-pressure may be recognised in certain societies and this legitimacy disappears with the change both in social structure and in the relations between classes.

A further discrimination, I would suggest, is the recognition that there are conventions of violence. It is their erosion and disappearance which very largely creates our problem. They are of two kinds: inter-cultural, that is to say between cultures and within a given culture and they define the degrees of legitimate violence, this is to what extent violence is supposed to be proportionate to the object of the action. The best example of the cultural difference in violence I know comes from that eminent historian, Walter Scott, in his marvellous story of *The Two Drovers*. It is the story of a Scots highlander and a north English drover who drive the cattle down, essentially to the London market and for some reason they come to dispute over which of the drovers is entitled to pasture his cattle in a farmer's field somewhere in Cumbria. The Englishman thinks that the Scotsman has done him out of his pasture and, in the pub in the evening when they meet, the Englishman says, 'Come outside and settle this'; the Scotsman says, 'No,' and the Englishman knocks him down. After this he offers his hand and thinks everything is solved, but it is not solved, because for the Scotsman there is only one thing to be done and that is to exact blood. He has no option about it: the man is a friend, the two have long been friends, but the rules of his game require that he be killed and he is killed and tried and there is a marvellous passage where the eighteenth-century judge understands, as it were, what he is doing and says, 'We must see that this man is not a criminal in any sense, he is simply doing what in his society he was morally expected to do. It is different from what we in England do, it is different from what the English law allows, but we must not see him as anti-social. Nevertheless as a representative of the law of the land I am obliged to sentence him to death.'

This brings out the subjective historical setting of what we are discussing as 'violence' extremely well. As for the discrimination within a specific culture, here I think we are on much more concrete ground, for it does seem, to judge by nineteenth-century England, that in traditional societies there was a very considerable degree of correlation between the aim of an action and the degree of permitted or necessary violence which was applied to it. The best known case I know is that of British farm labourers in the early nineteenth century. There, for certain purposes, violence against property was almost always legitimate, the killing or maiming of animals was almost always legitimate, violence against people was much less legitimate and only under certain circumstances, although under such circumstances beating people up, driving them out or violent acts – such as running them out of town, tarring and feathering them and so on – were quite legitimate as regular actions. What was hardly ever legitimate was killing people and indeed you find that in these violent movements very few people indeed are killed normally. This has often been pointed out: the people that are killed are killed by the other side, by the forces of order. The interesting point is that these discriminations were made by people who were not in themselves opposed to killing people. The very same men who, in a different situation such as if they were poachers confronted with gamekeepers, would fight and shoot to kill and expect to be fought and shot to be killed, refused to kill or even badly to wound if they were part of a mob demanding higher wages or destroying threshing machines. I think the mechanism of making violence proportionate to the aim is rather similar to making the penalty proportionate to the crime in official law. It is very widespread. In the customary codes of law which have been analysed by Italian observers, say in the Sardinian highlands, it is very clear that certain types of offence like stealing a goat must call for certain action, but not more than a certain retaliation, whereas more serious actions are met by escalating retaliation up to the most extreme. How then do these conventions which govern violence break down, how far have they broken down, how far are they being reconstructed? I think there are actually some signs that they are being reconstructed today, when we are once again living in a society with very widespread and endemic interpersonal violence as well as structural and political violence. I merely want to suggest two possible methods: first there is the kind of breakdown of older societies and structures in which, as one might say, the rules get out of hand, a phenomenon which is very well known in the history of blood feuds. The mechanisms which exist normally to correct and conclude blood feuds fairly rapidly rely on a basic framework of social relations and when that breaks down blood feuds get out of hand and you have long generation-lasting civil wars between kinship groups and families, which nobody knows quite how to conclude.

The second I suggest is destruction by liberalism. Nineteenth-century liberal society in rejecting all violence abolished the distinction between limited and unlimited violence, for when anything which is not actually writing a leading article in the paper or putting a cross in the ballot box could be defined as a violent action or the use of force, the very significant difference between killing somebody and threatening somebody or even going on strike may get destroyed. I think it has been destroyed. One final element I would like to mention. In the absence of institutional expressions and group interests, violence, that is to say illegal action, is often the only way open, because whatever people do who have no legal way of expressing their demands must be defined as illegal, even if it is not very violent. For we have to bear in mind that the definition of violence is administrative and legal. It is what is not allowed by law which is defined as a violent act, never mind whether it is simply a public meeting or an assassination. The traditional peasant rising in nineteenth-century Russia consisted largely of a policeman and a priest haranguing a gang of sullen *mushiks* in the village square and no more. It was defined administratively as an 'insurrection' and not clearly distinguished from a real insurrection.

Now all this changed in the nineteenth century. Social movements, the more conscious and organised, the more this happened to them, abandoned individual violence even when committed to revolution by insurrection and civil war as with Lenin, who looked forward to the breakdown of the old order which was to be replaced in direct confrontation by a new order. But of course he would have preferred to do without a civil war. But they resisted individual violence or terror or endemic violence of the kind that I have talked about, because in the situation they aimed at it was not very useful. Such violence for those new movements meant the lashing out of the weak against the strong, the mode of action of those who do not know any better and cannot do anything else. Hence, the at-first-sight surprising but deeply held difference between the classical movements of the left, including Marxism, with their rejection of individual terror, and movements such as the anarchists.

But finally at this point, we need to consider a completely different problem, namely what is the role of violence in revolutions as distinct from violence in defending oneself against counter-revolutions or even the violence of post-revolutionary states? How violent indeed are revolutions? My own feeling is that the actual mass revolutions in general, whatever happens afterwards, are on the whole relatively unviolent as indeed are very many of the mass movements of peasants and others. Insofar as their success is guaranteed they do not need it, indeed their object is not violence, or vengeance as such, but what is to be achieved by violence. This can be said of the relatively few groups in early nineteenth-century England who were committed to physical force and violence: what they wanted was not the violent action but its consequences. It seems to me that unless we consider some of these discriminations we may find it difficult to see the terrorism of the present in its proper perspective.

3 The Aims and Ideology of Violent Protest in Great Britain, 1800–48

Malcolm I. Thomis

The starting point for this paper, as it is indeed the starting point of all recent studies of violence in nineteenth century British history, is Eric Hobsbawm's article on the Machine Breakers.[1] In this, besides giving us that most quotable quotation 'collective bargaining by riot', he introduced us to the idea that violence in early industrial relations was not simply irrational and wild behaviour by thoughtless irresponsible workmen, but was frequently a deliberately selected technique of protest, perhaps the most effective one available at some times and in some places. My intention is to examine violent social and political protest in Britain in the first half of the nineteenth century by asking three questions about it: to what extent violence was consciously chosen as a means to pursue particular ends; to what extent violence was used as a means of implementing a particular ideology; and how successful violence was as a protest technique. The variety of examples chosen should help to confirm the willingness of Englishmen now to acknowledge that their country's history in modern times was not one of purely peaceful evolution under the custodianship of a benevolent parliamentary system.[2] Donald Read's contention that only in Britain would the death of eleven people, at Peterloo, constitute a massacre, and the perspective supplied by a further 150 years of history might incline us to see as almost benign the violence at work in these years.[3] Yet it was there and merits examination.

Categories of violent behaviour are not easy to establish, for any attempt to separate actions into their different groups according to the reasons why participants resorted to violence will probably break down because of the mixture of motives usually to be found. Nor is violence necessarily a marked characteristic of movements that have an avowedly violent intent. The revolutionaries of the period are interesting in this respect. Whilst there were undoubtedly a few, like the Cato Street conspirators, who plotted assassination, the majority of my acquaintance were strangely mild people, who seem to have wished for the end of revolution without accepting that violence was a necessary means to that end. The popularity of the notion that revolution would spontaneously occur from mass meetings simultaneously organised throughout the country, particularly strong in 1819 and 1839, seems to indicate a reluctance to anticipate the violence usually necessary to carry through a revolutionary coup. Even those people who took to the streets in 1817 and 1820 in what were certainly armed rebellions seem not to have contemplated violence very seriously. Neither the Pentrich rebels of 1817 nor those of the west of Scotland in 1820 were equipped with the necessary arms to subdue even a token force of opposition, and it was such a token force which in one case caused them to flee without a fight and in the other to engage in a tiny pitched battle.

Although the Pentrich rebels of 1817 were charged amongst other things with being 'armed in warlike manner', the authorities had taken from their prisoners only a dozen or so forks and picks, the latter 'manufactured out of old files or chisels sharpened applied to handles of considerable length'. Brandreth himself had acquired a gun. The Bonnymuir rebels of 1820 were similarly armed with '16 picks, a shaft without a head, a gun or two, and two pistols'. Thomas Bacon, perhaps the man most responsible for the Pentrich rebellion, believed that there would be no fighting, and he certainly made no serious effort to prepare his followers for such a thing. The gesture of rebellion was to be enough; the moral power of the rebels and the popularity of their cause would be sufficient to bring down the government, and the revolution would be achieved without violence. Indeed, the prevalence of notions among the rebels about pleasure trips on the Trent and feasts of plum pudding suggests that having a revolution was thought of more as a picnic outing than an occasion for fighting. The leader of the men on the day, Jeremiah Brandreth, was certainly violent to the extent of shooting a farm servant, almost accidently, but that was hardly the violence to cause governments to fall. He alone of the leaders was of intemperate disposition. The rest were men of good reputation and peaceful disposition. Their Scottish counterparts, particularly James Baird and Andrew Hardie, the two most important Bonnymuir rebels, were similarly men of great moral fervour and integrity for whom physical violence appears an anomalous activity. They too believed that the justice of their cause and the extent of its support would enable it to triumph. Calculations about the use and extent of violence necessary to achieve it played no part in their deliberations.[4]

It is worth noting, in contrast, that the middle class reformers, who threatened the Duke of Wellington with revolution in May 1832 if he formed a government, were at the same time the most unlikely revolutionaries for an industrialising society to throw up and yet the best organised and most able to deliver the violence necessary to bring down a government. Whether they would ever have been prepared to embark on revolution, knowing the threats to themselves that this could entail, has been a matter for endless speculation, but there is little room to doubt that they had more force at their command than any other groups that threatened British governments from within during the first half of the nineteenth century.[5] Their particular brand of political blackmail, a political demand backed up by a show of force and the threat to use it, was to recur during the Chartist period, when the violence of language rather than that of actions was to characterise the protest techniques of the parliamentary reformers.

Another category of violence is that associated with attacks upon objects of hatred, where targets are destroyed because they are themselves the object of the protesters' anger. Poorhouses and workhouses frequently feature as targets, both before and after the New Poor Law of 1834. Peacock records several such attacks in East Anglia in the late eighteenth and early nineteenth centuries, such as the destruction of 'Bulcamp Hell' and the attack on Nacton house by a mob of 400 labourers who were 'resolved the poor should be maintained in their own parishes'.[6] David Williams also records many such attacks during the *Rebecca* Riots in West Wales in 1839–43, on workhouses that were obnoxious for their own sake and because they were invariably chosen to accommodate soldiers who were sent to impose law and order.[7] They reached their most intensive form during the anti-Poor Law movement after 1834 when new workhouses were demolished, and attacks upon Poor Law Commissioners, guardians, and constables occurred. On 30 October 1837, Commissioner Power emerged from the Bradford Courthouse to a shower of mud, stones, and umbrellas, a treatment to which he was by this time quite accustomed. The following month a rioting crowd controlled the streets and possessed the courthouse despite the presence of special constables and troops.[8]

It would be difficult to say whether such incidents were ends in themselves or whether they were ever thought to be part of an assault upon a whole system that might be changed if a sufficient number of examples of its unpopularity were produced. Similarly, within machine-breaking, it is difficult to know if offensive machinery such as steam looms, gig mills, and shearing frames were thought to be possible candidates for total elimination by those who conducted their attacks upon them. There is no doubt that within a small industry such as the cloth-finishing trade, machine-breakers could for a short time, as in the summer of 1812, virtually eliminate the use of offensive machinery by maintaining a reign of terror, but in a larger operation like cotton-weaving the hold of the steam-loom was sufficiently strong and its use sufficiently widespread by the time of the major violent resistance of 1826 that destruction of steam looms was hardly a practical proposition.[9]

Threshing machines too were a frequent target of popular violence; the East Anglian machines of 4–5hp condemned by a Colchester correspondent in 1816 for their capacity to thrash as much corn in one day as 20 men working with the flail, were broken along with mole ploughs in the riots of that year.[10] The *Swing* riots of 1830 in the South East produced no fewer than 390 attacks of this kind.[11] Even more dramatically singled out were the toll-gates destroyed with much panache by the *Rebecca* Rioters in 1839–43, who also destroyed salmon weirs across rivers. Sometimes the rioters' target of hatred was a person, perhaps an election candidate, or an official responsible for implementing an unpopular policy. Richards records the contemporary view that there was 'a regular organised system of resistance to civil power during attempts to enforce the Highland clearances', during which Sheriff's officers could expect to be set upon, stripped naked, or otherwise humiliated.[12] Other possible targets for personal abuse were strike-breakers. The Glasgow Cotton Spinners' strike of 1837 produced incidents of vitriol-throwing and other unfriendly acts, but it was probably not typical of how industrial disputes were usually conducted.

A slightly different kind of hated target was that which was the property of the person currently the object of popular fury, as in the case of the Nottingham Reform Bill riots of October 1831. Here the best known incidents concerned Nottingham Castle, Colwick Hall, Beeston Mill, and Wollaton Hall, all property of well-known local opponents of the Reform Bill. Rioters were not concerned to demonstrate their hostility to castles, mills, or stately residences, all of which they tolerated happily enough in normal times, but to protest against the attitude of their owners by striking at their property.[13] This was scarcely 'collective bargaining by riot' unless the unlikely interpretation is accepted that participants were consciously and deliberately striking a blow for parliamentary reform by coercing their opponents into a situation in which they would be ready to concede reform rather than subject themselves to the risk of further outrages. That was not the outcome locally, and it was probably not intended that it should be. The attacks were negative in the sense that they were reprisals for grievances rather than positive in the sense that they were designed to achieve some particular good. They were acts committed in anger for past deeds rather than in anticipation that they would be productive of some good. To what extent the rioting crowds acted spontaneously and to what extent they received active leadership have recently been questioned, and this is an issue that clearly merits much more investigation.[14]

Sometimes violent deeds of an unexplained nature accompanied protest movements with otherwise clear causes and clear manifestations. The East Anglian riots of 1816, for instance, included a sequence of events in which a cottage was maliciously burnt down for no apparent reason, a haulm stack destroyed, other cottages pulled down, and farm buildings set alight. Such events were exceptional.[15] There were not many such cases to substantiate the traditional view of popular violence as a wild, irrational orgy of destruction.

It is often quite impossible to make a clear distinction between past grievance and future hopes. The labourers' risings in East Anglia in 1816 and in the South-eastern counties of England in 1830 are a mixture of angry response to an intolerable situation in the retaliatory form of arson, rick burning or assaults upon property. At the same time they have a more calculating aspect to them of collective bargaining by riot in attempts to fix wage rates, influence Poor Law administration, or the collection of tithes, not to mention the specific campaign waged against the threshing machine, which was rational enough to enlist the support of many farmers in that most curious phenomenon of nineteenth century protest, the readiness of some farmers to put out their own machines to be broken by the crowds.[16] With food-rioting, too, popular action is both an angry response, a lashing out at those who are supposedly responsible for the existing predicament, and a violent course directed towards positive objectives. These might be short-term ones of cheap or free food of a particular kind or the longer term ones of reminding government and society of their traditional values and traditional obligations, if one is to extend Edward Thompson's argument on the moral economy of the eighteenth-century crowd into the nineteenth century.[17] Whatever the acts of violence committed in moments of passion, it is unlikely that any historian would today be content to accept contemporary views of wanton disorder and destruction and refuse to look for pattern and purpose in what was being attempted. It may be that the rick-burning of the labourers is still seen as a primitive response in the sense that they were behaving instinctively rather than selecting from a variety of options open to them, for their options were indeed very limited, but their conduct would still be open to defence as an intelligible, even intelligent, resort to the means that were available and one not entirely unproductive of success.

Although violence has traditionally been ascribed to those engaged in protest of one kind or another, there have recently been salutory reminders that much of the violence in British political life at this time emanated from the authorities, who were frequently responsible for turning peaceful protest into something much more alarming. Indeed, it has been observed that 'the authorities have far greater control over the short-term extent and timing of collective violence, especially damage to persons rather than property, than their challengers do'.[18] Peterloo, 1819, is the classic case of this, though by no means a solitary one. Deaths and serious injuries in the Highlands, Richards reminds us, were almost entirely on the side of the protesters, and this would be true of food-rioting, machine-breaking, and the whole range of protest movements.[19] What seems particularly characteristic of the behaviour of those in authority in this period is their capacity to misjudge a situation and interfere with disastrous consequences. Popular political protest remained peaceful in the West of Scotland in the autumn of 1819, after Peterloo, except when the magistrates intervened, as they did at Paisley to seize a radical banner; then orderly crowds turned into rioting mobs and harmless people became menacing.[20] In July 1839, Birmingham experienced incendiary riots for nearly a week from an angered populace provoked by the actions of the local authorities, and during the Black Country coal strikes of 1842 actual clashes occurred only when mine-owners used regular soldiers, Yeomanry, and special constables to defend their pits against men on strike. In Wolverhampton, 1835, a hostile jeering crowd had been converted into a riotous one by a magistrate who read the Riot Act and ordered soldiers to fire on the crowd.[21]

In most of these cases violence has been seen as instinctive, retaliatory, or primitive behaviour, but rarely as a form of conduct consciously and deliberately chosen in preference to other forms or because other forms had been found wanting. A magistrate of Bury St Edmunds condemned rioters in 1816 for their failure to seek redress of grievance by 'peaceable, orderly, and legal application'.[22] The inadequacies of local protection and their ignorance of and exclusion from political processes ensured from the East Anglian labourers a pre-political response of resorting to violence, but such conduct was not always 'pre-political' in this period. In 1812 the war against cloth-finishing machinery was launched with the justification that 'we petition no more – that won't do – fighting must', and in all three areas of Luddite violence, the East Midlands, West Yorkshire, and East Lancashire, machine-breaking occurred only after a collapse of collective bargaining, petitioning and peaceful negotiation.[23] But this was a use of violence in its most sophisticated form, for not only was violence widespread and prolonged; it was also controlled in its application, as if violence were a legitimate and usable weapon that could be invoked as and when necessary by the working classes.

The most sophisticated operators were the East Midlands stocking-knitters, whose motives were quite different from those of their northern brothers who were involved in resisting machinery. The stocking-knitters were perhaps the best example of collective bargainers by riot, for they had developed by 1811–12, the years of their greatest violence, a traditional way of escalating their pressure upon employers if more peaceful methods proved unsuccessful. They were well practised in the arts of trade-union organisation and the conducting of strikes, and they were even experienced in working within the, admittedly fairly narrow, confines of the political system and petitioning parliament for a redress of their grievances. But when all these tactics and techniques proved useless, which they sometimes did, the stockingers still had one sanction remaining to them, the property of their employers, the hosiers, the stocking-frames on which they worked, which were kept not in a factory where they could be protected by the owner but in a small workshop, or more frequently in the workers' own homes, where they were almost totally vulnerable.

The breaking of stocking frames was an easy and obvious way of conducting a campaign. In 1778, on the failure of a petition for the parliamentary regulation of the hosiery trade, frames had been dragged out into the streets and smashed. In 1811 on the failure of negotiations to keep up wage rates and control production standards, stocking-frames were again destroyed, in large numbers, over wide areas, as the stockingers attempted to bargain by a policy of deliberate but controlled violence to fix wage rates and to impose other conditions upon their employers. And there is no doubt that machine-wrecking was a specifically chosen technique intended to achieve what could not be got by other means. Even in Yorkshire, where machine-wrecking was directed against the machinery itself rather than as a supplement to negotiation, there was an attempt to justify resort to the tactic on the grounds that all other avenues were now closed, including that trodden by the Prince Regent, who had been the focus of some hopes before 'falling in with that Damn'd set of Rogues, Percival & Co'.[24] In Nottingham, however, machine-breaking was a much more calculated policy, applied with a precision and degree of selectivity that almost anticipated the dictum that war is a continuation of diplomacy by other means. The most remarkable examples of this occurred in 1814, when machine-breaking is no longer the replacement alternative to trade-union organisation but appears to be under the careful and precise direction of the trade union itself, which selects the method of attack appropriate to the particular enemy.

After a succession of employers, Orgill, Needham, and Morley, had had their frames broken following resistance to the Union Society's claim for an increase in rates, Ray Brothers, who also resisted, were attacked by the more orthodox strike weapon. This last firm worked entirely on independent frames, not ones owned by themselves, as usually happened, and were in consequence not susceptible to coercion by frame-breaking. The punishment was chosen to fit not the crime, for all were charged with the same, but the criminal.[25] It might be necessary to look ahead to the years before 1914 to find such a dispassionate employment of violence as a technique of protest and resistance. Both the suffragettes who turned to acts of sabotage when their peaceful campaign had failed to achieve the required results and the Ulster Unionists who armed themselves to resist a legislative act of the British parliament which they were incapable of stopping by constitutional means were to make a conscious choice of violence as a means of gaining their wishes in the same way that the *Luddites* selected violence, not simply because it was the only way left but because it seemed the most effective way to operate in association with other techniques in particular situations.

If violence is often difficult to categorise, it is equally difficult to identify with any precise ideologies, let alone one particular one. When people resorted to violence in the first half of the nineteenth century they usually did so because they had specific and limited grievances, mainly against individuals, which could be satisfied by specific and limited remedies, again mainly supplied by individuals. Rarely was the grievance felt against a whole system, the state, the class-structure, capitalism, or industrialism, for example, and rarely was its remedy sought in some comprehensive solution that would involve a major shift of political or economic power within society. Violence tended to arise from discontents that could be accommodated. It was consequently often a serious problem but never a very serious problem.

This is not to say that the aims of those who resorted to violent social protest were totally devoid of ideological content. Invariably those who practised violence believed they were right to do so and justified themselves in terms of their pursuit of some ideal or high purpose, which was frequently expressed as justice, humanity, freedom, liberty, or some such concept. *Rebecca*, like Robin Hood, embodied natural justice, and her children were all those to whom it was denied:

> When I meet the lime-men on the road covered with sweat and dust, I know they are Rebeccaites. When I see the coalmen coming to town clothed in rags, hard worked and hard fed, I known they are mine, these are Rebecca's children. When I see the farmers' wives carrying loaded baskets to market, bending under the weight, I know well that these are my daughters. If I turn into a farmer's house, and see them eating barley bread and drinking whey, surely, say I, these are members of my family, these are the oppressed sons and daughters of Rebecca.

An army of principles, according to *Rebecca*, would penetrate where an army of soldiers could not, and *Rebecca* did all by principle and nothing by expediency, including the issuing of a xenophobic edict that no Englishman should be employed as a steward in Wales.[26]

The East Anglian rioters rose 'to fight for their liberties',[27] as they understood them, and the crofters of Sutherland for their traditional rights to their lands. Their thinking and their motivation were, it has been suggested, essentially backward-looking, directed towards lost rights rather than to-wards any future restructuring of the Highland economy or the old system of land-owning and land-holding.[28]

Similarly with the *Luddites*, neither their techniques nor their beliefs would be of interest to organised workers of the next generation; they advanced no new political ideology and insofar as they showed a common economic philosophy it was expressed in the desire to salvage what could be saved from the wreckage of the old paternalist, protective legislation, particularly to restore the state to its traditional role as protector of working-class jobs against new inventions. Such aims have been interpreted as the expression of an anti-capitalist ideology, and Luddism has been suggested by Edward Thompson as the crisis point for capitalism which it successfully survived.[29] Such a view almost certainly exaggerates the degree of coherence in Luddite attitudes and ignores the extent to which capitalism had established itself long before this date in all three industries which experienced Luddism in 1812. It is also an exaggeration to see the Luddites in unconscious revolt against the factory system or, conversely and paradoxically, to see them as standard bearers of the alternative social and economic philosophy for the future that will find expression in campaigns for the legal minimum wage, opposition to sweated labour, compensation for redundancy, trade unionism, and the ten-hour movement. The Luddites were machine-breakers with precise grievances who sought precise remedies, and their activities will not carry too heavy an ideological imposition.

George Rudé, it has recently been said, found that the rioting English populace of the eighteenth century acted in accordance with a coherent set of beliefs and values,[30] concepts of Englishmen's 'rights' and 'liberties', including the right and liberty to persecute Catholics and foreigners, and Edward Thompson's exposition of 'The moral economy of the English crowd' has ascribed an ideology to food rioters who are said to have acted in defence of principles long embodied in law and practice on how food ought to be marketed and what expectations the poor had of society.[31] This resistance to a market economy in food is a parallel to the resistance to a market economy in manufacture, and the coherence of principles and motives might well be overstated, but food-rioting, like almost every other aspect of working-class behaviour in this period, will never seem the same as a result of Thompson's exposition.

It has been the almost universal experience of those historians who have examined movements of violent social protest in the first half of the nineteenth century that they have been unable to detect any clear underlying political motivation or aspiration towards a particular political position. At the same time all have uncovered some statement of political intent amongst manifestos and formulations that deal with the particular matters that are the subject of the current protest. For example, Wigan food-rioters of 1800 threatened their local magistrates, in the imagery of the day, with the erection of the 'Tree of Liberty', whilst London rioters in September of the same year were urged to remember that sovereignty resided with them.[32] East Anglian rioters in 1816 talked of pulling down the Parliament House and marching to London to demand their rights like 'Sons of Liberty',[33] while the history of Luddism is spiced with references to extreme political designs, both from those who were concerned to suppress the movement and from documents that allegedly emanated from within Luddite ranks. The interpretation of this difficult material has been fraught with much controversy, but historians have been inclined to discount much of it as empty rhetoric or alarmist fears rather than see it as an accurate indicator of what the Luddites were really attempting.[34]

In my own work on the revolutionary movement in early-nineteenth-century Britain I found that the revolutionaries who took to the streets in 1817 were almost totally devoid of any ideological position. Their revolution would be all kinds of things to all men. It offered them what would give them most pleasure and it would be implemented by means that were understood by no man. The Scottish rebels of 1820 were at least thinking in terms of the acquisition of political rights as the basis for moving forward towards the just society, but their ideological position received no clearer definition than this.

Indeed, during this period of Industrial Revolution there emerged no common working-class ideology that could serve as a basis for either political or industrial action. In the 1790s working men were more inclined to form Church/King mobs and display their hatred of foreigners in celebration of war victories than they were to adopt a revolutionary political position or a class stance. Popular sentiment was crudely patriotic. When riots occurred they were more likely to be against the local baker than the system of government, the local employer rather than capitalism, the factory system, or the Industrial Revolution. And the continued failure of the working classes to evolve a common ideological position for themselves as workers remained a feature of working-class response into the second half of the nineteenth century. Perceived grievances remained immediate and able to be satisfied without the need for fundamental change within the social and political system. And when they had grievances they looked for their removal not to ideas by which a better system might be achieved but to leaders who might exploit the existing system to short-term advantage or expose them to the whims and fancies of the individual in command. It is interesting that William Lovett should have called for ideas, not leaders. In their absence, those who participated in movements of social protest, peaceful or violent, were never in a position to posit an ideological alternative to that which supported the system under which their grievances arose.

At the same time it must be acknowledged that when people rioted and committed acts of violence they frequently did so for the upholding of rights which they supposed they possessed. The notion of popular rights derived from somewhere, and if no consistent ideological position emerged in these years this was hardly because of any shortage of ideas. Perhaps their very abundance was part of the problem. This was the age of the Industrial Revolution, when workers were torn between backward glances towards Tudor and Stuart paternalism – under which monarchs themselves had occasionally intervened to ensure that British workers were not left unemployed by inventions and scientific advance – and the ideas and attractions of the new industrialism, to be developed possibly along Owenite lines but capable of being squeezed to some advantage even if economic individualism triumphed over co-operation. It was an age of political revolution when sons of liberty marched and trees of liberty were planted on both sides of the Atlantic and the rights of man were again enunciated, but man as the political animal he had long been rather than the industrial animal he was about to become. It was also an age of religious revolution when the Bible, over the centuries a bountiful provider of seditious ideas, once more left the hands of its professional interpreters and became for some an inspiration of radicalism, for others a justification for social and political conservatism. All the major changes of the age ensured an intellectual ferment, but they scarcely guaranteed a clear-cut ideology for social protest.

It has never been difficult to make out a case for the efficacy of violence as a protest technique. Food-rioters as yet unnumbered must have had dozens of successes to their credit in fixing prices and stopping movements of grain; the Luddites had a host of short-term victories whatever their long-term achievements; *Swing* rioters have been cited as the most successful of all machine-breakers;[35] Reform Bill rioters have frequently been given credit for the passing of the Great Reform Bill; anti-Poor Law rioters undoubtedly affected the course of the implementation of the New Poor Law; *Rebecca* ceased her activities when the government agreed to an enquiry into the Welsh turnpike system and won 'a substantial victory with the passing of Lord Cawdor's Act'[36]; 'Collective-bargaining by riot', deemed a rational and successful technique for pre-industrial trade unions, had its triumphs in the nineteenth century too; and the list could be continued.

Yet for all these successes, violence did not become institutionalised in Britain as a normal and acceptable form of protest and expression. Quite the reverse occurred as food-rioting disappeared from English life, though persisting longer in remote areas of Scotland; trade unions adapted to a peaceful role of negotiation, and political campaigners demonstrated their numbers and their strength in public meetings where actions spoke more softly than words. Britain had found by the middle of the nineteenth century the means to accommodate potential violence within the political system or to export it to Ireland. It is neither Whiggish nor bourgeois to note this or to regret only that Irish history was about to enter another violent phase.

Whatever future discoveries about the nature of pre-industrial society, it seems reasonable now to view the age of the Industrial Revolution as a period when British politics and society were prone to violence for all sorts of reasons. Demographic change and population redistribution placed an impossible burden on the traditional machinery of law and order, which was not appropriately adjusted until the middle of the nineteenth century. Industrialis-ation introduced a whole range of new problems and anxieties into people's lives and into social relationships, and it was not until the 1840s that British governments began to show any real awareness of these problems and the new society which they were governing. Like all ages it was an age of transition, but it was also an age of revolution, and it is possible that when we have satisfied the present urge to catalogue the violence and count the violent we shall revert to traditional attitudes and wonder at how successfully and peacefully Britain passed through these times.

NOTES

1. E. J. Hobsbawm, 'The Machine Breakers', *Past and Present*, 1 (1952).
2. R. Quinault and J. Stevenson (eds), *Popular Protest and Public Order* (London, 1974) p. 15.
3. D. Read, *Peterloo: the 'Massacre' and its background* (Manchester, 1958) p. vii.
4. M. I. Thomis and P. Holt, *Threats of Revolution in Britain, 1789–1848* (London, 1977) pp. 53–7, 76–9.
5. Ibid., pp. 90–1.
6. A. T. Peacock, *Bread or Blood* (London, 1965) p. 32.
7. D. Williams, *The Rebecca Riots* (Cardiff, 1955) pp. 224–5.
8. N. T. Edsall, *The Anti Poor Law Movement, 1833–44* (Manchester, 1971) pp. 110–11.

9. Hobsbawm, 'Machine Breakers'.
10. Peacock, p. 71.
11. E. J. Hobsbawm and G. Rudé, *Captain Swing* (London, 1969) p. 305.
12. E. S. Richards, 'Patterns of Highland Discontent, 1790–1860', in Quinault and Stevenson (eds), p. 93.
13. Thomis and Holt, p. 87.
14. J. Wigley, *Nottingham and the Reform Bill Riots of 1831*, Transactions of the Thoroton Society (Nottingham, 1973).
15. Peacock, p. 72.
16. Hobsbawm and Rudé, p. 363.
17. E. P. Thompson, 'The Moral Economy of the English Crowd in the Eighteenth Century', *Past and Present*, 50 (1971).
18. C. Tilly, quoted in Quinault and Stevenson (eds), p. 27.
19. *Ibid.*, p. 106.
20. Thomis and Holt, p. 66.
21. *Ibid.*, p. 106; Quinault and Stevenson (eds), pp. 157, 171.
22. Peacock, p. 72.
23. M. I. Thomis, *The Luddites* (Newton Abbot, 1970) Chapter 2.
24. Quoted in E. P. Thompson, *The Making of the English Working Class* (London, 1968) p. 644.
25. M. I. Thomis, *Politics and Society in Nottingham, 1785–1835* (Oxford, 1969) p. 92.
26. Williams, pp. 117, 226.
27. Peacock, p. 32.
28. Quinault and Stevenson (eds), p. 105.
29. Thompson, *Working Class*, pp. 594–604.
30. Quinault and Stevenson (eds), p. 21.
31. Thompson, *Moral Economy*.
32. Quinault and Stevenson (eds), p. 56.
33. Peacock, pp. 64–5.
34. See Thomis, *The Luddites*, Ch. 3.
35. Hobsbawm and Rudé, pp. 17, 19.
36. Williams, p. 291.

4 Collective Violent Protest during the German *Vormärz*

Hans-Gerhard Husung

Le Bon's prejudice on the destructivity of masses, seemingly 'guided from the spinal chord rather than from the brain'[1] seemed to have been monstrously confirmed in National Socialism. The following relatively non-violent 1950s and 1960s with the establishment of democratic forms of participation and an unprecedented economic boom gave little occasion in the Federal Republic for concern with violent mass action. The use of violence in the political and social process was regarded as a phenomenon of the past which had been overcome. Astonishment at the aggravation of race riots in the USA, the events of May 1968 in France, student unrest at home at the end of the 1960s and finally the terrorism of the 1970s[2] was therefore all the greater. In the ensuing discussion on violence and its role in society it almost seemed as if the historical dimension had been forgotten in a country with no conscious revolutionary tradition, especially since historical science itself had scarcely systematically examined the question.   /

In earlier works any reference to violence in the *Vormärz* period tended to highlight spectacular events such as the storming of the Frankfurt guardhouse or the Silesian weavers' revolts; however such occurrences failed to be interpreted as various facets of one overall phenomenon. On the other hand the Great 1789 French Revolution had long occasioned thematic debate on violent popular protest. The theory of the political and social development of England, allegedly free of violence, had the effect of a challenge which contributed to comprehensive research on numerous expressions of violence in revolutionary mass action and 'bargaining by riot' (Hobsbawm).[3] The methods and explanatory concepts successfully applied in the development of this theory provided a valuable example for recent German research on protest. Moreover further stimuli were provided by sociology and political science, above all from American sources, which in analysis of theories on revolution focused on acts of violence.[4] R. Tilly was the first to attempt an analysis of collective protest in Germany from an historical perspective, correlating it with economic and social change.[5] H. Volkmann was equally motivated by theories on modernisation and conflict – and concentrated initially on the forgotten revolutions of 1830–2 in the German Confederation; in his research he developed a system of categories based primarily on adequacy of source and method, the analytical application of which was confined to the German *Vormärz* period.[6] Even for this relatively short period research on protest has so far only succeeded in identifying a few regionally isolated islands within the terra incognita of protest which will not permit any general statements on the German Confederation as a whole.

One of these islands is formed by the former North German states of Hamburg, Bremen, Brunswick, Hanover and Oldenburg, partly including protest action in the Prussian province of Saxony from the Restoration to the eve of the 1848 revolution. The individual background to over ninety disturbances originally compiled as case studies from press reports and archive material will not be touched upon in the following considerations on the role of violence in North German collective protest. Instead we shall examine and try to typify the activists and the causes behind their action, the role of the forces of law and order and the features of violence. Alongside breach of the peace as an expression of the agitators' commitment a further characteristic of agitation selected is that it is always expressed collectively, thus indicating causes going beyond the individual.[7]

The basic concept of violence implies that violence has a discernible beginning, i.e. takes the form of a course of events, a process, manifesting itself on objects and carried out by an individual or a group of individuals; phenomena of structural violence are therefore excluded by definition.[8]

The following differentiation between the classes involved in agitation appropriately reflects source material:[9]

(i)   the urban bourgeoisie: their participation was considered by contemporaries as striking and was therefore recorded in source material;

(ii)   the craftsmen: a problematic category since boundaries are very fluid – upwards into the bourgeoisie in the case of master craftsmen and downwards towards workers and day labourers.

(iii)   workers, day labourers: classified according to the activity of the person concerned at the time;

(iv)   the rural population: differentiation according to property ownership, although not impossible, is virtually uninformative without reference to size of property.

I

Collective protest tended to be regarded by the authorities and in publications of the *Vormärz* period as a conspiracy or as mob rioting. These interpretations colour source material available; written reports by the protestors themselves are few and far between and can therefore not be systematically brought into consideration to balance our judgement. Press reports must also be regarded with some reserve: even a comparison of a number of newspapers hardly increased the information value. Precisely in the case of events in the provinces news was often compiled by a reporter – not infrequently a citizen who was simply fond of writing – whose portrayal of events was exchanged and printed by more than one newspaper.[10]

Reports and protocols drawn up by the lower administrative authorities, police and the courts must undoubtedly be accorded considerable importance, although the picture tended to be coloured by a prejudice against the lower social strata. In the case of the police, the army and the civic guard in particular a strategy of suspicion was evident whereby their action was determined by external characteristics of status.[11] However this prejudice on the part of the authorities in the *Vormärz* period only partly explains the fact that members of the bourgeoisie are relatively seldom mentioned as participants in reports on violent protest. With the exception of university students the bourgeoisie never appeared as the sole activists. If they became involved in violence, then only in coalition with other agitating classes and in situations where the size of the assembled crowds and the discernible passivity or unreliability of the forces of order – that is, the probable inferiority of their strength – were such that the personal risk factor involved was relatively low. Furthermore the motivation behind protest and its target objects tended to contribute towards strong feelings of emotion regardless of class distinction, from which the bourgeoisie could hardly escape.

In Brunswick in September 1830, craftsmen, workers and day labourers were the first to become involved in mass demonstrations and stone-throwing at the Duke's coach in an attempt to draw attention to their strained social situation and to remind the young Duke of his traditional duties to introduce public building projects and corn subsidies. It was only on the second day of demonstrations when the hated duke hastily left for abroad and the army became conspicuous by its deliberate inaction that the bourgeoisie, including members of the newly-formed civic guard, joined in the protest which was to climax in the storming and burning of the castle.

Sympathy for and subsequent participation in the protest stemmed from the general unpopularity among bourgeois classes of Duke Karl II's policy: the Duke had bypassed the estates and attempted to deprive them of their rights of representation; he had escalated a dispute with Hanover/England, his important neighbour both politically and economically, over the legitimacy of George IV's regency in Brunswick and the constitutional provisions decreed, as a result of which the English monarch and his minister Count Münster had initiated action throughout the Confederation to obtain redress. On top of this came the Duke's arbitrary domestic policy which had politically embittered and economically weakened the bourgeoisie. The storing of large quantities of gunpowder within the town walls and the placing of canons in front of the castle in connection with feared demonstrations aroused particular irritation and indignation. Rumours of plans to bombard the city centre not only incited protest action but made such action seem both necessary and legitimate. The fact that the ducal castle thereby went up in flames was presumably not the intention of the bourgeois participants. On the contrary: popular chastisement of the Duke as a means of redress for grievances was to give way the following morning to alarm and fear of the sudden prospect of riotous action also being directed at bourgeois property. In anticipation of this danger hundreds of houseowners enrolled in the newly-formed citizens' guards which now successfully sought forces to suppress further socially motivated protest from the lower classes.[12]

The attempted revolt in the Hanoverian town of Göttingen at the beginning of 1831 came close to a bourgeois revolution at local level. Encouraged by events in Brunswick and incited to action by similar endeavours in the town of Osterode in the Harz, university teachers, students and citizens set up an autonomous 'Gemeinderat' (Communal Council) in the university town with quasi legislative and executive powers which tried to justify its resistance in the traditional manner under the motto, 'Wilhelm, unser Bürgerkönig weiß nichts davon'. ('Wilhelm, our Citizen King, is ignorant of this'); the Münster ministry thereby became more and more the hated symbol of rigid feudal social and power structures. For more than a week the Gemeinderat was successful in upholding its rule both externally against growing military pressure and internally against its opponents loyal to the authorities and the lower classes, who saw the overruling of the usual institutions of law and order as an opportunity to launch their own protest action. Finally, however, the Hanoverian government's ultimatum for peaceful and unconditional capitulation was complied with.[13]

For the urban bourgeoisie and the majority of academics active violent resistance against the concentrated forces of the King seemed to have little realistic chance of success. As long as the mere threat of violence was enough to prevent the functioning of the State and municipal authorities, citizens had no qualms about taking up arms against State authority. However they were only prepared for violent action in retaliation against attempts at protest from the lower classes.

Members of the bourgeoisie were much more frequently involved in violent protest action as upholders of law and order than as activists. Whereas in a number of Hanoverian cities and in the Duchy of Brunswick they took action only when State authority had been undermined and the genuine forces of order overtaxed, in Bremen and Hamburg the *Bürgermilitär* (Citizen's Militia) was a permanent force of order. These armed civic guards were generally characterised by a certain restraint in the use of forceful bodily violence; their intervention was generally limited to arresting suspects. It was because of this, the fact that their social prestige was higher than that of the police and the army and their ability to relieve a given situation without the use of arms, that the Senates put the *Bürgermilitär* into action against demonstrators first and foremost whenever possible.[14]

Apart from the spectacular exceptions already mentioned, the bourgeoisie preferred petitionism as a means of voicing their discontent, for which education and insight into the structures and functioning of the political system were important prerequisites.

The overriding aversion of 'property and education' to all forms of violent breach of the peace stood in contrast to riotous popular protest which had its real origins in latent conflict and was brought to a head by short-term events which could then be favourably interpreted as reason for protest action. The Duchy of Brunswick for example went through a wave of this form of protest spreading from the capital to the provinces as a result of the events of September 1830. Provision by the State of employment and public relief considered insufficient, unfair trials, the alleged bad running of the administration and oppressive customs barriers formed the background to the attacks on civil servants and other 'scapegoats' who with their property were to a certain extent held liable for professional and social behaviour.[15]

The causes behind protest and the action itself primarily reflected accustomed habits and traditional expectations on how and when the authorities and well-to-do individuals should provide work and assistance in times of economic crisis. In their protest action the German lower classes in the first half of the nineteenth century were still guided by ideas similar to those outlined by E. P. Thompson on the 'moral economy of the English crowd in the 18th century'[16]; protest action was thereby morally justified and was quite in line with traditional means of expressing discontent in early modern times. Breaking windows, unroofing houses, knocking down fences and cutting down trees in the garden of the 'breaker of the law' were all widely-practised forms of revenge and chastisement.

They were also applied in cases of insult to the social sense of honour of individual members of the lower classes, interpreted collectively,[17] which could indeed lead to the escalation of widespread disturbances. A striking example is provided by events in Bremen in 1827: the arrest of a journeyman shoemaker, allegedly begging, triggered off a wave of spontaneous solidarity among passers-by who followed the arrested journeyman to the debtor's prison; troops were quickly called to the scene and soon attracted the crowd's attention. When the struggle with the injured and the arrested continued the following day the authorities were forced to release the journeyman to calm down the situation.[18]

Such spontaneous solidarity among members of the lower classes was of constitutive importance for many disturbances, and not least since the social prestige of police and milita was low among craftsmen and workers and the stimulus threshold also correspondingly low.

To resume, it can be said that traditional popular unrest was characterised by a high degree of spontaneity, a low level of developed organisation and leadership and divergence among the activists who often split into factions in the course of the protest over the aim and objectives of their action.

These features were to a certain extent also characteristic of anti-semitic actions concentrated in our field of study on Hamburg with a relatively high Jewish population; the main activists were to be found among the ranks of craftsmen and retailers. In the widest sense this protest was part of the progressive process of dismantling the social order based on the estates; the Jews, outside the estates and open to the new liberal economic order, were regarded as a symbol of this process.[19] Latent anti-semitism was brought to a head in 1819 when in a precarious economic situation external examples pointed to the Jews as scapegoats: they were leading in the financial circles of the Hanseatic city and as retailers and non-guild craftsmen seemed to pose fearfully overestimated competition. Emancipation policy, cautiously being followed by the Senate, and the will of many Jews for emancipation gave a highly emotive teint to the tension which began with shouts of 'Hep-Hep' and ended in acts of violence against Jewish property.[20] The same motives lay behind similar action in 1830 which marked the beginning of widespread social and political protest and for a time totally paralysed the rule of the Senate.[21]

In contrast to riotous popular protest the craftsmen as a specific group were in a position to use their existing trade association for protest. The craftsmen had a distinct tradition of protest, the organisational basis of which was provided by the journeymen's fraternities. Precisely in the *Vormärz* period, however, the world of the guilds was subject to increasing pressure from two directions: in the political sphere the Senate was resolutely increasing its efforts to dissolve autonomous legal and decision-making bodies and to carry out the development of individual competition on a free market in line with the progressing capitalist economic system; for itself it claimed a legislative monopoly which was incompatible with organisations with their own legal prerogatives. From a socio-economic point of view the crafts were going through a deep structural crisis. As a result of year-long population growth more and more workers were thronging into the crafts so that the employment and wages prospects for individual craftsmen declined; early stages of industrial manufacture in Germany and increasing imports from abroad were further essential factors contributing to the dissolution of the structures of the 'old trades and crafts'.[22]

In accordance with their traditional ideas of a moral craft economy, the reaction of the journeymen was consistently defensive and aimed at the restoration of the old system that was on the decline. The maintenance of the guild privileges was suspiciously observed and any breach punished in the traditional manner – destruction of the tool or product involved. In 1818 for example builders destroyed a newly built watchhouse in Hamburg since the work had been contracted for financial reasons to builders outside the city. Formally a violation of the law, the guild's action was evidently not totally denounced by the Senate since serious sanctions were not imposed.[23]

Competition between local and non-local journeymen for work often led to violent conflict. The locals tried to reserve potential earnings for themselves and force their non-resident colleagues into the role of a reservoir of labour, available at any time. And since the authorities and master craftsmen had little interest in lodging unemployed non-local journeymen in the town over lengthy periods of time, those seeking employment were exposed, relatively defenceless, to the massive intimidation of the guildsmen. The threat and use of physical force emphasised the right claimed by the craftsmen, in particular the journeymen's fraternities, to regulate the labour market themselves.

In 1839 within such a limited conflict 'foreign' journeymen masons, having had their lodgings attacked over a number of days, left Hamburg and called upon their fellow guildsmen in Lübeck, Copenhagen and Hanover to 'chastise' the Hamburg municipality for not having protected them.[24] Similar events in Bremen in 1840 finally led the governments of the German Confederation to 'take concurrent measures with regard to those journeymen craftsmen who have abused the laws of the land by unlawful journeymen's associations, courts, calls of ill repute and the like'. Journeymen's courts continued to be held outside the towns 'in the middle of nowhere' with occasional police arrests and charges of ill repute, thus demonstrating in the following years the persistence of the traditional structures and customs of the journeymen.[25]

Apart from some trades where craftsmen worked alongside workers and day labourers and shared common material interests, as for example in the building trade, coal mining in the Harz or arms manufacture in Herzberg,[26] these lower social groups had no involvement in the inner structures of the guilds. Whereas the journeymen craftsmen followed a traditional ideology interpreting the whole of society from a corporative point of view, within which the social role of their own group was defined, stimulating protest motivation, workers and day labourers on the other hand were guided by their direct material requirements. Their social status was already that of a disembodied class and as such they could not expect any improvement from the maintenance or the restoration of corporative structures. Their specific protest action was more based on safeguarding their own economic position without being any more offensive in the use of violence than the 'honourable craftsmen'. When workers or day labourers protested against existing or threatened unemployment or unjust wages they initially tried to achieve their aim by a demonstration of their numbers and by voicing their demands orally. At this stage the arrest or dismissal of a few of the presumed ringleaders was frequent enough to bring the protest to a standstill.[27] Unlike the journeymen who could use their guild organisation for protest in various sectors and regions, their scope for protest was restricted since it was action specific to an individual group and their place of work was a central condition for protest. Protest among members of the proletariat working on road, dyke, railway and other public building sites — where large numbers of their class were employed in the 1840s — largely occurred concerning the jobs available to them in the

Vormärz period.[28] On the other hand in our field of study the process of industrialisation had not yet set in and the use of agricultural machinery was not even widespread, which explains the virtual absence of attacks on machinery.[29]

Another form of violent protest, the fixing of prices for certain basic foodstuffs by collective action and active resistance to the *Kornabfuhr* (exporting of corn) precisely in times of crisis – as was common practice in England up to the early nineteenth century[30] – was only of peripheral importance in our area of study. Even throughout the price rises of 1846/47, only isolated food riots took place. In and around Hamburg women and youths were the main participants in attacks on traders and bakers at a point (June 1847) when the price of cereals in general had fallen considerably but continued to rise in Hamburg due to foreign demand.[31] In rural areas the 'hunger protest' was widespread, above all in the Prussian province of Saxony against potato and cereal exports. This was to voice the right claimed by the local population to preferential and sufficient supplies at an appropriate price before foreign demand was met and forced prices up. Meanwhile plundering served for direct supplies. Similar action was also carried out in rural communities in the catchment area of Magdeburg, the Elbe trans-shipment point, where an additional cause was provided by the hoarding of supplies with a view to profiteering.[32]

With the Elbe as an important transport route, this area was largely integrated into the supraregional cereals trade resulting in motives for protest hardly to be found in other regions. Here the stability of relative autarkies guaranteed minimum supplies for the lower classes in accordance with the 'moral economy'. Private charity and municipal and State assistance still seemed to function more or less traditionally in rural areas and the towns.[33] Nevertheless it would be wrong to conclude from the lack of collective protest in rural areas that the situation was a relatively satisfactory one. Overpopulation, the overburdening of agricultural structures, the negative consequences of the dissolution of common property, widespread underemployment and increased self-exploitation characterised the strained social situation of the rural lower classes, above all the large group of spinners and weavers; in this context it is evident that those groups whose existence was most threatened were not necessarily the first to protest. The occurrence or non-occurrence of protest was not only determined by the collective forms of perception and concepts of legitimacy of potential protestors, but also by the respective conditions for protest activities. Thus the low level of protest in rural areas was also a result of the continuation of the rural way of life and work, into which farmhands and parts of the lower rural classes were still integrated despite signs that traditional structures were crumbling. Other factors were involved, such as scattered settlement, dominant in certain regions, the rudimentary network of communications and last but not least the lack of objects of protest among the authorities. A high level of competition for every prospective job and the lack of structural organisation also counteracted protest, alongside the fact that the numbers of potential protestors were lower than in the towns. In such an environment collective protest had to be organised in advance, thus making it easier for the authorities and landowners to forestall agitation by concessions or preventative repression.

II

The forces of law and order – the police, the army and town militia – played a central role in the course of collective protest action and the extent of violence involved. The professional forces of order were recruited mainly from non-locals who could either find no job or make no livelihood in a 'respectable' trade. Their low social prestige impeded their perception of their functions, producing latent tension *vis-à-vis* the civil population. Their inadequate, one-sided, military-oriented training generally left both the police and the army with no sense of civic consciousness or respect for civic liberties. Their action was determined by the logic of the authorities, focused on orders and obedience and coloured by prejudiced strategies of perception. They thought they had the law and State authority on their side although the legitimacy of their behaviour was more than frequently called into question by the population; this was in fact the underlying driving force behind a number of disturbances.[34]

The civic guards on the other hand were formed by locals with full citizen's rights, the basic premise for their recruitment being that the possession of property also implied an interest in maintaining law and order; the lower classes were therefore excluded. Integrated into daily civic life, the social esteem and respect enjoyed by individual citizens was transposed into the militia itself, so that it was in a position to alleviate an acute situation of conflict by mere words of persuasion. Their social prestige, the calming effect emanating from the presence of the militia and their restraint in using violence were interdependent.

Police and the army were often reliant on their superior ability to use weapons. Whereas demonstrators were at best armed with stones and sticks, the former on occasions made rigorous use of their swords and firearms. As the course of the unrest in Hamburg showed in 1830, beginning with anti-semitic riots which expanded to symbolic public objects of protest, the intervention of the army in particular by no means had an intimidatory or a calming effect, but on the contrary led to an escalation of violence: when troops were brought in on the second day, the protest immediately focused on the forces of order. Embitterment grew the following day when mounted reinforcements were brought in who, 'thrashing their swords blindly', apparently violently scattered a crowd protesting against arrests in front of the town hall. This action provoked such rage that after ominous clashes between both formations the leaders of the town militia demanded the withdrawal of the hated soldiers from the town. This demand proved to be justified two days later when, on a Sunday afternoon, many Hamburgers went to look at an inn in the quarter of St Paul which had been pillaged the previous evening and was now guarded by a spectacular military presence. A number of stones were thrown from among the crowd and the ensuing massive reinforcement of troops created a situation of confrontation. After a short warning the soldiers shot blindly into the crowd, thereby and in the subsequent street-fighting apparently killing fifteen onlookers including two children; at least as many again were badly hurt.[35]

Apart from being prepared for such unscrupulous use of violence other features were evident: crowds, which often gathered precisely where there was an unusual police or military presence, were regarded as an acute danger to public order and security and were thus to be obstructed. Arrests and the use of violence aggravated the situation of conflict, often launching renewed escalation of violence and counter-violence.

On the other hand the police in particular could rationally react without the use of violence if faced with a crowd of demonstrators large in number and if military reinforcement was not on its way. This was often the situation in villages and rural communities. Arrests were then often carried out at a later date when the crowd had long dispersed, the feelings of solidarity had subsided and the local police forces had been reinforced by troops or town militia. Judicial inquiries into protest action led to arrests only days after the actual disturbances. It is of interest to note however that arrests after the event aroused hardly any demonstration of sympathy or attempts to free the prisoners; obviously such arrests provoked little feeling of emotion or solidarity. There was less risk involved for demonstrators in situations where the forces of repression showed little determination or sympathised with the activists, as for example the Hamburg *Bürgermilitär* in anti-semitic action.[36] Furthermore in periods of frequent protest the probability of sanctions being imposed also diminished considerably, since simultaneous protest in a number of places overburdened the *Vormärz* State's potential of repression: it could not make its presence felt everywhere with sufficient force.

Throughout the year of crisis 1846/47 the authorities deliberately raised the threshold of sanctions so as not to aggravate general dissatisfaction and to avoid creating unnecessary occasion for protest. Thus a charge against an alleged ringleader in a Bread Riot came rather inopportunely for the magistrate of Norden. Obliged to hold an enquiry, he tried to limit his action to a minimum since 'it was dangerous to increase agitation among the workers here – not to be underestimated – by pulling in too many of their accomplices'.[37]

The forces of order tended to mediate in cases of disturbances based on rivalry between members of a specific trade or craft or a social class.[38] However if journeymen and workers were in confrontation with their masters and entrepreneurs in disputes over wages or working conditions, the authorities' action was guided by formal legal interpretation of public order whereby the interests of the entrepreneurs and master craftsmen tended to coincide with the State's role of protecting property and upholding the peace. Furthermore, precisely in the towns, the magistrate had the task of either directly fixing working conditions and wages for individual trades or to a certain degree acting as guarantor for the regulations defined relatively autonomously by the guilds.[39]

The authorities were particularly attentive to the railway construction sites which, in view of the masses of workers concentrated *in situ*, were regarded as a constant latent source of threat, not only to public order but also to society as a whole. In dealing with conflict and labour disputes in larger factories the authorities followed a dual strategy: repression of all actionistic protest and at the same time examination of the social grievance involved, often recognised as justified, with the aim of initiating positive change; this, however, was confined to very narrow limits as a result of the virtually unrestricted authority and right of disposal of the entrepreneur in the factory or on building sites.[40]

Although repression by the forces of order was dominated overall by the use of violence against persons it must nevertheless be taken into consideration that in the *Vormärz* period there was only a very narrow range between inaction and the use of violence and by definition every act of violence could only be directed against persons. The fact that troops' use of violence was particularly intense can be partly explained by the point of their intervention in the disturbance: troops were called in when local civil servants and police forces were unable to bring the situation under control in accordance with the authorities' wishes and protest had mounted. Under such circumstances troops had little scope for not resorting to violence unless the protestors were immediately intimidated and demoralised by their superior show of arms.[41] In most cases however the presence of troops led to renewed escalation of violence on both sides.

III

In *Vormärz* society collective violence, of detrimental effect to the majority of its members, socially, politically and economically, was not a phenomenon concerning a mere fringe group. Violence, above all against objects, was part of a ritual of traditional popular protest. For the otherwise largely 'mute' social strata violent protest had a multiple function with regard to groups and situations: as a spectacular, out-of-the-ordinary event it promoted the formation of groups and feelings of solidarity, whereby the inner structure of the groups thus formed mostly remained rudimentary and fluctuating. The use of violence was a means of expressing social discontent and the weight of oppression. At the same time it was a means of punishing those allegedly to blame who, with their property and function as civil servants, were held liable for the policy of the government. Since the masses were largely incapable of abstract thinking this personification of abstract causes facilitated the articulation of discontent and the satisfaction of spontaneous feelings of revenge. In certain cases acts of violence directly obstructed the functioning of the institution considered as oppressive, for example if customs barriers were destroyed or tax rolls burned.[42]

The conscious selection of objects of collective protest and their symbolic content indicates a correlation with the causes which made the use of violence seem rational to the protestors. Finally violence was an infringement of the law, in all probability posing a challenge to the authorities, thus facilitating the input of discontent and demands for redress into the political system and demonstrating that they had to be resolved immediately. Frequently the use of violence was not seen by its initiators as the breaking of a norm, but as a traditional, legitimate and autonomous form of counterviolence which precisely in the *Vormärz* period came into collision with the monopoly of power increasingly being pushed through by the State and its tendency to 'objectivise' domestic violence as 'constitutionality'.[43]

Against the background of later developments, precisely in the field of the labour struggle, it becomes evident that constitutionality also implies institutionalised means of expressing conflict and reaching a consensus, its most important medium being legal organisation. As the behaviour of the guilds in the *Vormärz* period illustrated, organisation alone without an appropriate mechanism for settling conflict, tended to produce violence, hinder the emancipation of their members and serve no function in socio-political protest.[44]

NOTES

1. G. Le Bon, *Psychologie der Massen*, (Stuttgart, 1968) p. 10ff.
2. Cf. R. Quinault and J. Stevenson (eds), *Popular Protest and Public Order: Six Studies in British History, 1790–1920* (London, 1974) p. 15; A. D. Grimshaw, 'Interpreting Collective Violence: An Argument for the Importance of Social Structure', in *The Annals of the American Academy of Political and Social Science 1970*, pp. 9–20, in particular p. 11; J. Bronowski, 'Protest – Past and Present', in *The American Scholar 38* (1968/69) pp. 535–46.
3. Cf., for example, A. Soboul, *Les sans-culottes en l'an II: Mouvement populaire et gouvernement revolutionaire 2 juin 1793–9 thermidor an II* (Paris, 1958); G. Rudé, *The Crowd in the French Revolution* (New York, 1959); D. H. Pinkey, 'The Crowd in the French Revolution of 1830' in *American History Review 70* (1964), pp. 1–17; E. J. Hobsbawm, *Primitive Rebels: Studies in Archaic Forms of Social Movement in the 19th and 20th Centuries* (Manchester, 1959). E. J. Hobsbawm, *Labouring Men* (London, 1974); E. J. Hobsbawm and G. Rudé, *Captain Swing* (London, 1969); G. Rudé, 'English Rural and Urban Disturbances on the Eve of the First Reform Bill, 1830–31' in *Past and Present 37* (1967); E. P. Thompson,

The Making of the English Working Class (London, 1965); J. Z. Ward (ed.), *Popular Movements 1830–1850* (London, 1970).

4. Rather than reference to individual sources cf. the comprehensive debate by G. P. Meyer, 'Revolutionstheorien heute: Ein kritischer Überblick in historischer Absicht', in *GG*, Sonderheft 2 (1976) pp. 122–76.

5. R. Tilly, 'Popular Disorders in Germany in the 19th Century: A Preliminary Survey', in *Journal of Social History* 4 (1970) pp. 1–41; R., L. and C. Tilly, *The Rebellious Century 1830–1930* (Cambridge Mass., 1975).

6. H. Volkmann, *Die Krise von 1830. Form. Ursache und Funktion des sozialen Protests im deutschen Vormärz*, Habil. thesis Univ. Berlin 1975; H. Volkmann, 'Kategorien des sozialen Protests im Vormärz', in *GG* 3 (1977) pp. 164–89. R. Tilly (ed.), *GG 3: Sozialer Protest* gives a discussion of the premises for research.

7. Details on most of the individual cases may be found in H.-G. Husung, *Politische Krisen und kollektiver Protest in Norddeutschland zwischen Restauration und Revolution 1848*, Ph.D. thesis Univ. Brunswick 1978. This includes a discussion on selection criteria.

8. Cf. Ch. v. Ferber, *Die Gewalt in der Politik: Auseinandersetzungen mit Max Weber* (Stuttgart, Berlin, Cologne, Mainz 1970) p. 22ff.; J. Galtung, 'Der besondere Beitrag der Friedensforschung zum Studium der Gewalt: Typologien', in K. Röttges and H. Sauer (eds), *Gewalt, Grundlagenprobleme in der Diskussion der Gewaltphänomene* (Basel, Stuttgart, 1978) pp. 9–32.

9. On the class problem in general: A. Kraus, *Die Unterschichten Hamburgs in der 1. Hälfte des 19. Jahrhunderts. Entstehung, Struktur und Lebensverhältnisse: Eine historisch-statistische Untersuchung* (Stuttgart, 1965), p. 3ff.; W. K. Blessing, 'Zur Analyse politischer Mentalität und Ideologie der Unterschichten im 19. Jahrhundert: Aspekte, Methoden und Quellen am bayrischen Beispiel' in *Zeitschrift für bayrische Landesgeschichte* 34 (1971) pp. 768–816; F. D. Marquardt, 'Sozialer Aufstieg, sozialer Abstieg und die Entstehung der Berliner Arbeiterklasse, 1806–1848' in *GG* 1 (1976) pp. 43–77; P. Aycoberry, 'Der Strukturwandel im Kölner Mittelstand 1820–1850' in *ibid*, pp. 78–98.

10. On the problem of source material cf. Tilly, *Disorders* p. 6ff.; Blessing, p. 78; L. Uhen, *Gruppenbewußtsein bei deutschen Arbeitern im Jahrhundert der Industrialisierung* (Berlin, 1964) pp. 23, 27.

11. Cf. A. Lüdtke, 'Praxis und Funktion staatlicher Repression: Preußen 1815–50' in *GG* 3 (1977) pp. 190–211.

12. Staatsarchiv (State Archives) of Lower Saxony, Wolfenbüttel (StAWF), HS VI 9 No. 61; 12 A Neu Fb. 2 B 11 II; T. Müller, *Stadtdirektor Wilhelm Bode. Leben und Wirken* (Brunswick, 1963); O. Böse, *Karl II. Herzog zu Braunschweig und Lüneburg: Ein Beitrag zur Metternichforschung* (Brunswick, 1956) is tendentious; Husung, p. 78ff.

13. Hauptstaatsarchiv (Main State Archives) of Lower Saxony, Hanover (HStAH), Hann. Des. 92 XLI 137 vol. I, II; W. Löschburg, *Es begann in Göttingen. Protestation und Entlassung der Göttinger Sieben* (East Berlin, 1964) pp. 20ff.

14. See the Senate decrees dated 27 Sept., 7/8 Oct. 1830; Staatsarchiv (State Archives) of the Free Hanseatic City of Bremen (StAHB), 2-D-20. b.2.a.

15. StAWF, 12 A Neu Fb. 4 C 143; 12 A Neu Fb. 2 II B 4, vols 1 and 2, 13, 15; 133 Neu 2196; 34 N Fb. 1 No XXI 15.

16. *Past and Present* 50 (1971) pp. 76–136.

17. E.g. the abuse of a servant girl by her master in Hanover 1832; *The Augsburg 'Allgemeine Zeitung' (AAZ)* No. 270, 296, 1832.

18. StAHB 2-D-17.b.4.

19. On the situation in general, R. Rürup, *Emanzipation und Antisemitismus: Studien*

zur 'Judenfrage' der bürgerlichen Gesellschaft (Göttingen, 1977) pp. 22, 57, 76ff.;
M. Behnen, 'Probleme des Frühantisemitismus in Deutschland (1815–1848)' in
Blätter für deutsche Landesgeschichte 112 (1976) pp. 244–79.

20. Staatsarchiv (State Archives) of the Free Hanseatic City of Hamburg (StAHH),
CI. VII Lit. Lb. No. 18, Vol. 8 Fasc. 1. Cf. H. Krohn, *Die Juden in Hamburg
1800–1850: Ihre soziale, kulturelle und politische Entwicklung während der
Emanzipationszeit* (Frankfurt/Main, 1967) pp. 10–11, 20ff.; E. Sterling, 'The
Hep-Hep Riots in Germany 1819' in *Historia Judaica* 2 (1950) pp. 105–42, in
particular pp. 245, 266–7.

21. StAHH, CI VII Lit. Me No. 12 vol. 5; Polizeibeh.-Kriminalw. C, Jg. 1831 No.
469, 539.

22. Cf. in general G. Schmoller, *Zur Geschichte der deutschen Kleingewerbe im 19.
Jahrhundert: Statistische und nationalökonomische Untersuchungen* (Halle, 1870)
pp. 624ff., 647; W. Ritscher, *Koalition und Koalitionsrecht in Deutschland bis zur
Reichsgewerbeordnung* (Stuttgart, Berlin, 1971) in particular pp. 167–8; W.
Köllmann, 'Bevölkerung und Arbeitskräftepotential in Deutschland 1815–1865:
Ein Beitrag zur Analyse des Pauperismus' in *Jb. Landesamt für Forschung
Nordrhein-Westfalen* (1968) pp. 209–54; J. Bergmann, *Das Berliner Handwerk in
den Frühphasen der Industrialisierung* (Berlin, 1973) pp. 12ff., 47–8, 55ff., 91ff.

23. J. F. Voigt, 'Zerstörung des neuerbauten Wachthauses am Steintor durch
Hamburger Hauszimmerleute im Juli 1818', in *Mitteilungen Vereins für
Hamburgische Geschichte* 10 (1911) pp. 73–4.

24. StAHH, Polizeibeh.-Kriminalw. C, Jg. 1836 No. 1807; H. Laufenberg,
Geschichte der Arbeiterbewegung in Hamburg, Altona und Umgebung (Hamburg,
1911) p. 87. Göttingen students left the town in 1818 and 1823; cf. Hoppenstedt,
*Aktenmäßige Darstellung der Vorfälle, welche letztverflossenen Sommer auf der
Universität Göttingen stattgefunden haben* (Hanover, 1818). AAZ No 221 (9.8);
No 222 (10 Aug. 1823).

25. Quoted from H. Pelger and M. Knieriem, *Friedrich Engels als Bremer Kor-
respondent des Stuttgarter 'Morgenblattes für gebildete Leser' und der Augsburger
'Allgemeinen Zeitung'*, 2nd edition (Trier, 1976) pp. 24–5. See StAHH,
Polizeibeh.-Kriminalw. C. 1821 No. 354; 1831 No. 575; 1836 No. 1807; 1842 No.
469; *Leipziger Allgemeine Zeitung*, No. 263 (19 Sept.); No. 301 (27 Oct.); No.
363 (28 Dec. 1840); and *Die Verbindungen der Maurergesellen oder authentische
Darstellung der bei den Verbindungen üblichen Gebräuche.*, (Lübeck, 1841) pp.
48ff., 89.

26. HStAH, Hann. 74 Herzberg K 91; StAWF, 12 A Neu Fb. 2 II B 3, 4.

27. Existing or threatened unemployment was the cause of protest in Brunswick,
Wolfenbüttel and Holzminden in the winter of 1830/31; Zentrales Staatsarchiv
(State Archives) Merseburg (DZM), Rep. 77 Tit. 509 No. 8 vol. 1; StAWF, 12 A
Neu Fb. 2 B 4, 6, 14. Wage disputes resulted in protest among diggers in
Hamburg, building workers in Bremerhaven, dykers in Varel and Norden and on
various railway construction sites; StAHH, Hann. Des. 80 Hann. I Ba 100;
Staatsarchiv (State Archives) of Lower Saxony, Aurich, (StAAUR), Rep. 6 No
10499, 10505; Rep. 32 a No. 619; AAZ No. 287 (13 Oct. 1844); No. 295 (22 Oct.
1845).

28. Cf. R. Fremdling, *Eisenbahnbau und deutsches Wirtschaftswachstum 1840–1879.
Ein Beitrag zur Entwicklungstheorie und zur Theorie der Infrastruktur*
(Dortmund, 1975) in particular p. 98; W. Wortmann, *Eisenbahnbauarbeiter im
Vormärz. Sozialgeschichtliche Untersuchung der Bauarbeiter der Köln-Mindener
Eisenbahn in Minden-Ravensberg 1844–1847*, (Cologne, Vienna, 1972) in par-
ticular pp. 74ff., 225; F.-W. Schaer, 'Zur wirtschaftlichen und sozialen Lage der

Deicharbeiter an der oldenburgisch-ostfriesischen Küste in der vorindustriellen Gesellschaft' in *Niedersächsisches Jb* 45 (1973) pp. 115–44.

29. In 1833 in the Kingdom of Hanover even less than 0.1 per cent of the population was employed in factories with over 10 employees; only 21 steam engines were in operation at the end of the 1830s; F. W. v. Reden, *Das Königreich Hannover statistisch beschrieben* (with particular reference to agriculture, trade and industry), 2 vols (Hanover, 1839) Vol. 1, pp. 300–1, 310ff.; K. H. Kaufhold, 'Entstehung, Entwicklung und Gliederung der gewerblichen Arbeiterschaft in Nordwestdeutschland 1800–1875' in H. Kellenbenz (ed.), *Wirtschaftspolitik und Arbeitsmarkt* (Munich, 1974) pp. 69–85, with particular reference to State measures. The abolition of 'machines in factories' was called for in 1830 in Eilenburg; DZM, 2.2.1. No. 15012; the violent obstruction of shipping in Syke was directed against the replacement of human energy by animals in the hauling of ships; AAZ Beil. 121 (1831). On the storming of machinery in the province of the Rhine, see D. Dowe, *Aktion und Organisation: Arbeiterbewegung, sozialistische und kommunistische Bewegung in der preußischen Rheinprovinz 1820–1852*, (Hanover, 1970), p. 25ff.; a summary can also be found in E. Todt and H. Radant, *Zur Frühgeschichte der Deutschen Gewerkschaftsbewegung 1800–1849* (East Berlin, 1950) pp. 86–7.

30. Cf. Thompson, 'Moral Economy'.

31. StAHH, Protocollum Senatus Hamburgensis (1847) No. 1; Patronat St.Pauli II A 7596; AAZ No. 172 (21 June); No. 174 (23 June 1847). On the price movement see J. G. Gallois, *Geschichte der Stadt Hamburg*, vol. 3, (Hamburg, 1855) p. 275.

32. See DZM, 2.2.1. No 16413, 16448. Also J. Stevenson, 'Food Riots in England, 1792–1818' in Quinault and Stevenson (eds), pp. 33–74, which clearly illustrates that protest was distributed in accordance with London's 'supply lines'. In general Thompson, 'Moral Economy', pp. 76–136.

33. On these activities see StAWF, 39 Neu 4 46; 126 Neu 4298; 12 A Neu Fb. 13n 48833; StAAUR, Rep. 21 a No 2424; Staatsarchiv (State Archives) of Lower Saxony, Osnabrück (StAOS), Rep. 300 No 1007, 1008; W. Abel, *Massenarmut und Hungerkrisen im vorindustriellen Europa: Versuch einer Synopsis* (Hamburg, Berlin, 1974) pp. 383, 420ff.

34. In general on the Prussian example: Lüdtke, *Praxis*; A. Lüdtke, 'Die "gestärkte Hand" des Staates: Zur Entwicklung staatlicher Gewaltsamkeit – das Beispiel Preußen im 19. Jahrhundert', in *Leviathan* 2 (1979) pp. 199–226; Volkmann, *Krise*, pp. 143ff.; Tilly, *Disorders*, pp. 22–3. On the prestige question, cf. J. Calließ *Militär in der Krise: Die bayrische Armee in der Revolution 1848/49* (Boppard/Rhine 1976) in particular pp. 48ff.

35. DZM, 2.4.1. No 8172; StAHH, CI. VII Lit. Me no. 12 vol. 4; Details on the victims in AAZ Beil. No. 261 (1830).

36. Ibid.; StAHH, Polizeibeh.-Kriminalw. C. No. 574 (1831); StAHB, 2-D-20.b.2.a.

37. StAAUR, Dep. LX880; the Ministry of the Interior however demanded energetic proceedings; HStAH, Hann. Des. 80 Hann. IA 654.

38. StAHH, Polizeibeh.-Kriminalw. C. No. 354 (1821); No. 575 (1831); No. 1807 (1836); *Leipziger Allgemeine Zeitung* No. 301 (27 Oct. 1840); K. Helm, *Die bremischen Holzarbeiter vom 16. bis zur Mitte des 19. Jahrhunderts* (Bremen, 1911) pp. 37–8.

39. The position of the Arnsberg government was in contrast to this and typical for the situation in Prussia: the old guilds had been disbanded; the relationship between journeymen and masters was solely that of an employment contract. Journeymen now belonged to the 'class of other working classes'; Staatsarchiv (State Archives) of Koblenz, Reg. Arnsberg No I 181.

40.   Cf. StAAUR, Rep. 6 No 10499; Rep. 32a No 619; DZM, 2.2.1. No 15012. In general Lüdtke, *Praxis* p. 200.

41.   This is how the Göttingen 'Gemeinderat' was persuaded to capitulate; subsequently there was no resistance to the occupation of the town for which 4,500 infantrymen, 600 cavalrymen and 10 cannons had been assembled from the Göttingen area. HStAH, Hann. Des. 92 XLI 137 vol. I. In general, Volkmann, *Krise*, p. 149.

42.   The Hesse provinces of Hanau and Fulda were particularly affected; ibid. p. 95ff., 190.

43.   Cf. M. Weber, *Wirtschaft und Gesellschaft*, ed. J. Winkelmann, 2 vols., 5th edition (Tübingen, 1976) here vol. 1, pp. 29–30, 361; vol. 2, pp. 516, 822. Further on the problem of legitimacy and the significance of protest experience, Thompson, 'Moral Economy', esp. pp. 78, 95; D. V. J. Bell, *Resistance and Revolution* (Boston, 1973) esp. pp. 77ff.; Volkmann, *Krise*, pp. 52, 98; H. Medick, 'Die protoindustrielle Familienwirtschaft', in P. Kriedtke et al., *Industrialisierung vor der Industrialisierung: Gewerbliche Warenproduktion auf dem Land in der Formationsphase des Kapitalismus* (Göttingen, 1977) pp. 90–154, here p. 52; K. Gerteis, 'Regionale Bauernrevolten: Eine Bestandsaufnahme', in *Zeitschrift für Historische Forschung* 6 (1979), pp. 37–62, esp. p. 55.

44.   Cf. U. Widmeier, *Politische Gewaltanwendung als Problem der Organisation von Interessen* (Meisenheim am Glan, 1978) esp. pp. 11–12, 37, 78.

5 Violence and Terror in Russian Revolutionary Populism: the *Narodnaya Volya*, 1879–83[1]

Astrid von Borcke

I

'The nihilists', it was said in a contemporary memorandum on terror prepared for the heir to the throne, the future Alexander III, had achieved what 'a Bismarck or a Beaconsfield' had not been able to do: to drive the Russian state to the brink of dissolution.[2]

In the Russia of the 1870s, terror had appeared more or less spontaneously, first in the South, where organisational bonds were weaker. Its success, however, was immense. After the assassination in August 1878 of the Chief of Section III, N. V. Mezenchev, D. A. Milyutin, the Minister of War during the Reform Period, noted in his diary that the 'satanic plan conceived by the secret society to terrorise the entire administration' was beginning to be successful.[3] The explosion in the Winter Palace of 2 February 1880 and finally the assassination of the 'liberator tsar' Alexander II on 13 March 1881 as well as the ensuing trials made even Western Europe see the 'nihilists' in a new light. 'To attract the attention of the entire world, is that not in itself a victory?' asked Plekhanov, the former great antagonist of the *narodnovoltsy*.[4]

The revolutionaries had relentlessly exposed the autocracy's lack of social support. Under the impact of the terror, Marx and Engels declared Russia 'the vanguard of revolutionary action in Europe'.[5]

The achievement of *Narodnaya Volya*, the first really significant organisation of 'professional revolutionaries' in Russia, was the creation of a quasi-'revolutionary situation', even in the absence of a mass movement from below. The party's 'Executive Committee' was able temporarily to paralyse the world's apparently most powerful police state. This was the work of a tiny minority (among a population of 90 million), for the 'committee' consisted of no more than 20–22 individuals at any one time.[6] Forty-four people had belonged to the original nucleus;[7] in addition there were around 500 people in the provinces,[8] who at the height of its power were grouped around the 'executive committee', plus an estimated 3–4,000 sympathisers, especially among the student youth.

Narodnaya Volya's revolutionary techniques and achievements were not lost on future generations of revolutionaries. Lenin's concept of a 'new type of party', characterised by professionalism, 'democratic centralism' and using 'front organisations' and sympathisers etc., was directly derived from the techniques developed by *Narodnaya Volya*. They may indeed even have had their effect on Hitler, who had been familiar at least indirectly, by way of the Okhrana forgery of the 'Protocols of the Elders of Zion', with the *narodnovoltsy*'s (members of *Narodnaya Volya*) organisational concepts.[9]

With the assassination of the tsar, the *Narodnaya Volya* had expended itself without being able to derive any tangible political profit from it. The murder of Alexander II (1855–81) – probably the best tsar of modern Russia – might be seen as politically totally unreasonable for it was the prelude to the reaction which set in under his successor, Alexander III (1881–94) that cost the radical intelligentsia many of its ablest representatives.

Yet in another sense the *narodnovoltsy* were eminently successful: they initiated the active confrontation between Russian society and the State. And they did, under Loris-Melikov's 'dictatorship of the heart' (1880), in a race against time, forestall limited reforms. From then on, the autocracy knew that reforms would be interpreted as a sign of weakness; indeed that reforms would by themselves lead to revolution. The radical intelligentsia, on the other hand, retained a vivid memory of the revolutionary heroes and martyrs that made any co-operation with the old State appear as treason.

The victory of Pobedonostsev's reactionary line over proposals for liberalisation by the more enlightened members of the higher bureaucracy was in essence already a victory for *narodnichestvo* over constitutionalism, liberalism, political modernisation and a more middle-class way of life. Thus, under Alexander III, the work of the great reforms (emancipation of the serfs, increased administrative autonomy, legal reform) was halted instead of being completed in the direction of granting society genuine political participation. At a time when industrialisation in Russia began to take off rapidly, Alexander III returned to the principles of his grandfather, Nicholas I (1825–55) – autocracy, orthodoxy, nationality – principles that had already been put in question by the Crimean War.

Narodnaya Volya thus made its decisive contribution in the prevention of the urgently required reconciliation between State and Society in Russia. This in turn increased the instability of the old regime. In this sense *Narodnaya Volya*'s terror represented a milestone on the road to revolution that led directly to 1905 and 1917, however little the Bolshevic revolution may have corresponded to the notions of the older revolutionaries.

II

One of the main sources of terrorism sprang from the intelligentsia's revolutionary maximalism. Apart from the influence exerted by radical Western European ideas, this was nourished principally by the absence of actual responsibility which the political system enforced. If active *narodnichestvo* (populism), the time of 'implementing' radical theories, began in the 1870s, the movement's spiritual roots lay deeper. Already Alexander Herzen (1812–70), in the atmosphere of 1848, had asked the would-be revolutionary whether he was prepared to break totally with traditional civilisation, way of life, religion and morality.[10] N. Dobrolyubov (1836–68) denounced the forties' generation's lack of fanaticism as *oblomovshchina*. Pisarev (1840–68) demanded to strike out 'left and right'; 'What can be smashed, must be smashed.'[11] Chernyshevsky (1828–89), in creating his mysterious figure Rakhmetov, proclaimed the professional revolutionary as the 'salt of the earth'.[12] Tkachev (1844–85) described the 'people of the future' as totally dedicated to the triumph of their idea and not to be deflected by 'any secondary considerations'.[13] Even the strict moralist Lavrov (1823–1900) declared:

> What we need are energetic, fanatical people, who risk all and are prepared to sacrifice everything: what we need are men whose legend by far surpasses their true worth.[14]

For reasons of this sort, Bakunin (1814–76) admired in a man like Nechaev the 'pure strength', indeed 'the saint'.[15]

With the *nechaevshchina* (the misdeeds of S. G. Nechaev (1847–82)) the 1860s' movement of political conspiracy reached its climax and degenerated into a travesty.[16] Nechaev made the intelligentsia aware of the problem posed by 'revolutionary reason', by demonstrating that all ethical nihilism left in the end was the naked will to power. New approaches appeared to be necessary; hence the origins of *narodnichestvo* as a movement.

P. Lavrov, in his *Historical Letters* of 1868/9 proclaimed – instead of a nihilism trusting in the primacy of reason, as propagated by the 'enlighteners' of the 1860s – a new message to an intelligentsia thirsting for fresh values: their 'debt before the people'. At the same time Bakunin took up again Herzen's call of the early 1860s: 'Back among the people!'[17] A further source for the *narodniki*'s thinking was the famous Appendix A to Bakunin's *Statehood and Anarchy*.[18] The belief in the autonomous action of the people and the *narodniki*'s apoliticism and anarchism received a further impulse from the Paris Commune, that is to say, from its myth.

When in the spring of 1874 the police smashed the Chaikovtsy circle which, under the leadership of Nechaev's notable antagonist M.A. Natanson, had executed the preliminary organisational work for the move back among the people, the Bakuninists had a clear field. In a fit of mass Rousseauism, thousands of the young and not-so-young went among the people, to prove their faith, to 'reconnoitre', to get to know this 'sphynx', the people; to live 'decently', that is to say as workers, and finally also to stir up the people by 'lightning propaganda' from 'zero to infinite' (D. Rogachev).[19]

The movement ended in fiasco. The government did not sit idly by while the propagandists attempted to 'Proudhonise and Lassallise' the country, evidently bent on undermining the old civilisation completely. The entire police apparatus went into action and there followed mass arrests. Very soon the *narodniki* had only just over a dozen men left at large among the people. 'We were literally beaten by the government', as V. Debogory-Mokrievich recorded.[20]

The second attempt to popularise Western socialism and to create a basis of trust by 'settling' among the people was not much more successful. The confrontation with the State spared the *narodniki* from making an assessment of their defeat in all its implications. In a sense they had been defeated by the very people they fought for (V. Figner).[21] Western socialism bounced off the Russian peasants 'like a pea off a wall' (S. Kravchinsky).[22] The people were politically apathetic and met their 'benefactors' with mistrust. By 1876 morale in the radical camp was low: emigration increased, many were attracted to Serbia and Herzegovina, where they gathered their first combat experience in the service of the 'slav question'.

The government's policy helped the revolutionaries. In April 1877 Russia declared war against Turkey. Once again the weakness and inefficiency of the old regime fully revealed themselves. The peace of San Stefano was followed by the Berlin Congress (1878), which was felt to be a grave diplomatic defeat. In society oppositional and constitutional voices were raised: the famous publicist N. K. Mikhailovsky even predicted the emergence of a 'secret committee of public safety'.[23]

1877 was also the very year in which a number of great political trials took place, notably the so-called trial of the 193 (members of the movement 'Back among the people') which significantly contributed to the formation of precisely the kind of social-revolutionary party whose spectre the government sought to banish. The terror began with the shot Vera Zasulich fired at the commanding officer of St Petersburg, F. F. Trepov, on 24 January 1878, the day after the conclusion of the 'trial of the 193' (in order to avenge the flogging of a radical student). The enthusiastic reception of her acquittal by jury – the latter had rejected the mere fact of attempted murder – was bound to make it appear that society approved of terror.

Terror, however, made one thing clear: the radicals were not principally waging war against social injustice or the threat of incipient capitalism, but against the State.

This perception had already gained ground in the early 1870s in the South, under the influence of the *Zemstvo*-Movement and the Ukrainian nationalists. The aims, however, which V. Osinsky proposed to the Council of *Zemlya i Volya* (Land and Freedom) in the winter of 1877/78 were frustrated by the opposition of such orthodox *narodniki* as Plekhanov, who were not prepared to let the radicals get 'the chestnuts out of the fire' for the liberals and thus, as they saw it, simply work towards the rise of the bourgeoisie.

Osinsky, with the approval of Alexander Mikhailov, returned south early in 1878 in order to test the possibilities and limitations of terrorism in Kiev. On 23 February 1878 he attempted to assassinate public prosecutor Kotlyarevsky; on 24 May there followed G. Popko's attempt on the life of Baron Heyking, the town's police chief. (Both were known for their liberalism and were thus far from being embodiments of an autocratic regime of terror.) With this the name of a (fictitious) 'executive committee' of an alleged 'social-revolutionary party' gained some prominence. (The links with Nechaev's *Narodnaya rasprava* – People's Revenge – are evident.) At the same time, Osinsky, the 'Apollo of the Revolution', with his daring and his manifest death wish, gave terrorism an aura of romanticism, which was heightened further by his arrest and execution in 1879; under the impression of his testament, the 'executive committee' of what was to become *Narodnaya Volya* was formed in Lipetsk in 1879.

Meanwhile those in the capital had evidently no desire to lag behind the provinces. On 4 August, two days after the execution of I. M. Kovalsky in Odessa (who had been the first to offer armed resistance against his arrest) S. Kravchinsky (Stepnyak) murdered the Chief of Section III, N. V. Mezenchev, in broad daylight on the Nevsky Prospect and was able to escape abroad. In his brochure 'Smert za smert' (a death for a death) he already justified the assassination in purely political terms: until political freedom was granted the radicals would continue their acts of terror. This created· a profound impression. Secretary of State P. A. Valuev, one of the most intelligent statesmen of his day, already felt that the 'ground was shaking under one's feet'.

In effect, Mezenchev's assassination was followed by a wave of arrests, which almost numbered amongst its victims also the (second) *Zemlya i Volya* that had been formed in 1876/77 under the leadership of Natanson. The reconstitution of the organisation in October 1878 was primarily the work of Alexander Mikhailov, one of the great organisers in Russian revolutionary history. For the populists this meant a turning point, since their hitherto diffuse movement now acquired a tight central organisation. Linked to this was a return, in a sense, to the conspiratorial political activities of the 1860s, as it were on a higher level.

Under Mikhailov, the spirit of political terrorism gained ground. It was reflected in the organisation's new statutes and in its programme, which then listed the 'disorganisation of the state' amongst its declared aims.[24]

This resulted in tensions *vis-à-vis* the orthodox propagandists. Terrorism began to claim the movement's human and financial resources to an increasing degree. The propagandists, however, were also made to pay in their work 'among the people'. Hardly had they achieved their first results and 'bang! the intelligentsia goes and eliminates someone and everything is destroyed again', complained Khalturin, co-founder of the North-Russian Workers' Association. 'If only they'd give us some time. . .'[25]

It was the opponents of this new trend, G. V. Plekhanov and O. V. Aptekman, who were among the first to see through the immanent logic of the party's terrorism: it meant a turn to a fight for purely political objectives, disregarding the true socialist concerns of the *narodniki*, and thus, in their view, tantamount to a betrayal of the people in favour of the interests of the privileged classes and a new bourgeoisie. Mikhailov, on the other hand, countered this by arguing that the party was not strong enough for anything else.

When on 2 April 1878, Alexander Solovev, an old *narodnik* who had worked among the people for a long time, made an attempt on the life of the tsar, 'privately' supported by Mikhailov and a number of the organisation's members, the time had come to set out basic principles: this was the purpose of the Party 'Congress' of Voronezh in June 1879.

Before this, however, the 'innovators', who had to reckon with expulsion from the party, met in Lipetsk, a spa near Kiev, in order to coordinate their efforts and to be able to present a united front: this was the occasion when the 'executive committee' came into being, out of the group *Svoboda ili Smert* (Freedom or Death) which had been formed around 2 April 1878 (by A. Mikhailov, L. Tikhomirov, S. Shiryaev, N. Morozov, A. Kvyatkovsky *et al.*). They met while still under the immediate impact of the execution of several comrades. Morozov opened the proceedings by reading Osinsky's testament which culminated in a call to continue on the path of terrorism. Michaylov, in one of his rare speeches, demanded the death sentence for the tsar, irrespective of his 'two good deeds' (emancipation of the peasants and law reform) at the beginning of his reign. The death sentence on the tsar was carried unanimously. Looking back, A. Kvyatkovsky reflected however: 'All acts where sentiment is the guiding factor . . . lead one further on occasion than one would oneself have wished.'[26]

In Voronezh a break was avoided: these young people, who had fought and suffered together, were too close for that. Only Plekhanov left, whom many already considered a grumbler. After the return to St. Petersburg, however, separation became inevitable and took place in all amity in August, and *Zemlya i Volya* split into *Narodnaya Volya* and *Cherny Peredel* (Black Repartition): the land went with the one, freedom with the other, as one contemporary remarked philosophically. Plekhanov, the former spokesman of the orthodox *narodniki*, conceded later that in practical questions the narodnovolcy had been in the right.[27]

It was the politically terrorist *Narodnaya Volya* which, in the ensuing two years, managed to gather around itself all the movement's spiritual and material forces. The 'death sentence' on the tsar was confirmed in St. Petersburg. From then on, the hunt for the 'crowned game' (M. Pokrovsky) took up the organisation's entire strength: eight attempts on the tsar's life followed each other in rapid succession. Particularly spectacular was the explosion in the Winter Palace in February 1880, organised by S. Khalturin and causing a sensation throughout Europe. This made the government realise that the system of military dictatorship by six governors general –

which had been the response to Solovev's attempt of 1879 – was not leading anywhere. In the bureaucracy's top echelons old constitutional projects of the time of the Great Reforms were revived. This marked the beginning of Loris-Melikov's 'dictatorship of the heart' (Katkov). Originally conceived as purely repressive, it attempted, up to August 1880, by a clever combination of selective repression and reasonable concessions towards society, to create a 'vacuum' around the revolutionaries, in seeking to overcome the disastrous passivity of the moderate majority in the country. This new approach was not without success. In the face of this incipient 'betrayal by the liberals' began the *narodovoltsy*'s race against time; they now tried to forestall reforms which, while falling far short of their own ideas, would nevertheless endanger their revolution.

On 1(13) March 1881 Alexander II met his fate. It was precisely the day on which the tsar had signed Loris-Melikov's draft of a proto-constitution. But as Zhelyabov had anticipated, with this deed the revolutionaries had in effect shot their bolt. Alexander Mikhailov had already been arrested at the end of November 1880. At the turn of the year they lost N. Kletochnikov, their agent in Section III, to whom they largely owed their sensational successes; on 27 February, the eve of the assassination, the police apprehended the man who was probably the most important among the terrorists, A. I. Zhelyabov.

The 'Executive Committee' – or what was left of it – had not even been properly prepared for a successful attempt: an entire week went by before the letter to the successor, written by Tikhomirov (with the stylistic assistance of N. K. Mikhailovsky), was published. This document – 'of cunning moderation' (K. Marx)[28] – merely demanded the 'legalising of the supreme power', since 'we possess no government in the true sense'.[29] Not one word about revolutionary aims. And in effect the true addressee of this letter, several thousand copies of which were distributed, was liberal society. This, however, was the last time that a common front was made with the liberals – a line which Mikhailov and Zhelyabov had advocated.

During the period of decline, the Executive Committee fell to the leadership of the 'jacobins': the concept of conspiracy and *coup* – which, in the last analysis, was the true *raison d'être* of terrorism – gained the upper hand. The aim of terror had been, after all, that in the imagination of the people the party should replace the tsar 'as the symbol of power and legitimacy' (Tikhomirov).[30] The fact that, after the destruction of *Narodnaya Volya*'s Moscow branch in the autumn of 1881, the military organisation was left as the 'party's' main prop further militated in the direction of 'Blanquism'.

In the middle of 1882 Tichomirov, the party's ideologist, also emigrated. This in effect spelled the end of the 'Executive Committee'. There remained V. Figner, the 'Venus of the Revolution', who had retired to the South; as a result of Degayev's denunciation, she was arrested in Kharkov in February 1883. With Degayev's betrayal, the 'party' became an instrument of the police.

After Degayev, in order to rehabilitate himself as a revolutionary, had instigated the murder of the highly talented police chief G. Sudeykin in December 1883, the time was ripe for attempts to rebuild the party, made amongst others by G. Lopatin in 1884, by B. Irzikh in 1885, L. Bogoraz in 1885 and by '*Narodnaya Volya*'s Terrorist Faction' (whose most prominent member was Lenin's brother Alexander Ulyanov) in 1887.

In practice, however, with the attempt on the life of the public prosecutor at the Military Tribunal of Odessa, Strelnikov, in March 1882, political terror had come to an end until 1901. This served as confirmation that terror is only possible in liberal systems or in modified autocracies: in this respect, too, the reactionary movement under Alexander III had managed to put Russia once again 'on ice' (K. Leontev).

The revolutionaries had gone too far – or not far enough. Instead of 'legalising' the government they had in fact, just like the Decembrists towards the end of Alexander I's reign, aided the reaction (in a form they had not deliberately intended).

Yet in a certain sense it was nevertheless a victory: the *narodnovoltsy* had demonstrated what a united, professionally organised minority was capable of, if it organised itself well and husbanded its resources rationally. More than that, the victory of Pobedonostsev's reactionary line over the proposals for liberalisation made by Loris-Melikov and others was, as I have said earlier, a kind of victory for *narodnichestvo*, an option for the principles of populism, against liberalism and a constitutional system, and against Russia's turning increasingly middle-class.

III

J. Conrad, a brilliant expert on the psyche of radicals, interpreted the Russian terror as a reaction of 'senseless despair' against an absurd tyranny.[31] It is true that *Narodnaya Volya*'s terrorism must be seen against the backcloth of the old regime's policies, policies which had served to alienate an awakening society from the State, made it sympathise instead with revolutionaries and prevented the intelligentsia from gaining political experience, from learning. It would mean a gross oversimplification, however, if one were merely to follow the revolutionaries' own concept, which saw terror as solely enforced by the regime. It would mean indeed accepting the maximalist, social-revolutionary premises as the only realistic basis for the country's further development – ideological premises, at that, which had already been rendered highly questionable by the radicals' own experiences.

It is true, however, that amongst the *narodnovoltsy* there existed hardly any who were terrorists as a matter of principle, for whom terror was a truly serious political weapon: the only ones who might be called terrorist in the

narrow sense were the rather pedestrian G. D. Goldenberg, the murderer of
the governor general of Kiev, Kropotkin; and G. Romanenko, who later,
significantly, went over to the proto-fascist 'Black Hundreds'. N. Morozov,
the prototype of the 'liberal with the bomb', wrote his propaganda of terror,
which he saw as the means of revolution here and now, indeed as its very
essence, but was only able to publish it abroad with the aid of the jacobin
Nabat-Group; Zhelyabov even planned to write a reply.

Narodnaya Volya's programme declared explicitly that individuals and
groups standing outside its fight aganist the government would be treated as
neutrals; their persons and property were to be inviolate. It is indeed
remarkable that in the period of *Narodnaya Volya's* political terror – which in
an autocracy was of necessity (V. Figner) directed against the head of state, the
autocrat – the overall number of political murders declined.[32] In a
democracy, the *narodnovoltsy* rejected terrorism on principle, as their remarkable letter of condolence on the occasion of the murder of the American
President Garfield, in September 1881, showed:

> In a country where freedom allows the individual an honourable intel-
> lectual fight, where the free will of the people not only determines the law,
> but the persons in government; in such a country political murder as a
> combat method is *a manifestation of the very same despotic spirit we have
> made it our task to destroy.* The despotism of a person and the despotism of
> a party are equally to be condemned, and violence can only be justified if it is
> directed against violence.[33]

Indeed many *narodnovoltsy* – among them the most prominent of the
'terrorists', Zhelyabov – soon came to see terror as not even a very promising
fighting method; by the autumn of 1880 their faith in the omnipotence of
terror had already been shaken. A. Kvyatkovsky, for instance, said in prison
that terrorism which was directed against individual members of the
government could not form part of 'any programme intended to be taken
seriously':

> The activity of any individual within the government is merely a manifes-
> tation of a particular system of government. The elimination of individual
> people, in this case, only leads to their replacement by others.[34]

This was Plekhanov's logic, who had cynically predicted that all the
narodnovoltsy would achieve would be that the name of Alexander would
henceforth be followed by 'three strokes' instead of two (a logic, however, that
played down the role of the personality in an autocracy rather too drastically).

The *narodnovoltsys'* real insight did not concern the power of terror, but the
importance of politics, of organisation, of institutions and of the state for the
life of a society. Out of this in the end grew certain significant liberal

departures, once revolutionary hopes had been dashed. Zhelyabov, formerly an admirer of the liberal Baron Korff, thus came to the conclusion that the real aim was not the emancipation of the peasants, indeed not even of the working class, but the 'renewal in general of the entire people'.[35] Alexander Mikhailov reflected analogously that they were in effect fighting for the 'purely radical ideals of the educated classes', which are 'totally divorced from the mass of our peasants'.[36] In A. Kvyatkovsky's view the issue in Russia was not the antagonism between capital and labour: 'Here in Russia the people's cause is a purely political issue – the issue of the people's participation in political life.'[37]

Terror had begun spontaneously: 'as revenge, as sensation, in order to diminish society's faith in the government'.[38] It had not turned into the party's main concern through any formal resolution, but because it had developed a kind of momentum of its own. 'We were taken over by terror', as Zhelyabov confessed.[39] Terror was thus not based on a unified political philosophy and even less on clear objectives. New members, according to Morozov, were not asked for their political views 'on socialism, anarchism, constitutions, republics. . . . 'We only asked: are you prepared this instant to offer your life, your personal freedom and all you possess for the liberation of your country?'[40]

The psychology of life in the underground affected them also in this sense. As N. A. Bakh recorded: once he had taken the path of revolution, he was 'utterly determined not to try to decide anew issues that had already been decided'.[41] The life of a terrorist, in any case, did not leave much time for reflection: Zhelyabov, who had originally regarded the publication of a theoretical magazine as the party's main task, complained that he hardly found time to read even *one* book. In the end, the highly educated G. P. Isayev was able to speak of nothing but bombs and dynamite. 'The terrorists in general were not reflective people', was Tikhomirov's summing-up.[42] What held them together was their shared passion, their shared struggle and thus, not least, the particular psychological dynamic force operating within the microcosm of a peer group, for which revolution (as R. Pipes has remarked so perceptively) was essentially the symbol of its group loyalty.[43]

Under the name of *Narodnaya Volya* – consciously or unconsciously ambivalent in itself – were thus gathered representatives of quite diverse tendencies: radicals, 'jacobins', liberals, and even a social democrat (A. Zundelevich).

The motive of power was no doubt central for someone like Lev Tikhomirov, the 'jacobin' main ideologist, and for his closest associate, Alexander Mikhailov, the man of practice, who had started from the basic assumption that power does not lie 'in the elaboration of even the truest theories, but in perfect organisation'.[44] For this reason he made his ironical remark about the party organ (when someone complained about Morozov's apologia of terrorism in the paper's supplement, *Listok Zemli i Voli*), that a blank sheet of paper would be best! He considered debates about political objectives to be inappropriate at a time of struggle and in this followed the views of Tkachev and Nechaev. In effect 'jacobinism', i.e. the striving for a political *coup* and for the revolutionary-socialist dictatorship of an 'elite' gained increasing impetus within *Narodnaya Volya*. Tikhomirov indeed interpreted the terror as the beginning of a failed *coup d'etat*.[45]

Narodniki such as Perovskaya, on the other hand, initially regarded terror as the spark that would set off the great explosion (manifesting the influence of Bakunin's thinking). It would 'unfetter' the hands of the people.Made more cynical by experience, Perovskaya then thought that after repeated (!) assassinations of tsars the peasants would conclude that the government had fallen into the hands of the landowners and rise against them.[46]

But when the people even after the murder of the tsar still showed itself apathetic, indeed hostile and when even pogroms followed, the idea of a political conspiracy came to the fore once more. 'In the end, we, the members of the executive committee, thought like jacobins', recorded Chernyavskaya, M. Oshanina's girl friend.[47]

Nevertheless, the conspiracy idea was never thoroughly discussed within the party as a whole (V. Figner). It showed, however, that Akselrod had been an able prophet, when he predicted in 1878 that the revolutionary populist movement in the end would disintegrate into constitutionalism or jacobinism.[48] The same dilemma was also to be a mark of the revolutionary movement of the future, when Plekhanov – under changed social 'determinants' – created out of Marxism a new 'algebra of revolution': politics is evidently more than a mere epiphenomenon of social and 'class' conditions.

The political ambivalence of the *Narodnaya Volya* movement even had its tactical value, since for a long time it was considered as an ally by liberal society. And liberal support, as the 'jacobins' Tkachev and Nechaev had stressed, was vital: it provided connections, cover addresses, secret hideouts and, not least, financial backing, for the *narodnovoltsy*, as a rule, possessed no money. Kravchinsky estimated that the three attempts on the life of the tsar alone had swallowed up between 30,000 and 40,000 rubles.[49] It is significant that the loss of liberal support was one of the decisive factors which led to the party's decline.

The Russian liberals until 1917 tended not to recognise the existence of any enemies on the left. In reality, however, the *narodnovoltsy* were no constitutionalists at all (as one might be led to believe by the Executive Committee's letter to Alexander III); their watchword was not the constitution, but *Zemsky Sobor* the constituent assembly. This, however, was tantamount to demanding that the old regime should dissolve itself. Karl Marx very accurately called the constituent power the 'posited revolt' (*gesetzte Revolte*),[50] for it had been the legislative power which had not only made the French Revolution but every other 'great, organic, general revolution' as well. The legally well-versed Zhelyabov spoke, no less clearly, of a 'commission of liquidation'.[51]

Narodnaya Volya's aims may have been democratic, but they were certainly not liberal: the Executive Committee in its letter to Alexander III consistently argued that even civil liberties were merely a 'provisional measure' until the constituent assembly had been called.[52] The members of the party saw themselves essentially in the role of the historical jacobins at the head of a revolutionary popular movement: it was no accident that the phrase 'the year 1793 of the Russian peasants' was reiterated time and again. They assumed that no other organised social forces able to oppose them would remain. Indeed, the 'jacobins' among the *narodnovoltsy* went further and argued that already the provisional government would have to carry out the actual political and social revolution, which would then merely remain to be sanctioned by a national assembly – a national assembly, moreover, that was to be kept free of opposition elements. In the meantime all one could demand, according to Tikhomirov, was the 'appeal to the people' . . . 'But we need not now broadcast to all the world what we want to achieve with this appeal.'[53]

Of course, not all the members of the organisation were in agreement with such a programme. In the eyes of the *narodniki*, who were not least pupils also of Proudhon, jacobinism was purely and simply the revolutionary Fall of Man. At least it did possess political consistency.

These debates show how little *Narodnaya Volya*'s fight against the old regime reflected the aspirations of the socially under-privileged classes themselves. The progressive *Delo* in the end went so far as to denounce terror as 'being based on narrow party interests', as 'self-interested and hostile to the people'.[54] The oppositional 'Young *Narodnaya Volya* party', which formed around the middle-class poet P. F. Yakubovich in the winter of 1883 in St. Petersburg, regarded terror as the main and immediate reason for *Narodnaya volya*'s failure: it had alienated the party from the people.[55] The 'Young party' therefore advocated (as Plekhanov had done before) an allegedly more populist economic (as opposed to political) terror.

In brief, the rise of *Narodnaya Volya* stemmed precisely from the recognition that the revolution they desired possessed no social base, or that at best the people might have to be manipulated. Ever since the Great Reforms the number of recorded peasant disturbances had in fact declined drastically; at the height of these disturbances their incidence had been twenty times greater.[56] The gathering movement of an emergent urban industrial proletariat that followed in the wake of the industrial crisis of the early 1880s did not, for the time being, alter this picture in any essential way, even though this development prompted the *narodnovoltsy* in 1882/83 to turn towards the workers. The Great Reforms, for all their half-heartedness, had stabilised the old regime for years to come and this was the reason why revolutionary populism failed.[57]

Narodnaya Volya was an organisation of the young intelligentsia, a kind of new middle class, consisting of *raznochintsy* (intellectuals who had abandoned their original class) and the lower gentry. But even such men of the people as Zhelyabov (who had still grown up as a serf), S. Shiryaev (also from a peasant family) and M. Frolenko (the son of a washerwoman) had received an education which raised them socially and intellectually above their origins.

In reality, *Narodnaya Volya* had engaged in a duel with the autocracy, based on the recognition that the party's strength was simply insufficient for other efforts of propaganda, enlightenment or social work 'among the people'. In addition, there arose a new impatience to take part in determining the fate of the country: Zhelyabov, for instance, wished expressly to give history a 'push', in order to hurry it along.

In *Narodnaya Volya*'s 'heroic period', personalities, their aims and passions, played a decisive part. And without taking radical ideology into account, the motivations that led to terror would be difficult to comprehend. The autocracy, with its policy of hesitant ruthlessness – either too harsh or not harsh enough – contributed to the rise of terrorism, by merely alienating society without being able to liquidate the revolutionary opposition. The system itself was the reason that an extreme minority could appear as the sole voice of social interests and aspirations and thus acquire disproportionate political weight. The autocracy screened the intelligentsia from the experiences and disappointments of practical politics and thus nourished their maximalism. The 'autocrator' virtually offered himself as a target for their terror, since it was this institution which promoted the hope that the whole system might be destroyed at one stroke. Through its policies, the government created a number of prophets, martyrs and heroes, who made a great impression on the young and on the following generations, particularly at the time of their trials, not least because these men possessed considerable charisma. (This may explain why Stalin made sure that the defendants in political trials made a confession of their guilt.) The Russian political system fostered a 'patented heroism', for which only the 'heroic maximum' could suffice, as S. Bulgakov wrote in *Vekhi*, when he presented his reckoning with the radical traditions. In this connection it is significant that, even in the case of the *narodnovoltsy*, confrontation with the realities did not only give rise to jacobinism, but also to a new gradualism, to a new sense of the feasible, which prompted the realistic attitude of the 1880s, before the great hunger of 1891 revived the radical spirit once more, this time in the form of Marxism. When at the beginning of the new century large-scale peasant disturbances occurred, the tradition of militant populism reappeared in a new guise as well, this time in the shape of the Socialist-Revolutionary Party.

NOTES

1. The entire nexus of Russian revolutionary ideologies and movements during the nineteenth century, in terms of their specific political aims and implications, particularly the controversies about a possible revolutionary dictatorship, has been the subject of my book, *Die Ursprünge des Bolschewismus. Die jakobinische*

Tradition in Rußland und die Theorie der revolutionären Diktatur (Munich, 1977).
2. T. Szamuely in R. Conquest (ed.), The Russian Tradition (London, 1974) p. 341.
3. Ibid., p. 339.
4. Y. Trifonov, Neterpenie: Povest' ob Andree Zhelyabove (Moscow, 1973) p. 329. (I am grateful to M. Hildermeier for having introduced me to this, from the historical point of view, excellent story.)
5. K. Marx and F. Engels, Foreword to the second Russian edition of the Communist Manifesto, in: Werke, 4th edn., vol. 19 (Berlin, 1962) p. 296.
6. S. S. Volk, Narodnaya volya: 1879–1882 (Moscow-Leningrad, 1966) p. 96.
7. O. V. Aptekman, Obšćestvo 'Zemlja i volja' 70-ch godov. Po ličnym vospominanijam. 2-e, ispravlennoe i značitel'no dopolnennoe izdanie (Petrograd, 1924) p. 199.
8. Volk, p. 277.
9. A. Hitler, Mein Kampf, 2 vols. in one, 66th edn. (Munich, 1933) p. 337. Cf. R. Löwenthal, 'The Model of the Totalitarian State', in Royal Institute of International Affairs (ed.), The Impact of the Russian Revolution, 1917–1967: The Influence of Bolshevism on the World Outside Russia, (London/New York/Toronto, 1967) pp. 274–351, esp. p. 11.
10. A. I. Gercen (Herzen), 'Pis'ma iz Francii i Italii', in V. P. Volgin et al. (eds) Sobranie sočinenij v devjati tomach, vol. 3 (Moscow, 1955–8) p. 279. On the attitude of the main representatives of the intelligentsia to revolution and violence, cf. v. Borcke, chapter 5, pp. 139–228.
11. D. I. Pisarev, 'Skholastika XIX veka', in Sočinenija v četyrech tomach, vol. 1 (Moscow, 1955–6) p. 135.
12. N. G. Černyševskij, Čto delat'? Iz rasskazov o novych ljudjach (Moscow, 1960) p. 279.
13. P. N. Tkačev in B. P. Koz'min (ed.), Izbrannye sočinenija na social'no-politićeskie temy, vol. 1 (Moscow, 1932–7) p. 192.
14. P. L. Lavrov, 'Istoričeskie pis'ma', in: Filosofija i sociologija. Izbrannye pro-izvedenija v dvuch tomach, vol. 2 (Moscow, 1965) p. 121.
15. M. Confino (ed.), Daughter of a Revolutionary. Natalie Herzen and the Bakunin-Nechayev Circle (London, 1974) pp. 25, 244.
16. On the Nechaev affair see v. Borcke, chapter 7, pp. 281–326.
17. M. P. Dragomanov (ed.), Pis'ma M. A. Bakunina k A. I. Gercenu i N. P. Ogarevu (Geneva, 1896) p. 468.
18. M. A. Bakunin in A. Lehning (ed.), Gosudarstvennost' i anarchija. Archives Bakounine, vol. 3 (Leyden, 1967).
19. For particulars see v. Borcke, pp. 369–72.
20. V. Debogorij-Mokrievič, Vospominanija (St. Petersburg, 1906) p. 162.
21. V. N. Figner, Zapečatlennyj trud: Vospominanija v dvuch tomach, vol. 1 (Moscow, 1964) p. 135.
22. Krasnyj archiv 6/19 (1926) p. 196.
23. Letučij listok 2 (April 1878), in S. N. Valk et al. (eds.), Revoljucionnoe narodničestvo 70-ch godov XIX veka: Sbornik dokumentov i materialov v dvuch tomach, vol. 2 (Moscow-Leningrad, 1964–5) p. 57.
24. Cf. Programma 'Zemli i voli', ibid., vol. 2, p. 33; Tezisy narodnikov, ibid., vol. 2, p. 34.
25. Aptekman, p. 392.
26. S. N. Valk (ed.), 'Avtobiografičeskoe zajavlenie A. A. Kvjatkovskogo', in: Krasnyj archiv 1/14 (1926) p. 169.
27. G. V. Plekhanov, 'Socializm i političeskaja bor'ba', in Izbrannye filosofskie poizvedenija v pjati tomach, vol. 1 (Moscow, 1956) p. 52.

28. Karl Marx to Jenny Longuet, 11 April 1881, in K. Marx and F. Engels, *Werke*, vol. 35 (Berlin, 1967) p. 179.
29. 'Pis'mo Ispolnitel'nogo Komiteta Aleksandru III', in *Revoljucionnoe narodničestvo*, vol. 2, p. 195.
30. A. B. Ulam, *In the Name of the People: Prophets and Conspirators in Prerevolutionary Russia* (New York, 1977) p. 317.
31. Quoted by W. Laqueur, 'Interpretationen des Terrorismus: Fakten, Fiktionen und politische Wissenschaft', in M. Funke (ed.), *Terrorismus: Untersuchungen zur Struktur und Strategie revolutionärer Gewaltpolitik* (Düsseldorf, 1977) p. 58.
32. Volk, p. 227.
33. *Literatura social'no-revoljucionnoj partii 'Narodnoj voli'* (n.p. 1905) p. 401.
34. *Avtobiografičeskoe zajavlenie A. A. Kvjatkovskogo*, p. 172.
35. An. (L. Tikhomirov), *Andrej Ivanovič Željabov: Člen Ispolnitel'nogo Komiteta partii 'Narodnaja volja': Materialy dlja biografii*, foreword by V. N. Figner (Moscow, 1930) p. 10.
36. N. A. Morozov in B. P. Koz'min (ed.), *Povesti moej žizni: Memuary*, vol. 2 (Moscow, 1961) p. 350.
37. *Avtobiografičeskoe zajavlenie A. Kvjatkovskogo*, p. 170.
38. 'Načalo 1879 g. – Iz pokazanija F. Kuricyna o revoljucionnom narodničestvom dviženii na juge Rossii vo vtoroj polovine 70-ch godov', in *Revoljucionnoe narodničestvo*, vol. 2, p. 120.
39. E. S. (Pseudonym of Marija N. Ošanina), 'K istorii partii Narodnoj voli', *Byloe* 6/18 (1907) p. 7.
40. N. A. Morozov, comments on M. F. Frolenko, Kommentarij k stat'e N. A. Morozova 'Vozniknovenie "Narodnoj voli" ', *Byloe* 12 (1906) p. 27, note 2.
41. N. A. Bakh, 'Vospominanija narodovol'ca', *Byloe* 3/15 (1907) p. 229.
42. *Vospominanija L'va Tikhomirova* (Moscow/Leningrad, 1927) p. 104.
43. R. Pipes, *Struve: Liberal on the Left, 1870–1905* (Cambridge/Mass., 1970) p. 235.
44. *Vospominanija L'va Tikhomirova*, p. 160.
45. Cf. v. Borcke, p. 417.
46. Ulam, p. 353.
47. V. M. Černov, *Pered burej: Vospominanija* (New York, 1953) p. 122.
48. P. B. Aksel'rod, 'Perechodnyj moment našej partii', *Obščina*, 8 and 9 (1878) p. 21.
49. A. Yarmolinsky, *Road to Revolution: A Century of Russian Radicalism* (New York, 1962) p. 237.
50. K. Marx, 'Kritik des Hegelschen Staatsrechts', in *Werke*, vol. 1 (Berlin, 1961) p. 295.
51. M. P. Dragomanov, *K biografii A. I. Željabova* (Geneva, n.d.) p. 9.
52. *Revoljucionnoe narodničestvo*, vol. 2, p. 195.
53. *Pis'mo Ispolnitel'nogo Komiteta 'Narodnoj voli' zagraničnym tovariščam*, ibid., vol. 2, pp. 319–20.
54. B. Lenskij, 'Intelligencija, narod, buržuazija', *Delo* 12 (1881) p. 7. Quoted from V. A. Tvardovskaja, 'Problema gosudarstva v ideologii narodničestva', *Istoričeskie zapiski* 74 (1963) pp. 159–60.
55. Cf. v. Borcke, pp. 402–3.
56. Cf. Szamuely, pp. 336–7.
57. P. Struve, 'Betrachtungen über die russische Revolution', in J. Melnik (ed.), *Russen über Rußland* (Frankfurt a.M., 1906) p. 2.
58. S. N. Bulgakov, 'Geroizm i podvižničestvo', in *Vechi: Sbornik statej o russkoj intelligencii*, 2nd edn. (Moscow, 1909) p. 38.

6 Political and Economic Terror in the Tactics of the Russian Socialist-Revolutionary Party before 1914

Maureen Perrie

The Russian Socialist-Revolutionaries (SRs)[1] are best known as a terrorist party whose Combat Organisation (*Boevaya Organizatsiya*) accomplished a series of spectacular assassinations in the early years of the twentieth century. Their victims were carefully chosen as particularly repressive figures from the Tsarist bureaucracy; they included the Ministers of Internal Affairs, D. S. Sipyagin and V. K. Plehve; and the Tsar's uncle, the governor-general of Moscow, Grand Duke Sergei Aleksandrovich. These assassinations, undertaken against the background of a developing revolutionary situation in Russia, gained the party much sympathy and support not only in Russia, but also in Western Europe. The right of the SRs to employ terrorist tactics against the Russian autocracy was recognised by many European socialists, and in 1903, in a *cause célèbre* of its day, the leaders of the Second International, to which the SR party belonged, launched a successful campaign to prevent the extradition from Italy to Russia of M. R. Gots, the chief émigré organiser of the SR Combat Organisation.[2]

Yet the SR party was far from being an exclusively terrorist organisation. The SRs always insisted that terror was only one form of revolutionary action, and that to be effective terror had to be integrated with the mass movement. The SRs aspired to be a mass socialist party, and although they failed to achieve this status before 1917, they placed great stress on organising the masses, not only the urban industrial workers, but also the peasant majority of the Russian population. Their attempts to combine terrorism with mass forms of action led to many tactical dilemmas for the SR party, particularly at the time of the 1905 revolution, and led to splits in the party in 1906.

The Russian Socialist-Revolutionary party was formed at the end of 1901 as the result of the unification of various groups of neo-populist tendency which existed in Russia and in emigration at the turn of the century. The SRs were the chief socialist rivals of the Russian Social Democrats (SDs), who had held their First Congress in 1898, and who split into the Bolshevik and Menshevik factions at their Second Congress in 1903. Viktor Chernov, the party's main theoretician, derived the SRs' ideological heritage both from Marx and from the Russian Populists, especially Lavrov and Mikhailovsky. The socialism of the SRs differed from that of the SDs in several important respects. In the first place the SRs, while accepting the concept of the class struggle, rejected the SDs' identification of the 'working class' with the industrial proletariat. In SR theory the working class was a broad alliance of the exploited – including the socialist intelligentsia and the small peasant and artisan producers as well as the industrial and agricultural proletariat – who were united in the struggle for socialism against the exploiting classes, the landowners, bourgeoisie and bureaucracy. The SRs also differed from the SDs in their assessment of the character of the forthcoming Russian revolution: while accepting a two-stage perspective of the transition to socialism, the SRs rejected the SDs' term 'bourgeois-democratic' for the first stage of the revolution, believing that in agriculture at least the revolution would be anti-capitalist as well as anti-feudal.[3] The SR party programme, approved by the First Congress in January 1906, followed the SD pattern of a minimum and maximum programme, but the minimum programme incorporated, in addition to the conventional socialist demands for political, social and economic reforms, the demand for the 'socialisation' of the land. Socialisation of the land was a complex concept: private property in land was to be abolished; the land was to be administered by democratically elected organs of local and central government; and the land was to be used on an egalitarian basis by those who worked it themselves.[4] The socialisation of land was seen by the SRs as a major measure against the entrenchment of agrarian capitalism in Russia, and hence an important step against Russian capitalism in general.

The SRs differed from the SDs also in the use of tactics. Like many of their Populist predecessors, but unlike the SDs, the SRs favoured the use of terrorist tactics in the struggle against tsarism. Initially terrorism for the SRs meant political terrorism. From 1904, however, the question of 'economic' terror arose to confront the party. Debates over political and economic terror caused tensions and splits in the party during the revolutionary years 1905–6. In the course of these debates many important issues were raised concerning the value and significance of terrorist tactics, and the relationship between terrorism and the mass movement.

I

The terrorism practised by the SRs in the first years of the party's existence was regarded by them as a continuation of the terrorist traditions of

Narodnaya Volya (People's Will), the Populist party, formed in 1879, which had assassinated Alexander II in 1881. But not all of the neo-populist groups which united to form the SR party in 1901 shared *Narodnaya Volya*'s view of terrorism: some belonged instead to the rival *Chernyi Peredel* (Black Partition) tradition of Russian Populism, with its stress on mass agitation among the workers and peasants.[5] On 14 February 1901 a former student, P. V. Karpovich, assassinated the Minister of Education, N. P. Bogolepov, who had been responsible for the suppression of student disorders in the universities in 1899–1901. Although Karpovich called himself a socialist-revolutionary, he acted as an individual, independently of any party or group control. Nevertheless, the success of Karpovich's action strengthened the position of the terrorist faction within the newly-formed party. In 1901 the party formed its Combat Organisation, under the leadership of G. A. Gershuni. The first terrorist act organised by the Combat Organisation was the assassination of Minister of Internal Affairs D. S. Sipyagin in St. Petersburg on 2 April 1902 by Stepan Balmashev. This was followed by the wounding of Prince Obolensky, the governor of Kharkov province, on 29 July 1902, by Foma Kachurov. On 6 May 1903, N. M. Bogdanovich, the governor of Ufa, was killed by Egor Dulebov. Soon after the assassination of Bogdanovich, Gershuni was arrested: he was replaced as head of the Combat Organisation by Evno Azef, an *agent provocateur* in the employ of the tsarist security police. On 15 July 1904 the party accomplished its most spectacular terrorist act with the assassination of Plehve, the Minister of Internal Affairs, in St. Petersburg, by a group including Egor Sazonov. Equally successful was the murder of the Grand Duke Sergei in Moscow, on 4 February 1905, by a bomb thrown by Ivan Kalaev.[6]

In the early years the SR party's attitude towards terrorism was somewhat defensive, and articles in the party press justifying the use of terrorist tactics were concerned to defend terrorism against criticism, especially from the Russian Social Democrats, and also from Western European socialists.[7] The party leadership argued that terrorism was necessary and inevitable, in the context of government repression of the growing mass movement, as a means of self-defence by the masses. The SRs produced two further justifications for terrorism. Firstly, it had an 'excitative' or agitational function – that is, a terrorist act attracted attention and provoked discussion, thereby serving to popularise the cause which it was intended to further. In the second place, terrorism created fear and disorganisation in the ranks of the government. But on this second point the SRs added some qualifications: terrorism was most effective when it was integrated with other forms of revolutionary action, such as the mass movement of workers and peasants. The SRs stressed the need for the organisation and control of terrorist action: it was the role of the party to integrate terrorism with the other forms of revolutionary activity.[8] The organisation of SR terrorist activity, however, was separate from that of the party as a whole. From its foundation, the Combat Organisation enjoyed

considerable autonomy within the party, and its independence of the Central
Committee was considerably enhanced in 1904, in the aftermath of the
assassination of Plehve.[9] The organisational separation of terrorism from the
rest of the party's activity was justified in terms of the 'division of labour' and
the need for secrecy and conspiracy,[10] but it created problems of control for
the party leadership.

In 1905, with the outbreak of the mass revolutionary movement, acts of
political terrorism moved from a predominantly 'central' to a 'local' level.[11]
The party itself increased its membership, and many local committees formed
their own terrorist groups, which were variously known as 'combat bands'
(*boevye druzhiny*) or 'flying combat detachments' (*letuchie boevye otryady*).
The revolutionary movement of 1905 achieved its greatest success with the
publication of the Tsar's Manifesto of 17 October which promised full civil
liberties and the election of a legislative assembly, the State *Duma*. Although
this concession fell short of the Constituent Assembly demanded by the
revolutionary parties, it was sufficiently important to cause the parties to
reassess their tactics. The SR Central Committee decided to disband the
Combat Organisation, on the grounds that it was no longer necessary now
that political freedom had been achieved.[12] Although 'central' terror was
suspended, many local committees continued to organise and carry out
terrorist acts.[13] The suspension of central terror itself was to prove shortlived.
By the end of 1905 the counter-revolutionary offensive by the government was
in the ascendant, and the promised political freedom seemed very elusive. The
First Congress of the SR party, which met in Finland from 29 December 1905
to 4 January 1906, resolved to resume political terrorism at both central and
local levels, and the Combat Organisation was re-formed.[14]

Although the SRs boycotted the elections to the First *Duma*, terrorist
activity was again temporarily suspended, by a resolution of the First Party
Council in May 1906, to coincide with the opening of the *Duma*, 'until the
political position and the tactics of the government are more fully clarified for
the mass of the population'.[15] Again, the suspension was not adhered to by all
local committees, and even some acts of 'central' terror continued.[16] When
the *Duma* was prematurely dissolved by the government on 9 July 1906,
however, terrorism was again resumed.[17] In February 1907 the Second Party
Congress met to consider the party's attitude to the Second *Duma*. Having
decided to participate in the *Duma*, the SRs nonetheless resolved to continue
with terrorism, but to place, as a temporary measure, all central and local
terrorist acts under the control of the Central Committee.[18] The early
dissolution of the Second *Duma* in June 1907 saved the SRs from the problems
which would undoubtedly have arisen for a party which sent deputies to the
Duma and at the same time conducted terrorist acts against the government.

Various reorganisations of the SR terrorist bodies took place in 1906–7. In
October 1906, after the failure of the Combat Organisation to assassinate their
chief target, Stolypin, the Chairman of the Council of Ministers, Azef and his

chief aide Boris Savinkov resigned from the leadership of the Combat Organisation, which was re-formed as the 'Combat Detachment of the Central Committee', headed by Lev Zilberberg, and under the close control of the Central Committee.[19] At the end of 1907, however, the old Combat Organisation was reinstated, under the leadership of Azef, who undertook to organise the assassination of the Tsar.[20] At the end of 1908, however, Azef was unmasked as an *agent provocateur*. The effect on party morale was shattering. The Fifth Party Council, which met in May 1909 to assess the implications of the 'Azef affair', decided to continue with terrorism, but to grant greater autonomy to the combat detachments of local party committees.[21] The new Combat Organisation was headed by Savinkov; but in practice very few terrorist acts were accomplished by the SRs in the years before the war.[22]

In the years 1907–14 the question of terror caused divisions in the party. On the left, the group which published the journal *Revolyutsionnaya Mysl'* (Revolutionary Thought) demanded the return to a more exclusive use of terrorism, including regicide, on the pattern of *Narodnaya Volya*. On the right, the group associated with the paper *Pochin* (Initiative) wished to abandon terrorism and conspiratorial organisation.[23]

In 1914 the SR party published an interesting compilation of statistics relating to the party's acts of political terror. Intended as a contribution to the debate on terrorism in the aftermath of the Azef affair, these statistics showed, according to the compiler, 'that terror exists, develops and is nourished by the mass movement'.[24] This, he believed, was demonstrated by the increase in the number of terrorist acts in the years 1905–7 (*Table 6.1*). An analysis of the social composition of the terrorists might also suggest that SR terrorism was integrated with the mass movement – more than half of the terrorists were workers (*Table 6.2*).[25] This conclusion may be modified, however, if one notes that most of these terrorists were very young at the time they made their

TABLE 6.1:   SR Terrorist Acts, 1902–11

Year	No. of acts
1902	2
1903	3
1904	1
1905	51
1906	78
1907	62
1908	3
1909	2
1910	1
1911	2
Total	205

TABLE 6.2:   Occupations of SR Terrorists

Occupation	No.
Worker	90
Intellectual	37
Peasant	20
Student	13
School-pupil	10
Teacher	3
Soldier	2
Sailor	2
Officer	1
Doctor	1
Total	179

TABLE 6.3:   Age of SR Terrorists

Age	No.
15–19	16
20–24	33
25–29	11
30–34	9
35–39	3
over 40	1
Total	73

Median age 22.1 years

Note: Figures in all three tables are calculated from Ivich, pp. 8–20.

attempt (*Table 6.3*).[26] In terrorism we seem to be dealing with a phenomenon which appealed particularly to young people, both students and workers. In fact the great majority of the 'worker' terrorists (about 70 per cent) committed their acts in the western provinces of the Empire which comprised the Jewish Pale of Settlement.[27] The Jewish workers in this area were mostly artisans employed in small workshops, rather than industrial proletarians, and this may partly explain their apparent willingness to resort to individual rather than collective forms of action. There is no unambiguous evidence, therefore, that SR political terrorism was ever fully integrated into the mass movement of the workers or peasants.

The development of SR political terrorism in the years 1902–14 did not proceed along the lines laid down for it in the party's statements on the topic in the years before 1905. The degree of party control over terrorist activities was less than ideal. The relative autonomy of the Combat Organisation from the

Central Committee, of local combat groups from their local party committees, and of the latter from the Central Committee, made it difficult for the party leadership to exercise control over terror. The conspiratorial character of the party's organisation intensified this problem, and rendered the Combat Organisation fatally vulnerable to police infiltration. The party's only response to this problem was to make endless attempts to reorganise its terrorist activity, but these appear to have had little practical effect. The inability of the leadership to exercise control is hardly surprising in the light of the party's circumstances before 1914: the organisation in Russia was illegal, and the party leaders were mostly in emigration. But since the SRs believed that terror was justified only in the absence of political freedom, it is difficult to see how they could have avoided this dilemma.

The impossibility of central control of terror was clearly demonstrated on the two occasions when the Central Committee attempted to suspend terrorism, after the October Manifesto of 1905, and at the opening of the First *Duma* in 1906, when the suspension was virtually ignored by the local terrorist organisations. Local terror in 1905–7 may have represented a popular form of revolutionary activity, but the gain in terms of the integration of terror with the mass movement was outweighed by the loss of that central party control which represented a major justification of terrorism in the eyes of the SR leadership.

In fact one may argue that SR terrorism was more effective in the years 1902–4, when the mass movement was only in its early stages, than in the revolutionary years 1905–7. The victims of 1902–4 were well chosen to symbolise repression by the state. There is evidence that the assassinations of Sipyagin and Bogdanovich gained some popular support for the SRs.[28] The murders of Pleve and the Grand Duke Sergei led directly to concessions by the Tsarist government: Pleve was replaced as Minister of Internal Affairs by the comparatively liberal Prince Svyatopolk-Mirsky; and an announcement of political reforms followed immediately after the Grand Duke's death, in February 1905. From 1905, however, although the number of SR terrorist acts increased dramatically, their impact was somewhat diffuse. Partly because of Azef's double role, the Combat Organisation failed to assassinate either of its main targets, Stolypin and the Tsar. By 1906 terrorism was already proving counter-productive: the need to combat revolutionary terror was adduced by Stolypin as justification for the introduction in that year of emergency measures of counter-revolutionary repression.

II

Political terrorism as practised by the SRs from the time of the formation of the party was defined by them as attacks on government officials, including spies and informers. From 1904, however, groups emerged within the party who favoured the use of *Economic Terror* as a means of integrating terrorist activity more closely with the mass movement. Economic Terror assumed various forms: *Agrarian Terror*,[29] Factory Terror, and Expropriations.

At the time of the formation of the party in 1901, only a minority of SRs favoured propaganda activity among the peasantry as an immediate task of the new party. Indeed, the prevailing mood of the SRs towards the peasantry was so hostile that the Agrarian-Socialist League, a body formed in Paris in 1900 to publish and distribute propaganda literature in the Russian countryside, remained aloof from the party until 1902.[30] The outbreak of widespread peasant disturbances in the Ukrainian provinces of Poltava and Khar'kov in 1902, however, caused the SRs to reassess the revolutionary role of the peasantry, and the party formed its Peasant Union to organise the peasants.[31]

Initially no clear distinction was made between forms of action which were later to be classified as 'political' and 'economic' terror. The first pamphlet of the SR Peasant Union, 'To All the Russian Peasantry' recommended peaceful means of economic struggle, such as wage strikes and rent boycotts, but added that if these were unsuccessful the peasants should resort to 'their own means'. The examples provided of such means were destructive violence against the landowner – illegal pasturing of animals and chopping of wood, and also arson, and violence against officials.[32] The problem of 'agrarian terror' was discussed at the First Congress of the Agrarian-Socialist League in August 1902. The League stressed that peaceful means of economic struggle should be recommended to the peasants, and the main speaker on the issue condemned agrarian terrorism because of the difficulty for the party of controlling such acts and accepting responsibility for them. The League recognised that the peasants themselves often resorted to violence against the property or person of the landowner, and in such cases, they concluded, the party's local peasant organisation would have to accept responsibility for such acts.[33] Thus from the outset the SRs' ambivalent attitude towards agrarian terrorism derived from their recognition that such tactics were the peasants' traditional 'own means' of struggle against the landowners. The party also feared that it might become isolated from the 'spontaneous' peasant movement if it condemned all forms of economic struggle other than peaceful and organised ones.

These considerations seem to have influenced the group of 'agrarian terrorists' which formed in Geneva in 1904.[34] The leaders of the group were M. I. Sokolov ('Cain', or 'The Bear') and E. Ustinov (Lozinsky). Sokolov argued that methods of agrarian terrorism had been employed by the Russian peasantry since the risings led by Razin and Pugachev in the seventeenth and eighteenth centuries; the role of the party should be not to condemn but to coordinate and organise these acts. Ustinov compiled a resolution along these lines, which was supported by a majority of 25 to 16 of the SR émigrés in Geneva. The advocates of agrarian terrorism were the youngest and most recent contingent of émigrés, including some who had experience of propaganda among the peasantry in 1902–3.[35] The counter-resolution was signed by the older generation of party leaders. It condemned agrarian terrorism, mainly on the grounds that it was difficult for the party to control and regulate such acts.[36]

The 'agrarian terrorists' were permitted to remain within the SR party and advocate their views, but they were forbidden to preach agrarian terror to the peasantry.[37] When Sokolov returned to Russia, however, he began to advocate not only agrarian but also other forms of economic terror. His views gained particular support in the Western provinces of the Empire (the Ukraine and Belorussia) which comprised the Jewish Pale of Settlement. In Minsk in November 1904 Sokolov issued a proclamation 'To the workers and peasants' which called on them to 'beat up the Tsarist officials, capitalists and landowners!', thereby breaching the undertaking he had given to the Central Committee.[38] Sokolov continued his attempts to convert the SR Peasant Union to agrarian terrorism, but in April 1905 the police raided a congress of the Peasant Union in Kursk which was attended by all the leading agrarians.[39] The arrest of Sokolov and his followers virtually destroyed the agrarian terrorists as an organised faction within the party. Agrarian terrorism was a plank in the Maximalist programmes of 1906, but SR-Maximalism was in practice more concerned with economic terror in an urban rather than a rural context. The question of agrarian terrorism did however continue to dog the SR party's debates on tactics after 1905.

At the First Party Congress Rakitnikov ('Bazarov') introduced a resolution on tactics which condemned agrarian terror in the conventional manner, but at the same time he admitted that there were occasions when agrarian terror was inevitable, and it was 'better than nothing'.[40] Resolutions approved by the First Party Conference and by the Fourth Party Council in 1908 again condemned agrarian terrorism.[41] The issue was complicated, however, by the simultaneous adoption of a resolution 'On Political Terror in the Countryside'. This resolution considered the case of landowners who hired cossacks to protect their estates, and encouraged them to attack the peasants. 'Revolutionary punishment of these men', the resolution stated, 'which is in its essence a manifestation of political, not economic terror, does not contradict the principles of the party'. Such acts of political terror, however, were only to be undertaken with the permission of a representative of the Central Committee and of the regional party committee.[42]

It is hardly surprising that such fine distinctions between political and economic terror were misunderstood or ignored by the party's peasant supporters. A survey of peasant opinions conducted by the party in 1907–8 showed that the peasants favoured all forms of agrarian terror, especially arson against landowners, as well as acts of political terror such as the murder of policemen and officials.[43]

And in fact agrarian terror was the main form of peasant action against the landowners in the revolution of 1905–7. Statistics relating to the peasant movement in these years reveal that the most common forms of action were those which the SRs classified as'agrarian terrorism': arson, destructive raids on estate buildings, seizure of crops, foodstuffs and fodder, illicit woodcutting and pasturing of animals. Such instances constituted over 70 per cent of all forms of action against landowners, whereas the peaceful and organised forms of action recommended by the SRs, such as strikes and withdrawal of labour, were less than 25 per cent of the total.[44]

The concept of _Factory Terror_ appears to have originated as a logical extension of agrarian terror. In Geneva, Chernov tells us, Ustinov rejected the analogy, but in Ekaterinoslav in 1904 Sokolov gained support for a resolution which favoured both agrarian and factory terror.[45] By 'factory terror' was meant the use or threat of violence against the life or property of a factory owner in order to further the economic interests of the workers. 'Factory terror' was most popular in the North-West (Belorussia), especially in Belostok, where the SR-Maximalists issued a proclamation calling on the workers to 'beat up the bourgeois', and adding that 'only with bombs can we make the bourgeois grant concessions'.[46] These views gained considerable support among a section of the working class in Belorussia, particularly among the younger Jewish workers.[47]

The advocacy of tactics of economic terror by groups within the SR party in 1904–5 developed in 1905–6 into the broader movement of Maximalism. Chernov has noted that both chronologically and logically SR-Maximalist ideas followed from the acceptance of economic terror.[48] If political terror against the government was accompanied by economic terror against the propertied classes, then the property-owners would become hostile to the revolutionary movement. Society would be polarised, and the possibility of compromise would be eliminated. The SR-Maximalists therefore rejected any agreement with the liberals, and many of them rejected parliamentarism altogether. They called for the expropriation of the factories by the workers, along with the expropriation of land by the peasantry (the simultaneous socialisation of industry and land), and hoped thereby to achieve an immediate socialist revolution in Russia. In the course of 1906 most Maximalist groups broke away from the SR party to form the Union of SR-Maximalists. Its existence as a separate organisation was however shortlived, as it was virtually destroyed at the end of 1906 by the arrest and execution of Sokolov and other Maximalist leaders. Many former Maximalists adhered in the following years to various groups of anarchists or Makhaevists (who rejected the revolutionary role of the intelligentsia).[49]

In practice factory terror appears to have been a less frequent tactic of the Maximalists than expropriations of money (see below) – possibly because acts of factory terror were less common as forms of the spontaneous and traditional working-class movement than were acts of agrarian terror by the peasantry. The SRs attached less significance to factory terror than to agrarian terror, simply condemning it in resolutions which were analogous to those on agrarian terror.[50] At the First Party Congress, the only example of factory terror practised by an SR committee was offered by the delegate from Baku. In Baku in August 1905, in the context of racial clashes between the Tatars and the Armenians, the party committee had ordered acts of arson against the oil-wells, and threatened the life and property of the capitalists if they did not close down their works to protect their workers.[51] The main speaker on tactics at the congress, however, decreed that this example was not strictly factory terror, since it occurred in the context of an incipient civil war in Baku. He stressed that terror could be used against a capitalist if, for example, he closed down his factory for political motives, but not if the factory was closed for purely economic reasons.[52] A more detailed resolution condemning factory terror was approved by the First Party Conference and Fourth Party Council in 1908.[53] But the party still maintained its distinction between factory terror, on the one hand, and acts of political terror against capitalists, on the other. Factory terror was forbidden, but acts of political terror against capitalists who 'systematically and blatantly breach their neutrality in the war between the government and the revolutionary people' – for example, by employing police or troops against their workers – were permitted with the sanction of the regional party committee.[54]

In the conditions of late Tsarist Russia, in fact, the distinction between political and economic terror was peculiarly difficult to apply. The forces of the state were liable to intervene in all economic disputes – both between workers and employers and between peasants and landowners – on the side of the propertied elements, thereby giving a political colouration to conflicts which originated from purely economic interests. By classifying as 'political terror' violent acts of self-defence by workers and peasants against police and cossacks called in by the capitalists and landowners to protect their property, the SRs recognised the political aspect of certain economic conflicts. But this did not help them to make their distinction between political and economic terror any more comprehensible to their rank and file supporters.

The tactic of *Expropriation* (robbery of money or property) by SR party members originated, like factory terror, in the Western provinces of the Empire. In 1904–5 SR elements in Ekaterinoslav and Belostok conducted a campaign against the property-owners, demanding money from wealthy individuals, reinforced by threats and sometimes acts of violence.[55] The question of 'the revolutionary expropriation of land, state and private property (in particular banks)' featured on the agenda of the First Party Congress,[56] but apart from condemnation of 'private expropriations' by the delegates from the North-West, little attention was paid to this aspect of economic terror.[57] The question of financial expropriations was brought to a head for the SRs when in the spring of 1906 members of the Moscow 'opposition' faction of the party, headed by Vladimir Mazurin, accomplished the robbery of almost one million roubles from the Moscow Merchant Bank. This robbery gave the opposition financial independence from the party, and enabled them to set up a separate organisation, with support not only in Moscow, but also in St Petersburg, Ekaterinoslav, Ryazan' and Stavropol'. These oppositionists later joined the Union of SR-Maximalists.[58]

The Second Party Council, meeting in October 1906, noted that expropriations had reached epidemic proportions, and sometimes involved party members. The resolution warned that expropriations had a demoralising effect on the party. They attracted undesirable elements, and lowered party prestige. Participants in private expropriations were to be expelled from the party. Only expropriations of money and arms belonging to the state were permitted, and even these with qualifications: only policemen and gendarmes could be killed in the course of the expropriation, and these 'state expropriations' could only be carried out with the permission and under the control of the regional committee of the party.[59] After a fairly lengthy and often heated debate on the issue at the Second Party Congress in 1907, this resolution was tightened even further: state expropriations were to take place only under the control and direction of the Central Committee, and no lives were to be sacrificed.[60] In practice no major state expropriations were carried out by the party itself.[61] The most spectacular state expropriation was the armed robbery by the Maximalists on 14 October 1906 of several hundred thousand roubles being transported from the Customs Office to the State Bank in St Petersburg.[62]

The SR party attempted to model its distinction between private and state expropriations on its distinction between political and economic terror: state expropriations were permissible because they were directed against the government, but private expropriations, being directed against individual members of the bourgeoisie, were forbidden. As might have been expected, these distinctions were not understood by the SR rank and file. The party's survey of peasant opinion in 1907–8 showed that the peasants were in favour of both private and state expropriations.[63]

The issue of expropriations of money was further complicated by the party's ambivalent attitude towards a particular form of 'private expropriation', land seizures by the peasants. Before 1905 the SRs welcomed all attempts by the peasants to take over and work gentry land, seeing in this a spontaneous attempt by the peasantry to socialise the land 'from below'. In response to the formation of the 'agrarian terrorists' in 1904, however, and to the development of the spontaneous peasant movement of 1905, the party clarified its views on the 'revolutionary expropriation of the land'.[64] Peasant land seizures, the SRs stressed,

> should consist not in the arbitrary seizure of particular plots by particular individuals, but in the abolition of the boundaries and borders of private ownership, in the declaration of the land to be common property, and in the demand for its general, egalitarian and universal distribution for the use of those who work it.[65]

At the First Party Congress this issue was raised by the group of 'legal Populists', Annensky, Myakotin and Peshekhonov, who were later to split with the party to form their own Party of Popular Socialists (*Narodnye Sotsialisty*). The legal Populists argued that the SRs' perspectives of socialisation from below were utopian.[66] In the debates, many other SR delegates expressed similar concern that peasant land seizures would lead simply to the transfer of land from the private property of the landowners to that of individual peasants or individual communes.[67] Although a compromise resolution on agrarian tactics was adopted by the congress, the party continued to stand for the 'revolutionary expropriation of the land'.[68] This gave rise to charges of inconsistency from the Maximalists, who wondered why the party permitted expropriation of land but not of other forms of private property, such as money. They wondered, too, why the SRs called on the peasants to seize the land, but refused to call on the workers to seize the factories.[69]

Chernov's reply was that there was no inconsistency. Socialisation of the land was not a socialist measure, since agricultural production would not be socialised, but would remain on an individual basis. Socialisation of the factories, however, would involve socialisation of industrial production, which was a socialist measure – for which, Chernov argued, objective conditions in Russia were not yet ripe.[70] The Maximalists, however, rejected Chernov's two-stage scenario for socialist revolution as a mere imitation of the Social Democrats; they advocated an immediate socialist revolution.[71] In their own terms, therefore, the Maximalists' tactics of expropriation of land and factories were consistent with their perspective of an immediate socialist revolution, while Chernov's advocacy only of land socialisation was consistent with his two-stage view of the transition to socialism in Russia. This consistency at the level of high theory, however, did not translate very effectively into consistency at the level of mass propaganda and agitation. In fact the seizure of factories was not a major demand of the working-class movement in the 1905 revolution. At the First SR Congress only Altovsky ('Goretskii'), the delegate from Saratov, claimed that the workers wished to seize the factories.[72] And we are told that some workers in the Maximalist stronghold of Bryansk believed that 'it's a very tempting prospect that the factories and mills should be ours'.[73] As for the popularity of private expropriations of money, this probably derived from its apparent legitimation of theft in the eyes of criminal elements who kept the stolen money for their own purposes rather than handing it over to party funds.[74]

The SR party attempted to integrate political terrorism with the development of peaceful methods of economic struggle. In order to achieve this integration, the SRs insisted that political terror must be conducted under strict party control. A major argument in the party literature against the use of economic terror was the difficulty of exerting adequate control over such acts.

But the party found that in practice it was impossible to exert the required degree of control even over political terror. There was thus considerable logic in the position of the future Maximalists in the party who argued in favour of economic terror, that party control was neither possible nor desirable. It was impossible because of the underground character of the party, and it was undesirable because of the danger of isolating the party from the 'spontaneous' revolutionary movement of the masses.

In 1902–3, and again in 1905–7, the SR party had to come to terms with the emergence of a mass revolutionary movement which developed largely outside its control. Although the spontaneous movement was uncoordinated and inchoate, it involved far greater numbers of people than any existing political party in Russia could realistically have hoped to organise, and it had a greater impact on the Tsarist government than any movement since the 'peasant wars' of the seventeenth and eighteenth centuries. In the countryside in particular, the peasants favoured methods of economic terror against the landowners, and it was difficult for the SRs to condemn such methods out of hand. The party was faced with an awkward dilemma: how to preserve standards of socialist morality and organisation compatible with its membership of the Second International, without risking the alienation of its potential base of popular support in Russia. It is not surprising that the SRs failed to square the circle. Their distinctions between political and economic terror, and between state and private expropriations, were often absurd and virtually impossible to translate into practice.

It might be argued that the logic of political terrorism led directly to the advocacy of economic terror within the SR party; that once the principle of terrorist violence against life and property was conceded, it was impossible to place limits on its application. The development of the views of many SRs in this period through Maximalism to anarchism might seem to demonstrate this logic. Yet abstract logic in itself seldom plays a role in history; the 'logic of events' is more important. At the time of the party's formation the SRs hoped that political terror would have the agitational effect of arousing a mass revolutionary movement. In 1905–7 the emergence of the mass movement, largely as a spontaneous phenomenon, caused the party to reassess its tactical directives on terror. But the SRs could not agree on the lessons to be drawn from the events of 1905. Some wanted to abandon terror, others to extend it. The intermediate position adopted by the party leadership, with all its inconsistencies, represented a compromise, not only between the different factions in the party, but also between neo-populist theory and the reality of the Russian revolution.

NOTES

1.   The secondary literature in Western languages on the SR party before 1914 is
      comparatively small. The account by a former Tsarist policy chief, translated
      from the Russian, is still a valuable compilation: A. Spiridovitch, *Histoire du*

terrorisme russe, 1886–1917, (Paris, 1930). There is a brief account of the pre-war years in the first three chapters of: O. H. Radkey, *The Agrarian Foes of Bolshevism: Promise and Default of the Russian Socialist-Revolutionaries, February–October 1917* (New York, 1958). In the past decade, the history of the party before 1914 has been the subject of research by Maureen Perrie in Britain and Manfred Hildermeier in Germany: Maureen Perrie, 'The Social Composition and Structure of the Socialist-Revolutionary Party before 1917', *Soviet Studies* 24 (1972), pp. 223–50; M. Perrie, *The Agrarian Policy of the Russian Socialist-Revolutionary Party: From its Origins through the Revolution of 1905–1907* (Cambridge, 1976); Manfred Hildermeier, 'Zur Sozialstruktur der Führungsgruppen und zur terroristischen Kampfmethode der Sozialrevolutionären Partei Russlands vor 1917', *Jahrbücher für Geschichte Osteuropas*, N.F. 20 (1972) pp. 516–50; Hildermeier, 'Neopopulismus und Industrialisierung: Zur Diskussion von Theorie und Taktik in der Sozialrevolutionären Partei Russlands vor dem Ersten Weltkrieg' *Jahrbücher für Geschichte Osteuropas*, N.F. 22 (1974), pp. 358–89; Hildermeier, 'Neopopulism and Modernisation: the Debate on Theory and Tactics in the Socialist Revolutionary Party, 1905–14', *Russian Review* 34 (1975) pp. 453–75; Hildermeier, *Die Sozialrevolutionäre Partei Russlands: Agrarsozialismus und Modernisierung im Zarenreich (1900–1914)* (Cologne, 1978).

2. V. M. Chernov, *Pered burei: Vospominaniya* (New York, 1953) pp. 150–3.

3. For a fuller discussion of these issues, see Perrie, *The Agrarian Policy*, passim.

4. *Protokoly pervogo s"ezda Partii Sotsialistov-Revolyutsionerov* (n.p., 1906) pp. 355–65.

5. For a review of the views on terror of the SR groups of the 1890s, see S. N. Sletov, *K istorii vozniknoveniya Partii Sotsialistov-Revolyutsionerov* (Petrograd, 1917) pp. 61–6.

6. On the terrorist acts committed by the Combat Organisation in 1902–5, see: Spiridovitch, pp. 149–260; Chernov, *Pered burei*, pp. 162–90; B. V. Savinkov, 'Vospominaniya', *Byloe* 1 (1917) pp. 149–95; 2 (1917) pp. 68–110; 3 (1917) pp. 68–120.

7. See, for example: 'Terroristicheskii element v nashei programme', *Revolyutsionnaya Rossiya* 7 (June 1902), pp. 2–5; 'Terror i massovoe dvizhenie', *Revolyutsionnaya Rossiya* 24 (May 1903) pp. 1–3; 'Terroristicheskaya taktika pered sudom sotsialisticheskoi pressy', *Revolyutsionnaya Rossiya* 52 (Sept. 1904) pp. 6–11; D. Khilkov, 'Terror i massovaya bor'ba', *Vestnik Russkoi Revolyutsii* 4 (March 1905) pp. 225–61.

8. 'Terroristicheskii element', pp. 3–5.

9. Spiridovitch, pp. 186–90; Savinkov, *Byloe* 2 (1917) pp. 69–75.

10. 'Terroristicheskii element', p. 5.

11. Spiridovitch, pp. 233–8. See also M. Ivich (comp.), 'Statistika terroristicheskikh aktov', *Pamyatnaya knizhka Sotsialista-Revolyutsionera*, no. 2 (n.p., 1914) pp. 8–9.

12. Spiridovitch, pp. 266–8; Savinkov, *Byloe* 3 (1917) pp. 116–20.

13. Spiridovitch, pp. 286–7. Cf. Ivich, pp. 9–10.

14. *Protokoly pervogo s"ezda*, p. 314; Savinkov, *Byloe* 1 (1918) pp. 68–74.

15. A. Kubov (comp.), 'Svod postanovlenii obshchepartiinykh Sovetov i S"ezdov', *Pamyatnaya knizhka Sotsialista-Revolyutsionera*, no. 1 (n.p., 1911) p. 65.

16. Spiridovitch, pp. 367–72; Savinkov, *Byloe* 2 (1918) p. 4; Ivich, pp. 11–12.

17. Spiridovitch, p. 372; Savinkov, *Byloe* 2 (1918) p. 26.

18. *Protokoly vtorogo (ekstrennogo) s"ezda Partii Sotsialistov-Revolyutsionerov* (St Petersburg, 1907) p. 162.

19. Spiridovitch, pp. 372–6; Savinkov, *Byloe* 2 (1918) pp. 30–1.

20. Spiridovitch, pp. 483–8; Savinkov, *Byloe* 2 (1918) pp. 44–5.
21. Spiridovitch, pp. 587–9; Savinkov, *Byloe* 3 (1918) pp. 31–55; 6 (1918) pp. 89–110. For the discussion on terror at the Fifth Party Council, see: 'Vopros o terrore na V Sovete Partii, Mai 1909 god', *Sotsialist-Revolyutsioner* 2 (1910) pp. 1–52.
22. Spiridovitch, pp. 624–5, 627–8.
23. For a discussion of these groups, see Hildermeier, 'Neopopulism and Modernisation', pp. 457–8, 468–71.
24. Ivich, p. 5.
25. The evidence from the party's own statistics concerning the occupations of SR terrorists was confirmed by an analysis by the present writer of the biographies of over 1,000 SRs active in the party before 1914. Of 293 SRs who had been involved in terrorism, 154 were workers or artisans: Perrie, 'The Social Composition and Structure of the Socialist-Revolutionary Party before 1917', p. 246.
26. My analysis of SR biographies suggested that the terrorists were even younger, with a median age of 20 in 1905: M. Perrie, 'The Social Composition and Structure of the Socialist-Revolutionary Party, and its Activity amongst the Russian Peasantry, 1901–7', M.A. thesis (University of Birmingham, 1971) p. 46b.
27. Ivich, pp. 8–20. The suggestion that many of the 'worker' terrorists in *Table 6.2* may have been Jewish artisans was made at the GHI Conference by Eric Hobsbawm: their regional distribution certainly supports this hypothesis.
28. Even their Social Democratic critics recognised that terrorism gained popular support for the SRs in this period. See: A. Egorov, 'Zarozhdenie politicheskikh partii i ikh deyatel'nost'', in L. Martov, P. Maslov and A. Potresov (eds), *Obshchestvennoe dvizhenie v Rossii v nachale XX-go veka*, vol. 1 (St Petersburg, 1909), p. 420; P. Maslov, 'Narodnicheskie partii' in ibid., vol. 3 (St Petersburg, 1914) p. 105.
29. For a fuller discussion of the issues covered in this section, see Perrie, *The Agrarian Policy*, pp. 91–7, 165–6.
30. Ibid., pp. 24–33, 42–50.
31. Ibid., pp. 58–69.
32. *Ko vsemu russkomu krest'yanstvu ot Krest'yanskogo Soyuza Partii Sotsialistov-Revolyutsionerov* (n.p., 1902) p. 24.
33. 'Pervyi s"ezd Agrarno-Sotsialisticheskoi Ligi', *Revolyutsionnaya Rossiya* 12 (Oct. 1902) pp. 21–3.
34. For a fuller discussion of this group, see V. Chernov, 'K kharakteristike maksimalizma', *Sotsialist-Revolyutsioner* 1 (1910) pp. 184–203.
35. Ibid., pp. 185–90.
36. Ibid., pp. 191–2.
37. Ibid., pp. 194–5.
38. Ibid., pp. 197–8.
39. Spiridovitch, p. 224.
40. *Protokoly pervogo s"ezda*, p. 336.
41. *Protokoly pervoi obshchepartiinoi konferentsii Partii Sotsialistov-Revolyutsionerov, avgust 1908* (Paris, 1908) pp. 230–1; Kubov, p. 48.
42. *Protokoly pervoi obshchepartiinoi konferentsii*, p. 230; Kubov, pp. 46–7.
43. I. Ritina (ed.), 'Iz materialov krest'yanskoi ankety (prodolzhenie)', *Znamya Truda* 27 (1910) pp. 19–20. See also the English translation by Maureen Perrie (ed.), 'The Russian Peasantry in 1907–1908; a Survey by the Socialist-Revolutionary Party', *History Workshop Journal* 4 (1977) pp. 189–90. There were also replies in favour of agrarian terror in response to a survey of Ukrainian peasant organisations, published in an SR-Maximalist journal: 'Otvety

krest'yanskikh organizatsii (Ukrainskikh grupp)', *Trudovaya Respublika* 2 (1909) p. 16.
44. Perrie, *The Agrarian Policy*, p. 119; taken from S. M. Dubrovskii, *Krest'yanskoe dvizhenie v revolyutsii 1905–1907 gg.* (Moscow, 1956) p. 67.
45. Chernov, 'K kharakteristike maksimalizma', p. 197.
46. 'Koe-chto o maksimalistakh (Pis'mo iz Smolenska)', *Partiinye Izvestiya* 8 (1907) pp. 3–5.
47. Ibid., pp. 3–4.
48. Chernov, 'K kharakteristike maksimalizma', pp. 188, 229–30.
49. The secondary literature on Maximalism is very slight. See Spiridovitch, pp. 392–412; B. I: Gorev, 'Apoliticheskie i antiparlamentskie gruppy' in L. Martov, P. Maslov and A. Potresov (eds), *Obshchestvennoe dvizhenie v Rossii v nachale XX-go veka*, vol. 3 (St Petersburg, 1914) pp. 511–22.
50. *Protokoly pervogo s"ezda*, pp. 332–3.
51. Ibid., p. 334.
52. Ibid., p. 337.
53. *Protokoly pervoi obshchepartiinoi konferentsii*, pp. 234–5; Kubov, pp. 48–9.
54. 'Ot Tsentral'nogo Komiteta. Po voprosu ob agrarnom i fabrichnom terrore', *Znamya Truda* 3 (1907) p. 12; Kubov, pp. 49–50.
55. 'Koe-chto o maksimalistakh', pp. 3–4; Chernov, 'K kharakteristike maksimalizma', p. 198.
56. *Protokoly pervogo s"ezda*, p. 25.
57. Ibid., pp. 271, 311.
58. Chernov, 'K kharakteristike maksimalizma', pp. 210–16; Spiridovitch, pp. 392–4.
59. 'Vtoroe sobranie Soveta P.S.-R'., *Partiinye Izvestiya* 2 (1906) p. 3.
60. *Protokoly vtorogo (ekstrennogo) s"ezda*, pp. 147–60.
61. For a list of party expropriations in 1906, see Spiridovitch, p. 391.
62. Ibid., pp. 402–3.
63. Ritina, pp. 18–19 (Perrie (ed.), pp. 188–9). The replies of the Ukrainian peasant organisations to the Maximalist survey also favoured private expropriations: 'Otvety krest'yanskikh organizatsii', p. 16.
64. Perrie, *The Agrarian Policy*, pp. 102–4.
65. 'Reaktsionnaya demagogiya i revolyutsionnyi sotsializm', *Revolyutsionnaya Rossiya* 67 (May 1905) p. 3.
66. *Protokoly pervogo s"ezda*, pp. 89–96.
67. See especially the speeches of Shvetsov ('Pashin'), ibid., pp. 184–6, 205–12.
68. Ibid., pp. 312–32.
69. See the speech by the Maximalist 'Poroshin', ibid., pp. 105–7.
70. Ibid., pp. 147–52.
71. Ibid., pp. 272–6.
72. Ibid., p. 116.
73. 'Koe-chto o maksimalistakh', p. 4.
74. Spiridovitch, p. 388.

7 The Terrorist Strategies of the Socialist-Revolutionary Party in Russia, 1900–14

Manfred Hildermeier

As successor to the populist social movement of the 1870s, the Socialist-Revolutionary Party (SRP) represented the most important non-Marxist trend within the Russian revolutionary movement at the beginning of the twentieth century. It differed from the Social Democrats not only in its subjectivist social theory, which held the initiative of the 'creative individual' (P. L. Lavrov, N. K. Mikhailovsky) to be the driving force of the historical process, but also in its aim at a decentralised, agrarian-socialist society, and it maintained that the autocratic regime it was fighting could only be removed by popular insurrection under the leadership of the peasantry. Its particular nature manifested itself even more clearly in the forms of action it favoured, inherited from *Narodnaya Volya* and closely linked to the latter's subjectivist-voluntarist principles. Just as the call for 'socialisation of the land' was the distinguishing feature of the SRP's programme, the so-called 'individual terror' was to become the characteristic of SR strategy. The following comments are confined to an attempt to throw some light on the peculiarities of their political tactics as well as on some aspects that are of interest beyond the merely Russian context.[1] They will deal with (1) the theoretical justification of 'individual terror' and the form it took; (2) its political effectiveness; and (3) its organisation.

I

It was particularly in the Russia of the late 1870s that political terror began to form part of the revolutionary movement's action programme. It arose in a period characterised by disappointment about the failure to mobilise the peasants to revolt against the autocratic regime. The adherents of *Narodnaya Volya* regarded attempts on the life of leading representatives of the State apparatus, and indeed the tsar's own life, as the only means left to them, if they were still to accomplish their revolution. Deliberate use of violence seemed to

80

hold out the hope, as expressed in one of their pamphlets, of retrieving the failed popular insurrection 'with the least possible sacrifice and in the shortest possible time'.[2] Political terror was perceived as an alternative to the revolutionary action of the masses that had failed to materialise. It was both a consequence and a mark of the existing gulf between a conscious elite and the so-called 'dark' people. Yet the contrast between the use of violence and the tactics of peaceful enlightenment, which had been practised in the early 1870s, was only a superficial one. It might with greater justification be described as complementary to it, since both strategies revealed the helplessness of the self-appointed avant-garde.

Political terror, thus rationalised, constituted in Russia a mode of action specific to the intelligentsia and was in the last resort, in the words of Lenin's brother, Alexander Ulyanov, 'a conflict between government and intelligentsia'.[3] The terrorist, belonging to the educated class, took up the fight against oppression and exploitation as a deputy of the people and, as that deputy, he also chose his objectives: the revolutionary struggle turned into a kind of duel. Legitimacy and usefulness of terrorist attempts were expressly linked to this representative and personal character of the conflict: 'In our country', stated the *Narodnaya Volya* pamphlet already referred to, 'the terrorists conduct their fight against individuals and their personal interests – against the head of the dynasty and its most important pillars'. Where 'terror is not directed against individuals, but against whole institutions, classes or, even more importantly, the economic interests of an entire category of people, it is simply inappropriate'.[4]

In later SR-declarations this form of terrorist action was given additional justification by moral and ethical arguments. These showed a marked irrationalism and an almost pseudo-religious glorification of 'the avenging heroes' – as they tended to be called. It was not political motives which determined the acts of the assassin, but 'hatred', 'a spirit of sacrifice' and a 'sense of honour'. The throwing of bombs was declared to be a 'holy cause'. Thus the SRP shrouded its terrorists in a special aura, placing them far above what might be termed its civilian party members. They embodied, as it were, the ethical principle of the revolution, for they were prepared to give their lives for the revolutionary cause. A prominent SRP-member summarised this view as follows: 'In terms of moral philosophy, the act of killing must at the same time be an act of self-sacrifice.'[5] A few years later this was precisely the argument employed in order to distinguish the SR's legitimate tyrannicide from the Bolsheviks' execrable terror: the former, wrote the left-wing Socialist-Revolutionary who later became the Soviet government's first People's Commissar for Justice, Isaac Steinberg, sprang from personal effort which did not shrink from self-sacrifice, the latter from 'the comfort of bureaucratic chambers'.[6]

Populist theory and practice of 'individual terror' in the form described was closely linked to the structure of the autocratic state. The following considerations are of particular interest in this connection:

(1)   Even *Narodnaya Volya* had considered terrorist acts to be necessary or justified only as long as the autocratic regime refused to grant the people the right of political participation in the shape of a democratically elected parliament. Where representation of the people or a constituent assembly already existed the use of force was rejected. The famous letter of protest by the executive committee condemning the assassination of the American President Garfield in 1881 expresses this view very clearly.

(2)   The justification of so-called 'individual terror' corresponded to a concept of an order of state and society, which could still see dependence and injustice as being embodied in a few symbolic figures – the tsar, the governor, the landowner. At the same time this form of calculated use of violence corresponded to the markedly centralist system of rule that was a feature of tsarist autocracy and more generally of the type of society, which has been called an 'agrarian bureaucracy'. It was only in this context that the explicitly formulated assumption that the killing of a civil servant meant at the same time the destruction of some portion of autocratic rule, could make any sort of sense. And only in a state and a society of this kind could revolutionaries, such as the *narodnovoltsy*, seriously believe that by assassinating the tsar they would automatically destroy the system and bring about the freedom they aspired to.

(3)   The substitute character attaching to 'individual terror' reflects in some way Russia's social underdevelopment. Until the turn of the century the tsarist empire lacked the basic pre-conditions for organised collective social protest on any scale. No broad social stratum existed capable of supporting such a protest. Although peasant unrest broke out repeatedly, this remained limited, spontaneous and short-lived, and no revolutionary group was able to harness it for its own aims. Only in the course of industrialisation, from the 1870s onwards did an urban proletariat begin to emerge. Nor were the conditions propitious for the development of a middle class strong and independent enough to make political claims on the State. The revolutionary intelligentsia in an autocratic state was thus, to a much greater degree than in western European societies, thrown back on its own resources. It therefore seemed reasonable for them to compensate for their inadequate numerical strength by a strategy which, even without the backing of a mass movement, held out some prospect of success.

II

For the Socialist-Revolutionaries, terrorist attempts were to fulfil three main tactical functions: firstly, to protect the revolutionaries. It was expected that the forces of the State would be cautious in the certain knowledge that each of their repressive measures would elicit retaliation. Secondly, great hopes were placed in the propaganda effects of terrorist acts, since these would 'awaken even the sleepiest philistines . . . and force them, even against their will, to think politically'.[7] Thirdly and lastly, the assassination of the regime's most prominent representatives was to have a 'disorganising effect'. Guns and bombs were, if not to destroy the State, at least to force it to make concessions to 'society'.

It cannot be denied that in the initial phase, in what was later to be called the 'heroic period' of Socialist-Revolutionary terror preceding the 1905 revolution, all three main objectives were largely realised. The successful assassinations of one minister of education, two ministers of the interior, one governor-general and one member of the tsar's family, did indeed strike both anxiety and terror among the rulers, and evidently caused utter panic within the security forces. They were even greatly applauded by the liberals. With the onset of revolution this run of successes came to an abrupt end. To the dismay of the party leadership, the number of terrorist acts and violent incursions by local committees increased, yet the weapon of so-called 'central' political terror, which was the particular feature of SR strategy, nevertheless remained a blunt one, especially after revolutionary unrest had come to an end. Even the central committee's unceasing appeals and efforts at reorganisation could not alter that fact.

The causes of this development were, from 1909 onwards, a matter of heated debate among the SRP leadership. Roughly speaking, two positions began to emerge. The members of the central committee had a very convenient answer to this. They sought the sole explanation for the failures in the treason of an agent of the secret police who, as was discovered late in 1908, had for years been an active member of the inner group of the so-called 'combat organisation'. There is no doubt that this *agent provocateur*, Evno Azef, did untold damage to the party. But the central committee conveniently overlooked the fact that Azef's career had only been possible because he had equally cheated his paymasters and had committed a double treachery which, to his contemporaries, appeared incredible.

A less superficial explanation was offered by the representatives of the opposing right wing of the party. According to them, the unsuccessful terrorist attempts only proved that these tactics had become inappropriate and anachronistic. 'The people, or rather the exploited working class itself', they argued, 'had during the revolution entered into the arena of political struggle.' To challenge the government on their behalf was thus no longer necessary, and the individual struggle of the intelligentsia would have to cease.[8] Russia's social and political development, in other words, had irrevocably removed the basis of *Narodnaya Volya*'s strategy of 'individual terror', for it had changed the premises on which this had been founded.

This argument, reasonably sound in itself, may be complemented by the following more general thought. In so far as political terror is a symbolic act[9] it derives its efficacy from the fact that with relatively minimal expenditure of personal and material means, it is possible to achieve maximal political effect by creating fear and setting an example. This, of course, is only the case if certain preconditions exist. As a rule, it has been argued convincingly, terrorists tend to be particularly successful if, in an already unstable society, they are able to muster a small degree of actual, and a large degree of potential support. And this was precisely the position of the SRP on the eve of the revolution and comes closest to an explanation of the impact of the assassination of the two ministers of the interior, Sipyagin and Plehve. On the other hand, terrorists risk failure if they carry out attempts as already established political groups, which have gained at least partial social acceptance, since they then put their moral credibility at risk. This, too, the Socialist-Revolutionaries came to experience when, in the course of the revolution, they lost the support of the liberal intelligentsia and thus important financial backers. In other words, the graph depicting the rise and fall of SR terror suggests that political violence of this kind has its greatest impact in a still unstructured situation of diffuse ferment, where different and conflicting political currents still come together on a common front.

As soon as the contours of political parties have become more clearly defined in the next phase of the revolutionary movement, the impact of terrorist acts is diminished, since then their authors can less readily count on the support of fellow travellers of no fixed political position or from other political camps. The SR leadership failed to appreciate sufficiently the degree to which terrorist strategy depends on its being appropriate to a given situation. They did not recognise that political terror is unsuitable as a continuous strategy, that in the long run it did not serve to integrate the masses they were courting, and that at best it could mobilise them only for a short while, as it had done in 1904–5. The SRP, therefore, failed not least because it accorded absolute priority to a strategy which proved to be inappropriate in practice, and continued to cling to it, long after the preconditions for its usefulness had ceased to exist.

III

The SRP, in contrast to *Narodnaya Volya*, was a mass party, claiming to be open to anyone who supported its programme. As a result, its necessarily conspiratorial terrorist activities had to be strictly separated from its work of agitation. The former were entrusted to a so-called 'combat organisation', especially formed for this purpose. While *Narodnaya Volya*'s theoreticians, organisers and terrorists had been largely one and the same people, the SRP introduced a division of responsibilities. For the first time a whole group of revolutionaries existed whose sole function it was to prepare and carry out assassinations. Making terror organisationally independent, however, was not to remain without consequences. Even at an early stage it became evident that the party leadership was beginning to lose control over the 'combatants'. According to party statute it was the sole prerogative of the leadership to determine the target and timing of any attempt. In practice, however, the terrorists chose their victims themselves and also carried out their assassinations when they considered the situation to be propitious.

Still more damaging was the fact that members of the combat organisation often lived for years in complete isolation from the party. Under the strain of an illegal existence and exposed to constant persecution by the tsarist secret police, they developed their own values and their own elitist *esprit de corps*. With few exceptions, they adopted the arrogant view that it was they who accomplished the truly revolutionary deeds. Their inclination to take orders from a 'civilian' party leadership was correspondingly slight. Solidarity amongst themselves ranked higher than their obligation of loyalty to the party. This alienation went so far that one terrorist, during the investigations against Azef, the police agent and leader of the combat organisation, threatened to shoot the entire central committee, if it dared to prosecute him.

At the same time, most of the 'combatants' showed a marked scepticism towards any kind of theory and hardly bothered about the party's internal political debates. For them terror had become a 'craft', as one speaker at a party conference in 1909 remarked critically.[10] What counted in the combat organisations was organising ability, daring, histrionic talent and skill in the forging of passports and construction of bombs – not socialist-revolutionary theory or ideological staying power. And not least for this reason, it was possible that a police agent like Azef, whose theoretical indifference was no secret to anyone within the party leadership and who was therefore dubbed the 'liberal with the bomb', could on account of his organising ability rise to be the head of the combat organisation. Seen from this angle, the Azef affair, which shook the SRP to its very foundations, appears not merely as a nasty misfortune. It was surely also the consequence of growing organisational independence and insufficient ability to control terrorist tactics.

Any attempt to draw conclusions from the record of Socialist-Revolutionary terrorist actions, which might serve as a more general illustration of the calculated use of force as an instrument of political struggle, would require a degree of caution. It would be almost impossible to divorce the fundamental preconditions of 'individual terror' from the autocratic, agrarian-bureaucratic system of rule in Russia, from concrete political circumstances and from the socio-psychological situation of the Russian *intelligentsia*. It is possible, on the other hand, to detect certain phenomena which appear to represent, beyond the different historical contexts, certain related forms of political violence, that is to say in so far as they typify its deliberate use by small groups against the leading representatives of a State and society they are challenging, and not a mass phenomenon akin to civil war. The following in particular should be mentioned here, without claiming systematic categorisation.

＊Terrorist acts of the kind described above, seem to require a large degree of political and especially ethical legitimisation. Its function consists, on the one hand, in presenting assassinations as politically meaningful acts and differentiating them from criminal homicide, and on the other, apparently also in reducing psychological inhibitions about the act of killing. To the Russian terrorists at least, who had grown up in the humanist traditions of an educated middle class or belonged to an *intelligentsia* informed by German idealism, the deliberate destruction of human life posed a major moral problem. To assuage these qualms by invoking a natural right of opposition, as it were, and to construct on this a *theodicy* of violence, as did the Socialist-Revolutionaries, appears to have been an obvious and widespread solution to the problem. There are some indications, however, that the qualms and with them the deeply felt need for justification evaporate to the degree that terrorist groups, because they are forced into an illegal existence, lose contact with their political and social environment.

＊Small terrorist groups appear to emerge not infrequently – as for instance in Russia in the 1870s and at the beginning of the twentieth century, or in West Germany in recent times – during a (provisionally) final phase of comprehensive social movement. In this situation they attempt to prevent the failure of that movement. Violence is to bring about what peaceful means were not able to achieve; and at the very least it is hoped to revive the movement. Yet the success of such 'defensive' acts of terror appears to be limited, since a latent, widespread political dissatisfaction – which may be said to be an essential precondition for the mobilising effect of 'individual' terrorist attempts – exists only for a limited time. This, of course, does not mean that the 'destabilising' effect on the political system thus challenged may not occur.

＊Members of terrorist organisations, as a rule, are compelled to make a complete and lasting break with their previous existence, unless they are firmly tied in to larger national or religious minorities, or indeed form part of an 'alternative society'. They enter into a state of war which cuts them off from their previous life and largely insulates them against the world outside. They live under conditions of illegality and constant persecution, in an exceptional situation which produces specific behaviour patterns and causes considerable psychological strains. A consequence of this isolation and tension appears to be the progressive loss of the faculty to evaluate the political effect of their own deeds with any degree of realism. Acts of terrorism become an end in themselves. All the more so, as a return to non-violent methods of political conflict is often impossible and to continue on the chosen path remains the only way to safeguard the cohesion of the group and to shield it from the realisation of having resorted to inappropriate means that do not serve their intended purposes. The calculated use of political violence – contrary to the ideas of groups such as the Socialist-Revolutionaries – is tactically inflexible, since it is subject to the law of 'all or nothing' and, once embarked upon, can hardly be employed in a manner appropriate to the situation. This, too, may be regarded as proving the thesis that acts of terror of the kind described – which admittedly represent merely a small aspect of the whole phenomenon of terror – can only be a short-term and, in the end, ineffective means of revolutionary political struggle.

NOTES

1. Cf. more extensively: M. Hildermeier, *Die Sozialrevolutionäre Partei Russlands: Agrarsozialismus und Modernisierung im Zarenreich (1900–1914)* (Cologne and Vienna, 1978) p. 58ff, 340ff, 358ff.
2. Cf. L. Ja. Sternberg, *Političeskij terror v Rossii* (n.p., 1884), pp. 16, 18, 21. Similarly V. Tarnovskij and G. G. Romanenko, *Terrorizm i rutina* (London, 1881) p. 15; N. Morozov, 'Terrorstičeskaja bor'ba', *Da zdravstvuet Narodnaya Volya: Istoričeskij sbornik* 1 (Paris, 1907) p. 18.
3. Cf. A. I. Ul'yanova-Elizarova, *A. I. Ul'yanov i delo 1-go marta 1887 g.* (Moscow and Leningrad, 1927) p. 379.
4. Cf. Sternberg, *Političeskij terror*, p. 34.
5. Cf. V. M. Zenzinov, *Perežitoe* (New York, 1953) p. 108.
6. Cf. I. Steinberg, *Gewalt und Terror in der Revolution (Oktober-Revolution oder Bolschewismus)* (Berlin, 1931) p. 180f.
7. Cf. 'Terroristčeskij člement v našej programme', *Revolyucionnaya Rossija: Izd. Partii Socialistov-revoljucionerov* 7 (Geneva, 1902) p. 2.
8. Cf. 'Dokumenty po istorii partii S.-R.: Vopros o terrore na V. sovete Partii', *Socialist-Revoljucioner: Trechmesjalnoe literaturno-političeskoe obozrenie*, Pod. red. V. M. Černova, 2 (Paris, 1910) p. 21f.
9. Cf. T. P. Thornton, 'Terror as a Weapon of Political Agitation' in H. Eckstein (ed.), *Internal War: Problems and Approaches* (Glencoe, 1964) p. 73.
10. Cf. Dokumenty po istorii Partii S.-R., p. 23.

8 The Strategies of 'Direct Action' and Violence in Spanish Anarchism

Walther L. Bernecker

Dedicated to Joseph Becker on his 50th Birthday

I

The link between the working-class movement and Anarchism in nineteenth- and twentieth-century Spanish history is a far more tangible one than in any of the other modern European societies. Until the Civil War of 1936–9, Anarchism in Spain represented a significant revolutionary force which, in alliance with the Syndicalist movement, showed remarkable organisational stability. From the outset – when at the beginning of November 1868 the Italian Guiseppe Fanelli, as Bakunin's envoy, brought the news of the creation of an International Workers' Association to Spain – Iberian Anarchism was concentrated socially and regionally in two areas: in the feudal, latifundist South, where Anarchism took root among Andalusian agricultural labourers and artisans, and in the relatively industrialised North-east of the peninsula, where Catalan Anarcho-Syndicalism established itself. This social (industrial/agricultural) and regional (Andalusia/Catalonia) differentiation has not only prompted scholars to produce a variety of explanatory hypotheses about the causes that gave rise to Spanish Anarchism, but in the course of its history has also presented the movement itself with virtually insoluble structural problems. It determined its strategy and tactics, exercised a decisive influence on the anarchist concept of revolution and may even have been one of the main reasons for the movement's failure and ultimate eclipse as a social-revolutionary force.[1]

All libertarian authors who have taken a self-critical look at their movement and its role in the social conflicts during the last third of the nineteenth and the first third of the twentieth century, have pointed to the lack of accord between the different Anarchist wings on essential programmatic issues.[2] The Anarchists' internal disputes and their inability to reach consensus on questions of principle can be traced right back to the beginning of the movement: even at the first Workers Congress of 1870 in Barcelona the programme presented by the Spanish Section of the International ('in politics anarchist, in economy collectivist, in religion atheist') was only accepted after several crucial votes, and then only in an extremely diluted form. The disagreements during this congress set the pattern for the dissent that was to develop between 'reformists' and revolutionary activists. Significantly, even then the majority of Catalan delegates advocated a more moderate wording of individual proposals, but on the whole to little avail.[3]

The differing social and regional composition of the Spanish Anarchist movement had a very direct impact on such central issues as 'direct action' and the use of violence. Consideration of the social, economic, political, socio-historical preconditions for the rise of Anarchism and its development into a revolutionary mass movement implies at the same time the question of the different strategies of 'libertarian socialism'. In this context strategies are taken to mean the rational and objective aims of violent acts, while bearing in mind that especially in Spanish Anarchism irrational patterns of violence were also frequent and widespread.

For the Spanish Anarchists, the First International's motto – 'the emancipation of the proletariat must be the work of the proletariat itself' –could only mean consistent rejection of political parties or associations exerting an influence when it came to formulating political objectives or decisions. This 'anti-political' stance, as distinct from an 'apolitical' one,[4] also prevented them from forming (expedient) coalitions with Republican or Socialist parties and constituted one of the movement's essential traits. For the workers organised in the Federación Regional Española (FRE), antipoliticismo not only meant the rejection of all political parties, but hostility towards a republican form of government and the refusal to take part in elections. The debate about the appropriateness of these tactics – which had already flared up in 1870 and was two years later to lead to the Spanish labour movement splitting into a larger 'anti-authoritarian' (Bakuninist) and a smaller 'authoritarian' (Marxist) wing – as far as the Anarchist workers were concerned, was settled in favour of antipoliticismo, after the Paris Commune in 1871 had been bloodily suppressed by a republican government. For the Anarchists it was now proven beyond doubt that all politics, no matter under what form of government, were pernicious for the workers and therefore to be rejected.[5]

In place of 'political' action, the Anarchists put 'direct' or 'anti-political' action, which they originally conceived of as being the direct conflict between opposing social forces (labour and capital). It meant independent action of the people without recourse to parliamentary representatives, and, in direct reference to Bakunin, the intention to reach their ultimate aim, social revolution, 'not by way of formal use and dissemination of ready-made theories, but only through the spontaneous deed of a practical autonomous spirit'.[6] Initially, 'direct action' was thus by no means to be equated with the use of physical force, even if an extremist wing had always considered acts of sabotage and terror to be legitimate means in the fight against capital; 'direct action' meant activities such as collective bargaining, propagandist agitation and strikes. And, during the lifetime of the International's Spanish Regional Federation (1870–88) it was indeed the strike weapon which represented the preferred strategy of organised labour; in terms of their eventual goal it was considered a revolutionary weapon, yet in terms of the prevailing law it was a perfectly legal one. An anarchist pamphlet of 1872 expressed the International's objectives as follows:[7]

> It must gradually change the economic situation of the working class . . . improve working conditions, curtail, diminish and eliminate the privileges of capital, make these every day more dependant and precarious, until capital surrenders and disappears . . . This can be achieved by *resistance*, with the legal and open weapon of the *strike*.

The objectives to be attained by strikes, however, were not to be reformist improvements in the conditions of the working class – improvements that would render the ultimate remedy of social revolution superfluous – but a maximisation of the starting position from which to set out towards the final, inescapable act that would overthrow the existing political and economic order and bring about a stateless society. Targets such as the eight-hour day, wage improvements, freedom of speech and association, or the release of political prisoners were thus not justified as ends in themselves, but as purely tactical means, in order to weaken the position of the opponent and to strengthen one's own.[8]

The strategies developed by Spanish Anarchism during its 'heroic years'[9] can only be explained in the context of the movement's genesis. During the decades preceding the creation of the Anarcho-Syndicalist trade union *Confederación Nacional del Trabajo* (CNT) – different conditions prevailed in the subsequent period – the activities of Anarchist groups can be said to fall broadly into three patterns:

(1)   The initial concern of the International's Regional Spanish Federation was to gain a foothold in the labour movement. To this end, it made use of already existing workers' circles, peasant associations, cultural centres, etc., always careful to emphasise the legality of its actions. In the period from 1868–74 and again (after its re-admission by the liberal Sagasta government) from 1881–4, the (peaceful) strike developed into its main tactical instrument.

(2)   When, at the beginning of the era of restoration (1874), the International was proscribed and forced underground, this led, in view of the failure of peaceful tactics, to a radicalisation of a section of the Anarchist movement and, as a result, to a split within the FRE. In the ensuing conflict between syndicalists, standing for peaceful strategies, and extremists, advocating terrorist measures, a form of actionism asserted itself, particularly among the agrarian proletariat of Andalusia, which turned terrorism, as 'propaganda by deed', into one of the manifestations of Anarchism. During the 1880s, the

debate between Anarcho-Collectivists and Anarcho-Communists in Spain (a debate, which also took place on an international level) turned on the usefulness of violence. The fact that the landless agrarian proletariat of the South came down on the side of Anarcho-Communism resulted in the use of individual violence. Individual acts of terror were to continue throughout the 1890s and the first decade of the twentieth century.

(3) Ever since Anarcho-Collectivists and Anarcho-Communists had reached an historically viable compromise in Anarcho-Syndicalism, the general strike developed more and more markedly into the main strategy of the libertarian movement. Anarcho-Syndicalism's main postulates were federalism, the exclusively syndicalist struggle, and 'direct action' as the only method, culminating in the general strike.[10] The latter, apart from economic aims, was to further political ones as well: it was the means whereby the State could be overthrown and society be given a syndicalist organisation. The general strike, as the most effective form of direct action, was perceived as an instrument in the class war, which would bring about a new order of society. But the concern here was not to conquer political power, but to destroy it.

If we look at the Spanish labour movement's various strategies, that is, its calculated long or medium-term activities, as well as its more irrational forms of violence, in historical perspective, the question arises as to their respective causes. The central issue in this is the problem of violence in its various forms. In the following, I shall attempt to relate the different forms of collective social protest and individual acts of violence to the Anarchists' social situation and hence to the motives that prompted that behaviour. Is it possible to relate individual, historically definable types of violence to different ideologies and their supporters' differing socio-economic situations? In other words, can the use of violence be linked to the intellectual traditions and the specific interest of the working class? We shall have to ask what were the socio-political constellations that gave rise to the emergence and spread of the Anarchist movement in Spain and to its use of violence. In this connection, we shall have to take a closer look at the function of the institutional counter-violence of ruling groups and its effect on Anarchist forms of violence. This aspect is closely connected with the legitimisation of violence in the anarchists' perception of themselves. An analysis of the forms of violence thus also requires an investigation of how this violence tended to be explained and justified.

The development of the general strike into a strategy initiated a new phase in the evolution of Anarchism and for this reason can only be briefly touched on in the present contribution.

II

As soon as the International's Anarchist wing had gained a footing in Spain, the FRE initiated numerous activities with the objective of fully emancipating the working class. At the FRE's first congress in Barcelona (1870) a resolution was passed, recommending the strike as the most promising strategy of 'direct action' for the realisation of the workers' interests. In the internationalist press of the time, the term 'scientific strike' very soon became the accepted expression; this provided also some indication of the problems connected with this strategy: local strikes were not to be called until the entire machinery of the workers' organisation had been included in a 'scientific manner' in their planning and organisation. The bureaucratic mechanisms that needed to be set in motion from the moment a local sector made a strike application until its approval by the *Comité Federal* would thus have taken almost two months.[11] If one looks at the legalistic course pursued by the then predominantly Catalan FRE-leadership, one is led to conclude that the implementation of a strike was made dependent on compliance with numerous regulations, not out of a desire to achieve the greatest impact and to ensure solidarity and support of other sections of workers – as officially proclaimed – but because the Syndicalist-oriented wing wished to prevent strikes altogether. Until it was declared illegal in 1874, and again after its re-admission in 1881, the FRE also fought against the many 'wild cat' strikes which took place with particular frequency in agrarian Andalusia. Despite the opposition of the *Comité Federal*, during the first phase of the International strikes continued to be the strategy most frequently employed by the workers' movement. Rank-and-file workmen urged ever new strikes, embarked on unco-ordinated and ill-prepared protest actions, which mostly ended in failure, and thus provided the authorities with sufficient pretext to persecute and suppress the FRE. Because of lack of success and increasing tensions, most of the workers, particularly during the years the International was banned (1874–81), either sank into the apathy of despair or, much more frequently, took the radical path of violent action.[12]

Between 1868 and 1874 the organised labour movement in Spain pursued an invariably legal course: it intended to achieve its objectives by association, propaganda and peaceable strikes. On occasion it was even claimed that it was possible to achieve the social revolution by peaceful means, within the framework of the existing constitutional and political order. The inter-nationalist press of that time constantly reiterated its motto: 'Peace towards mankind, war against institutions'. And even the FRE's participation in the cantonal insurrection of 1873 did not, by any means, possess the significance which both Friedrich Engels and the conservative press of the day imputed to it with polemic intent.[13] Only the massive repression of the internationalist movement by the republican Castelar government towards the end of 1873 and the simultaneous recognition that the strike-strategy pursued so far had been a failure, caused the FRE to revise its hitherto mainly peaceful strategies and to come down – albeit reluctantly – on the side of violent measures. The excess of repressive violence on the part of the state had not made the workers more tractable, but had, on the contrary, resulted in an escalation of resistance and counter-violence. Even then the organisation attempted to ensure that its means remained commensurate: it merely announced 'retaliatory measures' in response to particular incursions on the part of the bourgeoisie. The movement intended to confine itself to retaliatory violence, and in its proclamations left no doubt that it regarded its actions merely as a violent response to government persecution and the bourgeoisie's institutionalised terror. In this phase, violence was less strategy than reaction and self-defence. When the International was legalised again in 1881, the workers' movement's first phase of violence came to an abrupt end; it had in any case consisted more in theory or threats, than in spectacular 'retaliatory measures' or acts of terror.

After 1881 it was again the 'legalist' wing which continued to determine the movement's course for a number of years; this, however, now showed obvious reformist traits. Not only the means, but the objectives as well had been shorn of their revolutionary dynamic and been replaced by servile recognition of the status quo. 'Their Excellencies, the Ministers' and 'their Honours, the Civil Governors', were respectfully asked to do something about the excesses perpetrated by the organs of the state. The *Revista Social*, the FRE's official mouthpiece, vigorously rejected the use of violence by workers. The Valencia Congress of 1883 expressly stated that those workers who still advocated a strategy of violence ought no longer to be able to count on the solidarity of the movement.

It would certainly be wrong to interpret the anarchists' perception of their own role as a reflection of their actual impotence during those years, or as the pre-emptive response to their fear of being banned again. It was rather that from the beginning it had been an unquestioned tenet of Spanish Anarchists that the social revolution was not to happen against the will of the majority of the people. They were vividly conscious of the fact that there existed an indivisible connection between ends and means; these had to remain reconcilable with each other, lest the means should destroy the end and finally replace it.[14] The constant call for organisation and propaganda, and the clear rejection of violent measures were thus not an expression of impotent resignation but a deliberate reiteration of one of Anarchism's basic postulates.

The climax of these legalistic tactics coincided with the period of the severest persecution the Anarchists were subjected to during those decades: the suppression of the organised labour movement after the *Mano Negra* cases (1883) led to a crisis and finally to the dissolution (1888) of the *Federación de Trabajadores de la Región Española* (FTRE). As legalistic tactics had failed and indeed ended in complete fiasco, the extreme left groups, which already in the period of illegality had carried out violent actions and were again advocating much more radical combat methods, found it relatively easy in the 1880s to gain greater influence within the Federation. Finally 'illegalism' completely won the day and this initiated a new phase in the history of the Spanish workers' movement.

If, after this brief chronicle of events, one were now to trace and analyse the ideological pattern underlying the actions of anarchist groups, the question as to the motives for the legalist-syndicalist tactics of the FTRE-leadership in Catalonia on the one hand, and for the numerous strikes and insurrections of agrarian anarchist groups in Andalusia on the other, must be extended, to inquire more generally into the reasons why Anarchism in Spain was able to gain so much ground. The relevant literature of recent decades has provided several partial answers, which allow us to come a little nearer to the complex subject of 'Spanish Anarchism'. The conceptual and socio-historical deficiencies of research into anarchism in general have recently been deplored; it is characterised by a lack of precision on the one hand and by a too narrow historical definition of the phenomenon of anarchism on the other and has thus, because it fails to provide explanatory models for the rise and the history of Anarchism, merely tended to reproduce the latter's absence of theory.[15] In the Spanish case, however, this is only true in the reverse sense: repeated attempts to explain Iberian Anarchism in monocausal terms have led to very diverse interpretative approaches, sometimes complementary, sometimes cancelling each other out.

One of the most frequent explanations traces Anarchism's mobilisation back to the movement's milleniarism. Constancio Bernaldo de Quirós[16] was one of the first Spanish scholars to describe Anarchism as a secular religion, founded on an apocalyptic belief in an equal society. When Juan Díaz del Moral in 1929 published his still authoritative study of the peasant movements in the province of Córdoba he was able to draw on Bernaldo de Quirós' theories.[17] The periodicity of anarchist rebellions, and the tremendous passions that were aroused during insurrections, have led Díaz del Moral to explain Spanish Anarchism in terms of social psychology. He argued that Anarchism, as other pre-modern religious movements, had a magic rather than a rationally scientific concept of time and historical evolution. The fact that anarchist insurrections repeated themselves at ten-year intervals (1873: cantonalist rising; 1883: harvest strike in the Cádiz province; 1892: rebellion at Jerez de la Frontera; 1902/3: general strike of coopers, agricultural and textile workers in western Andalusia) appeared to corroborate his thesis.

Gerald Brenan, in his masterly analysis of the social and political background to the Spanish Civil War, based himself on the findings of Bernaldo de Quirós and Díaz del Moral.[18] He argues that the radicalism of Andalusian Anarchism corresponds to the Spanish temperament, and that Spanish individualism and pride provided the ideal soil for a doctrine 'which, in a more extreme form than even the Protestant religion, places on each individual the responsibility for his own actions'.[19] Anarchism as a dynamic mass movement with a social-revolutionary thrust had come together in Spain with the emotions underlying a traditional attitude to life which it had only needed to stimulate.[20] The unparalleled vitality of Spanish Anarchism was deeply rooted in the mentality of the simple people; the coincidence of passionate individualism and a no-less-intense sense of community had fused into a social-revolutionary idealism, which constituted the 'Hispanic' nature of Anarchism.

Gerald Brenan's, and later Franz Borkenau's,[21] interpretative approach in terms of national psychology, romanticising and mysticising the Spanish soul, has found many followers. Brenan saw the reason for the anarchists' popular success in their pronouncedly idealistic, religious and moral character; he explained Spanish Anarchism as a 'religious heresy', which took the social content of the Gospels seriously and interpreted it as 'the expression of class-consciousness'.[22] The gap left by the diminishing influence of religion on the working people during the nineteenth century had been filled by Anarchism; the new world was to be founded entirely on moral principles.

Already Brenan pointed out in his study that the anarchic opposition to the norms of a liberal-capitalist industrial society must be seen as complementary to the endeavour to return to pre-capitalist agrarian conditions which, until the *desamortización* of the nineteenth century, and locally even up to a later date, had found their expression in collectivist communalism. The Anarchists, starting from the basic and comprehensible unit of the *pueblo*, were opposed to, for them, incomprehensible and uncontrollable economic forces and the many profound changes which the law and technical innovations in industry had brought in the nineteenth century. For many landless labourers and artisans of Southern Spain these represented a danger to their livelihood. Basing himself on Brenan's study, Eric Hobsbawm[23] has pointed out that the Anarchism of agrarian labourers and artisans in Southern Spain was a local and endemic spontaneous revolutionary protest both against exploitation and oppression and the consequences of 'the introduction of capitalist legal and social relationships into the Southern countryside'. He argues that in its early phase it was an 'archaic social movement', almost without organisation, representing collective opposition against the intrusion of new, less favourable living conditions for the landless masses. The anarchist revolts of the second half of the nineteenth century were thus an attempt to reinstate the 'agrarian collectivism'[24] that had been lost as a result of the sale of common and ecclesiastic land (*desamortización*) and its attendant consequences – abolition of guilds and their statutes, of brotherhoods, mutual-help organisations, social and health welfare, of granaries and hospitals, of communal arable land, pastures and woods. Apart from the abolition of the forced rotation of crops, 'with the advent of individual ownership of land, communal co-operative institutions and the mechanisms and rules which regulated the life of village communities have been destroyed or undermined'.[25] For this reason, the idea of *reparto* (division of land), taken up by the Spanish section of the International, gained ground among the rebellious agrarian proletariat in Andalusia and led to chiliastic-anarchist movements. Hobsbawm interprets their 'messianic' strikes, with the sole object of bringing about an immediate and fundamental change, as millenarian mass movements (their advantage

was spontaneous unanimity of action, their disadvantage lack of organisation, strategy, tactics and patience) and as the revolutionary attitude of
peasants that was a product both of modern conditions and of the inability to
adapt to these.

The liberalisation of the property laws and the establishment of a capitalist
legal system not only worsened agrarian conditions, but also robbed many
artisans of their basis of existence: Andalusia in the nineteenth century went
through a process of de-industrialisation, since it was unable to protect itself
against competition from Northern Spain and from abroad. Thus it appears
entirely comprehensible that the local leaders of anarchist revolts should have
been very often craftsmen; as *obreros conscientes* (conscious workers) they
were instrumental in the propagation of anarchist ideas among the illiterate
agricultural workers. In terms of social structure the characteristics of the
participants in the 1861 insurrection of Loja (Province of Granada),
organised by the veterinary surgeon and blacksmith Ramón Pérez del Alamo,
already point to the social structure of the later Anarchist movement.
Although the rebellion[26] was in the main one of illiterate wage labourers, and
to a lesser extent of skilled agricultural workers (*peritos agrícolas*), its leaders
belonged to the lower middle classes and possessed a far higher degree of
political consciousness than the mass of the labourers, who were merely
fighting for their physical livelihood. Class background and the level of
political consciousness of the leaders of the revolt, as well as the varying
objectives of the participants, already show that ambivalence which a decade
later was to become a characteristic of the artisan and agrarian Anarchism
that developed in Andalusia.

In contrast to the millenarian interpretations of previous research
(Constancio Bernaldo de Quirós, Díaz del Moral, Gerald Brenan, Eric
Hobsbawm *et al.*) a new approach has lately gained ground, which sees the
numerous anarchist strikes not as irrational, millenarian actions, but as the
perfectly rational strategy of a libertarian movement. This new interpretation
has been put forward in particular by Temma Kaplan,[28] who, while drawing
on the studies of Hobsbawm, Brenan and the social anthropologist Pitt-
Rivers, concentrates her research on the question as to the conditions under
which anarchist ideology and strategy developed and eventually became a
mass movement. Kaplan restricts her investigation to the viticultural province
of Cádiz; she shows that in the 1880s as a result of exogeneous (notably
economic, trade and fiscal) difficulties the lower middle class, mainly involved
in the Sherry trade, and the province's artisans and skilled workers,
threatened by social decline, entered into a populist alliance with the agrarian
proletariat, seeing their mutual enemy in the latifundist grain producers, the
Bourbon monarchy and the centralised State machinery. Thus Anarchism
was by no means a movement consisting exclusively of 'poor' agricultural
labourers. The threat of a loss of autonomy, the mechanisation of the vat-
production, the drastic decline in good-quality sherry exports as well as the

unimpeded influx of all kinds of goods contributed to the economic decline of hitherto independent and relatively prosperous artisans. The situation of wine-growers and small tradesmen worsened as a result of the government's fiscal policies, which unilaterally favoured the latifundist agrarian bourgeoisie and imposed luxury taxes and special municipal levies, so-called *consumos*, on the wine. Eventually, the broad mass of agricultural workers was also affected. The decline in trade reduced the number of jobs, thus further aggravating the endemic problem of unemployment, while the special wine levies brought a general increase in the cost of living.

Anarchist doctrines came to Spain[29] just at a time when the agrarian system was 'capitalised' and the old feudal society was transformed into a bourgeois one. These ideas produced a complex amalgam between the wish for full (professional) autonomy and self-determination in 'free communes' and the institutional challenges posed by urbanisation and industrialisation. The Anarchists articulated the deep dissatisfaction with the social status quo felt by the broad mass of the population and did not, as in so many other countries, have to 'run up' against 'all national traditions'. 'Anarchism in Spain was precisely the expression of federalist and freedom-loving traditions common to the people as a whole.'[30] Doubtlessly anarchist theories of social organisation, 'based on the primacy of the local unit, which is also, in the Anarchist view, the natural unit',[31] fitted in with a Spanish attitude to life and a *patria chica* tradition. The concept of a federalist State was tied to that of social revolution.

The large-scale destruction of co-operative traditions, caused by the intrusion of capitalist economic reforms and the modern State's centralist trends into the traditional way of life of scarcely developed regions around the middle of the nineteenth century, led to a demand for decentralisation and administrative autonomy. Anarchism provided the 'ideological re-inforcement' to this indigenous form of communalist thinking in terms of the traditional, autonomous *pueblo*, so that in Spanish Anarchism, too, one can observe the phenomenon of *Schichtenverdickung*.[32] Anarchism was the *pueblo*'s response to the intrusion of bureaucratised and centralised forms of government, and the movement was markedly influenced by the *pueblo*'s social background. Opposition to centralised rule by foreigners and the abolition of the *pueblo*'s communal and professional autonomy brought together various strata into the populist alliance between workers, artisans and small tradesmen, peculiar to Andalusian Anarchism.

Not only did the populist alliance spring from the rational deliberations of the inhabitants of the *pueblo*, but their collective measures as well. In times of greatest want the powerful weapon of the harvest strike could not be used; in such years of famine it was the individual acts of violence and terror (theft, murder, arson) that were most frequently committed. In good years, on the other hand, when the need for labourers increased suddenly at harvest time, these stood a far better chance of furthering their interests through a 'general strike'. Taking advantage of such opportunities in the form of organised strikes constituted a perfectly rational strategy of 'direct action', whereby the rural labourers clearly showed that they aimed at a change in social relations. The periodic insurrections of Andalusian anarchists appear to have occurred at times of relative prosperity or good harvests, which allowed the organised workers to play their cards to best effect. Many of these outbreaks of violence were no doubt based on a deliberate strategy of protest, although this was certainly not the only element.[33]

This 'rational' explanation of the strikes of Andalusian rural labourers as a deliberate strategy of collective social protest tends to generalise far less than the 'millenarian' interpretation. The former is able to include in its analysis the social basis of individual protest actions and interprets the strikes as the thought-out responses of precisely definable social groups to concrete socio-economic situations. Yet it is doubtful whether this approach can have general application; its validity remains to be tested by further local and regional studies. The fact that both the collective and individual protest actions of Andalusian anarchists contained 'millenarian' elements is linked to the wider problems of structure and strategy within the libertarian movement, which were, in the last third of the nineteenth century, to lead to a split of the Anarchist movement into ideologically opposed camps, that is to say to the conflict between Anarcho-Collectivists and Anarcho-Communists.

III

From the time the Anarchist movement emerged in Spain, there existed parallel to the FRE's strategy of legalism an inclination to employ violence, particularly among the Andalusian proletariat. In the 1870s, while the International was outlawed, vehement conflicts arose within its ranks between the Catalan leadership, of legalistic and syndicalist orientation, and the Andalusian representatives, who advocated 'revolutionary actions'.[34] After the re-admission of the International, these debates reached a crisis point, reflected in the organisation's transition from *Federación Regional Española* to *Federación de Trabajadores de la Región Española* (FTRE). The advocates of legalism emerged as the clear victors; revolutionary insurrections were eliminated from their 'official' strategic stock-in-trade, even if the inclination to violence was never altogether quelled in certain sections of organised labour, particularly in western Andalusia.

The legalist and reformist course pursued by the FTRE's leadership after 1881, however, was not rewarded in the expected manner by the authorities. No doubt this had something to do with the fact that even within the Anarchists' organisation, especially in the South, legalism never fully prevailed. As early as the mid-1870s so-called anarchist 'action groups' agitated, as already indicated, as 'combat units' (*unidades de guerra*) against the rule of the bourgeoisie. In 1873/74, at the time of the Geneva Congress, the influential Andalusian Anarchists Farga Pellicer and García Viñas had visited Michael Bakunin in Switzerland, and it is probable that he encouraged them to violence. In addition, reports about acts of violence abroad and the outcome of the discussions at the London Congress of the 'Black International' in 1881 did not remain without effect in Spain. Eventually some left 'deviationists', who did not agree with the FTRE's official appeasement policy, early in the 1880s founded their own opposition organisation – *Los Desheredados* (The Disinherited) – and regarded terrorist methods as a legitimate weapon in the struggle against state and capital.[35] These groups' continuing acts, or threats, of terror provided the government with a welcome pretext for a ruthless persecution of the entire labour movement, even after its organisations had been once more legalised. No distinctions were made between terrorist underground groups and legal workers organisations, such as the Andalusian *Unión de Trabajadores del Campo* (UTC). Several murders committed at the turn of the year 1882/83 were used as an excuse for the massive persecution of the workers. Even to be found reading a (legally distributed) anarchist publication was sufficient reason to be condemned as a 'member' of a terrorist gang. Every unexplained death, every kind of damage was automatically attributed to the FTRE or one of its adjuncts. Even the workers organisations' demand for collective bargaining was regarded as a revolutionary act by employers and authorities and punished accordingly.

Hunger and unemployment among the landless proletariat, blind rage against the institutional terror of local authorities, and against the murder of alleged ringleaders as well as disappointment within the ranks of the Spanish workers about the social and political developments provoked a climate of considerable tension and violence. Anarchist terror only becomes comprehensible if seen in the context of the social violence that gave rise to it. This also featured largely in the Anarchists' justification of violence, for it was argued that the bourgeois society is itself based on violence. All forms of force occurring in this society are founded on the basic principle of authority – in itself a form of violence; the social organisation of the bourgeois State produces class and race hatred, poverty, injustice, despotism and consequently violence. Hence, the way bourgeois society is organised is interpreted as a 'state of war', and this violent condition also justifies the use of violence, which, since it is used in conditions of war, merely serves defensive purposes. The prevailing conditions thus enforce the use of counter-violence. From 1883 onwards, as a result of repressive measures against the FTRE and the failure of the strike strategy, the International became more radicalised, extremist groups gained greater influence, and there appeared the first signs of what was later to be called the phase of terrorist attempts. The internationalist press – *Revista Social, El Eco de Ravachol, El Grito del Pueblo, Acracia, La Cuestión Social*, etc. – increasingly called for acts of violence, while some, for instance *La Revolución Social*, even started special columns for 'propaganda by deed'. This, in the anarchist language of the time meant:[36]

> to fight in writing, by word and by deed against property, government and
> religion; to awaken a spirit of rebellion in the proletarian masses; . . . to
> take advantage of every opportunity, every economic or political event, in
> order to get the people to attack property and to seize it, to insult and
> despise the authorities and to break the law . . . to incite everyone to take
> what they need from the bourgeois and to convert into deeds everything
> their sense of their own rights, of justice and solidarity towards others tells
> them to.

Apart from physical force, 'propaganda by deed' also meant all forms of
civil disobedience, as well as desertion from the army, rent strikes, assaults,
thefts, etc. In the early 1880s the debate about the strategies appropriate to the
working class movement was overlaid and exacerbated by two further issues:
one, the conflict between Anarcho-Collectivists and Anarcho-Communists;
the other the relation between the workers' federation and the secret society
Mano Negra.

The discussion that had already flared up during the *Jura Congress* at La
Chaux-de-Fonds (1880) between Bakuninist Anarcho-Collectivists and
Kropotkinist Anarcho-Communists, was continued in Spain at the second
national congress of the FTRE in Seville (1882) and brought out the clear split
in the libertarian movement between a more reformist-syndicalist and a more
communal-terroristic wing. The FTRE leadership, which had its seat in
Barcelona, and was composed of a delegation, the majority of whom came
from Northern Spain, insisted on a collectivist course for the national
federation. It aimed at collective ownership of the means of production,
communication and transport as well as syndicalist control over the profits of
their own labour. This concept, that the right to disposal of the wealth
produced did not belong to society as a whole but only to the producers
amalgamated into individual syndicates, appealed particularly to the industrial workers of Catalonia, to skilled workers organised into syndicates and
trade associations, as well as to middle-class farmers in the northern regions;
but it met with vehement opposition from Andalusia's numerous seasonal
labourers, its many unemployed and its women who only found work at
harvest time; their communalist traditions led them to regard the *pueblo* as the
natural unit of their whole existence.

While the collectivists advocated syndicalism, the mass movement, the
general strike and a certain degree of centralisation, in order to achieve social
conditions, where only the means of production were collective property and
each worker was paid according to his output, the communists rejected any
form of organisation, praised the autonomous group, the individual revolutionary deed and terrorism, and aimed at a society in which the private
ownership of consumer goods no longer existed, where each worked

according to his abilities and would be rewarded according to his needs. The dissent between collectivists and communists was in reality nothing but a dispute between Catalan and Andalusian Anarchists. However, it will be necessary to define this more precisely, since the ideological battle lines cut right across the ranks of Andalusian anarchists as well. As Temma Kaplan has shown for the province of Cádiz, the economic depression of the 1860s forced artisans, wine-growers, smallholders and (skilled) workers to organise themselves. Those threatened by social decline resorted to the corporate models of old and formed co-operatives, protection societies and syndicates. Around 1870 in Jerez alone there existed about fifty such societies, whose protest and strike actions were coordinated and mutually supportive. These *uniones* or *secciones de oficio* formed the basic structure of Andalusian Anarchism, into which the Anarchists endeavoured to integrate small producers and wage earners, peasants and rural proletariat, skilled and unskilled workers in a populist alliance. Contrary to its name, the *Unión de Trabajadores del Campo*, for example, comprised not only landless day labourers and independent smallholders, but bakers, coopers and carters as well. Here the Anarchists were able to ally their movement to militant syndicalism – although the term itself is of a later date – and to the traditional working-class culture. In this fashion the movement was not only able to survive long periods of illegality, but also to gain a large influx of new members. These *uniones* aimed not so much at economic reforms that would improve the conditions of the working class as at the destruction of capitalism and the extirpation of the bourgeoisie. Their strategy did not consist in reformist strikes but in the preparation of the final overthrow, of social revolution.

Within the ranks of Andalusian Anarchists there also developed considerable tensions between the syndicalistically organised workers of the *uniones* and the agrarian proletarians who had begun to form secret cells. The former clearly favoured the anarcho-collectivist line, while the latter, barely able to scratch a livelihood, did not orient themselves on a particular trade but on the commune as a whole. When at the Seville Congress the Anarcho-Communists failed to assert their views, one group, advocating the autonomy of the commune and the socialisation of production and consumption, split off.

The ideological differences between collectivists and communists were directly reflected in the movement's strategy: while the collectivists rejected any form of physical violence, for fear of repressive government measures and a renewed ban on workers organisations, the communist advocates of terrorism expressed themselves in favour of violent acts against the large landowners and other representatives of the system of exploitation. The Congress was unambiguously reminded that there were 30,000 unemployed in Andalusia, who had nothing to lose but their poverty; 14,000 of these were claimed to be Anarchists. The radical group which split from the FTRE's parent organisation held several 'congresses of the disinherited' and possibly even amalgamated with existing terrorist secret societies.

While the rejection of terrorist and violent methods on the part of the syndicalistically organised workers of Catalonia had become the 'official' FTRE-strategy, the Andalusian supporters of anarcho-communism opposed the Federation's legalist course and, through the actions of rural terrorist groups, kindled the fire of agrarian Anarchism. In the years that followed southern Anarchism split off more or less completely from the workers movement, dwindled into sectarianism and lost itself in minority activism.

In contrast to 'instrumental' justifications of violence, which to some degree can be explained by the Anarchists' social conditions, the form of individual terror which now emerged seems rather remote from the social and political situation of its authors. An irrational cult of violence makes this appear not as a means to achieve morally justifiable ends, but as an end in itself. Violence ceases to be a rational strategy and degenerates into actionism.

Apart from Andalusia it was in Barcelona especially where individual terror began to spread in the two decades following the dissensions between collectivists and communists. The anarchist terror of those years became the practice of individual revolutionaries in a non-revolutionary situation, and in the mind of the population associated – to this day – the concept of terrorism with that of Anarchism.[37] The prelude to this violent phase of anarchist attempts and police repression was the agrarian workers' insurrection at Jerez (1892) and the uncommonly ruthless repressive measures by the government; as a revenge for the executions of Jerez there followed in 1893 Paulino Pallás' assassination of General Martínez Campos; in order to avenge Pallás' execution, Santiago Salvador threw two bombs into the crowded Liceo-Theatre in Barcelona. Reacting to these assassinations, the government in 1894 and 1896 passed two 'Laws for the Suppression of Terrorism' and created a new police corps, the notorious *brigada político-social*. In 1896 an unknown man threw a bomb at a Corpus Christi procession in Barcelona. About 400 Anarchists were arrested and cruelly tortured in the fortress prison of Montjuich; this provoked vehement protests not only in Spain but particularly from abroad. The last action that has so far been linked with the Montjuich case was the assassination in 1897 of Prime Minister Antonio Cánovas del Castillo by the enraged Italian Anarchist, Michele Angiolillo.

This first phase of concentrated terrorist violence (1893–7) was followed a few years later by a second one (1904–6) of no less spectacular individual violence: Joaquín Miguel Artal's assassination of Premier Antonio Maura (1904), the bombs thrown by anonymous terrorists in the Rambla de la Flores in Barcelona and Mateo Morral's attempt to assassinate King Alfonso XIII on his wedding day.

The aim of these outbreaks of predominantly 'communicative' violence is difficult to determine. They may have been intended as a warning or an appeal and, in a more functional sense, as the exemplary punishment of the system's representatives (king, prime minister, etc.) or of its manifestations (theatre, church, etc.). As a rule, the object was probably to draw attention to the social grievances of the under-privileged classes through acts of physical violence by people who belonged to them. From the Anarchists' point of view, the society of their time was structured quite unjustly and by their protest actions they wished to bring this injustice to public notice. Anarchist texts of that time on the topic of violence frequently began with indictments of the social status quo that required change. Yet the Anarchists were perfectly aware that they would not in any way change the system they were fighting, simply by eliminating a few of its representatives. The object of their attempts was rather to shake society into awareness, to draw the public's attention to social injustice and to wield a fierce blow against a 'society of banditry'. These attempts certainly did not receive the support of the entire labour movement of Barcelona, as in the years around the turn of the century 'the Anarchists concerned themselves primarily with the working-class struggle and the creation of unions, rather than with the throwing of bombs'.[38] Joaquín Romero Maura has characterised the psychological situation of the bomb-throwers as follows:[39]

'The situation in which the Barcelona anarchists found themselves at this time was almost bound to generate the kind of lunatic fringe terrorism we have seen. Without the support of the workers; the movement was reduced to a nucleus of militant veterans (like Herreros, Basons, Castellote, Lorenzo, Prat, Ferrer) and a pleiad of young unknowns, many of them without professions, pedantic, jacobinical, enamoured of intolerance, men who preferred Nietzsche to Tolstoy . . .'

The struggle between collectivist Anarchism and insurrectionist Anarcho-Communism did not end until the beginning of the twentieth century, and then in a compromise whereby the Bakuninist ideas were to provide the basis for the class struggle and for the organisation of the workers, and 'libertarian communism' the final goal of revolutionary Syndicalism. These principles provided a welcome resolution for the discrepancy between the practice of the revolutionary Anarchist wing of the Spanish labour movement and the need to create an organ for collective action.

In a certain sense, employing Charles Tilly's typology, one may say that the collective violence of Anarcho-Communists took a 'primitive' communal form, and that of Anarcho-Collectivists a 'modern' corporate one, and thus see the changes in the organisational forms of violence as the criterion of historical change.[40] In other words, the debate between Anarcho-Collectivists and Anarcho-Communists clearly shows the interplay between changed production methods, requiring different skills from workers, on the one hand, and more differentiated patterns of organisation and strategy on the other. While (anarcho-collectivist) industrial and skilled agrarian workers had already organised themselves into syndicates and thus were able to exert collective pressure in the form of strikes and to pursue a more or less rational strategy, the (anarcho-communist) agricultural labourers possessed no solid organisational structure and thus saw themselves subjectively as isolated loners whose only weapon – since collective measures were out of the question – was individual acts of terror.

The term 'irrational violence', frequently used in the relevant literature to describe local agrarian insurrections in Andalusia, poses certain problems, if 'irrational' violence is taken to mean the discharge of aggression without discernible purpose as opposed to 'rational' violence as a means to a particular end. It would perhaps be more appropriate to use the term 'communicative' violence that aims at drawing the public's attention to conditions that require reform, while constituting at the same time a strategy of both threat and appeal. For despite the spontaneous and emotional nature of their insurrectionist acts of violence, the Andalusian anarchists also operated to some extent in a rational and certainly in a selective manner. Rational insofar as they possessed at least a vague idea of their ultimate aim – to be free of government; and selective, insofar as they mainly, albeit not exclusively, attacked persons and targets which for them were the particular symbols of the prevailing system of exploitation and repression.[41]

While the internal disputes within the FTRE between Anarcho-Collectivists and Anarcho-Communists were still in full swing and the Spanish International was threatened with a complete split into two warring factions, the organisation's unity and perception of itself came further under pressure through the *Mano Negra* cases. *Mano Negra* (Black Hand) was an anarchist secret society, which mainly operated in the provinces of Cádiz and Seville. It was probably formed in the years of prohibition following 1874 and it is likely that it was behind at least some of the daily acts of violence in the South, which towards the end of the 1870s began to take on an almost breathtaking momentum. Arson, the destruction of harvests, land occupations, strikes, assaults and murders were the order of the day. There appeared to be no end to this state of violence. The situation of the agricultural labourers worsened from day to day. Bad harvests increased unemployment and forced many day labourers to emigrate. As a consequence of increases in the price of bread the population no longer had adequate amounts of basic foodstuffs and this led to numerous deaths from starvation. Spontaneous land occupation provoked massive repressive measures by the police and exacerbated the vicious circle of violence and counter-violence. The imprisonment and execution of workers, arbitrarily arrested, increased the tensions among the agrarian proletariat and provoked acts of revenge. Even the FRE's *Comisión Federal* called on the workers to use open violence, claiming that it was the duty of all revolutionaries to rise against injustice and to fight for the social revolution. The illegally assembled *Conferencias Comarcales* in 1880 unanimously advocated armed struggle and retaliatory measures as a means in the fight against State and capital.[42]

In 1883, when the food crisis was at its height, the public was startled by a series of crimes, alleged to have been committed by the rural secret society *Mano Negra*. The authorities accused this 'secret association of kidnappers, murderers and arsonists' of wishing to overthrow the government, to destroy the state and to eliminate the landowning aristocracy of Andalusia. The hunt for individual murderers once again provided the government with a pretext for a destructive campaign against the International in Andalusia. *Mano Negra* was alleged to have nearly 50,000 members and between February and March the prisons were filled with thousands of workers. The authorities were firmly convinced that *Mano Negra* belonged to the International (FRTE). The latter hastened to deny any connection between it and the *Mano Negra* and even claimed that the 'Black Hand' had been invented by the government, in order to be able to oppress the workers' movement as a whole.[43] The FRTE's vehement denials are partly explained by its anxiety to protect the (legally operating) International against retaliatory measures or potential renewed prohibition, but arose partly also out of the deep differences of interests between the agrarian workers of the South and the industrial workers in the urban regions. The fact that the International emphatically distanced itself from the *Mano Negra*'s 'thieves, kidnappers and murderers' contributed to those latter's defeat and extinction.[44]

As can be seen from numerous libertarian sources, the *Mano Negra*'s terrorist acts were largely conceived as responses to 'structural' violence, or to repressive measures by the state. The concept of 'structural violence' covers all degrading living and working conditions.[45] This reaction to the authorities' repressive measures shows that the State's monopoly of force was not recognised. It is quite clear that the security organs of the State and the economically dominant class, by their behaviour, were to a great extent themselves responsible for the outbreak and escalation of violent excesses. The use of violence may thus be interpreted as a process of interaction between those in power and those who are subjected to it. Significantly, the majority – although not all – of the acts of terror were directed against the representatives of the political system and less against capitalist incumbents of positions of economic power (as one might have assumed, in view of the proclaimed objectives of the social revolution and the economic emancipation of working class); the nature of the targets of anarchist terror thus lends emphasis to the interpretation that anarchist terror was revolutionary violence consciously juxtaposed to institutional violence. In its conflict with terrorism, the socially and politically ruling class, on the other hand, did not concern itself with the motives of the terrorists and the social conditions that gave rise to them, but from the outset identified Anarchism with terrorism, in order to discredit a potent social movement which threatened their class rule and to banish it into the limbo of common- criminality. Anarchists were not represented as belonging to a social and political movement that aimed at a total transformation of society, but as madmen or criminals.

The secret underground groups formed in the South during the 1870s, although formally belonging to the Spanish Section of the International, from the outset employed methods that differed from that of the *Comisión Federal* in Barcelona. The radical stance of the Southern sections, which saw (individual and collective) terror as the only possible weapon in the struggle against the economic power of capital and the political power of the State – embodied for them in the person of the local *cacique* – was inevitably bound on a collision course with the legalistic principles of organisation of syndicalistically oriented *uniones* and industrial workers. Anarchism, with its emphasis on the worker's individuality and autonomy, very soon became the spiritual home for different social groups; but it was unable to bring together in a convincing common strategy the industrial and agrarian proletariat and their differing interests, which resulted from the unequal development of industrial centres and rural areas. The contrast between town and country, which became more and more marked as soon as a modern industrial sector began to develop, had a disastrous effect on the organisation and strategy of the workers' movement. The effective split of the anarchist workers, organisationally into secret cells and open trade unions, and strategically into terrorism and legalism, the failure of the FRTE's reformist tactics and massive repression on the part of the authorities led in the 1880s to the decline of the International and eventually (1888) to its formal dissolution.

The ideological crisis within the International reflected the uneven development of its members' diverging interests. The dissolution of the FRTE in 1888 clearly showed that the Anarcho-Collectivists legalistic-syndicalist course did not cover the movement's entire spectrum of interests. The terrorist secret organisations of the agrarian South became part of a long tradition of revolts, revolutionary conspiracies, armed insurrections and sporadic overthrows that was a feature of Spain throughout the nineteenth century. The hope for radical change, which these spontaneous outbreaks reflected, the Republicans, with their predominantly political and reformist orientation and their lack of success, were unable to contain. The mass of the peasants therefore turned to internationalism. The 1880s marked the climax, the crisis and also the turning point in the fortunes of this development. Now Anarchism, by a shift in the emphasis of its action, had to prove that it was capable of co-ordinating the interests of the rural labourers with those of the urban industrial workers and that it could integrate these into a common strategy, with the unanimous aim of social revolution.

IV

In order to put an end to the disorganisation of workers influenced by Anarchism, a group of militant Anarchists resolved in the first years of the new century to form a federation of working-class organisations, with the aim to improve both their objective conditions as a class and to foster at the same time the class consciousness needed to carry out revolutionary acts, destructive of the existing system. In Catalonia this proposal met with an unexpectedly enthusiastic response and in 1907 the regional federation *Solidaridad Obrera* (Workers' Solidarity) was formed, followed in 1910 by the *Confederación Nacional del Trabajo* (National Confederation of Workers). Syndicalism, in the words of G. D. H. Cole,[46] 'was both a policy for direct action in the present and a vision of a society in the future'.

The revolutionary syndicalists followed anarchist traditions, in the sense that they put their faith in a 'spontaneous' movement of the masses and saw in any 'authoritarian' organisation a hindrance to the development of a revolutionary consciousness. The anarcho-syndicalist CNT kept up the consistent rejection of any party or corporative influence on the processes of decision, so characteristic of Anarchism. Its anti-political attitude reflected the concrete experiences of the working-class movement with political parties and the parliamentary system.

Also in its attitude to the question of violence, the CNT became the successor to the legalism of the First International, and just like the latter, this anarcho-syndicalist trade-union federation was unable completely to eradicate terrorist actions from within its own ranks. The tensions inherent in its membership structure, between its industrial-progressive and agrarian-archaic sector, remained and were reflected in their divergent attitude to the question of the use of physical force.

In principle, it can be said nevertheless that the Anarchists perceived their own violent measures usually as being 'derived' from the violent structure of the state that ruled them: at issue was the destruction of a society characterised by the violent nature of its class relations; on its ruins they would build an unviolent and stateless anarchist society. In order to achieve this morally justified goal, it seemed to them legitimate to use violence in a bourgeois society held together by force. Anarchist violence thus derived its main justification from its aim of social transformation. Most of their forms of violence undeniably contained an element of strategy, that is to say of deliberation, even if their authors were not always fully conscious of it. But if we ask what was the practical effect of such violent actions, the answer must be that at best it produced short-term successes only; in the long term its value was relatively minimal. Since on the other hand they possessed few other means of asserting their aims, violence, although ultimately a failure, represented in most cases the only adequate method for the *Desheredados* and *Descamisados* of the rural South to articulate their dissatisfaction and their demands.

The history of the CNT, however, belongs to a later phase of Spanish Anarchism. The rise of a powerful rival in the socialist *Unión General de Trabajadores*, the economic changes brought about by the First World War and particularly the influence of the Russian Revolution created completely different circumstances and as a consequence the organised labour movement developed completely new militant strategies.

The workers organising themselves into the revolutionary-syndicalist CNT marked the beginning of a new phase in the history of the Spanish Labour movement – that cannot be gone into here – a phase that was to come to its (temporary) conclusion under the hail of fascist bullets in the Civil War of 1936–9.[47]

NOTES

1. On the disputes within the anarchist movement cf. (for example) A. Elorza, *La utopía anarquista bajo la segunda república española* (Madrid, 1973); S. J. Brademas, *Anarco-sindicalismo y revolución en España (1930–1937)* (Barcelona, 1974); C. M. Lorenzo, *Los anarquistas españoles y el poder* (Paris, 1972).
2. On this issue extensively W. L. Bernecker, *Die Soziale Revolution im Spanischen Bürgerkrieg. Historisch-politische Positionen und Kontroversen: Mit einer Bio-Bibliographie* (Munich, 1977).
3. Cf. the memoirs of one of the participants of the congress and 'father' of the Spanish anarchist movement, A. Lorenzo, *El proletariado militante*, 2 vols. (Toulouse, 1946); also J. Termes, *Anarquismo y sindicalismo en España: La Primera Internacional 1864–1881* (Barcelona, 1972).
4. The opponents of anarchism, in particular, do not differentiate in their usage of the terms 'anti-political' and 'a-political', in order to ridicule anarchist attitudes. Anarchists never regarded themselves as 'apolitical'; their *antipoliticismo* exclusively referred to their refusal to keep to the bourgeois-parliamentarian rules of the game. On this extensively (with documentary evidence) J. Alvarez Junco, *La ideología política del anarquismo español (1886–1910)* (Madrid, 1976) p. 411ff., esp. p. 416f.
5. The Anarchists did however make a qualitative distinction between republic and monarchy and preferred the former as being more progressive. A unanimous view on this issue does not appear to have existed; but when the republic was proclaimed in 1873 they initially assessed it cautiously but positively.
6. M. Bakunin, 'Die Reaktion in Deutschland' in: R. Beer (ed.), *Michael Bakunin: Philosophie der Tat* (Cologne, 1968) p. 77.
7. Quoted according to Alvarez Junco, p. 455.
8. Thus at the Barcelona Congress (1870) 'resistance', as a strategy of the workers' movement, was justified with the argument, that the working class would thereby gain a better 'intellectual and material' position in their struggle against capital. Cf. the congress resolutions in A. Lorenzo, vol. 1, pp. 85–120.
9. M. Bookchin, *The Spanish Anarchists: The Heroic Years 1868–1936* (New York, 1977).
10. Cf. the 'classical' description of the methods of direct action in E. Pouget, *Le sabotage* (Paris, 1910).
11. Cf. A. Lorenzo, pp. 106–8; commentary by Termes, pp. 67–76.
12. Statistics about the strike incidence of those years in M. Nettlau, *La première Internationale en Espagne (1868–88)*, 2 vols. (Amsterdam, 1968).
13. F. Engels, 'Die Bakunisten an der Arbeit: Denkschrift über den Aufstand in Spanien im Sommer 1873', *MEW* 18, pp. 476–93; on the general context see the balanced account by C. A. M. Hennessy, *The Federal Republic in Spain, Pi y*

Margall and the Federal Republican Movement (1868–1874) (Oxford, 1962).

14. On the identity between ends and means in the anarchist concept of revolution and on the Marxist critique thereof cf. W. L. Bernecker, Anarchismus und Bürgerkrieg: Zur Geschichte der Sozialen Revolution in Spanien 1936–1939 (Hamburg, 1978) pp. 27–44.

15. P. Lösche, 'Anarchismus – Versuch einer Definition und historischen Typologie', PVS 1 (1974) pp. 53–73.

16. C. B. de Quirós, 'El espartaquismo agrario andaluz' in Revista general de legislación y jurisprudencia (Madrid, April 1919). (Re-published, together with other writings by J. L. García Delgado and with the participation of de Quirós, 'El espartaquismo agrario' y otros ensayos sobre estructura económica y social de Andalucía (Madrid, 1973).)

17. J. Díaz del Moral, Historia de las agitaciones campesinas andaluzas: Antecedentes para una reforma agraria (Madrid, 1929).

18. G. Brenan, The Spanish Labyrinth: An Account of the Social and Political background of the Spanish Civil War (Cambridge, 1969); on Brenan's interpretation of Spanish anarchism, see M. L. Berneri, 'The Historical Background: Brenan's Spanish Labyrinth', Anarchy 5 (1961) p. 137–43.

19. Thus, continuing Brenan's approach, J. Joll, The Anarchists, 2nd edn (London, 1979) pp. 227–8; cf. also H. Matthews, 'Anarchism: Spain's Enigma' in N. Greene (ed.) European Socialism Since World War I (Chicago, 1971) pp. 110–16; national-socialist interpreters like D. J. Wölfel, So ist Spanien (Leipzig, 1937) explain the Spaniards' inclination to Anarchism by their 'national character'. On interpretations in terms of national psychology cf. P. Heintz, 'Die Struktur der spanischen Persönlichkeit', KZSS 1 (1955) pp. 101–18, who, basing himself on A. Castros' La realidad histórica de España, sees the Spaniards, from the point of view of cultural anthropology, as non-alienated personalities, whose fundamental basic structure (as a configuration of 'permanent behavioural dispositions') predisposes them for Spanish personalism, 'with its frequently markedly anarchist traits'.

20. A. von Borries, Introduction to G. Brenan, Spanische Revolution (Berlin, 1973) p. XI; cf., also von Borries, 'Der spanische Anarchismus', Neues Hochland 4 (1973) pp. 339–50.

21. F. Borkenau, El reñidero español (Paris, 1971) p. 229, argues that the Anarchists 'in the workers' camps are the genuine representatives of the Spanish resistance to Europeanisation'; according to him the anarchists also belong to the anti-commercialist and anti-capitalist tradition in Spain, which has continued to be influential well into the twentieth century. The opposition to capitalist evolution was directed against the material progress achieved by European industrial countries; it was thus also opposed to the Marxist theory of historic determinism. For the Spanish anarchists, the bourgeoisie did not represent a temporary revolutionary force; they did not see the capitalist development of productive resources as a necessary phase of economic development; for them, centralisation and accumulation were not the inevitable imperatives of industrialisation, but a means to reinforce and perpetuate a State they were fighting against. The Spanish anarchists accepted the inevitability of capitalist development no more than they did its material fetishism.

22. Brenan, Spanish Labyrinth, pp. 188–97.

23. E. Hobsbawm, Primitive Rebels – Studies in Archaic Forms of Social Movement in the 19th and 20th Centuries (Manchester, 1959).

24. On collectivist agrarian traditions in Spain cf. esp. J. Costa, Colectivismo agrario en España (Buenos Aires, 1944).

25. J. Hellwege, 'Genossenschaftliche Tradition und die Anfänge des Anarchismus

in Spanien', *VSWG* 59 (1972) pp. 305–49, here p. 329.

26.   For the following cf. R. Pérez del Alamo, *Apuntes sobre dos revoluciones andaluzas* (Seville, 1872, reprinted Madrid, 1971).

27.   While the leaders were mainly concerned with the abolition of the monarchy and with political democratisation, the mass of artisans and agricultural labourers, for whom *desamortización* meant the direct threat of proletarisation, gave to the rising a primarily social content; for them it was understood that the rebellion would lead to the abolition of the existing distribution of property and bring the hoped-for *reparto*, or communal ownership. They probably had in mind mainly the common land, which *desamortisación* had removed, since no protest has come to light against Pérez del Alamos' proclamation urging that private property should be respected.

28.   T. Kaplan, *Orígenes sociales del anarquismo en Andalucía. Capitalismo agrario y lucha de clases en la provincia de Cádiz 1868–1903* (Barcelona, 1977); also C. E. Lida, *Anarquismo y revolución en la España del XIX* (Madrid, 1972); she opposes the argument that the Spanish Anarchists were religious millenarians and that the members of the secret societies were isolated within Spanish society.

29.   Cf. Hobsbawm, *Primitive Rebels*; and P. Lösche, 'Probleme der Anarchismusforschung', *IWK* 19/20 (1973) pp. 125–44. Lösche concludes: 'Andalusian anarchism was a movement of the poor, and with uncanny clarity it showed up the interests of the village'; this needs to be qualified and modified by referring to Kaplan, *Orígenes sociales*, and to the findings of studies in social anthropology, which have pointed to the discrepancies that existed between anarchist and village interests. Cf. J. A. Pitt-Rivers, *The People of the Sierra* (London, 1954) pp. 220–3.

30.   H. Ruediger, *El anarcosindicalismo en la revolución española* (Barcelona, 1938) p. 44.

31.   G. Woodcock, 'Anarchism in Spain', *History Today* 12 (1962) pp. 22–32, here p. 23.

32.   On the same phenomenon in Russian Communism, cf. W. E. Mühlmann, *Chiliasmus und Nativismus: Studien zur Psychologie, Soziologie und historischen Kasuistik der Umsturzbewegungen* (Berlin, 1964) p. 395ff.

33.   In 1883, in Jerez, for instance, a good harvest was expected after several years of drought. The agricultural labourers promptly began to strike at the beginning of June (i.e. before the harvest) and provoked a massive intervention by the regional authorities. On this see Kaplan, p. 257.

34.   For numerous examples of this see Nettlau, p. 313ff.

35.   This form of justifying violence, however, is not characteristic for other trends of Anarchism; on the whole anarchist doctrine remains sceptical towards active physical force; this may be attributable to its anthropological optimism, its faith in the natural harmony of things, its criticism of bourgeois violence. From within anarchist ranks the advocates of violence are reminded of the virtues of propaganda, of peaceful means and especially education and training. Cf. C. E. Lida, 'Literatura anarquista y anarquismo literario', *Nueva Revista de Filología Hispánica*, vol. XIX, 2 (1970), pp. 360–81.

36.   La Revolución Social No. 6, quoted from Alvarez Junco, p. 494.

37.   On this issue generally cf. P. Lösche, 'Terrorismus und Anarchismus – Internationale und historische Aspekte', *Gewerkschaftliche Monatshefte* 2 (1978) pp. 106–16.

38.   J. Romero Maura, 'Terrorism in Barcelona and its impact on Spanish politics 1904–1909', *Past and Present* 41 (1968) pp. 130–83, here p. 147. From the turn of the century onwards, however, after the failure of the Catalan general strike of

1902 and as a result of the economic crisis, the calls in anarchist publications to violence and to 'propaganda by deed' increased again.

39.   Ibid., p. 152.
40.   C. Tilly, 'Collective Violence in European Perspective' in I. K. Feierabend, R. L. Feierabend, T. R. Gurr (eds), *Anger, Violence and Politics* (Englewood Cliffs, N. J., 1972). Cf. also P. Waldmann, *Strategien politischer Gewalt* (Stuttgart, 1977) pp. 14–18.
41.   Cf. Waldmann, p. 43.
42.   Already in 1872 the Regional Federation had threatened 'civil war, class war, a war between the poor and the rich' if it were to be declared illegal. Cf. Lida, *Anarquismo y revolución*, p. 255 and Lida, *La Mano Negra (Anarquismo agrario en Andalucía)* (Madrid, 1972) p. 46.
43.   For decades this was also claimed by scholars; the last was G. A. Waggoner, 'The Black Hand Mystery: Rural Unrest and Social Violence in Southern Spain, 1881–1883' in R. J. Bezucha and D. C. Heath (eds), *Modern Social European History* (Lexington, Mass. 1972) pp. 161–91. Since the statutes of the *Mano Negra* have come to light, there is now no doubt that this secret organisation did indeed exist, although the authorities certainly exaggerated its importance.
44.   It is not possible to establish exactly what the relations were between *Mano Negra* and *FTRE*. Lida, who has the greatest knowledge in this matter, points out that there existed a clear affinity between *Mano Negra*'s statutes and programme on the one hand, and vocabulary and revolutionary objectives of the International on the other. The *Mano Negra*'s own statutes indicate such a connection: 'Since the International Workers Association has been placed outside the law by the bourgeois governments and is thus prevented from approaching the social question which requires solution by peaceful means, it had to become a secret organisation, in order to carry out the social revolution by force.' Lida, *Anarquismo y revolución*, p. 255.
45.   The concept of 'structural violence' goes back to J. Galtung, Gewalt, Frieden und Friedensforschung', in D. Senghaas (ed.), *Kritische Friedensforschung* (Frankfurt, 1972).
46.   G. D. H. Cole, *Self Government in Industry*, 3rd edn (London, 1918) p. 216.
47.   On anarchist and anarcho-syndicalist developments in Catalonia at the beginning of the twentieth century cf. J. Connelly Ullman, *The Tragic Week* (Cambridge, 1968); J. Romero Maura, *La Rosa de Fuego* (Barcelona, 1975); X. Cuadrat, *Socialismo y anarquismo en Cataluña (1899–1911): Los orígenes de la CNT* (Madrid, 1976); for the period of World War I and after, see G. H. Meaker, *La izquierda revolucionaria en España (1914–1923)* (Barcelona, 1978).

9 Nationalist Violence and Terror in the Spanish Border Provinces: ETA

Gerhard Brunn

There has always been a tradition of political violence and individual terror in Spanish history. Yet the form both have taken since the 1960s, in combination with a movement towards nationalist autonomy – or separation – seems to be new. My task here will be to provide an analytical outline of the disintegrative trends in the Spanish unitary state by looking at regional processes of segregation, confining myself however to the two most significant movements – those in Catalonia and the Basque country. After examining the question of the extent to which these movements are nationalist ones, and what their strategic aims and political methods are, I shall inquire into the political constellations during the Franco Regime that gave rise to the sudden employment of strategic terror, into the underlying ideological patterns and into the form in which terror is being practised and how it is organised. Whereas in the first part the accent will be on Catalanism, the second part will focus on the Basque movement, and in particular on the organisation of ETA, which is responsible for the terror in the Basque country.

I

Spain is a country where, from the Napoleonic Wars until the present time, internal political and social conflicts have repeatedly been marked by both collective use of violence and individual terror. Thirty-seven of the sixty-nine years between 1808 and 1876 were characterised either by civil war or by conditions akin to civil war. Social protest in rural areas as well as class conflicts were accompanied by aimless revolutionary violence. From the 1880s onwards the 'philosophy of the bomb', and the pistol, played a dominant role. In the period between 1897 and 1921 three Spanish prime ministers became victims of anarchist assassinations. The bloody bomb attacks in the 1890s in Barcelona, the strategic Anarcho-Syndicalist terrorism at the beginning of this century, the flood of individual murders by anarchist 'pistoleros' and the

112

businessmen's hired assassins employed to fight them, came to a temporary halt and climax, when opposing camps liquidated thousands of political adversaries in the prelude to, during and at the close of the Civil War of 1936–9.[1]

In the light of this tradition of violence and terrorism, the terror that has now lasted for years, particularly in the Basque country, acquires new weight. One ought to be careful, however, not to assume uncritically that this is merely a heritage of the years up to the end of the Civil War. Indeed, present-day terror is something quite novel inasmuch as it is perpetrated by different groups, in the service of a new idea and new objectives – objectives that have long since been pursued by significant groupings within Spanish politics, but whose realisation formerly did not include the means of violence.

II

According to Hobsbawm's concise definition, the Iberian Peninsula has many problems, but no solutions to them.[2] And one of the unsolved problems, at the very least since the turn of the century, has been the national question. The Spanish nation that emerged from the national war of liberation was, admittedly, able to take over the unitary state created by the absolutist monarchy and develop it further in the first half of the nineteenth century without encountering significant opposition. From the second half of the century onwards, however, with the emergence of internal structural, economic and social conflicts, a counter-movement began to take shape, which tended towards the dissolution of the apparently so solidly established Spanish state. At a time of national unification movements and the emergence of nation states elsewhere, tendencies developed in Spain to question the existence of the Spanish nation and, instead of expanding the existing state into a fully fledged nation state, to limit the specific community of solidarity within the nation solely to historic regions. It became evident that while Spain had been capable of state-building, this state in the long run was not able to ensure that its citizens identified themselves with it sufficiently for it to be followed by the building of a nation that encompassed all the state's territories.[3]

The historic tradition of former political autonomy, of specific political and social structures, of a particular culture, symbolically and actually documented by a different language – Catalan or Basque – the development of separate economic and social structures in the course of partial industrialisation confined to a particular region, the formulation of a nationalist ideology oriented towards the region and based on Herder's concept of the people – all these were the constituent elements of a movement which a regional elite of young intellectuals used deliberately in order to effect political change while the Spanish state was in a crisis. The effect of this spread from Catalonia to other regions, but initially produced similarly significant political consequences only in the Basque country, where comparable traditions obtained.[4]

<h2 style="text-align:center">III</h2>

Catalanism and the Basque movement regarded themselves as national movements, standing for the right to national self-determination of specific, historically established nations within the framework of the Spanish state. They regarded their nations, in a conservative sense, as organically grown supra-individual individualities, possessing a territory, the continuity of their own language, their own history, their own particular social institutions, a distinct national character, their own moral and historic destiny. Out of this concept of the nation grew logically, at least in their theoretical formulations, the demand for their own state, although until recently actual separatism played only a secondary role; and in contrast to the – in theory – logical claim for a state of their own, in practical politics they contented themselves with the demand for the greatest possible autonomy within the borders of the Spanish state, so as to fulfil their own national aspirations within an autonomous region.[5]

<h2 style="text-align:center">IV</h2>

In their political practice these peripheral nationalisms – as Juan Linz has called them – conformed to the prevailing system.[6] They operated in a peaceful, evolutionary manner and rejected revolutionary use of violence. The protection of their movement through a network of local associations, parliamentary practice and the exertion of public pressure through mass demonstrations were the main methods employed to secure their interests.

In Catalonia, for instance, the Catalanists organised the largest demonstrations known so far, they created Spain's first modern party, the *Lliga Regionalista*, and, at a time when elections in Spain were no more than a gerrymandering instrument in the hands of the ruling party, they were able to press for an electoral system that gave the elected representatives genuine democratic legitimacy and offered the chance of influencing the decision-making process within the framework of the Spanish constitutional system. In this way, the Catalanists, much more so than the Basque nationalists, were able to field a large number of deputies on all three parliamentary levels – in the communes, in provincial or regional parliaments and in the *Cortes*.[7]

Well into the period of the Franco Regime, the use of the threat of violence played only a peripheral role. It ought not to be overlooked, however, that in *Catalanism* at least there have been attempts in specific situations to resort to the strategic use of violence. The cases that might be cited in this connection, such as the attempt by the later president of an autonomous Catalonia, Francisco Maciá, to build up a paramilitary, revolutionary youth organisation in 1922/23,[8] the miserable failure of his dilletante attempt at a military intervention in 1926, during Primo de Rivera's dictatorship,[9] the effortlessly repressed insurrection by militias and sections of the police under the Catalan Minister of the Interior Dencás in October 1934,[10] found no popular echo, however, and showed up how impossible it was, given the prevailing conditions, to win over Catalans to the use of violence in order to further nationalist ideas.

V

During the time of the Second Republic, proclaimed in 1931, both movements – *Catalanism* in 1932 and Basque nationalism in 1936 – were conceded a considerable degree of autonomy, and were given their own parliament, government, cultural administration and police force,[11] but with Franco's victory in the Civil War in 1939 these statutes were repealed. Franco, his political allies and the armed forces were strict adherents of a unitary, centralist nation state and had also fought the Civil War under the banner of national unity and territorial integrity; they had left no doubt that they would not tolerate special regional aspirations, whether political or cultural, and thus forced even conservative, Catholic Basque nationalists to fight on grimly for the survival of the anti-clerical Republic.[12] After the defeat of the Republicans, both the Basque and the Catalan movements were made to suffer the same unbridled and bloody persecution as all the other defenders of the Republic. All institutions and associations of both movements were forbidden, the special provisions for the regions abolished, monuments destroyed, language and culture in Catalonia and the Basque country suppressed. For three decades both provinces were dubbed the 'traitor provinces' in official parlance.[13]

The attempt of *Francoism* to solve the problem of Catalan and Basque nationalism by rigorous repression ended in complete failure, indeed it became a model for a misguided policy achieving the opposite of the desired effect.[14] Repression strengthened the will to oppose and was one of the causes for the emergence and legitimisation of violence in the Basque country. The first signs of liberalisation showed that, although the movements had been subjugated in the Civil War and been held down by the repression that followed, they had not been defeated. Now they even acquired a model character for other regions – such as Andalusia – which, before Franco, had shown no sign of aspiring to autonomy.

In structural and social terms their situation had, if anything, worsened. The wide gap in the development between the major part of Spain and the regions, as far as their industrial economic structure and the resulting social structure was concerned, had been narrowed by the developments in other parts of Spain. This meant that neither the feeling of superiority, stemming from their greater modernity, nor the complaint that a rich region was being exploited in a colonial manner by the backward, work-shy parts of Spain, on which a good part of the nationalists' self-perception was based, were justified to the same degree as before. Moreover, the continuing massive influx of people from other Spanish provinces has meant that these regions now contain so many 'foreigners' that a unified national identity *vis-à-vis* the rest of Spain can only be maintained with difficulty.[15]

On the other hand, these tendencies towards a levelling-off of contrasts and Madrid's conscious policy in this direction, even employing the rich tax revenues of the peripheral regions for this purpose, have fostered a counter-movement to safeguard the regional particularities in nationalist terms.[16] Conversely, for the architects of democratic, post-Franco Spain, the levelling-off of structural differences and the lessening of the danger of even greater alienation between the different regions, have facilitated a shift away from the rigid centralism of a nation state.[17] In a radical departure from the tradition of the *one* Spanish nation, the Spanish constitution of 1978 now recognises the different nationalities[18] and the possibility of a large degree of autonomy for them within the framework of the Spanish state. In October 1979 both Catalonia and the Basque country approved of the first autonomy statutes by referendum.[19]

In the Basque country meanwhile, as a legacy of Francoism, a radical terrorist movement lives on and demands the complete separation of their country, beyond the existing regulations for autonomy. In this struggle it employs the means of terrorist violence with increasing intensity. How and why did this violence come about? What are the reasons for the direct or indirect support – or at least passive toleration – it enjoys, and for its escalation?

VI

After Franco's victory, the Basque and Catalan movements in their exile initially followed parallel paths. Their governments-in-exile collaborated with the Allies in underground activities and after the end of the war organised actions of propaganda, resistance and protest in Spain, in the hope that the Allies, after their victory over Hitler's Germany, would also turn against Franco's Spain and thus help to re-establish Basque and Catalan autonomy within a Spanish democracy.[20] When the United States recognised Franco and collaborated with him, this proved to have been an illusion and the old guard nationalists, disappointed, disillusioned and exhausted, resigned themselves and to all intents and purposes gave up any further activities in Spain.[21] Yet at home a new generation of nationalistically minded young

Basques and Catalans was thirsting for new deeds. In contrast to the Catalan youth after the end of the First World War, who rebelled against an allegedly lukewarm party leadership, founded a new radical, nationalist party and were even able to develop a rich cultural life under Primo de Rivera's dictatorship,[22] the young people of the 1950s possessed no legal means to articulate their aspirations. Activities of the most harmless kind, such as the hoisting of Basque or Catalan national flags or the painting of slogans, were considered as 'subversive' or 'separatist' acts and met by brutal repressive measures – torture, imprisonment and relegation from the university.[23]

Under these auspices, there followed in the Basque country – but only there – a qualitative leap in youthful nationalist opposition to the Franco Regime. Out of various tentative preliminary organisations there emerged in July 1959 a new association called ETA – *Euskadi Ta Askatasuna* (Basque Country and Freedom). In the course of a few years it developed an internal structure, ideology and action programme of such efficacy that it was able, by the new means of strategic use of violence, to turn itself into the most spectacular opposition group against the Franco Regime.

There is a certain amount to be said for Payne's thesis that the main determining factors for the particularly radical path the Basque movement has taken lay in the serious threat to Basque identity, the decline in the Basque population and language, the disintegration of traditionally Basque social structures through progressive urbanisation, the participation of a clergy equally bent on preserving traditional structures and the ties to Catholicism, in a world caught up in the process of modernisation. In Catalanism, on the other hand, the same degree of radicalisation was not necessary, since Catalanism and modernisation were considered as twin movements, and on the way to a modern society it was thus able to hold its own.[24]

The Catalans' power of assimilation shows itself clearly superior to that of the Basques. Their language, as a romance idiom closely related to Spanish (Castilian), offers few obstacles to comprehension, it is an established language of literature; the openness of Catalan society promotes cultural and psychological 'Catalanisation'.[25]

In the Basque Country, and especially in the rural, petty bourgeois milieu where Basque nationalism continues to find its strongest support, people have always been more inward-looking, more particularist. Moreover, the Basque language is a totally alien body among its romance neighbours and difficult to adapt to modern requirements. During a survey conducted in 1966 in Catalonia, 90 per cent of those interviewed declared that they understood Catalan, and 62 per cent that they could read it; the comparative figures for the Basque country are 49 per cent and 25 per cent respectively.[26] In addition, Catalan is firmly rooted in the trend-setting middle class and knowledge of the language thus means a passport to social advance in Catalonia. The Basque language, by contrast, is mainly spoken in the country and a whiff of the backwoods attaches to it. Catalan nationalists publish and are understood;

Basque nationalists must continue to articulate their ideas in Spanish or French if they want to reach an adequate audience.[27]

That the specific situation of the Basque country has contributed to ETA's attraction and to its success among Basque youth, in terms of its perception of itself and its ideology, is beyond doubt, but does not provide an adequate explanation. ETA, with its heightened consciousness and its over-reaction, represents only a minority within Basque nationalism and an even greater minority of the Basque population as a whole.[28] It was not as a hyper-nationalist association that it achieved its true impact, but as a spectacular, effective, legendary opposition group against a hated regime. Secondly and irrespective of its nationalist claims, it belongs in its extreme form to the youthful movements of renewal, searching for a better world in opposition to the Establishment, which other Western industrial nations also witnessed during that period, such as the anti-Vietnam War movement in the United States and worldwide, the Paris May movement of 1968 and the Extra-Parliamentary Opposition (EPO) in West Germany.

There are many indicators that this is indeed the case. The same supporters (the young intelligentsia), the same idols (freedom fighters and freedom movements of the Third World and the spiritual fathers of the new European Left, Lelio Basso, André Gorz, Ernest Mandel), the same ideological pattern of belief in the socialist betterment of the world, eclectically assembled from many sources. For this reason, the causes for ETA's development will have to be sought in the structural and ideological patterns underlying the radicalisation of the young intellectuals in those other movements.[29]

On the other hand, one is bound to agree with Laqueur who, in view of the impossibility of finding a general explanation for the emergence of terrorism, argues that historical accident also plays a part,[30] and accept also for Basque terrorism a singular coincidence of a variety of factors. One of these is surely the specific situation under the Franco Regime, whose elements of rule included terror as a means of physical and psychological warfare against any opposition, and pushing such opposition into criminality.[31] Inherent in the Francoist system of rule was thus the chance that an opposition branded as criminal would be forced to employ 'criminal' methods of counter-terror. This process of self-fulfilling prophecy, as the example of other opposition movements to the Franco-system has shown, did not necessarily have to set in, but did so where ETA was concerned, in constantly escalating form.

VII

ETA was formed in 1959, as a nationalist organisation in the tradition of Basque nationalism as represented by PNV.[32] Very soon, however, far-reaching political objectives were added to the purely nationalist ones.

ETA has not produced any notable ideologists or theoreticians of its own, nor a consistent ideology. Its ideological evolution tends to be marked by eclecticism, heterogeneity, leaps and internal conflicts which have led to numerous splits and the hiving-off of individual groupings.

To a large extent this was due to the particular conditions of underground activity which, amongst other things, prevented any personal continuity amongst its members and fostered disintegration into groups; it was also due to the interplay between theory and practice and to the fact that ETA did not rigidly adhere to a theory, but, in the light of positive and negative experiences in its combat practice, reacted flexibly to internal discussion, as it did in the pursuit of new models of thought, in its adoption of examples from other countries and their practical transposition to Basque conditions.[33]

What gave ETA's tentative efforts at defining its own position support and direction initially and what turned it into a completely novel manifestation of peripheral nationalism in Spain and at the same time determined its programme of action was the example of Castro's Cuba and of other national liberation movements, from Palestine to Vietnam, that followed it.[34] Of the remarkable exemplary role Fidel Castro played for the modern youth of the world, Baran and Sweezy have stated that Castro in fact did what they all dreamed of doing.[35] In the Basque country, ETA attempted to apply Castro's example to its own situation, to the perception of its role and to its transposition into an action programme.

As a first step, ETA therefore defined itself as a movement of national liberation waging an anti-imperialist fight against a Spain which exploited and occupied the Basque country like a colony; it compared its struggle with that against the Moors during the *reconquista*, or against the French at the time of the Napoleonic Wars.[36]

As a consequence of seeing themselves as a national liberation movement, they now aimed at a complete separation of the Basque provinces from Spain and the creation of a sovereign Basque state. Linked to this and prompted by a new kind of irredentism was the demand for a sovereign Basque state that would also include the French Basque provinces beyond the Pyrennees, which in turn meant that ETA's struggle in the long run would have to be directed against France as well.[37]

After several years it became clear, however, that the concept of a national war of liberation, on the pattern of similar struggles in the Third World, was not appropriate to the Basque situation; influenced by classical models of Socialism in the Third World and the writings of the new Left, this resulted in a shift from national-revolutionary to social-revolutionary objectives. The anti-imperialist fight against an occupying force was re-interpreted as an anti-oligarchical class war against the dominant middle class in Spain, amongst which they also counted the 'denationalising' Basque middle class that was associated with it.[38] Consistently thought through, this path was bound to lead away from the isolated Basque class struggle and merge into the joint struggle of the working class in Spain as a whole against a common class enemy, the Spanish bourgeoisie. Indeed, ETA's internal controversies from the mid-1960s to the mid-1970s were marked by antagonism between the advocates of the superior claims of the class war and, going even further, its merger with the struggle in Spain as a whole, and those who were unwilling to relinquish their nationalist objectives. After several splits, the nationalists predominated against the universalist left, without however abandoning the idea of the class struggle.[39] It was argued that in the specific Basque situation, where class oppression and national oppression were one and the same, nationalism and socialism would also have to be identical. The nationalist and socialist revolution would have to take place simultaneously, and a national Basque path to socialism would have to be pursued. It is thus consistent that in the Basque country they frequently do not talk of a working class, but of a 'Basque working *people*' – the *'pueblo trabajador vasco* (PTV)'.[40] It is superfluous here to dwell on the finer points of ideological discussion and dissent. Whether, beyond the inner circles, these have been of importance for the history of ETA, or at least for its outward image, is open to doubt. What is certain is that the combatant, 'military' activism of ETA has outshone all ideological considerations or its attachment to specific policies, and that the mythos surrounding the protagonists of this activism within ETA – the so-called 'military front' or 'special commandos' – has, through the offices of the media, determined its image, ensured its appeal as well as the constant intake of young members to replenish the cadres decimated by repression, and thus also ensured constancy despite all persecutions.[41]

VIII

The advocacy of the principle of the use of violence and terror, in order to achieve the desired political aims, soon began to distinguish ETA from other opposition movements in Spain. The use of violence, in view of the impossibility of legal opposition and the state's own use of violence, was legitimised as the continuation of politics by other means.[42] This violence, however, was constantly threatening to become uncontrollable, to develop its own dynamic, to turn into an end in itself and, next to the ideological deliberations, the controversy surrounding the use, the function, the subordination or the abandonment of violence in favour of other political strategies turned into the other general topic of discussion within ETA.

Under the influence of Third World liberation movements, Krutwig in 1964 formulated the credo of the revolutionary war as a quasi-religious war.[43] There had been a call to violence already two years earlier: 'Violence is necessary. A contagious, destructive violence, which supports our struggle, the one the Israelis, the Congolese, the Algerians have taught us.'[44]

According to the theory formulated by Krutwig which, with modifications, remained the guideline until the early 1970s, the purpose of violence was to provoke repression – seen strategically as the creation of a spiral of repression and revolutionary action. The more intense the repression, the greater the number of innocents affected, the greater the degree of solidarity between population and the revolutionaries who fight against repression, thus spurring further revolutionary action. In terms of a strategy of violence, the 'spiral of repression-action-repression' is considered to be the driving force of revolutionary action. The final outcome of this escalation, according to this theory, would be a general revolution.[45]

Very soon after the first terrorist experiences of 1967/68 it became clear that the notion of the possibility of a guerilla war, of an armed revolution of the masses and a victory in military terms was illusory as far as the Basque country was concerned. Yet years went by before this was finally accepted.[46] New terrorist models were adopted – violence instead of guerilla warfare; the South American urban guerillas, whose techniques had been publicised in the manual of the Brazilian Carlos Marighella, and the Palestinian organisation Black September, which had caused a sensation with the assassination of the Jordanian Prime Minister Wasfi Tall and their attack during the Munich Olympics, now took the place of former Third World models.[47] It is no longer the function of this form of strategic violence – still practised in the democratic Spain of today – to prepare for a military victory, but supposedly to weaken and destabilise the 'power of the oligarchy' and to force it, worn out by a 'war of attrition', to accede to the concessions demanded from it in political terms.[48]

Within ETA, the use of violence has always been a matter of controversy. In 1967 one group split off because of this turn to guerilla methods,[49] and in subsequent years arguments have flared up time and again between members working legally or semi-legally and who, according to the organisational concept of a global approach obtaining since 1967, did not work on the so-called military front but agitated in the political and cultural sphere and at the workplace in order to prepare the revolutionary ground in a wider social context.[50] While the military activists, after they had carried out their actions, were able to escape abroad, those members who worked more openly in the Basque country had to suffer the entire weight of repression and to see the results of their efforts destroyed. For this reason, they argued for the abandonment or at least the sharp reduction of military actions, and for concentration instead on the building up of mass organisations. Not least because of the 'legal ones' ' failure to create an organisation of any size in the Basque country itself, the advocates of the autonomy of violence were able to gain the ascendancy. In the course of these controversies, however, two new and different approaches began to take shape, which led to the split of ETA into two organisations, still operating today, the *ETA militar* and the *ETA politico-militar*, or *poli-mili*. *ETA militar* took the view, and still does, that armed struggle – that is, the use of violence – and political action must be separate from each other, and that it is the task of the military cadres to create a revolutionary situation which can then be exploited by the political organisations in getting through the national movement's political demands. *ETA politico-militar*, on the other hand, advocated – and still advocates – the unity of violence and political activity; faithful to the principle of 'democratic centralism' it puts both under the strict, unified direction of an executive committee and is still today willing to use violence only if and when political actions achieve too little.[51]

From 1974 onwards it looked for a time as if the strategy of violence would take a secondary place in favour of purely political action. In view of the overthrow of the regimes in Greece and Portugal – both declared to be fascist – and of Franco's death and the subsequent process of democratisation in Spain, such hopes did not appear unreasonable; more so, since Debray in his 'Critique of Weapons' had ascribed the failure of Latin American guerillas to mistaken strategies and tactics; in the meantime the Tupamaros had failed in Uruguay and parties or party coalitions had developed, with links to both wings of ETA – the *Euskadido Eskerra* in the case of *ETA politico-militar* and *Herri Batasuna* in the case of *ETA militar* – and had received a considerable number of votes in the elections. These hopes, however, were not fulfilled. The question now is whether the present terror is still under political control or indeed controllable.[52]

IX

Even though the theoretical call for violence as a strategy in the military struggle for liberation had been formulated as early as 1962, or 1964 respectively, it was only in 1967 that internal structure and logistics were sufficiently developed to enable ETA to embark on its first terrorist campaign.[53]

Ever since, such campaigns have been renewed, as it were in waves. One wave of terror was followed by a counter-blast by the organs of the state, smashing ETA's cadres and its organisation. Once the phase of internal reconstruction was successfully completed, there followed a new wave of terror and counter-terror. In the course of these terrorist cycles, terror itself also escalated from relatively harmless acts such as violence against property, via manslaughter in self-defence, to cold-blooded systematic murder campaigns against specific groups of persons. It always required some time for the psychological barriers to break down that had previously prevented the transition to the next higher level of brutality.[54]

In the course of its evolution, ETA has developed an ample range of terrorist methods, suiting them to different purposes; its numerous murders can thus be said to represent merely the tip of the iceberg.

One form of systematic terror, which began in 1967, regularly reappeared in later years and was further amplified, was the bomb attacks on the institutions and emblems of Franco's state, such as police stations and barracks, town halls, the offices of Francoist syndicates, public buildings in general, monuments, Francoist newspapers, television relay stations as well as in later years the leisure institutions of the Basque middle class, such as sailing clubs and travel agencies and the business venues (bars) of suspected police spies.[55]

If the year 1967 had marked the turn to terrorist bombing campaigns, 1974 brought an even more drastic watershed, a new qualitative leap in ETA's terrorist evolution, the transition to a new type of action: the systematic and cold-blooded 'execution' of particular individuals. There certainly had been deaths before, but these had occurred in clashes with the police and ETA had declared them to be self-defence.[56] Other instances were the murders of two men who both possessed a certain symbolic character: the first of them took place in 1968, when one of the top police chiefs of the Basque region, Malitón Manzanas, was killed both to avenge the death of an ETA member, and at the same time as a representative of all the torturers in the police force; the second was in 1973, when Prime Minister Carrero Blanco, Franco's successor-designate, was assassinated.[57] What distinguished the new tactic, however, was the almost bureaucratic, systematic murder of officials on the lower levels of the state apparatus, or their agents. This was done by a new, technically perfect and ruthless generation of terrorists, who 'executed' police officers, police spies, mayors, and who still pursue these same tactics to the present day.[58]

Another sphere of activity is the kidnapping of entrepreneurs and – quite recently – politicians as an instrument of political blackmail, either in industrial conflicts or to effect the release of imprisoned terrorists. This method was first used in 1971/72 in the kidnapping of the manager of a large company which had refused to accede to the demands of striking workers but gave in under the pressure of the imminent murder of its representative.[59]

In general, these kidnappings end without lethal consequences for the hostages; the year 1974, however, brought the first murder of a kidnapped Basque industrialist, which was soon followed by a second one.[60] The taking of hostages remains a favoured tactical instrument to this day. In 1978/79, for instance, *ETA politico-militar* took eleven hostages who were all released after negotiations, usually having been shot through the legs.[61] The most recent climax in this development was the kidnapping of the Christian-Democrat politician Ruperez in 1979.[62]

It is one of the characteristics of ETA terror that it is confined to the Basque territory and deliberately limited either to individuals or groups identified with Francoism or to representatives of the upper middle class. This has tended to legitimise its terror beyond the narrow circle of radical nationalists.[63] In 1979 a sudden new qualitative leap seemed to have occurred, when ETA embarked on exploding bombs in Spanish coastal resorts, in the so-called 'holiday war', designed to keep away tourists by creating a climate of uncertainty and thus to deprive the Spanish exchequer of a vital source of foreign currency.

While in the 'holiday war' care had still been taken that no one was hurt, the three combined attempts in Madrid last July for the first time resulted in innocent bystanders being killed. It appears, however, as if ETA, in the face of massive criticism, even from within its own ranks, and under threat of impending total isolation has once more confined itself to its older types of target.[64]

The means to finance organisation, actions and full-time terrorists – the *liberados* (the liberated ones) – ever since 1967 have been obtained by regular robberies, usually involving the theft of large sums of money, but also of weapons, explosives, passport forms, duplicating machines and motor cars. It is only since the start of such systematic raids that ETA has been at all able to embark on terrorist campaigns or actions requiring large expenditure, such as the assassination of Carrero Blanco. After the first years of armed raids, perfected security measures made this method of obtaining financial means increasingly difficult. For this reason ETA came to prefer extortion, either by taking hostages or, more effectively, by levying a so-called 'revolutionary tax' – payments extracted by threats from companies or individuals.[65]

X

Despite ETA's secret nature, the main structural outlines of its organisation are known. Just as it did in its ideology, strategy and tactics, in its organisation structures it also tried out the examples provided by other movements – for instance by communist models – and adapted them to Basque needs in a dialectic interplay of theory and practice. Yet here, too, problems of continuity arose, since accumulated experiences perished with the dead, the arrested, the exiled. The inexperienced younger generation thus tended to repeat the old mistakes.[66] The structural principles on which ETA's present organisation is based were already established in its early days and have since been merely modified or perfected, if we take for the time being the organisational reform of 1974 as marking the last stage. Until that date a unified structure cannot be said to have existed and central direction was exercised only imperfectly. The various organisational areas, the 'military' sphere and the so-called 'fronts', operated autonomously and relatively independent of each other. At this stage decisions were still taken by groups of colleagues, the so-called *mesas de dirección*.[67] This has come to an end with the introduction of the principle of 'democratic centralism' in 1974.[68] While the general or national assembly (*Biltza Nagusia*), composed of representatives of the various branches of the organisation, still remains the supreme organ and decides on ideology and strategy, the top executive organ nevertheless plays a dominant role, despite the tendencies of this executive committee to become too independent – something that has been watched with mistrust. It is this committee which controls ETA activities, selects active combatants – the *liberados* and those 'responsible' for the different areas of organisation. Until 1974 it was the task of the 'fronts' to establish pioneering organisations among students and workers, generally to influence the social *ambiance* by agitation and organisation, to make it receptive to ETA's ideas and to create the familiar and protective conditions under whose umbrella violent action and the recruitment of new members became in the long term possible. Now the fronts were abolished, or rather dismissed as independent from the immediate ETA organisation, and replaced by sections that are under the direct rule of the executive committee. These sections are completely separated from each other, according to a by-now-well-established cell principle, so as to avoid the danger of a chain reaction when one cell is discovered. Now only individuals, those 'responsible act as link men'.[69] The organisational pattern, as of September 1975, pieced together by Kaufmann, reveals a somewhat more complex picture (Fig. 9.1).

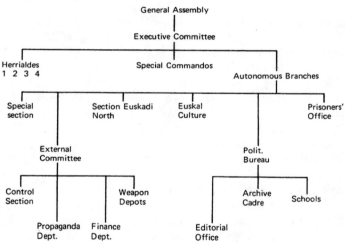

Figure 9.1

This organisational structure indicates that ETA consists of more than just a small nucleus of terrorist cadres. It possesses a developed organisational network which permits it to safeguard its terrorist activities within a wider social context and to make political use of them far more effectively than would be the case if it commanded no more than a diffuse, unstructured circle of sympathisers. It becomes clear that it was not merely the attested professional incompetence of the police and the fact that it was an alien body in hostile surroundings which prevented it from waging a successful battle against ETA, but also the fact that ETA, by means of its organisational structure, was able both to react flexibly to repressive measures and to find new catchment and recruitment areas as soon as the active terrorist spearhead and parts of the organisation fell victim to repressive measures.

ETA's organisational structure was capable of meeting a great variety of demands and also of accomplishing a great number of tasks, ranging from the political training of new recruits, the production of pamphlets and several regular publications, such as the theoretical magazine *Zutik*, to contacts with foreign organisations and governments willing to support ETA.

According to the organisation chart above, the political bureau is responsible for political education or training of members, for activities within mass organisations and for publications produced within the country. The special section is closely involved with terrorist activities. It organises the secret intelligence service, the smuggling of material and persons across borders. The external committee, finally, looks after foreign relations, particularly with other friendly associations, such as the IRA or, before their elimination, with the Argentine *Montoneros*, and the Uruguayan *Tupamaros*, from whom ETA copied the institution of 'people's prisons' for kidnapped 'capitalists'. ETA's connections with Cuba and Algeria are known, and very recently the Spanish government accused both these countries of having instructed the Basque terrorists in the techniques of guerilla warfare.[71]

Other independent branches are the prisoners' service, which looks after imprisoned ETA members, and the cultural department, *Euskal Culture*, responsible for trying to infiltrate cultural organisations and to transform them into centres of nationalist propaganda; it also arranges folklore performances and looks after the *Ikastolas*, the centres for the dissemination of the Basque language among children and adults.

For tactical purposes the Basque country is divided into zones, *herrialdes*, each of these being the responsibility of one man, the *herrialdeburu*, who is nominated by the executive committee. The responsibility of these men is essentially concerned with the logistic infra-structure in the Basque country. They organise weapon caches, hideouts, the securing of escape routes, etc.[72]

ETA's actual nucleus consists of the 'special commandos' – formerly the 'military front'; these, on the immediate orders of the executive committee, carry out raids, kidnappings and 'executions'. They are organised as revolutionary cells, consisting of 3–4 members, and have no direct link with each other. They are given an alias or *nom de guerre*, do not know their principals and are deployed in surroundings unknown to them – all protective measures taught by experience, aimed at avoiding the danger of largescale discovery.[73]

The members of these cadres are recruited after long observation of their work in legal organisations, such as students' associations or mountaineering clubs; in a process lasting several years they are gradually selected, via discussion circles, *charlas de formación*, and trained by being tried out in auxiliary expeditions.[74] This was done relatively undisturbed in the French Pyrennees until the French authorities took counter-measures. Special forces, however, at an early stage passed through courses conducted in the camps of organisations with extensive experience in guerilla warfare, such as the

Algerian FLN. After such training they become *liberados*, exclusively designated for combat, absolved from all other activities, and renumerated as such by ETA.[75]

Their limited size is a necessary structural principle of secret terrorist organisations. Correspondingly, ETA's terrorist nucleus has only a limited number of members, never exceeding more than a few hundred.[76] ETA's inner circle has thus always been a marginal organisation, albeit of considerable political weight. Its combatant spearhead consists of young people, intellectuals and for a large part former students, who regard themselves as a national avant-garde engaged in a class war.[77]

ETA had no need of *peones*, but of thinkers, of conscious, trained people, who know what they are doing.[78] It thus shares the fate of other organisations who claim to represent the interests of the proletariat, but in their social composition are far removed from it.

XI

How then is it to be explained that ETA, as a terrorist organisation, has been able to survive all waves of repression and thus continuously to sustain its concepts of the revolutionary struggle in an ever intensified and extended form?

It was possible because its strategic assessment of action and repression proved to be – at least partially – correct. The state's security organs responded to calculated attacks by waves of arrests, torture and the murder of genuine or alleged ETA activists, by extending and openly displaying an omnipresent police apparatus, as well as by public brutality against any form of suspected recalcitrance or any attack on the integrity of the Spanish nation. The *guardia civil*, as the merciless instrument of central government, reinforced the impression among the population of living in an occupied country, of being subject to the oppression of an alien power. At a time when, despite the continued despotic use of force on the part of the state, the call for political liberalisation became more and more clamorous throughout Spain, ETA presented itself as the most active fighter against the regime and was thus able to mobilise sympathies, not so much under the nationalist or socialist banner as under that of freedom and democracy.

An essential contribution to this was an extremely skilful use of propaganda, mobilising the domestic and foreign media, by presenting themselves in the romantic aura of freedom fighters and the dead, the imprisoned and the tortured as martyrs of a regime of violence. Beyond that, ETA was able to channel the general discontent in Spain as well as the social discontent of the workers towards its own interests.

How successfully ETA was thus able to acquire legitimacy in the eyes of the Basque population was shown by a survey conducted in 1975 by the magazine

Cambio 16, when 38 per cent of those interviewed agreed with the proposition: 'I condemn terror, but I can understand it', and 74 per cent believed that terror was directed only against people of a particular ideology.[79]

The breakthrough for ETA came in 1970, when the regime, in a show trial in Burgos against the first generation of actual ETA terrorists, was attempting to destroy the source of agitation. A wave of indignation, unknown in this form since the end of the Civil War, swept through the country and dealt the first severe blow to a regime on the way towards its decline. The German magazine *Stern* wrote at the time that this show trial had turned into the Stalingrad of the Franco Regime.[80] An even more disastrous defeat for the regime came with a hitherto unknown wave of demonstrations and general strikes, with the mobilisation of world opinion against Spain as a response to the government's second major attempt to eliminate ETA once and for all, by employing every means of repression at its disposal.[81]

It became evident that the Franco Regime had in part nourished terrorism and also made it possible; and that now, because of domestic developments and the ties to Western democratic countries and the consequent vulnerability to domestic and external criticism, repression could not be kept up as rigorously and absolutely as in the early days of the regime.[82]

A further factor in ETA's success was the open border with France, where the underground fighters could find shelter with sympathising French Basques and where, thanks to the practice of the French government (until 1979) of regarding them as political refugees, they were safe from persecution, expulsion or extradition.[83]

XII

How should the results of ETA terrorism be assessed? One may agree with Letamandía's judgement that the Basque movement has been a catalyst in the regime's decomposition and that in this process ETA has played the role of the explosive charge.[84] The assassination of Carrero Blanco, probably the only man capable of filling the gap left by Franco's death, certainly shortened the survival of the regime by several years at least.[85]

Beyond that, and contrary to Maravall's argument – which ascribes the decisive role in the process of replacing the Franco Regime to workers and students alone, and to their mobilising public resistance against it by strikes and demonstrations – one will have to concede that ETA and its terrorist and propagandist activities, as far as the Basque country is concerned, certainly achieved at least some significant initial impact.[86] One will also have to ascribe to the work of ETA, in both its manifestations, a large part of the nationalist radicalisation that has gripped the Basque country. The result of this has also been that the schematisation of the political spectrum into right, middle of the road and left, usual elsewhere, has acquired only secondary significance compared to the division into Basque or nationalist orientation and an all-Spanish one. A further mark of ETA's remarkable, continuing success and the assimilation of its ideas into the country's politics, is the success of the parties (or party groupings) close to both its wings – *Herri Batasuna* (Unified People) and *Euskadido Eskerra* (Basque Left) – in the Basque elections of 1979 and 1980. They proved that the parties of an all-Spanish persuasion – at least in the situation of 1979/80 – lost ground in favour of nationalist parties. Although PVN's socially and politically moderate nationalism of Christian orientation in the elections to the Basque parliament was able to attract the majority of electors (25 seats), the *Herri Batasuna* party, close to the violent *ETA militar*, nevertheless extended its vote and became the second largest grouping (11 seats). Taken together with the deputies of *Euskadido Eskerra* (6), a third of all representatives in the Basque parliament now belong to parties maintaining close links with terrorist ETA organisations. The latter, according to their own statements, can be expected to continue their violent actions, since they aim at complete independence for the Basque country and believe that this can only be achieved by terrorist activities.[87]

Beyond its immediate effect on the Basque country itself, ETA has placed a vast burden on democracy in Spain and is the cause, directly or indirectly, of the latent danger of a reactionary counterblow. In its wake, radical groups of left and right have come into being which employ the terrorist methods ETA has used in the Basque country, in order to pursue their objectives on a nationwide level. In the Basque country, too, ETA terror since 1975 has provoked constantly increasing counter-terror by radical right-wing groups which, under the auspices of Francoist ideas and in order to preserve the Spanish nation and its territorial integrity, have embarked on a new form of civil war against ETA members, institutions and suspected sympathisers. They do not confine their murderous attempts to Spanish territory, but extend their Spanish-nationalist motivated private justice to ETA representatives living in the French Basque region as well.[88] Just as the sorcerer's apprentice invoked spirits he could no longer control, ETA has opened the floodgates to a spate of terrorism of very diverse origins. The viability of democracy in Spain will depend on its ability to master terrorism.

NOTES

1. On the chronic state of war during the nineteenth century, cf. N. Sales, 'Servei militar i societat a l'Espanya del segle XIX', *Recerques* 1 (1970) pp. 145–81. On the tradition of anarchist violence, cf. W. L. Bernecker's contribution in this volume.

2. E. J. Hobsbawm, *Revolutionaries: Contemporary Essays* (London, 1973) p. 106.

3. G. Brunn, 'Regionalismus und sozialer Wandel: Das Beispiel Katalonien', in O. Dann (ed.), *Nationalismus und sozialer Wandel* (Hamburg, 1978) pp. 157–85.

4. G. Brunn, 'Die Organisation der katalanischen Bewegung 1859–1923', in Th.

Schieder and O. Dann (eds), *Nationale Bewegung und soziale Organisation* (Munich, 1978) pp. 281–339.

5. Because of their restricted practical political aims, both movements are usually described as autonomist or regionalist. In terms of ideology, however, they are nationalist movements. For an analysis of the ideology of Catalanism during its emergence see J. Solé-Tura, *Catalanismo y revolución burguesa* (Madrid, 1970). For the Basque country, cf. J. J. Solozábal Echavarria, *El primer nacionalismo vasco: Industrialismo y conciencia nacional* (Madrid, 1975); J. C. Larrouche, *El nacionalismo vasco: Su origen y su ideologia en la obra de Sabino Arana Goiri* (San Sebastian, 1978).

6. J. Linz, 'Early State-Building and Late Peripheral Nationalism against the State: The Case of Spain', in S. M. Lipset and S. Rokkan (eds), *Building States and Nations*, vol. 2 (Beverley Hills, 1973) pp. 32–116.

7. Cf. Brunn, *Organisation*, pp. 341–539.

8. Ibid., p. 312f., 382f.

9. Cf. the reports of the trial of Macía in France. Estat Catalá, *La Catalogne Rebelle: Tout le procès des conjurés catalans, précédé d'une notice sur la Catalogne et son mouvement national et suivi de quelques documents officiels* (Paris, 1927).

10. On the tying in of this attempted insurrection into the framework of the more general revolutionary movements in October 1934, P. Preston, 'Spain's October Revolution and the Rightist Grasp for Power', *JCH* 10 (1975) p. 571. Critical remark by R. Carr, *Spain 1808–1939* (Oxford, 1966) p. 633f. More recent descriptions from the Catalan point of view, J. Ma. Poblet, *História de l'Esquerra Republicana de Catalunya 1931–1936* (Barcelona, 1976) pp. 211–24.

11. Text of the statute in J. A. Gonzáles Casanova, *Federalismo i Autonomia a Catalunya (1868–1838): Documents* (Barcelona, 1974) pp. 745–54 and 851–60.

12. W. Haubrich and C. R. Moser, *Francos Erben: Spanien auf dem Weg in die Gegenwart* (Cologne, 1976) p. 110. The socially conservative Catalan bourgeoisie, organised in the *Lliga Regionalista*, on the other hand, sympathised with the Franco side. Cf. the indications in J. A. Parpal and J. M. Lladó, *Ferran Valls y Taberner: Un politic per la cultura catalana* (Barcelona, 1970) p. 223ff. They were nevertheless discriminated against after 1939 and remained excluded from political influence.

13. Haubrich, p. 110; N. L. Jones, 'The Catalan Question since the Civil War' in P. Preston (ed.), *Spain in Crisis: The Evolution and Decline of the Franco Regime* (Hassocks, 1976) p. 236ff; S. G. Payne, *Basque Nationalism* (Reno, 1975) p. 177ff.

14. Haubrich, p. 110.

15. On the socio-economic development of the Basque country under the aspect of post-war nationalism, cf. Payne, p. 230ff; for a comparison between Catalonia and the Basque country see S. G. Payne, 'Regional Nationalism: The Basques and the Catalans' in W. T. Salisbury and J. Theberge (eds), *Spain in the 1970s: Economics, Social Structure, Foreign Policy* (New York, 1976) pp. 76–102; cf. also Jones, p. 252f, 257.

16. For the Catalan case cf. Jones, p. 252f, 257.

17. Thus the correspondent of *Le Monde*, Ch. Vanhecke, *Le Monde* (26/10/1979).

18. How many true 'nationalities' there are in Spain, apart from Basques and Catalans, or might be resusciated or even created, will probably be a matter of controversy for many years. Nationality and the desire for regional autonomy need not be identical. This is shown by the example of Andalusia, whose wish for autonomy was for the time being not to be realised by the referendum of 2 March 1980. Cf. the report by W. Haubrich in *Frankfurter Allgemeine Zeitung* (4/3/1980).

19. Extensive reporting, with the necessary topical and background information, by Ch. Vanhecke, in *Le Monde* (26/10 and 27/10/79).
20. Catalans and Basques, however, did not develop the intensive maquis activities as for instance did the communists. On Catalan opposition activities, see Jones, p. 241ff. On those of the Basques see L. de Ibarra Enziondo, *El nacionalismo vasco en la paz y la guerra* (n. p., n. d., ca. 1975) p. 119ff; cf. also J. Elosegi, *Quiero morir por algo* (Bordeaux, 1971) p. 290ff.
21. Elosegi, p. 314ff; Ibarra Enziondo, p. 227f; cf. also the interview with the *PNV*'s leading theoretician, X. Arzallus, *Der Spiegel* 44 (1979) p. 147.
22. Brunn, *Organisation*, p. 311f, 381f; Parpal, p. 115f.
23. Jones, p. 247ff. The motives of ETA's founders are explained by one of them, J. Alvarez Emparanza, in an interview in R. C. Pastor, *Euskadi ante el futuro* (San Sebastian, 1977) p. 124f.
24. Payne, *Regional Nationalism*, p. 98ff. A corresponding analysis also in J. I. Paul and K. Otaegui, 'Diversas respuestas ante la questión nacional en Euskadi', *El Cárabo* 4 (1977) pp. 49–68. The idea of the threat to Basque identity is amply recorded in the Basque nationalists' own accounts. Cf. amongst others Elosegi, p. 20, or Gaurhuts, *Sobre nacionalismo revolucionario, socialismo abertzale y marxismo nacional* (Hendaye, 1976) p. 26ff; other records could be added at will.
25. Ibid., p. 85ff; Jones, p. 257.
26. Payne, *Basque Nationalism*, p. 237.
27. Payne, *Regional Nationalism*, p. 86; id., *Basque Nationalism*, p. 237f. On the situation of language and culture in the Basque country, cf. also the quantifying study by L. C. Nunez (Astrein) *Opresión y defensa del Euskera* (San Sebastian, 1977). On the Catalan language, for the first time in the 1960s, A. M. Badia i Margarit, *Le Llengua dels barcelonins* (Barcelona, 1969); a short summary of the pioneering sociological FOESSA-study of 1970 in Jones, p. 262.
28. This was last shown during the referendum on the autonomy statute, when ETA, despite vigorous propaganda, was not able to achieve massive abstentions from voting.
29. In this direction also the interpretative approaches in Payne, *Regional Nationalism*, p. 88ff. On the general categorisation of terrorist movements as youth movements of idealist character, see W. Laqueur, *Terrorismus* (Kronberg, 1977) p. 170.
30. Ibid., p. 170ff.
31. L. Maier, *Spaniens Weg zur Demokratie. Formen und Bedingungen der Opposition im autoritären Staat,* (Tübingen, 1977) p. 32ff.
32. The predecessors can be traced back to 1952/53. It is not the intention here to write a history of ETA, but simply to describe certain typical structural traits. A detailed, informed and sympathetic description (up to 1975) by Ortzv (i.e. Francisco Letamandía), *Historia de Euskadi: El nacionalismo vasco y ETA* (Paris, 1975). The quotations here are from the French edition, *Les Basques: Un peuple contre les états* (Paris, 1976). Letamandía is closely connected to ETA and is today deputy for *Herri Batasuna*, a party grouping close to *ETA militar*. A detailed chronicle (up to 1970) from the opposing camp, the *guardia civil*, obviously drawing on its archive material, by F. Aguado Sánchez, 'La E. T. A.: Apuntes para su historia', *Revista de Estudios Históricos de la Guardia Civil* IX/17 (1976) pp. 9–54 and IX/18, pp. 13–47. Valuable for the subsequent period A. Amigo, *Pertur: ETA 71–76* (Donostia, 1978) (with an appendix of documents). A good journalistic account, based partly on interviews with ETA members, by J. Kaufmann, *Mourir aux Pays Basques: Le combat impitoyable de l'ETA* (Paris, 1976). An informed account of its evolution by J. L. Hollyman,

'Basque Revolutionary Separatism: ETA', in Preston (ed.), *Spain in Crisis*, pp. 212–33.

33. On this thesis cf. Txabi, 'ETA y la questión nacional vasca', *Horizonte Español,* 2 (1972) pp. 78, 82; Gaurhuts, p. 20.

34. Letamandía, p. 162f; G. Halimi, *Le procès de Burgos* (Paris, 1971) p. 192f.

35. Quoted in Letamandía, p. 163.

36. Cf. the circular which ETA sent to the wives of *guardia civil* members. Aguado Sánchez, no. 18, p. 23f; see also Letamandía, p. 168; ibid. a theoretically sound critique of the colonialist argument, p. 233. When ETA was already on the point of abandoning this proposition, Jean-Paul Sartre formulated it for a still wider public, foreword to Halimi, p. 10f, 16f.

37. In this context note the vigorous opposition by *ETA militar* and the party grouping *Herri Batasuna* (Unified People) connected with it, against the passing of the autonomy statute, and its announcement that the struggle for an independent Basque country would continue. *Le Monde* (19/10/79 and 24/10/79). For tactical reasons, the demand for unification with the French Basque provinces is not stressed to the same degree. On this demand cf. for instance Pertur (i.e. Eduardo Ma. Moreno), 'Porqué estamos por un estado socialista vasco', in: Amigo, pp. 155–60 and the *declaración de agosto*, ibid., pp. 161–70; Haubrich, p. 111.

38. Gaurhuts, p. 20f, 29, 43; Letamandía, p. 174, 196; Txabi, p. 80ff.

39. Sartre, p. 24. Description of the formation of the various groups in Letamandía, p. 182ff; Aguado Sánchez, no. 18, p. 39ff; Txabi, p. 82ff; Amigo, p. 29ff, 46ff, 51ff, 68ff; Hollyman, p. 224ff.

40. On this Txabi, p. 80ff; Pertur, in Amigo, p. 155ff; Letamandía, p. 221ff, gives a theoretical substantiation with a historical dimension, entitled: *Patriotisme basque, socialisme et internationalisme (La théorie socialiste et les minorités nationales)*. More generally also the study by Gaurhuts.

41. Amigo, p. 22ff, 63f.

42. The first theoretician, Krutwig, of German descent, had also read Clausewitz, Letamandía, p. 164.

43. Ibid., p. 166ff.

44. Kaufmann, p. 54.

45. Ibid., p. 137ff; Letamandía, p. 169, 174; J. P. Mogui, *Révolte des Basques* (Paris, 1970) p. 65f.

46. On Third World influences and on the provocation of a revolutionary people's war by guerilla activities cf. Kaufmann, p. 135ff; Letamandía, p. 166f. In 1967 one group split off from ETA and tried to establish guerilla groups in the mountains; ibid., p. 171; Mogui, p. 72f. In 1971 the arming of the 'people's army' was still so ridiculously inadequate that in a direct confrontation it would have been defeated within minutes; Amigo, p. 25f.

47. Marighella's writings remained for years the preferred theoretical reading for many ETA militants, Amigo, p. 93; further Aguado Sánchez, no. 18, p. 19, 21; Letamandía, p. 196; Mogui, p. 47f.

48. Letamandía, p. 203, 205, 207; Pastor Castillo, p. 166. On ETA's theory of violence and its justification during the 1970s cf. Amigo, p. 161ff; (documentary appendix) and the documents in: *Operation Menschenfresser: Wie und warum wir Carrero Blanco hingerichtet haben – ein authentischer Bericht und Dokumente von E. T. A.* (Spanish title: *Operación ogro*), (Hendaye, 1974) p. 166ff. Most recently the declarations of both wings of ETA on the autonomy referendum, *Le Monde* (19/10/79).

49. Sartre speaks of the withdrawal of the 'humanist right', Sartre, p. 24. On the

motives of those who withdrew cf. the interview with one of them in Pastor Castillo, p. 126ff.

50. Cf. Amigo, p. 30f, 47ff, 54ff, 68ff; Letamandía, p. 200, 204f.
51. This split, prompted more than anything else by questions of strategy and tactics, is described and documented in detail in Amigo, p. 78ff and 201ff; Letamandía. p. 205ff. In the meantime however, different political weightings have evolved. Whereas *ETA politico-militar* pursues primarily social-revolutionary aims, *ETA militar* sees its struggle essentially as one of national liberation. Xavier Arzallus in *Der Spiegel* 44 (1979) p. 147. On the assessment of both wings cf. also *Frankfurter Rundschau* (16/11/79).
52. On ETA's public pronouncement at a press conference that in a democracy political mass organisations must take precedence, cf. Pastor Castillo, p. 166. This statement was made in connection with the prospective foundation of a party with close links to *ETA politico-militar*. The leading ideologist of this party, Pertur, exerted political and ideological pressure in favour of political activity instead of violence. It is possible that his disappearance without trace in 1976 is connected with this. Cf. Amigo, p. 93f; also Letamandía, p. 205.
53. The first wave was connected with the Basque 5th assembly, after which ETA was sometimes called ETA V. The new ETA, oriented on more universalist and class-war lines (1970), on the other hand, was called ETA VI. On this turn of events, Letamandía, p. 175ff; Aguado Sánchez, no. 18, p. 14ff. The prosecution at the Burgos trial (1970) for the three previous years listed nine armed raids, three murders and 46 officially recorded bomb attempts, Halimi, p. 261.
54. The first great wave of arrests had followed the first two assassination attempts. The next followed in 1963. After a lengthy phase of conscious reconstruction and quiessence on the part of ETA (Mogui, p. 65ff.), ETA's first murder (in August 1968) was answered by the most ruthless measures of persecution hitherto, so that in 1970 ETA – also because of the split – had to begin again virtually at zero (Halimi, p. 190f; Mogui, p. 75; Amigo, p. 23). After it had been restructured, action and repression followed in ever more rapid cycles (Amigo, p. 27f., 50, 71ff.). A similarly brief phyrric victory as in 1969/70 the security authorities achieved again in 1975, with an unprecedented deployment of resources. ETA's infra-structure was smashed almost completely. Only one commando remained intact (Amigo, p. 101ff.), yet in 1976 the series of attempts and murders nevertheless continued unbroken, cf. Equipo Cinco, *Victimas del postfranquismo. 55 muertos: Balance trágico de un año de terror* (Madrid, 1978) p. 19ff. 1979/80 saw a new climax of terror, after a comparatively peaceful previous year. With 19 lethal attempts between January and March 1980 alone, ETA embarked on the most bloody wave of terror so far. Cf. V. Mauersberger, 'Francos Erben vor dem Richter', *Die Zeit* 10 (29/2/1980). On the question of the psychological barrier cf. Amigo, p. 70.
55. A detailed chronicle of terrorist activities between 1967–1970 by Aguado Sánchez, no. 18, p. 14ff; also from November 1975–February 1977 in Equipo Cinco.
56. On the first lethal clashes Aguado Sánchez, no. 18, p. 22ff, 34ff; Letamandía, p. 177; Amigo, p. 28, stresses the involuntary nature of the murders of policemen during the first years.
57. On Melitón Manzanas, the 'operación Sagarra' cf. Aguado Sánchez, no. 18, p. 24ff; Letamandía, p. 177f; Kaufmann, p. 9ff; ibid., p. 115ff. on Carrero Blanco. Also Letamandía, p. 201f; especially *Operación ogro*, the perpetrators' own chronicle of events.
58. Cf. Amigo, p. 70; Gaurhuts, p. 66, stresses ETA's new 'technical perfection' since

1974. On the murders from this time onwards, here and there Letamandía, p. 209ff. From the autumn of 1975 onwards, Equipo Cinco, p. 9 passim. Until 1976 army officers were not among the targets of ETA's terror, after that they were attacked all the more vigorously. Between November 1976 and September 1979 13 officers were murdered by ETA; cf. *Le Monde* (21/9/79).

59. An extensive account of the first two kidnappings in Kaufmann, p. 151ff; Letamandía, p. 195, 199. On the criticism within ETA's ranks and by illegal Spanish workers' commissions, the *comisiones obreras*, Amigo, p. 43ff. The kidnapping of the German consul Behl in 1970 had other reasons, Aguado Sánchez, no. 18, p. 42ff.

60. Kaufmann, p. 189ff; *Archiv der Gegenwart*, p. 21062 ((22/6/1977); Amigo, p. 124ff, claims that the first murder had been a matter of controversy also within *ETA politico-militar*.

61. *Frankfurter Rundschau* (16/11/79).

62. On the background to this kidnapping, *Frankfurter Allgemeine Zeitung* (14/11/79).

63. Equipo Cinco, p. 42.

64. *Le Monde* (1/8/79, 4/8/79, 19/10/79).

65. Amigo, p. 25ff, 121f. The first extortions were modelled on the example of the Algerian FLN, Mogui, p. 69. On the numerous bank raids until the end of 1970 cf. Aguado Sánchez, no. 18, p. 15ff, 22, 33, 38f.; Letamandía, p. 199. On the revolutionary levy see Kaufmann, p. 174. On the continuing of this practice to the present day, *Le Monde* (27/9/79). The first significant arms purchases on the international market were initiated in 1971, Amigo, p. 28; Kaufmann, p. 79ff.

66. Amigo, p. 109f.

67. Halimi, p. 272; Aguado Sánchez, no. 18, p. 31. On the basic traits of this organisation until the reform of 1974, which was subject to numerous modifications, cf. Letamandía, p. 163f, 167f, 174, 177, 180; Aguado Sánchez, no. 17, p. 27, 30f, 47, 51f, and no. 18, p. 13f; Halimi, p. 186.

68. Gaurhuts, p. 34; Amigo, p. 53; Pastor Castillo, p. 166.

69. On the executive committee see Kaufmann, p. 69. On the reform of 1974, Gaurhuts, p. 58, 64ff; Pastor Castillo, p. 166. On the principle of fronts, an attempt to adapt the Vietnamese example to Basque conditions, cf. Aguado Sánchez, no. 18, p. 13f; Sartre, p. 25; Halimi, p. 189, 285; Mogui, p. 74f; Letamandía, p. 172, 174. Apart from its work in cultural, political and workers' organisations, ETA also tried to build up local branches. Cf. P. Celhay, *Consejos de guerra en España: Fascismo contra Euskadi* (Paris, 1976) p. 25. For reasons of security, greater mobility and in order to control the executive committee and to give important actions a broader membership base, the 'small committee' (BT = Biltaz Txikia) was established in 1967 as the highest authority between general assemblies; its members were *liberados* and the men with overall responsibility for branches of the organisation or zones, Halimi, p. 186, 268ff; Letamandía, p. 124.

70. Kaufmann, p. 68.

71. *Ibid.*, p. 78ff; *Archiv der Gegenwart*, p. 21901 (11/7/1977).

72. Kaufmann, p. 87f. On the earlier period cf. Letamandía, p. 164; Mogui, p. 76f. These were established as organisational units after the wave of arrests in 1963. Halimi, p. 86; also Aguado Sánchez, no. 17, p. 29f., 47. The number of herrialdes obviously varied in the course of time from seven to six to four.

73. Kaufmann, p. 85, 92ff. The Basque name for these commandos is *irurko* (three). The immediate instigation for the establishment of this kind of combat cell came from the Algerian FLN. Cf. Letamandía, p. 166, 177; also Mogui, p. 68; Aguado Sánchez, no. 17, p. 31 and no. 18, p. 13.

74. On methods of recruiting members, ibid., p. 36f; Mogui, p. 66; Halimi, p. 289; Kaufmann, p. 91ff.
75. *Liberados* were introduced after the wave of arrests of 1963, *ibid.*, p. 186; Kaufmann, p. 91ff. On the gradation of members from simple sympathisers to *liberados*, cf. Mogui, p. 68; Aguado Sánchez, no. 17, p. 30f.
76. Kaufmann, p. 93. At the fifth assembly for instance, where the active nucleus was represented, 40 participated in the first phase and some 70 in the second phase, Halimi, p. 282.
77. Kaufmann, p. 69ff. Biographies of the defendants in Burgos in Halimi, p. 262ff. A detailed biographical sketch of a leading member of the 70s, Pertur, who vanished without trace in 1976, in Amigo.
78. Quoted in Kaufmann, p. 91.
79. Equipo Cinco, p. 42. On the stylisation of killed ETA members into martyrs, see Mogui, p. 267f; Halimi, p. 190f; on the feeling of living in an occupied country, cf. the situation report in *Frankfurter Rundschau* (28/6/75). ETA's popularity interpreted as the consequence of its fight against repression in *Le Monde*, (27/10/79).
80. Quoted, along with many foreign press comments, by Halimi, p. 217. On the Burgos trial there exist both sympathetic and condemnatory accounts. Condemnatory of ETA, F. de Arteaga, *'ETA' y el proceso de Burgos* (Madrid, 1971). Sympathetic, K. Salaberri, *El proceso de Euskadi en Burgos* (Paris, 1971).
81. A detailed chronicle of the turbulent year 1975 by Celhay. On this cf. also *Archiv der Gegenwart* (28/10/75) pp. 19796–8. The fact that the combined acts of violence by the security forces and the trials with their death sentences in the end did not achieve their desired result, despite short term successes, is proved by the chronicle of terror in subsequent years. Cf. Equipo Cinco and *Archiv der Gegenwart* (22/6/77) pp. 21080–2.
82. On the thesis that repression of terrorism must be absolute if it is not to fail, cf. Laqueur, p. 180. The question is, whether the increased professionalism of the police, partly with German aid, and rooting it in the Basque country, as has recently been tried, will make the fight against ETA more successful. Cf. Arzallus, p. 147; Ortots, *Die Basken* (Munich, 1979) p. 79ff. The brutal methods employed by Spanish security forces are documented and have been frequently described. Cf. the *Report of an Amnesty International Mission to Spain: July 1975*; Mogui, p. 79ff; Batasuna, *Le répression au pays basque* (Paris, 1970). Basque publications tend to deplore police repression and to remain silent on ETA terror. Cf. for instance J.-K. Narbarte, *Mil días de la dictadura a le pre-autonomia en Euskadi* (San Sebastian, 1978).
83. *Archiv der Gegenwart* (31/1/79) p. 22357; Ch. Vanhecke, 'La France et ses ressortissants au pays basque payennt cher l'appui donné au gouvernement Suarez', *Le Monde* (27/9/79) p. 7.
84. Letamandía, p. 218.
85. This is also the opinion of foreign observers, quoted ibid., p. 202.
86. Thus for instance J. Maravall, *Dictatorship and Political Dissent: Workers and Students in Franco's Spain* (London, 1978) p. 11. Emphasis on ETA's catalyst character during the mass demonstrations and general strikes of 1974–6 in Paul and Otaegui, p. 65.
87. Maier, p. 247. A brief and subtle analysis of the political situation in the Basque country at the beginning of 1980 by H.-J. Puhle, 'Ein Kunstwort für das Baskenland: Ein Spezialfall des Separatismus und seine Wurzeln', *Das Parlament* XXX/3 (19/1/80) p. 13. The immunity of two *Cortes* deputies, members of *Herri Batasuna*, who refused to take part in the sessions of, in their words, a foreign parliament, while however claiming its privileges, was removed at the end of

November 1979, on the grounds of 'apologia of terrorism'. Cf. *Frankfurter Allgemeine Zeitung* (29/11/79).

88.   On the beginnings of right-wing terror in the Basque country, Celhay, p. 27ff. Further cases in the chronicle of Equipo Cinco, p. 187ff. Also a list of Spanish terror organisations existing in 1977, with characterisations. On the right-wing terror early in 1980, cf. *Frankfurter Allgemeine Zeitung* (31/1/80, 4/2/80). The spread of terror into France is documented in *Le Monde* (4/8/79, 27/9/79). There have been no parallel terrorist nationalist organisations of any significance in other Spanish regions, and ETA always appears to have remained largely isolated in Spain. On the complaint about its isolation cf. for instance *Operación ogro*, p. 25f. The Catalan FAC – *Frente de Liberación de Catalunya* – has made no notable appearance on the scene, cf. Equipo Cinco, p. 69.

10 Traditions of Violence in the Irish National Movement

Peter Alter

I

The dynamiting of a prison in the London borough of Clerkenwell in December 1867 and the assassinations in Dublin's Phoenix Park in May 1882 were among the most spectacular acts of political violence committed in the United Kingdom during the nineteenth century.[1] The bomb explosion in London, intended to free imprisoned Irish nationalists, killed twelve people and injured more than a hundred. In Phoenix Park both the newly appointed Chief Secretary for Ireland, Lord Frederick Cavendish, a relation of Gladstone's, and his deputy were murdered. Both events brought home to a shocked British public the existence of organisations within the Irish national movement, which, in the pursuit of their political objectives, were prepared to use violence and terror against people and property. Along with organisations seeking to agitate for the repeal of the Act of Union of 1801 or for Home Rule for Ireland by political and legal means, these groups represented the other end of the political spectrum and constituted an essential element of nineteenth-century Irish nationalism.

In their assessment of the 'Irish question' – which in the nineteenth century represented one of the greatest challenges to the British liberal system – and of the eventual political status they sought for Ireland, Irish nationalists of all shades and persuasions were in broad agreement. According to nationalist ideology, the Act of Union of 1801 was the source of Ireland's political, social and economic evils. Nevertheless, there existed significant differences of opinion between the various organisations and movements about the methods of achieving the nationalist programme. These differences about methods of agitation and means to be employed – rather than those about the nationalist programme as such – have led modern historians to speak of a revolutionary wing and a constitutional or legalistic-reformist wing within the Irish national movement, into which all national organisations and associations in Ireland up to the end of the nineteenth century can be fitted, despite the many overlaps that existed in practice. From the time of Daniel O'Connell, the constitutional wing was represented by a number of prominent parliamentary leaders and political associations. The political objective of constitutional nationalism was Irish autonomy, without, however, challenging in principle Ireland's affiliation to the English Crown.[2] The older revolutionary line of Irish nationalism, by contrast, justified its position by pointing to the superior goal of an independent Irish republic whose realisation set no limits as to the choice of means for its achievement.

In the present, necessarily brief, sketch attention will be focused on the revolutionary wing within the Irish national movement. My primary aim here is not to examine what significance individual organisations may have had for modern Irish history, but to give a rough outline of the manifold organisational forms revolutionary nationalism took in Ireland, based on the recorded data about all known organisations of more than regional importance within the Irish national movement since the eighteenth century.[3]

Under the heading of revolutionary nationalism I shall include all those bodies which have either stood for socially or politically revolutionary programmes or which, in the pursuit of their objectives, employed illegal means or indeed violence. On the basis of this material, sometimes inevitably incomplete, I shall outline, in the second part of my paper, the revolutionary political practices of this particular variant of Irish nationalism and, in the interests of making the evidence more generally relevant, deliberately abbreviate, simplify and categorise. However, the typological method employed here does not mean that particular features in individual cases will be excluded – if for no other reason than to avoid the risk of forcing the historical evidence into a rigid, abstract pattern. Sketching on a third aspect – that is, the social structure of revolutionary Irish nationalism – is something I shall have to forego here.[4]

Before going any further, one point about the history of the Irish national movement from the late eighteenth century onwards needs to be made first. If we consider the entire course of the Irish national movement up to the creation of the Irish Free State in 1921/22, we find that it was undoubtedly constitutional nationalism in its various forms which played the dominant role. Only the constitutional organisations were able to pursue their – from today's viewpoint – moderate aims by legal means, while the organisations of revolutionary nationalism automatically provoked counter-measures by the police, thus setting a time limit to the existence of such bodies or forcing them underground. For this reason, the long periods of agitation on the part of constitutional nationalist groupings, as for instance on the issues of Catholic emancipation, the repeal of the Act of Union and Home Rule, were interrupted only intermittently by unsuccessful, if spectacular, manifestations of revolutionary nationalism, as for example the attempted rebellions of 1803, 1848 and 1867 or during the plots of 1867 and 1882, already referred to. They provided incontrovertible indications that ever since the last third of the eighteenth century the chain of revolutionary nationalist organisations in Ireland had in effect never been broken. Irish nationalism, and particularly its constitutional variant, owed a good deal of its political effectiveness to the existence of this revolutionary groundswell, which lasted well into the twentieth century, and to the frequent pointers to the 'men of the hillsides'. The 1916 Easter Rising in Dublin, despite its rapid suppression, led directly to the emergence of an Irish national state.

II

Feliks Gross, in his study of *Violence in Politics,* observed that terror can last for a long time and can even become institutionalised within a society.[5] This observation is based particularly on the historical evidence of terrorism in Eastern Europe in the nineteenth and twentieth centuries, but can equally be applied to the Ireland of the same period. Irish revolutionary nationalism ever since the late eighteenth century can be said to fall into three main categories: Secret Societies, Revolutionary Agrarian Societies and Paramilitary Organisations. They established a tradition of violence which extends directly into our own times. Here follows a brief outline of the rise of these societies and their organisation.

From the eighteenth century onwards *Secret Societies* and *Brotherhoods* of regional or supra-regional dimensions were able to exert an influence on Irish politics and Irish nationalism to a degree probably unequalled elsewhere in Western Europe. These societies, which existed in many countries, have so far been the subject of only limited research. Eric J. Hobsbawm has recently urged the desirability of this type of study,[6] which is rendered more difficult, because source material about the development, organisation and the activities of such societies is scant and has been handed down in a somewhat random fashion.[7] On the basis of more or less reliable literature – which still remains to be supplemented by detailed local and regional studies – and of printed sources it is nevertheless possible to make some general observations about Irish secret societies.[8]

(1) In contrast to other European countries, the early secret societies in Ireland from the mid-eighteenth century onwards were almost exclusively agrarian in origin. They emerged particularly in times of economic depression or rising rents, whereas the later, supra-regional secret societies had predominantly political objectives and started in the cities.

(2) Well into the middle of the nineteenth century, the overriding aim of most secret societies of the proletarianised Irish rural population was the struggle against, or the removal of pressing economic and social grievances, resulting from the prevailing agrarian structure. The secret societies were

principally concerned with the protection of tenants, farm labourers and smallholders against arbitrary acts by landowners and against the payment of dues, which were felt to be 'illegal', such as certain taxes, or the tithes for the established Protestant Church.[9] They organised a violent form of self-defence against the injustices of their time and conditions, which merely favoured the interests of a small social group.[10] To what extent they also pursued a political aim is difficult to establish in individual instances. In the case of the Defenders in Ulster during the late eighteenth century, a somewhat sectarian secret society of Catholics established in response to the formation of the Protestant *Orange Order* (1795), as well as of the various *Ribbon Societies* since the beginning of the nineteenth century, such political and nationalist overtones are however unmistakeable. Their declarations speak of 'freeing Ireland' and 'liberating our country'. But it was the *Irish Republican Brotherhood*, which from the second half of the nineteenth century onwards aimed at an all-embracing revolutionary change of political conditions in Ireland, while at the same time paying little heed to the people's traditional social demands.

(3) Being protection societies of the rural population, whose support or at least approval they usually enjoyed, or political societies, pursuing revolutionary objectives, the primary orientation of these secret organisations was not anti-clerical. But since landowners and Anglo-Irish ascendancy belonged almost exclusively to the Protestant denominations, the formation of confessional fronts was a secondary consequence, although it would be wrong to see the Irish Catholics and Protestants as monolithic blocks. In Ulster the function of sectarian protection was nevertheless a dominant one. Individual priests excepted, these secret societies were in general not approved of by the Catholic clergy, who – certainly from the time of O'Connell's agitation – had only supported constitutional organisations and repeatedly condemned secret societies, threatening their members with religious sanctions.[12]

(4) The earliest important example of an agrarian secret society, which in many ways served as a model for all those that followed, was that of the *Whiteboys*, founded around 1760.[13] The name derived from the white shirts or white cockades the members wore as a badge of identification on their nocturnal forays. The *Whiteboys* first appeared in the relatively prosperous Co. Tipperary and subsequently spread, under the same or a similar name,[14] into other south-western counties, but it is frequently difficult to determine with any degree of certainty whether they or other *ad hoc* self-help organisations, formed independently of them, were responsible for cases of so-called 'agrarian crimes', 'agrarian outrages' or 'agrarian unrest'.[15] The existence of a link, however, between the emergence of the *Whiteboys* and their successor organisations on the one hand and agrarian crises – enclosures of common land, rapid economic change, increased rents for tenant farmers – on the other, cannot be denied. Significantly, the *Whiteboys* frequently called themselves 'Levellers'.[16]

As soon as economic conditions eased, and consequently also the latent conflict between landlords and tenants, these societies disappeared, only to re-emerge some time later under the same or a new name. Thus, from 1785 onwards the *Rightboys*, whose aims were similar to those of the *Whiteboys*, were much in evidence in the south-west of Ireland. From the early nineteenth century onwards the *Ribbonmen* (from 1826: *Ribbon Society*), taking their name from the white hat-band which they wore as a mark of identification,[17] continued the tradition of the *Whiteboys* far beyond the middle of the century. Elements of 'ribbonism' could still be detected in the *Irish National Land League* of the late 1870s.[18] In addition, there is evidence of a great number of local organisations during the first half of the nineteenth century, whose usually somewhat fanciful names[19] do not indicate any potential connection with larger regional organisations.

(5) The organisation of local secret societies of the *Whiteboy*-type was usually very simply structured. There was a leader, whose name is only occasionally known, and frequently a deputy leader. The bond between members, and their mutual recognition, was ensured by passwords or certain marks of identification.[20] Only rarely did these small secret societies have branches; contacts with analogous groups in the neighbourhood or in other parts of the country tended to be accidental and improvised. Their minimal organisational structure was, as a rule, quite sufficient for the pursuit of their limited objectives. At the same time, the fact that their organisation was so extremely rudimentary, and was hardly ever consolidated, rendered the police's fight against secret societies more difficult. Only the *Ribbon Society,* founded in 1826, was based on a loose union of already existing local 'lodges', which nevertheless continued to remain organisationally independent, only intermittently co-ordinating their activities with a central authority.[21] It is thus extremely difficult to date with any accuracy the emergence and disappearance of such local secret societies. One usually revealing indicator of their appearance are police reports about agrarian unrest in certain parts of the country, and about efforts on the part of local organisations to win new members and to 'swear them in'.[22] The oath all new members had to swear upon admission into a secret society thus tended to provide the strongest and most effective organisational bond.[23]

In most cases, the question as to the degree to which the endemic appearance of such organisations of the Irish rural population may be ascribed to national associations cannot be clearly answered. As a type, they occupied an intermediate position: in terms of their organisation and methods they belonged to the category of Secret Societies, while their aims were identical with those of subsequent tenant leagues, which sought the reform of the laws of land tenancy in Ireland.[24] Organisations such as the *Whiteboys*, which in the sense of the established laws were criminal, can probably best be understood if one views them in the light of archaic social movements, of the sort described by Eric J. Hobsbawm, taking his examples mainly from southern and south-western Europe from the time of the French Revolution onwards.[25] At best, these early secret peasant societies represented political programmes of the most rudimentary sort. Their members were still largely 'pre-political'.[26] For the Irish national movement, however, these societies were of considerable importance. Not only was their tradition as organisations for the protection of tenants – reflected in their heroic idealisation in the tales and ballads of folklore – continued by subsequent national organisations, but by their acts of violence against social and political conditions, which were felt to be oppressive, and by demonstrating the efficacy of joint action, they also helped to mobilise the population politically: 'The significance of these rural movements in the shaping of a national consciousness appears to have been considerable, for . . . they helped, in particular, to preserve a sense of group identity.'[27]

The earliest instance of a secret society with primarily political and national aims was the *Society of United Irishmen*, which until it was banned in 1794, claimed to be a constitutional association.[28] Its objective was the removal of British rule in Ireland in favour of an independent Irish republic. The realisation of this goal, as the attempted rebellion of 1798 was to prove amply, did not preclude the use of violence. It was a characteristic feature of the *United Irishmen* that their main bases were in Belfast and Dublin and that they were hardly able to gain a foothold in the countryside. They were the first in Irish history to discover that, given the existing social problems and the means of communication at that time, it was extremely difficult to mobilise the rural population with a purely political programme.

What the *United Irishmen* had attempted in vain, i.e. to extend their organisation throughout the entire country, the *Irish Republican Brotherhood* (IRB) sixty years later was able to achieve to a considerable degree. The IRB was the most important secret political society of nineteenth-century Ireland, whose activities continued up to the second decade of the twentieth century.[29] It was founded in 1858 in Dublin by Irish Americans, immediately after the establishment of its sister organisation in the US, the *Fenian Brotherhood*.[30] The connection between the American and the Irish organisations was always a close one and this led eventually to the name 'Fenians' being extended to the members of the *Irish Republican Brotherhood* as well.[31]

The IRB was notable for four characteristics:

(1) For a time it possessed a well-developed organisation in many parts of the country, modelled mainly on traditional agrarian societies and on the hierarchical organisational patterns of French and Italian secret societies. For the IRB, too, the chief element for its cohesion was provided by the oath all members were obliged to swear.[32] Its basic organisational unit was the 'circle', organised along lines similar to military command structures. The 'circle' usually covered one or several counties, or a town or part of a town, and was led by a 'centre', or 'A', or 'colonel'. An 'A' commanded nine 'B's or 'captains', one 'B' nine 'C's or 'sergeants', and one 'C' in turn commanded

nine 'D's or 'soldiers'. Thus a 'circle', fully structured on this pattern, would contain a total of 820 members.[33]

Organisational pattern of an IRB 'circle':

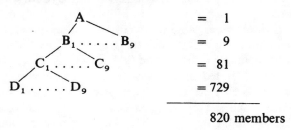

$$A \quad = \quad 1$$
$$B_1 \ldots \ldots B_9 \quad = \quad 9$$
$$C_1 \ldots \ldots C_9 \quad = \quad 81$$
$$D_1 \ldots \ldots D_9 \quad = 729$$

820 members

In theory, a rank and file member of the IRB (a 'D') was supposed to know only the eight men of his own section and his immediate superior. In practice this was impossible to achieve, and thus neither the system of circles – which appears more like a game of arithmetic – nor the oath provided adequate protection against the police or traitors within their own ranks. Leon O Broin's study in particular has shown very clearly how remarkably well the police were informed about IRB activities.[34] Moreover, the size of the circles varied considerably: on occasion some of them were claimed to have numbered over 2,000.[35]

After the abortive rebellion of 1867, the new head of the *Irish Republican Brotherhood* was the Supreme Council.[36] As the only overall head of a national association in Ireland, the Supreme Council claimed comprehensive political authority. According to the IRB's revised statutes, it constituted 'in fact as well as by right the sole government of the Irish Republic', and its decrees 'shall be the laws of the Irish Republic until the territory thereof shall have been recovered from the English enemy and a permanent government established'.[37] As a consequence, the IRB immediately formed provisional Irish governments during the insurrections of 1867 and 1916, but it is not entirely clear whether the Supreme Council expressly constituted itself as such or whether it continued to exist parallel to it. The local circles in Ireland and those of the Irish immigrants in England and Scotland were grouped into seven 'electoral divisions' under 'provincial centres',[38] each of which was represented by a delegate elected for a two-year term. The seven delegates in turn coopted four 'honorary members', so that the Supreme Council numbered eleven members in all. Since, for geographical reasons alone, this body could only meet occasionally (as a rule twice yearly), the actual command of the IRB was in the hands of an executive committee, elected from among the Supreme Council's eleven members.

(2) The IRB affirmed unconditionally that it would use every kind of violence in order to gain its political objective: an Irish republic independent of Britain. Both insurrection attempts during the lifetime of the IRB, the

Fenian Rising of 1867 and the Dublin Easter Rising of 1916, were inspired and supported by it. It was this extremism with regard to both political objectives and choice of means, which was the main reason for the Church's opposition to it; the fact that it was a clandestine society bound by oath constituted only a secondary reason.[39]

(3)   In contrast to all previous nationalist organisations in Ireland, the IRB could claim support not only from the Irish at home but also from Irish immigrants, particularly in the US and Britain. As has already been indicated, the latter were integrated into the organisation at home, while the Irish Americans not only provided the IRB with valuable political support but also with considerable financial backing. Moreover, without this almost ceaseless flow of American funds from about 1860, the agitation of virtually every other nationalist group in Ireland would not have been possible either. No evidence has come to light so far which would indicate that the IRB maintained links with revolutionary movements in Europe.[40]

(4)   The IRB had an exceedingly long life, beginning in 1858 and lasting until 1924. Although it lost importance after the 1867 rising and temporarily almost ceased to exist as an organisation, it experienced a revival after the turn of the century. The longevity of some of its founder members no doubt was one of the reasons for its long existence.[41]

Revolutionary Agrarian Societies included all those organisations and associations within the Irish national movement which sought to bring about fundamental changes in Irish agrarian conditions by close co-operation and collective action of tenant farmers. In this context, the term 'Revolutionary Agrarian Society' is intended to be a broad one, since very diverse tenants' leagues, in terms of their programmes, will be included under this heading. Their scale ranged from societies pursuing moderate objectives of agrarian reform – which might be increased, if circumstances were favourable – to those aiming at a radical reconstruction of land tenure in Ireland and, in order to attain their objectives, employing methods, which, at least by the standards of their time, were regarded as revolutionary.[42]

The model for revolutionary, or potentially revolutionary, agrarian societies, particularly in the last third of the nineteenth century, was provided by British trade unions, whose practices in pressing for the workers socio-political demands were referred to time and again. What distinguished the revolutionary agrarian societies from older secret ones, such as the *Whiteboys*, was their open organisation and the obvious political emphasis of their objectives. Yet this did not prevent them from forming links with secret agrarian societies still existing, to make the latter's demands their own and, to a certain extent, even to employ their methods in their conflict with landowners and the forces of the State. The organisational structure of the revolutionary agrarian societies hardly differed from that of the associations for political agitation existing at the same time. Like them, their structure was centralised, hierarchical and clearly modelled on that of the Catholic Church. This imitation of the Church's organisation, frequently noted by contemporary observers, not only suggested itself because it had proved its efficacy in extremely difficult political circumstances, but also because the nationally conscious lower clergy had played a leading role in virtually all non-revolutionary associations ever since the agitation for Catholic emancipation in the first half of the nineteenth century. The revolutionary agrarian societies were led by central bodies sitting, almost without exception, in Dublin, with local branches being directly responsible to them. As in the case of associations for political agitation, the boundaries and spheres of activity of local branches as a rule coincided with the parish boundaries.

The best known, most influential and at the same time most radical example of this type of Irish association was the *Irish National Land League*. Founded in 1879, at the height of a severe agrarian crisis, it had spread rapidly in Ireland's rural areas and had swallowed up the local tenants' societies, formed at the same time or slightly earlier.[43] Its demands for an adjustment of rents to the decrease in the price of agricultural produce, for a ban on landowners' giving arbitrary notice to tenants and finally for converting rented land into tenant's property, resulted in political and personal links with the Irish Parliamentary Party which had been demanding Home Rule in the British House of Commons since the late 1870s. For the first time in the history of the Irish national movement between 1879 and 1882 revolutionary and constitutional nationalism united for joint action. The Parliamentary Party made itself the voice of Irish tenant farmers in the House of Commons, while the *Irish National Land League*, with its tight and all-embracing organisation, brought Ireland's political and social order to the brink of chaos.[44]

Paramilitary Organisations, which did not have a national programme of their own but merely appealed to the patriotism of the Irish people, were a characteristic of the years immediately preceding the First World War, when agitation for Home Rule gained new impetus by the introduction of a third Home Rule Bill in the British parliament. In the past, too, the Irish national movement had on occasion brought forth militarily organised and armed volunteer groups. An early example were the *Irish Volunteers* between 1778 and 1782 who had originally been intended to replace Irish regiments sent to fight in North America in the defence of Ireland against a potential French invasion;[45] another early group was the already more strongly nationally motivated Volunteer Corps of the *United Irishmen* in 1792/93.[46] At the turn of the year 1844/45 O'Connell planned to set up a volunteer corps 'to smite all who invade our land or liberties',[47] and in 1848 the national association of *Young Irelanders* discussed the formation of a 'National Guard' modelled on French lines.[48]

The new and characteristic feature of the years since 1912 has been the militarisation of the great political groupings in Ireland. In an atmosphere of increasing violence, brought about mainly by the prospect of imminent Home Rule, the various national and anti-national groupings in Ireland set up their own paramilitary organisations. It was characteristic that from the beginning these militia-type forces were not conceived as clandestine commando units, but as private armies, which appeared quite openly, wore uniforms, held parades and actively recruited new members. These organisations very soon exchanged their cudgels and their fake guns for small arms by engaging in smuggling and raids.

This development had its origin in Ulster, where the Unionist opponents to Home Rule resolved in January 1913 to resist the nationalists' demand for Irish autonomy by every means at their disposal. The *Ulster Unionist Council* decided on that occasion to establish a 100,000-strong volunteer army, the *Ulster Volunteer Force*, and by the middle of the same year this plan had met with unforeseen success.[49] Initially, the nationalists did not take the Ulster Unionists' military efforts very seriously, but as the *Ulster Volunteer Force* came ever closer to its target strength,[50] nationalist groups outside Ulster began preparations for the establishment of an analogous organisation. Thus the *Irish National Volunteers* were set up in November 1913 and regarded themselves expressly as a counterpoise to the *Ulster Volunteers* and as a 'national defence force'.[51] Their purpose was 'to secure and to maintain the rights and liberties common to all the people of Ireland'.[52] In the beginning, the *Irish National Volunteers* were quite independent of the Irish Parliamentary Party and other nationalist organisations, although from the outset numerous adherents of the Home Rule movement were among their members. In the autumn of 1914, i.e. after the outbreak of the First World War, the *Irish Volunteers*, who were closer to the more radical positions within the national movement than the adherents of the *National Volunteers*, split off from the latter. Behind the *Irish Volunteers* stood the IRB and this explains their participation in the rebellion of 1916.[53] After 1916 the *Irish Volunteers* were the 'army' of the Irish revolutionary government, and as such played a leading role, as did the *Irish Republican Army*, which grew out of their ranks, when the guerilla war against Britain was resumed with renewed force in 1919.[54]

Along with the *Irish Volunteers* the *Irish Citizen Army* took a prominent part in the Easter Rising.[55] The latter had been formed in the autumn of 1913, at the height of a serious labour conflict, in order to defend Dublin workers against police excesses. Thus it was not originally a nationalist organisation, although it subsequently supported the pronouncedly nationalist programme of the Irish labour movement. Only the simultaneous existence of volunteer corps both on the nationalist and the unionist side, as well as the delaying tactics of Whitehall towards the tense situation in Ireland, prevented the banning of all these organisations, which were not just an expression of the sharpening political antagonism in pre-war Ireland but also exerted a decisive influence on the violent final phase in the process of Irish independence.

III

Needless to say, the political practice of constitutional and revolutionary nationalist organisations differed widely. Whereas their political objectives permitted the constitutional organisations to agitate openly, the formation and the activities of secret societies had to be conducted in the face of constant pressure from the authorities and therefore usually underground. As a consequence, their scope for agitation was far more limited than that of constitutional groupings. But even within this narrow framework it is possible to detect characteristic variations with regard to the revolutionary agitation of individual societies.

Agrarian secret societies, such as the *Whiteboys*, *Rightboys* and *Ribbonmen*, had primarily claimed to be the 'champions of the oppressed'.[56] In order to give violent expression to their protest against the living conditions of the Irish rural population and against the near absolute despotism of the landowners, they had committed themselves to a fairly primitive actionism, which manifested itself in very diverse and yet, ever since the eighteenth century, repetitive forms. During nocturnal expeditions with frequently several hundred participants, some of whom were armed, they pulled down fences, filled in ditches, assaulted landowners and their agents or 'collaborators', as well as police stations and State institutions, in order to lend force to such demands as the equitable fixing of rents, the abolition of tithes and certain communal taxes, the removal of enclosures to preserve arable land etc.[57] In this context arson, self-administered justice and varying degrees of intimidation and terror, even murder – acts which no doubt also contained an element of revenge – played a considerable role until the 1880s.[58] Arthur Young and Alexis de Tocqueville, who both visited Ireland in the late eighteenth and early nineteenth century respectively, observed there a specific lawlessness, which was not only reflected in the relatively high incidence of violent acts and offences against the law, but also in the degree to which the established law was held in disrespect, and a rival 'system of justice', local or indigenous, prevailed among the population.[59] In 1834 the then Lord Lieutenant of Ireland wrote about the phenomenon of '*Whiteboyism*': 'A complete system of legislation, with the most prompt, vigorous, and severe executive power, sworn, equipped, and armed for all purposes of savage punishment, is established in almost every district.'[60]

The agrarian societies' extensive 'social' agitation, which forced the government to adopt sharp counter-measures and on occasion even to declare a state of emergency in individual counties, was a lesser feature in the case of political secret societies. Thus, the *United Irishmen*, after their reconstitution in 1795, concentrated their efforts exclusively on the clandestine preparation of a rebellion.[61] The main task the political secret societies set themselves was to recruit new members, obtain arms, set up their organisation, to carry out bomb attacks, acts of sabotage and repeatedly to establish contacts abroad, notably with the French around 1800 and 1848, with the American Irish from the middle of the nineteenth century onwards, and finally with the Germans just before and during the First World War.[62] Apart from that, propaganda activities were to create unrest and a willingness to rebel among the population.

The sphere of activity of minor secret political societies was even more narrowly circumscribed. In the main, these were concerned with the violent *geste*, Franklin L. Ford has spoken of,[63] with an appeal to the public through some spectacular act. One secret society in Dublin, with the ironic cover name of *Philanthropic Society*, in 1793 concerned itself exclusively with the planning of an attempt on Dublin Castle, the seat of the Irish executive.[64] This was to provide the signal for a popular insurrection. Around 1848/49 some societies existed, preparing for rebellion, sometimes on quite unrealistic assumptions, seeking to procure the necessary weapons by raiding isolated police stations.[65] The *Irish National Invincibles*, who in 1882 were responsible for the Phoenix Park murders, limited themselves exclusively to dynamite plots and calculated political assassinations, without possessing any concrete notions about the shape an independent Irish state was to have. It has been argued from time to time that a similar lack of clarity about political objectives and the methods by which these might be achieved was also a characteristic of the IRB. Yet, this certainly cannot be said as far as its methods were concerned. It is true that for a period the IRB tried to establish an Irish republic by dynamite,[66] yet from its early days it concentrated its conspiratorial activities on four main targets: (1) the development and strengthening of its organisation throughout the country; (2) the planning and preparation of an armed insurrection, which they indeed attempted twice (1867 and 1916); (3) occasional assaults on persons and property, i.e. demonstrative gestures, yet without adopting the method frequently employed by other contemporary organisations – the assassination of leading representatives of the 'system';[67] (4) the infiltration of other nationalist organisations, and, in particular, to manoeuvre IRB members into their ruling bodies.[68] This kind of infiltration was in several instances highly successful, as in the case of the *Ribbonmen* (from 1860), the *Irish Home Rule League*, the *Irish National Land League*, the *Gaelic Athletic Association*, the *Gaelic League*, minor separatist organisations just before the First World war and finally the new *Sinn Fein* organisation from 1917 and the *Irish Republican Army* from 1920 onwards.

The social element was almost completely absent in the IRB's political theory and practice. It failed to take up the question of land reform and tenancy laws, which up to the beginning of the twentieth century had been an issue of overriding importance to the Irish tenantry. For the IRB, concern with the revolutionary struggle against British rule, which was to culminate in rebellion and in the foundation of an independent Irish state, relegated issues of social reform to second place.[69] It was the *Irish National Land League*, which took up the agrarian secret societies actionism, perfected it in an unprecedented manner and employed it in the furtherance of its socio-political objectives.[70] In the 'land war' of 1879–81 it attempted, as the declared self-help and protection society of Ireland's rural population, to obtain a fundamental change of the status quo in the agrarian sector. Although it, too, resorted to methods of intimidation, terror and physical force – familiar since the days of the *Whiteboys* – its most effective weapon was the boycott of landowners, agents, 'collaborators', etc., organised by its local branches. Boycott, i.e. the social and economic isolation of individuals or groups, as a tactical weapon in a situation of political or social conflict, was certainly no new discovery, even though the term was only coined at that time.[71] What was new, however, was the degree to which the *Irish National Land League* extended such boycott tactics to all spheres of life, and the consistency with which it employed them. Related methods were the collective refusal to pay rents, organised by the *Land League*, mass demonstrations against rents that were felt to be excessive, prevention of the forcible eviction of tenants by joint resistance of all neighbouring tenants and unilateral fixing of new rents by *Land League* 'courts', setting aside the prevailing laws.[72] Beyond that, the *Land League* organised demonstrations against evictions and mobilised the local population against tenants willing to take over tenancies others had been forced to leave. The *Land League* kept up this often violent agitation, as did its successor, the *Irish National League*, although in a somewhat diluted form, until the late 1880s; after that it dwindled away.

Not until the years immediately preceding the First World War did militancy and violence, on another level, again become a feature of Irish nationalism. Now it was the various paramilitary organisations, which took over the role of secretly or openly planning and executing violent and illegal acts. They also recruited their members publicly, wore uniforms, were partly armed and held military exercises and parades under the guidance of officers who had served in the British army.[73] As the militia arm of the various Irish nationalist and unionist groupings, they represented a fast growing force with which to intimidate and terrorise political adversaries. By 1913/14 their marches dominated the street scene of both Dublin and Belfast.

But major acts of violence against each other, against the police or the regular army were not yet a feature of those years. However, the increasing militarisation of the political conflict in Ireland created the climate for the events of 1916 – in which apart from the IRB and the organisations it had infiltrated, both the workers' *Irish Citizen Army* and the *Irish Volunteers* played a major role – as well as for those in the years leading up to independence and the civil war that followed it. After the Easter Rising, the *Irish Volunteers* in particular increasingly took on the character of an underground army conducting a guerilla war against the police, the British army and administration in Ireland.[74] Finally, the *Irish Republican Army* (IRA), which grew out of the *Irish Volunteers* in 1919, turned exclusively to ruthless guerilla tactics against the institutions and organs of the State.[75] Its terrorist methods, an extension and refinement of the instruments developed by Irish revolutionary nationalists ever since the eighteenth century, were to bring about by force in a short time what 120 years of apparently unsuccessful agitation had failed to achieve – an independent Irish republic. Although it did not realise this goal,[76] there is no question that revolutionary nationalism and the violence it institutionalised in Ireland, played a considerable part in the creation of the Irish Free State in 1921/22.

NOTES

1. T. Corfe, *The Phoenix Park Murders* (London, 1968); L. O Broin, *Revolutionary Underground: The Story of the Irish Republican Brotherhood 1858–1924* (Dublin, 1976); id., *Fenian Fever: An Anglo-American Dilemma* (London, 1971); about the Irish bombing attempts in Britain in the 1880s most recently K. R. M. Short, *The Dynamite War: Irish-American Bombers in Victorian Britain* (Dublin, 1979).
2. F. S. L. Lyons, *Ireland since the Famine*, 2nd ed. (London, 1973); id., *Charles Stewart Parnell* (London, 1977); P. Alter, *Die irische Nationalbewegung zwischen Parlament und Revolution: Der konstitutionelle Nationalismus in Irland 1880–1918* (Munich-Vienna, 1971).
3. Cf. more extensively, and about the Irish national movement as a whole, my study: 'Nationale Organisationen in Irland 1801–1921' in Th. Schieder and O. Dann (eds), *Nationale Bewegung und soziale Organisation I. Vergleichende Studien zur nationalen Vereinsbewegung des 19. Jahrhunderts in Europa* (Munich-Vienna, 1978) pp. 1–129.
4. Cf. J. S. Donnelly, Jr., 'The Whiteboy Movement, 1761–5', *Irish Historical Studies* 21 (1978/79) pp. 20–54; S. Clark, 'The Social Composition of the Land League', ibid. 17 (1970/71) pp. 447–69; T. W. Moody (ed.), *The Fenian Movement* (Cork, 1968); Alter, *Nationale Organisationen*, pp. 79–83.
5. *Violence in Politics: Terror and Political Assassination in Eastern Europe and Russia* (The Hague and Paris, 1972) p. 94.
6. *Primitive Rebels: Studies in Archaic Forms of Social Movement in the 19th and 20th Centuries* (Manchester, 1978) p. 173.
7. About the problem of source material with regard to Irish conditions: T. D. Williams (ed.), *Secret Societies in Ireland* (Dublin and New York, 1973) pp. 4–5; B. Mac Giolla Choille, 'Fenian Documents in the State Paper Office', *Irish Historical Studies* 16 (1968/69) pp. 258–84; T. W. Moody and L. O Broin (eds), 'Select Documents: XXXII The IRB Supreme Council, 1868–78' ibid. 19 (1974/75) pp. 286–332.
8. Cf. also the introduction in Williams (ed.), *Secret Societies*, pp. 1–12, as well as B. C. Pollard, *The Secret Societies of Ireland: Their Rise and Progress* (London, 1922).
9. For this reason, the agrarian secret societies were once described as 'a vast trades union of the Irish peasantry' (G. C. Lewis, *Local Disturbances in Ireland* (London, 1836) p. 99, quoted by G. Broeker, *Rural Disorder and Police Reform in Ireland, 1812–1836* (London and Toronto, 1970) p. 8.)

10. The best summary of this unrest is contained in K. B. Nowlan, 'Agrarian Unrest in Ireland 1800–1845', *University Review* 4 (1967) and Broeker, *Rural Disorder*.

11. R. Kee, *The Green Flag, A History of Irish Nationalism* (London, 1972) p. 25 and 299.

12. E. R. Norman, *The Catholic Church and Ireland in the Age of Rebellion, 1859– 1873* (London, 1965); D. McCartney, 'The Church and the Fenians', *University Review* 4 (1967) pp. 203–15; Williams (ed.), *Secret Societies*, pp. 9–10, pp. 68– 78; O Broin, *Revolutionary Underground*, pp. 71–3; D. Bowen, *The Protestant Crusade in Ireland, 1800–70: A Study of Protestant-Catholic Relations between the Act of Union and Disestablishment* (Dublin and Montreal, 1978) pp. 3–4; p. 9.

13. Precursor organisations to the Whiteboys can be traced back to 1711 (Kee, *Green Flag*, p. 24). On the Whiteboys most recently: Donnelly, *Whiteboy Movement*.

14. E.g. 'Oakboys', 'Hearts of Steel', 'Steelboys', 'Levellers', 'Corkboys', 'Shanavests'.

15. It was under these headings that the authorities described particularly the offences against the property of landowners and acts of violence against individuals. Their increase or decrease was taken to be an indicator of social and political unrest in the country. Cf. J. V. O'Brien, *William O'Brien and the Course of Irish Politics, 1881–1918* (Berkeley, 1976) pp. 249–52.; J. S. Donnelly, Jr., *The Land and the People of Nineteenth-Century Cork: The Rural Economy and the Land Question* (London and Boston, 1975) p. 282, p. 295; P. Bew, *Land and the National Question in Ireland 1858–82* (Dublin, 1978) pp. 34–8, 206.

16. Donnelly, 'Whiteboy Movement', pp. 21–3.

17. Kee, *Green Flag*, p. 299.

18. Cf. ibid., p. 25. In nineteenth-century Ireland 'Ribbonism' became a synonym for agrarian disorders, behind which stood the secret societies.

19. E.g.: 'Rockites', 'Terry Alts', 'Molly Maguires', 'Threshers', 'Whitefeet', 'Blackfeet', 'Lady Clares', 'Carders', 'Caravats'.

20. On the rites of the 'classical secret society' cf. Hobsbawm, *Primitive Rebels*, pp. 165–7.

21. Kee, *Green Flag*, p. 299; E. D. Steele, *Irish Land and British Politics: Tenant-Right and Nationality 1865–1870* (Cambridge, 1974) pp. 3–4.

22. ' "Swearing-in" of other peasants took place (under threat or persuasion) on isolated farms at night or on estates before the general expiration of leases or, most commonly of all perhaps, after Sunday mass, when all in the parish were collected and particularly vulnerable to demands to constitute a common front.' (O. MacDonagh, *Ireland: The Union and its Aftermath*, 2nd. ed. (London, 1977) pp. 144–5).

23. One version of the Whiteboys' oath of 1762 is reprinted in Donnelly, 'Whiteboy Movement', p. 27: 'I do hereby solemnly and sincerely swear that I will not make known any secret now given me, or hereafter may be given, to anyone in the world, except a sworn person belonging to the society called Whiteboys . . . Furthermore, I swear that I will be ready at an hour's warning, if possible, by being properly summoned by any of the officers, sergeants, and corporals belonging to my company. Furthermore, I swear that I will not wrong any of the company I belong to, to the value of one shilling, nor suffer it to be done by others, without acquainting them thereof. Furthermore, I swear that I will not make known, in any shape whatsoever, to any person that does not belong to us, the name or names of any of our fraternity, but particularly the names of our respective officers. Lastly, I swear that I will not drink of any liquor whatsoever whilst on duty, without the consent of any one or other of the officers, sergeants, or corporals; and that we will be loyal one to another as in our power lies.'

24. See below pp. 144–5.

25. Hobsbawm has coined the term 'social bandit' in order to distinguish the agrarian bandit from the common criminal, and also to indicate his function as a 'social avenger' (Hobsbawm, *Primitive Rebels*, pp. 13–29; id., 'Social Banditry' in H. A. Landsberger (ed.), *Rural Protest: Peasant Movements and Social Change* (London, 1974) pp. 142–57.

26. Hobsbawm, *Primitive Rebels*, pp. 110 and 123.

27. K. B. Nowlan in Williams (ed.), *Secret Societies*, p. 188.

28. R. Jacob, *The Rise of the United Irishmen, 1791–1794* (London, 1937); Williams (ed.), *Secret Societies*, pp. 58–67.

29. Moody (ed.), *Fenian Movement*; O Broin, *Revolutionary Underground*; D. Ryan, *The Phoenix Flame: A Study of Fenianism and John Devoy* (London, 1937); id., *The Fenian Chief: A Biography of James Stephens* (Dublin, 1967); H. Senior, 'The Place of Fenianism in the Irish Republican Tradition', *University Review* 4 (1967) pp. 250–9.

30. W. D'Arcy, *The Fenian Movement in the United States, 1858–1886* (Washington, 1947); B. Jenkins, *Fenians and Anglo-American Relations during Reconstruction* (Ithaka and London, 1969).

31. 'Fenians' was the name of an army in celtic mythology famous for its bravery (Kee, *Green Flag*, p. 310). Originally the IRB had no fixed name. It was called 'The Society', 'The Organisation', 'Our Movement', or 'The Brotherhood', the latter often with the adjective 'revolutionary' or 'republican'. Only after its reorganisation in 1873 did 'Irish Republican Brotherhood' become the official designation (cf. Lyons, *Ireland*, pp. 125–6; P. S. O'Hegarty, *A History of Ireland under the Union 1801 to 1922* (London, 1952) pp. 414–15).

32. The 1859 version: 'I, (name), in the presence of Almighty God, do solemnly swear allegiance to the Irish republic, now virtually established, and that I will do my utmost, at every risk, while life lasts, to defend its independence and integrity, and finally, that I will yield implicit obedience in all things, not contrary to the laws of God, to the commands of my superior officers. So help me God! Amen.' (E. Curtis and R. B. MacDowell (eds), *Irish Historical Documents 1172–1922* (London, 1943; reprint, 1969) p. 309.)

33. Cf. Williams (ed.), *Secret Societies*, p. 93; Moody (ed.), *Fenian movement*, p. 17; O Broin, *Fenian Fever*, p. 2. On Bakunin's concept of the nameless soldier, which evidently exerted some influence here, see W. Laqueur, *Terrorismus* (Kronberg/Ts, 1977) p. 29.

34. *Revolutionary Underground*, passim.

35. Moody (ed.), *Fenian Movement*, p. 17.

36. The first statute of the Supreme Council of August 1 1869 is reprinted in Moody and O Broin (eds), *Select Documents*, pp. 303–7.

37. Reprinted in ibid., pp. 315–16.

38. These were: Leinster, Munster, Connaught, Ulster, North of England, South of England, Scotland. Thus the IRB included the whole of the UK in its organisation. This was an exception, since other national organisations founded sister organisations in Britain.

39. Moody (ed.), *Fenian Movement*, p. 108.

40. Cf. P. O'Farrell, *Ireland's English Question: Anglo-Irish Relations 1534–1970* (London, 1971) pp. 143–4.

41. Moody (ed.), *Fenian Movement*, pp. 110–11.

42. Cf. especially agitation in the countryside during the 'land war'. N. D. Palmer, *The Irish Land League Crisis* (New Haven, 1940); J. E. Pomfret, *The Struggle for Land in Ireland 1800–1923* (Princeton, 1930; reprint New York, 1969); Bew, *Land and the National Question*; Donnelly, *The Land*, esp. pp. 251–307.

43. Clark, *Land League*, pp. 464–5; P. Alter, 'Nationalismus als agrarische Massen-

bewegung in Irland 1879–1886' in O. Dann (ed.), *Nationalismus und sozialer Wandel* (Hamburg, 1978) pp. 49–75.

44. Cf. Alter, *Die irische Nationalbewegung*, pp. 50–3, 103–51.
45. Kee, *Green Flag*, p. 31f; M. R. O'Connell, *Irish Politics and Social Conflict in the Age of the American Revolution* (Philadelphia, 1965) pp. 68–70.
46. G. O Tuathaigh, *Ireland before the Famine 1798–1848* (Dublin, 1972) p. 12.
47. The Nation 7/12/1844 (quoted in: Kee, *Green Flag*, p. 323).
48. Kee, *Green Flag*, pp. 266–8.
49. Ibid., pp. 478–83; P. Buckland, *Irish Unionism*, vol. 2: *Ulster Unionism and the Origins of Northern Ireland 1886–1922* (Dublin and New York, 1973), pp. 58–60; A. T. Q. Stewart, *The Ulster Crisis* (London, 1967).
50. By July 1913 it numbered 50,000 members (Kee, *Green Flag*, p. 478).
51. O'Hegarty, *History of Ireland*, p. 671; F. X. Martin, 'MacNeill and the Foundation of the Irish Volunteers' in F. X. Martin and F. J. Byrne (eds), *The Scholar Revolutionary: Eoin MacNeill, 1867–1945, and the Making of the New Ireland* (Shannon, 1973) pp. 99–179.
52. Quoted in Lyons, *Ireland*, p. 322.
53. F. X. Martin (ed.), *The Irish Volunteers 1913–15: Recollections and Documents* (Dublin, 1963).
54. J. Bowyer Bell, *The Secret Army: A History of the IRA 1915–1970* (London, 1972); Ch. Townshend, *The British Campaign in Ireland 1919–1921: The Development of Political and Military Policies* (London, 1975).
55. J. W. Boyle, 'Connolly, the Citizen Army and the Rising' in K. B. Nowlan (ed.), *The Making of 1916. Studies in the History of the Rising*, (Dublin 1969), pp. 49–68; D. Ryan *The Rising: The Complete Story of Easter Week*, 4th ed. (Dublin, 1966).
56. Williams (ed.), *Secret Societies*, p. 14.
57. A. Macintyre, *The Liberator: Daniel O'Connell and the Irish Party, 1830–1847* (London, 1965) pp. 176–8; Kee, *Green Flag*, pp. 24–6; MacDonagh, *Ireland*, pp. 146–7.
58. During the 'land war' around 1880, in which the Irish National Land League was involved, the police for instance registered a marked increase in 'agrarian crimes'. In the period January–March 1880 the police recorded 294 cases, for the same period in 1881 796 cases and in 1882 1 417 cases (Bew, *Land and the National Question*, p. 36 and p. 206; M. Brown, *The Politics of Irish Literature: From Thomas Davis to W. B. Yeats* (London, 1972) p. 269.)
59. See also MacDonagh, *Ireland*, p. 146. On the traditional 'faction fights' in Irish agrarian society see L. H. Lees, *Exiles of Erin: Irish Migrants in Victorian London* (Manchester, 1979) pp. 213–15.
60. Quoted in M. Davitt, *The Fall of Feudalism in Ireland or the Story of the Land League Revolution* (London and New York, 1904) p. 38.
61. Williams (ed.), *Secret Societies*, pp. 64–7.
62. On German-Irish contacts, see K. Wolf, *Sir Roger Casement und die deutsch-irischen Beziehungen* (Berlin, 1972) pp. 12–55; B. Inglis, *Roger Casement* (London, 1973); B. L. Reid, *The Lives of Roger Casement* (New Haven and London, 1976); R. R. Doerries, 'Die Mission Sir Roger Casements im Deutschen Reich 1914–1916', *Historische Zeitschrift* 222 (1976) pp. 578–625; id., *Washington-Berlin 1908–1917: Die Tätigkeit des Botschafters Johann Heinrich Graf von Bernstorff in Washington vor dem Eintritt der Vereinigten Staaten von Amerika in den Ersten Weltkrieg* (Düsseldorf, 1975) esp. pp. 180–2; W. Hünseler, *Das Deutsche Kaiserreich und die Irische Frage 1900–1914* (Frankfurt/M, Bern, Las Vegas, 1978); F. M. Carroll, *American Opinion and the Irish Question 1910–23: A Study in Opinion and Policy* (Dublin and New York, 1978) pp. 26–36,

46–54; Th. Gundelach, *Die irische Unabhängigkeitsbewegung 1916–1922* (Frankfurt/M, Bern, Las Vegas, 1977) pp. 141–82, 196–231.

63. See above, p. 4.
64. Kee, *Green Flag*, p. 70.
65. Ibid., p. 291.
66. Marx and Engels, by the way, condemned the IRB's use of violence. Marx called the bombing in Clerkenwell an act of stupidity; cf. Laqueur, *Terrorismus*, pp. 60–1.
67. As propagated, for example, by the German anarchist Johann Most in the 1880s and as practised by the Russian *Narodnaya Volya*. The IRB certainly discussed these tactics. (Cf. O Broin, *Revolutionary Underground*, p. 27).
68. Cf. also the more generalised observations about the activities of secret societies in Hobsbawm, *Primitive Rebels*, pp. 150–74.
69. J. C. Beckett, *The Making of Modern Ireland, 1603–1923* (London, 1966) p. 359.
70. Bew, *Land and the National Question*; Lyons, *Ireland*, pp. 160–77; Palmer, *Land League*; Promfret, *The Struggle for Land*; Davitt, *Fall of Feudalism*.
71. Lyons, *Ireland*, p. 168; J. Marlow, *Captain Boycott and the Irish* (London and New York 1973).
72. Cf. Lyons, *Ireland*, p. 170.
73. Kee, *Green Flag*, p. 523, 526.
74. T. Bowden, *The Breakdown of Public Security: The Case of Ireland 1916–1921 and Palestine 1936–1939* (London and Beverley Hills, 1977); id., 'The Irish Underground and the War of Independence 1919–21', *Journal of Contemporary History* 8 (1973) pp. 3–23; Bell, *Secret Army*; Gundelach, *Die irische Unabhängigkeitsbewegung*, pp. 462–653.
75. See Bell, *Secret Army*; Townshend, *British Campaign*; also the article by Michael Laffan in this volume pp. 155–74.
76. The republic was not proclaimed until 1949; at the same time Ireland left the Commonwealth. Since then the country's official designation has been 'Republic of Ireland' or 'Eire'.

11 Violence and Terror in Twentieth-Century Ireland: IRB and IRA

Michael Laffan

Twentieth-century Ireland has had a long history of small groups using force to undermine the established order and overthrow the power of the state. Its experience has been unusual on two counts. With rare exceptions the aim of such groups has been purely nationalist and political, they have had little interest in ideological, social or economic questions; and, again with rare exceptions, they have belonged to what was effectively one organisation, the *Irish Republican Brotherhood* (IRB) and the *Irish Republican Army* (IRA). These bodies have successively (the IRB until 1916, the IRA since 1919) exercised a near monopoly of the use of violence on any large scale or with any consistency.

Other groups, such as the two *Ulster Volunteer Forces* (one between 1912 and 1914, the other since 1966) or the *Blueshirts* in the 1930s, have used force or the threat of force to further their objectives, and in the case of both the UVFs have achieved important results, but they have never seriously challenged the central role of the IRB/IRA. Agrarian unrest, often leading to violence and intimidation, was endemic until the 1930s but it was on a small scale compared with the land wars of the nineteenth century. Left-wing groups prepared to use force have appeared from time to time but, most notably in 1916 and in the early 1930s, were subsumed into the nationalist movement, while with the exception of the great Dublin lock-out of 1913/14 industrial unrest has tended to be non-violent. In contrast, ever since its formation in 1858 the *Irish Republican Brotherhood* has planned or waged war on the British presence in Ireland.

This consistency of aim has been matched by flexibility of means. The forms which IRB/IRA violence have taken in this century have varied from a set-piece rebellion in 1916, through widespread guerrilla warfare in 1920/21, civil war in 1922/23, a bombing campaign in England in 1939/40, attacks on British forces in Ulster in the 1950s and a terror campaign in the 1970s, to isolated outbursts of intimidation and assassination. Despite its 120-year-old suspicion of politics and politicians the IRB/IRA has occasionally co-operated uneasily with constitutional movements, though it has only been happy when playing a dominant role.

Since the 1790s when French revolutionary ideas inspired Irish radicals, Irish rebel and terrorist movements have been concerned almost single-mindedly with ending British rule in Ireland. From then until the withdrawal of British forces from most of the island in 1922 their objective was a simple one, however frequently other issues such as the struggle for the land might become enmeshed in the national, political question, sometimes sharpening and strengthening it, sometimes blunting and deflecting it. As will be argued below, with the establishment of the Irish Free State in 1922 and the relegation of those nationalists still living under British rule to the role of a beleaguered minority, the IRA's targets became more diffused.

Wolfe Tone, the father of Irish nationalism in the 1790s, denounced the connection with England as 'the never-ending source of all our political evils', and over a hundred years later one of his disciples declared that 'it is not bad government that ails Ireland, it is foreign government, and till foreign government is ended Ireland cannot prosper'.[1] In the intervening century most Irishmen showed a remarkable consistency in their distaste for the British connection and the *Act of Union* of 1800, associating them, sometimes fairly, with British exploitation and duplicity. In the course of the nineteenth century the removal of other grievances, economic, social and religious, merely focussed attention on the fact that most Irishmen felt different from Englishmen and wanted to have a much louder voice in running their own affairs. Ireland developed a tradition of discontent, although as far as the great majority was concerned this was far from being a tradition of insurrection.

The proclamation of the Irish Republic in Easter Week 1916 referred to the Irish people having risen 'six times during the past three hundred years'. The first two such risings, in 1641 and 1690, could be fitted into such a pattern only with considerable difficulty, the third, in 1798, was a major catastrophe in which as many as 30,000 may have perished, while the remaining three, in 1803, 1848 and 1867 were botched, pathetic farces.

In the long run, for those who demanded Ireland's separation from Britain, this record of failure was unimportant.[2] What mattered to them was that subjection to British rule was not accepted passively, that there was a tradition of resistance, and that they themselves should carry on the tradition. The dead hand of the past pointed out to the living what their task must be. In the peroration of the most famous of his speeches Pearse, twentieth-century Ireland's leading exponent of the nationalist tradition, proclaimed that 'life springs from death; and from the graves of patriot men and women spring living nations. . . . they have left us our Fenian dead, and while Ireland holds these graves Ireland unfree shall never be at peace'.[3] Soon afterwards he was to argue 'that the national demand of Ireland is fixed and determined; that

that demand has been made by every generation; that we of this generation receive it as a trust from our fathers; that we are bound by it; that we have not the right to alter it or to abate it by one jot or tittle'.[4] Two years later de Valera told his followers 'Sinn Fein wished to keep the people true to the ideals sanctified by the blood of twenty-five generations – ideals which the mass of the Irish people at no time really compromised'.[5]

Historically this was utter rubbish, politically it was a powerful myth which legitimised and ennobled the activities of the IRA and its political counterpart, *Sinn Fein*. Most of the country was prepared to follow the moderate *Irish Parliamentary Party* and seek its limited goals, and until after 1916 views such as those expounded by Pearse and de Valera were held only by a small minority – but they were held passionately and fiercely. To this minority compromise was anathema, politics and Irish politicians were suspect, and they believed firmly that the British government, always treacherous in its dealings with Ireland, would yield only to force. These men plotted, talked or dynamited, or else waited for the time when they or their successors in the next generation could strike again. From 1858 onwards most of them were members of the secret *Irish Republican Brotherhood* which sought a fully independent Irish republic and regarded force as the only means of bringing this about.

By the early years of this century the IRB had fallen on hard times. The most recent rebellion receded further into the past, the organisation was infiltrated by government spies, numbers and morale were falling, and the Land Acts were bringing about a social revolution in Ireland while the political revolution remained as far away as ever; in fact the removal of so many material grievances – the policy of 'killing Home Rule with kindness' – seemed likely to blunt the demand for separation and independence. There was no sign that the Irish people were prepared to follow radical leaders using radical means. The situation worsened after 1910 when the Liberal government, dependent on Irish votes in the House of Commons, committed itself to the prompt introduction of *Home Rule*. For many IRB men this lack of widespread support, this clear absence of a pre-revolutionary situation, were reasons enough for postponing indefinitely any new rising; all the more when one clause of the 1873 IRB constitution declared that the organisation should 'await the decision of the Irish Nation, as expressed by a majority of the Irish people, as to the fit hour of inaugurating war against England'. This was an extraordinary self-denying ordinance for a revolutionary body, and it reflected awareness that lack of public support had helped doom earlier insurrections.

One example of the condition to which the IRB had sunk was the P. T. Daly affair. In 1908 Daly, the secretary of the supreme council, on being given £600 for IRB purposes by the Irish-American organisation *Clan na Gael*, pocketed half the money for himself and his family. He was eventually found out, but instead of being executed he was allowed to keep the money and was merely dismissed from the council.[6] There were extenuating circumstances, but such gentleness boded ill for the Irish revolution.

About this time, however, the IRB's fortunes began to revive. The key figures in this development were Tom Clarke, a middle-aged veteran of the dynamite campaign of the 1880s and of a subsequent 15-year penal sentence, and two young Ulstermen, Bulmer Hobson and Denis McCullough. They began purging the hive of drones, and the story has it that McCullough even forced out his own father. Soon the IRB was better placed to avail of improving circumstances, and by 1912 its numbers had increased to over 1500.[7]

The opportunity for action came from an unlikely source. The Ulster unionists, who dreaded the prospect of subjection to a Catholic-dominated *Home Rule* parliament in Dublin and were unreconciled by the limited powers such a parliament would enjoy, formed their own private army, the *Ulster Volunteers*, and threatened to rebel against the Crown so that they might remain the Crown's most loyal subjects. Their leader Sir Edward Carson declared 'we will shortly challenge the Government to interfere with us if they dare, and we will with equanimity await the result. . . They may tell us if they like that that is treason. It is not for men who have such stakes as we have to trouble about the cost.'[8] His claim that the government would not dare to interfere with what was illegal was vindicated; it temporised and compromised.

This action by their deadly enemies appealed to the imagination of many Irish nationalists both inside and outside the ranks of the IRB, it made physical force once more respectable, made it seem daring, heroic and successful. Carson brought guns back into Irish life, and the IRB was determined that some of the guns should be in its hands. At the IRB's instigation a rival *Irish National Volunteer* force was formed in November 1913, and Carson's example was also followed by the Dublin Transport Workers' Union which established its own defensive organisation, the *Irish Citizen Army*. Within a short time the Irish Volunteers' numbers had risen to about 180,000, and small quantities of arms were provided for them. But despite the IRB's infiltration of the Volunteers' higher ranks the force's unrevolutionary temperament was revealed when it split in two in 1914 and 170,000 of its men followed Redmond and the constitutional leadership, only 10,000 remaining loyal to those (including the IRB men) who had founded the movement.

The formation of a private army under IRB influence was followed closely by the outbreak of war in Europe, and this provided a further incentive to action. A key group within the IRB, in close collaboration with like-minded men outside the organisation but excluding IRB members who adhered to the constraints of the 1873 constitution, decided that as in the past 'England's difficulty was Ireland's opportunity' and that a rebellion must be staged while

Britain was distracted by war with Germany.[9] The patience of those who had waited years, even decades, for the right moment to strike was to be rewarded at last. The awkward facts that in economic terms Ireland did well out of the war, and that spreading disillusionment with the Irish Parliamentary Party was not transformed into support for a rising, did nothing to deter men like Pearse and Clarke who felt that they, rather than the majority of the population, recognised and represented the national will.

Although they prepared the rising carefully and secretly and were naturally anxious to maximise its chances of success, the rebels did not regard success as essential. When at a late stage their plans miscarried, an arms shipment from Germany was intercepted, Volunteer leaders outside the plot learned of it and tried to stop the insurrection, and it became clear that the British authorities were on their guard, they went ahead even though they knew that, in James Connolly's words 'we are going out to be slaughtered'. For most of them their determination that a rebellion should take place, that their generation should not betray the tradition of the 'protest in arms', was the most important consideration. Pearse, the rebel commander-in-chief, courted martyrdom.

Only about 1,500 Irish Volunteers fought for the newly-proclaimed Irish Republic, and apart from a few incidents in the countryside the rising was confined to Dublin. 450 people were killed and 2,500 wounded. Initially it was rejected with horror by the great mass of the Irish population, a common reaction being 'the British will never grant Home Rule now!' When the rebels surrendered and were marched off under arrest Dublin housewives rushed into the streets with food and drink, not for the prisoners, but for their guards. Gradually opinion changed. Realisation that the rebels had fought bravely and honourably and that the rising had not been an ignominious fiasco like its predecessors inspired pride as well as condemnation. Even John Dillon, the deputy leader of the Irish Parliamentary Party who had been dismayed by the insurrection, taunted British members of the House of Commons that 'it would have been a damned good thing for you if your soldiers were able to put up as good a fight as did these men in Dublin'.[10] As the leaders of the rising had intended, the Irish people were jolted out of their complacency and were forced to re-examine tactics – violence and rebellion – which they had come to associate with unhappy phases of the past.

Even more than the fighting itself, the government's response swung public opinion behind the rebels and helped redeem the tarnished image of violence. Over three thousand people were arrested, many of them having little or no sympathy with the insurrection. Sixteen men were executed, a few at a time, over a period of ten days. The result was instant canonisation. While the executions were still taking place George Bernard Shaw argued that the British government had ensured that each of the rebel leaders would be regarded as a martyr 'even though the day before the rising he may have been only a minor poet. The shot Irishmen will now take their place beside Emmet and the Manchester martyrs in Ireland, and beside the heros [*sic*] of Poland

and Serbia and Belgium in Europe; and nothing in heaven or on earth can prevent it'.[11] Nothing did prevent it. A month later T. P. O'Connor of the Irish Parliamentary Party wrote to Lloyd George telling him that a little girl had been heard in the street praying to 'St Pearse'.[12]

The Easter rising was itself partly the result of a myth, of a distorted image of Ireland forever renewing the struggle against British oppression. Its leaders soon became mythological figures themselves, their images sacrosanct and inviolable. Their cult still thrives. Within a short time not only the young but also the staid and the cautious began to gloss over their initial opposition to the rising and to give it their retrospective support, even veneration.

This development is one of the most important in modern Irish history. A small group of men, deciding that they represented the national interest and the national will, struck against the system supported, or at least accepted, by the overwhelming majority of the people. After their deaths their aims and methods won widespread approval. This posthumous success inspired others to emulate their achievement, and it has been the model for all subsequent Irishmen committed to the use of violence. Today the *Provisional IRA* likes to see itself as following the example given by Clarke and Pearse, confident that public opinion will support it eventually, however belatedly. Another objective of later rebels and terrorists, also modelled on the pattern of 1916 and also successful at times, was to force the government of the day into such repressive measures that the repression would seem, and would be, an even greater evil than the initial provocation; the public's resentment would shift from the IRA to the government. Their traditional dislike of alien rule had led the Irish people to sympathise with those who defied authority and the IRA could benefit from the national tendency to be 'agin' the government'.

However successful the rising had been in transforming Irish opinion, in military terms it was a failure and for the rest of the Great War it was clear that another rebellion was impossible. It was also unnecessary. From a military standpoint the best way to pursue the struggle begun in 1916 would be to consolidate and build on the newly won public sympathy so that when the time came for the next round Ireland would experience a genuine national uprising. One immediate problem was that the obvious means for doing this were repugnant to many of the rebels. When *Sinn Feiners* in Ireland decided to contest by-elections as a way of building up an organisation and arousing support and enthusiasm, the surviving imprisoned Volunteer leaders were hostile. They had long regarded politics as a demeaning activity and, accustomed to disparaging their own generation, they were not prepared to put their trust in the electorate's change of heart. De Valera complained that 'we are not willing that what has been purchased with our comrades' blood should be lost on a toss throw with dice loaded against us',[13] and when one of the prisoners was run – successfully – against the Irish Party candidate, he and virtually all his colleagues raised strong objections.[14] Their supporters back home were not deterred, and they won a series of spectacular election victories. Their success disarmed the purists, even though many continued to regard politics with suspicion and to feel it was no more than a tactical expedient, a second-best to fighting. Nonetheless the Volunteers proved remarkably successful politicians, a mass *Sinn Fein* party was built up in 1917, and in the 1918 general election it eliminated the Irish Party. Redmond's successors could win only two seats in the whole country against *Sinn Fein*.

De Valera and other Volunteers were elected to the highest posts in the party, and de Valera soon showed himself temperamentally more of a politician than a soldier. The effective takeover of the political leadership by the fighting men was a return to an old Irish pattern in which violence and political activity often interacted on each other. On the whole the political and the military wings of the movement co-operated harmoniously, although the soldiers' contempt for mere politicians was matched by some *Sinn Feiners'* alarm at the Volunteers' bellicosity. Dan Breen, one of the most active guerrillas in the Anglo-Irish war, remarked that in his district the first military display was an even bigger shock to the *Sinn Feiners* than it was to the British.[15]

The political phase which lasted throughout 1917 and 1918 overlapped with a steady revival of the Irish Volunteers (soon more widely known as the Irish Republican Army, or the IRA) and also, though on a small scale, of the IRB. In the eyes of most of the Volunteers the establishment of a large-scale force committed to rebellion made a secret society like the IRB redundant, and many were influenced by the Catholic Church's hostility towards secret societies. Nonetheless the IRB survived, its head still nominally president of the Irish Republic (a title later to be enjoyed by de Valera after his election as president of the Dáil, the Irish parliament established by Sinn Fein MPs in January 1919).[16] After the Easter rising the IRB played a relatively minor role and was significant mainly because Michael Collins, its guiding force, controlled so much else as well.[17] From 1919 onwards the active units of the IRA, a small minority of the total, occupied a position comparable to that held for so long by the IRB and shared many of its claims and attitudes.

The Anglo-Irish war of 1919–21 was basically a guerrilla campaign in which the use of terror played an important part in removing dangerous enemies, weakening British morale and deterring civilians from helping the government forces. Unlike the Easter rising it was a modern war, dirty and ungentlemanly. Policemen were shot in Dublin streets and in country lanes. Most of the IRA's victims were, like their killers, Irish Catholics (the police suffered far more heavily than the army; in the two and a half years of fighting the losses were respectively 405 and 150).[18] Many were well-known and popular in their neighbourhoods, and initially the normal response to what were seen as brutal and cowardly murders was revulsion and condemnation. *Sinn Feiners* felt that a few gunmen in Dublin and Tipperary were blackening the movement's good name. As Breen complained – oversimplifying and distorting the results of the 1918 elections – 'the people had voted for a

Republic, but now they seemed to have abandoned us who had tried to bring that Republic nearer, and who had taken them at their word'.[19] (He included many of the IRA in this denunciation, and as fighting spread and British pressure increased most volunteers lay low and only a small fraction took part in military operations.) Collins shared Breen's frustration and urged that 'the sooner fighting was forced and a general state of disorder created, the better'.[20]

The war began on a small scale and escalated slowly; in the first eighteen months, from January 1919 to June 1920, only sixty members of the crown forces were killed. Gradually the IRA's scale of activities was extended. In November 1920 Collins's 'squad' killed twelve officers in Dublin, most of them engaged in intelligence work, while sixteen policemen were killed in a battle in Co. Cork. Over a hundred IRA men were captured after the destruction of the Dublin *Custom House*, the centre of local government, in May 1921. Isolated killings continued, sometimes representing the settling of private grievances rather than attacks on 'enemies of the Republic'. Assassination was not a policy characteristic of the IRA, although there were exceptions: Cathal Brugha, later minister of defence, is reported to have planned to shoot down the British cabinet if conscription were imposed on Ireland in 1918; the viceroy narrowly escaped death in an ambush in December 1919; and in 1922, long after the formal ending of hostilities, two IRA men killed Sir Henry Wilson in London, probably acting on Collins's orders.

The IRA was delighted by the government's response to its attacks, a response criticised by *The Times* as 'collective punishment'.[21] When policemen and soldiers were ambushed the whole neighbourhood was often proclaimed a military district, fairs and markets were banned, curfews imposed, and the innocent were punished with the guilty. In retaliation for the killing of a policeman Limerick was subjected to military rule and to the imposition of permits needed for entering and leaving the city. The failure of a general strike in protest against these measures in no way diminished local resentment. There was little to choose between the terror imposed by the IRA and that imposed by the crown forces (the latter often in the form of 'official reprisals'), but the IRA had the double advantage of being the under-dogs and of being 'our lads'. Among many Irishmen, though certainly not all, the IRA acquired a romantic image which was enhanced by the panache and courage often shown in incidents such as prison escapes and arms raids. In late 1919 the police inspector general lamented that 'the general public is apparently prepared to suffer rather than condemn the criminal acts of the rebel fanatics'.[22]

Long before the end of the war Irish public opinion had been radicalised yet again. After 1916 the government's clumsy response to the rising encouraged widespread support for the rebels' aims and a sympathy with the idea or the memory of violence. The reality of violence, when it returned in less romantic circumstances in 1919, shocked people initially, but once again the authorities' blind and indiscriminate reaction (summarised by the viceroy's remark after one police inspector had been shot in Tipperary, that the government was convinced 'Sinn Feiners in this district are an organised club for murder')[23] closed the nationalist ranks behind the IRA. By and large people supported the IRA, or at least did not support the government, and fallen volunteers such as Kevin Barry were promptly incorporated into the republican mythology and became the heroes of ballads. In some cases, as Ernie O'Malley relates of himself, the fighting men could go to dances and hear songs being sung about their own exploits.[24] Between them, the IRA and the British government succeeded in identifying the IRA with nationalism and patriotism.

The authorities went to extreme lengths in polarising Irish opinion between the British army and the IRA. Late in 1919 the *Dáil*, the *Sinn Fein* party and other political bodies were banned. They continued to function underground, and particularly in 1920 succeeded in playing a significant political and administrative role in the conflict, but unable to act with their earlier effectiveness they could not rival the power and appeal of the IRA.

In its first issue *an t-Óglach*, the volunteers' journal declared

the Irish Volunteers are a military body pure and simple. They are the army of the Irish Republic, the agents of the National will . . . volunteers are not politicians . . . Let us accept the words of a great Prussian – adapted by Ruskin – 'I desire for my own country to secure that her soldiers should be her tutors, and the captains of her armies captains also of her mind' – as our motto'.[25]

While few IRA men could have quoted Ruskin, most would have shared the view that the soldiers were the elite of the nation, that they embodied the national will.

Despite the important role played by the Sinn Fein politicians and administrators, ultimately it was the IRA, the flying columns in the South and Collins's squad in Dublin, which undermined British determination and drove Lloyd George's government to the truce of July 1921 and the lengthy negotiations which followed.

The signing of a compromise treaty in December 1921 created new problems for the IRA. Until then its task had been uncomplicated – the achievement of an independent republican Ireland – and the means were the defeat of the British government and its agents. Even though the treaty conceded merely a Free State with a governor general representing the crown instead of an Irish Republic, and even though it left the island partitioned, it was good enough for the great majority of Irishmen who wanted nothing more than peace. The Church, the middle classes and the press were solidly in its favour. However most of the active units of the IRA were opposed to the treaty, as was a large minority of the political leadership (three out of seven members of the *Dáil* cabinet, including de Valera, and 57 out of 121 in the *Dáil*). The IRB command, probably through Collins's influence, threw its weight behind the settlement, although most of the rank and file were opposed to it.

Those who had been reared in the Fenian tradition, who had been 'out' in 1916 or else wished they had been, who had seen the change in public opinion after the rising, who had seen the people rally around those 'gunmen' who had been denounced at the beginning of the Anglo-Irish war, who had seen these gunmen extract concessions from the British which mere politicians could never have won, and who were yet dissatisfied with these concessions, could not be expected to accept a cabinet majority of one in favour of the treaty or a *Dáil* majority of seven. Later, in June 1922, popular endorsement in a general election also left them unmoved. Rejecting compromise they continued to demand a republic free of any formal connection with Britain, and majority disapproval deterred them no more than had similar opposition deterred Clarke and Pearse in 1916 or Collins and Breen in 1919.[26]

The section of the IRA which rejected the treaty now reverted to its normal role, that of a minority prepared to resort to arms to impose its vision of Ireland on the short-sighted majority. De Valera had told the *Dáil* during the treaty debates 'whenever I wanted to know what the Irish people wanted, I had only to examine my own heart and it told me straight off what the Irish people wanted',[27] and many IRA men throughout the country had a similar faith in the messages of their own hearts.

Collins, the most dangerous of all the 'gunmen', emerged as the chairman of the provisional government which began taking over power from the British in January 1922. Despite all his attempts to control the country it gradually slid towards anarchy, with rival groups of soldiers seizing barracks, munitions and strategic points. De Valera's verbal sniping did not help. In March 1922, for instance, he warned the new Irish government that the volunteers of the future might 'have to wade through Irish blood, through the blood of the soldiers of the Irish Government and through, perhaps, the blood of some of the members of the Government in order to get Irish freedom'.[28] But by now de Valera was effectively a civilian and in 1922 it was the soldiers who made the running. Their old distaste for politicians was illustrated by a remark made by one of the leaders of the anti-treaty garrison which seized the *Four Courts* in Dublin; when asked if he intended setting up a military dictatorship he replied nonchalantly 'you can take it that way if you like'.

Full-scale fighting broke out in June, and with 1916 still in mind the anti-treaty rebels holed themselves up in buildings in Dublin and waited until they were blasted out. But this time, although a considerable minority of Irishmen opposed the treaty with passion there was no swing of public opinion in their favour. Soon the anti-treaty IRA was forced to retreat to the hills where it waged a guerrilla war. In the course of the fighting Collins was killed in an ambush.

The republicans refused to acknowledge the legitimacy of the *Free State*, and saw the members of the government as traitors and British agents;[29] in return, they were viewed as anarchists, utterly negative and destructive. As the killing and devastation dragged on, both sides' ferocity increased, surpassing that of the recent fight against the British. The IRA launched an assassination campaign against members of the *Dáil* and in response the government began executing its prisoners. In all 77 were shot, three times the number executed during the Anglo-Irish war. Naturally this ruthlessness intensified existing opposition to the government and the treaty, but surprisingly it did not make such opposition more widespread; in general public opinion was prepared to acquiesce in executions and atrocities by an Irish administration which it would never have accepted from the British. For the third time in seven years the IRA had succeeded in provoking the government into repressive measures, but this time the tactic failed to mobilise support for the rebels.

The gradual consolidation of the government forced the anti-treaty IRA command to look more kindly on politicians, and in October 1922 the army executive called on de Valera to form a republican government whose members and activities would be subject to army ratification.[30] Little attention was paid to it, and towards the end of the war de Valera was driven to complain of his treatment by the IRA; 'the old contempt for civil or semi-civil work apparently persists'.[31]

By early 1923 the IRA rebels were defeated but instead of surrendering they buried their weapons and waited for a suitable time to resume the struggle. This did not come about until 1939, the campaign was then abandoned within a year and the IRA had to wait until 1956 for the third round. This in turn petered out after five years, and not until the 1970s did the IRA again become a significant force. The heroic decade between the formation of the *Irish Volunteers* in 1913 and the end of the civil war in 1923 was followed by a return to the traditional policy of waiting patiently for better days.

The IRA regarded itself, with much justification, as heir to the IRB tradition.[32] It was significant that it had retained its title, just as the republicans' political wing retained the name *Sinn Fein*, both of which had been abandoned by the majority who accepted the treaty. Their task was now much harder than it had been. The British had left most of Ireland, and in the six counties remaining under their rule nationalists of all kinds were outnumbered two to one by unionists. The citizens of the *Free State* seemed content with a government which did not share the IRA's zeal for a united Irish republic, and in the 1923 elections *Sinn Fein* won only 44 of the 153 *Dáil* seats. (The imprisoned IRA writer Peadar O'Donnell could interpret this result as meaning that 'the mass of national opinion was still resisting the Treaty'.[33] National opinion was clearly not to be confused with the electorate's vote.)

In the early 1920s the IRA was not a secret army, rather an open army defeated in the field whose members were known to the victorious government. It engaged in sporadic acts of violence – in 1924, for instance, some of its members tried to provoke a confrontation between the British and the Irish governments by attacking British sailors from the naval base on Spike Island – but these reflected frustration in the aftermath of defeat, not the beginning of a new campaign.

Relations between the IRA and the republican 'government' headed by de Valera worsened gradually. The anti-treaty politicians wanted power, but their policy of abstention from the *Dáil* doomed them to impotence. The IRA purists became suspicious that the *Sinn Feiners* might compromise their principles; in 1925 an army convention accused the republican government of developing into a mere political party and it set up an independent executive which was 'given the power to declare war'.[34] Aiken, the chief of staff who doubled as 'minister of defence', was distrusted as being too close to de Valera and was deposed.

In the course of the next two years de Valera and his more pragmatic colleagues left *Sinn Fein*, formed their own *Fianna Fail* party, entered the *Dáil* and became the official opposition, while the rump *Sinn Fein* went into a prompt decline and became no more than an adjunct of the IRA. De Valera and his followers were denounced as compromisers and traitors who had succumbed to the fatal lure of politics.

The 1920s witnessed a small but steady series of violent incidents. The IRA carried out arms raids, attacked and sometimes killed policemen who investigated them too closely, and later began intimidating prison warders, court witnesses and jurors. To a large extent these were spontaneous and uncoordinated measures and were often defensive in intent, designed to prevent the movement being destroyed by the *Free State* authorities. The IRA was not waging a campaign to bring down the *Cumann na nGaedheal* government or the political system, much though it hated both. Even the assassination in July 1927 of Kevin O'Higgins, the strong man of the Irish cabinet, was probably the work of IRA men acting on their own initiative and not on the orders of the army command.

In the early 1930s the tempo of IRA attacks increased dramatically, illegal drillings, arms raids and assaults (several fatal) on the police became more common. The government was forced to adopt harsh measures; the IRA and many allied organisations were banned, their members were rounded up in larger numbers and special military tribunals were established to try cases of politically motivated violence. This response to increased IRA provocation made the government look awkward and ridiculous as well as repressive and probably contributed to its defeat by *Fianna Fail* in the 1932 elections.[35] In a way this could be seen as another success for the policy of goading the authorities into unpopular, self-destructive actions, but there were many other causes of their defeat. The impact of the Depression, *Cumann na nGaedheal's* bungled and negative campaign, *Fianna Fail's* superior organisation and the simple desire for a change all played a part.

The 1932 elections and the peaceful transfer of power to those who had been defeated in the civil war less than ten years earlier were decisive events in the consolidation of Irish democracy. They were also significant in the history of the IRA.

Most IRA men regarded de Valera as a renegade, but at least he had recently been a fellow-rebel against the treatyite government and he still shared their rhetoric and many of their views. As soon as *Fianna Fail* was installed in office Aiken, now the real minister for defence, went to negotiate with the imprisoned IRA leaders whose chief of staff he had been until 1925, and he released them the next day. The ban on the IRA was lifted, the military tribunals were suspended and police surveillance was eased. De Valera intensified the previous government's policy of whittling away at the restrictions imposed on Irish sovereignty by the treaty, and one by one he removed its more obnoxious clauses. But he made it clear that he was going to move cautiously and peacefully, and he no longer talked about 'the Republic' which remained, along with reunification, the IRA's main objective.

IRA members were in a dilemma. De Valera was achieving many of their aims by peaceful means, and while they could and did reject his argument that with *Fianna Fail* in power they were no longer necessary, they realised there was no point in fighting another round against so sympathetic a government. Under the circumstances it is not surprising that the IRA was tempted to settle old scores, and applying the principle of 'no free speech for traitors' some of its members turned on the now powerless *Cumann na nGaedheal* party, attacking its leaders and disrupting its meetings. Feeling that the new administration was working hand-in-glove with a terrorist organisation, some *Cumann na nGaedheal* supporters formed a fascist-style *Blueshirt* movement which played a colourful if transient and ultimately unimportant role in Irish affairs in 1933 and 1934. Its main significance was as a catalyst in the relations between de Valera's government and the IRA.

By 1933 de Valera, the poacher turned gamekeeper, was securely in power. In his new position he resented his former colleagues' lawlessness but he found it difficult to turn on them; after all, he had deserted them, not they him, and they still held many objectives in common. In its rejection of majority rule and democratic procedure the IRA was firmly in the 1916–19 tradition, and de Valera's support of the anti-treaty forces in 1922 showed that he shared the IRA's view that violence was justifiable against an Irish as well as against a British administration. In a *Dáil* speech some years earlier he had made remarks which were to be used against him for decades to come:

we are all morally handicapped because of the circumstances in which the whole thing came about. The setting up of this State put a moral handicap on every one of us here . . . Those who continued on in that organization which we have left can claim exactly the same continuity that we claimed up to 1925.[36]

The IRA may have been a small minority but it was the direct successor of that other small minority whose resort to violence had established the state. Democratic politicians democratically elected occupied their positions because in 1921 the British had yielded to force when earlier they would not yield to reason.

While de Valera was understandably reluctant to suppress the IRA he was able to move freely against the *Blueshirts*, and did so. This simplified his problem. Once he had asserted the government's authority against one of the country's two private armies it was easier for him to turn on the other, which had all along been a far more powerful threat to stability and democracy. Gradually the basic incompatibility between de Valera's methods and those of the IRA became clearer, especially when some IRA elements began flirting with socially radical ideas, involving themselves in land disputes and in attempts to stop government strike-breaking. Once again policemen who harried the IRA were killed, and the crisis came when the IRA alienated itself decisively from public opinion by acts of stupid brutality. In March 1936 in County Cork the retired Admiral Somerville, who had acted as referee for local men wanting to join the Royal Navy, was shot dead on his own doorstep by an IRA group which had taken literally authorisation by the local command to 'get him'. Not long afterwards a 'traitor' was killed. The government's much-criticised indulgence of the IRA came to an end, and within a short time it was banned and its leaders arrested. Police pressure increased as its sympathisers in the cabinet lost their patience, and by the end of the decade the IRA's situation was no better than it had been under the *Cumann na nGaedheal* government before 1932. De Valera was now seen as another British collaborator, even more dangerous than his predecessors in office.

Some IRA men felt that as long as the Republic or a United Ireland remained distant goals the organisation should concern itself with economic and social problems and that only in this way could they acquire a mass following. (A mass following, of course, was viewed by the leadership with grave suspicion; in that direction lay the danger of becoming yet another political party.) Throughout the 1920s and 1930s the more radical members of the IRA, in particular Peadar O'Donnell, tried to move the organisation to the left. In 1927 he launched a campaign in Donegal against paying the annuities due to Britain under the Land Acts, and in 1931 he won the support of the IRA army council for *Saor Eire*, a new radical movement which would combine republicanism and socialism, overthrow capitalism and solve unemployment. Nothing came of this – the Church and the government attacked the new body, and de Valera's assumption of power a year later shifted people's minds back to 'the national question'. In 1934 the IRA radicals made another attempt to form a left-wing political party, the *Republican Congress*, but the army council opposed the move bitterly and warned that 'this Party will, in course of time, contest elections and enter the Free State Parliament'.[37] The *Republican Congress* soon followed *Saor Eire* into oblivion. As had been the case with the mass *Sinn Fein* party in 1917, and even with the *Irish Parliamentary Party* before it, divisive issues which would distract from a single-minded concentration on nationalist objectives were suspected and condemned. First and foremost the IRA remained an organisation dedicated to resuming, some day, the struggle with Britain.

By 1937 the Irish political system had been consolidated and opponents as well as supporters of the treaty were quite content to work within the framework established in 1922. The *Free State* had been officially ended and the treaty had been so dismantled that only the formal acknowledgement of the 'republic' was missing; this step (delayed until 1949) lost much of its importance once the crown had been removed from the constitution. Attacking the Southern state no longer seemed worthwhile and from the late 1930s onwards the IRA began to concentrate on the continuing British presence in Northern Ireland.

All Irish nationalists, North and South, regarded partition as the latest example of British cunning, and the border itself as a blatant gerrymander. Few Irishmen could understand why Britain was so appalled by the prospect of a united Ireland containing a Protestant minority of 26 per cent and so satisfied with an artificial Northern Ireland containing a Catholic minority of 33.5 per cent. A justifiable sense of grievance at how Ireland had been partitioned between 1920 and 1925 helped lure many young men into the IRA's ranks, but for many years its attention was centred on the easier target in the South rather than on the North.

This relative neglect of the North is one of the main ironies of Irish history during the inter-war years; after all, as the imperfections of the *Free State's* position were gradually removed, one might have expected a concentration of energies in an effort to drive out the 'British occupying forces' from Ulster. But *Sinn Fein* and the IRA had always been weak in the North, Ulster had played only a minor role in the Anglo-Irish war, and the great majority of killings since 1922 had been in the course of traditional sectarian conflict. Incursions across the border died down after 1923, and for most of the 1920s and 1930s the Northern units of the IRA saw their role as a defensive one, protecting the Catholic minority against the Protestant majority. The violent riots of 1935 showed the necessity of such protection.

North or South of the border, no-one could deny that the IRA's record since 1922 had been pitiful. It had survived and preserved its much-valued continuity, and if circumstances should improve there were men prepared to utilise them. The more active spirits felt that this was quite insufficient, and that more drastic steps were called for. In the late 1930s these men won the day and, led by Sean Russell, took over the leadership of the organisation.

For years Russell had demanded an attack on Britain, arguing that this

would both intimidate the British public into abandoning Northern Ireland
and unite Irishmen behind the IRA. One of his followers described his attitude
as follows. De Valera

> would not dare interfere with the IRA men going out to take part in the
> campaign or their return for shelter. The British would blame him for such a
> policy and very soon he would be forced to take his stand with us and the
> 1920–21 position would be restored. Alternatively he *would* interfere with
> us. The people would rise in anger against him and rally round us.[38]

Many of Russell's colleagues argued that Northern Ireland was a more
natural as well as an easier target – after all, the IRA's grievance was the
presence of British troops in Ulster, not in England. He paid no attention,
purged his opponents, and went ahead with his plans. Apart from the Anglo-
Irish war, Russell's bombing campaign in 1939–40 was to be the IRA's only
sustained exercise in terror until the 1970s. It was an utter failure. The
preparations, training and finance were all inadequate, little respect was paid
to the master plan, and local IRA units in Britain decided on the targets. From
January 1939 onwards bombs went off at electrical lines, power stations, left
luggage offices, the London underground, banks, cinemas and other public
places. Even *Madame Tussaud's* did not escape. Care was taken not to attack
individuals, and in the first seven months of the year, in the course of 127
attacks, only one person was killed and 55 injured.[39] But in Coventry in
August a bomb went off in the wrong place killing five people and injuring
sixty. The British government introduced emergency legislation, Irishmen
were deported and checks made on travellers between Britain and Ireland.
The bombers were steadily rounded up (in separate raids the arrests included
the 16 year-old Brendan Behan and his 77 year-old grandmother) and the
campaign faded out in early 1940.

The outbreak of the Second World War created new difficulties for the IRA.
De Valera was anxious above all to preserve Irish neutrality and he regarded
the bombing campaign in England and the IRA's links with Germany as a
grave embarrassment. This was compounded by a flamboyant, melodramatic
coup in December 1939 when the magazine fort in the Phoenix Park in Dublin
was raided and a million rounds of ammunition were seized. The government
and the Irish army were mortified, but so were the local IRA commanders who
could not cope with such an unexpected windfall. The government's response
was immediate and effective – so much so that it is said more weapons and
ammunition were recovered from raids on IRA arms stores all over the
country than had been taken from the magazine. From then on the army and
police were relentless in their attacks on the IRA. Its leaders were on the run
until they were rounded up and imprisoned or interned; during the war over
five hundred were interned and six hundred convicted under the *Offences
against the State Act*, six IRA men were executed and three died as a result of
hunger strikes. IRA action dwindled away.

The *coup de grace* came with the Stephen Hayes affair. Hayes succeeded Russell as chief of staff, but under the special wartime circumstances proved spectacularly ineffective[40] – to such an extent that some of his more impatient and aggressive colleagues in the North decided that he was a British agent deliberately destroying the organisation. In June 1941 they kidnapped him, held him prisoner for ten weeks, tortured him, tried him and sentenced him to death, but allowed him write out a lengthy confession, in the style of the Stalinist purges, before his execution. Hayes lingered over the extravagent details of this confession. Eventually he managed to escape and fled, his legs still chained together, to the sanctuary of a Dublin police station.[41] He was safe from his former captors, but spent the rest of the war in prison. Once the full, farcical details were made public it was hard for people to view the IRA seriously any longer. The arrests continued and by the end of the war, for the first time, continuity in the IRA's leadership had been broken. De Valera, the rebel of the civil war, had done what the British and the *Cumann na nGaedheal* governments had been unable to do.

The postwar history of the IRA, which will be treated briefly, almost as a postscript, was one of mixed fortunes in which the problems and opportunities encountered in the 1920s and 1930s repeated themselves. The main change, mentioned above, was a new concentration on Northern Ireland. The lure of politics continued. In 1946 Sean MacBride, one of the most prominent IRA leaders of the inter-war years, formed a new party, and two years later joined in coalition with the survivors and successors of the 1920s treatyite government. As in 1932 there were short-term gains for the extremists when one of their former colleagues came to power, and the remaining IRA prisoners were released, but the fact remained that once again a republican had 'sold out', had recognised the status quo and its institutions.

Between 1956 and 1962 a new attack was launched against British forces in Ulster. By this time the benefits of the welfare state and the lessening of sectarian tensions had weakened Northern Catholics' faith both in a united Ireland and in the IRA as their protector, and significantly the driving force for the new campaign came from South of the border. Once again it proved a miserable failure. In the five years it lasted 18 people were killed (in gruesome contrast the total during the 1970s would be over a hundred times as great) and the IRA statement calling off the campaign admitted that 'foremost among the factors motivating this course of action has been the attitude of the general public whose minds have deliberately been distracted from the supreme issue facing the Irish people – the unity and freedom of Ireland'.

There followed, in the 1960s, a return to the minority position of the 1920s and 1930s, a flirtation with left-wing ideas. Attention turned to questions such as housing and trade union organisation, and the IRA gave its support to the civil-rights movement, but this attitude was dropped promptly when national and sectarian problems re-emerged at the end of the 1960s. In August 1969 the Catholics' old fears were revived as Protestant mobs attacked their ghettoes and rendered 3,000 of them homeless. The *Provisional IRA* was formed a few months later when the traditionalist rank and file, disenchanted with the way in which their leaders' pacifism and social conscience had led to the Catholic areas being undefended (and the embarrassing slogan IRA = I Ran Away) decided to revert to the time-honoured aim of driving the British out and reunifying the island. All questions of social reform would be left aside until those first objectives had been achieved. As ever, the fact that the revived IRA was soon rejected by most Irish nationalists, on both sides of the border, carried no weight; what was new in the 1970s was the IRA's inability to win any parliamentary seat in any election, North or South.

The *Provisional IRA* has shown a new ruthlessness which had been lacking in the half-hearted campaign of 1956–62, or in Russell's bombing attacks in 1939/40; lacking often in the Anglo-Irish war of 1919–21. No matter how much the IRA might be sustained by its long tradition its tactics have naturally more in common with those of modern terrorist groups such as Irgun, EOKA, the FLN or the PLO than with those of its Irish predecessors. One former member describes the *Provisionals'* attitude most revealingly:

The Army Council's first target was to kill thirty-six British soldiers – the same number who died in Aden. The target was reached in early November 1971. But this, the Army Council felt, was not enough: I remember Dave [O'Connell], amongst others, saying: 'We've got to get eighty'. Once eighty had been killed, Dave felt, the pressure on the British to withdraw would be immense. I remember the feeling of satisfaction we had at hearing another one had died.[42]

However brutal and politically blind the *Provisional IRA* might be, however far removed its members are from the self-sacrifice of Pearse or the pragmatism of Collins, they remain unworthy heirs to an unbroken tradition going back to the mid-nineteenth century. Even their political obtuseness is a result of their divorce between Ireland and Irishmen, of their contempt for majority opinion and in particular for those who pander to majority opinion, politicians; and such attitudes have a long history in the IRB/IRA. However much ordinary Irishmen might disapprove of their actions, the mere fact that the *Provisionals* represent, however misguidedly, the present generation in the age-old fight against the British enemy has won them a certain sympathy; they are regarded as stupid and cruel, but their hearts are felt to be in the right place. This sympathy is felt at the highest levels. In 1970 the Irish *taoiseach*, Jack Lynch, dismissed Charles Haughey and Neil Blaney, the two most powerful ministers in his cabinet, for running guns to Northern Ireland. Both men were arrested, but charges against Mr Blaney were dropped and Mr Haughey was acquitted after two trials. Years later Mr Blaney told the *Dáil* about the role he had played.

Not only did circumstances bring the freedom fighters into existence but so did the promised support of help, not just by me but by a whole lot of others, who helped bring into existence shortly after those who are now condemned as terrorists, murderers – the gunmen of the Provisional IRA.[43]

Irish attitudes are ambivalent. The same person will deplore the *Provisionals* when they plant bombs in restaurants or kill children in crossfire, but applaud them when they escape from jail. Almost all non-unionist Irishmen regard British policy towards Ireland, at any period, with a well-merited distrust,[44] and any movement which can identify itself with the long tradition of active opposition to the British presence in Ireland can draw on latent support.

As an Irish political scientist has argued,

it seems reasonable to admit the claim of the Provisional IRA . . . as the true descendant of the unreconstructed Irish republican tradition of the mid-nineteenth century . . . they have a legitimacy of sorts . . . in politics you do not have to be illegitimate to be a bastard.[45]

NOTES

1. B. Hobson, *Defensive Warfare* (Dublin, 1909) p. 8.
2. Conor Cruise O'Brien even argues that the Irish republican movement is 'distinguished from other revolutionary movements in being *failure-proof*. Its greatest blunders are successes if they produce more martyrs, the guarantors of ultimate victory, in however remote an epoch' (*Herod: Reflections on Political Violence* (London, 1978) p. 47).
3. P. Pearse, *Political Writings and Speeches* (Dublin, 1922) pp. 136–7.
4. Ibid., p. 230.
5. *Irish Independent* (29 April 1918).
6. L. O Broin, *Revolutionary Underground* (Dublin, 1976) p. 134.
7. B. Hobson, *Ireland Yesterday and Tomorrow* (Tralee, 1968) p. 36.
8. I. Colvin, *Carson*, Vol. II (London, 1934) p. 129.
9. The details of the planning of the rising are complicated, and are beyond the scope of this paper. Particularly valuable are K. B. Nowlan (ed.), *The Making of 1916* (Dublin, 1969); R. Dudley Edwards, *Patrick Pearse: the Triumph of Failure* (London, 1977); and W. I. Thompson, *The Imagination of an Insurrection: Dublin 1916* (New York, 1967).
10. F. S. L. Lyons, *John Dillon* (London, 1969) p. 382.
11. G. B. Shaw, *The Matter with Ireland* (London, 1962) p. 112.
12. Lyons, p. 394.
13. T. P. O'Neill and P. O. Fiannachta, *De Valera*, Vol. I (Dublin, 1968) p. 78.
14. S. O'Luing, *I die in a good cause: a study of Thomas Ashe* (Tralee, 1970) p. 122; Lord Longford and T. P. O'Neill, *De Valera* (London, 1970) pp. 56–7.
15. D. Breen, *My Fight for Irish Freedom* (Dublin, 1924) p. 9.
16. In February 1919 Collins rescued both presidents of the Irish Republic, de Valera and Sean McGarry of the IRB, from Lincoln Jail (O Broin, p. 182).
17. Collins was minister for finance, director of organisation, director of intelligence, and head of the terror 'squad' in Dublin. His influence exceeded these official responsibilities.
18. Ch. Townshend, *The British Campaign in Ireland 1919–1921* (Oxford, 1975) Appendix V, p. 214.

19. Breen, p. 52.
20. D. Figgis, *Recollections of the Irish War* (Dublin, 1927) p. 243.
21. *The Times* (12 December 1919).
22. Public Record Office, London, CO.904/110, inspector general's report (15 October 1919).
23. Townshend, p. 26.
24. E. O'Malley, *On another man's wound*, 2nd edn. (Dublin, 1979) p. 317.
25. *An t-Óglach*, I, i (15 August 1918).
26. Curiously enough, the questions of the Crown and the *Free State's* constitutional relationship with the empire were the key issues in the treaty debates and the civil war. All sides assumed that, sooner or later, the North would be forced to merge with the South.
27. Dáil Eireann Official Report: Debate on the Treaty, p. 274 (6 January 1922).
28. F. S. L. Lyons, *Ireland since the Famine*, 2nd edn. (London, 1973) p. 454.
29. This attitude persisted. In 1933 Sean MacBride, one of the IRA leaders (in later phases of his career to become Irish foreign minister and Nobel peace prize winner), tried in vain to convince de Valera, now in power, that 'most of the high Government officials are merely British secret service agents' (MacBride to Joe McGarrity, 19 October 1933, McGarrity papers, National Library of Ireland MS 17,456).
30. Longford and O'Neill, p. 207; J. A. Gaughan, *Austin Stack: Portrait of a Separatist* (Dublin, 1977) p. 220.
31. Longford and O'Neill, p. 207.
32. Although the IRB lingered on until 1924, in the words of a recent authority 'from February 1922 the IRB as a national organisation ceased to function' and by 1923 it 'had become the servant and not the master of the military forces in the state' (J. O'Beirne-Ranelagh, 'The IRB from the treaty to 1924', *Irish Historical Studies* xx, no. 77 (March 1976) pp. 32, 39).
33. P. O'Donnell, *The Gates Flew Open* (London, 1932) pp. 178–9.
34. J. Bowyer Bell, *The Secret Army* (1970) p. 53.
35. Fianna Fail, whose first leaders had thrice resorted to arms in defiance of the people's views, has held power democratically for all but ten years since 1932.
36. Dáil Eireann Official Report, 28, cols. 1399–1400 (14 March 1929).
37. T. P. Coogan, *The IRA* (London, 1970) p. 80.
38. S. Hayes, 'My Strange Story', *The Bell* (Dublin) xvii, 4 (July 1951) pp. 12–13.
39. Bell, p. 160.
40. He later admitted his responsibilities were 'entirely beyond my experience and ability. I looked on myself merely as a recording caretaker clerk' (Hayes, p. 14).
41. Bell, pp. 201–7; Hayes, *The Bell*, xvii, 5 (August 1951) pp. 42–51.
42. M. Maguire, *To Take Arms* (London, 1973) pp. 74–5.
43. Dáil Eireann Official Report, 264, col. 668 (1 December 1972); cited in Cruise O'Brien, p. 139. Both men have retained widespread support and influence. In June 1979 Mr Blaney was elected triumphantly to the European parliament, and in December 1979 Mr Haughey succeeded Mr Lynch as *taoiseach*.
44. Nowadays, of course, unionists share this distrust, for opposite reasons.
45. T. Garvin, 'The Discreet Charm of the National Bourgeoisie', *Third Degree*, I, i (Dublin, Spring 1977) pp. 16–17.

12 Anarchism and Individual Terror in the German Empire, 1870–90

Andrew R. Carlson

There is a sizeable body of opinion that there was little anarchism in Germany and that those anarchists that were there contributed nothing to anarchist thought. A similar view contends that the German anarchist movement was ineffectual and meaningless so far as producing any lasting results are concerned.[1] The author of this article is of the opinion that German anarchists did more than sit around beer gardens discussing the theoretical aspects of anarchism. There were German anarchists active in both Germany and the International long before the assassination attempts of 1878. Anarchists did play a role in shaping the destiny of Germany in the nineteenth and twentieth centuries. However, this influence cannot be seen if one examines only the positive attainments of the anarchists in Germany. If, on the other hand, one examines their negative influence he will soon discover that many suppressive measures were enacted as a result of an anarchist deed. The Socialist Law, prompted by two attempts on the life of Wilhelm I in 1878, was the first such measure. This repressive law affected not only the anarchists, but everyone who was interested in developing a responsible parliamentary government in Germany. In the following I am not going to deal with the philosophical or theoretical aspects of German anarchism, but will limit myself to the period of the 1870s to 1890 when violence and 'propaganda by deed' dominated the scene.

Anarchism in Germany in the early 1870s has to be treated in conjunction with the International. It is not until the 1870s that it is possible to pick up the thread of an anarchist movement in Germany. By 1875 there were adherents of anarchism in Berlin, Leipzig, Magdeburg, Munich and other places.[2] The German anarchists of this period exerted most of their influence on the international scene rather than in Germany. The German influence in the international movement during these years was exerted by three individuals: Erich Otto Rinke (1853–99) usually called Otto Rinke: Emil Werner (1845–192?); and Friedrich August Reinsdorf (1849–85) who usually used the name August. Werner and Reinsdorf were compositors by trade while Rinke was a locksmith.

Reinsdorf was perhaps the most famous German anarchist of this period. At the outset of 1874 Reinsdorf, who was an anarchist before Johann Most came around to such a point of view, wrote to Most that 'the only way to realize their goals and aspirations would be through a second St. Bartholomew's Night', this according to Reinsdorf 'was the only possible solution to the social question'.[3]

On 2 October 1875 the first German anarchist program was drawn up in Bern at Werner's suggestion, and signed by the 25 members of the group which also included Rinke. The program stated that the existing society was based on personal property and had as its political organisation the state, which it declared was nothing more than a weapon in the hands of the ruling class. The state, it went on to say, must disappear and make room for the society of the future, which would be a society based on the principle of the free formation of groups of individuals. Such a society would have as its economic foundation the common possession of the soil, the mines, capital, the great lines of communication, and the tools of work. History, the program contended, demonstrated that a violent solution was necessary in order to achieve the transition from the unjust society of the past to the just society of the future.[4]

A newspaper, the *Arbeiter Zeitung*, was formed by the members of the group for the purpose of spreading anarchist propaganda into German speaking areas. The *Arbeiter Zeitung* was published in Bern from 15 July 1876 to 13 October 1877. Reinsdorf, Rinke, and Werner were among the founders of the paper. The first issue notes that it would take too long to bring about a change in society through achieving a legally constituted majority in parliament. They wanted quicker results – advocating more violent methods because:[5]

For he who possesses nothing
Freedom of the press is a lie
Freedom of speech is a lie
Freedom of thought is a lie
Freedom of assembly is a lie
Freedom of participation is a lie
All theoretical freedoms are open lies
For he who possesses nothing freedom means nothing, for the lame the freedom to walk, for the blind the freedom to see, for it is not enough to permit something to happen or to only have laws which allow it, one must also have the necessary means by which possessions can be obtained.

Reinsdorf was active in this period smuggling copies of the *Arbeiter Zeitung* into Germany and attempting to form small anarchist cells there. Werner and Rinke were also active. Naturally the efforts of the anarchists to spread their propaganda in Germany brought them into conflict with the Social Democratic Party (SPD). At the Universal Socialist Congress, held in Ghent 9–16 September 1877, Werner, in a speech, indicated that the anarchists intended to increase their activity in Germany, thus jeopardising gains that the SPD had made there. His remarks so infuriated Liebknecht, that he jumped to his feet and offered a counter challenge to Werner, 'If you dare to come to Germany and attack our organization, we shall annihilate you using any means necessary'.[6]

During 1876/7 Reinsdorf spent a good deal of time in Leipzig where he attended Social Democratic meetings to present the anarchist point of view. Converts came slowly, but after a while Reinsdorf managed to gather a small circle of adherents. One member of Reinsdorf's group was Max Hödel. It is highly possible that Reinsdorf also came in contact with Dr Carl Nobiling, who was still a student in Leipzig at the time. Nobiling appears to have known Werner. Most claims that both Hödel's and Nobiling's attempts on Wilhelm I were inspired by Reinsdorf, but the connection is tenuous as will be pointed out.[7]

The plan which the German anarchists were following was to invade meetings of the Social Democrats and use the opportunity to speak at these meetings to make converts to anarchism. In general, then, the anarchists did not seek out new territories but went to the industrial centers and cities of Germany where the Social Democrats had already made considerable inroads. The principal centers of anti-authoritarianism and anarchism in Germany in the years 1876–8 were Leipzig, Munich, and Berlin; Southern Germany, in general, was more receptive to anarchist ideas than Northern Germany.

The situation in Germany in the spring of 1878 found Reinsdorf in Berlin, Werner in Leipzig and Rinke in either Munich or Cologne. Anarchist groups had been formed in Leipzig, Munich, Berlin and a number of other places. The stage was set for a series of events which would change the entire course of the socialist movement in Germany.

Anarchism in Germany prior to the attempt, by Hödel, on the life of the German Emperor, was more of a source of annoyance to the Social Democratic Party than anything else. The threat that the anarchists would take over the leadership of the labor movement was never close to being realised. As far as the government and the middle-class citizenry of Germany were concerned the anarchists were nothing more than a part of the odious socialist movement. The confusion is not surprising because the majority of both the socialists and anarchists were not certain themselves of their respective positions. Part of the task of the next decade was to define their ideologies and clarify their differences.

Saturday, 11 May 1878 was a usual warm spring day in Berlin. The sun was shining and the water vendors were busy plying their trade on the city's main thoroughfare, Unter den Linden. The German Emperor, Wilhelm I (1796–1888), as was his daily habit, was out taking his afternoon constitutional in an open carriage accompanied by his daughter, the Grand Duchess of Baden. The aged emperor, fondly called by the people the 'greise Kaiser', was a man of fixed habits which varied little from day to day. Even though it was a common event to see the German Emperor, a crowd gathered along the sides of Unter den Linden hoping to catch a glimpse of their beloved Kaiser. He was returning from a ride in the Tiergarten about 3.30 in the afternoon. As the carriage was passing number seven Unter den Linden, which was the site of the Russian Embassy, located about half way between the Brandenburg Gate and the Royal Palace, a tall, rather good-looking young man pushed himself into the line of spectators and fired several shots at the Emperor, all of which missed the mark. The twenty-year-old man, Max Hödel, was a tinsmith by trade, who had been caught up in the workers' movement in Leipzig.[8] He was active in the SPD but after receiving a vote of censure was expelled from the party by the Central Party Committee. After this he joined Reinsdorf's small circle and worked at various meetings in conjunction with Werner speaking out on behalf of the impoverished people of Germany.[9]

It appears that Hödel's attempt on Wilhelm I was planned in Leipzig in conjunction with Werner, without the knowledge of Reinsdorf. Evidence indicates that Hödel's attempt was well financed and that someone had attempted to instruct him in the use of a pistol, probably Nobiling. The evidence is not as conclusive as one would like, but it does point in the direction of Werner and the *Jura Federation*.

Bismarck's attempt to pass a Socialist-Law following the Hödel attempt was unsuccessful, however; the Nobiling attempt on 2 June 1878 aroused the nation and the Reichstag sufficiently to force them to capitulate to Bismarck's demands. Nobiling's attempt, while being unsuccessful, nevertheless inflicted serious wounds to the Emperor. Nobiling's attempt on Wilhelm I immediately turned Berlin into a city that was garrisoned as though it were in a state of siege. The measure for the suppression of socialism was revived. The heavy hand of the law fell on anyone who suggested by word or deed that he sympathised with Hödel or Nobiling.

The Berlin police uncovered evidence that the German section of the *Jura Federation* was responsible for the plot against the Emperor, and that both assassination attempts has been directed from Leipzig, but this evidence was never followed up.[10] Some additional revelations were turned up, the significance of which it does not seem the Berlin police could have overlooked. But they did, perhaps intentionally. Louis Pinday, a former communard and friend of former communard Leo Frankel, received a letter from Frankel dated 20 May 1878 in which Frankel related that after the unsuccessful attempt by Hödel a meeting had been held in Neuchatel in which the German section of the *Jura Federation* decided to make another attempt on the life of the Kaiser.[11] It was also reported (date not specified) to the Berlin police that James Guillaume, living in Switzerland, had remarked, 'we know very well that Nobiling is one of us'.[12]

It is almost beyond belief that the Berlin police did not attach greater importance to an undated letter Emil Werner, living in Leipzig at the time, wrote to Paul Brousse who was serving as editor of *L'avant-Garde* in Chaux-de-Fonds, Switzerland. The contents of this letter revealed that Leo Frankel had been arrested and that, 'it would be in the best interest of the cause if Nobiling would soon die'. The letter went on to say that Nobiling was to have been initiated into the International but his sponsor, Paul Dentler, had died in Berlin five to six weeks previously.[13] The tone of this letter leads me to believe that Werner was aquainted to some extent with Nobiling, which is very possible considering the time Nobiling spent in Leipzig. It is amazing, almost beyond belief, that the police did not investigate Emil Werner more thoroughly in view of the fact that their investigations had demonstrated that Hödel had associated with him in Leipzig.[14] There is nothing in the letter to connect Werner directly with Nobiling but the implication is there both in Werner's statement, that it would be in the best interest of the cause if Nobiling would soon die, and also in his statement that Nobiling had been slated for membership in the International. The Berlin police were cognisant of Nobiling's trips to Leipzig. Upon his return to Berlin from these trips he talked to a number of people about the International. The police had enough circumstantial evidence to pick up Werner for questioning but did not.

It is doubtful if Leo Frankel (1844–96) was actually involved with the attempt on the life of the Emperor even though his name is mentioned several times. Frankel was, it is true, a former communard and both Hödel and Nobiling were imbued with enthusiasm for the ideas of the Commune. However, after the Commune Frankel became prominent in founding the Social Democratic Party in Hungary and was quite closely associated with Marx. Frankel attended the Universal Socialist Congress in Ghent from 1–15 September 1877, where he came in contact with Rinke and Werner. At the congress Frankel stood in opposition to the anarchists. He was forced to leave Belgium a day before the congress adjourned and returned to his native Hungary where he took part in the first socialist congress held in Hungary during the period 21–2 April 1878. According to his biographer, Frankel was in Hungary during the period of the two attempts; nowhere in the biography is any mention made of the attempts. There is also nothing to indicate that Frankel was arrested at the time.[15]

The Leo Frankel who was reported to the Berlin police supposedly was living at the time in Frankfurt-am-Main. It is quite possible that when Werner related to Paul Brousse, also a former communard, that Leo Frankel had been arrested he was actually referring to Otto Rinke. Werner does not say where he was arrested. Victor Dave a number of years later related that Rinke had been arrested in 1878 in the city of Cologne while using the name Otto Rau. It was a common practice for anarchists to use the names of well known Social Democrats as aliases. Reinsdorf at this period called himself Bernstein.[16] It is quite reasonable to assume that Rinke might have used the name Leo Frankel.

At Ghent, Frankel had sided with the Social Democrats against the anarchists. Liebknecht had openly attacked Rinke at Ghent with the approval of the rest of the Social Democrats. One way for Rinke to retaliate against the Social Democrats and at the same time to hide his identity would be to use the name of a Social Democrat as an alias. He could not use Liebknecht's name because Liebknecht was much older and also his face was reasonably well known because it was the practice of the time to sell pictures on the street of prominent Social Democratic Party leaders. Frankel, a Hungarian, was not popularly known and was close to Rinke's own age.[17]

It can be said with some degree of certainty that there was some connection between Hödel and Nobiling. At least both of them were associated with the German section of the *Jura Federation*, whose titular head in Germany was Emil Werner in Leipzig. Another connection between Hödel and Nobiling and the Germans who helped found the *Arbeiter-Zeitung* in Bern is evident upon reading the lead article in Paul Brousse's *L'avant Garde* (17 June 1878) entitled, 'Hödel, Nobiling and Propaganda by Deed', in which the acts of Hödel and Nobiling are praised. The article also implies that in some way *L'avant Garde* should claim a share of the glory for these two attempts. Brousse helped found the *Arbeiter-Zeitung* along with Werner, Rinke, and a number of others. He continued to be a good friend of Werner and Rinke and, as has already been noted, *L'avant Garde* took the place of the defunct *Arbeiter-Zeitung*. The Geneva section of the *Jura Federation* following Hödel's execution passed a resolution declaring Hödel to be a martyr for the rights of mankind.[18]

The general tenor of the Nobiling documents tend to indicate that the Berlin police were aware that the Nobiling and Hödel attempts were connected, but they never succeeded in actually getting enough concrete evidence to prove it. They spent too much time looking in the wrong places. If they had concentrated their efforts in Leipzig, Frankfurt-am-Main, and Switzerland, they probably would have found more information. Instead they seemed to be looking for some sort of international conspiracy, on a more grandiose scale, and Nobiling's travels pointed them in this direction. They conducted no investigation in Frankfurt and the investigation in Leipzig was limited to Nobiling's student associates and his land lady. For some unknown reason they failed to investigate Emil Werner whose name appears in both the Hödel and Nobiling documents. The German police network in Switzerland does not appear to have been very well-developed in 1878. The documents give the impression that they were primarily dependent upon Swiss sources for information.

Actually, as events proceeded after the Nobiling attempt, it became less and less desirable to find the group guilty of masterminding the two attempts or to establish a connection between the two. A scapegoat was named the night of the Nobiling attempt, as it was after the Hödel attempt and the burden of police efforts were aimed not at solving the Nobiling case, but at proving that

Nobiling had connections with the Social Democratic Party. The Hödel and Nobiling investigations were very similar; however, the police demonstrated beyond the shadow of a doubt that Hödel was an anarchist and that the SPD was not to blame for his crime. Nevertheless, an attempt was made to force through anti-socialist legislation on the false premise that Hödel was a socialist. In the Nobiling investigation the police turned up enough evidence to demonstrate conclusively, as in the Hödel case, that Nobiling had attended Social Democratic meetings and had connections with the Social Democratic Party. They also turned up conclusive evidence that Nobiling's act could in no way be attributed to the Social Democratic Party, but this evidence, as in the Hödel case, was not made public.

The afternoon extras which came off the presses announcing the second attempt on the German Emperor did not imply that the assassin was connected with the socialists. The evening editions of the *Post* and *Berliner Tageblatt* though carried information that Social Democratic writings were found among Nobiling's possessions. During the night of 2/3 June, or more precisely in the early morning hours of 3 June, a bombshell was exploded which would do irreparable damage to the image of the Social Democratic Party in Germany. At 2 am the Wolff Telegraph Bureau in Berlin sent out over the wires a message which was described as an 'official' government release on the Nobiling attempt. The next morning Germans awoke to read in their newspapers the text of the Wolff telegram which said:[19]

Subsequent interrogation of the assassin Nobiling has revealed that he holds socialist inclinations, also that he repeatedly attended socialist meetings here and that he has intended for a week to shoot His Majesty the Kaiser, because he maintains that it would be beneficial for the common welfare to eliminate the head of the state.

The arrival of this telegram at the news office of *Vorwärts* in Leipzig sent a feeling of consternation through Bebel, Liebknecht and Hasenclever who had gathered there on the morning of 3 June to determine if any of them knew Nobiling. The Wolff telegram shocked them out of their earlier feeling of security which they had achieved by receipt of an earlier telegram which carried no mention of Nobiling being connected with the socialists. Bebel had remarked, 'now they can't hang us on his coattails'.[20] This feeling of safety vanished when the Wolff telegram arrived and they became aware of the implication it could have for their movement.

Both Bebel and Bernstein on a number of occasions pointed out that this telegram was nothing more than a bold-faced lie.[21] Bernstein maintained that Nobiling was in no physical shape to be questioned or to reveal any information after his capture because of his wound. Bebel claimed that Nobiling was too severely injured to be examined and that he was unable to speak.[22] Bernstein's opinion is the same as that of Bebel, and it was probably

Bebel's defense of the Social Democratic Party in the *Reichstag* which so firmly established this opinion in his mind. This story, that Nobiling was too severely injured to be examined and to explain the reason for his action has been accepted without reservation by virtually everyone who has written on the subject.[23]

The truth of the matter is that nothing could be further from the realities of the case. Nobiling was questioned at length after his capture by the Public Prosecutor Johl and the Judge of Inquiry Schramm. In his answers to their questions Nobiling not only revealed his reasons for the attempt but also said he was not a Social Democrat. Nobiling said he wanted to kill the Kaiser because he thought it would be for the benefit of all to get rid of the head of the state. This part of the Wolff telegram is taken almost verbatim from Nobiling's answers. Only a few verb tenses are changed. Nobiling admitted having attended socialist meetings, but he did not admit, as the Wolff telegram claimed, having socialist inclinations. Johl asked Nobiling if he planned the attempt alone and he replied that he had planned it with a number of accomplices whom he refused to name. Nobiling further added that it was a follow-up to the unsuccessful attempt by Hödel. Johl asked if the Social Democratic Party was involved in the plot and Nobiling answered simply 'nein', but he did admit that he had associated with Social Democratic Party members and that he had attended Social Democratic Party meetings, but that he was not interested in politics. Nobiling also related that he had spoken at Social Democratic Party meetings. When asked to name a Social Democratic Party member with whom he had associated, he named Friedrich Wilhelm Fritzsche.[24]

The Wolff telegram then was not a complete fabrication. It was basically true, and what was not true could be implied from Nobiling's statements. The telegram was written in vague language and did not refer to the Social Democratic Party specifically, but only to the socialists. The Wolff telegram was a fabrication to the extent that it did not give the complete details of Nobiling's answers. If it had included the fact that Nobiling had said that the Social Democratic Party was not involved in the plot against the Emperor, it would have gotten the SPD off the hook immediately. If this fact had been included it would have altered the entire meaning of the telegram. But the telegram was so vaguely worded that the public could draw its own conclusions. It said Nobiling was a socialist and he was to the extent that an anarchist is a socialist of sorts. It said Nobiling had attended socialist meetings. Nobiling did attend Social Democratic meetings in Berlin as he had in Halle, Leipzig and Dresden. There is evidence which proves that he often entered Social Democratic Party meetings for the explicit purpose of putting forth his own ideas. His purpose in attending was not to hear Social Democratic theories propagated, but to dispute them. The telegram said he had socialist connections. He did, but they were not responsible for the plot.

Why was the fact that the SPD was not responsible for the attempt not included in the telegram? Why was this official news release so vague? We must conclude that someone wanted the telegram to imply that Nobiling was connected with the Social Democratic Party, so therefore the entire Social Democratic Party was responsible for the crime and should be punished. Who would benefit from such a scheme? It is obvious that the telegram had as its intention to heat up the fires of outrage against the Social Democratic Party in Germany. In most minds in Germany socialist referred to only one thing, the German Socialist Democratic Party. It did not have to be written out, the term 'Socialist' was sufficient.

Who then is responsible for this telegram which may properly be called the *second Ems telegram* because the same thing was done with it as with the Ems dispatch and it achieved a similar success. The results of Nobiling's interrogation appear in the telegram in such a way that no lies are told, but the truth was not revealed either. The real heart of Nobiling's testimony is that he acted with others in a plan to follow up the unsuccessful Hödel attempt and that the Social Democratic Party was in no way connected to the plot. This information was all missing in the Wolff telegram. The falsification was greater than Bebel or Bernstein ever imagined because they worked on the assumption that Nobiling's physical condition would not permit questioning.

It can be assumed that the Wolff telegram was authorised by someone who wanted deliberately to place the Social Democratic Party in a position of jeopardy. In the Nobiling documents there are both a handwritten copy of the telegram and a printed copy. The handwritten copy of the telegram is not signed, but it is written in the same handwriting as the extracts from the Nobiling interrogations which are signed by Lothar Bucher (1817–92).[25] The document signed by Lothar Bucher is a summary of the interrogation of Nobiling by the *Untersuchungsrichter* Johl. It is not a verbatim account but it is accurate. It is greatly reduced in size which leads me to believe that it was shortened for the purpose of telegraphing it to someone. Numerous abbreviations are also used. The news of the Nobiling attempt was telegraphed to Bismarck, and although it cannot be proven, probably the telegram which was sent contained the summarised version of the Nobiling interrogation which Bucher had extracted. Surely Bismarck must have been aware that if the second attempt were used properly it could open up new avenues to accomplish what he had failed to do after the Hödel attempt, namely the passage of an anti-socialist law. He saw this possibility when Hödel made his attempt on the Kaiser. At that time he was also at Friedrichsruhe and the evening of the Hödel attempt he telegraphed Bülow telling him that the incident should be seized on as a pretext for introducing a law against the socialists. Bismarck must have realised that if he managed the Nobiling affair properly he could make a great deal of political capital out of it, whip up feeling among the German public and in the end achieve his objectives, the suppression of the Social Democratic Party and the breaking of the power of the National Liberals who had voted against his bill to suppress the socialists after the Hödel affair. The original draft of the Wolff telegram, written in Bucher's handwriting, was more than likely transmitted to Berlin from Bismarck after he had read the telegram he had received which contained the summarised version of Nobiling's interrogation. Bismarck probably sent the text of the telegram to Bucher, authorising him to release it as an official statement on the assassination attempt. Bismarck was actually the only one in a position to release an official statement. William I could not, and until the Crown Prince could return home, Bismarck, as Chancellor, was the only one in a position to authorise such a statement. In view of the fact that the original draft of the telegram, which was probably transmitted in cipher, is in Bucher's handwriting, it is almost certain that Bismarck wrote it and authorised that it be released.[26] This time Bismarck was successful in obtaining passage of an anti-socialist law.

Following the passage of the Socialist Law, Johann Most (1846–1906), who was rapidly moving in the direction of the anarchist camp, was to be drummed out of the SPD in 1880. Most was set free from prison on 16 December 1878 and the SPD was relieved when he left Germany for London; however, once there he started to publish *Freiheit* which was originally intended to be a Social Democratic paper, published for the purpose of smuggling it into Germany. *Freiheit*, in unrestrained language called for the violent destruction of the state, the church, existing society, and above all kings. *Freiheit* played a role in helping Bismarck renew the Socialist Law four times. The SPD wished to disassociate themselves from Most and his flamboyant newspaper, which became anarchist in tone in 1880 with Reinsdorf playing the crucial role in Most's conversion.

The smuggling of *Freiheit* into Germany is an interesting and colorful part of German anarchist history. Table 12.1 gives an idea of the number of copies published and the number sent into Germany.[27]

TABLE 12.1: Publication and distribution of *Freiheit*

Date	No. of Copies Printed	No. of Copies Sent to Germany
1879	1,000–1,500	800–1,200
1880	2,000	1,800
1881	500–1,200	400–1,000
1882	2,000–2,700	1,800–2,500
1883	5,000	4,500 (incl. Austria)
1884	5,000	4,500 (incl. Austria)
1885	5,000	4,500 (incl. Austria)
1886	5,000	4,500 (incl. Austria)

Freiheit, both in its home office and in its distribution agents and correspondents in Germany was infiltrated with police spies. There were correspondents living in Germany who were in the pay of the Prussian Minister of the Interior and the Berlin Political Police. Two outstanding examples are August Rudolf Wolf and W. Wichmann.[28] Wichmann served as a correspondent for *Freiheit* in the Hamburg area. The articles he sent to *Freiheit* were actually written by August Engel (1840–1910), Police Commissioner and Criminal Police Inspector in Altona.[29] The articles were highly volatile, intended to fan the flames of police and popular oppression against the socialists and anarchists living in Germany. They were placed in *Freiheit* so that the Minister of the Interior, Robert von Puttkamer (1829–1900), could introduce them in the Reichstag as evidence to substantiate the need for the renewal of repressive measures against the socialists and anarchists.

Some examples of the types of articles attributed to Wichmann will help to demonstrate how they could be used to promote their campaign against the socialists and anarchists. In one of his first articles he says that it is like throwing money out of a window to spend it campaigning for votes; it would be better to spend it on arms. The socialists should take up arms and kill everyone who stands in their way or who hinders them from carrying out the socialist revolution. The King, religion, and all capitalists should be destroyed.[30] Following the assassination of Tsar Alexander II he wrote, 'May the day not be far off when a similar occurrence will free us from tyranny. We only regret that the other scoundrels did not receive their deserved reward at the same time'.[31] He went on to say that before very long the other monarchs of the world would receive the same treatment given Alexander II because the social revolution was about to break out. Wichmann's article amounted to a verbal threat on the life of William I.

Again in 1881 he called William I, whom he referred to as Lehmann, 'the perjured hero of Rastatt' who was now 'shaking for his life' as a result of an 'unbroken chain of villainous actions and cruelties'.[32]

Articles of this sort had their effect and were used by von Puttkamer to force a renewal of the Socialist Law in the Reichstag, because, as he argued, if stringent measures were not taken against the socialists, then 'throne, altar, and *Geldsack*' would fall under the social revolution as Wichmann claimed. The value of such articles cannot be overestimated because German authorities interested in suppressing socialism could show, printed in black and white, what could be expected if the socialists and anarchists were allowed to multiply.[33]

The anarchist cell organisation, which had been developing in Germany, was broken up in December 1880 when police arrested 44 members in Darmstadt, Bessingen, Bockenheim, Lechhausen, Offenbach, Augsburg, Pforzheim, Mannheim, Hanau, and other places. An interesting sidelight of the case were the fantastic stories which were concocted by the press, some of which were actually believed by the police. It was assumed by the Berlin police that an attempt would be made to throw a bomb from the gallery of the Reichstag down onto the deputies while they were in session. It was also believed that someone would try to blow up the police station in which the records of the accused were stored. Police investigation, however, did not turn up any evidence to substantiate these wild claims. All of the paraphernalia of a typical anarchist trial was introduced as evidence to condemn the 15 who were accused of high treason: letters written in invisible ink, secret printing presses, revolvers, ropes, cipher writing, poison, rifles, daggers, dynamite cartridges, sulphuric acid, strychnine and other assorted destructive chemicals, poems glorifying dynamite, and issues of *Freiheit*. The person the judges would like to have had on trial was Johann Most, because his name cropped up more often than any other at the trial. Most and his newspaper *Freiheit*, were the primary reasons behind the trial: thus Most was probably correct when he claimed that his name was mentioned in every treason trial in Germany and Austria during this period.[34] It.was not empty bragging when Most made such a statement. During the decade of the 1880s his name was known to most German officials as well as a household word synonymous with violence. During the period of the Socialist Law Most was better known than some of the less significant members of the SPD who have since been enshrined.[35]

The German scene in the decade of the 1880s is a muddled and confused one. The outward impression is that the government wanted to suppress the anarchists completely, yet there is evidence to demonstrate that when the anarchists reached a low point, the German government itself subsidised the movement through *agents provocateurs*. The cases of Wichmann and Wolf who wrote for *Freiheit* have already been referred to above. In 1881 the merchant Elias Schmidt from Dresden was hired by the Dresden *Kriminalrat* Weller and Kommissar Paul, as well as Police Inspector Kaltenbach in Mülhausen. Schmidt was sent to Switzerland and in Zürich he established an assassination fund for the purpose of carrying out acts of 'propaganda by deed' in Germany. The first 20 francs donated to the fund were given by Schmidt which came from police funds. He was not exposed as a police agent until November 1882. The plumber Weiss, from Dresden, who in Liestal bei Basel in Switzerland distributed anarchist literature glorifying robbery, murder, and 'propaganda by deed', was also, like Schmidt, a paid police agent.[36]

In a personal memorandum early in April 1881, Bismarck noted delightedly that the English were going to do something about Most for his story on the death of Alexander II. He hoped that they would impose more stringent measures against *Freiheit* and the followers of Most in England.[37] On the other hand one the English got *Freiheit* on the run for the publication of an article glorifying the assassination of Lord Cavendish, forcing the paper to leave England for Switzerland, there is considerable evidence to show that the Berlin police may have paid for the printing of *Freiheit*. During the period that *Freiheit* was in Switzerland the Berlin police made considerable use of a cabinet-maker named Karl Schröder whom they had hired in 1881 as a spy. He was paid 250 marks a month. His duties were to gather socialist and anarchist literature in Switzerland which he mailed to von Madai in Berlin; he was also to attend socialist and anarchist meetings and send accounts of these meetings to Berlin, as well as the names of anyone involved in the smuggling of anarchist or socialist literature into Germany. In Switzerland Schröder came in close association with many of the leaders of the German-speaking anarchist movement including Josef Peukert, Hermann Stellmacher, Josef Kaufmann, Friedrich Kennel, and Anton Kammerer. He also wrote to Julius Schwab in New York, John Neve and others. Schröder was able to supply Berlin with information which led to the arrest of some anarchists in Germany, but more important was his ability to infiltrate the *Freiheit* organisation in Switzerland, where he had the confidence of both anarchists and socialists, not being exposed until late in 1887.[38]

Another spy active in Switzerland was the foundry moulder Christian Haupt, born in Bernburg (Anhalt). He was employed by Adolf Hermann Krüger in 1880 and after 1884 worked for the Polizeirat of the Berlin Political Police, Gustav von Hake. Fricke maintains that Haupt was a Social Democrat with anarchist tendencies. He entered the service of the Berlin police in 1880 because he hated Bismarck and wanted to register a protest against the Socialist Law, by being a spy for the Social Democrats within the Berlin police system, but once he got into the service of the police he sank deeper and deeper into police activities and spied on, and turned in many of his former comrades. He started out at a salary of 100 marks a month but quickly rose to 200 marks a month. Haupt and Schröder were exposed as spies at the same time. The total cost of the services of Haupt and Schröder to Germany in wages alone was 24,000 marks, of which Schröder received 10,000 marks and Haupt 14,000.[39]

If the German police had been intent on putting *Freiheit* out of business or stopping the flow of the newspaper into Germany, they more than likely could have accomplished either goal with the help of the spies they had within the *Freiheit* organisation. It seems that after 1881 the only time that the German police moved with force against *Freiheit* or the cells in Germany was to capture an important person in the structure. One thing appears certain; the police in Germany seemed to be able to regulate, at a desired level, the amount of anarchism they wished to have in Germany. To a great extent they were able to control the flow of *Freiheit* into Germany; the notable exception being the overland route through Belgium headed by John Neve. The German government appeared to operate on the premise that a little anarchism was good, as long as it was not permitted to get out of hand. Some anarchism was necessary to keep Puttkamer's 'Zittersack' full for presentation to the Reichstag and the country whenever the debate came up on the renewal of the Socialist Law. There can be no doubt that the German government used the actions of the anarchists to enforce stringent measures against the socialists.

'Propaganda by deed' played an important role in the German movement of the 1880s. It had an obvious appeal to Johann Most. Late in 1880 articles started to appear in *Freiheit* which were intended to instill in the readers the value of terrorism and 'propaganda by deed' often giving explicit instructions in the manufacture and use of explosives including dynamite and nitroglycerin. Detailed instructions were also given on how to use fire, poison, and knives in the most effective way.[40] Most told his readers that 'the revolution has no respect for things or people who are connected with the existing system of robbery and murder. Such people are condemned and will sooner or later receive their just fate'.[41] He called for the destruction of the means of communication, the dynamiting of homes, offices, churches, stores, and factories, saying that 'lead and dynamite, poison and knives are the weapons with which our brothers will open the skirmish'.[42] 'All methods are justified to achieve the social revolution'.[43] And 'it was time for the atonement of the crimes committed against society using the principle of "an eye for an eye" '.[44] To people of the temperament of Hödel and Nobiling living in Germany, Most advised 'Ready, aim, fire'.[45]

Most warned the German aristocracy that:

> Every prince will find his Brutus. Poison on the table of the gourmet will cancel out his debt. Dynamite will explode in the splendid, rubber tyred, coaches of the aristocracy and bourgeois as they pull up to the opera. Death will await them, both by day and by night, on all roads and footpaths and even in their homes, lurking in a thousand different forms.[46]

> Shake you dogs, you blood suckers, you violators of young girls, you murderers and executioners – the day of retribution, the day of vengeance draws near.[47]

Most said quite frankly:

> We will murder those who must be killed in order to be free . . . We do not dispute over whether it is right or wrong. Say what you will, do what you do, but the victor is right. Comrades of 'Freiheit', we say murder the murderers. Rescue mankind through blood, iron, poison, and dynamite.[48]

> We believe once and for all in powder and lead, poison, knives, dynamite, and fire. With these the people will be able to argue more loudly and stronger; with these our goals will be attained more surely and quickly.[49]

The columns of *Freiheit* for the period from late 1880 through July 1885 are literally full of articles urging workers on to perform acts of 'propaganda by deed'. Much of the information contained in these articles on the production and deployment of bombs, explosives, poison, knives and so forth were incorporated into a 74-page book by Most entitled *Revolutionäre Kriegswissenschaft: Ein Handbüchlein zur Anleitung betreffend Gebrauches und Herstellung von Nitroglyzerin, Dynamit, Schiessbaumwolle, Knallquecksilber, Bomben, Brandsätzen, Giften, usw.*[50]

Space does not permit a detailing of anarchist attempts at 'propaganda by deed' undertaken by Hermann Stellmacher, Anton Kammerer, Michael Kumics, and others. These henious crimes had the effect of turning the workers against 'propaganda by deed'. Another effect of the adoption of 'propaganda by deed' was the suppression of anarchism in both Switzerland and Austria which had served as bases for the German movement. In general the articles in *Freiheit* advocating violence and terrorism had the effect of frightening the bourgeois and aristocratic elements of society, at whom most of the articles were aimed. These segments of society possessed the power to demand protection and repressive measures against such fanaticism. Being frightened out of their wits they were not about to quibble over the differences between the SPD and the anarchists. The violent articles in *Freiheit* were voraciously devoured by the police and read with great trepidation by the people at whom the crimes were aimed. The government reaped great propaganda benefits as well by releasing to the press alleged attempts against the life of the aged Emperor. It did not take many terrorist acts to create a general atmosphere of uneasiness among the people who were the intended victims of the crimes – those in positions of authority or those who possessed substantial amounts of material goods. The mayor's home in Walsenhausen was completely demolished by two bombs; two policemen were shot in Wattenscheid; in Erfeld a factory owner was stabbed to death. These were not the only crimes which took place. Some which occurred and which were planned actually shocked the imagination of everyone.

August Reinsdorf hatched a number of grandiose plans to carry out acts of 'propaganda by deed'. For example late in July 1880 he went to Berlin to kill the Berlin Police President von Madai.[51] In September of that same year he wrote to Most of a plan he had to blow up the Reichstag building while the Reichstag was in session. The plan called for Reinsdorf to dig a tunnel under the building and set charges at the points of maximum stress. If the charges could be placed at these critical places the entire structure would be brought down because, as Reinsdorf pointed out, much of the building was only a façade, with only a few points supporting the weight of the structure. This plan and that of his attempt to kill von Madai were relayed to the Berlin police by the spy Oskar Neumann in London, and Reinsdorf was quickly apprehended on 14 November 1880 in the vicinity of von Madai's home carrying a long dagger and was sentenced to three months in prison.[52]

Reinsdorf planned other attentats, but the most spectacular was his plan to set off an explosion at the dedication of the Niederwald Monument on 28 September 1883. All of the celebrities of the reign of Wilhelm I were to be assembled at the dedication including the Emperor himself; his son the Crown Prince ('Unser Fritz'); His Nephew Wilhelm the 'Red Prince'; Prince Albrecht of Prussia; the King of Saxony; the Grand Duke of Baden; the Grand Duke of Hesse-Darmstadt; Prince Luitpold of Bavaria; von Moltke; Bismarck; the surviving military leaders of Königgrätz, Wörth, Mars-la-Tour, Sedan and Metz, as well as numerous other members of the aristocracy, government officials, and dignitaries. Reinsdorf intended to place a charge of dynamite which would kill as many of them as possible, however, because of a leg injury he was unable to carry out the plan himself and had to rely on two accomplices who were completely inept and bungled the job.

It was not until 11 January 1884 that Reinsdorf was arrested for questioning on the dynamite explosion which had occurred at the Police Station in Frankfurt a/M on 29 October 1883. The remainder of Reinsdorf's small Elberfeld circle were also rounded up. As each member of the group was arrested it was given the usual publicity. Now the stage was set. All of Germany had been made aware of the explosion which had occurred in Frankfurt and the several explosions which had taken place in the Elberfeld area in the summer of 1883. The police had gathered the cast, each of whom was given full press coverage as they were apprehended.

Information on the attempt to kill the Emperor at the dedication of the Niederwald monument was first made public on 24 April 1884. It had been withheld by Bismarck, Wilhelm I, and Puttkamer until the proper time. On 23 April Wilhelm I wrote to Minister of the Interior Puttkamer that they were about to make political capital out of the Niederwald attempt in conjunction with the debate on the renewal of the Socialist Law in May 1884. The dramatic manner in which the renewal of the Socialist Law and the passage of the Dynamite Law was accomplished resulted in a wave of hysteria which swept across Germany, especially among the aristocracy and the bourgeois who had been frightened by Most's propaganda. Now they had their worst fears reinforced by the public exposure of Reinsdorf and his group.[53]

The trial of the Niederwald conspirators opened in Leipzig on Monday, 15 December 1884. The eight defendants were charged with the explosions which had taken place in the Wilhemsen Restaurant, the dynamiting of the Police Headquarters in Frankfurt a/M, the explosion at the *Festhalle* in Rüdesheim, and the attempt on the life of the Emperor at the unveiling of the Niederwald monument. There were 54 witnesses. The chief Crown witness was the weaver Palm, a police spy, who testified that he knew in advance of the Wilhelmsen bombing and of the attempt that was going to occur at the Niederwald. Reinsdorf tried to shield, rather than incriminate his accomplices. He put on an admirable show admitting that he had planned the Niederwald attempt, regretting his inability to carry it out himself because of an injured ankle.[54] He also admitted to being associated with Hödel.

Later in the trial, after the sentence had been handed down, Reinsdorf responded to the remarks of the judge that the hand of providence had saved the Emperor from death.

> I tell you the bungling hand of Rupsch saved him. I am sorry to say that I had no one else at my disposal. The only thing I have to regret is that the attempt failed . . . In the factories the workers are used for the benefit of the stockholders. These honest christians swindle the working people out of

half of what they earn. My lawyer wanted to save my head, but for a hunted proletarian as myself, the quickest death is the best.[55]

He went on to point out that the excessive use of house searches by the German police and the paying of police spies such as Palm and Weidenmüller demonstrated how corrupt society had become. He told how Police Commissioner Gottschalk, who had employed Palm and Weidenmüller, knew in advance of the Niederwald attempt and did nothing to stop it. Reinsdorf claimed that it was Gottschalk who was responsible for Küchler being on trial because he had instructed Rupsch to carry out the plan alone, but when Palm gave Küchler 40 marks there was enough money for Küchler to go along and keep an eye on the younger Rupsch. Reinsdorf maintained that the use by the police of such people as Palm was sufficient evidence of the decadence and corruption of society: 'against such corruption are not our deeds justified?' 'If I had ten heads I would offer them gladly and lay them on the block for the cause of anarchism.'[56] He ended his moving speech with 'The social revolution will never be abandoned, even if there are a hundred tribunals. The people will one day have enough dynamite to blow up all of you and every other member of the bourgeois.'[57]

For his part in the Niederwald attempt Reinsdorf was beheaded on 7 February 1885. His last words were 'I die for humanity, down with barbarism, long live anarchism.'

The murder of the Frankfurt Police Chief Rumpf on 13 January 1885 can best be thought of as a corollary to the Niederwald attempt. Most called for revenge to atone for the sentences handed down by the tribunal in Leipzig. It was never proven conclusively that Julius Lieske murdered Rumpf. The most incriminating evidence against him was again, as in other trials, paid police informers. He maintained his innocence until he was put to death. The importance of Lieske's trial for the murder of Rumpf is that it helped to bring into the open the widening split in the German anarchist movement. In the *Freiheit*, Most claimed that Rumpf had been condemned and ordered killed by the command of an executive committee.[58] *Le Révolté* replied by asking if the German anarchists were still institutionalised.[59] *Der Rebell* answered *Freiheit* by saying that the German anarchists did not follow the orders of any executive committee, but undertook such ventures on individual initiative. Such acts were spontaneous and committed at the discretion of the individual and were not influenced by other members, groups, or executive committees. *Der Rebell* maintained that they sought to achieve the complete suppression of all authority and for that reason would never acknowledge that an executive committee had the right to order anything.[60]

These statements point out the disparity of views in the German anarchist camp, which were eventually going to shatter what solidarity the movement had.

The arrest of John Neve on 21 February 1887, a central figure in the German anarchist movement of the 1880s, assured that the wounds of the

Bruderkrieg would never be healed. His arrest was the catalyst which triggered an eruption in the German anarchist movement that had been seething since 1884. The long simmering pot boiled over extinguishing what flame remained in the movement. The passionate exchange of charges and counter-charges which followed the arrest of Neve consumed what energy remained in the movement when it could least afford it, as well as discrediting the leadership of the movement. His arrest was a blow to the movement in another respect, because it was impossible to replace him with an equally competent and dedicated person. The movement was running out of men of his stature and new men of talent were not being recruited to replace those lost. The arrest of Neve cut off the key route by which literature and explosives were smuggled into Germany and distributed there. It brought the *Bruderkrieg* to a climatic struggle in which the leaders of the movement fell victim to the senseless exchange of vile allegations.

For all practical purposes the early German anarchist movement was dead by late 1887. Nevertheless it was not in the best interest of the German government to have anarchism completely downtrodden, because it would eliminate an important whipping boy who could be brought out as evidence of the need for more stringent measures against the anarchists and socialists. When it became apparent that the German anarchists did not plan to send a delegate to the anarchist congress being held in Verviers on 21 April 1889, the Chief of Police in Elberfeld, Kammhoff, informed the Minister of the Interior, Ludwig Herrfurth, that he had sent an agent to the meeting representing the German anarchists. This person sent by Kammhoff was the only German delegate at the congress. He presented a plan at the meeting to assassinate the German Kaiser.[61] In effect an artificial anarchist threat was created where none existed. That is not to say that anarchist attempts at 'propaganda by deed' were no longer carried out in Germany, they were and would be for several decades, but these acts were only residual effects of the old movement because the new movement, which was finding its footing around 1890, was not committed to a policy of 'propaganda by deed', but none the less they had to live with the reputation that the old movement had given to anarchism.

Why did the early German anarchist movement wane in the late 1880s? One reason is the *Bruderkrieg* which resulted in the loss of the leadership of the movement, as well as diminished connections that the nerve center in London had with the continent. Another factor was the adverse effect of 'propaganda by deed' which undermined anarchist appeal to the mass of German workers. Still another reason was the fact that in the period 1830–90 Germany had become an industrialised nation. The great majority of the followers of anarchism came from the handicraft occupation which by the late 1880s were either being absorbed into industry or were being replaced by machines.

The adoption of a policy of violence and 'propaganda by deed' on the part of the anarchists insured the renewal of the Socialist Law as well as the passage of more stringent measures against the use of dynamite. The adoption of 'propaganda by deed' was soon followed by the introduction of Bismarck's program of State Socialism designed to wean the workers away from socialism and anarchism. Although the connection is perhaps tenuous, it should be noted that Bismarck did not push for such legislation until the stepped-up campaign of terrorism and violence on the part of the anarchists.

The German anarchists also discredited the Social Democratic Party. The public was confused over the difference between the Social Democratic Party and the anarchists, and Bismarck and other public officials capitalised on the confusion, using it to suppress the SPD. By the end of the 1880s the Social Democratic Party was still in the process of attempting to clarify the differences between themselves and the anarchists, with mixed results. They were not able to accomplish this until the decade of the 1890s.

The anarchists played a role in forcing the Social Democratic Party into supporting a policy of parliamentarianism that it continued to follow down to the outbreak of the First World War; a policy which concentrated on capturing as many seats as possible in the Reichstag. Unfortunately, such a policy was a futile one from the start, for under the existing system of government in Germany the Social Democratic Party had no prospect of ever playing an important role in the government of the Reich. Another factor which should be stressed was the development of a secret police force by Bismarck which came into being largely as a result of anarchist activities. This set a precedent in Germany for various types of secret paramilitary police forces which reached their culmination in the Third Reich.

As a force, the anarchists in Germany exerted power all out of proportion to their numbers. Prior to 1890 they achieved little in the way of success, in numerical strength, but nevertheless they aroused sufficient anxiety to bring into being repressive legislation which restricted the activities of everyone interested in reforming the monarchial system in Germany. Credit for improving the social conditions of the poor in Germany is usually given to either the monarchial government or the socialists, depending on one's point of view. If credit is to be given, some of it must go to anarchists, who though unsuccessful in their immediate objectives of creating a new society either by revolutionary or peaceful means, nevertheless made it apparent to the government that concessions had to be made to assuage the masses.

Even though there were differences of opinion among the German anarchist groups, there was nevertheless general agreement that social conditions in Germany needed to be changed. They were of the opinion that meaningful reforms could not be accomplished through parliamentary means. In this respect, perhaps, the anarchists were able to see more clearly than the Social Democrats that Germany could not be reformed by electing representatives to the *Reichstag*. The system needed to be changed, but the anarchists offered no feasible alternatives.

The actions of Bismarck and the German government in the period under study are anything but admirable. Surely one could not agree with the methods and tactics of the anarchists, but on the other hand neither should the policy followed by the German government be condoned. Bismarck emerges from this study greatly tarnished; he rigged the Nobiling affair to make it appear that the Social Democratic Party was responsible for the assassination attempt; he hired numerous spies who wrote inflammatory articles for anarchist newspapers, articles which were introduced as evidence for the necessity of renewing the Socialist Law; he made use of *agents provocateurs* to insure that the level of anarchist activity would be maintained at a level necessary to insure the continuance of repressive measures against the socialists. It was in the interest of Bismarck and the German government always to maintain the visible appearance of a potential anarchist threat. The bourgeoisie and the aristocracy, at whom the anarchist threats were directed, were frightened by the violence preached in the columns of the anarchist newspapers and were willing to accede to practically anything to insure their own safety. Bismarck realised this and played on their fears, by creating an artificial anarchist threat.

There are many historians who praise the accomplishments of Bismarck. They readily point out that he was able to avoid a general European war after 1871, but how do you explain his domestic policy, which was based on lies, duplicity and suppression. How do you rationalise using a spy to infiltrate an anarchist meeting for the apparent purpose of obtaining information that a crime is going to be committed, and then once you have the knowledge not only do nothing stop it, but in fact assign agents who assist in the preparations for the crime to insure that it would be carried out so as to make use of the propaganda value that could be obtained from it? Is there any way to give a satisfactory explanation of why a government should subsidise a man through a spy, to take part in a plot to kill the head of state, and then put him on trial and execute him as an example? Should not a responsible government put down immediately any threat to its citizens to insure their peace of mind, rather than create an artificial threat to keep them in a state of uneasiness?

Much has been written about Bismarck, and there are thousands of volumes which try to explain what happened to Germany in the twentieth century. One theme, which runs through much of this literature, is that Bismarck had the Reich on the proper course and William II steered it onto the shoals. One thing that is wrong with this line of reasoning is that Bismarck, before his fall from power, created the image of the Emperor and established the foundation stones on which the Reich was to be built in the next two and a half decades. If William II possessed more power than one man should have, it was to Bismarck that he owed his omnipotence. Bismarck's selection of the foundation stones of the Reich was unfortunate as his dealings with the anarchists demonstrate, because here he followed a deliberate policy of lies, duplicity and suppression of all opposition. This is not a firm basis on which to develop a government. Perhaps Bismarck was able to avoid a general European war, but what did his policies do to Germany?

Bismarck ran a tight ship and steered a straight course, but the German ship of state foundered in the storm of the First World War; it came unglued and attempts to put it back together in the Weimar period ended in failure, followed by dictatorship. There are many factors involved in the failure of the Weimar Republic, but one stands out: the inability of the German electorate and politicians to replace the monarchy with a viable form of government. The immaturity of those in political life played a part in this because power was thrust into the hands of those who were not prepared to deal with it. The real cause of the failure of the political immaturity of the Weimar period is to be found in the decades of the 1870s and 1880s. At this critical juncture in German development, Bismarck seized upon opportunities presented to him by the anarchists to suppress political life, especially the Social Democratic Party, forcing them to follow a policy of parliamentarianism. This policy was followed by the SPD to the outbreak of the First World War. The goals of the Social Democratic Party were unrealistic because they did not come to grips with the essential problem that faced Germany – the concentration of power in the hands of the Emperor.

NOTES

1. For example see G. D. H. Cole, *Socialist Thought, Marxism and Anarchism, 1850–1890* (London, 1961) p. 330; *Der Grosse Brockhaus* Vol. I (Wiesbaden, 1953) p. 261; J. Joll, *The Anarchists* (London, 1964) p. 140; B. W. Tuchman, *The Proud Tower: A Portrait of the World Before the War, 1890–1914* (New York, 1967) p. 119; *Handwörterbuch der Staatswissenschaft*, 4th ed. Vol. I (Jena, 1924) p. 290; *La Grande Enclopédie* Vol. II (Paris, o.t.) p. 953.
2. *Le Révolté* (10 December 1881).
3. J. Most, *August Reinsdorf* (New York, 1885) p. 13.
4. Quoted in M. Nettlau, *Anarchisten und Sozialrevolutionäre* (Berlin, 1931) p. 131f.
5. *Arbeiter Zeitung*, 1 (15 July 1876).
6. Quoted in *Le Révolté* (10 December 1881).
7. Most, p. 28f.
8. A. R. Carlson, *Anarchism in Germany* (Metuchen, 1972) p. 115f.
9. Brandenburgisches Landeshauptarchiv Potsdam, Pr. Br. Rep. 30 Berlin C, Tit. 94, Lit. A., No. 248 (8626), Hödel Attentat, Folder 108.
10. Staatsarchiv Potsdam (Brandenburgisches Landeshauptarchiv Potsdam) Acta der Königlichen Polizei Präsidii zu Berlin, Geheime Präsidial-Registratur, Pr. Br. Rep. 30 Berlin C, Tit. 94, Lit. A., No. 242, Nobiling-Attentat, vol. IV (8616), Folder 33. Hereafter cited as: Brandenburgisches Landeshauptarchiv Potsdam, etc.
11. Ibid., vol. I (8613) Folders 154–5.
12. Ibid., vol. I (8613) Folder 154.
13. Ibid., vol. I (8613) Folder 155. The Social Democrat Paul Dentler died on 24 April 1878, which means that Werner probably wrote the letter sometime between 6 and 13 June, or after Nobiling's attempt.
14. Brandenburgisches Landeshauptarchiv Potsdam, Pr. Br. Rep. 30 Berlin C, Tit. 94, Lit. A., Hödel-Attentat, Folders 108–10. After Werner's arrest in Berlin on 25 December 1879, in connection with the publication of *Der Kampf, Der*

Sozialdemokrat (18 January 1880), carried an article which said that Werner had been breaking laws for years and that the police had done nothing about it. The article also asserted that Werner's name was prominently mentioned in the documents concerning the Hödel attempt. The writer of the article claimed that the police did not arrest him at the time because they were waiting for Werner to commit a serious crime to press for more repressive measures in the Reichstag. Rudolf Rocker, *Johann Most*, S. 113, said that this charge was baseless. An examination of the documents proves that Rocker was wrong and substantiates the article in *Der Sozialdemokrat*, but they do not contain any clue why Werner was not arrested. The implication of the article in *Der Sozialdemokrat* is that Werner was an unwitting tool of police repression. One fact not explained by the article is their source of information. It would appear that either the Social Democrats had a spy in the government who had access to the *Geheime Präsidial-Registratur* which contained the Hödel documents, or that the writer of the article made a brilliant assumption that Werner's name figured prominently in the documents. However, the fact remains that there was sufficient evidence connecting Werner with Hödel and Nobiling that he should have been, at the least, picked up and questioned by police, but they chose to do nothing. Reinsdorf claimed that the reason the Berlin police did not arrest Werner at the time was because they did not know his whereabouts, a story that is difficult to believe.

15. M. Aranyossi, *Leo Frankel* (East Berlin, 1957) pp. 116–40, 390. Often times his name appears as Fränkel; however, for the sake of consistency I have used it as does his biographer.

16. There is also evidence stating that the Berlin police were interested in a man named Bernstein who had been seen associating with Nobiling. Reinsdorf at this time was in Berlin so it is very possible that the Bernstein reported to the Berlin police was Reinsdorf. On this point see: Brandenburgisches Landeshauptarchiv Potsdam, Pr. Br. Rep. 30 Berlin C, Tit. 94, Lit. A., No. 242, Nobiling-Attentat, vol. I (8613) Folders 87–8.

17. Another piece of information which Pinday is supposed to have allowed to leak out to police agents in Switzerland, where he was living in exile after the Commune, is that Leo Frankel masterminded the Nobiling attempt on William I. More than likely this piece of information was a pure fabrication thought up by some police informer. But it is possible that Pinday, who was an anarchist, let the information out to discredit Frankel who was a Marxist. However, this explanation does not seem plausible if they continued to correspond. But no police agent in Switzerland ever saw the letter from Frankel to Pinday; they only knew of its contents indirectly from hearing Pinday talk. Perhaps there never was a letter. Probably he knew that whatever he said was bound to end up in the police records so he included the name Frankel to confuse the police. Ibid. vol. I (8613) Folders 154–5.

18. *Avant-Garde* (7 October 1878).

19. Brandenburgisches Landeshauptarchiv Potsdam, Pr. Br. Rep. 30 Berlin C,Tit. A., No. 242, Nobiling-Attentat, vol. III (8615) Folder 84 contains a printed copy of the telegram bearing the number 2512 assigned to it by the Wolff Telegraph Bureau and the date 3 June 1878. Folder 10 contains a handwritten copy of the telegram with no identification number assigned to it and it is dated 2 June 1878, so it is assumed that the handwritten copy is the original.

20. A. Bebel, *Aus meinem Leben* (East Berlin, 1964) pp. 593–4.

21. Ibid., p. 594; Bernstein, p. 365.

22. Bernstein, p. 365.

23. For example see: W. Pack, *Das parlamentarische Ringen* (Düsseldorf, 1961) p. 15;

E. Eyck, *Bismarck and the German Empire* (New York, 1964) p. 230f; W. Richter, *Bismarck* (New York, 1965) p. 219.

24. Brandenburgisches Landeshauptarchiv Potsdam, Pr. Br. Rep. 30 Berlin C, Tit. 94, Lit. A., No. 242, Nobiling Attentat, vol. III (8615) Folders 11–12. Naturally Fritzsche denied that he knew Nobiling. Evidently the story leaked out though and Fritzsche felt obligated to give a public denial. In the *Volks-Zeitung*, 164 (16 July 1878) Fritzsche said that he did not know Nobiling and that he had not participated in any meeting with Nobiling on the theme of 'Schutzzoll und Freihandel', as Nobiling claimed. According to an account which appeared in the *Berliner Tageblatt*, 157 (7 July 1878) such a meeting had taken place in the late fall of 1877. It was held in the Andreasgarten in the Andreasstrasse and the meeting ended with Nobiling speaking on the glories of the Paris Commune. Fritzsche replied in the *Volks-Zeitung*, 164 (16 July 1878) that, if someone had gotten up from the audience to speak and announced himself as Dr Nobiling, the title doctor would have stood out in a workers' meeting and he would have remembered it. More than likely Nobiling did, as he claimed, have some association with Fritzsche, but perhaps he was more of a thorn in his side than anything else.

25. Bucher was *Vortragender Rat* in the Foreign Office, 1864–86. The part he played for Bismarck in the Hohenzollern candidacy has been treated in detail by R. H. Lord, *The Origins of the War of 1870* (Cambridge, Mass., 1924); and L. D. Steefel, *Bismarck and the Hohenzollern Candidacy and the Origins of the War of 1870* (Cambridge, Mass., 1962) and need not be repeated here. Bismarck, according to Holstein, regarded Bucher as a tool and 'used him to carry out all kinds of strictly confidential and personal business'. N. Rich and M. H. Fisher, *The Holstein Papers*, vol. I, Memoirs (Cambridge, 1955) p. 52f. For the Congress of Berlin, which convened less than two weeks after the Nobiling attempt, Bismarck named Bucher the Senior Counsellor of the Political Division of the Foreign Office. N. Rich, *Friedrich von Holstein: Politics and Diplomacy in the Era of Bismarck and William II*, vol. I (Cambridge, 1965) p. 101f. Bucher resigned when Herbert Bismarck became Under State Secretary in 1885. Herbert corrected some of Bucher's work in such a rude way that Bucher demanded his release which was granted but Prince Bismarck saw to it that Bucher received a handsome pension of 2,000 marks a year. Later in life Bismarck sought, and received, the services of Bucher in writing his memoirs. Ibid., p. 122; Rich and Fisher, vol. I, p. 68. There can be no doubt that Bismarck used and trusted Bucher. Erick Eyck relates that Bucher was one of the few persons for whom Bismarck felt something like friendship and that Bucher knew more of Bismarck's most intimate secrets than any other man. Eyck, p. 164. The obvious question now has to be asked: was the appointment of Bucher as Senior Counsellor in the Political Division in the Foreign Office a reward for services performed in Nobiling affair? The question has to remain open: there is no answer, but the fact remains that the original draft of the Wolff telegram is in Bucher's handwriting which means that it had to come from Bismarck.

26. Brandenburgisches Landeshauptarchiv Potsdam, Pr. Br. Rep. 30 Berlin C, Tit. 94, Lit. A., No. 242, Nobiling-Attentat, vol. III (8615) Folder 11.

27. Brandenburgisches Landeshauptarchiv Potsdam, Pr. Br. Rep. 30 Berlin C, Tit. 94, Lit. S., Nr. I (13,087), Folders 137, 287; vol. II (13,088) Folders 46, 106; Anonymus, *Sozialismus und Anarchismus in Europa und Nordamerika während der Jahre 1883–1886* (Berlin, 1887) p. 38; Bismarck, Die gesammelten Werke, vol. 6 c (1871–90) p. 210.

28. D. Fricke, *Bismarcks Prätorianer: Die Berliner politische Polizei im Kampf gegen die deutsche Arbeiterbewegung 1871–1898* (East Berlin, 1962) p. 393, gives

Wichmann's first initial as A., but J. Jensen, *Presse und politische Polizei* (Hannover, 1966) p. 70 prints a facsimile of the first page of Wichmann's (unpublished) memoirs, *Um Ehre, Recht und Wahrheit oder wahre und Erwiesene Erlebnisse des damaligen Geheimpolizisten W. Wichmann*. On this basis I have used W.

29. Laufenburg, *Geschichte der Arbeiterbewegung im Hamburg* (Hamburg, 1931) vol. II, p. 230; I. Auer, *Nach zehn Jahren: Material und Glossen zur Geschichte des Sozialistengesetzes* (Nuremburg, 1913) p. 183; Jensen, p. 71; E. Ernst, *Polizeispitzeleien und Ausnahmegesetze 1878–1910* (Berlin, 1911) p. 26; R. Lipinski, *Die Sozialdemokratie von ihren Anfängen bis zu Gegenwart* (Berlin, 1928) vol. II, p. 97f. Engels was rewarded for his service with the *Kgl. Adlerorden 4. Klasse* in 1881, and the *Roter Adlerorden 4. Klasse* in 1904. Jensen, p. 180.

30. *Freiheit*, 46 (13 November 1880) p. 4.

31. Ibid., 23 (4 June 1881) p. 4.

32. Ibid., 39 (24 September 1881) p. 2.

33. Wichmann, like Wolf, received no reward for his services. The decorations were reserved for the superiors for whom they worked. The Altona workers eventually discovered that Wichmann was a spy, and being of no further use to the Berlin police he was dismissed without a pension or any other form of compensation. Like Wolf, Wichmann, too, wrote his memoirs, but once again as in the case of Wolf, they were never published. It cannot be established that he was intimidated by the Berlin police, or if they paid him not to publish them, but nevertheless the handwritten copy of his memoirs, *Ehre, Recht und Wahrheit oder wahre und erwiesene Erlebnisse des damaligen Geheimpolizisten W. Wichmann*, is found in Akten des Senats der Freien und Hansestadt, Staatsarchiv, Hamburg. How did it get there?

34. Hessisches Hauptstaatsarchiv Wiesbaden, 407 Polizeipräsidium Frankfurt, 174 'Untersuchung gegen den Sozialdemokraten Joseph Breuder und Genossen in Frankfurt a.M. wegen Hochverrats, 1880–1881'; G. Künzel (ed.), *Der erste Hochverrathsprozess vor dem Reichsgericht* (Leipzig, 1881) pp. 11–28, 92–5, 101–18; 'Geschichte der Freiheit', *Der Sozialist*, No. 43 (24 October 1896) p. 255.

35. In Chemnitz early in 1880 the police, in a search to Julius Vahlteich's (1839–1915) house, found the entire first quarter of *Freiheit* including the first number. R. Strauss and K. Finsterbusch, *Die Chemnitzer Arbeiterbewegung unter dem Sozialistengesetz* (East Berlin, 1954) pp. 43–6; one file on Most, which contains some interesting material, but nothing new, is in Staatsarchiv Ludwigsburg, 664, *Die Freiheit*; another file, which contains nothing new, but which reveals the significance contemporary officials attached to Most, is in Hessisches Hauptstaatsarchiv Wiesbaden, 407 Polizeipräsidium Frankfurt, 177 Sozialdemokratisches Organ *Die Freiheit* von Johann Most. Intus: Verschiedene Zeitungsexemplare, 1879–1894; a good example of police interest in the activities of Most in England and the United States is found in Geheimes Staatsarchiv Munich, Ministerial-Extradiction 1921 II, Deutsches Reich, Abteilung West I, Tit. II Polizeiwesen A, Sozialdemokratie und Anarchismus, MA 76512, 'Die sozialdemokratische und anarchistische Bewegung' Folders 46–56, 94–110.

36. Lipinski, vol. II, p. 99; Ernst, p. 20f.

37. Bismarck, vol. 6 c, p. 210f.

38. Fricke, p. 235. Schröder, representing Lausanne, took part in a high level conference in Bern on 18 June 1882. The purpose of the conference was to discuss ways to improve the smuggling of *Freiheit* into Germany and Austria. Others present were: Kennel (Freiburg), Otter (Vevey), Schmelzbach (Zürich), Heilmann (Biel), Deschner and Czerkauer. Brandenburgisches Landeshauptarchiv Potsdam, Pr. Br. Rep. 30 Berlin C., Polizeipräsidium, Tit. 94, Lit. S., Nr. 442, vol.

9 (12,808), 'Die politische Zustände in der Schweiz 1882'.
39. Ernst, p. 19; Langhard, p. 318. On 16 December 1901, Haupt, who at the time was living in Buenos Aires, prepared a memorandum, at the request of Julius Mottler, detailing his activities as a police spy. This memorandum is preserved today among Mottler's papers in the International Institute of Social History in Amsterdam. Haupt was a miserable man for having betrayed his former friends. Fricke, p. 158.
40. A partial listing of articles of this nature contained in *Freiheit* is as follows: 'Durch Terrorismus zur Freiheit', 50 (11 December 1880) p. 1; P. Knauer, 'Die Taktik der revolutionaeren Arbeiter-Partei', 29 (10 July 1881) p. 1; E. Nathan-Ganz, 'Die Chemie und die Revolution', 33 (13 August 1881) p. 2; Publicca, 'Die Propaganda durch die That', 42 (15 October 1881) p. 1; 'Die Propaganda durch die That', 38 (11 November 1882) p. 2; 'Wissenschaftliche Winke', 3 (20 January 1883) p. 3f. and 5 (9 February 1883) p. 1f.; 'Praktische Winke', 15 (14 April 1883) p. 1; 'Dynamit', 18 (5 May 1883) p. 1; 'Ein Salon-Blatt über Dynamitpolitik', 19 (12 May 1883) p. 1f.; 'Das Nitroglyzerin', 26 (30 June 1883) p. 1f.; 'Zur Propaganda der That', 47 (24 November 1883) p. 1f.; 'Revolutionäre Kriegskunst', No. 52 (29 December 1883) p. 2; 'Zur propaganda der That', 2 (12 January 1884) p. 1; 'Zur Propaganda der That', 7 (16 February 1884) p. 1f.; 'Neue Kriegstaktik der Revolution', 10 (8 March 1884) p. 2; 'Die Propaganda der That', 23 (7 June 1884) p. 1. Also on the masthead of *Freiheit* starting on 25 March 1882 was carried the admonition 'Gegen die Tyrannen sind alle Mittel gesetzlich'. Evidently someone pointed out to Most that the word gesetzlich had no meaning for an anarchist and it was later changed to berechtigt. In a letter of 5 November 1881, Sebastian Trunk proudly proclaimed to Victor Dave: 'Today *Freiheit* is what it should be. A newspaper that is completely for the revolutionary worker.' Brandenburgisches Landeshauptarchiv Potsdam, Pr. Br. Rep. 30 Berlin C, Polizeipräsidium, Tit. 94, Lit. D., Nr. 398 (9582), 'Victor Joseph Louis Dave 1880–1907'.
41. 'Dynamite', *Freiheit*, No. 18 (5 May 1883) p. 1.
42. 'Neue Kriegstaktik der Revolution', Ibid., No. 10 (8 March 1884) p. 2.
43. Ibid.
44. 'Die Propaganda der That', Ibid., No. 23 (7 June 1884) p. 1.
45. 'Hödel und Nobiling', Ibid., No. 34 (23 August 1884) p. 2.
46. Ibid.
47. 'Justizmorderei', *Freiheit*, No. 40 (4 October 1884) p. 1f.
48. 'Mord contra Mord', Ibid., No. 11 (14 March 1885) p. 3.
49. Ibid.
50. Some examples of articles which appeared in *Freiheit* in the first half of 1885 are: 'Zur Propaganda der That', No. 1 (3 January 1885) p. 2; 'Theorie und Praxis der revolutionären Kriegswissenschaft', No. 3 (17 January 1885) p. 1; 'Kriegs-wissenschaftliche Praxis', No. 4 (24 January 1885) p. 2; 'Zittere Kanaille', No. 4 (24 January 1885) p. 1; 'Taktische Winke', No. 4 (24 January 1885) p. 1f.; 'Dynamit', No. 5 (31 January 1885) p. 1f.; 'Bomben', No. 6 (7 February 1885) p. 2; 'Stoff und Kraft', No. 7 (14 February 1885) p. 2; 'Spreng-Uebungen', No. 8 (21 February 1885) p. 1f.; 'Einfache Chemie', No. 10, (10 March 1885) p. 2; 'Mord contra Mord', No. 11 (14 March 1885) p. 3; 'Schiessbaumwolle und Nitrogelatin', No. 12 (21 March 1885) p. 1f.; 'Knallquecksilber', No. 13 (28 March 1885) p. 2f.; 'Kampf mit allen Mitteln', No. 14 (4 April 1885) p. 2; 'Weitere chemische Winke', No. 26 (27 June 1885) p. 2; 'Dynamit', No. 27 (4 July 1885) p. 1; 'Die Propaganda der That', No. 30 (25 July 1885) p. 1. After this there is a marked change in *Freiheit*, as noted previously the number of articles advocating violence practically ceases.

Ironically 'Revolutionäre Kriegswissenschaft' was published at a time when Most was already starting to doubt the usefulness of 'propaganda by deed' as an instrument to bring about the social revolution. Although he does not renounce 'propaganda by deed', Most's actions and words in *Freiheit* point out that by the middle of 1885 he had lost his confidence in violence. This facet of Most's character was not brought out into the open at the time, even though many of his close friends suspected it, until Alexander Berkman's assassination attempt on the life of Henry Fricke in 1892.

51. Brandenburgisches Landeshauptarchiv Potsdam, Pr. Br. Rep. 30 Berlin C., Tit. 94, Lit. S., Nr. 1255, Bd. I (13,087) Folder 184; Pr. Br. Rep. 30 Berlin C., Tit. 94, Lit. G., Nr. 548 (10196), 'Der Schriftsetzer Joseph Alfred Gfeller', recte: Friedrich August Reinsdorf 1880–1902.

52. Ibid.; Most, p. 37f.; Ernst, p. 57. The arrest of Reinsdorf added to the battle taking place between *Freiheit* and *Der Sozialdemokrat*. On 21 November 1880, *Der Sozialdemokrat* printed a short piece stating that Reinsdorf, alias Bernstein, alias Gfeller, had gone to Germany to meet Fleuron, alias Peterson, for the purpose of carrying out an act of 'propaganda by deed', and that they had received 30 pounds (600 marks) from London. Reinsdorf was already locked up when the article appeared, but it was still considered by the anarchists a journalistic low to print such an item.

53. Fricke, p. 160f.; K. Braun-Wiesbaden, 'Das Attentat auf dem Niederwald und der Hochverrathsprozess vor dem Reichsgericht', *Nord und Süd*, XXXIII (1885) S. 66; P. M., 'Das Verbrechen am Niederwald', *Preussische Jahrbücher*, LV (1885) p. 116–23.

54. 'Der Anarchistenprozess Reinsdorf und Genossen', pp. 17–22, 55–8. Expert opinion confirmed that the place where the dynamite had been planted was such that if the explosion had gone off as planned it would have doubtlessly killed all the intended victims. Ibid., p. 31f. Bismarck, claiming ill health, did not attend the ceremony. His absence leads me to the speculation that, if he had already been informed of the plot in advance by the police spy Palm – he obviously did nothing to stop it – and if Küchler and Rupsch had been successful, this would have put Bismarck in charge of Germany. This is only a wild conjecture on my part, but the Emperor was 86 years old and could not hope to live much longer and Bismarck was aware by this time that Wilhelm's successor, Friedrich, felt a deep seated animosity for him so there was no hope that he could ever control him the way he had the old Emperor.

55. Ibid., S. 88.

56. Ibid., S. 89.

57. Ibid.

58. No. 27 (4 July 1885) p. 3.

59. No. 8 (14 July–2 August 1885) p. 3.

60. October 1885, p. 1.

61. Lipinski, Bd. II, p. 100.

13 'Propaganda by Deed' and 'Direct Action': Two Concepts of Anarchist Violence

Ulrich Linse

The following remarks should not be understood as an attempt to equate terrorism with anarchism. Such a conclusion would be contrary to the findings of recent research. Anarchism in the nineteenth and twentieth centuries was imbued with the activist maxim that society was not only to be explained but to be changed. However, the means designed by anarchists to bring about change were varied and included the bomb as well as 'free love', the general strike as well as the land commune. Both psychopaths and political philosophers were to be found amongst supporters of anarchism. However, most anarchists died neither on the barricades nor on the guillotine. There were undoubtedly criminals amongst their ranks and yet it is just as legitimate to imagine the anarchist as a cultural revolutionary fighting the battle armed merely with words and writings in an attempt to 'enlighten'. Anarchism as a 'cultural movement' (Rudolf Rocker) still awaits to be studied, and any such study would have to take account of such phenomena as anti-authoritarian (non-violent) pedagogy, libertarian pacifism and militant anarchic anti-militarism.

I

The precise meaning of the term 'propaganda by deed' has changed since it was originally conceived as a concept in the 1870s.[1] The leaders of Italian anarchism, Errico Malatesta, Carlo Cafiero and Emilio Covelli, had formulated the idea of 'propaganda by deed' in personal discussions from July to October 1876 in Naples and introduced it into the Anarchist International thereafter; they understood their concept to mean insurrection, and not political assassination. On 3 December 1876, Malatesta wrote in the bulletin of the 'Federation Jurassiene' of the International:

> The Italian Federation (of the International) believes that insurrection, reinforcing socialist principles through deeds, is the most effective means of propaganda; and, without deceiving or corrupting the masses, it is also the only means of reaching ever the lowest social classes and to involve these strongly alive forces of mankind in the struggle of the International.[2]

Malatesta's summary of the experiences of the Italian Federation must be seen against the background of agrarian social protests which the Federation, strongly influenced by Bakunin, had been organising and, in parts, been putting into action in 1874 amongst the agrarian population of Romagna, Apulia and Sicily. It was hoped that this would spark off an Italian revolution.

Similarly, Cafiero's article entitled 'L'Action' in Peter Kropotkin's organ *Le Revolte* on 25 December 1880, often misinterpreted as proof of Kropotkin's support for 'dynamite terrorism', must be seen in this social and intellectual context: 'Our action must be permanent revolt, in words and in writing, with fists, guns and bombs . . . We are dedicated and principled, and we will use any means to carry out insurrections. All means that are illegal are right for us.' The question was posed: 'How do we initiate action?' Answer: 'You must look for the opportunity, and it will soon present itself. Wherever the air is filled with revolt and gunpowder, we must be at hand.'[3] Action therefore was equated with armed and conspiratorial insurrection, as the precursor to revolution.

The Bakunist element and the southern agrarian experience defined the idea of 'propaganda by deed', and it also dominated the London Congress of the Anarchist International in 1881. 'Propaganda by deed' was held to be a far more effective tool of advertisement for anarchism than the written or spoken word. Significantly, however, the following clarification was added:

> Given the fact, that the agrarian worker still stands outside the mainstream revolutionary movement, it is absolutely essential that every effort is made to win him over and to understand that any action against existing institutions is far more likely to grip and find the support of the masses than thousands of leaflets and a stream of words. Furthermore, 'propaganda by deed' is of greater importance in the countryside than in the town.[4]

While Bakunin's teachings clearly lie at the heart of these words, the International, in a further paragraph, stressed the important contribution technology and chemistry could make to the revolutionary movement in the future; it encouraged its members to dedicate themselves to the study of science. It would be wrong to conclude that it was Kropotkin's fault, dominating the London Congress, that anarchism was moving towards the questionable path of political assassination. In the explanation of this shift that was to overshadow the failure of anarchism and 'propaganda by deed' for the next hundred years from the idea of armed insurrection of the Italian Bakunists to individual acts of terrorism against the representatives of the state and the leading classes, we must look for changes in circumstances. In an ironic twist, the basis for the adoption of 'dynamite terrorism' in London was not to be found in any tradition of anarchism, but in the powerful impression the successful assassination of Csar Alexander II by Russian Nihilists had left on Europe. Individual acts of terrorism became the new revolutionary hope for anarchists. The international dissemination of this form of 'propaganda by deed' shows that the reasons for this shift in emphasis were not to be found in national peculiarities (even less so in individual biographies!) but has to be viewed in a larger context.

Bakunin – representative of a mystic and apocalyptic revolutionarism, conspirator and professional revolutionary – died in 1876 without his life's objective – the social revolution in Europe – having been achieved. Spending the last phase of his life in the Tessin (1869–76),[5] a period that coincided with his retreat from the propaganda centres of the Russian Exiles in Geneva and Zurich, his mood wavered between resignation and renewed faint hopes of revolution. In 1869, Bakunin left Geneva, apparently in search of a quieter and cheaper place to live, free of police harrassment and for the sake of his expectant wife. In 1870, he temporarily returned to Geneva hoping for the outbreak of a social revolution in France, and even in Europe as a whole, in the wake of the French defeat in the Franco-Prussian war. Aged fifty-six, he travelled to Lyon to lead the commune that had been proclaimed in the aftermath of the French defeat at Sedan and 'to perhaps wage his final gamble'. The armed anarchist insurrection in Lyon failed, and Bakunin had to flee. His plans for the 'Committee to Save France' had thereby collapsed, and he predicted that Prussian-Russian hegemony in Europe would lead to a long-term setback for revolutionary movements in Europe. And yet, when in 1873, revolutionary hopes were raised in Spain, once again, pressurised by friends, he decided to go there.

The republic, proclaimed in Spain in 1873, collapsed, just as preparations for an anarchist insurrection amongst peasants in Andalusia also came to nothing. In fact, Bakunin could not even raise the money for travel to participate in these abortive actions. Friends then acquired the Villa Baronata near Minusio-Locarno overlooking the Lago Maggiore, to serve as his retirement home and a revolutionary centre. Bakunin declared publicly that he would in future refrain from taking an active part in revolutionary politics. But as serious conflicts arose over the enormous amounts of money used to finance the rebuilding of the Villa Baronata and his financial situation was nearing catastrophe, the Italian insurrections in 1874 once again fed new hopes of a general revolution in him, and he decided to go to Bologna – the predicted centre of the uprising – to make his final stand, to perish or triumph there. Both the insurrections in Southern Italy and Bologna collapsed.

Bakunin described the decisive hours during the night of 7 August 1874 in his diary: 'Disappointment; a terrible night; pistol, two feet from death.'[6] He planned his suicide for four o'clock next morning, but was dissuaded by friends. Homeless, Bakunin, while taking flight once again, planned another uprising in Florence which met a similar fate. This was Bakunin's last revolutionary activity. The rest of his life he spent putting his private life in order and securing a home for his family. In October 1874, he settled in Lugano, physically and psychologically a broken man, spending most of his time gardening. The revolutionary dream of 1848, which Bakunin had kept alive until 1874, had not just for him but also for the anarchist movement as a whole come to an end.

This did not stop the Italians Cafiero and Malatesta from introducing the idea of 'propaganda by deed' for the first time at the Berne Congress of the Anarchist International in October 1876. Yet already the moderate attempt – even without aspiring to the perspective of the Italian insurrections of 1874 as an inspiration for a general uprising – to spread socialist propaganda amongst the Italian peasantry through the uprising of Benevento failed miserably. 'Conspiracy . . . cannot achieve social revolution',[7] Andrea Costa concluded. New ways to influence the masses had to be devised.

The Anarchist International only survived for a short period. It had grown out of the ideologically divided First International in which first Marxism and Proudhonism, and later Marxism and Bakunism had quarrelled bitterly. As a prelude to its collapse, the Latin Federation had seceded at the Congress of Chaux-de-Fonds in April 1870, and, at the Hague Congress in September 1872, the International split altogether. Formally, it was an argument over the 'dictatorship' of the General Council which non-Marxists opposed, refusing to recognise the principle of authority in the International. In actual fact, however, the expulsion of Bakunin and James Guillaume, only showed up the deeper reasons why the International had been in the process of dissolving ever since 1869: the Federations of the Italian speaking part of Switzerland, Spain and Italy had opted for Bakunin, the Belgian and Italian Federations were inclined that way. The opposition convened a counter-congress at Saint-Junier in September 1872, rejected the decisions taken at The Hague and refused to recognise the newly elected General Council: the Congress proclaimed itself the legitimate representative of the International. This Saint-Imier-International had been created by anarchists from the Swiss Jura, Spain and Italy but it also included non-anarchist federations. It hence came to be known as the anti-authoritarian International as distinct from the strictly anarchist International of which, after the schism of the anti-authoritarian International of the Socialist World Congress at Gent in September 1877, a mere torso had remained. From 1877 onwards, the anarchist International disintegrated rapidly, and attempts to revive it at the London Congress of 1881 proved fruitless. While in the years 1872 until 1877 Bakunin could count on stronger support than Marxists, this was no longer the case after the collapse of the anarchist International. Political assassination therefore became an option at the very moment time when anarchism had to abandon all hope of influencing a wide mass of peasant and industrial workers in Europe.

The collapse of the International also resulted in the disintegration of national anarchist federations for similar reasons. These reasons were a combination involving their opposition to any formal organisation and the effects of increasing state persecution in the aftermath of the Paris Commune. Until the First World War, there were to be no national federations in Spain, Italy and France with anarchism having retreated to organise on a more local or regional level. For legal reasons, there had been no German federation in the International, only individual members. From 1900 onwards, the German 'Anarchist-Federation', with its local and regional federations, was organised, benefiting from the SPD-like fetish for organisation of its members. Nevertheless it failed ever to rise above the status of a political sect.

Max Nettlau[8] and George Woodcock[9] have drawn attention to the fact that the decline of Bakunism and the rise of Kropotkin did not merely constitute an ideological shift in anarchism. Proudhon's mutualism and Bakunin's collectivism, whereby a future society would reward the individual according to how much work he had actually invested, was superseded by Kropotkin's anarchist communism based on the principle of 'everyone according to his needs'. This re-orientation, however, was accompanied by a new attitude towards the question of organisation. In the tradition of the First International, the collectivists had primarily thought to organise the working masses, led, it is true, by an elite of firmly committed anarchists (often secretly organised), without demanding the same kind of devotion from the mass of its members. Anarchist communists in Italy, France and Spain, on the other hand, felt it to be vital to organise in groups which exclusively consisted of zealous anarchists, in word as well as in deed. Anarchism was closing itself off against the masses because they had turned to social reformism, and furthermore the danger of infiltration by police and *agents provocateurs* necessitated a closing of ranks. Thus a hitherto formal organisation was replaced by the formation of independent groups.

As a result of anarchist opposition to formal organisation after the 1870s, decisions as to future actions were no longer taken by the representatives of larger organisations, but – as anarchist assassinations show – were carried out by fanatic individuals or small undercover groups. The collapse of earlier organisations meant the loss of control over their members.

One of the main reasons for the wave of assassinations after the repression of the Paris Commune was the harsh retaliation of European governments against the insurrections of the Bakunist International. Anti-terrorist measures were taken both on a national as well as international scale. Already in 1871, on Bismarck's initiative, a conference of European governments had outlined a common approach, and decided upon a European alliance against the International. England had refused to participate but separate German-Austrian negotiations in 1872 considered legal as well as political measures to oppose the International. This policy continued throughout the 1880s and 1890s with bilateral agreements amongst European states designed to stamp out anarchism. There were also international agreements which in the past had failed because of English and Swiss resistance, two countries which traditionally had welcomed exiles. Germany was also highly critical of American attitudes in this respect.[10] At the Rome Conference in 1898, German, Russian, Austrian and Turkish pressure finally succeeded in forcing the conference (against the opposition of France, Portugal, Sweden, Norway and Switzerland; England was not even present) to adopt, amongst other measures, the death penalty for assassins of heads of state. In the Secret Petersburg Protocol of 1904 (not signed by Switzerland) further administrative details for the fight against anarchism were worked out. Ironically, these policies came into existence after the wave of terrorist attacks in the 1880s and 1890s. Apparently, the government in Berlin hoped to continue to use the fight against anarchism as a foreign policy instrument.

The violent repression of Bakunist insurrections in the 1870s by state authorities had resulted in the wave of assassinations thereafter. The vicious circle of assassination – police repression – assassination had brought the anarchism of 'propaganda by deed' to the brink of self-destruction. Successive terrorists sought to avenge their executed predecessors. 'Terrorism is infectious', writes James Joll with some justification.[11] Political murder became personal vendetta.

State resistance and the unholy alliance of anti-democratic monarchies had brought about the failure of Bakunist insurrections and had reduced anarchists to a sectarian minority; the majority of socialists had chosen the legal and parliamentary paths to social reform. According to Nettlau, Malatesta's first definition of 'propaganda by deed' in 1876 was already an attempt to stem the tide of social reformism. As has been shown earlier, he considered 'propaganda by deed' to be the only strategy that did not 'deceive' or 'corrupt' the masses. This was his answer to a suggestion by anarchists from Bari in October 1876 at the Italian anarchist meeting in Florence that, for propaganda reasons, they should participate in elections.[12] Italy also provided a powerful example of the attractiveness of parliamentarianism even amongst anarchist circles: Andrea Costa had originally been one of the most fervent supporters of the politics of insurrection, and, next to Malatesta and Cafiero, the leading Italian anarchist. But already in 1877, he had tried to persuade the latter to desist from the planned uprising at Benevento because he thought social revolution only possible through the organisation of the masses and not through political conspiracies. Costa's high-flying activism in the years 1871 to 1878 had apparently been inspired by hopes of quick revolutionary success. These hopes were crushed, and, while still in prison in 1879, he denounced anarchism and voiced his support in favour of political action and parliamentary socialism. In 1882 he entered the Italian Parliament, and proceeded to become one of the leading personalites of the Italian Socialist Party. Small wonder therefore, that anarchists, in an Italian pamphlet in 1883,[13] were called upon to fight against 'the reformist and parliamentary illusions which present the greatest dangers to socialism today'. Similarly, Jules Guesde and Paul Brousse in France had converted from anarchism to become leaders of French socialism. The First International of 1871 had recommended the founding of national socialist parties to the workers of industrialised societies. Socialist parties were successfully founded in Germany in the 1860s, and in the rest of Europe in the 1870s and 1880s. This generation of workers had experienced significant if slow economic improvement of their conditions, largely due to corrective social legislation on the part of governments. It was the pressure of workers' parties and their affiliated trade unions which had brought about this state intervention.

Political terrorism constituted a desperate attempt on the part of the anarchist movement to escape the isolation which parliamentary socialism had sidetracked it into. And yet the politics of violence only reinforced this ghetto position into which anarchism had been driven by the successful co-operation of state and workers. Anarchists' opposition to the state rendered them impotent to answer the growing feeling amongst the working class that the social question, caused by industrialisation and accentuated by liberal practices, could only be solved by influencing, and ultimately conquering, the state. The negation of the state by anarchists appeared to them as a political cul-de-sac. Thus political violence became the substitute revolution of anarchists, and signified their protest against parliamentarianism.

The insurrectional phase of anarchism is, sociologically speaking, identical with agrarian anarchism, and can therefore be interpreted as the ideological manifestation of what Eric Hobsbawm has described as the tradition of social brigandage and banditry resulting from the failure of the defeudalisation of agriculture.

'Propaganda-by-deed'-style political violence by artisan anarchists co-incided with the transition period of a pre-capitalist economy to the establishment of organised capitalism. Increasing industrial production foreshadowed the end of traditional craftsmanship, and this social crisis led to artisans resorting to violence to express their grievances. Agrarian insurrections and artisan acts of terrorism can therefore be interpreted as two forms of violent social protest.

Historically speaking, 'propaganda by deed' falls between old forms of anarchism – Peter Lösche[14] defines agrarian and artisan anarchism as such old forms – and a new form of anarchism as embodied by organised syndicalism, prominent amongst workers in large factories and mines. 'Propaganda by deed' therefore marks an important sociological dividing line in the history of anarchism.

This turning point of the movement also witnessed the rise of anarchism amongst the European intelligentsia and artists at the end of the 1880s until 1900. Hobsbawm suggests that the artists of the time were also declining artisans. Bohemian anarchism hallowed the heroic deeds of the assassins because – as they saw it – both devoted themselves to an elitist cult of the ego, influenced, in the latter case, by Max Stirner and Nietzsche. The bohemian rebel, struggling against the authoritarian state and the self-satisfied bourgeoisie, was drawn to the lonely terrorist. Political and aesthetic revolt seemed to coincide. Bohemian anarchism by the sons of the bourgeoisie, inspired by youthful revulsion against society, resulted in a messianic cult of the 'Super Man', a glorification of the criminal and a fascination with conspirators and terrorists: 'The totally subjective agression of terrorists impressed by its stark contrast to the "golden mean of society".'[15] And yet, while these bohemians were eulogising violence, they refused to participate actively themselves.

It is important, however, to point out that there was also opposition to this literary lauding of anarchist murders and bomb throwers[16] amongst the anarchist intelligentsia. While in Germany for example, Erich Mühsam was rejoicing in violence,[17] his paternal friend, Gustav Landauer denounced this form of 'propaganda by the deed'. Its aim should be the intellectual renewal of man creating the conditions for the regeneration of society: 'This is how I understand "propaganda by deed", everything else is passions run wild, desperation and total madness. It is not the aim to kill human beings but to bring about the rebirth of mankind. . . . '[18]

'Propaganda by deed' indicated the end of older forms of anarchism. Meanwhile, in the hour of its final decline, its total destructiveness was hailed by this new bohemian anarchism. This politics of terror, however, delivered the final kiss of death to old-style anarchism because it subjected the movement to relentless state persecution, and alienated the working masses. In this situation, the ideals of anarchism vanished into meaningless utopia. The revolutionary destruction of the state had failed; it was time to retreat from politics and society. The hopes of revolutionising the political and socio-economic status quo gave way to feelings of resignation, and vague desires for cultural and intellectual revolutionary change. Rural communes and anti-authoritarian schools were the new starting point for creating an alternative subcultural milieu. With some justification, the German anarchist leader Rudolf Lange could argue that anarchism would only regain contact with the masses if it participated in parliamentary politics. Anarchist social democracy, however, found no support.[19] Only libertarian syndicalist anarchism – in a new form – would once again provide the chance to seek mass working-class support.

In the 1880s and the beginning of the 1890s, anarchism was primarily characterised by acts of political assassination. Dividing anarchist activities periodically will bring out certain national differences and variations: in France, anarchist assassinations were concentrated in the years 1892 to 1894, even though the beginnings of terrorist propaganda can be traced back to 1880;[20] in Germany and Austria anarchist activities were concentrated in the first half of the 1880s,[21] and again in 1893 when renewed activity, however, was quickly repressed by the police.[22]

In an account of German speaking anarchism it is important to remember that, when anarchism developed into an organised movement in Austria and Germany crucial international developments had already taken place: It had proved futile to stimulate an uprising of the rural population through armed insurrection. Also, neither German anarchism nor anarcho-syndicalism had attempted serious propaganda amongst the peasant population.[23] Furthermore, from the beginning anarchists were faced with a powerful social democratic movement. Their only hope consisted in exploiting the persecution of socialists by Bismarck and converting the verbal radicalism of the social democratic working-class movement into radical actions. These arguments reflect the international development of anarchism as has been outlined above; there are, however, a number of specific points that need to be related to German-speaking anarchism.

It has been argued that there were special personal circumstances contributing to the development of German anarchism: in his memoires, Johann Most traced his own fanatical hatred of tyrants to his heartless and cold stepmother which he claimed caused a 'negative emotional development' in his personality.[24] Or, the deeprooted desire of August Reinsdorf to contribute decisively to the freeing of mankind before tuberculosis would take his own life.[25] It seems, however, that for an explanation of anarchist violence there are more important structural factors than these merely individual-psychological reasons.

In an article in Kropotkin's *Le Révolté* in 1880, the following interesting sociological thesis was put forward:[26] the state-centralist and 'authoritarian' socialism of the SPD was the product of an industrialised North Germany; in Southern Germany, on the other hand, the mentality of the population was far more suited to the autonomist-federalist tendency in anarchism. And thus we are reminded – in comparing it to rural, mediterranean insurrections – of the tradition of peasant wars, and in particular of one of their leaders, Florian Geyer. Nevertheless, the strong artisan element in this historic movement has been overlooked. Further research would be needed to show whether artisan violence reached its final climax in the German anarchist movement of the 1870s and 1880s, as an expression of resistance on the part of artisan employees against large scale organised capitalism and its organised working class.

Furthermore, German and Austrian terrorism can only be termed anarchist within a limited sense. The anarchist movement had developed out of the schism in German and Austrian social democracy which had led to the formation of a verbally radical but legalist and reformist wing, on the one hand, and a social-revolutionary wing, on the other hand. The fusion of this social revolutionary direction with the theoretical tradition of anarchism produced the dynamics of terrorist violence.

Nettlau arrives at an alternative – if apologetic – conclusion. He argues that the reaction of social democracy to state persecution during the period of anti-socialist legislation disappointed the workers and had to lead to a revolutionary mood. And yet because these newly radicalised social democrats had *not* absorbed the ideas of libertarian socialism, their radicalism,'while still basically being authoritarian socialists . . . was inclined towards violence against society, favoured political and social terrorism, and was imbued with hatred against the parties and representatives of peaceful social democratic tactics'.[27] People seemed to revel in this 'cult of naked violence' underlying revolutionary terrorism: 'Political terrorism, and not anarchism, had come to replace social democracy, anarchism having been relegated to a goal in the far distance.'[28] Nettlau's distinction between 'anarchists' and 'social revolutionaries' seems questionable, even though it is true that in the aftermath of the anti-socialist laws they did remain separate for a few years, only to unite later.

A major cause of German-speaking terrorism was undoubtedly the suppression of the working-class movement by the state through the emergency laws of 1878. This repression meant that anarchists were prevented from operating in the open. Anarchists therefore had to resort to Mazzini and Blanqui-type tactics in order to avoid infiltration of their organisation by police agents. 'The movement thereby became restricted to secret groups and could only reach the masses through the infrequent distribution of newsletters and pamphlets.'[29] Naturally, these underground groups therefore became increasingly militant.

Added to this, was the outrage of anarchists who had been forced into exile by the authorities. The Swiss lawyer Eduard Müller wrote in 1885 complaining about German political pressure against what they regarded as the liberal immigration policy of Switzerland: 'Again and again, we are reminded of the fight against the anti-socialist laws of these countries (Germany and Austria) which cause extreme hardship amongst the exiled and fills them with unending bitterness for their institutions at home.'[30] Thus, August Reinsdorf who had organised the Niederwald assassination and was hunted from village to village, wrote to a comrade in America in 1882, that only the bomb could 'bring vengeance': 'Revenge for all the dirty tricks and atrocities, complete and utter revenge – I want to inject the whole bourgeoisie and their slaves with total terror, even if I myself get hung, drawn and quartered.'[31]

The political goal of these social revolutionaries was to bring about a 'localized collapse' of society. This intended revolutionary goal was tied to the hope that individual, heroic acts would sharpen the already revolutionary mood of the masses to this end.[32] The assassin Anton Kammerer wrote in a letter: 'We must not rest until the weak foundations of capitalist society have crumbled under the pounding of social revolution.'[33]

The chiliastic hope of these persecuted activists willing their own martyrdom, has been described in a contemporary report with reference to their mental state:

> The continuous persecution we were subjected to and the enormous sacrifices we had to bear nearly every day, produced in us a quite abnormal state of mind which it is difficult to describe. The most curious effect, however, was that these persecutions did not cause any discomfort: far from it, many longed for them because we were convinced that our cause which seemed so close to fulfillment would be best served in this way. . . . We perceived the world through coloured spectacles, and wherever we looked there were signs of miracles which only we could comprehend. Our hatred of the system led us to regard everybody with contempt who supported the system.[34]

The atmosphere became even more frenzied as convicted anarchists were executed. It led to renewed acts of revenge, stimulated by the police themselves, who, having been informed by their undercover agents of planned terrorist attacks, did not stop them but in fact helped with their preparation. Terrorism was used as a propaganda tool to justify the repression of social democracy and bring about a 'de-liberalisation' in the attitudes of liberals.

It is all the more remarkable that despite these specific structural circumstances, the politics of 'propaganda by deed' could in fact be 'exported'. While amongst the Austrian and German working class, anarchism remained a marginal phenomena, amongst the German speaking (and Italian) workers who had emigrated to America (often victims of anti-socialist legislation) this revolutionary cult of violence became quite widespread in the 1880s. Most, who himself had moved to America in 1882, became the inspired leader of this movement. It culminated in the Chicago Haymarket attack in which for the first time in American history, a bomb, aimed at human life, was thrown in peacetime. Here, much more clearly so than in Germany and Austria, economic grievances lay at the heart of terrorist attacks: Euphoria about the bomb was largely due to the extremely sordid situation of recently arrived, frustrated immigrants in the crowded habitat of Chicago and the brutal methods of repression by capitalist entrepreneurs.[35] The radicalisation of the working class in Germany and Austria had only been indirectly the result of the economic depression of the 1880s. A consequence of this, however, had been that the effective integration of the working class through social democratic parties and their reformist policies was wearing off.[36]

Widely different assessments have been made of the significance of political assassinations in Germany (concentrated in the first half of the 1890s) for an understanding of German anarchism. Andrew R. Carlson has emphasised the spectacular aspects of German anarchism by adding the Hödel and Nobiling assassination attempts on Wilhelm I's life to the list of anarchist activities. The present author attributes less importance to these acts for the anarchist movement and instead prefers to stress other forms of illegal activity, including the smuggling of censored newspapers and the formation of secret reading and discussion groups. For the majority of anarchists, even during the high point of anarchist attacks, were not involved in either the planning or carrying out of political assassinations; they were at the most 'sympathisers'.

If it had been the intention of anarchist assassins to signal the outbreak of the revolution through their symbolic attacks against political institutions, their activities can only be judged a complete failure. Not a single prominent representative of the state – unlike in other countries – was killed in Germany. There were a few minor successes amongst the lower ranks of the bureaucracy. Only terrorist attacks against private individuals and their property showed any kind of results at all. And because there was no spectacular political success, worse, innocent people were affected, the propaganda value of these acts was negligible, or, was in fact counterproductive.

Furthermore, the resources of state repression and counter-violence proved enormous; the Prussian police headquarters in Berlin kept a file on every known anarchist. Despite the anti-socialist legislation, the working class continued to be represented in Parliament, and the very fact that social democracy was not subject to open and direct persecution made the task of the anarchists even more difficult. In addition, there was no effective tradition of anti-state opposition in Germany. The 'enemies of the Empire', like Great Germans, particularist and dynastic patriots and Catholics, were not opposed to the political system as such. Finally the anarchists did not succeed – as they were to attempt during the November revolution in 1918/19 in Bavaria – in exploiting particularist and regionalist tendencies in Southern Germany because the idea of national unity, as enacted by the federalist constitution of the German Empire, had succeeded on all accounts. These were the reasons for the relegation of organised anarchism to a political *quantité negligeable*. Anarchist terrorism was a mere bogey which the government used to frighten the bourgeois National Liberals, inducing them to abandon their liberal ideals, and ensure the prolongation of anti-socialist legislation. While organised anarchism was politically insignificant, anarchist subculture in Wilhelmine Germany (cf. the Stirner renaissance of the 1890s),[38] as an expression of bourgeois intellectual opposition to the state, has to be taken far more seriously.

II

The concept of 'direct action' embraces anarcho-syndicalist violent and non-violent forms of struggle. Its principles were outlined in the statement of the founding congress of the syndicalist International in Berlin in December 1922:

Revolutionary syndicalism is based on direct action and is ready to join in all popular struggles whose aim is the destruction of monopolist economies and the tyranny of the state. Strikes, boycotts, sabotages, etc. are legitimate means in this struggle. It is in the general strike that direct action attains its fullest realization . . .[39]

The general strike was not a syndicalist invention. The idea had been developed much earlier, and anarchists had propagated it in the 1880s. (Even Bakunin has been associated with the idea.) It had also been discussed and recommended at French anarchist meetings since 1888. According to Nettlau, the idea was so widespread amongst international anarchists that in contemporary international discussion some warned that it should not be seen as a miracle solution.[40]

The idea gained strength when it began to infiltrate and finally revolutionise the French trade-union movement. This was largely due to Fernand Pelloutier.[41] He had adopted the concept of the general strike in September 1892. He finalised his view in a pamphlet written with Henri Girard in 1895 entitled 'Qu'est ce que la Grève Générale?' The general strike is defined as a 'revolutionary strike' ('la grève-révolution'), and hence distinct from previous forms of strikes: 'The general strike will not be a peaceful movement because a peaceful general strike would result in failure'. For it to succeed it would above all have to win over the workers in key sectors of the economy. Especially, if the strike fails to spread quickly, a paralysis of the transport system (in other words, a railway strike) would become vital. In this way, strike-breaking soldiers would be immobilised, industry would grind to a halt because of lack of coal, food imports would be cut off and energy supplies would collapse. A miners' strike by itself would be quite senseless if the railways continued to run. Workers, however, stationed at the neuralgic points of the economy, could achieve extreme effectiveness by exploiting the present system of division of labour to their own ends.

Pelloutier believed that the general strike would succeed because its participants would remain widely dispersed and thus force a similar splintering of the armed forces. It would render the army ineffective, and the collapse of the transport system would mean that any large troop concentrations would soon find themselves without food. The general strike should be 'revolution from everywhere and nowhere'. The strikers would remain in their parts of the town, and it is there 'that the appropriation of the means of production will take place, area by area, street by street, house by house'. Small groups of strikers, consisting of the workers at the most, would take over the workshops of each street, first the smaller ones, like bakeries, the larger ones, and finally after the victory of the strike movement assured, large-scale industries. Thus 'free production' could be initiated without the interference of a revolutionary government or a proletarian dictatorship.

The general strike would be rehearsed in small revolutionary strikes. As

Pierre Monatte explained at the International Anarchist Congress in August 1907 in Amsterdam:

> The strike is the most basic, or rather, visible form of direct action. A double edged weapon, if you like. It constitutes a most reliable and effective weapon when handled with skill by the worker capable of destroying the entrepreneur. The strike will involve the mass of workers in class struggle, and they will become aware of its implications. The strike will lead to their revolutionary education, and they will be able to measure themselves against their foe, capitalism. They will gain self-confidence and learn the art of taking risks.[42]

Thus the strike would become the training ground for the revolutionary proletariat. The strike would not merely be a means of improving their material condition but also would provide the opportunity to rehearse heroic virtue in their moral struggle. Boycotts would strengthen the effectiveness of strikes, especially in the case of industries which rely on mass markets: 'A strike by producers will be more decisive if it is supported by loosely organised consumer action, sympathetic to the striking workers.'[43]

Another form of 'direct action' was sabotage. Arnold Roller explained the meaning of 'Sabots' in a pamphlet entitled *Direct Action* in 1903. 'Sabots' had become a German term at the turn of the century, and simply meant violence against property: It implied 'damaging property, material objects and the means of production of the entrepreneur', a tactic that should be used especially if a strike proved impossible. There would be various options: deliberate wastage and destruction of raw materials, the deliberate production of faulty and damaged goods and finally the slow but persistent vandalisation of tools and materials, so that eventually only faulty products could be manufactured.

Roller also included in this form of 'direct action' the tactic of 'Go-canny'. It required a 'go-slow' by workers and would be especially effective if the workers were paid on a daily or hourly rate (i.e. not piecework).

Finally, Roller introduced the idea of 'obstructionism', or 'work to rule'. This tactic should be used in all those industries where the production process was closely tied to an exact time schedule. This of course would be particularly true in all transport and communication industries, including the railways, the postal service and the press. 'Go Canny' and 'Work to rule' would have the distinct advantage that there would be no serious financial consequences to the worker as a result of his actions because he would continue to receive his wages.

Those who favoured 'direct action' also pointed to its dangers: these actions could only mobilise the working masses if they were based on concrete goals like the demand for higher wages and a shortening of working hours. This might lead in turn, however, to people simply accepting reformist short-term aims as an end in itself. Woodcock points out that even anarchist leaders learned 'to compromise deeply with the actualities of a pre-anarchist world'.[44] A hard core of syndicalists (once again Bakunin's idea of a revolutionary elite appeared in anarcho-syndicalist theory)[45] had to oppose the merely short-term aims of its supporters and instead point to the ultimate revolutionary goal, the revolutionary general strike. Roller wrote:

'Direct action is not confined to achieving improvements for the working class here and now. Its aim is the destruction of capitalist society, and the organisation of a free society. . . . General strike and expropriation are the ultimate realization and climax of direct action by the working class.'[46]

Already here, the general strike was seen as a signal for revolution. It had attained the status of a social myth, a theme which was to be developed further by Sorel in his *Reflections sur la Violence*.

The consequences of political assassinations had been far more devastating for the anarchists themselves than for the society they had been directed against. The politics of terror led to co-ordinated efforts on the part of the states that had been affected in tracking down anarchists. The anarchist movement was forced to go underground and resort to clandestine activities. Many of their best supporters wasted away in prisons, and the remaining anarchist groups found themselves isolated from the working masses. Anarchism had 'barricaded itself off from reality'.[47]

This situation led Fernand Pelloutier to conclude in 1895:[48] 'I know many workers who are disenchanted with parliamentary socialism but who hesitate to support libertarian socialism because, in their view, anarchism simply implies the individualistic use of the bomb.' It was indeed true that many workers idolised the assassin Francois-Claudius Ravachol, and, as Rocker recorded in his memoires, the ribald song 'La Ravachole' with the memorable refrain 'Vive le son/de l'explosion!' became one of the most popular mass songs in Paris after Ravachol's execution in 1892.[49] 'But none of them would in fact dare to pronounce himself an anarchist. He does not wish to give the impression that he has abandoned collective revolt in favour of individual revolt.' Pelloutier argued that anarchism could and should 'disregard the individualistic use of the bomb . . . if [its teachings] are to find any support'.

'Direct action' of anarcho-syndicalism was not an alternative to terrorism; it was merely its continuation in a different form. Thus Pierre Monatte declared at the International Anarchist Congress in Amsterdam in 1907 that in 'direct action' 'the spirit of revolution is revived and regenerated through its contact with syndicalism. And for the first time, since the mighty sound of anarchist bombs had died away, the bourgeoisie is gripped by fear.'[50] Roller emphasised the continuity between violence against persons and violence against property even more strongly: 'direct action' operates both through 'economic' and 'social' terror. The former he defined as a 'terrorist revolutionary strike' designed to frighten the capitalist by damaging or destroying his means of production and property. The aim of the latter would be the assassination of capitalists. Both forms of terrorism were justified, for as an old saying goes: 'Those who beg receive nothing, those who threaten receive something and those who commit violence receive everything.' Roller explicitly drew a line of comparison between this new form of terrorism and the previous phase of political assassinations:

> It [social terrorism] is merely a new form of murdering tyrants. The socialised killing of tyrants is justified because the bourgeoisie is the collective tyrant of the proletariat. Economic and social violence against economic tyrants follows in the footsteps of political terrorism. Even if such terrorist actions can only be carried out by courageous *individual* comrades, they are nevertheless of the greatest significance because they are an expression of the bitterness of the masses who often will follow the brave examples of a few individuals . . . [51]

Despite this emphasis on the continuity of terrorist actions, it is obvious that revolutionary syndicalism countered the disintegration of anarchism into small groups with its own idea of mass workers' organisation. And the extreme individualism of 'propaganda by deed' in the form of political assassinations was replaced by the idea of 'direct action', designed to arouse the solidarity of the masses in its attempt to achieve its revolutionary goal. Indeed, as James Joll has pointed out,[52] the idea of direct revolutionary action was so attractive because the syndicalist movement itself was very weak. Furthermore, it is by no means certain, whether the myth of 'direct action' did in fact change the economic struggle of the workers, or merely re-interpret it.

In its concept of 'direct action', pure syndicalism was advocating a theory and practice for industrial action. It was clearly contrary both to individual terrorist actions and Bakunin's ideas of conspiracy and insurrection. It is true that Woodcock and Nettlau[53] have both tried to trace syndicalist emphasis on the economic struggle of the masses to Proudhon, and above all, to Bakunin. But these arguments tend to overlook the fact that it is difficult to re-connect syndicalism and its 'direct action' with Bakunin's own ideas. For the core of Bakunin's revolutionary theory had been insurrection, and not the general strike. The starting point for syndicalism, on the other hand, had been purely economic. In short, Bakunism had quite simply not been a trade-union movement.

The divergence between old-style Bakunists and new revolutionary syndicalism was the subject of a famous debate between Pierre Monatte and Errico Malatesta on the occasion of the Amsterdam Congress in 1907.[54] Malatesta had always denounced the reduction of anarchism to mere individual acts of revolt in the previous years always holding out 'hope for real general revolutionary action'.[55] In Amsterdam he defended the tradition of the First

International claiming that even when the International was dissolved he had refused to enter 'the ivory tower of speculations'; in fact, he had always tried to fight 'this arrogant mentality of sectarianism'. He argued that anarchists should be active in trade unions because the working class movement was indeed 'a meeting place between the masses and us'. But the true anarchist could never accept the general strike as the only means of struggle. He conceded that the general strike might indeed be a most effective means in the initiation of revolution. 'But', Malatesta warned his audience, 'we must be aware of the fateful illusion that the general strike has made armed insurrection obsolete.' The point was well taken because there were obvious weaknesses in the idea of the general strike as developed by Pelloutier. He had indeed expected miracles from a decentralised revolutionary strike in bringing down capitalism and its armies. Malatesta countered that the general strike was 'pure utopia' and 'nonsense'. For, once production has stopped, the first people to face starvation would not be the bourgeoisie, but the workers, and it would force them to give in. Defeat could only be averted if the worker – against predictable resistance from police forces – would, through force, take possession of the products: 'The moment of insurrection has arrived, and the stronger will carry the day. Let us therefore prepare for this inevitable uprising, instead of relying solely on the general strike as the ultimate answer to all our misery.'

I cannot agree with James Joll who argues that Monatte's tactic proved to be more effective than Malatesta's.[56] Malatesta himself was able to show that it was not only in theory realistically possible to guide strikes into armed insurrection (the revolutionary events in 1917/18 also support this view): I am referring to the 'Red Week' of Ancona in June 1914, one of the most important revolutionary events in Europe during the syndicalist phase of anarchism. Malatesta played a leading role during the 'Red Week', and later emphasised[57] that this had been a 'strike with a tendency towards insurrection'; and yet, at the very moment, when 'the revolution began to grow', the withdrawal of moderate trade unions led to defeat.

Experiences like these help to explain why the anarcho-syndicalist International refused to adhere to the general strike as the only means of struggle in its policy statement in 1922: 'Direct action finds its ultimate realization in the general strike. The general strike must also, at the same time, be the beginning of social revolution thus assuring victory in the tradition of revolutionary syndicalism.'[58] This formula vindicated Malatesta's opposition to equating the general strike with revolution. The old idea of insurrection was at least indirectly integrated into the concept of 'direct action'. For, Malatesta himself had already put forward the following motion at the Amsterdam Anarchist Congress:

Anarchists regard trade unionism and the general strike as the most effective means of revolution but not as a substitute for

revolution . . . Anarchists believe that the destruction of a capitalist and
authoritarian society can only be brought about by armed insurrection and
violent expropriation. Support for a more or less general strike and the
trade union movement must not lead us to abandon direct violent means in
the struggle against the military power of governments.[59]

It was only during the Russian Revolution that these ideas re-surfaced, and
hence, according to Nettlau,[60] Malatesta remained isolated within the
movement from 1900 until the First World War. It had simply been forgotten.

(that) the only man who did not believe in the slow propaganda of ideas or
in the automatic or incidental collapse of the whole system [as, for example,
syndicalists did at first] and, who, as Bakunin himself had done, continued
to believe in the possibility of truly revolutionary action, was right there
amongst them.[61]

Arnold Roller[62] argued that one of the reasons for the importance of 'direct
action' was the failure of peaceful wage struggles. In his case, the miners' strike
in the Rhineland in 1905 assumed particular importance, but there were many
other examples too. He also referred to the failure of the fight for the eight-
hour day, a demand that in Germany was only fulfilled with the November
Revolution of 1918. In criticising the policy of social democrats and trade
unions during the abortive Ruhr strike in 1905, he expressed his fear that
the reformism of the trade union movement – he called it a 'strike of
resignation' – could only mean the abandonment of social revolution
altogether. Indeed, it could be argued that the very integration of the workers
into the present political and economic system led to a policy of peaceful wage
struggles. Furthermore, the ideal of revolution was being undermined by a
fetish for organisation and bureaucracy. Trade unions should not just feed
their bureaucrats but should uphold the old revolutionary spirit for heroic
actions. The defeats of workers' movements were largely due to a spirit of
legality and obedience. 'Peaceful strikes exhaust the energies of the strikers;
their confidence, their personal courage and initiative are stamped out as they
rely on their leaders, on arbitrators, on parliaments, and, in particular, on
financial contributions.'
    While the 'negative integration' of the working class into state and society
was correctly analysed, he listed further reasons why peaceful strikes would
only have a limited chance of success: in an economy where small manu-
facturers and artisans were competing against each other the peaceful refusal
to work actually made sense because strike action threatened their very
existence and forced them to give in. This weapon had been blunted since
businesses were now more concentrated, organised in employers' organisations and supported each other with the aim of ensuring continuing

production. The anonymous and elusive stockholder, his investments widely spread, could no longer be fatally wounded, and his dividend would only fall marginally. The capitalists had recently thought up a most oppressive weapon designed to disrupt the organisation and the strike funds of the workers: they had locked the workers out of the factories. Pushed to an extreme, the general lock-out would even prevent the uninvolved workers from supporting the strikers in solidarity. All this could only go to prove that circumstances had shifted decisively in favour of the capitalists. 'Direct action' would be the only option in this situation; that is, of course, if one did not want to move the field of action altogether from the economic sphere into Parliament, as social democrats and socialist trade unions have done.

'Direct action' became the rallying point for opposing 'the political pre-occupation of comfortable working class up-starts with their plush German and Austrian sofas'.[63] It was an attempt to rescue the tradition of economic class struggle and the goal of expropriating the expropriations from an embourgeoised workers' aristocracy and the modern nation state into which the working class had become integrated, a fact that was to become most evident on the eve of the First World War.

By the very logic of its term, 'direct action' should be direct, and unmediated: 'Workers' demands should be pushed through directly *without* the consent of entrepreneurs and authorities, and, more importantly, without holding ballots or elections.'[64] The emancipation of the worker should be of his own doing, and, on this point, the view of revolutionary syndicalism coincided with that of the First International: 'Direct action means acting oneself and only trusting oneself.'[65] Syndicalism opposed the deflection of the working-class struggle onto the political level and instead maintained that only economic and industrial action, i.e. the economic fight, could lead to a revolutionary movement. It was thought that the ideological and organisational cement of a party was insufficiently strong for revolutionary action; such lasting bonds could only be forged through communal activity in the factory from which common economic interests would evolve. Thus syndicalism and 'direct action' can be seen as an attempt to oppose the legal mass organisations of the socialist parties and their hierarchic workers' bureaucracies with a revolutionary mass movement of industrial workers. It was hoped that in this way the trade-union movement could be rescued from just becoming a mere subsection of socialist workers' parties; the trade unions could thus become the revolutionary alternative. Fernand Pelloutier wanted to recruit all those workers for the syndicalist movement who had so far mistrusted all trade unions 'as the breeding ground for future parliamentarians.' The struggle against social reformism and its revisionist belief in the powers of voting and social legislation set in here.

Even in the Germany of 1905 'the fresh breeze from Czarist Russia resulted in a widespread discussion of the general strike'.[66] The reform socialists who were against the general strike[67] felt endangered enough by this discussion to expel their Berlin deputy and leader of the health insurance campaign, Raphael Friedeberg,[68] from the party in 1907 because he had supported syndicalism in a pamphlet entitled *Parliamentarianism and General Strike*. More positive steps followed: Bebel formulated the slogan 'political mass strike' at the SPD Party Conference in Jena in 1904. The Jena and Mannheim party conference, two years later in 1906, both showed that this new tactical slogan was designed to undermine the syndicalist call for a general strike. The 'political mass strike' was not conceived as a revolutionary alternative to parliamentary battles, but, nevertheless, as an extra-parliamentary if peaceful safety net to parliamentary work itself just in case the right to vote or form parties would ever be suspended.[69] This strike was a defensive rather than an offensive measure.

To avoid all confusion, the International Anarchist Congress at Amsterdam in 1907 expressly denounced the 'political mass strike' once again, which, according to Monatte's motion, was nothing 'but the attempt of politicians to deflect the general strike from its economic and revolutionary goal'.[70] And yet it soon became clear that the radical Marxists in the German social democracy followed the concept of 'the political mass strike' very closely, and adopted it as their means of revolutionary struggle.

This particular form of political struggle, untamed by parliamentary procedure, its effectiveness proven by the Russian Revolution of 1917, was so attractive that in the end syndicalists did finally fall prey to the communist party idea which so far they had opposed as vigorously as party socialism. For the syndicalists had always maintained that a minority should inspire and lead the masses, and after the war it seemed as if the communist party could just be that 'leading minority': 'It was the point at which revolutionary syndicalism, in its enthusiasm for the Russian Revolution, committed suicide.'[71]

In autumn 1920, the workers of Milan's steel factories created a new form of 'direct action'. Rudolf Rocker described it in his memoires:

> The incident had arisen because the employers' organisation had decided to lock out its workforce in order to nullify the concessions the workers had forced upon them. . . . The workers, however, simply turned the tables on them and occupied the factories in August and September 1920 so that they themselves could continue production without their employers. In order to prevent police and troops from forcefully expelling them, they dug trenches, armed with machine guns, around their factories, converting them into quasi-fortresses. The new strategy of this powerful movement which also spread to other industries echoed throughout the workers' movements of many countries.[72]

The origins of this tactic are not clear. Daniel Guerin has argued[73] that Italian left-wing socialists and anarchists followed the Russian revolutionary ideal and that the actions of steel workers in northern Italy imitated the Soviet model. In February 1920, the Italian workers had forced the employers to accept the election of so-called 'internal commissions' in the factories. The factory occupations in August and September were an attempt to transform these elected workers' commissions into factory councils. Despite the threat of force, they had failed to win the support of engineers and foremen, and hence were forced to hand over the running of factories to workers' councils. 'This', according to Guerin, 'was a first attempt at self-rule.'

While Guerin emphasised the aspect of self-rule through workers' councils, tracing them to the Soviet model, Nettlau (like Rocker) gave priority to the idea of factory occupation. He was thus able to show that with this tactic one of Malatesta's constant demands had been realised.[74] Malatesta had opposed the syndicalist vision of the general strike at the Amsterdam Congress of 1907: 'The point is not to ask the worker to stop working but to continue his work to his own benefit.'[75] This idea of 'stay in' rather than 'come out on strike' had been preached twenty years earlier by the anarchist shoemaker J. Harragan in London. Nettlau had to admit, however, that the idea had fallen on deaf ears then.[76]

The reasons for Guerin's and Nettlau's different emphases are obvious: the anarchists felt that the adoption of workers' councils would clear the way for the communist desire for more dictatorship and authority. In fact, the analysis of the Milan experiment gave rise to serious differences between Italian libertarians and Gramsci, the father of the Italian Communist party. The communist and anarcho-syndicalist alliance in the 'red trenches' (*trincea rosse*) of Milan's factories symbolised a short-lived unity of action between these divergent left-wing forces. The anarchist Erich Mühsam himself believed in the realisation of this hope during the days of the Munich Republic.[77]

The 'spontaneous strike movements' that preceded the German November Revolution in the years 1917/18 had not been the work of syndicalists but of socialist trade-union opposition. The 'direct action' workers were simply helping themselves, without as yet being influenced by syndicalist or communist workers' councils' ideas. This anti-bureaucratic, anti-centralist and spontaneous trade-union opposition, however, had sown the seeds from which, after the collapse of Germany, determined unionist and syndicalist trade unions could grow and recruit mass support. But it was only after the German syndicalist movement became primarily composed of supporters from the steel and mining industry, rather than the building industry, that it became practical and revolutionary. Towards the end of 1919, the syndicalist 'Free Workers' Union of Germany' could call upon 100,000 members of which 28,000 were miners and 10,000 steel workers. Significantly the first and largest syndicalist federation founded after the war in Germany, was a miners' union.

Miners in the Ruhr could look back on a pre-war tradition of syndicalism. For miners combined a syndicalist struggle against workers' bureaucracy in trade unions and parties and 'direct action' with a 'traditional pre-liberal determination and decision-making process peculiar to the miners' world'.[78]

The strong connection between syndicalism and 'factory workforce actions'[79] continued to be in evidence after the war in that the syndicalist federation of miners (cf. above) organised itself according to mines rather than, as syndicalist theory taught, according to professions.[80]

With the First World War, another important element was added to the workers in the Ruhr: a young generation of industrial workers[81] as yet unaffected by traditional working-class organisations, began to lead mass proletarian actions. This revolutionary working-class youth had opposed the war which had brought it into opposition with the Majority – SPD. They demanded organisational independence and protested against the 'bureaucratisation' of adult organisations. This 'class struggle between generations' was accentuated by the extreme youth cult underlying this proletarian youth movement. In 1918, Karl Liebknecht had celebrated youth as the saviour of socialism: 'she was the purest and brightest flame of the revolution; and she will be the most glowing, the purest, the eternal flame of the new revolution which will and must come'. The young working-class movement adopted this youth-oriented pathos in their songs: 'We are the young guards of the proletariat'; or 'The new era begins with us'. Their awareness of being the 'avant garde of the revolution' lay at the heart of the potential violence of Weimar working-class youth movements. They believed in themselves as the ultimate bearer of revolution, and thus rejected any organisational subjection to adult socialist and communist parties. Its most prominent example was Willi Münzenberg. It is therefore for good reasons that this phenomenon came to be known as 'youth syndicalism' because there was undoubtedly a close relationship with the anti-bureaucratic and anti-centralist ideology of syndicalism in general.

In a recent study, Klaus Tenfelde has stressed 'the link between spontaneous action of a united factory workforce with the syndicalist model for action', and has shown that unorganised mass activities usually led to syndicalist-type agitation.[82] Similarly, H. M. Bock had argued earlier, that even though the unofficial strikes of workers in the Ruhr during and after World War I were directly related to the syndicalist postulate of 'direct action' and spontaneous mass action, they were primarily characterised by spontaneous and direct self-help on the part of the working class.[83] And only by seeing the syndicalist movement against the background of this revolutionary situation can we understand how syndicalism, condemned to impotency before and after this period, rose to such great prominence in the early years of the Weimar Republic. For a short time, it was a regional mass movement, reaching its climax with 150,000 members at the end of 1921. According to Bock, proletarian action had been fused in this instance with the theoretical postulates of 'direct action'. The theory and practice of syndicalism underlined and strengthened spontaneous workers' self-help actions in strikes and uprisings.[84]

This 'symbiosis'[85] of workers' activism and syndicalism had a great impact on the great Ruhr strikes of 1919 and 1920. Rocker was able to state with some justification that the impact of syndicalism 'went far beyond just their sheer number, especially in the mining and steel industry of the Rhineland where in many places they played a leading role in the general strike of these years'.[86] Syndicalists were involved in the local Ruhr miners' strikes in December 1918,[87] as well as in the two great general strikes in February and April 1919, and they represented, in alliance with Communists and Independent Socialists, the radical wing of the movement.[88] Syndicalists fought against invading troops and helped with the management of mining companies. Syndicalists wanted to occupy their mines, run them and distribute the profits amongst themselves, inspired by the slogan 'The mines are ours'.[89] After the violent repression of the four-week general miners' strike in April 1919, many miners left their old trade unions, and thousands flocked to join syndicalism in the second half of 1919.

In December 1919, the *Free Workers' Trade Union* (of Germany) was founded. Its programme, written by Rocker,[90] proclaimed 'direct action' and 'general strike' as its principles, even though these German syndicalists refrained from propagating the destruction of the means of production.[91] Each local organisation independently determined the beginning and end of their strikes. As a result of the decentralised nature of their organisation, the local branches had to rely on their own strike funds. Hence their influence remained limited in comparison with large trade-union and employers' organisations, and independent strike action was quite impossible. They were forced to confine 'the deployment of their forces in spontaneous mass strikes and in the wage struggles decided upon by the general trade union council'.[92]

The potential impact of 'direct action' on the insurrections of 1920 and 1921 in the Ruhr and in central Germany was never fully realised because Rocker, while being in favour of the general economic strike, was opposed to armed uprisings. This was not only due to his idealistic pacifism but based on his belief – similar to Friedrich Engels before him – that there were practical difficulties: 'With the present state of military techniques, the time of old-style political revolution, where armed civilians fought the army, has passed for ever. The superiority of military leadership and their techniques will always ensure their victory,' Rocker concluded after the January battles of 1919.[93] It was for this reason that the leadership of the German *Free Workers Trade Union* – in any case opposed to the left-wing alliance of syndicalists and communists – condemned the battles in the Ruhr in March 1920, even though the syndicalists, in relation to the strength of their membership, provided the largest number in the 'Red Army' of the Ruhr. As late as 1920, Augustin Souchy had expressed the hope that in a new revolution the syndicalists in the Ruhr would be powerful enough to initiate the take-over of factories by workers.[94] Rocker, however, believed that the failure of the Ruhr rising in 1920 had vindicated his warning 'that armed action was incapable of defeating the military'.[95]

In 1923, the leaders of the *Free Workers Trade Union* proclaimed a general strike but in the face of shrinking membership this remained a fruitless gesture. The goal Rocker had envisaged for German syndicalism in 1919 to 'conquer workplace and factory'[96] remained unattainable.

Rocker had not conceived German syndicalism as a political force but, following Gustav Landauer, as a cultural movement aimed at the 'spiritual enlightenment of the masses'.[97] In reality, however, it had merely been a 'campaigning political sect'.[98] Rocker himself had to admit in retrospect that German syndicalism 'never did realise its practical aim which we had hoped it would fulfill'. Even at the best of times it was incapable of 'acting independently on a grand scale'.[99] Its main achievement had been the publication and distribution of 'libertarian literature' in its effort to enlighten.[100]

Once the revolutionary wave of the immediate post-war period had died down, resignation spread. Even the chances of success for 'direct action' seemed slim. In 1929, for example, the *International*, organ of the syndicalist International, published an article which underlined this development.[101] The author, U. Rath, apologised for the fact that his suggestions were 'devoid of revolutionary fervour' or 'a rousing call for personal courage and sacrifice' but were 'directed at a quite different set of intellectual qualities of the working class'. For in these times of economic crises, the worker was required not to be just a 'soldier' but also a 'thinker'. He was to be the 'official receiver of bourgeois society', and this would be a most 'prosaic task'. So far anarchism and anarcho-syndicalism had rejoiced in heroic action be it conspiracy, terrorism, insurrection or revolutionary strike; Rath proceeded to suggest a new path for 'direct action': continuing the tradition of co-operatives, workers should buy up bankrupt factories from capitalists in order to initiate, here and now, the socialist experiment. This would enable the worker 'to learn and practice the workings of economics at first hand', and thus acquire knowledge so vital for social revolution.

Helmut Rüdiger remarked in the editorial introduction that Rath's ideas – 'who is an outsider in our movement in any case' – were indeed 'new to the anti-authoritarian movement'. He pointed out that a factory, still functioning within the capitalist economy, could hardly be called 'socialist', and yet Rath's suggestion that socialism after the revolution was impossible 'without knowledge of the workings of production and management', should be taken to heart: 'The working class must gain experience in the running of factories, and must cease to be merely the object of the capitalist economy.'

A critical reader[102] at the time commented ironically that Rath's idea did indeed have a distinct attraction 'doing away with social revolution, the revolutionary general strikes and similar means, because they demand sacrifice and commitment from the masses and are therefore unpopular, and replacing it with economic measures which require no sacrifices leading sanguinely to socialism'. This was not, however, revolutionary syndicalism but mere social-democratic reformism.

Criticism was also levelled[103] against Rath because he refused to recognise violent destruction of capitalism as a prerequisite for a socialist society. Rath had stressed that 'direct action' had been far too one-sidedly propagated as a weapon against capitalism failing to integrate the concept into 'a constructive idea for the development of socialism'. It was indeed Rath's achievement to have extended the meaning of 'direct action' in this sense.

It is interesting to notice that both Rath as well as his sympathetic critic, in emphasising the constructive aspect in the growth of socialism, were indebted to Gustav Landauer and his idea of 'the realisation of socialism'. In the final analysis, Helmut Rüdiger's postulate that the worker should stop being the mere object of capitalist economy left an important mark on the last surviving representative of this idea, August Souchy, the best known old-style German anarchist today. Souchy wrote in his memoires in 1977: 'The present trade union demand for workers' participation and self-rule in factories had been an original goal of anarcho-syndicalism.'[104] Thus 'direct action' – both in its violent (factory occupation) and non-violent (buying the factory) seizure of factories – became the model for workers' democracy, workers' participation and self-rule. At the same time, leading German syndicalists de-mythologised the cult of violent revolution after the Second World War.[105] And yet, the eventual breakthrough to 'pragmatic anarchism' did not take place in Germany, but in the Anglo-Saxon countries.[106]

NOTES

1. For the history of the term anarchism see W. Laqueur, *Terrorism* (London, 1977) p.
2. M. Nettlau, *Die revolutionären Aktionen des italienischen Proletariats und die Rolle Errico Malatestas* (reprinted Berlin, 1973) p. 66f.
3. E. Oberländer (ed.), *Der Anarchismus* (= Dokumente der Weltrevolution, vol. 4) (Olten und Freiburg im Breisgau, 1972) p. 231f.
4. A. R. Carlson, *Anarchism in Germany: The Early Movement*, (Diss. Michigan State University, 1970) p. 367.
5. R. Broggini, 'Anarchie und Befreiungsbewegungen um 1870 in der Gegend von Locarno' in H. Szeemann (ed.), *Monte Verita* (Milan, 1978); also H. Bienek, *Bakunin, eine Invention* (Munich, 1970) p. 46f.
6. Nettlau, *Malatesta*, p. 53.
7. J. Joll, *The Anarchists,* 2nd edn. (London, 1977) p. 105.
8. Nettlau, *Malatesta*, p. 64ff.
9. G. Woodcock, *Anarchism* (London, 1962) p. 345f.
10. Cf. the official document: *Sozialismus und Anarchismus in Europa und Nordamerika während der Jahre 1883 bis 1886* (Berlin, 1887; reprinted 1974).
11. Joll, p. 111.
12. Nettlau, *Malatesta*, p. 67.
13. Ibid., p. 91f.

14. P. Lösche, *Anarchismus* (Darmstadt, 1977) p. 31f.
15. H. Kreuzer, *Die Boheme* (Stuttgart, 1968) p. 309.
16. For an example see Kreuzer, p. 307ff.; Woodcock, p. 285ff.
17. E. Mühsam, *Ascona* (Locarno, 1905); id., 'Terror', *Polis* I/10 (1.9. 1907) pp. 160–2.
18. G. Landauer, 'Der Anarchismus in Deutschland', *Die Zukunft* 10 (1895) now in G. Landauer, *Erkenntnis und Befreiung* (Frankfurt/Main, 1976) p. 13.
19. U. Linse, *Organisierter Anarchismus im Deutschen Kaiserreich von 1871* (Berlin, 1969) p. 378f.
20. J. Maitron, 'Die Ära der Attentate' in W. Laqueur (ed.), *Zeugnisse politischer Gewalt. Dokumente zur Geschichte des Terrorismus* (Kronberg/Ts, 1978) pp. 79–82.
21. Carlson, p. 249ff.
22. Linse, *Organisierter Anarchismus*, p. 162; G. Botz *et al.*, *Im Schatten der Arbeiterbewegung: Zur Geschichte des Anarchismus in Österreich und Deutschland* (Vienna, 1977) p. 47.
23. Linse, 'Anarcho-syndikalistische Landarbeiteragitation in Deutschland (1910–1933): Uber die soziale Kluft zwischen Stadt- und Landproletariat' in S. Blankertz (ed.), *Auf dem Misthaufen der Geschichte*, No. 1 (Münster/Wetzlar, 1978).
24. R. Rocker, *Johann Most, Das Leben eines Rebellen* (Berlin, 1924) p. 14.
25. Carlson, pp. 428 and 455.
26. 'Le Fédéralisme-Anarchiste dans l'Allemagne du Sud', *Le Révolté*, Organe socialiste, II/7 (1880).
27. M. Nettlau, *Anarchisten und Sozialrevolutionäre der Jahre 1880–1886* (Berlin, 1931) p. 146.
28. Ibid., p. 163.
29. J. Peukert, *Erinnerungen eines Proletariers aus der revolutionären Arbeiterbewegung* (Berlin, 1913) p. 201 describes August Reinsdorf's actions in this way.
30. E. Müller, *Bericht über die Untersuchungen betreffend die anarchistischen Umtriebe in der Schweiz an den hohen Bundesrath der schweizerischen Eidgenossenschaft* (Bern, 1885) p. 176.
31. J. Langhard, *Die anarchistische Bewegung in der Schweiz von ihren Anfängen bis zur Gegenwart und die internationalen Führer* (Berlin, 1908) p. 258.
32. Botz *et al.*, p. 32f.
33. Rocker, *Most*, p. 189.
34. Ibid., p. 189 footnote.
35. See also H. Karasek, 'Amerika oder die deutschen Gastarbeiter greifen zur Bombe' in id., *Propaganda und Tat: Drei Abhandlungen über den militanten Anarchismus unter dem Sozialistengesetz* (Frankfurt/Main, n.d.).
36. Botz *et al.*, p. 169f.
37. Linse, 'Die Anarchisten und die Münchner Novemberrevolution' in K. Bosl (ed.), *Bayern im Umbruch: Die Revolution von 1918, ihre Voraussetzungen, ihr Verlauf und ihre Folgen* (Munich and Vienna, 1969) pp. 37–73; Linse (ed.), *Gustav Landauer und die Revolutionszeit 1918/19* (Berlin, 1974); E. Lunn, *Prophet of Community: The Romantic Socialism of Gustav Landauer* (Berkeley, 1973) pp. 291ff.
38. M. G. Helms, *Die Ideologie der anonymen Gesellschaft: Max Stirners 'Einziger' und der Fortschritt des demokratischen Selbstbewusstseins vom Vormärz bis zur Bundesrepublik* (Cologne, 1966) p. 295ff.
39. Quoted from the 2nd International Workers' Association, Amsterdam, March 1925, in: *Die Internationale*, Organ der Internationalen Arbeiter-Assoziation,

II/5 (June 1925) p. 55.

40. M. Nettlau, 'Fernand Pelloutiers Platz in der Entwicklung des Syndikalismus', *Die Internationale*, Zeitschrift fur die revolutionäre Arbeiterbewegung, Gesellschaftskritik und sozialistischen Neuaufbau, I/4 (February 1928) p. 22.
41. For the following Nettlau, p. 22f.
42. Oberländer, p. 332.
43. R. Rocker, Streik und Boykott, *Die Internationale* (cf. footnote 40), III/1 (November 1929).
44. Woodcock, p. 256.
45. Ibid., p. 302.
46. A. Roller, *Die direkte Aktion* (reprinted Bremen, n.d.).
47. D. Guerin, *Anarchismus* (Frankfurt/Main, 1967) p. 69.
48. Oberländer, pp. 316, 321.
49. R. Rocker, *Aus den Memoiren eines deutschen Anarchisten* (Frankfurt/Main, 1974) p. 106.
50. Oberländer, p. 333.
51. Roller.
52. Joll, p. 184.
53. Woodcock, pp. 109, 269, 299; M. Nettlau, 'Michael Bakunin und der Syndikalismus', *Die Internationale* (cf. footnote 37), I/8 (June 1928).
54. Oberländer, p. 339f; see Nettlau, *Malatesta*, p. 127f.
55. Nettlau, *Malatesta*, p. 107.
56. Joll, p. 188.
57. Nettlau, *Malatesta*, pp. 135–7.
58. See footnote 39.
59. Oberländer, p. 342.
60. Nettlau, *Malatesta*, p. 128.·
61. Joll, p. 185.
62. Roller.
63. F. Brupbacher, *60 Jahre Ketzer, Selbstbiographie* (reprinted Zürich, 1973) p. 107; for a comparison between the German and French trade union movement, see p. 119.
64. Brupbacher, p. 107 footnote.
65. Oberländer, p. 332.
66. Brupbacher, p. 118.
67. W. Röhrich, *Revolutionärer Syndikalismus: Ein Beitrag zur Sozialgeschichte der Arbeiterbewegung* (Darmstadt, 1977) p. 16f.
68. F. Tennstedt, 'Sozialismus, Lebensreform und Krankenkassenbewegung, Friedrich Landmann und Raphael Friedeberg als Ratgeber der Krankenkassen', *Soziale Sicherheit* 26 (1977) pp. 306ff., 332ff.; H. M. Bock and F. Tennstedt, 'Raphael Friedeberg: Arzt und Anarchist in Ascona' in Szeemann (ed.), *Monte Verita*.
69. Linse, *Organisierter Anarchismus*, p. 56.
70. Oberländer, p. 344f.
71. Brupbacher, p. 243.
72. Rocker, *Memoiren*, p. 349.
73. Guerin, p. 94f.
74. *Malatesta 1889 – Malatesta 1920*: see Nettlau, *Malatesta*, pp. 98 and 156, 160.
75. Oberländer, p. 349f.
76. Nettlau, *Malatesta*, p. 163f footnote.
77. E. Mühsam, *Von Eisner bis Levine: Die Entstehung der bayerischen Räterepublik* (Berlin, 1929); H. Hug, *Erich Mühsam: Untersuchungen zu Leben und Werk*

(Glashütten im Taunus, 1974) pp. 42ff. and 173ff.

78. K. Tenfelde, 'Linksradikale Strömungen in der Bergarbeiterschaft an der Ruhr 1905 bis 1919' in H. Mommsen and U. Borsdorf (eds), *Glück auf, Kameraden! Die Bergarbeiter und ihre Organisationen in Deutschland* (Cologne, 1979) p. 223.
79. Ibid., p. 203.
80. H. M. Bock, *Syndikalismus und Linkskommunismus von 1918–1923* (Meisenheim am Glan, 1969) pp. 134, 138.
81. For the following: Linse, 'Lebensformen der bürgerlichen und der proletarischen Jugendbewegung: Die Aufbrüche der Jugend und die Krise der Erwachsenenwelt', *Jahrbuch des Archivs der deutschen Jugendbewegung*, vol. 10 (Burg Ludwigstein, 1978) pp. 24–55; id., *Die anarchistische und anarchosyndikalistische Jugendbewegung 1919–1933* (= Quellen und Beiträge zur Geschichte der Jugendbewegung, vol. 18) (Frankfurt a. M., 1976) id., (ed.), *Ernst Friedrich zum 10: Todestag* (= europäische ideen, vol. 29) (Berlin, 1977).
82. Tenfelde, p. 221.
83. Bock, p. 82.
84. Ibid., p. 118.
85. Ibid., p. 120.
86. Rocker, *Memoiren*, p. 300.
87. Bock, p. 119.
88. P. von Oertzen, 'Die grossen Streiks der Ruhrhergarbeiterschaft im Frühjahr 1919', *Vierteljahreshefte·für Zeitgeschichte* 6 (1958) pp. 243–5; Bock, p. 120f.
89. Oertzen, p. 255 with footnote 101.
90. Cited in Bock, p. 363ff.
91. Ibid., p. 164, footnote 52.
92. Ibid., p. 164f.
93. *Keine Kriegswaffen mehr!* Speech by comrade Rocker (Berlin), on the occasion of the National Conference of the German armament workers, held in Erfurt from 18–22 March 1919, Erfurt (1919) p. 11f.
94. Bock, p. 292.
95. In *Der Syndikalist*, II/16 (1920) quoted from Bock, p. 292f.
96. *Keine Kriegswaffen mehr!*, p. 5.
97. Ibid., p. 12.
98. Bock, p. 169.
99. R. Rocker, *Zur Betrachtung der Lage in Deutschland. Die Möglichkeiten einer freiheitlichen Bewegung* (New York-London-Stockholm, 1947) p. 10.
100. Rocker, *Memoiren*, p. 303.
101. U. Rath, 'Direkte Aktion?' *Die Internationale* (see footnote 40), II/10 (August 1929) pp. 14–20.
102. H. W. Gerhard, 'Direkte Aktion? Zu dem Artikel von U. Rath', ibid., II/10 (September 1929) pp. 7–9.
103. H. Beckmann, 'Die Übernahme der Produktionsmittel durch die Arbeiter', ibid., II/11 (September 1929) pp. 10–12; II/12 (October 1929) pp. 16–18.
104. A. Souchy, '*Vorsicht: Anarchist!' Ein Leben für die Freiheit. Politische Erinnerungen* (Darmstadt-Neuwied, 1977) p. 261.
105. R. Rocker, 'Revolutionsmythologie und revolutionäre Wirklichkeit', *Die freie Gesellschaft, Monatsschrift für Gesellschaftskritik und freiheitlichen Sozialismus*, IV/36–7 (November 1952); Souchy, *Erinnerungen*, p. 259ff.
106. Cf. Lösche, p. 148: 'The old anarchist slogan of "propaganda by the deed" has a new meaning to the pragmatic anarchists, and becomes "propaganda through the deed": these include all forms of civil disobedience and living an exemplary communal life. Thus "direct action" becomes "a theory and practice striving to

achieve the active participation of a vast majority of people in all political decisions . . . " ' i.e., a direct-plebiscitary democracy; for English anarchism see J. Quail, *The Slow Burning Fuse: The Lost History of the British Anarchists* (London, 1978); for German anarchism after 1945 see G. Bartsch, *Anarchismus in Deutschland*, vol. 1, 1945–65 (Hannover, 1972); vol. 2, 1965–73 (Hannover, 1973).

The following books were published only after the completion of this article and could therefore not be taken into consideration: J. Wagner, *Politischer Terrorismus und Strafrecht im Deutschen Kaiserreich von 1871* (Berlin, 1981); R. Theisen, P. Walter, J. Wilhelms, *Anarcho-Syndikalistischer Widerstand an Rhein und Ruhr* (Meppen, 1981).

14 Syndicalism, Strikes and Revolutionary Action in France[1]

F. F. Ridley

'Once simply economic, the strike has become revolutionary – the workers have made of it a weapon of war.' 'The union is a militant formation organised for the class struggle, and the strike is the most common weapon.' Thus two French historians of the labour movement, one sympathetic, the other hostile, writing in the first decade of this century when revolutionary syndicalism appeared to dominate French trade unions.

Whatever the facts about the strike record during the period, militant syndicalists certainly presented strikes in this way. Government, press and middle class tended to share their view. Thus an American historian on the great strike movement of 1906, writing a few years after the event:

> The 1st May found Paris in a state of siege. Clemenceau had collected numerous troops in the capital. Since the days of the Commune, Paris had not seen so many. Among the bourgeoisie real panic reigned. Many left Paris to cross the Channel. Those who remained spoke of the coming revolution which the unions were to let loose on society.

This feeling reoccurred during the 1909 public service strikes. In the words of the *Spectator* at the time:

> Englishmen lately returned from Paris tell us that respectable French people are alarmed at the frequency and viciousness of labour riots, shake their heads at the sign of the times, and speak of another revolution. We cannot help feeling that there will be no revolution. Paris would not be Paris if it were not on the verge of one; it generally has been; and we have come to understand that in the clear atmosphere of quick and vivid thought there things seem much nearer than they are.

It was right, of course. Revolutionary syndicalism made no revolution. Indeed, it now appears that syndicalists did not even stimulate French

230

workers to anything very extraordinary in the way of everyday strikes. Recent labour historians have analysed the evidence to show that the number and character of strikes during the period did not differ significantly from the strike record of other times or in other countries. Which is not to say that a fair number of workers may not have seen their action through 'revolutionary' eyes.

The revolutionary syndicalists preached direct action to achieve their aims, whether immediate improvements in their conditions of employment or the final emancipation of the proletariat. They rejected the 'constitutional' channels of democracy: parties, elections, parliament, legislation. Nor did they wish to act as a pressure group within the system, pursuing the alternative line of democratic politics through negotiation and compromise. Their short-run aim was to win concessions from employers and government by war and, more important, to overthrow capitalist system and state through war. The war fought by workers is the class war, the strike its weapon par excellence. In syndicalist theory, therefore, the strike was a form of permanent revolution. It is with the strike in this sense, a form of direct action outside and against the constitutional order, that this article is concerned.

Interpretation of the strike as a form of revolutionary direct action can only be understood by putting the strike in the context of syndicalist theory. But what is syndicalist theory? Syndicalism was a movement rather than a philosophy, a trend within the French labour movement. In one sense it was the principles adopted by the *Confédération Générale du Travail* (CGT) in the first decade of the present century; in another it was the practice of militant workers. How widely believed the principles really were, how distinctive the practice of those who believed them, is another matter. The point here is that no doctrine entitled 'revolutionary syndicalism' was ever officially adopted by the CGT. Nor was it the creation of an identifiable group of political theorists. There were a number of 'theorists' among the militant leadership but their ideas are scattered in newspapers, pamphlets and speeches. There is no authorised, coherent body of writing. Principles were adopted by the CGT at different times, sometimes with little reference to one another, often little supported in practice. The meaning attached to them (notably to the doctrine of the general strike) also changed over time. In my view syndicalism is best understood as a particular temper, reflected in sentiments and expressed in action. For the moment, however, we are concerned with theory. The theory, then, is a bit like a patchwork quilt: bits added now here, now there, gradually built up, but in accordance with no prearranged plan, thus forming no logical pattern. The logic, to some extent, has to be read into syndicalism, or imposed upon it, for the sake of exposition. It follows that the study of syndicalism falls between two stools, history and political theory. This partly explains the unsatisfactory nature of much that has been written on the subject. The absence of records of what rank-file syndicalists actually thought and did led commentators to interpret the movement in terms of its pamphleteers. While taking the latter at face value makes for bad labour history, it may not be entirely unreasonable at first sight for the historian of political thought. Union declarations and articles by union leaders can be taken at their face value to construct a theory of syndicalism without the political theorist worrying too much about the representative character of his sources.

Even for the political theorist, however, there is a serious problem of the relationship between theory and practice in the case of syndicalism. Syndicalism was often called a 'philosophy of action' by its exponents. This meant more than that they advocated action, central though this was. They used the phrase to describe the nature of syndicalism itself, though in an ambiguous way. They often stressed the spontaneity of syndicalism: it was not a matter of 'think first, act later' but of 'act first'. Sometimes this only meant that syndicalism was supposed to be an *interprétation clairvoyante* of working-class action, itself intuitive: principles were drawn from the lessons of life rather than ivory-tower speculation and centred on strategies of action rather than the solution of theoretical problems. Sometimes they went further, claiming that syndicalism was action itself, what the workers did, deeds not words. Syndicalist workers, so the argument runs, need not consciously subscribe to the doctrines of revolutionary syndicalism at all. The writings of militant syndicalists, even if they claim to do no more than make explicit the experience of the movement, can then be thought of as 'meta-syndicalism' and it is the action of workers that needs to be considered if one is to study the essence of syndicalism. If that is true (though it does not seem a very satisfactory way of defining any 'ism'), it places the study of the subject back even more firmly in the field of the historian. Recent labour historians have certainly looked at it this way. Claiming to find nothing very distinctive about the activities of the French labour movement during the period, either in the number of strikes or in their character, they have argued that syndicalism never existed at all. But, again, the situation is more complicated because the theorists of syndicalism maintained that action has a subjective as well as an objective aspect: what mattered was not so much what the workers did but the way they did it. I do not mean here whether their strikes were more violent than other strikes (that claim of the time has also be undermined by recent historians) but how they perceived their action. The syndicalist worker did not articulate a philosophy, he felt it. It is hard to see how the historian can test this.

For the moment I want to put together – briefly and somewhat selectively, picking out the ideas that are particularly relevant to the doctrine of direct action through strike – the theory of syndicalism as found in the writing of its leaders. I shall return to the obvious questions. First, did it correspond to the ideas of the movement, or at least its rank-and-file militants? While certainly not articulating such ideas in a systematic way, the militants probably had some sort of picture in their mind into which, at least as slogans, they probably fitted quite well. Second, did it correspond to the practice of the movement?

As in many other movements, the Christian churches for example, there does seem to have been a considerable gap between apparent belief and practice: syndicalism was later described by one of its own leaders as having been little more than *verbalisme révolutionnaire*.

At the root of syndicalist theory lay the idea of the class war. Though the terminology was marxist, the concept was reduced to a simple slogan and taken as a fact experienced every day by workers, requiring no theoretical foundation. No legislative reforms, no agreements with employers, could free them from the double yoke of oppression and exploitation. Only complete overthrow of the existing order, abolition of property and destruction of the state, could emancipate the proletariat. Emancipation meant revolution and syndicalism was essentially a strategy of revolution. The capitalist order would be replaced by an anarchist society geared to the working class: the 'administration of things' would be undertaken by industrial unions and local inter-union trades councils; without 'government of men', the state was superfluous. In fact Utopia played almost as small a part in syndicalism as in marxism although its outlines were a little clearer and, more important, it was based on a harmony between means and ends.

Syndicalism made little of marxist theories about the automatic intensification of conflict, inevitable revolution and predestined victory of the proletariat. It tended to see the class war as a war like any other: victory would depend on the fighting spirit – élan – of the workers, on will not the forces of history. *Vouloir, c'est pouvoir* was a favourite slogan. There were, however, attempts to have it both ways. Syndicalists sometimes balanced free will by historical forces, maintaining that workers' participation in the class struggle was an 'intuitive' reaction to their circumstances and that strikes objectively furthered the revolutionary cause even if, subjectively, strikers did not see themselves as revolutionaries.

If the war was to be won, it must be fought; and if it was to be fought with spirit, its existence must be constantly reaffirmed. As in any war, this meant an absolute breach between the contestants. The proletariat must not only oppose bourgeois interests at all points, it must isolate itself from bourgeois institutions and bourgeois state. In order that the division of society into hostile camps might be seen clearly by all, any overlap between classes must be prevented. Collaboration with socialist intellectuals only blurred the issue. Moreover, as the basis of class war was the conflict of interest between workers and employers, the support of middle-class socialists was likely to be superficial: in practice they fraternised with the enemy and tended to compromise with him; if allowed to influence the working-class movement, they would divert it. To maintain its revolutionary spirit, in other words, the movement must restrict itself to those bound by immediate ties of common exploitation and organise itself entirely within the formations proper to its own class. Syndicalism proclaimed itself proletarian.

Rejection of what the syndicalists called 'politics' followed from this.

Political action, whether democratic or revolutionary, led to the confusion of classes and thus undermined the class war whatever the intention. Political parties, even when they claimed to represent a class interest, cut across class lines in their membership. Socialist parties, reformist and revolutionary alike, were dominated by men who were not workers. Because they rested on philosophy rather than directly experienced interest, they were an artificial form of organisation, lacking the genuine bonds necessary for battle formations. Political action, even for soi-disant revolutionary parties, was primarily electoral, appealing to workers as citizens, a role they shared with other classes. The normal terrain of politics – parliament – was common to all parties and all classes: it tended to associate rather than differentiate proletariat and bourgeoisie. Even revolutionary politics could not escape the fact that its battle ranks were not rigorously class-based because its methods (e.g. barricades) were not specific to the working class.

Democracy, above all, contradicted the idea of class war. Its essential character was agreement. Even under the banner of a revolutionary programme, it involved parties in *formal* collaboration with the bourgeoisie and thus recognition of the existing order. Worse: the parliamentary milieu inevitably led to *real* collaboration with the bourgeoisie; democratic politics meant bargaining, concessions and ultimate betrayal of the working class. Whatever immediate benefits the workers may gain from this process, they could not compensate for its dangers. Democracy was a system designed for bourgeois domination, a facade to hide the real nature of social conflict under capitalism, a game that diverted the energy of the working class into harmless channels. Social reforms, moreover, were merely attempts to undermine the class war, palliatives that did not alter fundamental property relations. Again, an ambiguity, for syndicalists campaigned for such reforms, describing them as partial expropriations of the capitalists, thus steps towards the final revolution. Such gains, however, were not achieved through parliamentary politics but were won in battle, obtained by the direct action of the working class in the class struggle.

In place of the party, the syndicalists put the trade union. This was the autonomous organisation of the working class, wholly proletarian in character. The union clearly differentiated the classes, organising the workers not on the basic socialist ideas they might share with others but in their essential quality as workers. This was also its strength compared to the party: members were not asked to make an intellectual commitment, they simply entered a relationship forced upon them by their economic situation and the lessons of life: while the party was an association of choice, the union was an association of necessity. The union, finally, stood at the very point where the class conflict arose: it organised the worker in the direct struggle against the immediate class enemy. It was here that the class war was best fought.

In place of the state, syndicalists also put the union. With anarchists, they believed that power corrupts and that freedom cannot be established from above. They rejected the revolution that was simple a coup d'état, just another form of political action, believing that the state would not wither away under a marxist dictatorship of the proletariat. Just as parliament was the natural form of government in a bourgeois society and dictatorship in a marxist, so they believed that unions, horizontally and vertically federalised, were the natural form of administration in the free society of the future.

The union therefore linked the present and the future. It organised the worker in his everyday struggle against the employer, obtaining material concessions of immediate value and preparing him for the revolution. Battle formation, it was at the same time cell of the new order. This allowed syndicalists to declare their movement self-sufficient. Every action that reinforced the union, every action that strengthened its will and increased its power, was at one and the same time a step towards the final revolution and a brick built for the society to come. The seeds of destruction carried within capitalism were also the seeds of construction: the final revolution would bring no problems of transition.

The revolution could not be achieved through democratic political channels, but only by the workers acting for themselves. This was the doctrine of direct action. The syndicalists interpreted the formula that the emancipation of the proletariat must be the work of the proletariat itself literally: it must be achieved by workers acting as workers (through unions not parties) and it must be achieved without intermediaries (through direct action not electoral politics). Direct 'political' action – insurrection – was not feasible, however, because the class enemy controlled the powerful forces of the state. Just as the union was the proper form of organisation for workers, so industrial action was their proper sphere of action. The syndicalists advocated various forms of industrial action such as boycott, sabotage and work to rule. The strike, however, was direct economic action par excellence. It was the clearest expression of the class war, placing the workers in an immediate conflict with the employers and thus illuminating most sharply the antagonism between capital and labour. It was also the most effective weapon available. It had the advantage of involving the immediate and inescapable interests of the working class, mobilising energies that political issues failed to sustain. It drew those lacking revolutionary consciousness into forms of action that could be used for revolutionary ends by a militant leadership. Its battle formations were ready made, requiring no fragile political organisations.

The strike had a double aspect, conveniently linking reformist and revolutionary goals. Even if the workers were only pursuing some immediate concession from the employer, such as a wage increase, it automatically furthered the cause of revolution. If it was successful, the gain was a partial expropriation of the capitalists and a weakening of the power of the bourgeoisie. At the same time, every strike – whether successful or not – increased the hostility between the classes and thereby stimulated further conflict, sharpened the war that had to be fought. It encouraged working-class solidarity, stimulated revolutionary élan and served as a training ground for the greater battles yet to come. Syndicalism was sometimes called a philosophy of the strike and, certainly, its central feature was the advocacy of strikes as revolutionary direct action outside and against the political order of the time.

The strike also lay at the centre of the logic of syndicalism. The outcome and climax of a long series of such strikes, growing ever larger, becoming better organised and at the same time increasingly bitter, would be the general strike. It would finally overthrow the capitalist system and emancipate the proletariat. The concept of the general strike completed the syndicalist strategy. Capitalism would never voluntarily surrender its power and privileges: the general strike was thus the corner stone on which all else had ultimately to rest, for it alone could bring the class war to a victorious conclusion. The general strike, however, was closely linked to the strike of every day. The revolution would not be an isolated event but the outcome of a continuous intensification of the regular struggle of the working class. Although it would mobilise more workers, last longer and involve more violence than previous strikes, it would not differ from them in essence. It was to be the last battle, not the entire war. The syndicalist programme of action was thus able to claim a remarkable degree of unity. Tactics and strategy – strike and general strike – were links in a single chain. The union, natural formation of battle, was also the natural cell of the new society, bringing means and ends into the same link.

Above we have put syndicalist doctrine of the strike in its theoretical context. Strikes were considered a form of direct action. Direct action meant by-passing electoral politics. Even when the immediate aim was reformist legislation (as on the eight-hour day), this was seen as pressure against, rather than within, the constitutional order. Strikes were links in the chain leading to the general strike and thus a form of permanent revolution.

How did this interpretation, put on strikes by the militant theorists of the movement, correspond to the reality of strikes? In practice, the labour movement undoubtedly pursued reformist aims, primarily concessions from employers, in the manner of trade unions elsewhere. It was sometimes said, therefore, that the syndicalist doctrine of the strike was a rationalisation. Syndicalist leaders, in a period of 'revolutionary romanticism', as the CGT leader of the time was himself to call it later, interpreted reformist practice to fit the programme of revolutionary syndicalism – as its theory so conveniently allowed. What, however, did the rank and file think when they took part in the everyday struggle of the labour movement? A clear answer, as I will suggest below, is impossible. Most strikes pursued specific reforms and were settled on that basis – win or lose. But even if the motivation was not revolutionary, that does not mean that many workers did not see the strike in some such way, their quite ordinary actions acquiring a romantic tinge as a result. It seems likely that notions of the general strike, even hazier notions of the emancipation of the workers, formed part of the stock of mental images of part of the working class. Most of the time they were probably no more than hazy pictures at the back of their minds but occasionally, at the height of battle, in the nation-wide movements of strike and agitation or in particularly bitter local conflicts, when the class war was seen most sharply, these pictures doubtless grew brighter, suddenly giving a wider significance to their campaigns, perhaps even acting as a morale booster pushing such movements further than they would otherwise have gone. On several occasions, certainly, there was a feeling, shared by workers and bourgeoisie, that revolution or something very similar was about to occur. This article opened with reference to the strike movements of 1906 and 1909. Despite the talk of militants, the workers entered those strikes without any real revolutionary intent. The picture of revolution may have been vivid enough – one gets the feeling that it was – but that does not necessarily mean that revolutionary slogans were believed, much less that anyone seriously intended to act them out.

Can the strikes of the period nevertheless be interpreted as direct action with the anti-democratic implications suggested above? Direct action was the syndicalists' most popular slogan. But, again, it was something of a theoretical construct. The practice of direct action was simply what the workers did. Though a necessary part of their programme, syndicalists described it as spontaneous, pursued, in other words, without reference to syndicalist doctrines. Workers usually struck because of the pressure of economic conditions. One must not fall into the trap of treating their activities as a consequence of syndicalist theory, a trap that syndicalist theory itself, though sometimes ambiguously, tried to avoid. The fact remains, however, that interpretations of the strike as direct action seem to have had wide currency, that a fair number of workers seem to have talked and thought in this way. Whatever the reasons for their action, whatever its real character, it could be seen by participants as action outside the democratic process. In that sense the secretary general of the CGT could describe it at its 1912 congress as 'permanent illegality'.

Strikes are part of the normal behaviour pattern of workers, not specifically syndicalist. I have made the point that images may have attached to them in the first decade of this century in France, even if they did not affect the strikers' practice. One could refer to the revolutionary tradition of France, part of the political culture into which succeeding generations were socialised. As one historian of political thought put it: 'On the least provocation the French visualised themselves as overturning something; there have perhaps been too many pictures of revolutionary heroes storming the barricades. The Marseillaise, with its call to arms, was in their blood.' In that tradition, images of the strike were a substitute for the barricades. Such images fill a need: they can be attached to action with no more than marginal influence upon it. Another aspect of French culture has also been invoked. Thus a historian of the labour movement: 'For the French it was not sufficient to act under necessity – the act had to be generalised into principle, the principle systematised, and the system compressed into concise and catching formulae.' These formulae had their place at mass meetings, filling a need, again, without necessarily affecting action very much.

One may nevertheless ask whether syndicalism had a practical influence on the trade-union movement during the period of its supposed hegemony. Were there more strikes in France then than at other times, more strikes than in other industrialised countries at the same time, more strikes than can be satisfactorily explained by socio-economic conditions? Were unions that voted syndicalist principles at national congresses more strike-prone than reformist unions? Did strikes show characteristics that distinguished them in any way? Were they more 'revolutionary', more violent for example, when practiced by syndicalist unions than otherwise? Recent students have answered these questions negatively and concluded that syndicalism did not really exist. Before turning to these analysts, let me say a few words about the strike record as it appeared to me. Workers certainly appeared strike-prone during the period and there was a tendency to see strikes not as once-and-for-all affairs, designed to achieve some particular concession that would satisfy the workers, but as part of an ongoing conflict. The general hostility of the CGT towards the whole idea of collective agreements was evidence of this. There was little feeling that the settlement of a strike restored social peace, even if it was to the workers' advantage. And if results were not obtained quickly, the unions went back to work, ready to try again as soon as circumstances permitted. Strikes were sometimes declared for quite trivial reasons. As one commentator later noted, these short but frequent strikes kept the working class in a state of alert. Employers and government also, one might have added. Syndicalists were prone to attribute the strike record to the growing combativeness of the working class, stimulated by the battles fought and by their own efforts to raise workers' understanding of the struggle. There were, however, other adequate explanations of the strike record. French unions were too weak at the time to negotiate successfully with employers and resorted to strikes in desperation. A policy of numerous short strikes was the only one possible, given the unions' limited funds and their inability to pay much in the way of strike benefits. The picture, in any case, is one now familiar to us and we are less likely to resort to ideological explanations unless we also attribute current strike waves in Britain to Trotskyite influence.

But what of the character of strikes? While reformist unions during the period were often willing to negotiate with employers, even to accept arbitration, syndicalist leaders called for direct action. This was an ambiguous phrase, however. Any strike meant action rather than talk, the use of 'force', at least to the extent that strikes are inescapably an attempt to bring pressure on the employers. In general, however, it meant more than that. One commentator in 1907 saw the distinction between syndicalist and reformist strikes in terms of the tactics employed rather than of the ends pursued. He claimed that despite much talk of direct action, no new tactics had appeared that could really intimidate employers or bourgeoisie except for the use of violence: the only contribution of syndicalist theory to direct action, in other words, was the principle of violence and the only distinguishing mark of syndicalism in practice was its use.

He denied – and his view has been confirmed by recent studies – that violence was often used by unions, thus implying that there were in fact few distinctively syndicalist strikes. Violence, when it occurred, was no syndicalist monopoly. It can break out spontaneously, without the inspiration of syndicalist theory, as the Encyclopaedia of Social Sciences pointed out: 'It is obvious that violence in the form of physical assault or destruction of property may easily arise in the course of a strike, particularly if it be prolonged or if bitter feeling is engendered'. That said, syndicalism gave it a theoretical justification and its polemical writings cannot have been entirely without influence.

Syndicalists, then, claimed that direct action distinguished the revolutionary strike from the passive – and legal – withdrawal of labour advocated by reformist unions. They tended to do so in military terms. The unions were short of soldiers as well as material: only a small proportion of the working class was unionised, so that a simple withdrawal of labour was likely to be ineffective even if, given their limited funds, it could be sustained for any length of time. More drastic action is called for to intimidate the bourgeoisie and thus wring concessions from it. In longer-term perspective, violence, by sharpening the conflict, deepens the split between proletariat and the forces of capitalism, including those of the state that come to its rescue, illuminates the class war, strengthens the solidarity of the workers and their resolve to fight. In the manner of Sorel, syndicalist leaders occasionally praised violence for reasons more sophisticated than the simple fact that it might frighten employers into surrender. By the deep feelings it aroused, the shock it administered to both sides, violence helped to divide the classes: it was the most effective antidote to reformist and democratic efforts at glossing over the fundamental issues of the class war. Violence, moreover, was more like war than a straightforward strike: it brought out the heroic qualities of the proletariat and, in that sense, had an educative value.

In general, however, syndicalists developed no real justifactory theory of violence, even when they advocated it, nor did they develop any original tactics for its use. It would, of course, have been difficult to complicate so simple an idea as the *coup de poing*. For the labour movement as a whole, in any case, acts of violence were probably just acts of violence, not even part of some unformulated picture of war in their minds. Sometimes stimulated by agitators, they were more often neither premeditated nor even deliberate: mounting bitterness as a result of continual disputes, personal hostility towards individual employers, the frustration of weakness caused by lack of numbers and shortage of funds, fraying tempers and growing tension, the final explosion often set off by the introduction of blackleg labour or intervention of the police. At such times, in such moods, the use of fists, stones, arson, even dynamite, requires no special explanation.

Violence could take the form of destroying property of the employers. At Marseille, for example, the dockers smashed cranes, fired warehouses and destroyed goods, until the military commander of the area was forced to declare a state of siege. At Brest they threw overboard the cargo of one ship and emptied a number of warehouses in similar fashion, rolling fifty barrels of wine into the sea. At Mazamet workers burnt down a textile mill and exploded dynamite cartridges in several others. During the campaign for weekly-day-of-rest legislation, waiters, barbers and shop assistants smashed shop windows and threw acid at shop fronts. While the hope in these cases may have been to terrorise employers into surrender, frustration and revenge were as likely motives. At Meru, for example, workers sacked an employer's home as well as his factory and bricks were not infrequently thrown at employers' houses. More frequent, perhaps, were attacks on blacklegs, probably for similar reasons. Yet there may have been the occasional elements of anarcho-syndicalist propaganda by the deed, doubtless rare and now hard to isolate. One syndicalist, reminiscing fifty years later, said that the first thing he did on joining the labour movement in 1902 was to re-edit an anarchist pamphlet on the manufacture of bombs: whenever a strike appeared to be drawing out, one of his friends would leave for the scene of action to blow out a few of the employer's windows.

More often, violence involved assault on persons and attacks on property outside the place of work, as when the linen weavers of Armentières pillaged shops. The majority of violent incidents, conflicts with the police for example, had no direct connection with strikes at all, but demonstrations by strikers could also lead to scuffles with the police and escalate into more serious clashes. Whether brawl or riot, such incidents turned strikes into conflicts with the forces of the state and served to underpin syndicalist notions about the nature of the class war. In retrospect, the incidence of violence may not be high, but critics at the time certainly spoke of 'revolutionary vandalism masked as strikes' and of 'movements which degenerated from strike into insurrection'. 'Direct action means violence' was a phrase that ran through their accounts. The impressions of the time were coloured by a relatively small number of dramatic conflicts where strikes escalated into riots and conflict with the troops (e.g. at Monceau-les-Mines, Villeneuve-Saint-Georges, Narbonne) and by an even smaller number of strikers in the public services which involved cases of sabotage and seemed for brief periods as if they might paralyse the country. The sporadic violence which occurred in other strikes during the period did not add up to a tactic of direct action. On occasion, nevertheless, they must have allowed workers to see themselves in a revolutionary light and, on occasion, revolutionary images must have contributed to their behaviour.

Attempts have recently been made to show that revolutionary syndicalism had no influence on French workers and that, therefore, there was little that can be described as syndicalist action, notably by Peter Stearns in *Revolutionary Syndicalism and French Labor* and by Edward Shorter and Charles Tilly in *Strikes in France 1830–1968*.

'Most historians who know anything about the French labour movement between 1890 and 1914 . . . would claim that revolutionary syndicalism was its most striking attribute.' Few would dispute Stearns' opening. 'This view is at best a good guess, for it has never been seriously tested. Historians . . . too often look at the expressed ideas of a movement or organisation without checking the extent to which the ideas were held by participants or manifested in their behaviour.' That, too, is fair comment. It is true that syndicalism, as other socialisms, tends to get written up in intellectual terms. Histories of political thought are legitimate. The difficulties arise when one tries to pin ideas on movements. Three questions may be asked. Did the declarations of principle of the CGT and the writings of its leaders reflect rank-and-file opinion: what proportion of the CGT (itself organising only a minority of the country's labour force) subscribed to syndicalist doctrines? Of those who apparently subscribed, how many really believed these doctrines: were they merely surface slogans, an automatic ritual repeated on certain occasions, or did they form a permanent and deeply felt set of beliefs? Were even the true believers prepared to prove their faith by action, or was life divided into unrelated compartments of theory and practice? The CGT undoubtedly contained many non-syndicalists – marxists, reformists, even some straight anarchists, as well as workers with no 'ism' at all. The syndicalists themselves were quite capable of the same *verbalisme révolutionnaire* of which they accused socialist politicians: they had no difficulty in pursuing practical, i.e. reformist, goals while repeating revolutionary slogans. Even believers seemed capable of dropping one set of slogans when emotional pressures made another more appropriate, as in the overnight transition from anti-militarist internationalism to patriotic mobilisation in 1914.

The trouble is, we have no direct way of answering these questions. As Shorter and Tilly say, the attitude survey is an option foreclosed to the student of history. A negative test is less difficult than a positive identification of past beliefs. In other words, it is easier to show what the rank-and-file cannot have believed very deeply by setting assumed beliefs against recorded practice. Revolutionary syndicalism preached intensification of the class war, advocated the strike as the only effective weapon and saw the general strike as sole means of emancipating the proletariat. The hold of syndicalism (if more than 'verbalisme') should therefore be reflected in the strike record of the labour movement during the period of apparent syndicalist hegemony. The studies mentioned show that there was nothing about the pattern of strikes – frequency, duration, size – which requires special explanation in terms of syndicalist leadership or syndicalist beliefs. Although there was an increase in strike activity during the period, it was matched by developments in other industrialised countries. High unemployment and a decline in living standards appear a reasonable explanation. The strike record of soi-disant syndicalist unions, moreover, was not different from that of French unions with other leadership.

The syndicalists, of course, never claimed that the strike rate was the most significant fact in the short run. They were well aware that poor and poorly organised unions, based on one trade in one town, could not mobilise workers on a large scale or for any length of time. As the secretary general of the CGT pointed out, it was the spirit that counted: syndicalist strikes were defined by their revolutionary character. What external indicators there might be, the manner in which strikes were settled, for example, or the use of direct action (for which read violence), do not substantiate this claim. Little appeared distinctive about syndicalist-led strikes: violence, for example, did not primarily occur in strikes at all and, where associated with strikes, were found as often in non-syndicalist unions. Violence, itself, moreover, could be adequately explained by other factors such as natural frustration, anger against blacklegs or clashes caused by the intervention of police.

There was another sense, however, in which syndicalist theorists might claim that their strikes were different in character from other strikes and this would not necessarily have been mirrored in the behaviour of strikers at all. For the revolutionary syndicalists – and this was the point Sorel picked up and dramatised – each strike was seen as a battle in the class war, each strike made the image of the general strike, the revolution itself, more vivid. The point, then, is that even if syndicalist strikes did not differ from others objectively, they may well have differed subjectively. It is hard to see what quantitative data could be used to test this claim. How can one determine what proportion of the population were genuine Christians at any given time in the past? If church attendance does not distinguish the true believer from the ritual attender, could one look at 'christian' behaviour in everyday life as an indicator? Surely not? Some of those who practice christian virtues will not be believers; some believers will not relate their faith to action. The same applies to the mythology of revolution. Sorel had the last word on this: 'We know that these myths in no way prevent a man profiting from the observation he makes in the course of his life and form no obstacle to the pursuit of normal occupations'. Stearns agrees that we cannot tell what the workers really thought, what myths they believed, for we cannot penetrate so deeply in their minds. 'Who then was really a syndicalist? We can never know for sure; but in terms of actual protest activity it does not seem to matter much.' That dismissal is too easy. It certainly mattered to contemporaries.

The rigorous method used in analysing the externally observable characteristics of strikes is not matched in these studies by a similar assessment of public opinion. This is shown in what is essentially a throw-away line: 'Neither the government nor the employers took syndicalism too seriously'. That, presumably, could be tested by a content analysis of contemporary newspapers and by study of contemporary commentators. In articles and books written at the time by employers' representatives, as well as more serious historians of the labour movement, one regularly comes across versions of the conspiracy theory, a small band of revolutionary leaders successfully inciting the workers to revolt. And there was a good deal of alarm in government circles and the middle class generally about the way things were going. The press shows this well enough. On that reading of the period, French strikes, whatever their real character, were played on a stage with a revolutionary backdrop: many strikes appeared to have a revolutionary potential, and thus presented a revolutionary image, to those on both sides of the class struggle. In retrospect, it is easy enough to see that there was no really likelihood of a revolutionary general strike, much less a successful one. But hindsight itself is a little too easy. The potential may have been real. Who then was really a syndicalist could have mattered a great deal.

The whole question of motivation, moreover, is not as simply dealt with as these studies would have one believe. Both tend to explain strikes as spontaneous reactions to environmental conditions. In this, though they do not seem to realise it, they echo syndicalist theory. The theorists of the movement argued that it did not matter whether strikes were syndicalist inspired nor, indeed, whether the rank and file consciously accepted syndicalist ideas. What mattered was that the labour movement should develop a revolutionary class consciousness. This they believed required no intellectual commitment on the part of the masses, not even the verbalised acceptance of certain doctrines. The revolutionary potential of the working class arose out of their industrial situation, their union membership and their conflict with the capitalist system. In one sense (though only one) syndicalism was a theory for the enlightened vanguard of the proletariat rather than for the masses – in that respect it closely resembled the position of marxist contemporaries. Syndicalists believed that the workers' will to action was more important than the inevitable contradictions of capitalism of orthodox marxism, but that will to action, nevertheless, arose out of their natural situation and, in the last resort, did not require of them that they should be syndicalists.

Of course the theorists, who were also militant leaders of the CGT, did not entirely believe this for it would have made nonsense of their own efforts. Their purpose was to enhance the workers' awareness of the class war and stimulate his will to action. Can one disentangle the two influences, environmental and propagandist, on the minds of the workers? But that is not the point I have in mind here. It is simply this. The studies discussed set out to prove that syndicalist ideas did not cause strikes or violence. But in the course of conflicts caused by other factors, did some workers see themselves as engaged in a revolutionary activity? Did action give rise to images, some translated into slogans, that influenced the pattern of reaction, if only at the margin? Or were such images already there, part of the political culture? Can one then disentangle the direct influence of environmental factors from the mediating influence of a language into which workers had grown?

One cannot, in other words, dismiss as easily as Shorter and Tilly 'the closet of psychological explanations'. An explanation of behaviour that does not seek to enter the mind of actors is necessarily incomplete. Action requires the will to act, and that requires psychological motivation. Correlation of environmental conditions with strike records does not explain the way in which environmental inputs are transformed into strike outputs in the 'black box' of the human mind. The causal relationship need not be straightforward. External stimuli are not automatic triggers: they act on a set of attitudes, beliefs and dispositions, and it is only through them that they are translated into motivations to act. It is no answer to this to rely on aggregate data, discounting individual attitudes 'because surrounding political, social, economic and industrial structures call forth and transform collective action quite independent on the psychologies of the individuals involved in group action'. It is not groups that act; it is individuals. All one can argue is that if they act collectively there must be a collective 'black box' with collective images.

This, of course, is the notion of political culture and political sub-cultures. Can one doubt that the cultures of the working class – the stock of images and the language of thought – differ from country to country as a result of the different historical experience of each? French, German and English workers, in other words, may have acted in similar ways for what are, in the last resort, rather different reasons. The trouble with cliometrics is that it brushes aside what it cannot measure. The direct action of French workers during the period of syndicalism may be 'explained' – and thus explained away – by environmental factors common to industrialised nations. The same events can be 'explained' by ideological factors, if not as rigorously because these are not amenable to quantification. Because the first set of explanations appears to make the second unnecessary is no conclusive proof of their irrelevance. The revolutionary tradition in France, for example, is not an invention of historians who prefer the history of ideas. One has only to get a feel for the French labour movement in the early years of the century – by reading, not counting – to acquire a sense of its force.

And syndicalist leaders undoubtedly had some influence on the thinking of militant workers. To say, as Stearns does, that past historians of the French labour movement have been wrong because they tended to assume that workers are easily motivated by ideas is surely to underrate the working class.

Whether images acquired through political socialisation or intuitively acquired in class conflict, whether ideas consciously picked up from speeches, newspapers and pamphlets – syndicalist notions appear to have had some currency among sections of the French labour movement. All contemporary commentators agreed on this and they cannot all have misread the situation. We shall never know how many syndicalists there really were. They cannot now be counted. Nor can we now determine the 'cash value' of such notions, what effect they really had on action.

As far as violence is concerned, however, if we mean by that more than the odd brawl, generalised data is not relevant in any case. It is marginal explanations that matter: what caused a particular person to act the way he did. It does not need an entire workforce to throw bombs for havoc to be caused; a single bomb will do. Such explanations must be largely psychological in the strict sense. Whatever the personal factors that produce an activist temper, there are enough case studies to show the influence of ideas on receptive minds. In that respect revolutionary syndicalism surely had its impact, like anarchism before it. To the broad sweep of the history of the labour movement that impact may appear marginal – but where real violence is concerned the margin is important. As those who live in societies where violent action occurs will only too readily understand.

NOTE

1. This article draws in part on my earlier book *Revolutionary Syndicalism in France* (Cambridge, 1970). The two works referred to are: E. Shorter and C. Tilly, *Strikes in France 1830–1968* (Cambridge, 1974); P. N. Stearns, *Revolutionary Syndicalism and French Labor* (Rutgers, 1971).

15 Georges Sorel and the Myth of Violence: From Syndicalism to Fascism

Wilfried Röhrich

Wyndham Lewis believed himself to be justified in saying: 'Georges Sorel is the key to all contemporary political thought'.[1] This dictum appears extreme and yet it contains a grain of truth. After all, Sorel did provide very disparate movements of his day with stirring slogans – albeit frequently unintentionally. And it was no accident that prominent leaders of these movements referred to him time and again. What they most often resorted to was his myth of violence. Two historic movements, in particular, made use of this idea, and Sorel's interpreters have dubbed him more than once the metaphysician of revolutionary Syndicalism and the pioneer of Fascism. Yet, possibly the most important trait of his intellectual attitude – his revolutionary conservatism – was brought out only rarely.

What argues for the hypothesis that Sorel's stance was essentially one of revolutionary conservatism is his deep-rooted hostility towards the French Republic and the ideology it was founded on, one which Sorel fought against alternately from the Left and the Right. Himself a member of the bourgeoisie, he detested his class, above all because he found it lacked the political energy and moral seriousness which it had once possessed. Sorel's criticism was directed against Liberalism and parliamentary democracy and he was never tired of reproaching the liberal enlightenment for having initiated the process of decay at the end of which there would be nothing but a void, unless some new faith replaced the old. One may see in this the true meaning of Sorel's attempt to secure for the myth of violence its due role in the dawn of a new age. And it was the latter which was the true concern of Georges Sorel, the 'revolutionary conservative'.

While this French thinker thus remained faithful to his cause, his public statements about the issues of his day changed with confusing speed. Let us here retrace some of these issues and Sorel's comments on them: Sorel was born in 1847 and reached the age of 45 before he gave up his profession as a civil engineer in order to devote himself to his private studies. He therefore experienced at first hand the period leading up to the Paris Commune and this no doubt helped to shape his hostility towards liberalism and parliamentary democracy. The June revolution of 1848 and the defeat of the proletariat were followed in 1851 by Bonapartism which, according to Marx's definition, represented 'the only possible form of government at a time, when the bourgeoisie had already lost its capacity to rule the nation, while the working class had not yet acquired that capacity'.[2] Thus, the bourgeoisie, which Sorel later described as lacking energy, had even at that time relinquished its political role in order to safeguard its social existence. Increasingly, the bourgeoisie longed for a period 'when it could rule without being responsible for its rule; when a bogus power, standing between it and the people, would have to act and at the same time serve as hiding place for it; when it would have a crowned scapegoat, whom the proletariat could hit at whenever it wanted to attack the bourgeoisie, and against whom it might make common cause with the proletariat, whenever the scapegoat became a nuisance or showed signs of establishing itself as a power in its own right'.[3]

This early observation by Marx characterises the situation of 1850/51 very accurately and at the same time reveals the indecisive attitude of the workers, who, as Marx noted in his 'Eighteenth Brumaire', denied themselves the honour 'of being a conquered force', but instead bowed to their fate and proved 'that the defeat of June 1848 had made them incapable of fighting for years to come'.[4] Even then that moral decline of the ruling classes, which Sorel later never ceased to deplore, revealed itself. But equally the French labour movement, which Sorel later turned to, was still far from assuming a historically significant role.

It is superfluous here to dwell on the details surrounding the rise of the Paris Commune, which was to weaken the labour movement very much further. As we know, after a siege of almost two months and an eight-day battle on the barricades, the Paris Commune was defeated. In the executions during the 'bloody week' that followed, the labour movement again, as in 1848, lost its most active members and its ablest leaders, not only in Paris, but also in Lyon, St Etienne, Marseilles, Toulouse, Narbonne, Limoges and all other places where the communard movement had awakened proletarian impulses.

The French labour movement was to recover only slowly from the defeat of the Paris Commune. Accompanied by heated internal controversies, it began to gain strength again in the period from 1880 to 1900.[5] Within the organised parties of the labour movement the greatest differences of opinion were provoked by the question as to the wisdom of a policy of electoral alliances with bourgeois democrats and gradual participation in the rule of government. In the somewhat overstated partisan terms of a prominent historian of Anarcho-Syndicalism, which could equally have come from Georges Sorel: 'Everything turned on a few, mostly illusory mandates to the Chamber of Deputies, on municipal mandates, rather agreeable to the incumbents, and on coveted jobs on daily papers, *Citoyen-Bataille*, etc.'. Only the Anarchists were dedicated to the 'economic struggle' and thus gained the sympathy of many workers; 'slowly there developed that absolute contempt for politicking, which was later, in the heyday of Syndicalism, to break through for a time with such elemental force'.[6]

Increasingly, this tendency was to find its expression in the new Syndicalist movement, which grew much more rapidly than the party organisations. In 1884 there followed the final abolition of the ban on coalitions with the passing of a new law on associations. Two years later, under the aegis of the *Parti Ouvrier Français* (Guesdists), the *Féderation Nationale des Syndicats* was formed. This, however, in contrast to the *Bourses du Travail* established soon thereafter, was to gain no lasting importance. The *Bourses du Travail* – the first was created in Paris in 1887 as combined employment agency, assembly point and training centre – were the seat of the local branch offices established by the trade unions, and provided a variety of new impulses. Certainly the most important of these was the suggestion made in 1887 by the Paris labour exchange to create a federation of labour exchanges, a plan that was to be realised that very year at St Etienne. Three years later, the *Féderation Nationale des Bourses du Travail* was to find in Fernand Pelloutier the organiser and secretary who probably exerted the greatest influence on revolutionary Syndicalism. With him originated the idea of the general strike, which Sorel later adopted. In revolutionary Syndicalism embodying this specific idea, both the democratic and reformist Socialism of Jean Jaurès and the 'orthodox' Marxism of Jules Guesde had acquired a rival that could not be matched by the 'putschism' of a Blanqui or the mere anarchism of a Bakunin.

Especially hostile towards parliamentary Socialism, Pelloutier's main concern – just as very soon thereafter Sorel's – was to disabuse Anarchism of its faith in the persuasive power of dynamite, and the trade-union movement of the hope it vested in social reforms. The trade-union movement of revolutionary-syndicalist persuasion would have to rethink the direction of its economic-revolutionary thrust. This new thinking was to be provided by the *Bourses du Travail*, as study centres where, as Pelloutier's brother Maurice noted, 'the proletariat could reflect on its situation and investigate the individual elements of the economic problem, in order to become capable of its own liberation, which is theirs by right'.[7] Intent on the 'anarchist education of man', the trade-union movement had to aim at transforming society. Revolutionary Syndicalism had to become the practical training ground for the class war, as Fernand Pelloutier reiterated more than once in his programmatic article 'L'anarchisme et les syndicats ouvriers'.[8]

In the context of this paper it is neither possible nor necessary to trace the phenomenon of revolutionary Syndicalism in France in great detail, since this is in any case the subject of another contribution.[9] Only certain phases and basic ideas will be briefly sketched in here, so as to bring out Sorel's attitude towards Syndicalism more clearly:

After the organisational accord reached at Montpellier in 1902 (a year after Pelloutier's death), an agreement of views was achieved at the Congress of Amiens (1906), which provided an essential precondition for the strengthening of the Syndicalist movement. The Congress of Amiens confirmed the separation of revolutionary Syndicalism from the Socialist parties and determined that every member of the CGT (*Confédération Générale du Travail*) was free to 'participate outside his trade organisation in such forms of struggle as correspond to his philosophical and political views', but it also laid down that these views were not to be carried into the trade unions. According to the *Charte d'Amiens*, the CGT comprised all workers 'who are conscious of the need to fight in order to abolish wage slavery and private enterprise'. It demanded the 'recognition of the class struggle, which on the economic level brings the worker into revolt against all forms of material and moral exploitation and oppression deployed by the capitalist class'.[10]

The *Charte* brought out the concept of the general strike as the syndicalists' guiding principle very clearly indeed: 'Il (le syndicalisme) préconise comme moyen d'action la grève générale'.[11] Proletarian solidarity had to develop on the basis of its strongest, i.e. the economic, bond. According to the Congress' resolution already referred to, the class war had to be conducted on the economic plane. It had to stress direct action, as opposed to parliamentary or indirect actions. This implied what was probably the most significant syndicalist demand, namely that the emancipation of the proletariat would have to be the work of the proletariat itself. In the explanatory words of Victor Griffuelhes, 'direct action means action by the workers themselves, an action carried out directly by the participant himself. It is the worker himself who makes the effort, carrying it out personally against the powers which rule him, in order to gain from them the advantages he claims. By this direct action the worker takes up the fight himself; it is he who carries it out, determined not to leave the concern for his emancipation to anyone but himself.'[12] This direct action, in the form of street demonstrations, sabotage, boycott, union label or strike, implied also an appeal to moral exertion by the individual.

Thus, the means for the overthrow of the capitalist social order was the general strike. It implied the rejection of the private annexation of any surplus in nationalised production and therefore represented for the revolutionary Syndicalist movement the means of action par excellence. 'The refusal to continue production within the framework of capitalism', declared Emile Pouget,

> will not be wholly negative. It will go hand in hand with the seizure of the means of production and reorganisation on a communist basis, originating from the trade unions as the social cells. The trade unions, having thus become the focal points of the new life, will supplant and destroy the focal points of the old order – the State and the municipalities.[13]

The CGT thus declared itself a revolutionary organisation, whose aim it was to seize economic and political power by direct action, culminating in a general strike.

The period during which revolutionary Syndicalism developed into *unité ouvriere* had come to a close – an end which very soon was to be accompanied by a loss of *élan*. The general strike in particular, which revolutionary Syndicalism had propagated as the signal for revolution, became less an aspect of revolutionary technique and instead increasingly a social myth mobilising the creative forces of the proletariat and implying an irrational ideal of 'perfection'. It gained a more symbolic significance, not least thanks to Sorel's attempt, in his 'Réflexions sur la violence', to provide the Syndicalist movement with a theoretical base. Increasingly out of temper with the bourgeoisie, Georges Sorel had turned to revolutionary Socialism and Syndicalism, prompted not by direct experience of proletarian misery, but by the spectacle of the ruling classes' moral decline. It is important to bear this in mind, since Sorel's stance bespeaks that of a revolutionary conservative who came to Marx by way of Vico.

It is not least this genesis which helps to explain the objectives contained in his 'Réflexions sur la violence'. They embody the philosophy of Sorel the Syndicalist and we must therefore now turn to them in greater detail. The 'Réflexions', a compilation of several articles previously published in *Mouvement Socialiste* contain the demand for a creative proletarian élite to grow out of the workers' movement, which would then be able to rise against parliamentary rule and at the same time, in order not to become weakened itself, stir a hostile bourgeoisie into militancy. The determining factor in this was the recognition that the proletariat's revolutionary energy would have to be mobilised by opposition from the bourgeoisie and that the movement could only be driven forward by *ricorso* to proletarian violence, in the sense of Giambattista Vico's theory of *corsi e ricorsi*. The 'diplomatic alliance' between State and party-socialists would have to be fought. Their amorphousness was to be defeated by the passionate nature of the action. This constituted an appeal to the heroism of the proletariat, combined with an absolute rejection of the 'optimistic school' of reformism which, as the elitist theoretician Vilfredo Pareto once expressed it, was under the illusion 'that the ruling class, inspired by pure charity', would exert itself 'for the benefit of the oppressed class'.[14]

Sorel, then, with the weapon of the general strike sought to counter party-socialism with bellicose proletarian solidarity. 'The syndicalist general strike', he wrote, 'is most closely related to the system of war: the proletariat organises itself for battle . . . by regarding itself as the great driving force of history and by subordinating every social concern to that of the struggle.'[15] For Sorel it was the great battle images which were to fire this struggle, it was the mythos of the *grève générale*, as the spontaneous expression of group beliefs, representing an intellectually irrefutable 'unity'. Socialist action was to be understood as an inner, spiritual imperative, as a philosophy of action akin to Henri Bergson's.[16] Sorel, who stressed the importance of the *élan vital*, took up this philosophy of creative evolution, which to him meant proletarian evolution. Socialism, 'une vertu qui naît', had to grow out of the working classes' dynamic impulses of will.

More than by Bergson, however, Sorel was influenced by Proudhon,[17] particularly with regard to the proletarian ethic, and the concept of justice connected with it. To be sure, many ideas of this 'first truly proletarian-socialist theoretician' (Edouard Berth) went unheeded by Sorel. Then, more than in Proudhon's day, the future of Socialism depended on the *scala del capitalismo* – and from this recognition flowed Sorel's demand, already referred to, to arouse the proletariat to engage as equals in the battle with a strong bourgeoisie.

Sorel, the anti-parliamentarian, sought to fuse Proudhon's work with that of Marx. Already in his essay 'Le procès de Socrate' (1889) he had begun to think in Proudhonist terms and even in his revolutionary Syndicalist phase he remained faithful to Proudhon's thinking. The idea of justice, just as the idea of the *bataille napoléonienne*, was an interpretation of Socialism based on Proudhon's concepts – a socialism conceived as a manifestation of the proletarian conscience, in the sense of a rugged, masculine moralism. Both men addressed themselves to the *homme révolté*, urging him to rise against the authoritarian forces; both emphasised the existential dialectic, in the sense of the *anima appassionata*. Sorel argued that the revolutionary energy of the proletariat alone 'could demonstrate the revolutionary reality to the bourgeoisie and spoil its pleasure in humanitarian platitudes'.[18] This French theoretician, who claimed to have 'moralised Marx a little',[19] interpreted Socialism as an inner tension, producing a combative spirit. Marx appeared not to have considered 'that there might occur a revolution whose ideal would be regression or at least the preservation of the social status quo'.[20] Marx was not able to conceive of such a 'revolution'. However, just such a revolution was now being sought, when the proletariat, originally perceived as a class on its own, began to develop, or rather its party organisation began to develop, into a vague community of interests. And in view of this phenomenon alone, the 'Reflections on Violence' would be heard on the other side of the barricades as well, in their intention to rekindle social antagonism. Not least for this reason, violence, in spontaneous action, was to arouse proletarian impulses of will, conscious that the struggle to come would be the 'most profound and sublime phenomenon of moral existence'.[21]

Violence, growing out of a revolutionary spirit and aiming at a napoleonic battle, was thus sanctioned. The proletariat appeared as the hero of the drama; the *grève générale* would become an 'accumulation d'exploits héroiques' (Sorel), corresponding to that freedom of will which Proudhon had stressed, providing the 'sentiments of the beautiful and sublime' that went with it.[22] In the place of 'force', as the bourgeoisie's instrument of power, 'violence', as the manifestation of the class struggle, indicated the method of the proletarian general strike. This violence, incomprehensible to a bourgeois society, aimed at the real possibility of a struggle, oriented on those great creative elements from which, according to Carlyle, 'truth' springs.

With the myth of the general strike it was intended to separate the classes; yet if it were only to make Syndicalism more heroic, that would already be an achievement of incalculable value. It was here that the significance of the myth of violence lay, and here also that of which Sorel said: 'One must invoke total images, capable in their entirety and by intuition alone . . . of evoking attitudes corresponding to the various manifestations of the war, which Socialism has begun against modern society'.[23]

With this I have outlined Georges Sorel's main ideas with regard to revolutionary Syndicalism. This conservative revolutionary entertained them only for a few years before he gradually came to hold the view – expressed on the publication of Croce's essay 'La morte del Socialismo' – that Socialism was dead.[24] By 1909, when Mussolini the socialist, in his comprehensive review of 'Réflexions sur la violence', stressed how much 'contemporary Socialism in Latin countries' owed to Sorel,[25] the latter had already completed his turn towards nationalism, which up to 1914 was to become increasingly emphatic. In this he was in harmony with the ideas of his time. The Syndicalist movement, too, had capitulated before the more powerful nationalist impulses. Everywhere, the idea of the nation superseded other hitherto dominant notions of solidarity. Several syndicalists in France turned to the *Action française*, while in Italy revolutionary socialists and syndicalists had come together with irredentists and nationalists already during the founding congress of the 'Associazione Nazionalista' in Florence (1910). And no less a man than Georges Sorel reached out 'his hand to the *Action française*, while his work proclaimed . . . the return of the fatherland'.[26] Together with Edouard Berth he became editor of *Cité Française*, a publication founded in 1910, and with the aid of the *Cercle Proudhon*, inspired by Sorel, the alliance between Sorelians and the Valoi-Group was to become even closer. A synthesis between nationalist and syndicalist ideas came about and it was possible to refer to Sorel, if for no other reason than that his general ideas were sufficiently vague to serve nationalist movements equally well.

Decisive above all was the myth of violence, now no longer implying a general strike, but a nationalist act of supreme solidarity. In the search, then, for revolutionary energy and spontaneous activity, one looked for a new combination of ideas, bearing in mind that, according to Sorel, the idea of the struggle would have to be preserved, if *élan* and existential impulses were not to be lost. In Italy he was remembered not least in terms of his 'exploits heroiques'. Here if was among the nationalists, as represented by Enrico Corradini, where 'the man of the national struggle . . . could hold out his hand to the man of the class struggle, as Sorel had done'.[27] Corradini, whom Mussolini was later to describe as 'the Fascist of the very first hour',[28] proclaimed, like Sorel, the myth of the nation. And if one takes a look in isolation at the ideology of big business at that time, close to both nationalism and Fascism, one realises that a considerable step in the direction of Fascism had already been taken.

Here again it would be beyond the scope of this paper to retrace the genesis of Fascism in detail. Without wishing to pre-empt the following contribution, it should nevertheless be borne in mind that Fascism could only acquire political power, because prominent factions within the economically dominant class and their political and ideological representatives desired this. Max Horkheimer's famous remark that those who don't want to talk about capitalism should also keep quiet about Fascism,[29] indicates the perhaps most relevant link between the two phenomena, namely of capitalist production and reproduction and the form of rule that goes with it. If one adds to this socio-economic function of Fascism the anti-communist ideology fostered by the revolutionary threat posed by the Italian maximalists, as well as the mass support provided by social groups of middle-class mentality[30] even before the Fascist seizure of power, it is possible to make out the historically significant contours of the epochal phenomenon of Fascism. These brief indications must suffice before we return once more to our more restricted subject: Sorel's relation to Fascism.

If Georges Sorel's relation to emergent Fascism – he died shortly before the march on Rome – is to be assessed correctly, it will be necessary to remember not only how dominant for his thinking were his anti-parliamentarian and anti-democratic views, but also his myths – the mythos of violence, of the general strike, of the nation. In this Sorel comes very close to Vilfredo Pareto's anti-democratic theory of the élite. Long before Sorel turned to politics, Pareto had recognised that parliamentary democracy, or at least the form it took at that time in Italy, was doomed. Already in his 'Trattato di sociologia generale' (1916) Pareto had advocated the energetic rule of the élite and condemned as demagogy any form of democratic government. Thus, in his later writings, we find the close intellectual relationship to Sorel emphasised; just like the latter, Pareto stressed the 'futility of parliamentary and democratic dogmas',[31] pointed to the 'absurd idea of one half plus one'.[32] As Mussolini had jibed: 'Oh, precious naïvety of an era that believes in the *metà più uno*'.[33] Both thinkers, in their advocacy of the elitist idea, aimed at a *trasformazione della democrazia*, according to the slogan with which Pareto headed his collection of articles, published in the *Rivista di Milano* in the historic year of 1920.

In the case of Sorel, his antidemocratic, elitist theory was combined with the element of myth. The characteristic features of this myth have already been referred to in connection with revolutionary Syndicalism and need now only be extended from the proletariat to the entire nation, in order to comprehend their impact. The social myth, directed at the creative proletarian energies and implying, as we have seen, an irrational idea of 'perfection', encapsulated the Socialist movement in images which – *en bloc et par la seule intuition* – were to stimulate individual acts in the proletarian struggle. The appeal to the heroic spirit of the proletariat needed only to be replaced by an appeal to the power instincts of national élites. These, as history has taught us, were equally able to spur fanaticised masses to unbridled violence by means of a mythos. This interpretation may sound a little harsh, but it pinpoints the constant ambivalence attaching to the mythos of violence, which after all, according to Sorel, could have a positive as well as a negative connotation – it could have revolutionary or reactionary application.

After all that has been said so far, it is hardly surprising that Italian Fascism invoked Sorel, and that he in turn did not hide his sympathy for Mussolini. The fact that Sorel had meanwhile written his 'Pour Lénine' (1918/19) and praised the 'heroic efforts' of the Russian proletariat[34] may appear to contradict this. But above all Sorel emphasised that he saw in Russia's national myth 'the heroic rise of a modern nation'; and since Sorel at the same time wished to see Mussolini kindling the national energies, and had become an advocate of Italian interests, he saw the kind of 'heroism' that creates nations equally in the rise of Fascism; in a letter to Benedetto Croce, he called it 'perhaps the most original social phenomenon of contemporary Italy'.[35]

Thus it was possible to come to Fascism by way of Sorel and even to quote him, if one wished to extend the myth, as the spontaneous expression of group beliefs, to the nation as a whole.

Mussolini himself, who, once he became *duce*, was to confess that even when still a socialist, touched by the tragic quality of violence, he had been a fascist at heart, never ceased to stress the myth of the nation and to underline the significance of concepts such as *azione* and *sentimento*, the latter indicating the dominance of the myth.[36] In this no doubt the tactical consideration of a need to nourish idealised hopes predominated, just as his vague programmatic statements were intended to appeal to extremely diverse groups. But independent of such tactical questions, the 'heroic epics' of the author of 'Réflexions sur la violence' remained vivid for Mussolini, and it was no accident that even in his *dottrina del fascismo* he was to stress the currents in Fascism that had flowed from Sorel: 'Nel grande fiume del fascismo troverete i filoni che si dipartirono dal Sorel . . . '.[37]

The dialectic tension between Mussolini's theory and practice is seen perhaps most clearly in his answer to a question posed by an editor of the Madrid publication ABC, about influences he considered to have been decisive in his life: 'Sorel's. The main thing for me was to act. But I repeat, it is to Sorel that I owe most.'[38] There can be no doubt that it was Sorel's myth of violence aimed at arousing national energies, to which Mussolini referred. However careful one ought to be in designating certain thinkers as 'intellectual fathers of Fascism',[39] it would nevertheless be impossible to deny that Sorel had opted for Fascism. In several of his post-war articles he welcomed the re-awakening of a national conscience in Italy; and when Sorel's friend Robert Michels met him in March 1922 for the last time, he was able to convince himself, as he noted in his diary, of Sorel's 'faith' in the new movement. 'Of

Benito Mussolini he spoke with great sympathy. "Do we know", he said, "where he will go? At any rate, he will go far." '[40] Sorel's remark characterises the hopes he vested in Mussolini. It shows also what he had recognised in Fascism: the will to act which, as Sorel clearly stressed, in contrast to the maximalist's revolutionary experiment, aimed at arousing national energies. Neither in the *red signorie* nor in the traditional *classe dirigente* could he, who still hoped to witness the 'humiliation of democracy', detect an awareness of the 'historic hour'. It was no accident that his statement 'le gouvernement par l'ensemble des citoyens n'a jamais été qu'une fiction; mais cette fiction était le dernier mot de la science démocratique'[42] was time and again used by Fascism as an argument against the 'corrupt parliamentary democracy'.[43]

NOTES

1. *The Art of Being Ruled* (London, 1926) p. 128.
2. K. Marx, 'Der Bürgerkrieg in Frankreich', *Marx-Engels-Werke* (MEW), vol. 17 (East Berlin, 1973) p. 338.
3. K. Marx, 'Die Pariser 'Réforme' über die französischen *Zustände*', *MEW*, vol. 5 (1973) p. 449.
4. K. Marx, 'Der achtzehnte Brumaire des Louis Bonaparte', *MEW*, vol. 8 (1973) p. 157.
5. This period was characterised by a remarkable development in French industrial production. Increased growth in basic industries and a rapid development of heavy industry determined the economic background. Typical for France remained the large share of agriculture in the overall economic development: it was that branch of the national economy which even at the turn of the century still employed a million more workers than factories, crafts, transport and mining taken together. It was a feature of French economic structure that there existed relatively few monopolies, very little horizontal or vertical concentration and initially also little modernisation, as a result of concentration on the domestic market and of protectionism, providing a shield against foreign competition. Small and medium businesses remained the dominant feature; as late as 1906 60 per cent of all workers were employed by enterprises with less than 10 employees.
6. M. Nettlau, 'Fernand Pelloutiers Platz in der Entwicklung des Syndikalismus', *Internationale* (a publication of revolutionary Syndikalism in Berlin, which appeared for a short time), 1 (1927/28) p. 50.
7. M. Pelloutier, *Fernand Pelloutier: Sa vie, son oeuvre (1867–1901)* (Paris, 1911) p. 62.
8. Fernand Pelloutier's programmatic article appeared in: *Les Temps Nouveaux*, 1 (1895) pp. 2–4; quoted here from the German translation by Ursula Lange, in: E. Oberländer (ed.), *Der Anarchismus* (Olten, 1972) pp. 316–25.
9. See the contribution by F. F. Ridley in this volume; for a detailed description see also W. Röhrich, *Revolutionärer Syndikalismus: Ein Beitrag zur Sozialgeschichte der Arbeiterbewegung* (Darmstadt, 1977).
10. Congrès National des Syndicats de France, *Comte rendu des travaux du congrès* (Amiens, 1906).
11. Ibid.
12. V. Griffuelhes, *L'action syndicaliste* (Paris, 1908) p. 23.
13. E. Pouget, *La C. G. T.* (Paris, 1907) p. 47f.

u

14. V. Pareto, *Les systèmes socialistes (1902–03)* (Paris, 1926) p. 421.
15. G. Sorel, *Über die Gewalt (Réflexions sur la violence)* (Innsbruck, 1928) p. 198.
16. Cf. H. Bergson, 'Sur les données immédiates de la conscience' in *Oeuvre* (Paris, 1959) p. 151.
17. 'Si l'on veut indiquer les inspirateurs véritables de Sorel, c'est Proudhon et Marx qu'il faut citer. Et, des deux, il me paraît incontestable que c'est Proudhon qui a été son plus authentique maître', G. Pirou, *Georges Sorel* (Paris, 1925) p. 56f.
18. Sorel, *Über die Gewalt*, p. 87.
19. Georges Sorel's letter to Benedetto Croce, dated 27/5/1899, *La Critica*, 25 (1927) p. 304.
20. Sorel, *Über die Gewalt*, p. 96.
21. P.-J. Proudhon, 'La guerre et la paix', in: *Oeuvres complètes*, vol. 13 (Paris, 1869) p. 38.
22. Ibid., 'De la justice dans la révolution et dans l'église', *Oeuvres complètes*.
23. Sorel, *Über die Gewalt*, pp. 136–7.
24. 'J'ai grand peur que vous n'ayez trop raison dans ce que vous avez dit sur la mort du socialisme', was what Sorel wrote about Croce's essay, in a letter to him, dated 19/2/1911, in *La Critica* 26 (1928) p. 347.
25. B. Mussolini, 'Lo sciopero generale e la violenza' (review), *Opera Omnia*, vol. 2 p. 167. Typical of Sorel's influence on Mussolini, the Socialist, were also remarks such as: 'We have to accomplish a work of great magnitude – the creation of a new world! As Sorel has emphasised, our mission is awesome, serious and sublime!' – B. Mussolini, 'Ai compagni', in: *Opera Omnia*, vol. 2 (1951) p. 255.
26. M. Freund, *Georges Sorel: Der revolutionäre Konservativismus* (Frankfurt/M, 1932) p. 220.
27. Ibid., p. 256.
28. B. Mussolini, 'Enrico Corradini', in: *Opera Omnia*, vol. 25 (1958) p. 69f.
29. M. Horkheimer, 'Die Juden und Europa', *Zeitschrift für Sozialforschung* 8 (1939) p. 115.
30. These social groups of middle-class mentality consisted of small property owners (artisans, small traders and peasants) and groups conscious of upward mobility (office employees, civil servants), who were determined to defend their 'middle-class' position against the lower social classes.
31. V. Pareto, 'Georges Sorel', *La Ronda* 4 (1922) p. 542.
32. Ibid., p. 546f.
33. B. Mussolini, 'Quando il mito tramonta', in: *Opera Omnia*, vol. 17 (1955) p. 323.
34. G. Sorel, 'Pour Lénine' in *Über die Gewalt*, p. 349–361.
35. Sorel's letter to Benedetto Croce, dated 26/8/1921, *La Critica*, 28 (1930) p. 195.
36. B. Mussolini, 'Discorso a Trieste (20/10/1920)', *Opera Omnia*, vol. 15 (1954) p. 218.
37. B. Mussolini, 'La Dottrina del Fascismo (1932)', *Opera Omnia*, vol. 34 (1961) p. 122.
38. According to Pirou, *Georges Sorel*, p. 53.
39. Such an interpretation, with Sorel in mind, was made by Georges Valois: 'Le père intellectuel du fascisme, c'est Georges Sorel.' G. Valois, *Le Fascisme* (Paris, 1927) p. 5.
40. Entry in Robert Michels' diary on 22/3/1922, in: 'Lettere di Georges Sorel a Roberto Michels', *Nuovi Studi di Diritto, Economia e Politica*, 2 (1969) p. 293.
41. Thus the closing words in Sorel's 'Pour Lénine,' *Über die Gewalt*, p. 361.
42. Georges Sorel, 'Avenir socialiste des syndicats et annexes (1914)' in *Matériaux d'une théorie du prolétariat (1919)* (Paris, 1921) p. 118.
43. B. Mussolini, 'Ne fasto! (10/6/1920)', *Opera Omnia*, vol. 15 (1954) p. 26.

16 Fascism and Violence in Post-War Italy: Political Strategy and Social Conflict

Adrian Lyttelton

I

My purpose in this article is to give an account of the context within which Fascist violence operated, the particular modes of its operation, and the interplay between the dynamic of the self-generating violence at the grass-roots of the movement, and the deliberate strategy of Mussolini's seizure and consolidation of power.

The first difficulty in writing about Fascist political violence is how to delimit the subject in such a way that it is not identical with the history of the Fascist movement as a whole. Violence was so inherent in the practice of the movement, and so prominent in its ideology, that it cannot be treated merely as one aspect among others of the history of Fascism. Certain political movements, such as terrorism, are defined by their commitment to a particular mode of violent action. Indeed, the decision to undertake such a mode of action may be the original project, logically and temporally antecedent to the creation of a political organisation. Mussolini announced[1] that the pro-gramme of the *fasci di combattimento* was 'contained in the name'. The Fascist movement from the beginning presented itself as a fighting organisation for civil conflict. The success of this formula, however, was not immediate. Although intelligent observers early noted the dangerous potential of a movement which could make a special appeal to ex-officers and other specialists in violence, the political situation during 1919 and most of 1920, as is well known, did not allow Fascist violence to achieve more than an episodic importance. To understand the reasons for the expansion of *squadrismo* it is necessary to examine both the context and the social sources of Fascist violence.

By context, I intend to refer to two different sets of conditions: firstly the social and political situation of post-war Italy, and the way which it generated and facilitated violence; and secondly, the legal and institutional order, and the constraints it imposed.

The simplest and oldest theory of Fascist violence treats it in origin as the manifestation of a class war of the bourgeois and propertied classes against peasants and workers. The evidence for this thesis is in fact very strong, and I do not think its fundamental truth should be questioned.[2] The character and success of Fascist violence, and its geographical distribution, cannot be explained except by reference to the pattern of social conflict existing already by 1919–20. Although in 1919 the strike level was lower than in England, France and Germany, in 1920 the level was higher than in any other country.[3] The incidence of Fascist violence was greatest in those regions where social conflict was already strongest. The only exceptions are parts of the south of Italy and Sicily where social conflict took the apparently more radical form of land occupations, and the incidence of Fascist violence was comparatively slight. Fascist violence was predominantly a response to the more modern forms of labour organisation and class conflict, and was relatively inapplicable to areas where older patterns of communal rebellion obtained. One problem which in this respect would repay investigation is the extent to which other forms of violence performed a substitutive function. At least in Western Sicily, the violence employed by *Mafia* gangs against peasant organisers can be viewed in this light,[4] although the problem of *Mafia* and violence as a whole is undoubtedly more complex.

However, when one says that Fascist violence was a response to the modern forms of labour organisation and class conflict, this conclusion needs to be qualified. Although Fascist violence was used against urban industrial workers, the relationship between class conflict in industry and Fascist violence was much less close than that for agrarian conflict. One should distinguish further here between 'urban' and 'industrial'. Large industrial cities offered a less favourable *ambiente* for Fascist violence than small towns and villages. The same is probably true of large firms or factories compared to small.

Compared with industrial, agrarian class conflict has inherently stronger tendencies making for violence. The seasonal nature of agricultural work means that on the one hand the effect of strikes during harvest-time or other peak periods of the year may be disproportionately disastrous to employers; on the other hand, the slack months offer the latter a good chance for a counter-offensive. In the lands of the Po valley, moreover, the existence of a permanent labour surplus posed a continual threat to stable trade-union organisation. By a remarkable *tour de force*, the Socialist peasant leagues had overcome this difficulty in the first two decades of the century. But their achievement had a price. The need to maintain cohesion in the face of the constant threat of blacklegging by unemployed or migrant workers made necessary extremely harsh methods of discipline. Boycotting and violent intimidation were frequent in the 'red' provinces. In the post-war climate of messianic revolutionary expectation, this often extended to an intolerance of political or religious dissent. Socialism in the Po Valley thus provides an exception to Raymond Carr's generalisation that 'an organised social-democratic labour movement cannot be formed in an area with high permanent unemployment'. But it is an exception which proves the rule, in the sense that the resulting problems both rendered the movement vulnerable and contributed to the prevalence of the mentality of *massimalismo*. Even where the local leadership professed reformist principles, their methods of control were scarcely compatible with the bourgeois liberal order.[5]

One aspect of the social and political conflict which had a peculiar importance for the rise of Fascism, and which can be directly linked to many of the movement's acts of organised violence, is the contest for local power. The Socialist conquest of the municipalities and the provinces in the autumn of 1920 was one of the factors which drove local élites to take action. In the eyes of the opponents of Socialism, the flying of the red flag from the town hall was an insult to the nation and an invitation to violence. The Socialists, on their side, by announcing their intention to use the communes as a springboard for revolution, presented their opponents with a fine excuse for illegal action. What Charles Tilly terms the 'nationalisation of politics'[6] was still, I would argue, incomplete in Italy. It is true that the war had contributed to a vast upsurge of identification with political programmes of national or international significance. However, in most of Italy, local conflict had a far greater immediacy. Other factors played their part in maintaining the small-scale, immediate character of politics. In a country where effective literacy could not be taken for granted, and before the rise of the modern mass media, propaganda had still to be conducted very largely by face-to-face and personal methods of communication. Violence was demonstrative as well as intimidatory. The contest for public space, in the piazza or the main street, was an important feature of politics. *Squadrismo* was not the product of a mass society of atomised individuals, but of closely knit provincial communities.

A second, obvious explanation for Fascist violence lies in the effect of the war. It is certainly incorrect to view Fascist violence merely as a kind of aberration or intoxication bred by wartime psychology. Class conflict had spilled over into serious violence even before the war.[7] However, the war contributed to the growth of violence both incidentally, by the political passions it aroused, and the hopes it awakened and disappointed, and also directly, by encouraging men already inured to combat to seek violent solutions. Neither the specific characteristics, nor the extent and effectiveness of Fascist violence could have been predicted without the war. The bewilderment of the opponents of Fascism is a sign of the radical novelty which the war had introduced into politics. Before, political violence was associated either with 'protest', or with repression by state organs; its deliberate large-scale use by a party to further political aims, was something which most pre-war politicians, even revolutionaries, did not seriously contemplate.

We must now turn to an examination of the constraints imposed on Fascist

violence by the legal and institutional order of Italy in this period. The modern
state, according to Weber's famous definition,[8] claims the monopoly of
legitimate forms of coercion. It follows that the growth of political violence is
circumscribed by the powers of the state, and by the way in which they are
exercised. The legal system as well as social *mores* define what violence is.
Particularly important, as Pareto pointed out[9], is the extent to which collective
violence is recognised as a phenomenon *sui generis*, which cannot be dealt with
by the ordinary processes of criminal law. Giolitti, often accused of leniency in
dealing with Socialist 'crimes' against property, put this very clearly in June
1921, when he replied to Socialist demands for more energetic action against
Fascist violence: 'I dati raccolti dall 'amministrazione dell' interno portereb-
bero il numero degli iscritti ai fasci a 187,000. Non è dunque una questione
pura di polizia, è una questione di politica altissima che va risolta dal
Parlamento.'[10]

When a state enters into crisis, other political groups occupy the space
which it has left open for their violent action. Two different explanations can
be advanced for this 'retreat of the state': collusion and weakness. The latter is
likely to give rise to the former, as representatives of the state seek to make
bargains with the likely winners. However, it is difficult to explain collusion if
one assumes an homogeneous ruling class. Otherwise, why should the holders
of state power endanger their own monopoly of force? In a liberal democracy,
however, collusion with illegal violence may be the means by which the
administrative apparatus can extend its power at the expense of the
legislature. Within the administrative structure itself, superiors may need to
resort to outsiders to compel compliance with their orders; or, more
frequently, subordinates may use the same methods to bring pressure on their
bosses and subvert the hierarchy of command. These observations may
appear unnecessary; but I believe that they contradict those explanations of
Fascist violence which treat it as merely an epiphenomenon, or as a mere
variant of a basically unchanging system of repression.

While one certainly cannot exempt political leaders from responsibility,
collusion with Fascist violence was more serious among magistrates, officials
and army officers. More controversially, I would argue that it was more
extensive at the lower levels of the hierarchy in the Army and in the civil
bureaucracy. As collusion grew more widespread, the ability of political
leaders to impose law and order on the Fascists was undermined. I will expand
this point in a later section of this paper. Yet Fascist political violence was
never entirely free and unfettered. Even after 1925, fear of the reactions of the
King, the Church, and foreign powers could restrain the temptation to resort
to wholesale terror.[11] However, the extent of the space left open to Fascist
violence was very considerable. In Germany, Hitler could only unleash the full
force of Nazi violence once he had captured the levers of official government
authority; in Italy, Mussolini did not need to adopt a 'legality tactic', and
could employ violence relatively openly not only to destroy his enemies but to

subvert the state itself.[12] This points to the conclusion that the ambiguities and weaknesses of the Italian legal order played a great part in facilitating Fascist violence. The key role of the prefects, officials who had to act according to political discretion rather than administrative precedent, certainly made for flexibility, but this flexibility could be dangerous. It meant that law very easily took second place to political expediency. Some of the critics of the Giolittian system, such as Einaudi and Albertini, even though their criticisms were often bound up with the defence of class interests, had identified this danger before the rise of Fascism.

More generally, confidence in the impartiality of law and the administration in Italy was insecure, and with good reason. Italian society, at the same time, preserved large areas of lawlessness and violence. In this situation, state authorities had resorted since unification both to collusion with crime and to arbitrary police action. More damaging still, both these responses to disorder were deliberately exploited against political opponents. Political violence to some degree became acceptable to public opinion, and to many of the custodians of law and order themselves. It is nevertheless true that all the blame cannot be laid at the doors of the state or of the heritage of Italian history. The verbal assaults of the Socialists on state authority did much to dispose middle-class opinion to justify Fascist violence. Initially, some of those who later protested vigorously regarded it as a 'legitimate reaction' against the excesses of revolutionaries and pseudo-revolutionaries.

II

Can Fascism be related to a previously existing national propensity for violence? In a provocative recent study[13] Emmanuel Todd draws a distinction between cultures of suicide, where aggression is turned inwards against the self, and cultures of homicide, where it expresses itself more directly. The Mediterranean countries, especially Italy and Spain, belong to the latter category.

In 1910, in Italy as a whole, there were 10.11 homicides per 100,000 inhabitants; but the national average conceals an immense variation. In the vast jurisdiction of the Naples appeal court the homicide rate (24.48) was ten times that of Milan (2.4). The south and the islands accounted for about 71 per cent of all homicides. Yet it was in the relatively more 'civilised' provinces that some of the leading centres of Fascist violence were to be found. It may indeed be true that in normal times political conflict acted as an outlet for aggressive feelings, particularly among the lower classes in the countryside, which elsewhere found outlet in outbursts of violence against persons. However, the explanatory role of such a hypothesis is clearly negligible. I believe, however, that something valuable may be learned about Fascist violence from comparing it with the general incidence of violence in Italian society. I have taken homicide as the main yardstick, because homicide figures are less affected by changes in law enforcement than are other crime indexes. For example, the incidence of crimes against public order (*delitti contro l'ordine pubblico*), and cases of *violenze, resistenze e oltraggi all' autorità* was lower in 1919 than in 1915;[14] it is reasonable to suppose that this decline indicates the greater reluctance of the authorities to prosecute, rather than an effective decrease in disorder.

Our direct knowledge of the casualties of Fascist violence and the counter-violence of their opponents is still fragmentary. However, official sources, which almost certainly err on the side of understatement, give figures of 102 dead and 388 wounded for the period 1 January to 1 April 1921, and 71 dead and 216 wounded in the period 16–30 May alone.[15] The total number of deaths resulting from Fascist violence during 1921 can probably be estimated at around 500–600. The official figures (which may err on the low side) show an increase in homicides in the northern and central provinces of Italy of about 350 between 1920 and 1921. In other words, the increase in violence between 1920 and 1921 is fully accounted for by Fascism.[16] The figures in fact show a marked contrast between North and South; in the south the number of homicides declined by about 240, only the Abruzzi showing a significant increase.[17] If, however, we look a little further into the pattern of post-war violence, a somewhat different picture emerges. First of all, the most rapid growth in violence in the post-war period took place not in 1921 but in late 1919 and 1920. The homicide rate for Italy as a whole jumped from 8.62 in 1919 (still below pre-war levels) to 13.95 in 1920 and reached a maximum of 16.88 in 1922.[18] This points to the conclusion that Fascism was responsible for only a part of the growth of violence in post-war Italy. It should of course be stressed that homicide figures do not distinguish between deaths due to political or collective violence, and those attributable to passion, vendetta, armed robbery, etc. A major work of collation of the evidence provided by newspapers and local studies is still needed before we can arrive at a true estimate of the extent of exclusively political violence during the period. The statistics of *cause di morte* show that 26 individuals were killed by the police or by the army in 1919, 92 in 1920, 115 in 1921 and 22 in 1922.[19] This is again probably an underestimate, since some doctors may have been reluctant to attribute responsibility to the forces of order. These figures reinforce the conclusion that 1920 already saw a dramatic increase in the gravity of political violence. They also show that the part played by the institutional violence of the state, though notable, nonetheless definitely took second place to Fascist violence in 1921–2.

In another sense, however, it may be unnecessary to distinguish between political and other forms of violence. Private as well as politically motivated homicide may be an index of disruption. Suicide, which had declined sharply during the war, increased from 1919 on, but did not reach pre-war levels till 1923. This lends confirmation to the argument that the wartime sanction for aggression against others continued to operate, though with gradually diminishing force. A commonsense explanation of suicide which did not take into account the factor of aggression would be hard put to it to account for its lesser incidence compared with pre-war. At the same time the distribution of suicide by age shows a relative increase from 1919 to 1923 of suicide among the younger age groups (10–40) who were most directly affected by the war and its immediate consequences.[20]

The war accustomed men to killing, and made them more likely to seek violent solutions to their problems in peacetime. Familiarity with lethal weapons was in itself important. Almost the whole of the increase in homicide between 1919 and 1921 is attributable to deaths inflicted by firearms. Moreover, the war multiplied the number of disputes. Individuals and classes alike had been encouraged to make competing and incompatible claims on resources. The promises made to the *reduci* contrasted with the inevitable fact that they returned to find others in occupation of their jobs and their land. The rise in violence can be linked fairly closely to demobilisation.[21] Whether the demobilised took out their resentment against the ruling classes or against the Socialists, it all in the end contributed to the growth of Fascism. The secret of Fascism's success is that it could both offer an outlet to the violent tendencies of the postwar era, and promise a restoration of order to those who feared them.

Secondly, if we compare northern violence to southern violence, the picture remains somewhat disconcerting. Between 1919 and 1920, the increase in homicides in Sicily (390) was greater than the total number of deaths which can be certainly attributed to Fascism in the first five months of 1921. In absolute terms there were more homicides in the four provinces of Western Sicily, than in the whole of the two regions of greatest Fascist terror, Emilia and Tuscany.[22] My purpose in making these comparisons is certainly not to minimise the gravity of Fascist violence. As we have seen, it involved a 'barbarisation' of regions of Italy which, unlike Western Sicily, no longer accepted violence as part of daily life. It seems to me that the comparison is revealing in another way, which points back to the conclusion I suggested earlier. The South and the North were very different societies. But they were ruled by the same state and indeed a disproportionate number of the staff of the administration and the police were from the South. Southern violence thus had its part in moulding the attitudes of administrators and politicians towards violence in general, and the lack of success of the liberal state in enforcing law was not the least of the motives which led ordinary citizens to look with favour on the possibility of dictatorship.

III

The interpretation of Fascist terror as the logical culmination of increasingly acute class-conflict retains much explanatory power. What is left that it does not explain? First of all, I do not think it offers an adequate explanation of why the terror was so successful. I should like to point here to the difficulties which the propertied classes had in organising their own defence. During 1919–20, their attempts to do so were on the whole unsuccessful. They needed the help of those with an aptitude for conflict. In 1918–19, Mussolini deliberately set out to win the allegiance of those skilled in using violence. His definition of combatant went 'from Diaz to the last infantryman'[23] but in practice the Fascists appealed mostly to the aristocracy of combatants, to those who fought from choice rather than from necessity, the *arditi*, the volunteers, many of the reservist ex-officers.

The *arditi* in particular formed a pool of potential users of violence whose susceptibility both to idealistic appeals and to hard cash transcended the bounds of ideology. Mussolini was one of the first to appreciate their importance, but throughout 1919 and much of 1920 he was forced to compete with the powerful rival attraction of D'Annunzio. The violence exercised by the *arditi* (excluding Fiume and Dalmatia from consideration) was sporadic and its immediate political effects were limited or even counter-productive. But the *arditi* and their ideological spokesmen, the Futurists, were extremely important in creating the image of the Fascist, the Fascist style, even though during 1919 their identification with Fascism was by no means total. What was later to be described as the first exploit of Fascist *squadrismo*, the burning of the Socialist newspaper *Avanti!* on 15 April 1919, was largely the work of the Futurists and the *arditi*. It was an unplanned spontaneous action carried out by young officer-students under the leadership of the Futurist Marinetti and the chief of the *arditi*, Ferruccio Vecchi.

In spite of their small numbers and bizarre programme, the role played by the Futurists in the psychological preparation of Fascist violence was significant, from the time of the interventionist campaigns of 1914–15 when they had led the field in verbal violence. The violence of the anarchistic Bohème has been mentioned in other contexts; through the Futurists the Fascists were able to tap this source. Marinetti himself, in a remarkable article written in 1919, preached a synthesis between nationalism and anarchism: the Futurists, he said, had glorified 'both patriotism and the destructive action of lovers of freedom'.[24] The notorious demonstration against the Wilsonian democrat Bissolati at the *Scala* in January 1919 could be described as a Futurist evening. The courage and irreverence of the Futurists attracted young officers, even when they had little real affinity with the movement's artistic aims. The founder of Fascism in Ferrara, Gaggioli, called himself a 'Futurist'; he had won three silver medals in the war, and once killed three Austrians in hand-to-hand combat.[25]

In 1921–2 being a Fascist bully was often easy work; but in 1919–20, at least in the 'red provinces', it still required considerable courage, and so men like Gaggioli were essential. During this period in fact, the attempts of elements among the propertied classes to organise for self-defence were on the whole unsuccessful. They needed the active support of those groups such as the *arditi*, the ex-officers, nationalist students and the 'heretics' of national syndicalism who were psychologically prepared to abandon legality. These marginal groups provided the leadership cadres for the later mass movement. The older generation of the bourgeois and the middle classes were mostly pacific by training, and easily intimidated by the apparently irresistible strength of the Socialists. In April 1920, the leader of the Bologna *fascio*, Arpinati, wrote, 'Certo è che questa borghesia bolognese . . . non si è mossa se non quando si è sentita, coll' ultimo sciopero, minacciata nella propria sicurezza e nel proprio portafoglio.'[26]

This sums up the contemptuousness with which the leaders of early Fascism conceded their services to their bourgeois backers. One can document a very important phase of preparation in the last half of 1920, during which the Fascist movement reinforced its para-military structures, and gave them clear priority over other aspects of the movement. The organisation and armament of the action squads was carried out in response to definite instructions from the central leadership of the *fasci*. On 26 October the Secretary of the *fasci* Pasella, wrote to Gaggioli, 'Un particolare plauso per la costituzione delle squadre fasciste d'azione che rappresentano – dato il momento e data la caratteristica della nostra organizzazione – il compito precipuo nostro'.[27] Another sign of the primacy given to para-military organisation was the instruction issued by the Central Committee to the *fasci* to choose demobilised officers wherever possible to occupy the key post of political secretary. The first great success of *squadrismo* was won in Trieste, a city still under army occupation, where the squads from the beginning followed regular military criteria for organisation. However, in the provinces of the rest of Italy, the squads had to rely at first on a much more informal structure.

It is true that the incapacity of the propertied classes to organise their defence directly was in part due to their continued faith in alternative strategies. Many industrialists, indeed, refused to give support to the squads even in 1921–2. The agrarians were much more determined and united in their support. For the agrarians, the great strikes of summer 1920 were the turning point. It was only then that the agrarians took effective steps to concert their action, and only then did the more aggressive elements decisively gain the upper hand over the more moderate leadership of the *Confagraria*, who had put their faith in conciliation and the intervention of the state. This division in the agrarian ranks goes back to the Giolittian period. It emerged clearly in the aftermath of the great Syndicalist strike of 1908 in Parma, when the agrarian organiser Lino Carrara, the man most responsible for breaking the strike, proposed the creation of 'un corpo di volontari interprovinciale', whose propaganda would be 'pacifica finchè ci permettano che pacifica sia, perchè talvolta potrebbe essere anche propaganda attiva'.[28] Active propaganda was clearly a euphemism for coercion.

It is significant that, as far as one can see, it was the more dynamic capitalist entrepreneurs in agriculture who took the lead in urging a more aggressive policy, while a more cautious attitude prevailed among the nobility and large landowners. The changes in landownership in the post-war period, though their extent has never been satisfactorily measured, clearly strengthened the former of these groups at the expense of the latter. But it should be emphasised that the major explanation of the commitment of the agrarians to violence lies in the circumstances of 1920. In particular the disastrous defeat of the agrarian organisations in the Bologna strike movement brought about a far-reaching crisis of confidence in the old leadership. In 1921, the old landowning aristocracy of Tuscany embraced the policy of terror with as much enthusiasm as the 'new men' of the Po valley. In regions where the aristocracy had retained a strong influence, the failure of paternalism came as a sudden shock which found the landowners unprepared to meet the crisis by any but the most brutal means. In such regions the aristocracy were fighting to re-establish their political supremacy as well as their control over land; the two aspects of power were regarded as inseparable. It should be mentioned that the *declassé* young aristocrat bent on restoring his fortunes was a characteristic figure among the leadership of the squads: men such as Arrivabene and Barbiellini in the Po valley, and Perrone Compagni in Florence.

The agrarians financed and armed the squads throughout the countryside of north and central Italy. In some provinces, the agrarian Federations were directly responsible for the creation of the local Fascist movement, for example in Alessandria, Pavia and Arezzo. The victims of the 'punitive expeditions', even when these were launched from the cities, were usually marked out by the local agrarians, who guided the squads to their destination.[29] To enforce subordination, even isolated acts of individual resistance to the agrarians' claims might be punished. In Cremona, 40 Fascists surrounded and beat up a Catholic peasant who had asked his landlord to pay off the arrears he owed him.[30] Even in the first phase of *squadrismo*, when most of the recruits still came from the provincial capitals, there was a strong agrarian element present. Apart from landowning families resident in the provincial cities, many *agrari* would have sent their sons to study there, especially in university towns like Bologna, Ferrara, or Pisa.

Faced with the phenomenon of agrarian Fascism, the historian must deplore the inadequacy of formulas which treat political violence *a priori* as a manifestation of 'protest' or aggression resulting from frustration.[31] The agrarian terrorism of the squads was highly organised, strategically effective, and employed for clearly defined goals. Its aim was nothing less than the piecemeal annihilation of its opponents' organisations (Socialist or Popolari). The destruction of the institutions and property of party branches, cooperatives, printing presses and even cultural circles, was the most visible and symbolic form of violence. But the 'conquest' of Socialist organisations and municipalities was reinforced and made possible by terror exercised against individuals. Beating was the usual form of violence, with more or less intentional homicide a frequent occurrence. Important also were forms of punishment involving the shaming of the adversary: the notorious castor-oil purges, or the practice current in Ferrara and Rovigo of kidnapping victims in the middle of the night and abandoning them naked by the roadside, or tied to a tree.[32]

The Fascists advertised their power and their opponents' weakness by publishing formal bans on the latter's re-entry into their home town or province. This practice, which started very early on in the history of *squadrismo*, once again emphasises the primacy of local concerns. At the same time, the mobility of the Fascists in their lorries, provided by the *agrari*, or sometimes directly by the military, gave them an overwhelming advantage of a classic military kind, by enabling them to concentrate their forces to crush any pockets of resistance. It is worth noting here that the half-hearted attempts of the prefects to check *squadrismo* concentrated particularly on trying to deprive the Fascists of their mobility, which soon revealed itself as a threat to the power of the state itself. By late 1921, when Fascism had assumed massive proportions, restricting the mobility of the squads posed severe difficulties in terms of police man-power and resources. But in any case, the extent of collusion in the police forces ensured the failure of such attempts. As the Fascists' star rose, self-interest, coercion and corruption became additional motives for officials to collaborate. The chief of police in Cremona in 1921/22, for example, became a client of the local *ras* Farinacci, and was eventually rewarded with a prefecture.[33] At a lower level, the ordinary *carabiniere* or *maresciallo* fully shared the Fascists' hostility to the Reds. He was often a drinking companion of the *squadristi*.

Agrarian terrorism was not the work of the *agrari* alone. The city squads, whose help was needed to break the initial resistance of the peasant league, drew most of their members from the petty bourgeoisie of shopkeepers and employees, and from the professional classes. Fascism as a whole was overwhelmingly a movement of the younger generations, and the emphasis on youth was naturally even more marked among the active *squadristi* than among the reserve of sympathisers. In addition, in the Po valley provinces, peasant proprietors, leaseholders and sharecroppers often turned against the day-labourers and joined the squads. Here it is impossible to overlook the contribution of socialist violence to the genesis of agrarian *squadrismo*. In Ferrara at least it was the small leaseholders who were most in danger of their lives; two were killed and three others wounded during the general strikes of July–August 1920.[34] Even in the 'pacific' province of Rovigo, where Matteotti was acknowledged to have done all he could to prevent intimidation, members of the Catholic peasant organisations were often set upon.[35]

While unquestionably this climate of intimidation helped to provoke the reaction and to justify it in the eyes of public opinion, an important distinction must be made between Socialist and Fascist violence. The former was usually unorganised, more or less spontaneous, and it seldom extended to deliberate murder. Except in the case of strike-breakers, violence against persons was usually considered unnecessary, as the Socialists believed they had numbers, right and History on their side. For the agrarian Fascists, on the other hand, planned terror was the essence of their activity. A confrontation in Lendinara, in the province of Rovigo, gives a typical example of the difference between the two types of violence. It seems that the Socialists may actually have started it after a row between Socialist councillors and Fascists in the *caffé dei signori* on the town's main *piazza*. A crowd of cudgel-bearing Socialists invaded the *piazza* and demanded that the owner of the *caffé* expel the Fascists. The latter had to fight their way out and left the Socialists in possession of the field, but later Fascist reinforcements arrived from other places in the province, and the Socialists eventually fled when the first revolver-shots were fired.[36] The Fascists, indeed, often deliberately provoked popular indignation in order to have an excuse to intervene in force. Finally, although at the beginning Socialist violence as in the incidents of the Palazzo Accursio in Bologna, and of the Castello Estense in Ferrara, was vitally important in legitimising Fascist reprisals, once the reaction was well under way it spared no one, however legal their methods.

As the squads lengthened the range of their operations, the objectives of their leaders became more ambitious. There was a natural transition from the expedition in aid of a distant *fascio* to the planned assault on cities, which increasingly served the dual purpose of demonstrating the impotence of the state and breaking the strength of the opposition. It is at this point that the explanation of *squadrismo* in terms of class war becomes partially inadequate. *Squadrismo* developed its own momentum, which carried it beyond its initial objectives. In part, this was due to the vested interests created by success: the military leaders of *squadrismo* faced the danger of unemployment or at least declining importance if pacification became a reality. Even after the March on Rome most of the *ras* saw their power and influence as conditional on the continuance of *squadrismo*, albeit on a much reduced scale. The agrarians themselves, though in many cases they had largely achieved their local aims by the end of 1921, still felt their gains to be insecure so long as the movement they had promoted was excluded from power. They were therefore more disposed than the industrialists to promote the violent seizure of power.

At the same time, the very success of agrarian Fascism opened up the possibility of conflict between the economic interests of the agrarians and the political interests of the Fascists. Although there was usually far more rhetoric than substance in the threats of Fascist leaders to 'turn their cudgels to the Right', where the agrarians tried to resist the *ras'* political control, they did on occasion become victims in their turn.[37]

From being purely and simply a means of winning the class war, rural *squadrismo* came in addition to serve a variety of local and personal interests and feuds. In many cases the commanders of the squads succeeded in taking over the political leadership of the movement. *Ras* like Ricci of Carrara and

Barbiellini of Piacenza kept their own squads for use against enemies and rivals, particularly within the Fascist movement. Balbo, with a more sophisticated technique resembling that of the criminal syndicates, employed thugs from Perugia to intimidate his local enemies. The continued exercise of violence by the *ras*, in spite of its sordid and personal aims, was also an element in their popularity with the ordinary *squadristi*. The mythology of *squadrismo* contrasted simple solutions imposed by force to the corruption of 'politics': the only true Fascists were those who knew how to 'menar le mani'. Many *squadristi* believed that they were engaged in a crusade for national revival whose true goals were still in the future. For the majority, however, the main motive for continued activity may not have been so much either cynical careerism or patriotic idealism as a kind of *camaraderie*. Photographs of the action squads show a striking similarity to those of football or sports teams. The punitive expedition, even if it involved breaking someone's head, for the participants was often an outing with the lads, an excuse to make a lot of noise, eat and drink without paying, and have a good time generally. The spirit of these gatherings has been described brilliantly (not without a certain sympathy) by Pratolini in his novel *Lo scialo*.

The squads had their own names and flags, frequently possessed their own membership cards, and owed obedience to their own leaders, chosen usually by informal methods. The origins of many squads can be found in groups of adolescents and young men united by primary ties of relationship or friendship. Like youth gangs, the squads provided ways of proving 'manhood' through violent action. Violence for the *squadrista* was the requirement for membership of a group of peers, and the squad was a powerful focus for attraction, loyalty and solidarity. Rivalry between squads in the same city or province often ended in hostilities. Challenges and duels between individual Fascists were also frequent, and the party had a 'court of honour' to deal with such disputes. This reflected not only the military ethos, but also the aping of aristocratic manners by certain groups in society, particularly journalists. Mussolini himself was an accomplished duellist. Although the small-group solidarity of the squads posed great difficulties for the leaders in terms of control, and the imposition of coherent strategy, on the other hand it had great psychological advantages. It seemed to protect the Fascists from the feelings of boredom and impotence common among the members of large organisations. Studies of armies and factories have shown the importance of informal group membership in mediating the demands of the organisation on the individual and making them tolerable. To a high degree, the informal loyalties of the squads survived even after the creation of the MVSN in 1922. The Consuls of the individual legions were usually at first chosen from among the old leaders of the squads: 'Mantenne (il Comando Generale) si può dire totalmente in carica i Consoli che essili raggruppavano. Il Console era l'uomo d'assoluta fiducia del gregario.'[38]

At all levels the Fascist movement made use of symbolic devices for 'bonding' well-known to students of social psychology, e.g. the salute, the use of uniforms, and the ritual mocking of opponents. Elementary as they may seem, the forms of Fascist violence themselves were not without their crude symbolism. The *manganello* or cudgel acquired the connotations of a virility symbol; caricatures of the *manganello* assimilate the shape to that of mock clubs used in carnival. Such episodes as the public humiliation of Misiano, the former deserter elected deputy, were presented as rites of national purification. The novelty of Fascist politics was not in violence or military organisation alone, but in the combination of these features with ritual, as in the cult of the movement's 'martyrs'. Party violence was thus disguised by both military and religious forms.

The Fascist regime did not institutionalise terroristic violence, as distinct from police oppression, in permanent forms. Even the semi-legal activities of the Militia were curbed once organised political opposition had been crushed. From 1926 on, *squadrismo* once again largely became a 'fringe phenomenon' of discontented groups of activists. But the myths and traditions of *squadrismo* survived as an important component of Fascism, which even the fall of the regime did not permanently eradicate. Neo-Fascism after 1945 has been associated with a sub-culture of violence. This can legitimately be described as an affair of 'fringe groups', locally circumscribed and limited to a relatively small number of youthful activists. It has flourished particularly in Rome, both in the university and in certain petty bourgeois *quartieri*. The cult of sport and physical force attracted recruits from a seedy world of second-rate gymnasia and boxing rings, where contacts with the criminal underworld were frequent. After a first peak in the early 1950s, *squadrismo* became a serious problem again in the 1970s, in reaction both to the advance of the PCI and to the activity of the extra parliamentary left. In the last years, the violence between extreme Right and extreme Left has seemed to take on a more factional character, in which political and class motivation take second place to contests for 'territory'. This is another example of the ambiguities of political violence and its tendency to degenerate into violence pure and simple. A movement such as the Fascist, with an ideology relatively weak in coherence and explanatory power and emphasising the positive value of violence *per se*, is particularly likely to give rise to phenomena of this sort. There are signs, however, that the mystical and irrationalist strains in Fascist ideology may also be having a revival; some of the latest 'action groups' of the extreme Right have taken to naming themselves after Tolkien heroes.[39]

IV

In trying to understand the meaning of Fascist violence, I believe one must take into account three different types of motivation: violence arising from frustration and social disorganisation, violence reacting against a threat to basic values, and violence deliberately employed as part of a strategy (both collective and individual) designed to secure definite ends. Fascism was, somewhat paradoxically, a movement founded on an irrationalist ideology which nonetheless pursued a strategy of violence which was calculated, planned, and unusually effective. One could, of course, question whether this violence always achieved the aims of the users of violence, the *squadristi* themselves. But one should not overlook the real if modest degree of social success attained by members of the rank and file through party office and the Fascist version of the spoils system. On a collective level, the social superiority of lower-middle class groups over the working-class was reaffirmed and income differentials widened.

However, it is doubtful whether the social groups interested in reaction could have mobilised or been mobilised for violence without the other, 'non-rational', motives. The organisation and extent of Fascist terror can only be explained by its political aims. However, the ability of Fascism to mobilise not only those most immediately affected, but also wider sections of the middle classes can reasonably be attributed to a situation of 'relative deprivation' and the resultant frustrations. These must be interpreted in the special sense that these groups were severely disappointed in their expectations, and that they found the social distance between themselves and the working classes to be narrowing.[40] Inflation and unemployment among the 'intellectual professions',[41] as well as the particular problems of demobilisation created a widespread sense of disorientation and uncertainty, particularly since the groups affected were also threatened by the slogans of an aggressively proletarian revolution. The uncertainty of career expectations and the discrediting of the economic ideals of thrift by inflation, together with the disappointment at the results of the war, created a particularly acute 'generation gap', which has much to do with the demand for a 'new order' which would carry out a reaction against socialism without purely and simply restoring the status quo. In the case of the agrarians, frustration arising from a feeling that the national political system had ceased to respond to their needs was an important element in predisposing them to violence.

The psychological features of post-war Italy which made Fascism so potent can also in part be recognised as corresponding to Merton's classic description of *anomie*. The general growth of violence in post-war Italy, of which Fascism was the most important but not the only manifestation, can indeed be seen as powerfully promoted by 'the perception that little can be accomplished in a society which is seen as basically unpredictable and lacking order'. Merton's observation that *anomie*, defined as the discordance between cultural norms and social structure, is characteristic not only of groups frustrated in their expectations of social mobility, but also of those who enjoy 'de facto mobility . . . without moral approval' is also important. 'Gainers' as well as 'losers' were certainly present in the Fascist movement.[42] However, we are still very far from being able to test Merton's hypothesis in any rigorous way, which would imply a contrast between both upwardly and downwardly mobile groups and a relatively static control group.

If Merton's categories may help to explain the reasons why certain groups in post-war Italy were easily mobilised for violence, they cannot explain the meaning and direction of that violence. It would not even be satisfactory to view material and status aspirations as the main source of psychological confusion contributing to violence. What Vivarelli has summed up under the heading of the 'psychological reality of the war'[43] was no doubt still more important. Italy's recent unification and the uncertainty of mass support for the war, or indeed for the nation, forced the defenders of patriotic causes into a defensive stridency and a desperate idealism which exceeded even that prevalent in other countries. It was difficult for supporters of the war to be entirely honest about its motives and results, or entirely realistic about the motives which made men fight, though a few succeeded. Consequently, a culture of war founded on myth opposed itself to peacetime values as embodying a 'higher' and more worthwhile alternative. Violence was not only justified in the name of these wartime values, but was a symbol of them.

This culture of war though it only claimed the active allegiance of a minority, could nevertheless command much wider sympathy and support because it was linked with the more permanent values of patriotism, which were seen as threatened by both external and internal forces. The historian of sixteenth-century France, Natalie Davis, has warned that violence should not be explained primarily in terms of 'how crazy . . . or frustrated the violent people are . . . but in terms of the goals of their actions and in terms of the roles and patterns of behaviour allowed by their culture'. 'Violence is intense' when 'it connects intimately with the fundamental roles and self-definition of a community'.[44] 'The nation' was clearly such a fundamental value; at the same time it should be stressed again that the war had created new roles and patterns of behaviour which permitted a higher level of deliberate violence than pre-war Italy would have sanctioned. The wartime culture produced a disposition to act violently; at the same time the approval of the official patriotic culture powerfully reinforced by bourgeois self-interest, removed the inhibitions on aggression by diminishing its moral and material risks.

The paradox of Fascist violence lies here: in the ability to harness anti-social feelings to the defence of the existing social order through a vocabulary which presented amorality and freedom from conventional standards as an attribute of heroic leadership, and which encouraged the identification of the ordinary rank-and-file member with such models.

NOTES

1. *Popolo d'Italia* (6 March 1919).
2. For a contrary view, see D. Settembrini, *Fascismo controrivoluzione imperfetta* (Florence, 1978) pp. 117–29, 149–66. In particular, Settembrini underrates the extent of complicity between the local leaders of Fascism and organised agrarian interests; see esp. p. 152.
3. A. Tasca, *Nascita e avvento del fascismo* vol. 1 (Bari, 1965) p. 131 (but the figure for 1919 is incorrect: 554,000 instead of 1,554,000): in 1920 there were 2,314,000 strikers in Italy, compared with 1,779,000 in England, 1,429,000 in Germany, 1,317,000 in France. 1,046,000 of the strikers in Italy were in agriculture (C. Seton-Watson, *Italy from Liberalism to Fascism 1870–1925* (London, 1967) p. 520).
4. A. Block, *The Mafia of a Sicilian Village 1860–1960: a study of violent peasant entrepreneurs* (Oxford, 1974) p. 140.
5. I. Barbadoro, *Storia del sindacalismo italiano dalla nascita al fascismo* vol. 1 *La Federterra* (Florence, 1973) ch. 4 passim., esp. 251–3.
6. C. Tilly, 'Collective violence in European perspective' in I. K. Feierabend, R. L. Feierabend and T. R. Gurr (eds), *Anger, Violence and Politics* (Englewood Cliffs, 1972) p. 345.
7. See L. Lotti, *La settimana rossa* (Florence, 1965) passim.
8. M. Weber, in W. G. Runciman (ed.), *Selections in Translation* (Cambridge, 1978) p. 41.
9. V. Pareto, *The Mind and Society: a treatise in general sociology* vol. 2 (New York, 1935) pp. 1530–2, 1878–9.
10. D. Novacco (ed.) *Storia del Parlamento italiano*, vol. 12 (Palermo, 1967) p. 195.
11. See N. A. O. Lyttelton, *The Seizure of Power: Fascism in Italy 1919–1929* (London, 1973) pp. 282–3.
12. See the article by G. Botz in this volume (Chapter 18).
13. E. Todd, *Le fou et le prolétaire* (Paris, 1979).
14. *Annuario statistico italiano 1919–1921* (Rome, 1922) p. 186.
15. G. De Rosa, *Storia del movimento cattolico in Italia* vol. 2: *Il Partito Popolare italiano* (Bari, 1966) p. 185.
16. See the article by J. Petersen (Chapter 17). I have constructed the estimate of deaths resulting from Fascist violence by combining the January–May totals with the figures for Fascist casualties in Table 17.2.
17. Istituto Centrale di Statistica, *Cause di morte 1887–1955* (Rome, 1957) p. 269.
18. *Annuario statistico italiano 1922–1925*, p. 124.
19. Ministero dell'Economia Nazionale, *Statistica delle cause di morte 1919–1923* (Rome, 1925).
20. Ibid.
21. Ibid.
22. See note 14 above.
23. R. De Felice, *Mussolini il rivoluzionario* (Turin, 1965) p. 406.
24. A. Lyttelton (ed.), *Italian Fascisms* (London, 1973) p. 217.
25. P. Corner, *Fascism in Ferrara 1915–1925* (Oxford, 1975) p. 142.
26. *Archivio Centrale dello Stato, Mostra della Rivoluzione Fascista*, b 100, fasc. Bologna (26 April 1920) q. Lyttelton, *Seizure of Power*, p. 58.
27. *Ibid.* b 102 fasc. Ferrara (26 Oct. 1920) q. ibid. p. 53.
28. *Resoconto del congresso agrario* (1909) p. 108, q. ibid. p. 215.
29. See Matteotti, in *Storia del Parlamento* cit., pp. 166–7.
30. F. J. Demers, *Le origini del fascismo a Cremona* (Bari, 1979) p. 194.

31.   See C. Tilly's criticism of Gurr and others, in C., L., and R. Tilly, *The Rebellious Century 1830–1930* (London, 1975) p. 297.
32.   See note 24 above.
33.   Demers, pp. 210–11.
34.   Corner, pp. 97–8.
35.   See F. Merlin, in *Storia del Parlamento*, pp. 171–2.
36.   *Ibid.* p. 165.
37.   E.g. in Brescia, even before the March on Rome the threat of violence was used to pressure independent agrarians into joining the Fascist organisation; in 1923 an employer was murdered by two officers of the Militia 'in the name of class collaboration', for failing to pay agreed wage rates: A. Kelikian, *Brescia 1915– 1926: from liberalism to corporatism*, unpublished. D. Phil. thesis (Univ. of Oxford, 1978) pp. 226, 250.
38.   E. De Bono, 'Le origini della milizia e i suoi primi ordinamenti', in: T. Sillani, *Le forze armate dell 'Italia Fascista* (Rome, 1939) pp. 288–91.
39.   For a remarkable portrait of this *ambiente*, see G. Salierno, *Autobiografia di un picchiatore fascista* (Turin, 1976).
40.   See W. G. Runciman, *Relative Deprivation and Social Justice* (London, 1972) pp. 154–6 for the concept as applied to the middle classes.
41.   See M. Barbagli, *Disoccupazione intellettuale e sistema scolastico in Italia* (Bologna, 1974) pp. 168–95.
42.   See R. K. Merton, *Social Theory and Social Structure* (New York, 1953) pp. 161–94.
43.   R. Vivarelli, *Il dopoguerra in Italia e l'avvento del fascismo (1918–1922)*, vol. 1, *Dalla fine della guerra all' impresa di Fiume* (Naples, 1967) p. 100.
44.   N. Z. Davis, *Society and Culture in Early Modern France* (London, 1975) p. 186.

17 Violence in Italian Fascism, 1919–25

Jens Petersen

Mussolini, hard-pressed by radical Fascism, both provincial and agrarian, and by the Aventino's intransigent opposition, in his parliamentary speech of 3 January 1925 proclaimed the breakthrough to the fascist one-party state. Answering his anti-fascist critics, he said:

> They say that Fascism consists of a horde of barbarians who have pitched their tents within the nation, that it is a movement of bandits and robbers! They raise the moral issues . . . very well, I hereby declare . . . that I alone take the political, moral and historic responsibility for everything that has happened . . . The fault is mine if Fascism has been nothing but castor oil and cudgels, rather than the noble passion of the flower of Italian youth! If all acts of violence have been the outcome of a certain historical, political, moral climate, then the responsibility is mine, for I created this climate . . . by a propaganda beginning at the time of the *intervento* and lasting to the present day.[1]

His words at this decisive moment gave an indication of the central importance then attaching to the problem of violence in the assessment of Fascism. For the victims of fascist violence – the labour movement, the parties of the Left and the trade unions – Fascism and violence seemed to have become virtually synonymous. The experiences of twenty years of fascist dictatorship and of the civil war of 1943–5, coinciding with the final stages of the Second World War, have shrouded the early phase of Fascism as well in an even darker light.

What has been the significance accorded to the question of violence in the discussions to date? Looking back, P. Togliatti called the Fascists and their *squadri*'s systematic illegal violence 'the great innovation in the conduct of leading political groups in Italy. In that phase of their history, it represented the only truly novel creation . . . of the Italian bourgeoisie.'[2]

Recent research is unanimous in regarding violence as 'a fundamental ingredient', indeed as the 'actual substance of Fascism'.[3] Among the elements which triggered the crisis in Italy's political system, social violence is seen as

275

the most important factor by far. Since the modern State, along with the monopoly of legitimate coercion, has taken over the function of securing internal peace and of guaranteeing an unbloody settlement of social conflict, 'the practice of private violence and its more or less open "toleration and approbation" . . . constitutes a break' with the traditional perception of the role of the State.[4] According to W. Schieder, Fascism did not set out 'to convince or defeat its opponents, but to destroy them. The will to *annihilate the opponent* is a constituent element of fascist rule'.[5] E. Nolte has called Fascism the realisation of the principle of war in peacetime, a continuation of war by other means. He argues that Fascism with its 'unbridled rule of force . . . in large parts of Italy', its campaigns of destruction and its 'massacres' precipitated Italy into a 'civil war' and terrorised the country to a degree, 'which had no equal in the history of modern European states'.[6]

While Nolte, as a liberal, still possesses a keen eye for the movement's idealistic impulses, capable of creating sympathy and consensus, many of the Left's accounts are entirely overshadowed by the violence, terror and common criminality which constitute the dark side of Fascism. Thus, an analysis of Fascism in Tuscany – particularly notorious for its ruthlessness – declares that it had been 'at the outset, and for a number of years after it became institutionalised, a murky and repulsive record of gangs of assassins, who attacked and overthrew the edifice of the State, the White Guard of a blind and merciless Vendée'.[7]

The unanimity of such judgements has its roots in the accounts of suffering by the victims of Fascism from 1920 onwards. 'Fascism', as one communist publication of that time put it, 'has established itself in Italy, on the corpses of thousands of workers and peasants, on the funeral pyres of workers' institutions and cooperatives; the prisons are full of workers and peasants . . . the cases of ill-treatment and enforced administration of castor oil run into millions.'[8] In the summer of 1921, A. Gramsci described the situation as follows:

In the 356 days of 1920, 2,500 Italians (men, women, children and old people) have been killed in streets and squares by the guns of police and fascists. In the past 200 days of the barbaric year 1921, about 1,500 Italians have been murdered by bullet, dagger or cudgel. About 40,000 free citizens of democratic Italy have been beaten, disfigured, injured; a further 20,000 of these ever so free citizens of this ever so democratic Italy . . . were forced by threats to leave their work places and their homes . . . about 300 local government representatives were forced to resign . . . hundreds of workers institutions, people's houses, cooperatives belonging to communist and socialist party branches have been looted and burnt; 15 million Italians in the Emilia, the Polesine, the Romagna, in Tuscany, Umbria, Veneto and Lombardy are being constantly subjected to the rule of armed gangs, who are allowed to pillage and loot and beat them up with impunity.[9]

The most impressive portrayal of what Gramsci described so tersely as the 'dilemma of life or death', a civil war of 'fire and sword' and the 'most savage and difficult guerilla war a working class ever had to fight',[10] has so far come from A. Tasca. His *Nascita e avvento del fascismo*,[11] first published in 1938, has exercised a lasting influence on all subsequent accounts. Under the heading of 'Civil War in Italy' he joined together all the elements indicated above, to describe the tragedy of the Italian labour movement. All subsequent local and regional studies have done no more than to supplement, or add local colour to Tasca's panoramic picture. Thus, the leading communist historian, P. Spriano, has described fascist violence from the autumn of 1920 onwards as 'a story that has meanwhile been told down to its minutest details',[12] one which may be summarised as a 'civil war, which the fascist *squadri* unleashed in countryside and towns throughout Italy for two years'.[13] It was a history which, according to all accounts, was characterised by the omnipresent threat, or actual use, of violence, by tens of thousands dead, and hundreds of thousands injured, by millions who were the victims of physical violence and, mocked and humiliated, found themselves deprived of their civil and human rights and even of their material livelihood; a history characterised also by the immense material damage inflicted on the labour movement and the economy in general, by the disintegration of a network of social, economic and organisational structures in the sphere of party politics, trade unions and co-operatives, which had taken years to grow up. Metaphor and symbol of this comprehensive reign of terror was the 'civil war', of which the Catholic author G. Papini said in 1922 that it had brought Italy more dead and wounded than any of the great battles of the World War, and that this, whether one wished to acknowledge it or not, was the reality which dominated daily life in Italy.[14]

II

Where, in the typology of political forms of violence, which conflict research has developed over recent decades, would one place the events of Italy after 1919? Eckstein distinguishes between

> relatively unorganised and spontaneous *riots* by crowds with low capabilities for violence and modest aims, *coups d'état* by members of an elite against other members of the elite, fullscale *political revolutions* to achieve largescale socio-economic as well as constitutional changes, and *wars of independence* to achieve sovereignty in a previous dependent territory.[15]

In the case of Fascism, the aim of changing the system, the high degree of organisation and mass participation might argue for classifying it under the heading of 'revolution'.[16] Although this has sometimes been done, it has vigorously been denied by the advocates of a positive, progressive concept of revolution.[17] The Italian example shows a number of special features which make any kind of typological classification difficult. For one, it was not a case of conflict between the forces of the State and an insurgent minority, but of a conflict within society, in which the State, threatened by a loss of legitimacy and efficiency, became partly accomplice and partly target of a fascist force, which considered itself as a legitimate 'alternative state'. Secondly, the fact that the violence of Left and Right existed both successively and simultaneously, that its causes and justifications are inextricably tangled, constitutes a very singular feature which so far has not been adequately studied, as witness the recent polemics between G. Amendola and P. Spriano about the 'red' or 'red-black' nature of the years 1919–20.[18] Those who argue that it represents a new type of revolution, in which the relation between State and revolution has been reversed, probably come closest to providing an answer. 'Where once upon a time making a revolution meant overthrowing the State, in the new situation it is the State which makes the revolution.'[19]

In the absence of suitable conceptual tools, the interpreters of the events in Italy after 1919 have spoken of a 'civil war'. This term, as I have partly shown already, has gained widespread acceptance both on the Left and the Right, even though they do not agree on its precise time scale. P. Nenni, for instance, dated the beginning of the 'six years of civil war' from 1919, but then wrote that 'precisely at the moment when there was a pause in the class war . . . the federation of major landowners began to take the initiative towards civil war, by employing the fascists as combat troops. A revolution of words was followed by a counter-revolution of blood.'[20] The communist and anarchist left, in particular, saw Fascism as the direct continuation of the war and – after the dramatic increase in class tensions up to 1918 (870,000 criminal proceedings by military courts, 190,000 cases against deserters and 4,000 death sentences) – as its transfer from an external to an internal enemy. Fascism appeared thus as a 'continuation of the war-regime'. 'Fascism is the war that is being carried from the trenches into towns and villages . . . into schools and families.'[21] But Fascism itself, when it wished to emphasise the revolutionary nature of its rise, also stressed the violent side of the events of that time. As Mussolini wrote in 1927:

'In reality, the bloody struggle between Fascism and Anti-Fascism began on April 15, 1919 and reached its climax in the early August of 1922. For precisely four years the nation lived in a state of almost general civil war . . . During this time . . . countless fascists fell. The news reports are spattered with the blood of young fascists.'[22]

In the fascist mythology of war and combat, war and civil war are inextricably linked. Mussolini announced as early as 1919 the defence of the 'Italian victory' – if need be, by force. 'We shall defend the dead . . . even if we have to dig the trenches in the squares and streets of our towns.'[23] 'For the greatness and well-being of the whole people', wrote D. Guardi in December 1920, 'the fascists today deliver their second declaration of war. War without armistice and without mercy.'[24] This 'last war of independence (and) national unity' (E. Corradini) was directed against the 'traitors', the 'enemy within', the bolshevik criminals,[25] and legitimised because it would prevent 'red barbarism' and the chaos of civil war which the social-bolsheviks wanted. Fascism as Italy's (supposed) saviour from the red peril was the epithet of glory which brought it, in terms of foreign and domestic politics, the greatest gain. The history of anti-bolshevik ideology in Italy has not yet been written. It would probably show that the images of the red enemy were closely connected to war propaganda.

But apart from the duration and intensity of, and the participation in, violent incidents in Italy at that time, it is the one-sided distribution of the causes of violence which appears to give the application of the term 'civil war' doubtful validity. In the definition of the *Brockhaus Lexikon*,

'civil war is held to be an armed struggle within a State between rebels (insurgents, insurrectionists) and government, or between hostile groups, for political power. Not every armed insurrection is a civil war; the latter is predicated upon rebels or hostile parties organising themselves on military lines and being capable of acting on a unified plan and under a unified authority of command'.[26]

Yet the Italian Left at the time possessed neither military organisation, active political leadership, nor authority of command. Certainly, the Socialists, in their maximalist programme of 1919 announced the beginning of 'a period of revolutionary struggle, to bring about the forcible suppression of the bourgeoisie within a short time' and demanded the 'armed insurrection of the proletarian masses and proletarian soldiers' in order to establish the dictatorship of the working class;[27] the Socialist leftwing theorised about the difference between progressive proletarian and oppressive bourgeois violence –

bourgeois violence is unlimited and constantly creates new preconditions for violence . . . [it] is disorder in permanence, it is 'civil war' . . . The violence of socialist revolutionaries is the force necessary, in order to drive out the robbers . . . it is temporary violence, because employed by the overwhelming majority against the few[28]

– yet *de facto* nothing had happened to give this rhetoric of revolution and violence a firm base on which to plan and to act.

The complete absence of any political or military plan is precisely the aspect which, in retrospect, has prompted the sharpest criticism from the communist side. In 1923 the PCI leadership produced a collection of 'Notes on the experiences with military forms of struggle during the "civil war of 1919–22" in Italy'[29] in which, in the face of the fascist campaign of violence, it no longer questions the legitimacy of proletarian use of violence, but merely criticises the inability of the Left, particularly the maximalists, to come to grips with the technical, organisational, psychological and military problems attaching to the conduct of a civil war by the proletariat. Today, it is from this position that a large part of the new Italian Left judges the political situation of that time.[30]

But it was, after all, a feature of the Italian situation after 1919 that two more or less evenly matched parties to the civil war did not in fact exist. Instead of action and counter-action, there existed (fascist) action and

TABLE 17.1:   Acts of Political Violence in Italy, 1 January to 8 May 1921

	Violent acts betw. fasc. & soc.	Reported to the courts	Not reported	Arrested fasc.	Arrested soc.	Fasc. reported but free	Soc. reported but free
Piemont	58	50	8	30	224	91	27
Lombardy	139	133	6	28	144	57	45
Liguria	15	15	–	6	34	2	. 6
Emilia-Romagna	317	265	52	162	274	219	255
Veneto	191	174	17	92	142	181	112
Venezia-Giulia	10	7	3	1	13	11	17
Total, Northern Italy	730	644	86	319	831	561	462
Tuscany	97	91	6	27	187	89	45
Umbria	74	74	–	6	46	31	1
Marches	23	20	3	5	20	22	42
Latium	15	14	1	9	28	2	3
Abruzzi	21	20	1	1	33	46	13
Total, Central Italy	230	219	11	48	314	190	104
Campagna	14	11	3	6	11	19	5
Apulia	59	59	–	15	191	45	35
Calabria	7	5	2	1	5	16	3
Basilicata	4	2	2	–	–	–	–
Sicily	24	20	4	5	53	41	23
Sardinia	5	4	1	2	16	6	–
Total, Southern Italy	113	101	12	29	276	127	66

TABLE 17.1 (*Contd.*)

	Violent acts betw. fasc. & soc.	Reported to the courts	Not reported	Arrested fasc.	Arrested soc.	Fasc. reported but free	Soc. reported but free
Cremona	13	13	–	2	28	–	–
Mantua	42	42	–	2	4	40	11
Pavia	49	48	1	5	11	9	21
Ferrara	49	49	–	33	110	26	79
Modena	93	52	41	5	6	46	57
Parma	18	12	6	2	11	8	4
Piacenza	29	27	2	9	35	4	7
Reggio E.	41	41	–	16	45	91	84
Rovigo	79	72	7	38	56	63	23
Bologna	73	73	–	84	52	40	24
Total, Po Valley							
Total	486	429	57	196	358	327	310

Source: R. De Felice, *Mussolini il fascista*, Vol. I. *La conquista del potere 1921–1925* (Turin, 1966) pp. 36–9 (revised).

(proletarian) suffering, and on the part of the lower and middle echelons of the State passivity, impotence or even complicity.

> In an amazing and often infuriating manner . . . the struggle [was] decided by the predominance of one party. Everywhere it was the fascists who were the aggressors. Socialist acts of violence, which may have been the immediate cause for retaliatory strikes, were for the most part no more than a response to fascist incursions. Everywhere fascist violence was systematic, deliberate and intent on destroying the opponent; socialist resistance on the other hand was inconsistent, sporadic and flagged soon.[31]

This defensive aspect of Left violence – regardless of whether it is judged positively or negatively – is almost completely absent in the accounts of the Left: Fascism is simply turned into the symbol of innocently suffered violence. If we follow these authors, there were virtually no instances where known men of violence were arrested, remanded in custody or indeed sentenced. Even minimal guarantees provided by a constitutional State had been wiped out. The socialist G. Matteotti, for instance, spoke of the 'absolute guarantee of impunity . . . for all (fascist) criminals',[32] and took the view that the whole state apparatus – up to the highest echelons of government – was in collusion with fascist private justice.

Research by G. De Rosa, R. De Felice *et al.* has shown that there can be no question of such complicity on the part of the Giolitti and Bonomi Governments (1920–2),[33] and that it was much more a case of many cogs within the state machinery no longer functioning properly, of central government directives, aimed at controlling violence, at enforcing the authority of the state, at maintaining the State's monopoly of force and at pacifying those regions that had slipped out of control, met with procrastination and sabotage at the intermediate level. The figures in Table 17.1, based on official data of the Ministry of the Interior about acts of political violence in Italy for the first half of 1921, show that the impressions formulated by the left are only correct with certain qualifications. The overwhelming majority of criminal acts were reported to the authorities (about 90 per cent). The ratio of arrests (1,421 'socialist' as opposed to 396 fascists) does show massive bias on the part of police and judiciary, but equally that there was no question of absolute impunity. The data indicate great local and regional variations. In Apulia the ratio was one of 191 members of the left for every 15 fascists, in Tuscany 187 socialists to 27 fascists. In Emilia-Romagna, on the other hand, the ratio was 274 : 162; in the province of Bologna, where the state had a particularly energetic prefect, the number of arrested fascists even exceeded that of their opponents by more than two dozen (52 : 84).

III

The Fascists always conceived of their violence as counter-violence, as a response to 'Red Barbarism', a legitimate reaction to the threat of a bolshevik overthrow and an answer to the 'nihilist violence of triumphant bestiality'. The concept of 'punitive expeditions' stems from this perception of their role. Many personal accounts about the early days of the futurist and fascist movements do however show how calculated the argument of counter-violence was. Even in this early phase the will to action and the readiness for violence were the most notable characteristics. A glance at fascist songs, which elevate cudgel, dagger, gun and hand grenade into pseudo-religious cult objects, and glorify the ill-treatment and killing of an enemy branded as criminal, shows this quite clearly.[34] The refrains run something like 'the dagger between my teeth, the bomb in my hand', or 'bash them, bash them, bash them all you can'. H. Heller has argued that this aimless ethos of violence, this apotheosis of violence influenced by Nietzsche and Sorel, represented by far the most significant feature of Fascism, whose hallmark was a 'fundamental contempt for ideas and a religion of violence'. 'Apart from this formal ideology of violence (there is) no single idea that (would link) the fascism of 1922 or indeed of 1915 with that of 1922 or 1929.'[35] E. Santarelli comes to a similar conclusion: 'The "philosophy of power", the theory and practice of violence, the doctrine of war respectively provided the ideological framework . . . for Mussolini's action.'[36] The prerequisites for this ideology of violence, both in terms of the history of thought and of social psychology, have been studied relatively thoroughly. They will be dealt with in other contributions.

In organisational terms, the fascist ideology of violence found its expression in *squadrismo*. What fascist combat units had in common was not so much certain objectives or political programmes, but rather being at one in feeling anti-middle class, sharing the dynamism, the primacy of action, of fighting, of physical violence. *Squadrismo*, as E. Beckerath wrote in 1927, 'was a spontaneous unity of will, youth, movement, activity for the sake of it, a kind of *l'art pour l'art* in the sphere of politics'.[37] The significance of *squadrismo* as an instrument consisted not merely in its acts of violence or in the terrorist threat to political opponents, but equally in the appeal and fascination the ideology and practice of violence possessed for large sections of Italian youth. According to the findings of conflict studies, the menace and the appeal of violence, its instrumental and communicative strategies are frequently evenly balanced.[38] This aspect of fascist violence has hitherto been wrongly neglected. A. Aquarone was the last to point out this aspect. 'In the punitive expeditions during the heyday of *squadrismo*, systematic use of violence, and its programmatic glorification served not only to annihilate the opponent, but also . . . for self-fulfillment as such.' Aquarone warned, however, that it would not do to postulate a too narrow and quasi-mechanical relation between violence and consensus as complementary phenomena of political rule. In his view, they represented two variables, relatively independent of each other. 'The regime needed violence not just to repress, but also in order to legitimise itself *vis-à-vis* its own rank and file.'

> A party which develops and gains ground as an anti-party and an alternative state . . . which not merely seizes power by the instrument of violence, but makes it its ideological programme and glorifies it as the basis of good government, for the better protection of the 'true interests' of the people – a party of this kind will not readily be able to renounce violence both as a means and a value.[39]

K.-P. Hoepke, in his study of the German Right and Italian Fascism, has pointed out that the appeal which the use of violence possessed for the pro-fascist section of the German public at that time was of far greater significance than any ideological or programmatic substance Fascism may have had.[40] These brief indications of the problems connected with the appeal exerted by fascist violence must suffice here. *Squadrismo* as a phenomenon of group psychology still appears to be a largely unresearched area of historiography.

IV

The debate about violence within the Italian Left, and the forms political violence of the Left took during the so-called 'two red years' (unrest caused by inflation, strikes, land occupations, mutinies, occupations of factories), can only briefly be touched upon here. In his work, G. Salvemini effectively exploded the legend of 'red chaos' and was able to show that the degree of social conflict in Italy at that time did not exceed that of victorious nations like France and Britain. It has meanwhile become an axiom of historiography that it was not 'red' violence which provoked fascist violence – which already existed latently and indeed in practice – but that it merely provided it with a convenient justification. 'The violence of Italian Socialists [produced] with a minimum of substance a maximum of false and evil images and no gain at all.'[41] At the party conference in Bologna in November 1919, F. Turati, the leading thinker of the Socialists' reformist wing, warned against the claim that the dictatorship of the proletariat could only be achieved by violence and called it 'a lackluster ideal of armed and brutal violence'.

> Violence is nothing else but the suicide of the proletariat . . . At present (our opponents) do not yet take us quite seriously; but if they should consider it useful to take us seriously, then our appeal to violence will be taken up by our enemies, who are a hundred times better armed than we are, and then it will be good-bye for quite a while to parliamentary action, to economic organisation and to the Socialist Party!

Turati foresaw a 'cruel reaction', the complete isolation of the proletariat, because of the hostility of all the middle classes, and 'the ruin of the labour movement for half a century'.[42] No one else among Italian socialists focused his thinking as much on the issue of violence and on a critique of the ideology of violence as did Turati. Shaken in his confidence in the persuasive power of reason and in constitutional legality and having lost faith in the progressive forces within the Italian middle class, he responded to the outbreak of fascist illegality with a desperate appeal to non-violence and the ethos of the 'heroism of cowardice': 'No retaliation, ever, not even when most justified. We must break this vicious circle, this rising spiral of violence . . . it is a thousand times better to be killed than to kill.'[43]

No one on the parliamentary scene has documented the fascist terror more convincingly and more accusingly in the matter-of-fact presentation of his material, than the democratic socialist G. Matteotti. In a series of parliamentary speeches and questions, which he himself rightly called 'an unending scream of pain from our provinces oppressed by terror', he noted that the emergence of an 'armed illegal organisation' which was carrying out private justice, was corrupting the fundamental principles of a constitutional

State. Matteotti called fascist illegality, and the reactions of both government and middle class public that accompanied it, a landmine which would cause civil war and the 'disintegration of the country'. He spoke of the tragedy of reformist socialism which, through the egotism and self-surrender of the bourgeoisie, was being deprived of its basis for political action. 'In a terrain of violence, which the complicity of the State helps to nourish, a Socialist Party that stands for cultural, civilisatory progress and for the masses, is deprived of its right to exist.'[45] The events of these months would bring it home to the people 'that now only violence would serve to defend them against violence and that, as an ultimate law of life, terror would have to be countered by terror.'[46]

V

It might be assumed from the foregoing that the phenomenon of social violence was at the centre of political debate in post-war Italy and that the 'civil war' – as Papini argued – dominated the daily life of every Italian. This assumption is certainly correct as far as certain months and certain Italian regions at that time were concerned. It is probably also true for certain sections of the political elites of the day, particularly for those who were in close contact with the labour movement and the parties of the Left, or indeed belonged to them. But on the other hand, the subject of political violence seems to have bypassed large sections of public opinion almost unnoticed. A look at the debates in the Senate during those years, for instance, reveals only scant and quite inadequate indications of this aspect of Italian reality.

If one reads the declarations of the Bonomi (1921) and Facta (1922) governments in Chamber and Senate, one is hard put to believe that one is dealing with a country in which the fascist seizure of power was only just around the corner. Bonomi, for instance, proclaimed in December 1921 that the policy of pacification pursued by him had already proved largely successful. That portion of Italy, where armed conflict still occurred sporadically, had been reduced to a fifth of the State's territory, and even in these still disturbed districts 'calm and order would be restored in the near future'.[47] Facta's *nutro fiducia* (I have faith in the future), with which he sought to calm his critics, has since become axiomatic for the helplessly blind optimism and the divorce from reality this politician, and the political forces of liberalism he represented, suffered from. While F. Turati declared in the Chamber that 'Italy today is in a state of full-scale civil war! The very existence of the constitutional State . . . is at stake . . . We are facing the collapse of a culture . . . At issue now is the decision between a civilised Italy and a re-barbarised one',[48] Facta felt able to state that 'the attempts . . . at violence and incursions against citizens and State' were by and large 'limited and isolated'. 'Our country is far from those conditions which it has pleased this or

that person to call grave.'[49] Recent studies have rightly emphasised the
inability of large sections of the ruling elites of the day and of public opinion to
comprehend the phenomenon of Fascism in all its danger and magnitude[50]
and this is evidently particularly true where the extent and implications of
non-constitutional, illegal use of violence were concerned. Relegated to the
local news pages, under headings similar to those of common crimes, it seems
that the events of that time were frequently not regarded as 'political' in the
strict sense, but as a 'brutta cronaca'.[51] In August 1922 a liberal conservative,
such as G. Sarrocchi, could speak of 'past episodes which have also been called
civil war', and even for a nationalist like Federzoni it was a question of
'occasional acts of violence' and 'disruptions of public order'.[52]

Depending on political viewpoint, personal fate or generation as well as
political and moral sensitivity, the events of that time have been felt in quite
different ways. This impression is confirmed on looking through evidence of
private reflections, in the form of correspondence, diaries, notes about
conversations, etc., now richly available. Anna Kuliscioff, for instance,
F. Turati's companion, already in the first months after the war, showed herself
deeply disturbed about the degree of destructiveness and verbal aggression
present in Italian society, about the 'overwhelming wave of hatred and blind
partisanship'. 'In Milan and Turin', she wrote in April 1919, 'we will hardly be
able . . . to escape from another 1898, certainly far more terrible and bloody
than those six days twenty years ago'. A few days later, after the destruction of
the *Avanti* offices, she writes, filled with a deep pessimism about Italy's future,
'I still hope that we may be able to get away with no more than one painful
experiment or another in revolutionary gymnastics and that it won't come to
the complete demolition of the entire social system, which for Italy, more than
elsewhere, would spell unmitigated disaster'.[54] The correspondence between
Turati and Kuliscioff between 1919 and 1922 reveals numerous instances of
seismographic sensitivity and a feeling for the extraordinary nature of the
political situation, that seem to be completely lacking in other records, such as
the diaries of Prezzolino or Ojetti.[55]

VI

What were the dimensions of political violence in the Italy of that time? What
was the extent, the limits, the regional distribution, the quantitative and
qualitative aspects? What was the relation between political and criminal
violence? What long-term average statistics about Italian society should be
taken into account in assessing the problem of post-war violence? The only
comprehensive data available so far – which still provide the stock references
for even the most recent accounts – are based on the studies by A. Tasca and
G. Salvemini. The fragmentary official statistics, published by G. De Rosa
and R. De Felice, help to throw additional light on the reality of that period.

In answering the question as to the number of deaths in the 'civil war', one must distinguish four groups:
(1) the parties of the labour movement (socialists, communists);
(2) fascists and ancillary groups (nationalists);
(3) representatives of the forces of the State;
(4) civilian bystanders.

The fascists surrounded their own casualties with a pseudo-religious cult of martyrdom and produced different statements as to their numbers at different times. Mussolini spoke of the 'countless dead' Fascism had sacrificed in the Italian cause,[56] of 'thousands of young fascists who died fearlessly, in order to save Italy from impending disintegration and chaos'.[57] In September 1924 Mussolini talked of the 'indescribable sacrifice of our three thousand dead'.[58] During the tenth anniversary celebrations of Fascism he even stressed the sacrificial and violent nature of the seizure of power in 1922 by asserting 'that among all the insurrections of modern times, the fascist had been the bloodiest'.[59] Other fascist publications mention figures of up to 50,000.[60] The last figures produced by the fascists list 672 as "fallen for the fascist revolution" in the period between 1919 and 1926.

Table 17.2 shows the chronological distribution. As to be expected, the year 1921 shows the greatest number of casualties. The figures for the first seven months – the period leading up to the 'pacification pact' – with an average of 22 deaths, are only slightly higher than the monthly average for the whole year

TABLE 17.2:   Number of Deaths on the Fascist Side (According to Fascist Accounts)

	1919	1920	1921	1922	1923	1924	1925	1926
January	–	–	6	8	14	2	2	–
February	–	–	10	6	8	3	5	1
March	–	–	20	10	7	9	2	2
April	–	4	14	10	3	9	7	2
May	–	1	53	19	6	4	8	2
June	–	3	20	8	3	4	–	1
July	–	5	33	15	3	6	1	2
August	1	5	15	23	4	4	6	2
September	–	4	22	13	3	10	5	6
October	–	6	16	41*	1	3	6	2
November	2	2	13	24	3	10	5	4
December	1	6	9	15	5	7	3	5
Total	4	36	231	192	60	71	50	29

* 27 of these between October 27 and 31 1922.

Source: *Panorami di realizzazioni del fascismo*, Vol. II: *I grandi scomparsi e i caduti della rivoluzione fascista* (Rome, n.d., ca 1942).

(19.3). May 1921 (parliamentary elections) and October 1922 (March on Rome) stand out as the months of greatest bloodshed. These data must be taken with considerable reserve, since they were inflated wherever possible (fascists killed as a result of accidents or illness, or even non-fascist middle-class notabilities were numbered among the 'martyrs' as victims of Left-wing violence) and should certainly be reduced by 20–30 per cent. Yet the fact remains that up to 1926 500–600 fascists were killed, either during violent actions of the *squadri*, in conflicts with the organs of the state or as victims of assaults. It is further revealing that until October 1920, i.e. in the months of 'red terror' and 'bolshevik anarchy', a total of 32 deaths are listed, among them a considerable number of 'liquidated' non-fascist citizens. One set of figures about the violence of the left, published by the fascist movement under the title 'Red Barbarism' and covering the period between 15 April 1919 and 21 June 1921, lists 33 deaths for the months up to October 1920.[61] For the period 1 October 1920–30 October 1922 again according to the fascists' own records, their dead numbered 359, of which 46 lost their lives in conflicts with the police. Again a certain number would have to be deducted as victims of accidents or illness, leaving around 300 fascist 'martyrs' for the two years leading up to the march on Rome.[62]

It is far more difficult to estimate the number of dead on the other side. According to Salvemini, during the fascist era all research into the number of anti-fascist victims was rendered impossible.[63] But even after 1945 no analyses of this kind were undertaken. The *enciclopedia dell' antifascismo* states tersely: 'There are no official statistics about the number of anti-fascists killed by the *squadristi*, by members of the fascist militia or the police before or after the march on Rome.'[64] A search through the columns of the *Corriere della Sera*, conducted at Salvemini's instigation, in order to establish the number of victims of political violence after 1919, has revealed that until September 1920, there were 65 acts of 'bolshevik' violence which resulted in killings. Of the 65 victims 35 were members of the police. 'In order to evaluate these data with greater precision', writes Salvemini, it ought to be kept in mind that:

'1) In Italy life counts for less than it should do in a civilised country; 2) in 1919/20 Italians had only recently returned from the war, where respect for human life was not among the things they had learned. On December 18, 1922, the Turin fascists killed 21 people in a single day. It would be as well to keep these facts in mind when one hears talk about the 'bolshevik's bloody and despotic rule in Italy during 1919 and 1920'.[65]

During the same period (January 1919–September 1920) according to Salvemini the civilian population and the labour movement lost 131 dead.[66] A collection of data about *Murders in Italy* by P. Secchia, covering the same period, lists 212 members of the labour movement as killed.[67] Without giving specific reasons, Salvemini later raised the total number of deaths to 300.[68] Whatever the reliability of the above data, it is clear at any rate, that the *biennio rosso*, the two red years, were relatively unbloody, if compared with the period that followed.

For the actual period of 'civil war' from October 1920 onwards, the records are patchy. According to statistics produced by the Ministry of the Interior, clashes between fascists and socialists between 1 January 1921 and 7 April 1921 (the day parliament was dissolved) resulted in 102 deaths (25 fascists, 41 socialists, 16 bystanders and 20 policemen) and 388 injured, 108 fascists and 123 socialists among them. From 8 April to 15 May (election day) 105 were killed and 431 injured, from 16 to 31 May the figures are 71 deaths (16 fascists, 31 socialists, 20 bystanders, 4 policemen) and 216 injured.[69] As far as the fascists are concerned, these data correspond roughly to the figures published by themselves. According to Table 17.2, 103 fascists died during the period January–May 1921. Properly adjusted, these figures coincide approximately with the 65–70 fascists listed in official statistics. For the total number of 'socialists' who perished (approx. 115–20 during the first five months of 1921), the data quoted offer valuable indications as well. The survey of the *Corriere della Sera*, referred to earlier, came up with the figure of 406 'socialists' who were killed by fascists between 1 October 1920 and 30 October 1922. Salvemini assumes that roughly a third of fascist acts of violence were not picked up by the *Corriere*. On top of that one would have to assume that a considerable number of injured only died weeks or even months after such clashes, as a result of the injuries or beatings they received. Salvemini therefore arrives at a hypothetical total of approximately 600 'socialist' casualties. In his estimation, to the 300 fascists and 600 socialists would have to be added the fascists and anti-fascists who lost their lives in clashes with the police as well as all 'civilians' involved. The two latter groups he estimates at 1,100, and for the period from October 1920 up to the march on Rome he arrives at a total of 2,000 victims.[70] 'If we compare the 2,000 killed during the civil war of 1921/22 with the 200 killed during the period of bloody 'bolshevik tyranny', it is clear that the casualties inflicted by civil war were worse than those inflicted by '"bolshevism".'[71] The fact that Salvemini later revised upwards his estimate of the victims of fascist violence for the years 1921/22 shows on how uncertain a base these data rest.

As for the extent, the chronological and the geographical distribution of violence against property and institutions again we have only partial and chronologically incomplete data. According to A. Tasca's survey (cf. Table 17.3) the fascists destroyed in the first half of 1921: 17 printing works and newspaper offices, 59 people's houses, 119 workers' institutions, 107 cooperative houses, 8 mutual insurances, 141 socialist and communist party offices, 100 cultural centres, 10 people's libraries and theatres, 1 adult education institute, 28 labour trade unions, 53 workers' and convalescent

TABLE 17.3: Record of Destruction by the Fascists in the First Six Months of 1921

	Newspaper offices & printing works	People's homes	Trade union head offices	Co-operatives	Peasant leagues	Mutual assurances	Local and regional branch offices of CPI and PSI	Cultural centres	People's libraries & theatres	Adult education institutes	Labour trade unions	Workers' and convalescent homes	Total
Latium	—	—	—	—	—	—	1	—	—	—	—	1	3
Romagna	3	11	1	11	—	2	70	—	—	—	1	24	137
Tuscany	—	—	15	3	—	—	—	—	—	—	—	—	17
Marches	1	—	—	—	—	1	—	—	—	—	—	1	—
Umbria	—	—	5	—	—	—	6	—	—	—	—	—	—
Sicily	—	—	3	—	3	—	4	—	—	—	9	5	24
Sardinia	—	—	1	—	—	—	—	—	—	—	—	2	3
Apulia	—	1	13	4	2	—	1	—	—	—	7	1	29
Southern Italy*	2	—	2	—	—	—	3	—	—	—	—	—	7
Piemont	1	4	9	3	2	1	9	—	2	—	10	8	49
Liguria	—	—	3	—	—	—	—	—	—	—	—	—	3
Venezia-Giulia	4	2	21	3	—	—	5	100	—	—	—	2	137
Lombardy**	3	—	1	2	—	—	6	—	—	—	—	1	13
Veneto***	—	1	9	8	1	—	7	—	1	—	—	1	28
Total, regions	14	19	83	34	8	4	112	100	3	—	27	46	450

Bologna	1	6	7	9	5	—	5	—	—	—	—	2	35
Cremona	—	—	—	—	—	—	—	—	—	—	—	—	—
Ferrara	—	3	9	1	19	—	5	—	2	—	1	—	37
Mantua	—	—	4	37	15	—	2	—	—	1	—	1	63
Modena	—	—	2	—	—	—	—	—	—	—	—	—	2
Parma	—	5	1	6	—	—	8	—	—	—	—	1	15
Pavia	—	21	7	9	25	4	8	—	4	—	—	2	80
Piacenza	1	2	—	7	—	—	3	—	—	—	—	—	13
Reggio Emilia	—	1	2	1	8	—	2	—	1	—	—	—	16
Rovigo	—	2	4	3	3	—	2	—	—	—	—	1	15
Total, Po Valley	3	40	36	73	75	4	29	—	7	1	1	7	276
Total	17	59	119	107	83	8	141	100	10	1	28	53	726

* excluding Apulia
** excluding Pavia, Cremona and Mantua
*** excluding Rovigo

Source: Angelo Tasca, *Nascita e avvento del fascismo* (Bari, 1965) p. 439.

homes – a total of 726 individual targets. At the same time, hundreds of leftwing representatives in communal, municipal and provincial government were forced to resign. Table 17.3 further shows how strongly at that time this storm of destruction was centred on the provinces of the lower Po Valley, Veneto-Giulia and Tuscany (550 out of the total of 726 targets). Data which would indicate what happened thereafter, for instance up to the time of the march on Rome, do not exist at all. Thus, surmise and phantasy have so far been boundless.

All data about the number of victims after 31 October 1922 are even more open to doubt. The hope that once the fascists were in power that would mean the end of all private and illegal violence was widespread. Yet in reality from that moment onwards the party's and the State's illegal social violence coincided, for now army, police, administration and judicature were in the hands of the fascist coalition government, while the *squadri* were not disbanded but merged with the MVSN, the party's militia organised on military lines. The data in Table 17.2 show that from the beginning of 1923, the number of victims on the fascist side decreased rapidly and even in the months of the Matteotti-crisis of 1924 did not reach the casualty figures of 1921 and 1922. Thus in the four years from 1923–6 less fascists were killed than in the single year of 1921 (210:31).

Does this decrease in the casualties on the fascist side correspond to a decrease also as far as the other groups were concerned? The hopes entertained by middle class and pro-fascists that fascism would become normalised and 'parliamentarised' and that fascist illegality would be kept in check, were only partially realised. The demise of the liberal system and the creation of a one-party dictatorship were accomplished under the protection and pressure of continuing fascist violence. A. Gambino, for instance, argues that the degree of fascist violence further increased after 28 October 1922, even though the majority of such incidents, for reasons of fear, ignorance or complicity, were no longer reported by the press.[72] G. Salvemini sets the number of victims of fascist violence for the period November 1922 until the end of 1926 at 1,000.[73] The Ministry of the Interior's fragmentary statistics, published by De Felice (Tables 17.4 and 17.5), for the year 1925 and January– April 1926 and 1927 respectively, indicate the surprising fact that the number of dead and injured in many of the months covered were supposed to be higher on the fascist side than on that of their opponents. For the year 1925 the ratio was 35:27. The number of persons reported to the authorities and arrested (740:934) are also more or less evenly balanced. It is difficult to reconcile these data, as far as numbers and ratios are concerned, with the picture of a by now impotent and outlawed opposition, increasingly exposed to the despotic rule of State and Fascism, painted by the literature to date. Only in one respect do these data confirm the traditional picture: in 1925, too, the initiative in actions against party offices, cultural centres and trade-union buildings rested entirely with the fascist side (1:89).

TABLE 17.4: Acts of Political Violence in Italy in 1925 (up to 29 Dec. 1979)

	Dead		Injured		Arrests, reported to the authorities		Violence against institutions		Other acts of violence	
	Fascists	*Opposers*	*Fascists*	*Opposers*	*Fascists*	*Opposers*	*Fascists*	*Opposers*	*Fascists*	*Opposers*
January	2	2	65	46	100	276	–	30	44	51
February	4	4	29	25	107	126	–	–	19	17
March	1	2	46	35	42	66	–	5	5	15
April	5	5	32	31	45	85	–	6	10	57
May	7	4	20	27	29	54	–	5	5	38
June	1	2	42	38	33	88	–	5	7	33
July	1	–	20	23	25	33	–	1	4	32
August	7	1	10	21	18	28	1	–	6	16
September	3	–	31	23	26	56	–	–	15	30
October	1	5	29	75	257	57	–	24	14	89
November	2	1	21	29	43	52	–	13	6	60
December	1	1	10	15	15	13	–	–	3	5
Total:	35	27	355	388	740	934	1	89	138	441

Source: R. De Felice, *Mussolini il fascista*, Vol. II: *L'organizzazione dello Stato fascista 1925–1929* (Torino, 1968) p. 125f.

TABLE 17.5: Acts of Political Violence in Italy in the first four months of 1926 and 1927

	Dead		Injured		Arrests		Charges		Other acts of violence	
	Fascists	*Opposers*	*Fascists*	*Opposers*	*Fascists*	*Opposers*	*Fascists*	*Opposers*	*Fascists*	*Opposers*
Jan.–April 1926	6	2	50	49	51	90	62	43	45	99
Jan.–April 1927	4	–	10	1	50	45	49	11	30	42

Source: R. De Felice, *Mussolini il fascista*, vol. II, cit., p. 191.

VII

What conclusions can be drawn from the statistics referred to above? The first phase of historical research into Anti-Fascism, still informed by direct experience of participation and suffering, was based largely on an identification of Fascism with violence. *Le terreur fasciste* (G. Salvemini), *Gli anni del manganello* (The years of the cudgel) (W. Tobagi)[74] appeared as the essential characteristics of one-party dictatorship. The concept of totalitarian rule became the symbol of evil and of pure negativity. In his *Goliath* – one of the key texts of the anti-fascist opposition – G. A. Borgese in 1937 called the fascist system 'a penitentiary for forced labour', 'a slavery harsher than any we know in ancient or modern history'. Although Borgese called the attempt to 'distinguish between black and pitch-black as absurd as it is repulsive', he formulated at the same time, with Nazi Germany in mind, a primacy of evil for the Italian case unsurpassed in its violent nature and its utter stupidity.[75]

The point of historical research, however, is precisely to distinguish between grey, black and pitch-black, that is to circumscribe the dimensions of a phenomenon and to penetrate past questions of guilt to causes and structural problems. The debate about the relation between power, violence and consensus in the fascist regime, prompted by the works of R. De Felice,[76] suggests that the problem of violence during the transitional period, i.e. from 1919–25, should be investigated more closely. What do we know so far about aims, objects, means, participants, extent, intensity and organisational forms of violence which emerged in Italian post-war society? What do we know about the distribution of the various social groups, their regional and historical patterns, what about the extent of material destruction and the distribution of the resulting costs? And what about the punishment of crimes of violence imposed by the courts?

In the thirties, K. Mannheim complained that sociology had 'failed to concern itself thoroughly with a theoretical analysis of the role of violence and the circumstances surrounding its appearance'. In the sixties, H. Arendt still spoke of the 'matter-of-course' way violence is accepted in politics, and that violence was being neither analysed nor questioned.[77] After a number of years of intensive research into the nature of conflicts and of critical studies on peace, which in the United States, for example, have taken political violence as one of the 'central topics' of investigation,[78] this criticism would hardly be reiterated today. The point here is, whether the methods and hypotheses developed in this connection might also be applied to the historiographical study of Fascism. The few attempts in this direction[79] show how much more work remains to be done, beginning with a comprehensive inventory of political violence in Italy, based on a systematic and thorough analysis of the press – an inventory which would finally do away with the practice prevalent hitherto, of each 'party' counting its own dead. It does not say much for the quality of research into Fascism that it must to this day depend on the findings of Tasca and Salvemini, by now forty years old. Such a broad-spectrum survey would also permit us to examine the concept of 'civil war' in its applicability to the Italian case.

And lastly an inventory of this kind would also greatly benefit the objectivity of historiographical debate. Certain unverified assumptions about the causes of political violence are, explicitly or implicitly, central to the judgements arrived at in most historical accounts. In this context, the continuing debate about who was responsible for the murder of Matteotti – which in Italy occupies a similarly central place to the one about the burning of the *Reichstag* in Germany – can be said to be emblematic. The reproach levelled at the De Felice school of historiography – that it tended to minimise or exculpate Fascism – is based especially on its interpretation of the problem of violence. Thus, someone like L. Valiani writes:

> In De Felice's 'Interview' there is no mention of Fascism's acts of violence and murders. . . . In the several volumes of his biography he does speak about it, but only sketchily and in a manner that minimises the significance of these crimes and exculpates Mussolini. . . . The violence of Fascism, which did not stop at murder, as well as its impunity, were among the essential reasons for its success. Thus it was able to turn *squadrismo* into a nationwide armed force of decisive political importance and later to establish a militia.[80]

The events in present-day Italy have given us a keener eye for the problem of violence. Yet there can be hardly anyone who would consider it legitimate to compare the Italy of 1920 with that of 1979. And yet, there are pessimists who speak of 'squadrismo 1979' and of the impending civil war of the 1980s.[81] A more exact knowledge of the problems of violence in Italian society then and now would prove useful.

NOTES

1. E. and D. Susmel (eds), *Opera Omnia di Benito Mussolini*, Vol. xxi (Florence, 1953ff) p. 238f (in the following cited as O.O.)
2. P. Togliatti, *Opere scelte* (Rome, 1974) p. 1030.
3. L. Salvatorelli and G. Mira, *Storia d'Italia nel periodo fascista* (Turin, 1957) p. 168.
4. P. Farneti, 'La crisi della democrazia italiana e l'avvento del fascismo: 1919–1922', *Rivista Italiana di scienza politica*, 5 (1975) p. 49f.
5. W. Schieder, 'Faschismus' in *Sowjetsystem und demokratische Gesellschaft* Vol. 2 (Freiburg/Br., 1968) col. 454.
6. E. Nolte, *Europa und die faschistischen Bewegungen*, (Munich, 1968) p. 12, 75f, 101.
7. R. Cantagalli, *Storia del fascismo fiorentino 1919/1925* (Florence, 1972) p. 230.
8. *Il fascismo in Italia* (Leningrad, 1926). R. De Felice (ed.), *Studio inedito per i quadri dell' Internazionale comunista* (Milan, 1965) p. 107.

9. A. Gramsci, *Socialismo e fascismo* (Turin, 1971) p. 248.
10. A. Gramsci, *La costruzione del partito comunista, 1923–1926*, (Turin, 1971) p. 18.
11. A. Tasca, *Nascita e avvento del fascismo* (Bari, 1965) (French original, edition 1938).
12. P. Spriano, *Storia del Partito comunista italiano*, Vol. 1: *Da Bordiga a Gramsci* (Turin, 1967) p. 123.
13. S. Colarizi, *L'Italia antifascista dal 1922 al 1940*, Vol. 2 (Bari, 1976) p. 300.
14. G. Papini, *Preghiere per la pace, 1922*, quoted from I. Silione, *Der Faschismus* (Zurich, 1934) p. 137f.
15. H. Eckstein, 'On the etiology of internal wars', *History and Theory*, 4 (1964/65) pp. 133–63, p. 135ff.
16. Cf. the typology in P. Waldmann, *Strategien politischer Gewalt* (Stuttgart, 1977) p. 36f., which in its turn is based on T. R. Gurr's typology.
17. Cf. R. De Felice, *Der Faschismus: Ein Interview mit M. A. Leeden* (Stuttgart, 1977) passim and the discussion sketched in my postscript, esp. p. 126ff.
18. Most recently P. Spriano, *Sulla rivoluzione italiana. Socialisti e comunisti nella storia d'Italia* (Turin, 1978); id., *Intervista sulla storia de PCI* (Bari, 1978); G. Amendola, *Storia del Partito comunista italiano, 1921–1943* (Rome, 1978); id. 'Lettera a Spirano sulla storia del PCI: su questo non sono d'accordo con te . . . ', *Rinascita* (2/3/1979).
19. E. Weber, 'Revolution? Counterrevolution? What revolution?', in W. Laqueur (ed.), *Fascism: A Reader's Guide* (London, 1976) pp. 435–67, p. 440.
20. P. Nenni, *Sei anni di guerra civile* (Milan, 1945) p. 97ff.
21. Thus the assessment in the anarchist publication *L'adunata dei refrattari* (4/8/1934), quoted in: S. Colarizi, *L'Italia antifascista*, cit., p. 194.
22. *O.O.*, xxiii, p. 50–3.
23. *O.O.*, xii, p. 233.
24. Quoted in G. A. Chiurco, *Storia della rivoluzione fascista*, Vol. ii (Florence, 1929) p. 218.
25. E. Corradini, *Discorsi politici (1902–1923)* (Florence, 1923) pp. 482, 484.
26. *Brockhaus Enzyklopädie*, 18th ed., Vol. 3 (Wiesbaden, 1967) p. 491.
27. Quoted from: M. Spinella, A. Caracciolo, R. Amaduzzi, G. Petronio (eds), *Critica sociale*, Vol. 1: *Politica e ideologia politica* (Milan, 1959) p. 448.
28. A. Gramsci, *Per la veritá: Scritti 1913–1926* (Rome, 1974) p. 89. (The assessment dates from November 1919).
29. R. De Felice (ed.), 'La 'guerra civile 1919–1922' in un dokumento del Partito Comunista d'Italia', *Rivista storica del socialismo*, 27 (1966) pp. 104–25.
30. Cf. for instance R. Del Carria, *Proletari senza rivoluzione, Storia delle classi subalterne italiane dal 1860 al 1950*, 2 vols (Milan, 1970); G. Quazza argues that in the situation after 1919 – as today – it was necessary to 'mantenere il "lavoratore" – lo "sfruttato" – sul piede di guerra in un pur sempre acuto scontro di classe, a tenere stretto il nesso fra lotta politico-sociale e lotta armata almeno come possibilità permanente della "violenza dal basso" '. (G. Quazza, *Resistenza e storia d'Italia: Problemi e ipotesi di ricerca* (Milan, 1976) p. 64.)
31. E. Nolte, *Der Faschismus in seiner Epoche* (Munich, 1963) p. 254.
32. G. Matteotti, *Scritti e discorsi* (Parma, 1974) p. 190.
33. G. De Rosa, *Giolitti e il fascismo* (Rome, 1957); R. de Felice, *Mussolini il fascista*, Vol. 1, *La conquista del potere 1921–1925* (Turin, 1966) p. 24ff.
34. Cf. most recently: A. V. Savona and M. L. Straniero, *Canti dell'Italia fascista (1919–1945)* (Milan, 1979) passim.
35. H. Heller, *Gesammelte Schriften* Vol. 2 (Leiden, 1971) p. 500.
36. E. Santarelli (ed. and intro.), *Scritti politici di Benito Mussolini* (Milan, 1979) p. 43.

37. E. von Beckerath, *Wesen und Werden des faschistischen Staates* (Berlin, 1927) p. 25.
38. Waldmann, *Strategien*, p. 43ff., 75ff.
39. A. Aquarone, Violenza e consenso nel fascismo italiano, *Storia contemporanea*, 10 (1979), pp. 145–55, p. 146f.
40. K.-P. Hoepke, *Die deutsche Rechte und der italienische Faschismus* (Düsseldorf, Droste, 1968) passim.
41. Nolte, *Faschismus*, p. 186.
42. F. Turati, *Le vie maestre del socialismo* (Bologna, 1921) p. 278, 295f.
43. Id., *Socialismo e riformismo nella storia d'Italia, Scritti politici 1878–1932* (Milan, 1979) p. 437.
44. Matteotti, *Scritti e discorsi*, p. 186.
45. Ibid., pp. 127, 134, 196.
46. Ibid., p. 205.
47. I. Bonomi, *Dieci anni di Politica Italiana* (Milan, 1923) p. 257.
48. (F. Turati), *Discorsi di Filippo Turati*, Vol. 3 (Rome, 1950) pp. 1938–40.
49. *Atti del Parlamento italiano*, Camera dei deputati, Legislatura XXVI, Vol. 8, p. 8249f.
50. Cf. for instance De Felice, *Faschismus*, p. 49ff.; J. Petersen, 'Die Entstehung des Totalitarismusbegriffs in Italien' in M. Funke (ed.) *Totalitarismus* (Düsseldorf, 1979) pp. 105–28.
51. Corradini, *Discorsi politici*, p. 459.
52. Atti del Parlamento italiano, Vol. 8, p. 8316f.
53. On 7 May 1898 General Bava Beccaria crushed a popular rising with great ruthlessness and by employing the military. For the Italian left the 'events of Milan' became axiomatic for military-reactionary rule.
54. F. Turati and A. Kuliscioff, *Carteggio*, Vol. 5, *Doppoguerra e fascismo* (1919–22) (Turin, 1953) pp. 78, 80, 82.
55. U. Ojetti, *I taccuini (1914–1943)* (Florence, 1954); G. Prezzolini, *Diario 1900–1941* (Milan, 1978).
56. *O.O.*, XVIII, p. 13.
57. *O.O.*, XX, p. 113.
58. *O.O.*, XXI, p. 70.
59. Quoted from: *Panorami do realizzazioni del fascismo*, Vol. 2: *I grandi scomparsi e i caduti della rivoluzione fascista* (Rome, n.d.) p. 152.
60. G. Salvemini, *Scritti sul fascismo*, Vol. 1 (Milan, 1963) p. 62.
61. *Barbarie rossa, Riassunto cronologico della gesta compiute dai socialisti italiani dal 1919 in poi, a cura del Comitato Centrale dei Fasci Italiani di Combattimento* (Rome, 1921).
62. Salvemini, *Scritti sul fascismo*, pp. 63, 554.
63. Ibid., p. 63.
64. *Enciclopedia dell'antifascismo e della Resistenza*, Vol. 1 (Milan, 1968) p. 414.
65. Salvemini, *Scritti sul fascismo*, p. 19.
66. Ibid., p. 19.
67. *Enciclopedia*, vol. 2, p. 181f.
68. Salvemini, *Scritti sul fascismo*, p. 523 (he did this in his 'Harvard lectures' of 1943).
69. Quoted from G. Candeloro, *Storia dell'Italia contemporanea*, vol. 8: *La prima guerra mondiale, il doppoguerra, l'avvento del fascismo* (Milan, 1978) p. 353.
70. Salvemini, *Scritti sul fascismo*, p. 63f. In 1943 Salvemini estimated the number of victims of fascism to be considerably higher. 'Circa 3,000 persone persero la vita per mano fascista durante i due anni die guerra civile.' (*Scritti*, p. 554.)
71. Ibid., p. 64.

72. A. Gambino, *Storia del PNF* (Milan, 1962) pp. 66–9.
73. Salvemini, *Scritti*, p. 348f and p. 554.
74. W. Tobagi, *Gli anni del manganello* (Milan, 1973).
75. G. A. Borgese, *Golia: Marcia del fascismo* (Milan, 1946) pp. 312f, 348f.
76. De Felice, *Faschismus*; id., *Mussolini il duce: Gli anni del consenso 1929–1936* (Turin, 1974).
77. Quoted in *Militärgeschichtliche Mitteilungen* (1/1977) p. 294.
78. Waldmann, *Strategien*, p. 39.
79. A. Szymanski, 'Fascism. Industrialism and Socialism: the Case of Italy', *Comparative Studies in Society and History*, 15 (1973) pp. 394–404; Ch. Tilly, L. Tilly, R. Tilly, *The Rebellious Century 1830–1930* (Cambridge/Mass., 1975) pp. 165–89.
80. L. Valliani, 'Osservazioni sul fascismo e sul nazismo', *Rivista Storica Italiana*, 88 (1976) pp. 509–30, p. 526f.
81. A. Ronchey, *Accadde in Italia 1968/1977* (Milan, 1977); G. Neppi Modona, 'Squadrismo 1979', *La Repubblica* (27/4/1979).

18 Political Violence, its Forms and Strategies in the First Austrian Republic

Gerhard Botz

This contribution deals with the concept of 'political violence' in so far as it concerns actions whereby human beings inflict (forcible) physical damage – injuries or death – on each other.[1] Political violence, in this context, is understood as one of the forms political and social conflicts may take in a given society. In a wide range of not-yet-violent methods for the articulation of interests and the settlement of conflicts, which vary according to conflict systems, violence represents the most extreme means.[2] It appears not merely in one area of conflict – such as politics and government – but is systematically linked to many conflict systems, within families, the workplace and the economy. It is, however, a characteristic of violence that at certain levels, or when the 'normal' sequence of escalation is blocked, it can, through external influence, shift from one conflict system to another; this accounts for its multi-dimensional nature that makes it so difficult to pin down.[3] Its study therefore also requires at least some examination of non-violent levels in the conduct of conflicts within a conflict system.

Seen from this angle, it is clear that violence must always be examined in conjunction with its (less active) counterpart in a given conflict. Thus political violence is not to be defined exclusively from the point of view of the modern state's monopoly of violence. It includes not only the illegal actions by persons and groups[4] in opposition to state and society, but also its use by the organs of the state.

However desirable it might therefore appear to link the following deliber-ations on the subject – violence in the context of 'striving for a share in the power or for an influence on the distribution of power . . . within a state'[5] – with the wider history of conflicts within Austrian society during the inter-war years, limitations of space and not least the present state of research into conflict,[6] do not permit this. In the following I shall therefore attempt to steer a pragmatic course between too narrow and too comprehensive an approach.

The treatment will be under the following headings:

I   The quantitative changes in political violence between 1918 and 1934 and the qualitative changes in the structure of political conflict;

II   the forms and patterns of political violence that emerged in this connection;

III   some explicit strategies of violence by individual political groupings;

IV   the social causes of political violence.

I

No more practicable indicator of the actual extent of violence exists than the number of victims it claims. Their number also represents that yardstick of violence which enables us to compare and thus to quantify different forms of political violence – at least with regard to its extent, although not in relation to the public's perception of violence, nor the degree of its deliberateness and thus moral reprehensibility. In the following I shall merely examine the annual numbers of dead and seriously injured, which throughout the years under review remained at a fairly constant ratio of 1 : 3.[7] A separate analysis of the different categories of physical injury would produce practically the same results.

The line traced in Fig. 18.1, by taking the number of victims (logarithmically transformed), shows the course of violence in Austria from 1919 to 1934.[8]

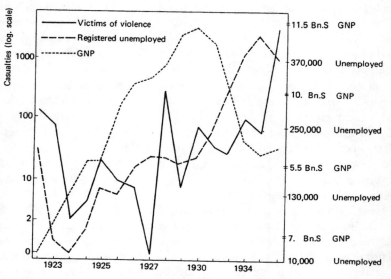

Figure 18.1:   *The Course of Political Violence, Unemployment and Gross National Product (GNP) in the First Austrian Republic.*

This shows that the years 1919 and 1920 (including the last quarter of 1918), with a total number of casualties ranging from 76 to 124, compared to the six years thereafter, stand out clearly as the period of 'Austrian revolution'.[9] This semi-revolutionary period saw the political and national reshaping of Austria, within a social and political structure broken up by the aftermath of the World War; at the same time however, in social and economic terms, the shift of political weight from the traditional power elites of the Habsburg monarchy to the industrial working class and the independent peasants as well as later to the industrial bourgeoisie, was only a limited one.[10] After a brief period of dominance by the Social Democratic working class, the 'Austrian revolution' ended up in a kind of 'balance of class forces'.[11]

In the subsequent period of comparative internal stability, the political and social distribution of power that had been established in 1918/20 remained still relatively intact.[12] Only once during the period up to 1926 – in 1923 – did the annual number of casualties of violence exceed 20. Compared to other periods of the First Republic these years thus appear relatively non-violent, although compared to the Second Republic they were distinctly violent.

The 89 dead and at least 266 seriously injured during the workers' unrest of 15 July 1927 (the burning of the Palace of Justice),[13] which led to a police massacre, mark the end of a state of comparative internal stability and of a still broadly even distribution of weight between the forces of Left and Right, before the first symptoms of the world economic crisis had even begun to be observed in Austria.

Although in 1928 the stabilising forces within the political system once again appeared to gain the upper hand, the first signs of the world slump of 1929 set in train a process of progressive destabilisation and the appearance of fascist forces – first in the shape of *Heimwehren* (home defence units), and from 1932 onwards in the form of National Socialism and an increasing marginalisation of the Social Democratic workers' movement.[14] Despite considerable variations in the annual casualty figures (between 27 and 104), the years between 1929 and 1933 were characterised by a marked tendency towards increased political violence. In 1934, this period of latent civil war finally turned into temporary open civil war (the *Schutzbund* revolt of 12 February, with a total of 320 deaths, and the National Socialist putsch of 25 July, with a total of 269 deaths)[15] and led to the replacement of a parliamentary-democratic system of political rule and control by a semi-fascist authoritatian one.[16]

A breakdown of the statistics on victims of violence according to political affiliation indicates the dominant lines of conflict within Austrian society along which political violence tended to occur.[17] *Table 18.1* below shows the total numbers of victims for each year as well as the political groupings which were mainly involved in violent conflicts, according to their share in the overall annual casualty figures. The casualties suffered by the state's organs of coercion are distributed among the various political and social 'camps' according to political weighting.

TABLE 18.1: Annual Levels of Violence (numbers of victims) and Percentages According to Political Affiliation.

	No. of victims	Percentages according to political affiliations
1918 (from 12 Nov.)	9	(1) 'Marxists' (78%); (2) Conservatives (22%)
1919	124	(1) Left-wing radicals (52%); (2) Catholic-conservatives (12%); (3) Social Democrats (11%)
1920	76	(1) Social Democrats (47%); (2) Communists (45%); (3) Catholic-conservatives (6%)
1921	2 ⎫	low incidence of violent conflicts
1922	5 ⎭	
1923	22	(1) Social Democrats (36%); (2) Catholic-conservatives (32%)
1924	10 ⎫	
1925	8 ⎬	low incidence of violent conflicts
1926	0 ⎭	
1927	274	(1) 'Marxists' (54%); (2) Catholic-conservatives (45%)
1928	8	low incidence of violent conflicts
1929	77	(1) *Heimwehr* (66%); (2) Social Democrats (25%)
1930	40	(1) *Heimwehr* (40%); (2) Social Democrats (35%)
1931	27	(1) Social Democrats (44%); (2) Catholic-conservatives and *Heimwehr* (30%); (3) National Socialists (26%)
1932	104	(1) National-Socialists (42%); (2) Social Democrats (22%); (3) 'Austro-fascist grouping'[18] (19%).
1933	69	(1) 'Austro-fascist' grouping (38%); (2) National Socialists (32%); (3) Social Democrats (16%)
1934 (only Feb. 12 and Jul. 25)	567[19] (deaths only)	(1) 'Austro-Fascist' grouping (39%); (2) Social Democrats (35%); (3) National Socialists (25%).

Source: G. Botz, 'Gewalt und politisch-gesellschaftlicher Konflikt in der Ersten Republik (1918 bis 1933)', *Österreichische Zeitschrift für Politikwissenschaft*, 4 (1975) p. 527.

Of the total figure of 859 victims of political violence (217 deaths and 642 serious injuries) for the period between 12 November 1918 and 11 February 1934, 16 per cent were Communists, 33 per cent Social Democrats, 15 per cent members of the *Heimwehr* and the Catholic-conservative 'camp', 10 per cent National Socialists; the remainder were other civilians (6 per cent) and members of the state's executive (20 per cent).

II

The annual variations in the levels of violence, set out in *Table 18.1*, broadly correspond to the internal political conflict potential in general.[20] The forms political violence took must therefore be seen against this background.

Politically, the conflict constellation of the 'Austrian revolution' was, typically, a three-cornered one: left-wing radicals–Social-Democratic workers–Catholic-conservative bourgeoisie. In 1919 the main battle lines of violence ran between left-wing radicals (mostly Communists) on the one hand, and Catholic-conservatives and Social Democrats, the coalition partners in the federal government, on the other. In 1920 the same conflict structure persisted, but was beginning to be superseded by a line-up of the middle class against Social Democrats and other left-wing forces.

The type of violence associated with the largest number of victims during the 'Austrian revolution' took the form of unrests with political or economic objectives, arising more or less spontaneously from demonstrations or offences against property, with significant incidents of violence resulting as a rule only from police intervention (as in the case of hunger demonstrations or price revolts in the winter and spring of 1919 and 1920 in Linz and Graz). A subsidiary branch of this type of violence were putschist actions – still of a spontaneous nature – by left-wing radicals and Communists.[21] The social base for such actions was provided in the main by the urban lower classes, particularly the unemployed, invalids and war veterans. Spontaneous unrests among the rural population, so-called 'peasant revolts', on the other hand, involved considerably less violence.[22] During the 'Austrian revolution' these types of violence were intimately linked to acute shortages of food and consumer goods and deficient social security provisions; thus their incidence, up to 1921, tended to increase during the winter and spring quarters.

Two less bloody forms of violent conflict were limited almost entirely to the first months of the 'Austrian revolution'; once the climax of the revolutionary movement had been passed by mid-1919, such actions also disappeared. One of them consisted in insults to officers and was mainly directed against members of the former imperial military apparatus, aristocrats and, to a lesser degree, industrialists; very rarely, however, did such attacks reach the degree of violence that might be described as serious bodily injury. Such acts, by small groups or individuals, often inflicting more symbolic and psychological than actual harm, were particularly frequent during the collapse of the Austro-Hungarian state apparatus in October and November 1918, an otherwise almost completely non-violent phase. During the power vacuum and the reshaping of the state's structures that followed, somewhat bloodier conflicts began to set in between the members and formations of competing sectors of the state apparatus, either as an accompaniment to the dissolution of the Habsburg empire – where the exchanges of fire by troops belonging to the emergent nation states constituted in effect a transitional form of international violence – or in the course of the formation of the new 'German-Austrian' state, whose apparatus of coercion contained very different political persuasions.[23]

The animosity between the gendarmerie and the federal police, who continued to be conservative-middle class in outlook, on the one hand, and the newly formed 'marxist' *Volkswehr* (people's defence units) on the other, found its direct expression in occasional shoot-outs between the two, but also existed as a groundswell in mass disturbances when, during conflicts with the police, parts of the *Volkswehr* took the side of the civilian population. But even within the military apparatus itself the dissent between Communist-dominated sections of the armed forces (*Rote Garde, Deutschmeister, Battailon Nr. 14*) and the Social Democrat majority tended to break out openly, and frequently very bloodily, during insurrectionist actions by left-wing radicals.[24] Acts of violence such as the disruption of meetings or joint assaults on political adversaries still belong chronologically, though not genetically, to the final phase of the 'Austrian revolution'. In the beginning it was the Social Democrat and the Communist workers who were mainly responsible for these.[25] The fact that their middle-class adversaries were able to come out with strong 'anti-Marxist' and anti-republican agitation – particularly during election campaigns – was a sign of the growing strength of counter-revolutionary forces. The Left, on the other hand, had few other means at its disposal beyond a barely organised but deliberate policy of forcible intimidation by a relatively small number and this circumstance signalled the end of its being able to mobilise a revolutionary rank and file. It was only during the next stage, the period of collision, that this particular form of political violence became the germinating cell for the prevalent type of violence.

If we summarise the most important trends in violence during the 'Austrian revolution', we can say that the increasingly revolutionary movement of the rank and file, until it reached its climax in the spring of 1919, had achieved its remarkable (but by no means total) political and social successes by non-violent or relatively unviolent means. Within a few weeks after the start of the 'Austrian revolution', the impact of revolutionary ideas had already begun to lessen; at the same time, however, rank-and-file support became both more radical and more narrowly based. Correspondingly, there was a trend towards a decline in mass support and spontaneity, and a greater degree of planning and organisation of violent conflicts, coupled with an increase in the danger of the weapons used. Numerous spontaneous forms of violence, difficult to categorise in party-political terms and usually directed against property, nevertheless remained a phenomenon of this period and disappeared only gradually. In inverse proportion to this, the executive's harshness in the repression of violence directed against the system grew.

The period of relative stability brought no change in the 'anti-Marxist' – 'Marxist' pattern of conflict, although until 1926 this remained at a relatively low level of violence. Left-wing radicalism had disappeared almost completely and become merged into the Social Democratic movement, which had meanwhile taken on the role of parliamentary opposition; and within the two 'middle-class' camps – Catholic-conservatives and anti-clerical German-Nationalists – the fascist threat to the parliamentary democratic system had not yet become a force in its own right. Even the climax of the stability crisis in 1923, following the inflationary upheavals of 1922, led only to a quantitative increase but not to a qualitative change in this balance of conflict. The same holds true even for the year 1927, although it was completely overshadowed by the July disturbances that took on dimensions little short of civil war and is usually considered to have been the turning point in Austria's internal political development during the inter-war era.

Soon after the beginning of the period of relative stability, new forms of violence came into being, or more accurately forms that had been developed from types of violence seen earlier. A series of individual acts of violence that now followed represented without doubt a new type of political violence in the Austrian Republic, which no later period in Austrian history was to see again in this accumulated form: acts such as the Nazi *Feme* murder of a young member of a National-Socialist secret society in 1923, the attempt on the life of the Christian-Socialist Federal Chancellor, Ignaz Seipel, by a Social Democrat worker in 1924, the murder of a liberal Jewish author by a Nazi fanatic in 1925, the attempt on the life of the Social Democrat Mayor of Vienna, Karl Seitz, in 1927 by a psychopath under the influence of a right-wing radical 'war veterans' association'. These and a number of other acts of violence, of less far-reaching consequences, were closely connected either with the desperate economic situation or the more or less marked mental anomaly of their perpetrators. A direct link with political organisations and their specific strategies of violence in these cases is only evident where the perpetrators were National-Socialists.

A specific form of violence already referred to as taking the form of disrupting meetings or joint assaults – developed towards the end of the 'Austrian revolution' and initially practised mainly by the Left – evolved into the typical form of violence of all subsequent pre-civil war periods: the street brawl between unequally organised political adversaries, or the armed clash. This type had arisen out of the following circumstances: the emergence of 'anti-Marxist', anti-democratic radical minorities, against whom the 'Marxist' workers, in the face of state authorities increasingly sympathetic to the Right, were forced to resort to 'self-help' violence; the minorities, in their turn, developed self-defence cadres, organised on strict military lines and armed with fire-arms and during meetings and demonstration marches very soon ceased to operate in a purely defensive manner and instead, in anticipation of attacks from the Left, took the offensive and resorted to extreme means of violence and the use of fire-arms. This constellation resulted in fierce clashes, at first more by accident than design, between the unequal partners in the conflict, with casualties, up to 1927, usually being incurred by the Left.[26]

The causes at work in the case of the workers' unrests of *15 July 1927* in Vienna, however, were different. Their complex further development into a general strike, traffic blockades and, in the western and southern regions of the Federation,[27] sections of the Federal Army and the *Heimwehren* preparing themselves to fight a civil war need not be gone into here. The start of the events of *15 July 1927* in Vienna thus appears as a clash between two uncoordinated violent strategies of threat and repression, the one represented by the Social Democrats' tactics of relatively non-violent, mass street demonstrations, the other by police tactics; the latter, as a result of the shift in political power since 1918/19, were now able to operate with more vigour, albeit no better prepared organisationally than before, against disturbances of law and order from the 'Left'.[28] After a typical process of escalation between initially non-violent demonstrators and the police, Austria stood within a few hours at the brink of a civil war – a development which was prevented mainly by the retreat of the Social-Democratic party leadership, a step that was to lead to its eventual political defeat.

As an exceptional case in the history of Austria since 1848, should be noted the murder caused by the lynching of a young Christian-Democrat gymnast by some members of the Viennese Prater sub-culture, who broke away from an 'anti-fascist' street meeting – an incident that throws some light on the extent of latent political tensions as early as 1925.

Compared with the 'revolutionary period' and the latent civil war that was to come, the interim phase, apart from its opening and closing years, showed a remarkable consistency in the forms of violence employed, a fact which might be taken to indicate that political conflicts had not yet taken on a self-generating dynamism strong enough not to be coped with by the stabilising elements within society – always presupposing the absence of external disturbances.

Although the relative calm of 1928, in terms of violence, still appeared to be untouched either by the events surrounding the *15 July 1927*, which deeply polarised public opinion, or by the accelerated rise of the *Heimwehr* movement, there now set in an almost unbreakable sequence of violent events that marked the period from 1928 to 1933 as one of latent civil war, which in 1934 finally turned into a state of open civil war. Already by 1929, the first signs of the world economic crisis had led to a significant sharpening of the existing conflict structure, and within the Catholic-conservative 'camp' the *Heimwehr* now began to be a politically dominant and increasingly independent auxiliary force. And in 1930 too, Austrian domestic politics were overshadowed by the violent conflict between middle-class and 'Austro-Marxism'.

The year 1931, however, saw the beginnings of a remarkable shift in the political battle fronts, as National Socialists joined the side of the Catholic-conservative, *Heimwehr*-fascist grouping in the struggle against 'Marxism'. Shortly before the world economic crisis had reached its climax, the year 1932 showed very clearly how profoundly the constellation of conflict had changed: the strongest enmity now existed between *NSDAP* and the so-called *System-Parteien* (parties supporting the state) with the Social Democratic Party continuing to carry the main burden of the battle against the German version of Fascism, while itself still caught up in a state of conflict with the *Heimwehr* (and the rest of the Catholic-conservative 'camp'). In 1933 the same main battle lines continued to exist, the only difference being that the weight of the anti-Nazi struggle had now shifted to the conservative, semi-fascist government 'camp', leaving untapped the powers of resistance of the Social Democrats, whom Chancellor Dollfuß had manoeuvred into a political corner.

In the civil war year of 1934, the same triangular conflict situation persisted. As we can see from *Table 18.1*, the government 'camp' came first in the league table of violence. This was the result of its double involvement in a civil-war-like struggle, first from 12–14 February with parts of the 'Marxist camp' and then from 25–9 July with the Austrian National Socialists.

Apart from individual acts of violence which continued to occur sporadically (such as a Communist and a Nazi *Feme* murder in 1931 and 1932 respectively) as well as the assassination of Engelbert Dollfuß in 1934 and the armed attack on the *Heimwehr*-leader Richard Steidle by the National Socialists in 1933), the period of latent civil war once more shows typical forms of violence. The armed clashes now indicated a more even match between adversaries than had been the case previously, since the 'Marxist' side had now adapted its organisation, tactics and armament to its adversaries on the Right. Instead of groups of workers operating relatively spontaneously, there now emerged the militarily well-organised *Republikanische Schutzbund* (republican defence league).[29] Clashes became more frequent, indeed were quite often provoked deliberately, they led to severe physical injury and occasionally, just as earlier in 1929 in the Styrian village of St Lorenzen, turned into pitched street battles. Increasingly, the state's forces of order were dragged into the conflict, as for instance during the bloody clash in the Viennese district of Simmering in 1932.[30]

The attempted putsch by the Styrian, the German Nationalist wing of the *Heimwehren* on 13 September 1931 represented a further notable form of violence that played an important role during this period, even though this attempt was confined to a single incident.[31] The military staff exercises and the preparations carried out by the *Heimwehren*, but equally the *Republikanische Schutzbund*'s defensive preparations, from 1928 onwards had gone in the direction of this form of violence. The Austrian *Heimwehr*-fascists frankly admitted that the 'march on Rome' had served them as a model for this.[32]

When it appeared probable that the *NSDAP* would be made illegal, the year

1933 brought a further form of violence into the political battle field, hitherto unknown in Austrian history: systematic bomb terror. Its objectives ranged from purely demonstrative purposes to deliberately lethal attacks.[33] During the months of impending illegality and also after the *NSDAP* had been proscribed as a party, this particular form of violence replaced the other most frequent one so far, i.e. clashes between paramilitarily organised private armies.

The logical final stage of latent civil war came with the two outbreaks of battles between the three 'camps', each lasting several days and involving large numbers of people. In formal terms, both civil wars show a certain resemblance: both cases were a mixture of spontaneity and long-term planning, of a high and a low level of organisation. In both cases, when the fighting began, an already proscribed paramilitary formation stood at the centre of the action. Yet there were also significant differences. The rather broad participation of the *SA* in the Austrian regions in July 1934 is thus to be regarded merely as the (unplanned) consequence of the *SS*'s operations in Vienna, which followed the classical pattern of a military putsch. The participation of the 'Marxist' workers' movement in the attempted insurrection of the Upper-Austrian *Republikanische Schutzbund* in February 1934, on the other hand, which would have been necessary to provide the required backing, did not occur to the extent the insurgents had hoped for.[34] In typological terms, the *12 February 1934* ought thus to be seên as a *defensive insurrection attempt*, the *25 July 1934*, on the other hand, as a *putschist attempt to seize power*.

Looking at the period between 1918 and 1934 as a whole, one finds that the groups in opposition to the system were usually also the ones most strongly involved in violent conflicts, for they, in trying to assert their social objectives, possessed few non-violent alternative means. Thus, from a position of weakness, they tended to take the offensive and resort to violence, only to be regarded as a serious threat by the social groupings controlling the state and to be held down all the more repressively by them.

Table 18.2 below provides a systematic listing of the most significant forms of violence which occurred in the First Republic, according to the number of participants (or duration of violence) and the conflicting parties' degree of organisation.

Acts of violence committed by individuals or very small groups, especially the merely structured or amorphous forms, were a feature throughout the entire period of the First Republic, even though the frequency of their incidence tended to vary. The 'Austrian revolution' was characterised in particular by forms of violence which, while involving mass participation, were marked by little or no organisation.

The period of relative political equilibrium saw forms of violence with every level of participation; the less they were organised, the greater the number who

TABLE 18.2:   Forms of Political Violence in Austria 1918–34

Number of participants: duration of violence: Degree of organisation	Few (– 5) short	Many (– 500) medium	Very many (500 +) long
organised	Assassination Feme-murder Bomb-terror	Clash	Coup d'état Putsch
structured	{ Assault Clash	Clash	Putschist action Insurrection
amorphous	Insults Political brawls	Lynching	Riot Unrests

took part and, conversely, the more highly organised they were, the smaller the circle of participants. The period of latent civil war, typically, showed highly organised forms of violence at all levels of participation.

The state authorities, as a rule, were the immediate target only of the forms of violence involving many participants; both workers and the urban lower classes, but also the peasants, were particularly active in mass violence of little or no organisation. Participation by the very young or the 'middle class', on the other hand, is a characteristic feature of all variants of organised individual violence, and this also corresponds to the prevalence of National Socialists in this type of violence.

In *sociographical terms*, the supporters of predominantly organised or structured forms of violence, ranging from a few to large numbers of participants, may be described in a rather compressed form as follows:

Over-represented among the supporters of political violence (in comparison to society as a whole and also to the non-'militants' within the individual 'camps') are urban and metropolitan youths and young men (under thirty), particularly in the case of the National Socialists, to a lesser degree in that of the Social Democrats. Because of the conflicting parties' paramilitary forms of organisation, women and girls are involved in this type of violence only in exceptional instances.

Particularly disposed towards violence also were the members of groups not (or not yet) firmly incorporated into working life, and therefore with the necessary time and mobility to take part in political violence, i.e. especially the unemployed, war veterans, invalids (and adolescents). The 'lower' strata of almost all social classes and groups, who appear as 'representative' for these classes or groups as a whole, appear to be particularly predisposed to political violence: students and youngsters in secondary education representing the liberal professions and civil servants, the sons of peasants, tradesmen and merchants deputising for their fathers, unskilled workers and apprentices for skilled workers and craftsmen. Workers in general are more numerous among the 'militants' than among the simple members of the individual 'camps'.

The generation of former soldiers, who had fought in the First World War as very young men, especially officers and non-commissioned officers, provided an important reservoir for the supporters of violence.[35]

III

As may be seen from the previous section, violence appears often associated with political radicalism and social fringe groups. Indeed, for violence on any scale between political and social 'camps' to occur at all, it requires a prior process of political marginalisation of at least one of the political 'camps' involved. This conclusion may be drawn from the Communists' putschist actions on the Maundy Thursday of 1919 and on 15 June 1919, but equally from the two outbreaks of civil war in 1934.

According to the three Tillys,[36] the causes for this must be sought in the following facts: for a powerful group, which, if it deserves this attribute, also stands in close relation to the apparatus of rule, active use of violence is hardly worthwhile. The incidental social costs of (direct) violence very frequently exceed its immediate usefulness, unless those in power are confronted by a serious challenge to their position. The converse holds true for groups which are either far removed from power or without it altogether, since, firstly, the signalling effect attaching to the use of violence, or being turned into the victim of violence, may evoke hidden sympathies or support from sections of the established power groups, and secondly, because those with little power have very few alternative courses of legal action open to them; consequently, the probability of coming to violence by way of illegality is great and — in view of the state's threat of sanctions — causes them to drift even further from the socially accepted rules of the political game. Finally, purposeful and bloody terrorism may well strengthen the power position of groups with little power, by discrediting the power of the government, especially in areas where the latter already suffers from a power vacuum, as was the case in the First Austrian Republic.

This general framework needs to be borne in mind when turning, as we do now, to the explicit strategies of violence developed by political parties and movements in Austria between 1918 and 1934. We may be unable to reach more than provisional conclusions, but this is inevitable, given the absence of any appropriate analyses that go beyond the mere examination of programmatic or theoretical declarations.

First of all we have to consider one strategy of violence which, while highly developed in practice, tended to be too easily overlooked, that is to say, the strategy and tactics in the deployment of the state's forces of order, especially the police. An actual or anticipated infraction of 'law and order', which by definition should precede any action by the police, would seem to impose a reactive strategy on the state in the exercise of its monopoly of coercion; this, however, was (and still is) not always the case. Yet even reactive strategies in the deployment of the police, and particularly the threshold where violence sets in, show a very broad range of variation, according to specific cultural particularities or the composition of the ruling social groupings and classes. Thus the police strategies *vis-à-vis* disturbances of order from Left or Right respectively varied considerably.[37]

As long as the state apparatus was still weak and the revolutionary movement unspecific but broadly based – which was the case until around April 1919 – the executive's response to spontaneous disturbances, even in cases of deliberate political infractions of law and order (such as setting fire to the parliament building on 17 April 1919) and during lethal attacks on the police, was a careful and defensive protection of property coupled with peaceful persuasion. The employment of Social Democratic leaders and of soldiers' and workers' councils to mediate, and to legitimise the means of violence deployed made it possible to settle even critical situations with little or no violence. By means of this strategy, Vienna's (German Nationalist) chief of police Schober was able to establish his reputation as a man of 'order', which later gave him access to the highest political offices. Even after the 'revolutionary' constellation of power had ceased to exist, Schober's police apparatus still tended to exercise restraint in the use of extreme measures.

Once the revolutionary movements had lost some of its breadth, but had gained in Bolshevik direction and radicalism that posed a threat to the system and also brought it into conflict with large sections of Social Democratic opinion, the police practices changed. Both during the Communist's putschist action of 15 June 1919 in Vienna and during hunger and inflation disturbances in the provincial capitals in 1920 they were given fairly indiscriminate orders to clear the streets and to shoot. When the events of 15 July 1927 escalated into the burning of the Palace of Justice and involved considerable loss of life (almost exclusively among civilians) this was due, at least to some extent, to an extremely forceful if uncoordinated and patchy deployment of the police with mounted and armed men.

The consequence of this trial of strength, which ended in a victory for the 'middle-class' government side, was that henceforth the executive's strategy against the Left became increasingly ruthless, while its attitude to threats to the constitution from the Right was one, if not of open cooperation, at least of compliance and tolerance. Thus, different strategies of repression and control were employed which varied according to the political and social origins of the disturbers of law and order.

The Austrian Communists' strategy of violence manifested itself during their spontaneous putschist actions of 17 April and 15 June, 1919 in Vienna. The earlier charge by 'Red Guards' on the parliament building, on the occasion of the proclamation of the Republic on 12 November 1918, already linked part of the left-wing radical movement – which at this stage still included the Bolshevik element that emerged only later as a separate entity – with putschist efforts. This concept of testing their strength by violence had the following background.

Its starting point was (of course) Lenin's successful revolutionary theory, particularly the notion that in a 'revolutionary situation' objective and subjective factors come together: for a revolution to take place, objective social elements (the weakening of the existing system of rule, increased distress among the masses, greater political mobilisation) would have to coincide with subjective ones. These subjective factors, which depended on human will, would find their expression especially in the working class's capacity for revolutionary mass action, under Communist party leadership.[38] Thus the 'correct' degree of consciousness and organisation were decisive elements, if a revolutionary change of power was to become a reality.

A large section of the Austrian Communists took the view in 1918/19, with some justification, that such a 'revolutionary situation' did indeed exist and that it required only minimal assistance in the form of agitation and organisation to set the powder keg alight. A temporary intake of people made 'rootless' by the Great War and its aftermath was claimed to have increased the Austrian Communist Party's membership to around 40,000 by May 1919, the highest figure recorded throughout the period of the First Republic.[39] This appeared to confirm the revolutionary perspective, as did also the proclamation of a republic of councils in both Hungary and Bavaria.

The spontaneous version of the Communists' putsch strategy now consisted in calling simultaneous meetings in different parts of Vienna and, if these meetings proved successful in terms of attendance and atmosphere, to issue orders for an immediate march on the parliament building in the city's centre, there to state their socio-political demands in the form of an ultimatum and to call for the immediate establishment of a republic of councils. Beyond the wave of excitement engendered by several thousand demonstrators, this also required support from units of the *Volkswehr* (people's defence units). Communist agitators therefore appeared in army barracks, seeking to arouse enthusiasm for their cause among Social Democratic soldiers and workers. These efforts were to result in the overthrow of the government, or at least lead to its reconstruction, and the elimination of the Social Democrats' bourgeois coalition partners.

Ernst Bettelheim, who had been sent from Hungary to revolutionise Austria, furnished with dictatorial powers over the Communist Party, after his arrest by the police made the following statement:

that the Communists (at any moment)[40] consider the proclamation of a republic of councils to be desirable, and that the question as to whether any

demonstration may result in such a proclamation can only be answered
during the demonstration itself, according to the will of the masses who
participate in the same, and according to the prevailing balance of forces.[41]

As early as April 1919, the Communist organisation repeatedly attempted
to drive the 'mass of the proletariat' towards revolution. However, the
Communist functionaries had either misread the political situation or been
guilty of organisational mistakes, for at the critical moment a large part of
the working population refused to follow them. An attempted storming of the
parliament building and exchanges of fire, although without mass
participation, created the impression of a putsch. A Communist workers'
council found the 'classical' formulation for this type of strategy: 'What today
is called a putsch, will, if successful, be a revolution tomorrow.'[42]

Another form of Communist putschism shows a marked resemblance to the
Blanquist concept of insurgence: when the attempted overthrow of April 1919
failed and the Hungarian government of councils came under increasing
pressure from abroad, Hungarian emissaries redoubled their efforts to force a
political change in Austria. This brought their financially extremely well-
endowed cadre organisation into conflict with sections of Communist opinion
back home. Undaunted, even though the police, backed by the Social
Democrats, carried out preventive arrests, a hard core around Bettelheim
nevertheless tried to use the not unfavourable mood among soldiers,
threatened by an impending reduction in their numbers, in order to carry out
their plan. This attempt, which started on 15 June 1919, found its bloody
conclusion under a hail of police bullets. In one of the barracks a central
authority had been established to direct military operations of sections of the
Volkswehr that had been originally envisaged but never came to pass. Military
staff exercises on the deployment of the Hungarian Red Army against Vienna
may have played a role as well.

As soon as the revolutionary tide ebbed towards the middle of 1919,
revolutionary expectations began to collapse rapidly. For a time, Communist
splinter groups turned their attentions to the blowing up of a railway bridge
(the so-called *Lumpi*-coup) and to obtaining money by breaking into shops
and churches[43] – as a curious precursor to the politically motivated bank
raids of recent times.

In the years that followed, the Communist Party was never again able to
develop its own strategy of violence. Realistically, it could only direct its
activities towards mobilising other, stronger proletarian forces and foster
armed clashes that might end in an insurrection by Social Democrats, as was
indeed attempted on 15 July 1927 and after the clash on 16 October 1932 at
Simmering.[44]

The Social Democrats' strategy of violence flowed from their party's
reformism which, while attentist in character, was nevertheless based on
principles of socialist reconstruction. While the majority of the Party did not

reject violence as a political instrument in principle, it nevertheless wished to restrict it to a merely defensive function. Even the ominous formulation in the 'Linz Programme' of 1926, which spoke of breaking the 'bourgeoisie's resistance with the instruments of a dictatorship', ought to be understood as a mainly defensive statement, intended in effect to force the bourgeois side to keep to the democratic rules, in case it should prove unwilling to give up political power peacefully, once the Social Democrats had won their expected overwhelming election victory.[45]

This strategy was also imposed on the *Republikanische Schutzbund*, founded in 1923 as the supposed armed executive organ of the Socialist 'camp'. Ever since the end of the 'Austrian revolution' the Social Democrats, after all, had had sound reasons for not believing the state apparatus to be absolutely reliable when it came to repulsing counter-revolutionary stratagems, monarchist putsch attempts, the influences of Bavarian and Hungarian right-wing extremists, etc. In these circumstances, the party leadership felt constrained to turn the 'proletariat's fighting fitness' into the reality of a counter-army – and this was precisely what the *Schutzbund* developed into after 1927. Strict military discipline, uniforms, weapon training, military staff exercises, the establishment of arms depots, etc., turned this organisation, which originally had been opposed to militarism, into a militarist one. This also meant that its strategy of violence began to resemble that of its opponents more closely.

Theodor Körner, a former general and the Social Democrats' defence expert, denounced this development in the sharpest terms and at an early stage predicted its consequences: it would have a soporific effect on the Socialist 'camp's' will to fight, compress in an indifferentiated way their various opponents into a single enemy image, produce an almost exclusive reliance on violent means, in the use of which the Social Democrats, despite their numerical superiority, would nevertheless always remain inferior to their opponents. Körner's suggestion to take account in their military concept of the possibility of mobilising the entire working population politically and of spontaneous passive resistance went unheeded, as did his exhortation to try every means available within a parliamentary, democratic constitutional state before resorting to defensive violence.[46]

In effect, the *Schutzbund* increasingly had its fighting methods imposed upon it by others, especially the *Heimwehr*'s strategy of marches, developed towards the end of the 1920s. From 1928 onwards, several thousand *Schutzbund* members tested and demonstrated 'the proletariat's readiness to defend itself', in large-scale manoeuvres and marches virtually every Sunday. It was in the nature of things that this led to collisions with the *Heimwehr*'s opposing strategies and frequently ended in bloodshed. The *Schutzbund*, at least, cannot be accused of directly provoking clashes on any scale, a charge which might with justification be levelled against its opponents.

It was, however, not by accident that the military spirit within the

Schutzbund prompted a modification of the conditions governing the use of violence – in order to prevent a legal takeover of government after a Social Democratic election victory. The *Schutzbund* leadership around Alexander Eifler and Julius Deutsch took the view that the *Schutzbund* would have to counter right-wing efforts to establish a dictatorship even before the Social Democrats had gained a parliamentary majority. As early as 1928, they reckoned with the ever-present possibility of a civil war breaking out for whatever reason.[47]

If there existed deviations from stated theoretical principles contained in the party programme of 1926 amongst the leadership of its paramilitary organisation, these were bound to be very much more marked and less differentiated among the rank and file. What tended to happen in the day-to-day practice of political conflict – during the 'class struggle with pitchforks' (K. Renner)[49] – was precisely what Otto Bauer, referring to the 'Linz Programme', had warned against: 'Violence does not mean a street brawl!' The defensive strategy of violence degenerated into partially offensive tactics of brawling. An example of this sort of thing is provided by the following report in a Social Democratic daily paper:

> Our *Republikanischer Schutzbund* of course was not content merely with preventing a scheduled meeting (of War Veterans), but decided to carry out a proper raid. So they broke up the lair of War Veterans in the 'Königswieser' pub . . . and scattered the whole bunch of them. They also took a look at the National Socialists' pub at the 'Grüne Baum' . . . Their thorough cleaning-up operation extends, of course, to the whole of Upper Austria.[50]

Even if some of this is merely verbal radicalism, the strategy of weakening and intimidating opponents by breaking up meetings and raiding the party venues of right-wing radicals did not stop short of active use of violence. The fact that the party leadership not only knew that their theoretical concepts were being bent, but indeed made occasional deliberate use of a dual political strategy, was proved by the momentous failure of this very strategy on 15 July 1927: using the rank and file to exert pressure on political opponents by stormy demonstrations, 'violence against property' and structured or amorphous forms of personal violence,[51] while as a party leadership pursuing a moderate course, recoiling from the consequences of their own policies. Much as the middle-class and fascist propaganda polemicised against the 'red peril', men like Seipel and Dollfuß, by contrast, were perfectly able to see through this game and to calculate unyieldingly and successfully the risks attaching to their own policies.[52]

For a long time the middle-class Catholic-conservative 'camp' did not develop its own strategies of violence. Ever since the foundation of the Republic, at first timidly and later with growing self-assurance, it had entertained close relations with virtually all levels of the state apparatus, the only exception being the Viennese municipal and regional administrations. The state's executive, or at least sections of it, had always been at its disposal. This may create the impression that this 'camp' had a strictly legalistic orientation throughout. No doubt, quite a few middle-class politicians recoiled from an open break with legality, even at a time when, as in the early 1930s, notions about 'true democracy', 'the authoritarian state', undemocratic, dictatorial forms of government had already gained strong currency also among Christian-Socialists (and German-Nationalists). This is not to say, however, that the same group of politicians had not already in 1920, in cooperation with Hungarian counter-revolutionaries, entertained serious plans for the overthrow of a coalition government that gave them only a half-share of power.[53] At various times in later years as well, plans for a coup d'état played an important role among large sections of the middle-class parties. When Dollfuß set aside parliamentary democracy in March 1933, this constituted in effect a sort of 'cold' *coup d'état*, carried out by stages.[54]

In the day-to-day political skirmishing of the inter-war period, however, this 'camp' did employ auxiliary troups which operated outside the law and used violent means: the early *Heimwehr* formations, the monarchist *Ostara*, the 'War Veterans' Association' etc., were without exception proto- or semi-fascist organisations. If these were able to operate as independently, as the heterogeneous collection of organisations that had come together in the *Heimwehr* had been able to do since 1927, and to build up their own party organisations, the essential criteria for a fascist movement were in effect already met.

These right-wing radical – and, later on, blatantly fascist – formations had already in the early 1920s practised an offensive version of the Social Democrats' defensive strategy of violence, especially in those regions of Austria where they could command a broad social base.[55] This indicates a constant interplay between the Left's and the Right's strategies of violence, which determined their further development. The *Schutzbund* later copied this strategy, thus provoking in its turn a further mobilisation of its opponents and a general exacerbation of the climate of violence. The fact that right-wing radical and fascist formations had taken the lead, at least initially, in the deadliness of their weapons and the readiness of their use explains why the casualties until 1927, as we have seen earlier, were so unevenly distributed among the warring factions.

As time went on, the *Heimwehr* developed – not least under the influence of Italian fascists and Hungarian reactionaries – a strategy of mass marches designed systematically to encircle 'Red Vienna' and other citadels of Social Democracy, and make them ripe for a takeover, along the lines of the Italian model. Such a provocative display of *Heimwehr* formations in the middle of industrial centres and working class districts (with the blessings of the

Catholic clergy and the protection of the state authorities), tightening their
formations in ever closer circles around Vienna, meant a symbolic breaking of
the 'Reds' monopoly of the street', and with it a psychological weakening of
the 'Austro-Marxists'. The latter did indeed perceive it in this way. Yet when
the Social Democrats took up the challenge and deployed their *Schutzbund*, it
often required only a minor incident for shooting and violent street-fighting to
break out. Virtually every Sunday during the late 1920s saw, by now almost
automatic, collisions between marchers and counter-marchers especially in
the industrial regions of Upper Styria and Lower Austria.

A planned putsch attempt by the *Heimwehr* may well have taken this
automatic triggering of violence into account. Sections of the middle-class
parties, for all their sympathy with the *Heimwehr*, were nevertheless hostile to
the idea of the latter establishing a dictatorship. For this reason, many
Heimwehr-leaders, as well as some of their Christian-Socialist backers (such as
Anton Rintelen in Styria) hoped that by provoking clashes with the
Schutzbund they might tempt the latter into larger-scale hostilities or even an
attempted *coup d'état*. This in turn was to be answered by a counter-blow from
the *Heimwehr*, acting in conjunction with police and army. The expected
defeat of the 'reds' was thus to lead to a reconstruction of Austria on fascist
lines, unfettered by any constitutional constraints.

This was also the political background to street fights such as the one at St
Lorenzen of 18 August 1929. On these occasions the *Schutzbund* acted with
restraint, while on the Christian-Socialist side there were reasonable men as
well who were able to curb the hotheads within their own and the *Heimwehr*'s
ranks. Without the active participation of the state executive, most of the
Heimwehr leaders did not in any case feel strong enough to attempt a putsch.[56]
When the leader of the radical, pro-Nazi Styrian *Heimatschutz* (home
defence), Walter Pfrimer, fearing a possible defeat of the Austrian variant of
fascism that was the *Heimwehr* decided, on 13 September 1931, to bring about
a 'march on Vienna' after all, his attempt failed miserably in the face of the
Schutzbund's counter-measures and the army's initial neutrality and subsequent hesitant intervention.[57]

The thesis that the *Schutzbund*'s attempted insurrection of February 1934
had been deliberately provoked by the *Heimwehr* remains a matter of heated
controversy among scholars of Austrian history, but is certainly not an
improbable one. What decided the issue in any case was that the *Schutzbund*,
weakened as it was by mass unemployment, the political retreat of the party
leadership, and by being banned for almost eleven months, was bound to be
defeated, if attacked jointly by the executive and the *Heimwehr*, even if
circumstances had been a little more favourable.[59]

If the *Heimwehr* from time to time showed signs of recoiling from the use of
the most brutal means of violence, this was not the case with the National
Socialists, who proclaimed and practised 'ruthless violence against bestial
terror',[60] both towards 'Marxists' and Jews. And it was National Socialism,

too, which produced the greatest variety in the forms and strategies of violence.

It was also the one political alignment which unreservedly proclaimed the use of individual terror for the realisation of its political aims, irrespective of what their party leaders at home and abroad declared. The fascists' very personalised perception of politics did, in effect, lead them to hope for profound political changes from their scarcely concealed calls to assassinate Social Democrat party leaders, Jewish authors or politicians and even Christian-Socialist Chancellors. As early as March 1925, a lone operator was to obey this call and carry out such an attempt, without implicating his party by having any direct accessory or collaborator. Thus from 1924 onwards, a full-blown murder campaign was conducted by the entire *völkisch* press, finding expression in the attempted assassination of Seipel, disguised as a carnival joke, by a Nazi gym-teacher from Vienna, Kaspar Hellering, as well as in murderous attempts on several Social Democrat politicians and the Jewish writer Hugo Bettauer. The latter eventually fell victim to a young Nazi who had obeyed the injunction. Other assassination attempts, like those on the life of Dollfuß and Steidle in the early 1930s, were carried out in a similar manner.

A strategy of more far-reaching consequence was the National Socialists' 'stormtroop terror'. This was embarked upon in an unmistakable manner in 1923, immediately after Hitler had begun to establish his influence also among Austrian National Socialists. The ostensible occasion for implementing this strategy was usually provided by Nazi rallies in working-class districts; their supposed protection against the rising anger of the 'Marxist' workers was to be provided by armed and partly uniformed gangs, who were not registered with the authorities. The resulting (unequal) clashes were thus part of a carefully worked out programme. The middle-class *Neue Freie Presse* reported such incidents as follows:

> The particular characteristic of these incidents in the outer districts (of Vienna) is that the National Socialists seek to penetrate the Social Democrats' headquarters . . . Tactics of such extreme boldness were bound to be regarded as a provocation and it was only to be expected that daring ruses of this kind would elicit an even fiercer response, and that in the face of this kind of offensive a counter-offensive is being taken.[61]

What the instructions were which prepared these 'disciplinary units', the *Vaterländische Schutzbund* (the patriotic defence league) and later the SA for their tasks, can be gleaned from National Socialist newspaper articles, amounting to a veiled call to murder:

> Instead of waiting until a Jewish hireling, under the protection of darkness,

bashes my head in with a cudgel or sticks a knife between my ribs, I prefer to shoot, and shoot as long as my bullets last. A life for a life. If my life is to end, so and so many of my attackers will have to go with me.[62]

The function of this strategy of violence, within the framework of the National Socialists' path to power, may be summarised – just as for other extreme right-wing organisations of the 1920s – as follows:

Demonstrative rallies and the display of large forces of right-wing paramilitary organisations in known 'Marxist' working-class districts, deliberately incurring the risk of armed clashes, were not primarily designed to smash and repress the opposition's organisations. This had been the case in the squadrist terror of Italian Fascism, where fascist militias would be gathered from a whole district to raid a single target – a tactic which turned them into a power factor against Social Democrats and Communists.[63] In Austria, the strength of the 'anti-Marxist' combat formations was inadequate for this kind of action, particularly in the eastern part of the country, nor was the Austrian state apparatus corrupted and weakened to the same degree as the Italian one in 1921/22. The strategy of early fascist and reactionary groups, particularly in Vienna, was thus many-layered.

If a demonstrative meeting in a 'red stronghold' went off without disturbance, it could be used for propaganda (and financial) purposes, since it gave proof of strength both to their own rank and file and to the middle-class in general, who still feared the extra-parliamentary power of the Social Democrats and considered them to be revolutionary.

If, however, demonstrative actions provoked the 'Marxist' workers into disrupting the meetings and into physical attacks which eventually ended in bloodshed, with the greater number of casualties on the Left – attacks, moreover, for which the fascist gangs were well prepared – the expected impact was twofold: on the one hand it would serve to intimidate vaccilating groups among the Social Democrats, and on the other it would prove once again to the bourgeois power elites and electorate how dangerous the 'Marxists' were, against whom the fascist cadres had merely acted in 'self-defence' – and thus offer themselves as the most effective instrument against the Left.

In 1933, when the National Socialists had shifted their main line of attack from 'Marxism' to the 'authoritarian system', composed of Catholic-conservative *Heimwehr*-fascists, the fragmented strategies of Nazi propaganda and violence were integrated into a single violent strategy for the seizure of power. The outbreaks of week-long waves of terror (by bomb attempts, assassinations, the explosion of blank shells, clashes), directed and sustained from Germany, signalled the last phase before an attempt was made to overthrow the government. A staged plan, decided on during a secret conference of Nazi party leaders in Linz on 6 December 1932, envisaged the following steps:

(a) Small-scale street terror against anything that stands for black-and-yellow in word, print or picture.

(b) Disruption of all meetings and conferences of this nature.

(c) To increase the emotional turbulence until conditions are ripe for 'everything'.

(d) A call to all would-be suicides, that if they wanted to die to choose a hero's death, taking with them a few of those responsible for their distress. Provided this propaganda is skilfully handled, the persons who should be the targets can be nicely pushed into the foreground.

(e) To blow up goods trains, for instance of wine or industrial products, etc.[64]

The object of these violent measures was to strike a death blow at an Austria already hard hit by the world slump and to combine this with external economic measures on the part of the German Reich (the 1000-Mark limit): 'The present government must not be allowed a quiet moment'.[65]

In the event, this strategy failed to achieve complete success, as did the attempted putsch of 25 July 1934. It was only the combination of three very different strategies for the seizure of power – the infiltration of government and adminstrative posts from the inside, the generation of pressure from below by relatively non-violent street demonstrations, but most of all the military intervention from outside – which eventually brought the National Socialists to power in March 1938.[66]

IV

The emphasis placed, so far, on the element of strategy and tactics might suggest that the acts of political violence which occurred in the First Republic can be adequately explained by the processes of political and strategic decision-making within organisations and groups capable of exercising power. In order to correct this impression, the following analysis of the causes of violence, by way of conclusion, deals with these in macro-historical terms.

In the process of transition from a predominantly agrarian to a predominantly industrial society, the First Republic occupied an interim position.[67] Transitional stages of this kind tend to be characterised by an uneven growth (or decline) of individual sectors of the economy, by concentration in the structure of ownership, and by changes in the distribution of incomes, etc; they are frequently marked also by great social tensions, political instability and a high level of violence. Highly developed as well as completely traditional countries, on the other hand, tend towards political stability and a low level of violence.[68] Social change, particularly if it takes place abruptly or is interrupted – which is the case in most societies at an intermediate level of development – may cause great socio-psychological and political tensions; in this connection the determining role in the shaping of political attitudes has been ascribed to 'relative deprivation'.[69] The high level of violence in the Austria of the inter-war period, compared with the last decades of the Habsburg monarchy and the Second Republic, may thus be linked to the country's accelerated process of modernisation that had already begun at the turn of the century.

If the revolutionary changes, both national and social, which the years 1918/19 had brought in the former empire were partly also a phenomenon of a critical transitional phase in the process of modernisation, the 'Austrian revolution', in its turn, provided a further element to heighten the conflict. Especially the (not unnatural) absence of consensus as to the structure of state and society resulted in the recently established political and social system being called into question – by the Left, for whom the revolutionary and evolutionary changes since the Great War had not been radical enough, and by the various groups of the Right, because these changes had gone much too far. This explains the attempt, made early on, by the large socio-political groupings to create their own armed formations and to arrogate themselves the right to use violence. The fact that they achieved this to a disastrous degree reflects the weakness of the young state, which in addition was being restricted by the peace treaties. For this reason, the representatives of the state, both middle-class and Social Democratic politicians, were neither able nor willing to prevent the accumulation and distribution of weapons left over by the World War.

A further factor in the fostering of violence, equally a result of the War, was that the veterans of this war as well as the rising generation had grown accustomed to the use of violence.[70] The greater inclination to employ violent means, the 'front spirit', played an important role throughout the First Republic when it came to giving violent expression to political and social discontent and tensions.

From an historical point of view, next to these long-term or constant causes of violence – their list might be even further extended – the medium-term causes of violence possess an even greater explanatory value. These concern the worsening, over a period of months or a few years, of economic or social conditions. There is no doubt that cyclical downswings, in the short term, produced both an increased degree of social discontent and a greater inclination to use violence. During the democratic phase of the First Republic – which is, strictly speaking, our subject here – periods of economic growth went hand in hand with low annual figures for the casualties of violence, unless there were strikes.[71] Conversely, any decline in GNP was accompanied by an increase in political violence (see Figure 18.1).

In all this, unemployment must be regarded as the key factor in transposing the area of conflict from the industrial-economic sphere to the extra-parliamentary political level (Pearson's correlation coefficient with violence:

0.40). For hundreds of thousands, a long-term and hopeless unemployment situation was the experience which, directly or indirectly, shaped their attitudes, mobilising politically those who had not yet suffered this fate, inclining them more towards the use of violence, while the unemployed tended to be depoliticised by it and alienated from the traditional Social Democratic workers' organisations, which had been opposed to violence.[72] This in turn explains the large percentage of unemployed in the paramilitary organisations of all political persuasions.

The link with unemployment appears significant in another respect as well: its negative effect both on the attitude to strikes and on trade unions may have blocked the settlement of primarily economic conflicts within the orderly confines of labour relations, and may thus have banked up a conflict potential on the economic level which spilled over into the political one. And it is this which, arguably, was the cause of the particular ferocity with which violent political conflicts were fought out in the First Republic.

The fact that in the First Republic, unemployment was of such long duration and made more acute because the slump caused by the world economic crisis further exacerbated an already high degree of long-term, structural unemployment,[73] plays a significant part in accounting for the casualty figures of violence. If one examines the degree to which violence was determined by the time lag between economic growth and a reduction in unemployment, one finds that a one-year time lag alone accounted for 20 per cent of the total violence.[74]

It is therefore only to be expected that political violence cannot be accounted for in purely economic or social terms. A quantitative explanatory model that would also include the organisational strength of the parties in the conflict might lead us in many respects into the area of political explanations. The numerical strength of political organisations engaged in hostilities and violence by itself played an important, albeit quantitatively not yet ascertainable, role. The aspect of the ratio of organisational strength must come into any explanation of the reasons why, in the First Republic, the statistical incidence of violence was subject to considerable annual fluctuations. This leads to the conclusion that a high incidence of political violence weakened the material and organisational potential of one of the parties to the conflict – the loser – to such a degree that the avoidance of political violence in the immediately following period became likely.

Perhaps even more important for the exercise of political violence in the First Republic, was the impact of the state's forces of repression. As has been mentioned before, a large percentage of the victims of violence was accounted for by the fact that – whenever the executive was involved in violent conflicts, which tended to happen somewhat automatically if these were on any scale[75] – police and army were more effectively armed and possessed superior organisation and direction.

Probably the most significant cause of political violence was that its very presence in political conflicts dragged the state's apparatus of coercion into the struggle, even if originally the executive had not been involved. This produced – as long as conflict potential existed within society and the necessary organisational preconditions were present – a tendency for the interplay of violence and counter-violence to escalate to dimensions approaching civil war. (For this reason, the statistical analyses given here in summarised form, do not use the crude data of the annual casualty figures, but their decadic logarithm, increased by a factor of 1).[76]

A quantitative explanatory model, certainly still incomplete, for the incidence of political violence in a particular year (O_t) in terms of economic growth (G_{t-1}), unemployment (U_{t-1}), incidence of violence (O_{t-1}) in the previous year and intervention by the executive (E_t) in the following multiple regression equation accounts for 82 per cent of the overall fluctuation of casualty figures:

$$O_t = 0.78 - 0.007G_{t-1} + 0.104U_{t-1} - 0.136O_{t-1} + 0.86E_t$$

While change in economic growth compared to the previous year does not produce a direct effect – albeit an indirect one by way of unemployment – the previous year's unemployment rate constitutes by far the most significant

TABLE 18.3: Casualties of Violence, Economic Growth and Unemployment in Austria, 1919–34 (values of the variables of the regression equation)

Year	Casualties of violence (deaths and serious injuries)	Log. of casualty figures increased by a factor of 1	Growth of GNP in real terms, in %, compared to previous year (= 100)	Unemployment rate (as % of labour force)	Strong involvement by executive (more than 1 death on the govt. side = 1, otherwise = 0)
1919	124	2.097	0.1	9.2	1
1920	76	1.886	6.9	2.0	1
1921	2	0.477	10.7	1.4	0
1922	5	0.778	9.0	3.4	0
1923	22	1.362	– 1.1	6.6	0
1924	10	1.041	11.7	5.8	0
1925	8	0.954	6.8	7.9	0
1926	0	0.0	1.6	9.4	0
1927	274	2.439	3.1	9.2	1
1928	8	0.954	4.6	8.5	0
1929	77	1.892	1.5	8.9	0
1930	40	1.613	– 2.8	11.2	0
1931	27	1.447	– 8.0	14.2	0
1932	104	2.021	–10.3	18.3	0
1933	69	1.845	– 3.3	20.3	0
1934	1932	3.286	0.8	18.8	1

single cause of violence. A positive casual effect on the incidence of violence in a particular year of roughly half this size is dependent upon whether or not the state executive was involved on a major scale in a violent conflict. At the same time, however, a high incidence of violence in the previous year – by weakening the violence potential – inhibits the tendency towards a renewed, equally strong outbreak of violence.

NOTES

1. Cf. K.-D. Knodel, *Der Begriff der Gewalt im Strafrecht* (Munich, 1962) p. 3; W. Fuchs *et al.* (eds), *Lexikon zur Soziologie* (Opladen, 1973) p. 247.
2. Cf. for instance L. A. Coser, *Theorie sozialer Konflikte* (Neuwied, 1972) p. 142ff., 178ff.; A. L. Nieburg, *Political Violence: The Behavioral Process* (New York, 1969) p. 13; H. Davis Graham and T. R. Gurr (eds), *The History of Violence in America: Historical and Comparative Perspectives* (New York, 1969); E. Zimmermann, *Soziologie der politischen Gewalt* (Stuttgart, 1977).
3. More extensively treated in my contribution 'Formen und Intensität politisch-sozialer Konflikte in der Ersten und Zweiten Republik' to the symposium 'Deux fois l'Autriche: Après 1918 et après 1945', Rouen, 8–12 Nov. 1977, *Austriaca, Cahiers universitaires d'information sur l'Autriche*, no. spécial 3 (1979) p. 428ff. as well as in my (unpublished) scenario *Bedingungen 'sozialen Friedens' und politischer Gewalt in Perioden wirtschaftlicher Krisen in Österreich* (Institut für Konfliktforschung, Vienna, 1978) (a more comprehensive publication on this subject is being prepared for the *Studienreihe Konfliktforschung*, Vienna).
4. T. Nardin, *Violence and the State: A Critique of Empirical Political Theory* (Beverly Hills-London, 1971) p. 66.
5. M. Weber in J. Winckelmann (ed.), *Wirtschaft und Gesellschaft.* (Cologne, 1964) p. 1042f.
6. The most comprehensive and most recent publication on Austria: B. Marin (ed.), *Wachstumskrisen in Österreich?*, vol. II: *Szenarios* (Vienna, 1979); cf. more generally also: *Geschichte und Gesellschaft* 3 (1977), especially the contributions by Ch. Tilly and H. Volkmann.
7. See G. Botz, *Gewalt in der Politik: Attentate, Zusammenstöße, Putschversuche, Unruhen in Österreich 1918–1934* (Munich, 1976) p. 235ff.
8. What argues for the use of the decadic logarithm in calculating annual casualty figures, increased by a factor of 1, are theoretical considerations (see also below, Section IV) and the demands imposed by the regression model (H. M. Blalock, Jr., *Social Statistics*, 2nd. edn. (Tokyo, 1972) p. 408ff; K. Holm (ed.), *Die Befragung 5* (Munich, 1977) p. 70f., 124ff.
9. O. Bauer, 'Die österreichische Revolution (1923)' in id., *Werkausgabe*, vol. 2 (Vienna, 1976) pp. 489–865.
10. Ibid., p. 743ff.; F. L. Carsten, *Revolutionen in Mitteleuropa 1918/19* (Cologne, 1973) p. 23ff. A comprehensive bibliography on this and the First Republic as a whole most recently, U. Kluge, 'Das Dilemma der Demokratie', *Neue Politische Literatur* 23 (1978) pp. 219–47; cf. generally also D. Lehnert, *Die Epoche der Revolution am Ende des Ersten Weltkrieges 1917–1920*, (schriftliches) Referat auf der 'Internationalen Tagung der Historiker der Arbeiterbewegung, 15. Linzer Konferenz', (Linz, 11–15 Sept., 1979).
11. O. Bauer, 'Das Gleichgewicht der Klassenkräfte', *Der Kampf* 17 (1924) pp. 57–67.

12. Cf. generally H. Hautmann and R. Kropf, *Die österreichische Arbeiterbewegung vom Vormärz bis 1945*, 3rd edn. (Vienna, 1978) p. 125ff.
13. See most recently: R. Neck and A. Wandruszka (eds), *Die Ereignisse des 15. Juli 1927* (Vienna, 1979).
14. Cf. N. Leser, *Zwischen Reformismus und Bolschewismus* (Vienna, 1968) p. 449ff.; H. Mommsen, *Arbeiterbewegung und Nationale Frage* (Göttingen, 1979) p. 345ff.
15. K. R. Stadler, *Opfer verlorener Zeiten* (Vienna, 1974) p. 44; G. Jagschitz, *Der Putsch: Die Nationalsozialisten in Österreich* (Graz, 1976) p. 167; cf. also L. Jedlicka and R. Neck (eds), *Das Jahr 1934: 12. Februar* (Vienna, 1975); id., (eds), *Das Jahr 1934: 25. Juli* (Vienna, 1975).
16. See E. Holtmann, *Zwischen Unterdrückung und Befreiung: Sozialistische Arbeiterbewegung und autoritäres Regime in Österreich 1933–1938* (Vienna, 1978) p. 42ff.
17. On the modus of the break down see G. Botz, 'Gewalt und politisch-gesellschaftlicher Konflikt in der Ersten Republik (1918 bis 1933)', *Österreichische Zeitschrift für Politikwissenschaft* 4 (1975) p. 526.
18. 'Austro-fascist' in this context is meant as a general designation of those political groupings that stood behind the Dollfuß government. On the term 'Austro-fascism' see in particular: W. Holzer, 'Faschismus in Österreich 1918–1938', *Austriaca* no. spécial 1 (1978) pp. 69–170. F. L. Carsten, *Faschismus in Österreich* (Munich, 1977) p. 211ff.
19. There exist only rough estimates as to the number of (seriously) injured, see Note 15.
20. On the absence of a social history of the Austrian Republic in the inter-war years see Ch. A. Gulick, *Österreich von Habsburg zu Hitler*, abbrev. edn. (Vienna, 1976); H. Benedikt (ed.), *Geschichte der Republik Österreich* (Vienna, 1977); K. R. Stadler, *Austria* (London, 1971); also G. Otruba, ' "Bauer" und "Arbeiter" in der Ersten Republik' in *Geschichte und Gesellschaft: Festschrift für Karl R. Stadler zum 60. Geburtstag* (Vienna, 1974) pp. 57–98; O. Leichter, *Glanz und Elend der Ersten Republik* (Vienna, 1964); B. Skotsberg, *Der österreichische Parlamentarismus* (Göteborg, 1940); K. Ausch, *Als die Banken fielen* (Vienna, 1968); see further literature also in P. Malina and G. Spann, *Bibliographie zur österreichischen Zeitgeschichte 1918–1978* (Vienna, 1978).
21. Botz, *Gewalt*, p. 44ff.; H. Hautmann, *Die verlorene Räterepublik*, 2nd revised edn. (Vienna, 1971), p. 145ff.; 179ff.; J. Deutsch, *Aus Österreichs Revolution* (Vienna, 1921) p. 54ff.
22. Carsten, *Revolutionen*, p. 252ff.; cf. also A. Staudinger, 'Die Ereignisse in den Ländern Deutschösterreichs im Herbst 1919' in L. Jedlicka, *Ende und Anfang* (Salzburg, 1969) p. 78; E. R. Starhemberg, *Memoiren* (Vienna, 1971) p. 37f.; A. Rintelen, *Erinnerungen an Österreichs Weg* (Munich, 1941) p. 40f.; K. Schuschnigg, *Dreimal Österreich* (Vienna, 1937) p. 67; more generally also Botz, *Gewalt*, pp. 22–86 (on the following also ibid., pp. 87–280).
23. L. Jedlicka, *Ein Heer im Schatten der Parteien* (Graz, 1955) p. 16.
24. Deutsch, *Österreichs Revolution*, p. 33ff., 47ff., 110ff.
25. Cf. for instance J. Deutsch, *Die Faschistengefahr* (Vienna, 1923) p. 12ff.; L. Kunschak, *Steinchen vom Wege* (Vienna, 1952) p. 78f.; Rintelen, *Erinnerungen*, p. 106, 110ff.
26. G. Botz, 'Bewaffnete Zusammenstöße und Strategie des frühfaschistischen Terrors in Österreich, Teil I und II', *Archiv. Mitteilungsblatt des Vereins der Geschichte für Arbeiterbewegung* (1973) pp. 41–50, 58–68.
27. Kriegsarchiv Wien (Bundesheer, 1927); Assistenzberichte; L. Jedlicka and R. Neck (eds), *Österreich 1927 bis 1938* (Vienna, 1973) p. 31ff.

28. Akten der Untersuchungskommission des Wiener Gemeinderates, Allg. Verwaltungsarchiv Wien, Christl.-soz. Partei Wien, box 16; R. Danneberg, *Die Wahrheit über die 'Polizeiaktion' am 15. Juli* (Vienna, 1927); *Ausschreitungen in Wien am 15. und 16. Juli 1927: Weißbuch*, (Vienna: Polizeidirektion, 1927).
29. E. C. Kollman, *Theodor Körner* (Munich, 1973) p. 191ff.; I. Duczynska, *Der demokratische Bolschewik* (Munich, 1975) p. 109.
30. R. Neck, 'Simmering, 16. Oktober 1932 – Vorspiel zum Bürgerkrieg', in: L. Jedlicka and R. Neck (eds), *Vom Justizpalast zum Heldenplatz* (Vienna, 1975) pp. 94–102.
31. J. Hofmann, *Der Pfrimerputsch* (Vienna, 1965); B. F. Pauley, *Hahnenschwanz und Hakenkreuz* (Vienna, 1972).
32. L. Kerekes, *Abenddämmerung einer Demokratie* (Vienna, 1966).
33. *Das Braunbuch: Hakenkreuz gegen Österreich* (Vienna: the Bundeskanzleramt, 1933); Jagschitz, *Putsch*, p. 31ff.
34. Cf. for instance K. Peball, *Die Kämpfe in Wien im Februar 1934* (Vienna, 1974); H. Fiereder, 'Der Republikanische Schutzbund in Linz und die Kampfhandlungen im Februar 1934', in *Historisches Jahrbuch der Stadt Linz 1978* (Linz, 1979) pp. 201–48; A. Reisberg, *Februar 1934* (Vienna, 1974); K. Haas, 'Der "12. Februar 1934" als historiographisches Problem' in Jedlicka and Neck (eds), *Justizpalast*, pp. 156–67.
35. G. Botz, 'Die "Juli-Demonstranten", ihre Motive und die quantifizierbaren Ursachen des "15. Juli 1927" ', in: Neck and Wandruszka (eds), *Ereignisse*, pp. 17–59; Botz, *Gewalt*, p. 238ff.
36. Ch. Tilly, L. Tilly and R. Tilly, *The Rebellious Century 1830–1930* (Cambridge, Mass., 1975) p. 283.
37. P. Waldmann, *Strategien politischer Gewalt* (Stuttgart, 1977) p. 78ff.; unless indicated otherwise, the following arguments are based on my work: *Gewalt in der Politik*.
38. W. I. Lenin, 'Der Zusammenbruch der II. Internationale' in id., *Werke*, vol. 21 (Berlin (GDR), 1968) p. 206f.; id., 'Was tun?' in Ibid. vol. 8 (Berlin (GDR), 1955) p. 467f.
39. H. Hautmann, *Die Anfänge der linksradikalen Bewegung und der Kommunistischen Partei Deutschösterreichs 1916 bis 1919*, phil. Diss. (Vienna, 1968) p. 48, 225.
40. Bettelheim rescinded the bracketed part of the protocol when it came to signing it.
41. Allg. Verwaltungsarchiv Wien, Bka, Inneres, 22/gen, Aktenzahl 29653/19.
42. *Der Abend* (14/6/1919) p. 2.
43. Allg. Verwaltungsarchiv Wien, Bka, Inneres, 22/gen, Aktenzahl 27612/19.
44. Bericht der Bundespolizeidirektion in Wien vom 20. Oktober 1932, ibid., Aktenzahl 100001/33; Strafsache gegen Johann Koplenig, Vr. 4472/27, Landesgericht für Strafsachen Wien; Ausschreitungen in Wien, p. 33ff.
45. K. Berchtold (ed.), *Österreichische Parteiprogramm 1966–1968* (Vienna, 1967) p. 251ff.; H. Feichter, 'Das Linzer Programm (1926) der österreichischen Sozialdemokratie', *Historisches Jahrbuch der Stadt Linz 1973/74* (1975), pp. 233–9; A. Schunck and H.-J. Steinberg, 'Mit Wahlen und Waffen' in W. Huber and J. Schwerdtfeger (eds), *Frieden, Gewalt, Sozialismus* (Stuttgart, 1976) p. 464ff.
46. Kollman, *Körner*, p. 208f; Duczynska, *Bolschewik*, p. 117ff.
47. Kollman, *Körner*, p. 204f.
48. In *Protokoll des sozialdemokratischen Parteitages 1926*, abgehalten in Linz vom 30. Oktober bis 3. November 1926 (Vienna, 1926) p. 265.
49. In *Parteitag 1927: Protokoll des sozialdemokratischen Parteitages*, abgehalten vom 29. Oktober bis 1. November 1927 im Ottakringer Arbeiterheim in Wien (Vienna, 1927) p. 132f., 139.

50. Tagblatt (Linz), 13/9/1925, Tagblatt-Archiv, Mappe "Sd-Gewalt", Arbeiter-kammer Wien, Dokumentationsabteilung.
51. See: Allg. Verwaltungsarchiv Wien, Soz.-dem. Parteistellen, Karton 6, Mappe 'Sitzungsprotokolle 1921–1928', Protokoll der Vorstandssitzung (der Vereinigung der sozialdemokratisch organiserten Angestellten und Bediensteten der Stadt Wien) vom 26. Juli 1927, Aufnahmeschrift mit Karl Reder; also Ausschreitungen in Wien, as above, p. 141f.
52. Leser, *Reformismus*, p. 413f.
53. L. Kerekes, Die 'Weiße Allianz', *Österreichische Osthefte* 7 (1965) p. 360ff.; see also H. G. W. Nusser, *Konservative Wehrverbände in Bayern, Preußen und Österreich 1918–1933* (Munich, 1973) L. Rape, *Die österreichischen Heimwehren und die bayerische Rechte 1920–1923* (Vienna, 1977).
54. P. Huemer, *Sektionschef Robert Hecht und die Zerstörung der Demokratie in Österreich* (Vienna, 1975).
55. Carsten, *Faschismus*, p. 63ff., 104ff.; Rape, *Heimwehren*, p. 116ff.
56. F. Winkler, *Die Diktatur in Österreich* (Zurich, 1953) p. 27f.; E. Ludwig, *Österreichs Sendung im Donauraum* (Vienna, 1954) p. 68.
57. Hofmann, *Pfrimerputsch*, p. 69ff.; Jedlicka, *Heer*, p. 90.
58. R. Neck, 'Thesen zum Februar' in Jedlicka and Neck (eds), *Justizpalast*, p. 154f.; also in Jedlicka and Neck (eds.), *12. Februar*, p. 21f.
59. Peball, *Kämpfe*, p. 19f., 37ff.
60. *Grobian* (Salzburg, 1/8/1923), p. 4.
61. *Neue Freie Presse* (5/5/1923), p. 1.
62. *Grobian* (15/8/1923), p. 3f.
63. R. de Felice, *Mussolini il fascista: I. La conquista del potere* (Turin, 1966) p. 34ff.; A. Tasca, *Glauben, gehorchen, kämpfen: Aufstieg des Faschismus* (Vienna, 1969) p. 129ff.
64. Dokumentationsarchiv des österreichischen Widerstandes, Wien, Dok. Nr. 2162; *Braunbuch*, as above, p. 23.
65. *Braunbuch*, as above, p. 15; Jagschitz, *Putsch*, p. 34ff.
66. For details see my study: *Vom Anschluß zum Krieg* (Vienna, 1978) p. 107ff.
67. K. W. Rothschild, 'Wurzeln und Triebkräfte der Entwicklung der Österreichischen Wirtschaftsstruktur' in W. Weber (ed.), *Österreichs Wirtschaftsstruktur gestern – heute – morgen*, vol. 1 (Vienna, 1961) p. 16ff.
68. I. K. Feierabend and R. L. Feierabend, 'Aggressive Behaviour within Politics, 1948–1962' in J. Chowming Davies (ed.), *When Men Revolt and Why* (New York, 1971) p. 236ff.; id. and B. A. Nesvold, 'Social Change and Political Violence' in Davis Graham and Gurr (eds), *History of Violence*, p. 653ff.; T. R. Gurr, 'A Comparative Study of Civil Strife' in ibid. p. 572ff.
69. See T. R. Gurr, *Rebellion: Eine Motivationsanalyse von Aufruhr, Konspiration und innerem Krieg* (Düsseldorf, 1972) p. 33ff.
70. P. H. Merkl, *Political Violence under the Swastika* (New Jersey, 1975) p. 154ff.; K. Renner, *Österreich von der Ersten zur Zweiten Republik* (Vienna, 1953) p. 117ff.
71. On this see my articles: 'Streik in Österreich 1918 bis 1975' in G. Botz *et al.* (eds), *Bewegung und Klasse: Studien zur österreichischen Arbeitergeschichte* (Vienna, 1978) pp. 807–31; and 'Politische Gewalt und industrielle Arbeitskämpfe in Wirtschaftskrisen', in Marin, *Wachstumskrisen*, pp. 260–306.
72. M. Jahoda, P. F. Lazarsfeld and H. Zeisel, *Die Arbeitslosen von Marienthal*, 2nd edn. (Allensbach, 1960) p. 42ff., 83f.
73. D. Stiefel, *Arbeitslosigkeit: Soziale, politische und wirtschaftliche Auswirkungen – am Beispiel Österreichs 1918–1938* (Berlin, 1979); see generally also K. W. Rothschild, *Arbeitslosigkeit in Österreich 1955–1975* (Linz, 1977) p. 20ff.

74. This value results from a comparison between the multiple defining quantity R^2 for regression equations of economic growth and unemployment, once inclusive once exclusive of the time lag in casualty figures.
75. Cf. also Ch. Tilly, 'Revolution and Collective Violence', in F. I. Greenstein and N. W. Polsby (eds), *Handbook of Political Science*, vol. 3 (Reading, Mass., 1975) p. 515.
76. The quantitative values used here are given in the Appendix (Table 18.3). Sources for them in Botz, *Politische Gewalt*, p. 261f. (Notes 7–9).

19 Anti-Democratic Terror in the Weimar Republic: the Black *Reichswehr* and the *Feme*-Murders

David B. Southern

'Direct action' is the renunciation of politics. Both individuals and groups may employ extreme forms of political protest. Individuals who resort to 'direct action' often feel themselves to be divorced from and superior to the society around them, like Hamlet who, as Harley Granville Barker observes, 'is a man adrift from old faiths and not yet anchored in new'.[1] They are Nietzschean individuals who by heroic efforts of will strive to create new values and so place themselves 'beyond good and evil'. 'Direct action' is likewise the expedient of social groups who have lost faith in received values and institutions, and run out of ordinary solutions. Arthur Rosenberg writes of the crisis of German government in 1916: 'If Germany's ruling classes now recognized the bankruptcy of the Imperial government but simultaneously rejected parliamentary government, what further possibility remained?'.[2] It was this disorientation of German conservatism in the late nineteenth and twentieth centuries which led stability-loving groups to espouse radical political action.

Political protest is conditioned by its social and historical context. Two sets of people are required to produce it: a wider section of conditional allegiants in society who oppose the system but do not engage in direct subversion; and a smaller group of declared opponents of the state who seek its overthrow.

The venture of fringe groups into direct subversion is profoundly apolitical. Politics is about the conciliation of conflicting interests. Marriage – the most intimate thing in our lives – is a daily compromise. Compromise is something which exists in life and without which life cannot go on. Yet extremists reject compromise and seek absolute solutions. They disdain also the means to achieve compromise: argument, discussion, negotiation, respect for legality, voting, elections. They seek not simply to defeat but to destroy their opponents. Politics is normally conducted against a background of force but force does not provide its principal subject-matter. Once fringe groups become committed to direct action, they elevate force into the main business of politics.

The pre-condition for the emergence of direct subversion is what Lyttleton calls 'the retreat of the state'.[3] The state fails to maintain its monopoly of the coercive power and instead shares power with private groups and individuals. This occurs when the distinction between the legitimate and illegitimate use of force is obscured. The results of the loss of this distinction are twofold. Those entitled to employ force become inhibited about using it:

> Thus conscience does make cowards of us all
> And thus the native hue of resolution
> Is sicklied o'er with the pale cast of thought.
> (W. Shakespeare)

By contrast outsiders become uninhibited about using force:

> The best lack all conviction, while the worst
> Are full of passionate intensity.
> (W. B. Yeats)

In the Weimar Republic the subversive potential of the German Communist Party (KPD) was limited because there existed a consensus that the use of violence and extra-legal methods by the Communists was illegitimate: politicians, administrators, the police, the armed forces, the judiciary all regarded it as self-evident that Communist activity should be suppressed when it moved outside the law and were ready to act on that assumption. The same measure of agreement, however, did not exist in respect of right-wing subversion. There was a widespread diffidence about regarding right-wing subversion as illegitimate and state action against it as legitimate. The distinguishing features of right-wing protest in Weimar Germany were its qualitative and quantitative uniqueness. It was nourished by tolerance and support from solid and respectable sections of German society. This in turn fostered that ambiguity with which it was regarded, and without which it would never have achieved its subsequent dimensions.

I

The precondition for the growth of direct action in Weimar Germany was the decline of the notion that the state should attract the automatic loyalty and obedience of all right-thinking citizens. The reasons for this development lay in the general dilemma of German conservatism, and the special circumstances of the Weimar Republic.[4]

Every conservative must ask himself Disraeli's question: 'What do you want to conserve?' By the opening of the twentieth century economic, social and political change threatened the status quo with which German conservatives identified their interests. Hence they had little left to conserve and became increasingly radical. The decline of European agriculture had everywhere undermined the position of the landed classes. Urbanisation produced new social groups which competed with and were not dependent on or attached to the old aristocracies. The growth of democracy threatened the position of political elites. In Germany the process of unification, in the course of which Bismarck superimposed a new German *Reich* on the old territorial states, dealt German conservatism a blow from which it never recovered.

Military defeat in 1918 and the establishment of the Weimar Republic intensified these threats to the social and political structure. By establishing a democratic Republic it put in office political groups which had been outsiders in the Empire: social democrats, Catholics and liberals. With its democratic franchise, concern for social welfare and proclaimed egalitarianism the Weimar Republic reproduced and compounded those features of the Empire which had excited conservative hostility. The Weimar Republic also shared the ills of the Empire which deprived the right of the anchor of a status quo: the inadequate sense of political integration; the breakdown of traditional regulating influences; nostalgia for a lost world of order combined with a set of post-liberal attitudes which ultimately manifested themselves in radical rebellion against tradition, morality and all humanitarian rules of conduct. Thus arose a revolutionary conservatism which sought to overthrow rather than preserve the status quo. Conservative classes did not reflect on the illogicality of basing a conservative creed on advocacy of revolution.

These factors led conservatives to deny to the Weimar Republic those attributes of statehood which normally entitle states to require the loyalty and obedience of citizens. Delegitimisation of the state organisation to which they were opposed made opposition to it morally obligatory. The Weimar Republic was delegitimised in two ways.

Firstly, the stab in the back legend was utilised to show that the Republic was the product of betrayal and high treason. The nation had not been defeated but betrayed. Hence the state did not serve the nation's greatness but was on the contrary anti-patriotic. Secondly, the constitution was declared to be a partisan one. The 'true' state was characterised by its superiority to society. The state should be a sovereign organ of decision standing above the conflicts of interest groups and parties. In the Weimar Republic the state was no longer a non-political organisation: it was party rule posing as a national constitution and could therefore no longer count on the automatic compulsory loyalty of good citizens. To affirm the state was, paradoxically, to deny the state.[5]

Both state patriots and radical nationalists could respond to these delegitimising arguments. It was this undermined loyalty of basically conservative groups which gave the real subversives their chance.

II

Conservatives and nationalists reacted to this vacuum in their pantheon by seeking to create a new state in their own image. Those parts of the old state which still had the capacity to draw their respect were separated from it and idealised as non-political. To this extent, they remained loyal to the state. Beyond this there was a proliferation of new organisations designed to fulfil the unsatisfied need for group identification and emotional loyalty. These organisations embodied the ideals and values to which conservatives transferred their allegiance, in the absence of a political and social status quo with which they could identify. Finally, members of these associations sought to purify the corrupt inheritance of the Weimar Republic by eliminating traitors.

Ironically the state itself called into existence potential counter-institutions. At the end of the First World War the old army was demobilised en masse. In the vacuum of public authority 'self-defence' (*Selbstschutz*) and 'self-help' (*Selbsthilfe*) organisations were formed all over Germany. The government also found that it needed some armed force. In cooperation with the old military authorities, volunteer forces were organised, of which the principal element was constituted by the *Freikorps*, which in 1919 totalled 200–400,000 men. These played a prominent role in suppressing left-wing dissent in Germany, fighting Polish insurgents on the eastern frontier, and conducting an independent campaign in the Baltic culminating in the capture of Riga on 22 May 1919. A provisional *Reichswehr* was established early in 1919 but never managed to bring the heterogeneous mass of *Freikorps* under satisfactory control. Attempts to amalgamate the *Freikorps* with the new *Reichswehr* foundered on the disarmament provisions of the Treaty of Versailles, which forced a reduction of the *Reichwehr* from 300,000 to 100,000 men. The semi-official military formations could not be integrated into the State. Hence there arose in postwar Germany what Diehl calls 'a pluralistic system of military forces'.[6]

The growth of illicit military formations was fuelled by the existence of a reservoir of unemployed ex-soldiers, unable to demobilise psychologically. The radical right in general was recruited from people whose social or economic position had been rendered precarious by social and economic progress. The First World War and its aftermath vastly increased the potential following of the radical right by leaving a whole generation of young men who, like Othello, yearned for the big wars and found that their occupation had gone. Professor Friedrich Grimm – prominent defence lawyer in the Feme-murder trials – recorded his impressions of 'these young activists . . . who had all missed the entrance to ordinary life'. Of Edmund Heines – Lieutenant in the First World War, member of the *Freikorps Rossbach*, Feme-murderer, SA-leader, *NSDAP Reichstag* deputy and finally victim of the purge of 30 June 1934 – he wrote: 'Heines . . . had missed the opening to middle-class life . . . an unbalanced man, full of storm and stress, with the understanding of a child . . . He had the character of a mercenary, completely spoilt for normal life'.[7]

III

The Kapp Putsch of March 1920 led to the disbandment of the remaining *Freikorps*. Official dissolution, however, did not mean actual disappearance. Successor organisations contrived to lead a clandestine existence. The *Reichswehr*, moreover, was anxious to use such organisations as secret reserves. In the wake of the Franco-Belgian occupation of the Ruhr in January 1923, Seeckt – the head of the *Reichswehr* – organised the Black *Reichswehr* from existing paramilitary formations, largely ex-*Freikorps*. In this scheme Seeckt had the cooperation and approval of *Reichswehr* Minister Gessler and Prussian Interior Minister Severing.[8] The illicit formations were called *Arbeits-Kommandos* (AK), and the principal organisers were Major Buchrucker and Leutnant Schulz. Their strength was about 20,000 men. On 1 October 1923 Buchrucker attempted to launch a putsch at Kustrin and thereafter the AKs were rapidly dissolved. The *Reichswehr* subsequently denied any connection with the Black *Reichswehr*. The reason for this disclaimer lay in the activities of the special section.

The link between the *Reichswehr* leadership and the Black *Reichswehr* was provided by Oberleutnant Paul Schulz, whom Grimm characterised as 'the veritable soul of the undertaking'.[9] Schulz formed a special section – *Kommando zu besonderer Verwendung* (KzbV) – consisting of three ex-warrant officers, Klapproth, Fahlbusch and Büsching. The purpose of this special section was to eliminate 'traitors' who might betray the existence of the Black *Reichswehr*. If the official *Reichswehr* leadership knew of the existence of the Black *Reichswehr*, they might also be thought to know about the special section. When the murders came to light, the *Reichswehr* disavowed its illicit formations of 1923 at the trial of Leutnant Eckermann before the *Landgericht* Schwerin in 1929, there was a confrontation between General Hammerstein on behalf of the *Reichswehr*, and the former Freikorps leader Rossbach about the *Reichswehr's* cognisance of the Black *Reichswehr*. Before his 1928 trial Fahlbusch alleged that he had killed Wilms on the direct orders of the *Reichswehr*: this Schulz denied but Professor Grimm nevertheless believed Fahlbusch's version to be correct.[10] It was also recorded that within the Black *Reichswehr* 'to send by transport' (*auf Transport schicken*) was a euphemism for 'liquidate' (*erledigen*). The true position was best summarised by *Landgerichtsdirektor* (= LGD) Siegert in the court's judgement in the Schulz case on 26 March 1927:[11]

The *Reichswehr*, which at that time organised the *Arbeits-Kommandos*, was and must have been aware, that it was creating formations which were to be kept secret. If it left the solution of the difficult problem of achieving this to the *Arbeits-Kommandos* themselves, it brought thereby a certain moral responsibility on itself, for the possibility of such an act as has been tried here lay in the lack of control by the organizing authority. Moreover, in the uprising in Upper Silesia in 1921–2 a similar lynch justice with the aim of liquidating traitors had established itself and this could not have remained unknown to the Reichswehr.

IV

A poem on the Black *Reichswehr* by Lampel was entitled 'Traitors fall victim to the Feme' (*Verräter verfallen der Feme*).[12] Feme was the name applied to the secret self-constituted tribunals in Westphalia in the Middle Ages. Hence the term *Fememord* was applied to the killings carried out by members of the Black *Reichswehr* in order to safeguard the existence of the formations.

The trials which ultimately followed on these homicides illustrated the dilemma of public authority in the Weimar Republic. The old machinery of the state continued to function. It was manned by stolid, unimaginative men who would not have had the jobs they did had they not been stolid, unimaginative men. The state could still assert itself if it could summon up the political will to do so. But its self-confidence and self-belief had been sapped by the official toleration of organisations which in the last resort challenged the state's monopoly of legitimate coercion. Moreover, the illegal actions of members of these groups were regarded as innocent of any criminality by right-thinking members of society and justified by involving a rival theory of political legitimacy.

Two trials may be singled out: (1) the trial of Schirmann and others for the murder of Pannier before the *Schwurgericht* of *Landgericht* III Berlin on 1–2 February 1926; (2) the trial of Schulz and others for the murder of Wilms before the *Schwurgericht, Landgericht* III Berlin on 11–26 March 1927.[13]

Pannier was a member of the Black *Reichswehr* killed as a potential traitor on 3 June 1923. This led to the trial of eleven accused in 1926 before a court presided over by LGD Bombe. The trial was held in camera, and resulted in the accused being found guilty and sentenced to long terms of penal servitude. The trial had an unexpected sequel. On 21 February 1926 the Prussian Minister-President, Otto Braun, speaking at the *Reichsbannertag* in Hamburg, declared that certain judges had placed themselves protectively in front of the ringleaders who were responsible for the Feme-murders. When challenged to substantiate this statement in the Prussian *Landtag*, Braun replied that his Hamburg speech referred to Bombe's decision to exclude the public in the Pannier trial; contrary to the express wish of the government, the case had been heard in secret.[14] Braun's attack unleashed a storm of controversy around the head of LGD Bombe and an investigation was at once started into the events which had led to the court's action.

The main proceedings had been fixed for 1 February 1926.[15] To prevent accusations that information about the Black *Reichswehr* was being suppressed, the Prussian government was anxious to ensure that the case was heard in public. On 22 January 1926 the Secretary of State in the Prussian Justice Ministry instructed *Oberstaatsanwalt* Sethe to oppose any motion for the exclusion of the public. On 26 January Bombe expressed himself anxious about the Foreign Office's attitude to the case. He asked the Prussian Justice Ministry to find out whether the Foreign Office regarded the case as politically sensitive. If no answer were obtained from the Foreign Office by 1 February, Bombe declared that he would prefer to exclude the public as a precautionary measure, rather than postpone the hearing.

Unbeknown to Bombe and the Prussian government, the *Reich* cabinet had that day held a meeting, at which the inadvisability of holding such trials in public was stressed because of its possible effect on relations with foreign governments. On 29 January, the Prussian government learnt of the attitude of the Foreign Office and *Reich* government and asked that the matter be reconsidered.

On 30 January a highly confidential meeting was held, attended by the *Reich*-Chancellor, *Reich*-President, Foreign Minister, *Reichswehr* Minister, *Reich* Minister of the Interior, Prussian Minister of the Interior and the Secretaries of State in the Prussian State and Justice ministries. Stresemann insisted that foreign-policy considerations, in particular the pending negotiations about the reduction in the strength of the army of occupation in the Rhineland, made it requisite that the court proceedings should be postponed for at least six weeks. The members of the Prussian government agreed, but pointed out that the principle of judicial independence prevented the government from giving direct instructions to the court. It was agreed that the Foreign Office should not reply directly to the court's inquiry: instead, the court would be told informally of the Foreign Office's reasons for wishing to postpone the hearing.

Straight after the meeting, the Secretary of State in the Prussian Justice Ministry informed Tigges, *Kammergericht* President, that the government wanted the main hearing of the Pannier case postponed. Tigges contacted the President of *Landgericht* III Berlin who in turn told LGD Bombe. On 31 January Sethe was given his instructions by the Secretary of State in the Prussian Justice Ministry. He was told to seek a postponement and inform the court confidentially that no reply would be sent by the Foreign Office.

Before the proceedings opened on 1 February, Sethe told Bombe in private of his instructions. When the request to delay the hearing was submitted in open court, the defence opposed the motion. The court withdrew to consider the request. Bombe did not know what he could tell the rest of the court of the government's reasons, which he himself only knew imperfectly; no answer had been received about the Foreign Office's attitude; the prosecution's reason for its request seemed inadequate. To Sethe's dismay, the court decided not to delay proceedings but instead to exclude the public. The committee of inquiry of the Prussian *Landtag* conceded that Bombe had suffered under 'considerable lack of clarity'.[16] Braun must have known of the secret consultations between his own and the *Reich* government. His Hamburg speech reflected the need to say something striking but unspecific. Called on to substantiate his charges, he picked on the unfortunate LGD Bombe. This was a horse that would not run.

The President of the *Landgericht* III, *Landgericht*-President Kirchstein, set down dates for *Schwurgericht* hearings to begin in 1927: 10 January, 21 February, 21 March, 25 April etc. *Kammergericht* President Tigges appointed LGD Bombe to be the presiding judge in the *Schwurgericht*, while Kirchstein appointed LGD Siegert to be his deputy. At the end of December 1926 Kirchstein became aware firstly, that Schulz's case would be ready for trial in March 1927; secondly, that two other major *Schwurgericht* trials would take place in January–March. Because of pressure of judicial business Kirchstein, with the approval of Tigges, arranged an additional *Schwurgericht* hearing – an extraordinary *Schwurgericht* – to open on 11 March under the presidency of LGD Siegert to conduct the trial of Schulz.[17]

Siegert was a member of the DNVP and had 'the reputation of being of the sternest and ultra-conservative in his views'. He was, however, 'known as a man of unusual determination'.[18] When the trial of Schulz, Umhofer and Klapproth for the murder of Wilms opened, all the defence lawyers sought to have the case transferred to the regular *Schwurgericht* sitting, on the grounds that the extraordinary *Schwurgericht* had been convened not because of pressure of business but to transfer the case from Bombe to Siegert, thereby depriving the accused of their regular judges contrary to the Judicature Act and the Constitution. When this was rejected, Schulz through his counsel Dr Sack unsuccessfully sought to have the professional judges removed for fear of bias. A subsequent appeal to the *Reichsgericht* failed to upset either of these determinations.

Schulz had already taken part in two earlier *Feme*-murder trials. With others he had been tried by the *Landgericht* Landsberg from 28 October to 3 November 1926 for the murder of Gröschke. Shortly afterwards the same court tried him from 8 to 12 November 1926 for the murder of Gädicke. Though both trials ended in acquittal for Schulz, the judgement in the Gröschke case had specifically found that shortly before Gröschke's disappearance Schulz had planned his murder by reliable people and, though Schulz could not be convicted of incitement, he bore moral responsibility for the deed.

Schulz's third trial, however, took a different course. Siegert's judgement outlined the position of Schulz as the true leader of the Black *Reichswehr* and the role of the special section. It was not contested that Klapproth, Fuhrmann and Umhofer had actually killed Wilms on 18 July 1923. The real question was – the judgement continued – who had ordered them to do it? It reached the conclusion: 'one will organized the perpetrators for the deed and awoke in them the resolve to kill Wilms . . . the fate of Wilms was decided upon in no other place than the headquarters of the Arbeits-Kommando'. Schulz 'intentionally produced in the perpetrators the resolve to kill and the murder was thereupon carried out'. Fuhrmann, Klapproth and Umhofer were sentenced to death for murder; Schulz received the same sentence for incitement to murder. On 1 December 1927 their appeals were rejected by the *Reichsgericht*.

These sentences were greeted with fury by right-wing circles. Siegert himself became the object of vehement personal attacks.[19] To large sections of the political right, it was clear that no crime had been committed. Patriotic men had liquidated traitors in the interest of national security. The former head of the *Reichswehr*, Seeckt, called the death-sentence against Schulz 'a miscarriage of justice in the light of a higher justice'.[20]

Two defending lawyers played a prominent role in the *Feme*-murder trials and numerous other cases involving Nationalist and Nazi accused: Luetgebrune and Grimm. Luetgebrune was rich, fat, led an extravagant lifestyle and demanded high fees. Grimm had a lean and hungry look and was motivated by his convictions rather than professional motives. Their fees and expenses were paid by an association incorporated under the name of *Nationale Nothilfe e.V.* which was headed by Wilhelm van Oppen and supported by members of the DNVP and other radical Nationalists. Luetgebrune had represented Umhofer in Schulz's 1927 trial. He was invited to appear on behalf of Schulz for the appeal. After this had been rejected Dr Meinardus, the Lutheran chaplain of the prison where Schulz was detained, asked Grimm to take up Schulz's case.

Grimm produced an argument in exculpation of Schulz and others convicted of *Feme*-murders which reflected the attitudes of the nationalist right to the Weimar Republic. It had been established that a plea of necessity could excuse the infraction of a criminal law in order to avert a greater evil either to oneself (*Notwehr*) or to others (*Notstand*). In 1927 the *Reichsgericht* had invoked the doctrine of supra legal necessity (*übergesetzlicher Notstand*) to exonerate two doctors who had illegally terminated a pregnancy to save the life of the mother.[21] If a person honestly but wrongly believed that circumstances existed which justified the violation of a criminal law (putative necessity, *putativer Notstand*), he was equally exempt from criminal guilt.

Grimm argued that if the state itself was a legal person which was entitled in emergency to the same protection as a natural person, it must be in contravention of the criminal law. If the *Feme*-killings had been actuated by the conviction that they were essential to protect the state, then these acts were exempt from punishment because they could be justified and defended on grounds of state necessity. If the conviction that the state was exposed to an exceptional danger was erroneous, those who violated the law, in reliance on this mistaken but honest belief, were immune from legal penalties, because they acted by virtue of a putative state necessity (*putative Staatsnotwehr, putativer Staatsnotstand*). Grimm's argument stemmed from the proposition that the true state was no longer embodied in the institutions of the Weimar Republic: its army, its police, its laws. Therefore one had a right and duty to disregard the obligations imposed by the existing state.[22]

The suggestion that the perpetrators could invoke some sort of extra-legal necessity had already been scouted by Siegert in his judgement. Nevertheless, Grimm submitted a request for a retrial to *Landgericht* I Berlin. On 9 January 1929 the court (presiding judge LGD Friedman) rejected Grimm's request along with his theory of 'extra-statutory state necessity'. The court argued that in a constitutional state the protection of the state was the exclusive responsibility of those organs on whom this duty was conferred by law. The individual was not free to decide what the state interest did or did not require. The law, not the personal conviction of individuals, was the measure of legality.[23]

Among German judges there were thus men of independence and a sense of justice. But the German state did not lend them its support. It was the standing policy of the Prussian State Ministry to commute all death sentences where the conviction was based on circumstantial evidence. This applied to Schulz. If Schulz's sentence was to be commuted to life imprisonment, the same must be done for his co-defendants. The 1928 *Reich* amnesty reduced the life sentences to seven-and-half years. On 28 June 1929 Schulz was released on medical grounds and the remaining men convicted in the case were released soon afterwards. Schulz became prominent in the SA, was left for dead in the purge of 30 June 1934 but managed to escape to Switzerland. He is reported to be alive, happy and living in West Germany.

The *Feme*-cases showed that the courts were by no means excessively reluctant to convict or lenient in sentencing right wing offenders. In cases which ended in conviction, the courts imposed on 22 defendants:

6 death sentences
1 sentence of life imprisonment
2 sentences of 15 years penal servitude
2 sentences of 10 years penal servitude
1 sentence of 8 years penal servitude

besides lesser sentences.[24]

As a result of incessant amnesties and individual acts of clemency, all these sentences were commuted or remitted, so that by February 1930 only two of those sentenced for their part in *Feme*-cases were still in prison.

Like other states reluctant to use force, the Weimar Republic found in the end that it had no force to use. In this sense its high-mindedness was its own undoing. The delegitimisation of public authority ultimately brought about its breakdown. Radical opponents of the status quo in liberal democracies have always claimed that the state is in a process of dissolution, at the end of which lie anarchy and nihilism. They are, of course, correct. But one can quote to them the words of Alexander Herzen to the Russian liberals: 'Gentlemen, you are not the doctors – you are the disease'.

NOTES

1. H. G. Barker, *Prefaces to Shakespeare* (London, 1972) p. 256.
2. A. Rosenberg in K. Kursten (ed.), *Entstehung der Weimarer Republik* (Frankfurt, 1961) p. 103.
3. A. Lyttelton, 'Fascism and Violence in Post-War Italy', ch. 16 of this volume.
4. On the phenomenon of revolutionary conservatism in Germany there is an enormous literature. See in particular: P. G. J. Pulzer, *The Rise of Political Anti-Semitism in Germany and Austria* (New York, 1964); K. Sontheimer, *Anti-demokratisches Denken in der Weimarer Republik* (Munich, 1968).
5. The most significant attempt to demonstrate the illegitimacy of the Weimar Constitution is: A. Freiherr von Freytagh-Loringhoven, *Die Weimarer Verfassung in Lehre und Wirklichkeit* (Munich, 1924).
6. J. Diehl, *Paramilitary Politics in Weimar Germany* (Bloomington, 1977) pp. 18, 24.
7. Bundesarchiv Koblenz (= B. A. Koblenz), Nachlass Grimm, pp. 25, 34.
8. F. L. Carsten, *The Reichswehr and Politics 1918–1933* (Oxford, 1966). C. Severing, *Mein Lebensweg*, 2 vols. (Cologne, 1950). O.-E. Schüddekopf, *Das Heer und die Republik: Quellen zur Politik der Reichswehrführung 1918 bis 1933* (Hannover, 1955).
9. B. A. Koblenz, Nachlass Grimm 5; F. Grimm, *40 Jahre Dienst am Recht: Politische, Justiz, die Krankheit unserer Zeit* (Bonn, 1953) pp. 96–100.
10. B. A. Koblenz, Nachlass Grimm pp. 38–9 F. Grimm, *Mit Offenem Visier* (Leoni, 1961) p. 113.
11. B. A. Koblenz, Nachlass Luetgebrune, No. 67.
12. Lampel himself was subsequently alleged to have perpetrated a Feme-type murder in Upper Silesia: *Die Weltbühne* (1929), p. 749.
13. From 1924 onwards a *Schwurgericht* consisted of three professional and six lay judges sitting and deciding together.
14. Drucksachen des Preussischen Landtags, 1925–6; Kleine Anfrage No. 809 (DVP) (23 February 1926): No. 2248 (KPD) (5 March 1927); No. 2706 (9 March 1927). Prussian Landtag 1925–6 (9), G.R. 700, pp. 9942–6 (23 March 1926), DJZ 31 (1926) p. 128.
15. The sequence of events is recorded in: Geheimes Staatsarchiv Berlin-Dahlem. Rep. 84a. No. 30315, f.1/48–69.
16. Teilbericht der 25. Kommission des Preussischen Landtages, Drucksache No. 2290: Prussian Landtag, 8927A (20 March 1928).
17. B. A. Koblenz, Nachlass Luetgebrune, No. 67.
18. B. A. Koblenz, Nachlass Grimm, p. 17; A. Apfel, *Behind the Scenes of German Justice* (London, 1935) pp. 93, 125.
19. B. A. Koblenz, Nachlass Grimm pp. 12, 18; Die Justiz IV (1928/9) p. 544.

20. F. von Rabenau, *Seeckt: aus seinem Leben 1918–1936* (Leipzig, 1940) pp. 424–6.
21. RGSt. 61, 242: cf. *Rv. Bourne* [1939] 1 K.B. p. 687.
22. F. Grimm, *Grundsätzliches zu den Femeprozessen* (Munich, 1928); B. A. Koblenz, R 43 I, No. 1243, ff. 259–83; Radbruch, 'Zum Fememordprozess Schulz' *Die Justiz* IV (1928/9) pp. 164–6; K. Siegert, *Notstand und Putativnotstand* (Berlin, 1931).
23. Dahlem, Rep. 84a, No. 11769, ff. 1–6.
24. Dahlem, Rep. 84a, No. 7922, ff. 36, 124.

20 The KPD in the Weimar Republic and the Problem of Terror during the 'Third Period', 1929–33

Eve Rosenhaft

For insurrectionary groups the use of violence as a political tool is not, in principle, problematic. When a revolutionary party aims to take an active part in the organisation of social and political life during periods preceding the moment of insurrection, however, the appropriate forms and occasions of violent action have to be continuously reviewed, debated and reassessed. The use of any kind of violence is made problematic at times like these by the contrast between the enormity of the threat that organised public violence is generally held to pose to civil society – and the corresponding harshness of official response to it – and the relative weakness of the party, as implied in the party's recognition of a non- or at best pre-revolutionary period: even where the party may recognise the tactical utility of certain forms of violence, it cannot allow an escalation of violence that might force it into the position of fighting a rearguard action in a premature civil war or result in its suppression by the police. These basic tensions can become acutely problematic in practice when the party's policy-makers have to contend with pressures for violent action coming from within the party itself and/or from its opponents. For the German Communist Party – the KPD – the question of political terror was a problem in both these senses during the better part of its existence; in the years between 1929 and 1933 the official analysis of the 'Third Period', with its combination of threat and promise, joined with conditions of social and political crisis to raise that question to the status of a central issue in Communist tactics.

The discussion of the uses of terror within the KPD revolved around two distinct but related questions: first, what sort of violent actions the Party itself ought to initiate in its efforts to hasten the approach of an 'acutely revolutionary situation', and second, how the Communists in particular and the working class in general ought to respond to the terrorism of Hitler's SA. 'Terror', legitimate and illegitimate, was explicitly at issue only in the debate

342

about the latter question, but it is necessary to consider both areas of policy in addressing the problem of terror. For one thing, conclusions reached in the more general discussion of proto-revolutionary violence provided the answers to most of the questions about the physical fight against the Nazis. More fundamentally, however, the Communists implicitly regarded every form of violence in a non-revolutionary period as terroristic, in that its value lay in its capacity to change the attitudes and perceptions of its agents, victims or audience, rather than in any possibility of directly effecting material changes in the immediate situation.

I

Official approval of this kind of violence grew directly out of the KPD's analysis of how and in what direction it ought to mobilise the masses in the 'Third Period'. The doctrine of the 'Third Period', as promulgated at the Sixth Comintern Congress in 1928, predicted a new wave of imperialist wars and class struggles. These presented both the threat of increased state repression and, eventually, the institution of a fascist regime, and the promise of general radicalisation of the oppressed leading to the victory of the revolution. The combined prospect raised in particularly acute form a fundamental problem of Communist strategy: 'the question of the conquest of the majority of the working class' –the essential precondition for revolution.[1]

The means by which the Communists aimed to win the leadership of the working class was the creation of a 'united front from below'. This meant separating the Social Democratic and trade-union rank and file from its traditional leaders. One aspect of this was a concerted campaign of exposing the corruption of the reformist leadership through propaganda and action. The other was the recruitment of disillusioned Social Democrats to the Communist cause.

The pursuit of the united front from below involved not only intensified application of traditional organisational techniques, but also a positive change in tactics. The Party itself had to provide an alternative leadership. It must prove its claim to be the only party of the working class by taking the initiative in organising the conflicts of the pre-revolutionary period:

> The working masses must be able to convince themselves, on the basis of deeds, that the Communist Party is not a fireproof safe for the accumulation of influence, or a bankbook in which they can deposit their revolutionary energies until the 'final decisive battle'.[2]

The difference between the tactics of the 'Second Period' and those of the 'Third' was the difference between agitation and propaganda, on the one hand, and the 'independent leadership of struggles' on the other.[3] The most important of these struggles were to be the industrial ones, since they had the greatest bearing both on the interests of the workers and on the stability of the capitalist system. The 'preparation, setting in motion, and carrying through of economic struggles, even against the will of the reformists' was the first major task to which the KPD applied itself after the Sixth Congress.[4]

But organised workers were not the only section of the population on which the Communist Party set its sights in the 'Third Period'. The need to organise the broad middle strata, along with the 'unorganised' sections of the working class, also became urgent in the crisis.[5] Strikes as such had little relevance to the situation of these people; the Party pledged itself to articulating their special needs, and to enforcing their demands through popular action outside the factory. By combining strikes and popular action, the Party could achieve a new alignment of class forces. And if the workers and other members of the 'labouring masses' were to see their causes as a single revolutionary struggle, the two forms of activity must be tightly coordinated on every occasion.

The 'indivisible connection' of strikes with 'revolutionary street-demonstrations, with revolutionary mass-meetings'[6] became a central tenet of Communist tactics. Organised support outside the factory meant that a strike was sustained and its impact widened, while the converse of politicising each economic conflict was the organisation of industrial action as the climax of every political campaign. Strikes and mass demonstrations were mutual guarantees of short-term success; in combination, they were the means to the long-range victory of the revolution. The Comintern Programme established a hierarchy of 'strikes, strikes combined with demonstrations, strikes combined with armed demonstrations, and finally the general strike combined with armed insurrection'.[7]

By the end of 1929, the mass-strike had moved to the centre of tactical discussion. This was largely the result of the events of the preceding May in Berlin: in spite of a long-standing police ban on public demonstrations, the KPD called its followers into the streets in traditional celebration of the First of May. When police moved to prevent demonstrators from proceeding towards their central meeting point, running battles developed in many parts of the city. In the working-class districts of Wedding and Neukölln, barricades were constructed against the police. The fighting, which continued intermittently into 4 May, left over thirty dead (none of them policemen), nearly 200 wounded, and some 1,200 under arrest. In its wake, the Communist press was banned for several weeks, and by 15 May the Party's paramilitary organisation, the *Roter Frontkämpferbund* (RFB) was illegal in all parts of Germany. On 2 May, the KPD issued the call for a protest strike, which was answered – the Party claimed – by 25,000 workers in Berlin and another 50,000 throughout the country.[8]

There was a whole series of lessons to be learnt from the Berlin events, all of which, as interpreted by the Communists, tended to confirm the expectations of the 'Third Period'. The feasibility of the political mass-strike was the most important of these. But the unexpected vehemence with which the residents of Wedding and Neukölln reacted to the actions of the police also stimulated discussion of the form and function of demonstrations as such. The article which summarised the conclusions of the Tenth Plenum of the Comintern Executive (ECCI) regarding the mass-strike ended with an analysis of the importance of the battle for the streets in a period when 'the masses learn propaganda and agitation primarily on the streets'.[9] And May Day 1929 had shown the conditions under which this battle would have to be carried on. In the context of the Party's deliberations on the problem of repression and legality, the demonstration took on an importance of its own as a tactical instrument.

The doctrine of the 'Third Period' held out the prospect of direct reprisals against the Communist parties and their auxiliary bodies as well as of continuous encroachments on the workers' freedom. It would be four years before the German Communists would have to face the concentration camps, courts martial and firing squads predicted by one Comintern publicist after May 1929.[10] But in the last years of the Weimar Republic, political activity was already encumbered by repeated local, provincial and national pro-hibitions on public gatherings and by bans on various radical publications and organisations. Aimed in principle at extremists of both left and right, these measures were applied with greater consistency and regularity to the Communists, as anti-subversive legislation had been throughout the Republic's history.[11] In the eyes of the Comintern, the German Party in 1930 was already only 'semi-legal'.[12]

. Questions of legality and illegality were thus a major preoccupation of the Communists from 1929 on. These questions were fundamental to the survival of the Party, and their solution was not simple. How was the Party to avoid being driven underground without abandoning its revolutionary activities, how carry on those activities without provoking all-out reprisals? For the Party itself, the tacticians' answer was twofold. The Communists must prepare in advance – rehearse and reorganise – for operation underground, and at the same time the Party must establish itself and its influence so firmly among the masses as to frustrate any ban.[13]

Important as were their implications for the way the Party operated, these were essentially precautionary measures. The long-range strategy of the KPD proposed another, more drastic answer to repression: to provoke it, to defy it, and in the process to forge a revolutionary mass-movement:

The slogan of the day is: construction of an illegal *Apparat*, but by no means becoming submerged in illegality. The slogan of the day is – not 'exploitation of all the legal opportunities', but development of the mass-struggle of the proletariat to burst the bounds of police and trade-union legality.[14]

Seen in these terms, the function of popular action in the 'Third Period' went beyond the simple manifestation of opinion or even the enforcement of concrete demands. Every action organised by the Communists was designed to instruct and engage its participants. The achievement of the stated aims of any individual strike or demonstration was of material importance, both to the prestige of the Party and to the welfare of the workers, and the Party celebrated its tactical victories as such. But in the light of history, it was the action itself that counted. The men of the 'Third Period' saw signs in the events of 1928/29 that the masses were ready to fight on just those terms. '*Hart gegen hart*', said Kuusinen at the Tenth Plenum, 'that is the mood of the broad working masses. Any partial defeats in this period no longer evoke depression; even serious setbacks can be more easily borne than cases of capitulation without a fight'.[15]

For a trade-unionist, to break through 'trade-union legality' in an unofficial strike, even a non-violent one, was to be radically divided from one's traditional allegiances and prejudices. The action in which people were led into direct confrontation with the forces of the state had the same effect on a 'higher' level; it was a purely political act. The ideal remained a combined assault on both levels. At the meeting of the ECCI Presidium in February 1930, Manuilski welcomed the fact that strikes were more and more often accompanied by 'street demonstrations, clashes with the police, with the constabulary, with the military, with strike-breakers, with social fascist spies'.[16]

But even when closely associated with a strike, the show of force was a distinct type of event, and one of the lessons of May 1929 was that a demonstration which exposed the brutality of the state could itself be the basis for a strike movement. In the view of the KPD, it had been the achievement of the Party in those days to overcome its own legalism, to the extent of openly organising and carrying out demonstrations in defiance of the police ban. The violent form the demonstrations took represented a breakthrough on the part of the masses: they had taken up the challenge of a direct battle with the state itself.[17] The fight against the police was of the essence of armed insurrection. Every demonstration was an exercise for the coming military struggle and a lesson in the civil-war character of the existing political order.

The discussion of how demonstrations should be organised so as to gain the maximum agitational profit from the political situation at the minimum organisational cost tended to detach itself from the broader strategic argument. The demonstration was studied as a weapon in its own right, aimed directly at the system. In April 1931, the clandestine KPD journal *Oktober* compared the various forms of public demonstration with the successive stages of insurrection – from the already obsolete legal mass-action, through demonstrations 'in which one has to reckon right from the start with some kind of incident', to the final armed march on the centres of power.[18] As District Leader of Berlin, Walter Ulbricht in mid-1931 initiated a programme of 'blitz' demonstrations: Small groups of demonstrators would appear without warning, prepared to dissolve and regroup just as suddenly if approached by the police. Their purpose was both to frustrate any ban and to confuse and exhaust the police.[19]

The problems encountered by the demonstrators in Berlin in May 1929 underlined the need for dependable groups of stewards to manage, protect and give point to large demonstrations.[20] The need was recognised by the Party and built into the functions of the RFB's successor organisations. The question of whether these cadres should be armed, also raised by the events of May, remained a difficult one. Armed demonstrations as such were rejected in principle, as long as no 'acutely revolutionary situation' existed. But the sentiment in favour of carrying and, if necessary, using weapons was strong; by the end of 1932 the view that demonstrations could no longer be carried out unless they were armed was widespread within the Party.[21] The use of guns did come to be approved conditionally, at least at the local level; in 1931 armed squads were a feature of several Communist demonstrations in Berlin.[22]

Finally, the calculated risk of confrontation was elaborated into an extended discussion of popular tactics against the police. This, too, grew out of the 1929 experience; at the Tenth Plenum, Ulbricht spoke of the workers' growing 'consciousness . . . that the police, in spite of their armoured cars, are not invincible'.[23] It was carried further in the context of the Party's technical preparations for insurrection. In the literature of the illegal military *Apparat*, whose leaders bore the responsibility for practical preparations for an eventual insurrection, discussion of the methods of self-defence against police terror was assimilated to the systematic propagation of the techniques of street-fighting.[24]

The tendency of all these discussions was to subvert the original purpose of the demonstration as a means for leading the masses into a functional confrontation with the system. Emphasis was more and more placed on mobility, technical preparation, and the effect on the 'enemy', rather than on mobilising large numbers. At the same time, the danger of an inappropriate and premature explosion of bloodletting was heightened as the Party slid into a futile arms race with the police. Both of these processes were implicit in the insurrectionary posture of the Party in the 'Third Period'. They were dictated by the logic of the terms in which the question of organising demonstrations was phrased: the more important the demonstration became in the Party's tactical arsenal, the more often it was used, the sharper and more frequent the repressive response, the stronger became the arguments for tight organisation and the precautionary distribution of firearms. But there is also an element here of despair of organising true mass-actions. When the Party leadership attempted to halt the slide into 'individual terror', it became clear that there existed very palpable limits to the policy of mass mobilisation, not only in the objective condition of the 'masses', but most obviously in the attitudes of a considerable section of the Communist membership. That attempt, and the ensuing debate, came in the context of the fight with the National Socialists, when the question of violence became sharply focussed as both leadership and rank and file were forced to work out the appropriate response to an immediate threat on ground not chosen by themselves, in a struggle which was so costly in human lives and so fraught with wider political implications as to place the Party in a very precarious position.

II

From the very beginning, 'terror' was identified as an integral part of National Socialist activity. When, in August 1929, the Communist press began to take notice of the Nazis as a force to be reckoned with, the occasion of the change was the series of SA attacks on workers and their institutions that accompanied the NSDAP Congress in Nürnberg.[25] This followed a spring and summer during which KPD organs, while predicting a major realignment and revitalisation on the right, had repeatedly denied any possibility of an independent political role for the Nazi Party.[26] It preceded an autumn crowded with violent signs of the NSDAP's resurgence; official sources confirmed Communist claims of a new wave of confrontations and direct attacks by the SA.[27] By the end of the summer, it had become clear that the 'white terror' predicted by Comintern analyses would wear a brown shirt. In August the Berlin District Leadership stated with some finality that the task of demoralising the proletariat had passed from the hands of the Social Fascists into those of the Nazis.[28] KPD observers, while they remained watchfully skeptical of the NSDAP's political significance, turned to analysing the terrorism of the SA as a key to its character.[29]

By the end of the year, a consensus had been reached. For the purpose of policy, the Nazi assault was henceforth treated as tactical, functional rather than instrumental – not as a military campaign aimed at the most efficient possible destruction of the workers' movement or the Communist Party, still less as the first stage of a seizure of power, but as a series of preliminary skirmishes designed 'to cripple their resistance to the capitalist offensive, to distract them from the central tasks of the class struggle'.[30] To the SA was assigned 'the same role as the cavalry in wartime', its purpose to undermine the workers' will to react decisively to a major assault on their rights by making 'a sort of customary law' out of terror.[31]

The terrorism of the SA could even be seen to have its uses for Communist agitation. On the one hand, it contributed to the general collapse of bourgeois society towards which the KPD itself was working. Like the tactical violence of the Communists, the fascists' 'policy of open violence batters the deeply-rooted prejudices of bourgeois legality'.[32] On the other, terror itself, in the con-text of the SA organisation, seemed to have a special attraction for the masses of uprooted young people for whose allegiance the parties were competing. Party writers and speakers pointedly contrasted the 'romantic fighting methods' of the Nazis – military parades, 'unsurpassable *Führer*-cult', uniforms, and, not least, 'bloody terror' – with the 'all too sober character' of KPD agitation among the young.[33]

In the light of all these considerations, a forcible response to Nazi violence – in KPD terminology, the '*wehrhafter Kampf*' – was desirable, its functions in KPD agitation mirroring the functions that fascist terror was seen to have. Passivity in the face of attack was repeatedly branded a moral and political weakness fraught with danger for the Party and the whole working class. In a speech to the Central Committee at the beginning of 1931, KPD Chairman Ernst Thälmann named 'shrinking back before murder-fascism' as 'the decisive deviation in this period'. He went on to enumerate the advantages of a vigorous response:

> There must no longer be a single act of terror by the Nazi murderers without the workers everywhere reacting immediately with the most aggressive physical [*wehrhaftem*] mass-struggle. What does this counter-action mean? It means: 1. a political security in the proletariat . . .; 2., that the Social Democratic workers gain confidence in us, because they see that we are there and fight back. 3. . . . that the fascist front is undermined and decimated. 4., that we strengthen, forge and steel our cadres together with the mass front for higher tasks in the revolution.[34]

In the context of the KPD's general line, the most valuable of these was the effect of the fighting on third parties, particularly on the Social Democrats. Within the SPD, dissatisfaction at the reluctance of party leaders to sanction violence was strong enough to provoke a crisis in the Berlin party in November 1930.[35] Such conflicts opened the way for an appeal to the Social Democratic rank and file on the basis of the visible preparedness of the Communists to fight the common enemy. More broadly, the *wehrhafter Kampf* was seen as yet another way to the heart of the 'labouring masses'. As such, it was entirely in keeping with the tactics of the 'Third Period', in which the KPD gave its approval to and in some sense took responsibility for the urge to action among ordinary people, hoping to broaden the movement under Communist influence, and to extend the Party's influence in propagating the movement. Thus Thälmann, somewhat optimistically: 'Today the outrage of the proletariat is already so great that one may almost say: If the KPD were to neglect this fight, the masses themselves would spontaneously begin to answer each new fascist murder with anti-fascist punitive expeditions.'[36]

Equally characteristic of the Third Period was the KPD's fear of its own populism, which constantly threatened to compromise the Party's theoretical position and hence its *raison d'être*. This too was voiced from time to time in the context of the *wehrhafter Kampf*, as in January 1932, when, at the beginning of a year of new initiatives in the wooing of Social Democrats, the Berlin District Leadership condemned

> tendencies towards exclusive concentration of the fighting energies of the workers against Nazi terror. . . . Such a false orientation means . . . concentrating the struggle on the neighbourhoods and the petty-bourgeois masses, where the Nazi influence is strongest. But the struggle . . . is above all a struggle for the factories.[37]

Ideally, of course, the *wehrhafter Kampf* should, like the other components of Communist agitation, provide a bridge between the factory and the street. Above all, if it was to fulfil the functions assigned to it, the fight against the Nazis had to be defensive in character and organised on a mass basis. Attacks by individuals or small groups were condemned as 'individual terror'. Against such terror the whole weight of Marxist-Leninist tradition was invoked; sabotage and provocation, systematic assault on the Party's enemies had their place only in an immediately revolutionary situation. This was put in the clearest possible terms in the Central Committee's Resolution of 10 November 1931. It described as 'a serious threat' the existence within the Party of 'left-sectarian states of mind, directed against the mass-work of the Party', characterised by 'the application of individual terror against the fascists . . . the carrying out of senseless isolated actions and isolated armed attacks . . . adventurist fooling-around with explosives'. Such tendencies, the Central Committee declared, had 'nothing in common with Communism':

> Without refraining for one moment from the use of all appropriate fighting methods, and without limiting in the slightest the Communist formula of organized proletarian mass-defence, the Central Committee declares the advocacy or toleration of terroristic ideology and practice in any form to be absolutely forbidden.

In explanation of this policy, the Central Committee adduced 'not . . . any considerations of bourgeois morality or "white moderation"', but 'compelling reasons of expediency': 'Individual terror' could only weaken and divide the proletariat, distract the Party from the task of organising the masses, and needlessly provoke repressive measures from the state.[38] A lead article in *Die Rote Fahne*, published at the same time as the resolution, closed with a text from Lenin: 'In the best circumstances, ["individual terror"] is appropriate as one of the methods in the decisive assault of the masses', and the conclusion: 'but at the present moment the preconditions for this assault do not exist'.[39]

The primary function of the *wehrhafter Kampf* was and remained the fulfilment of the first precondition for organising the revolution: the gathering-in of the majority of the working class. The alternative to 'individual terror' was thus the 'organised mass struggle', or what came to be called 'mass terror'. The fight against the National Socialists had to be so organised as to involve as many people as possible. Ideally, response to the incursions of the SA in working-class neighbourhoods should take the form of a gesture of community solidarity, beginning with the exercise of economic pressure through boycotts and rent-strikes, continuing through the organis-ation of collective self-defence on a united-front basis and the orchestration of mass demonstrations, and culminating in political strikes. Communist cadres should initiate and lead such actions, but the involvement of Party members alone, without mass participation, represented tactical failure.[40]

While the need to win over the working class and to steel it for revolutionary struggles dictated a policy of fighting back against the Nazis, the growing sense of a need to compete for popular support with the Nazis themselves dictated certain major modifications in the *wehrhafter Kampf*. The real threat posed by the NSDAP was a political one; this became clear to the Communists with the realisation that National Socialism was a true mass-movement, as one electoral sensation followed another. Although it was practically inconceivable, in the eyes of the Party, that Nazi propaganda could endanger the stability of the KPD's own constituency, the class-conscious proletariat, successes of the NSDAP represented a threat to Communist agitation because success in the 'Third Period' depended on the Party's ability to reach beyond the vanguard. The objective political function of the NSDAP in this context was to draw off the radicalised members of all social strata and to slow the process of revolutionary polarisation.[41] This analysis gained urgency as it became clear that proletarian elements were contributing to the Nazis' success. In particular, Communist observers began very early to see the SA as the focus of working-class recruitment to the NSDAP.[42]

Although the Communists recognised that violence itself could be a drawing point, and particularly among the type of youth that the SA could be seen to attract, the elements within the NSDAP and SA whom the KPD hoped to capture, or recapture, for the working-class movement were hardly to be won over by direct physical attacks on themselves. In order that potential allies among the Nazis' supporters should not be permanently alienated, Communist policy dictated that the physical fight be tempered with the methods of 'ideological struggle': argument and discussion and propagation of the Communist line among the National Socialists. An instructional circular of early 1931 tried to clarify the relationship between the ideological struggle and the properly organised, politically informed *wehrhafter Kampf*: rejection of 'individual terror' did not mean a complete turn away from violence,

> but what is needed is proletarian mass terror (in which a distinction must be made between the fascist cadres and the fellow-travellers), and this

has for its precondition under all circumstances a broad ideological and political propaganda and mass-agitation . . . a fight with the fists *alone* . . . can . . . once again become correct when the fascist movement is sufficiently eroded and undermined in the political struggle.[43]

This, then, was the KPD's answer to fascist terror: a self-defence movement vigorous enough to discourage attack and maintain the integrity of the Communist movement and so organised as to fulfil certain fundamental agitational functions, but not so aggressive or ideologically insensitive as to prejudice the chances for a broad front of the 'labouring masses'.

III

Although all of the elements of the KPD's line on 'individual' and 'mass terror' can be found in Party documents from 1929 on, in its totality it was only gradually articulated. Because the violence of the SA was both highly visible and highly disturbing to the Party's actual and potential constituency, the interest of the KPD lay in sustaining the call to action at its highest pitch, unless and until the threat to its existence arising from the consequences of that action appeared overwhelming. Moreover, the question of the *wehrhafter Kampf* was highly sensitive to shifts in the Party's general line, since the fight against National Socialism was secondary to the fight against Social Democracy in the context of the Party's long-range strategy and of its self-image, and the physical fight was, in turn, ancillary to both those struggles.

Five phases can be distinguished in the articulation of the KPD's policy on the *wehrhafter Kampf*, each corresponding to broader shifts in policy and/or perceived changes in the political atmosphere in Germany. The first phase, lasting from August 1929 to the spring of 1930, was characterised by the widespread use of the slogan, 'Schlagt die Faschisten, wo Ihr sie trefft!' ('Beat the Fascists wherever you meet them!')[44] The tendency of all KPD statements in this phase was to encourage a vigorous and violent response to the growing Nazi presence. The all-but-undifferentiated propaganda of violence reflected both genuine surprise at the sudden resurgence of the Nazi movement and uncertainty about how the movement might be expected to develop, as well as a lingering confidence that National Socialism, being an anomaly on the political scene, might yet be literally beaten back.[45]

The second phase began in mid-1930. By this time, Communist observers had already come to see National Socialism less as 'a military organisation of a few tens of thousands of mercenaries of German capital' and more as a mass movement.[46] There was another factor dictating a shift of line, however. In February 1930 the Comintern Executive met to reaffirm the importance of winning the confidence of the Social Democratic rank and file in preparation for the fast-approaching revolutionary crisis, and to condemn explicitly the tendency of certain KPD leaders to lump rank and file and functionaries together in their attacks on the SPD.[47] This had two consequences for the *wehrhafter Kampf*: first, new emphasis was placed on it as a political tool, an instrument of the united front campaign. At the same time, the language of the united front from below was reactivated and applied to the conflict with the Nazis. In May instructions were issued that 'Schlagt die Faschisten . . . !' should be withdrawn from circulation, as the elements of a new line were introduced into public speeches.[48] On 15 June, *Die Rote Fahne* published the first major Resolution on the Fight against Fascism. Dated 4 June, the Resolution described the 'schematic' application of the slogan 'Schlagt die Faschisten . . . !' as no longer appropriate and laid out systematically for the first time the prescriptions of mass action and the ideological fight. Where during the first phase the KPD had looked to broad political campaigns to cut into the NSDAP's electoral reserves, the Resolution emphasised immediate ideological confrontation with individual National Socialists, calling for new efforts in the 'work of differentiation and subversion within the camp of the labouring followers of the fascist organisations'.[49]

A third phase can be dated from the Reichstag elections of September 1930. In the light of the Nazis' electoral successes, the Party analysts anticipated a further sharpening of the political crisis, and by the end of the year their predictions seemed to be fulfilled. In October the cooperation of the SPD with the government parties in the Reichstag established the Social Democrats' policy of tolerating Brüning's presidential government, and thereby provided a basis for new attacks from the left. At the same time, while the KPD leaders predicted an 'unavoidable struggle', to follow within the coming year upon the deepening of the economic crisis and the sharpening of police terror, the Comintern's military-political expert reminded readers that 'the emphasis of this struggle does not yet lie on physical combat with the fascists'.[50] During these weeks, Thälmann referred for the first time directly to 'the propaganda, preparation and carrying-out of the political mass-strike against fascist attacks'.[51]

On 1 December Chancellor Brüning introduced the first of his blanket emergency decrees 'for the protection of economy and finances'. On the following day a lead article in *Die Rote Fahne* declared: 'The current policy of the government represents the fascist transformation of the country', and a *Polbüro* resolution a few days later confirmed that the Brüning government was officially regarded as the first stage of a fascist dictatorship.[52] This new situation, it was argued, placed the prospect of a People's Revolution (*Volksrevolution*) on the agenda; the Party must begin to propagate the idea of an uprising of the dispossessed of all classes. Of course, the revolutionary situation had still to be organised, as Thälmann was at pains to point out.[53] In concrete terms, this meant simultaneously an activation of the whole Party, including renewed calls for a vigorous *wehrhafter Kampf*, and more effective appeals to the Nazi rank and file. In the first three months of 1931 we find the first systematic explication of the value of the *wehrhafter Kampf* and, in mid-March – in the midst of an otherwise singularly bloodthirsty propaganda campaign arising out of the murder of Communist Deputy Henning in Hamburg – the first explicit public disavowal of individual terror.[54]

In April 1931, the Comintern Executive met again. It approved the general line of the KPD and held up the activity of the German Communists as a model for the other national parties. At the same time, though less publicly, the KPD was criticised for courting the Nazi rank and file at the expense of the working-class united front and for encouraging tendencies to terror and violence at any price. The Party's analysis of the German political situation was also corrected; Brüning's government was characterised as the government of 'the implementation of a fascist dictatorship', rather than as a fascist regime itself.[55] This, the Eleventh Plenum of the ECCI, may be said to mark the beginning of a fourth phase, although it was the approval rather than the censure they received in Moscow that was reflected in the activities of the German Communists during the following summer.

These continued to alternate between winning the Nazis over and beating them back, in the context of a general activation of the Party which increased the likelihood of violent clashes of all kinds. In Berlin between May and August, four police officers were shot to death and two severely wounded in clashes involving Communists. The most notorious of these cases, the murder of the police captains Anlauf and Lenk on the Bülow-Platz on 9 August, was carried out on direct orders from some member or members of the KPD leadership and welcomed in the locals for the intimidating effect it had had (or was expected to have) on the police force at large.[56] A wave of revolutionary expectation swept the membership, officially discouraged by the leadership but tacitly confirmed by the reissue of the Party's insurrectionary handbook, *Der Weg zum Sieg*. The Party began for the first time to make practical preparations for going underground. At the same time, fights between Communists and Nazis became more frequent and more deadly. In Berlin in September, the first attempt to put the policy of mass terror into practice, in the organisation of a united-front campaign around the presence of SA-taverns in working-class neighbourhoods, degenerated into a series of shooting raids.[57] By the autumn, the position of the Party was seriously compromised by the acts of its own membership.

As the year drew to a close, the KPD leadership found itself under threat from changes in the general political situation as well. The formation of the 'Harzburg Front' in October was seen to represent a major regrouping on the right, while the long-anticipated shift to a more openly repressive phase of 'presidential government' was signalled by the issuance of the third blanket emergency decree, the first to declare explicitly that the basic civil rights enumerated in Article 48 of the Weimar Constitution were 'inoperative'. Extraordinary police measures had already been sanctioned by the three decrees against 'political excesses' issued between March and August, but the fusion of the ministries of defence and the interior in the person of General Wilhelm Groener, confirmed on 9 October, augured worse to come.[58]

Again, however, the situation was not without promise. Under such obvious pressures from the right, Social Democrats were beginning to look around for ways to cooperation with the KPD.[59] At the level of street politics, too, evidence of increasing terror was accompanied by signs of hope. On 17 and 18 October the convention of the SA in Braunschweig led to violent clashes and attacks by the National Socialists on workers' quarters. The Communists took the concerted resistance of the Braunschweig workers and the protest strikes that followed as a sign of the feasibility of mass self-defence and a signal to begin a new campaign for the organisation of strikes and mass actions on a united-front basis.[60] Early in November word went out that fights with the SA were to be discouraged,[61] and on the 10th the Central Committee issued its Resolution condemning 'individual terror'.

In a series of statements in which they tried to impress upon readers and listeners that they meant what they said, the members of the Central Committee freely admitted that the legality of the Party was a primary consideration in the issuing of the resolution.[62] But there is no reason to doubt the genuineness of the other reasons adduced by the Party: the need, 'entirely independent of questions of legality or illegality', to concentrate all energies on the organising of mass actions, to foster 'clarity about the perspective of the Party' and end 'all adventurist ideas that the decisive battle is just around the corner', and to 'free the way' for 'ideological' agitation among rank-and-file Nazis.[63] Wilhelm Pieck's speech to the Central Committee Plenum the following February conveys something of the urgency that these tasks appeared to have at the time:

Without falling into a mood of panic, the Comrades of the Comintern are filled with grave concern . . . We have a situation in which fascism can come to power in Germany, without the Communist Party's being able even to begin a serious fight . . . in which it is possible for the Party to be beaten by the fascists without succeeding in leading the masses into the fight. Such a situation can break over the Party. What that would mean for the Comintern, anyone can count on his ten fingers.[64]

The November Resolution ushered in the fifth and final phase of the *wehrhafter Kampf.* During the year and a half that followed, the Communist leadership seized every opportunity to reaffirm its opposition to 'individual terror'. The line established by the resolution was maintained consistently in both internal and public discussion, and formed the basis for new initiatives in the united-front campaign. As late as May 1933 the Party was still explaining to anybody who was listening: 'Our motto, now as ever, is: Not through individual terror, but only through mass terror will we go forward in our fight . . . To follow the tactics of individual terror would mean the end of the Party.'[65]

IV

In fact, the November Resolution not only failed to suppress gang-style violence in practice, but also met with outspoken opposition from certain sections of the Communist movement. This could hardly have been unexpected. As early as May 1930, the Central Committee advised that the slogan 'Schlagt die Faschisten . . .!' be withdrawn and the elements of the new line introduced discreetly, in order to avoid provoking the membership. In Berlin, the publication of the full text of the resolution of 4 June 1930 met with strong disapproval from that quarter. People were even – it was said within the Party – refusing to turn out for public demonstrations because of their objections to the new line. At a meeting held on 23 June to mark the formation of a 'Fighting Committee of Red Berlin against Fascism', the main speaker felt compelled to explain that the disavowal of the old slogan 'should not be interpreted to mean that in future no hair of their heads should be touched, but you can just as easily take advantage of an appropriate opportunity'.[66]

In this light, the final assertion of Leninist orthodoxy in November 1931 appears as an act of extraordinary determination on the part of the Central Committee, and the leadership expressed both its anxieties and its sincerity in the extraordinary sanctions it invoked. The resolution declared: 'Anyone who breaks Party discipline is not worthy of the name of Communist' and threatened all such with 'the sharpest disciplinary measures up to and including expulsion from the Party'. The united-front initiatives of the following months were accompanied by vigorous attempts to enforce the resolution.

The most important of the KPD members to be disciplined in the name of the November Resolution was Heinz Neumann, Central Committee member and editor-in-chief of *Die Rote Fahne*. Neumann was removed from the Party Secretariat in May 1932. The following August, he was expelled from the Politbüro, and at the Twelfth ECCI Plenum in September he was publicly condemned for underestimating the Nazi threat and advocating 'individual terror'; as editor of *Die Rote Fahne* he was made responsible for all the tactical gaffes of the past two years.[67]

The extent to which the struggle within the KPD leadership was a conflict over substantive issues, in which Neumann maintained a distinct 'terroristic' line in opposition to Thälmann and the orthodoxy of the Comintern, remains a subject for debate. Neumann, who had earned a reputation as the Goebbels of the KPD, did personify the more sensational aspects of Communist propaganda, and there is evidence that in Berlin, at least, members of the Party rank and file were aware of the existence of a 'Neumann-tendency' and a 'Thälmann-tendency', and identified the former with extreme activism. Moreover, Neumann was an exceedingly popular figure within the Party, much in demand as a speaker. Whatever its value as a move in an internal power struggle, the disciplining of Heinz Neumann fulfilled the function of impressing on a fractious membership the seriousness of the Central Committee's intentions in the *wehrhafter Kampf*.[68]

Among other leading figures censured, removed from their posts, or brought publicly to recant in the course of the following year were Central Committee members Hermann Remmele and Leo Flieg, the Communist Youth (KJVD) leaders Alfred Hiller and Kurt Müller and the Organisational Leader for Berlin, Albert Kuntz. The extent of the resolution's organisational repercussions at the highest levels is suggested by Thälmann's remark, following the Twelfth ECCI Plenum: 'With the liquidation of the Neumann-Müller-Helmuth Remmele-etc. -Group the KJVD is delivering up a full dozen functionaries to the Party.'[69] Comparable measures were applied at the lower levels of the Party. Some members were expelled; others, probably the majority of Party-workers, preferred the lesser humiliation of carrying out a political about-face.[70]

Within a week of its formulation, the Party's decision was being expounded in the Berlin locals. Heinz Neumann himself was dispatched to speak to one of the series of Party-workers' conferences held around the city.[71] As the Party's instructors and local secretaries took up the task of advocating a policy which many of them had been directly contradicting the week before, voices of protest began to be raised. Members refused to take the new line seriously, speculating that it had been inspired by such diverse and trivial considerations as the Chinese war, fights among the Party's intellectuals, or the inability of the Communist Red Aid organisation to pay the costs of further prosecutions. Others saw the resolution as a genuine reflection of the Central Committee's views, but nevertheless balked at accepting it.[72] The meetings of some of the Berlin cells witnessed stormy debates and even fist-fights.[73] Even functionaries who had adopted the new line expressed doubts about its feasibility, 'in view of a situation in which the Nazis are openly arming for civil war',[74] while others returned within a few weeks to the open advocacy of terror. The organiser of the Neukölln local, still reeling from the effects of a misconceived gesture of mass terror which had left an SA tavern-keeper dying and twenty-two Communists in gaol, reportedly told his people: 'In my opinion, mass terror is a sheer impossibility.'[75] The Party's youth accused the leadership of cowardice and betrayal. A letter of protest from a KJVD group in the north of Berlin called the resolution 'a licence for the fascist terror-groups against the workers':

We, as revolutionary youth, have always seen the best defence against fascist attacks in retaliation. '*Not only mass-struggle — but also individual terror!*' We don't care for the idea that, if we are murdered by SA-men, a small part of the proletariat will carry out a half-hour's protest strike, while the SA laugh at having got off so lightly . . . We have come to the conclusion that the fear of illegality played an important role in the formulation of the resolution. To this we remark that we Young Communists carried out a large part of the illegal work of the Party at the time of the emergency decrees, without grousing or asking the consequences. But if illegality appears so frightful to the Central Committee, then we will of necessity stop all illegal work, so nobody can try to lay the blame on us in case of a ban on the Party. It's quite clear to us that that will cost us much in revolutionary energy and dynamism and we will lose our character as a revolutionary youth organization. Thanks to this resolution *the once purest flame of revolution will be reduced to a flickering oil-spot* — and we shall no doubt have to wait for the Soviet Germany that we all yearn for so passionately until it drops down as a gift from heaven.[76]

The KJVD remained a source of resistance to the resolution.[77]

The situation in the party's defence organisations was even more serious. There, many categorically refused to adhere to the Central Committee's ruling. Along with the familiar arguments, that the Party was neglecting the interests of its members and of the revolution, 'that the resolution . . . is a product of cowardice and calculated to make the cowardice of the Party leadership obligatory for the opposing party', leaders of the RFB (operating underground since the end of 1929) excused their recalcitrance with the view that the resolution was binding for the Party but not for its auxiliaries. Some left the defence formations; one RFB leader was quoted as saying: 'If the Party won't lead the fight against fascism, we'll just join the Nazis.' Others remained and carried on the fight with their accustomed violent methods, or maintained a truculent passivity in the face of all efforts to involve them in the Party's mass-actions.[78]

These groups continued to generate problems for the Party leadership for some time to come. At the end of 1931 it was reported that several Communist Reichstag deputies had proposed that the RFB be dissolved, in order to put an end to the embarrassing indiscipline of its members. The suggestion foundered on the threat of the RFB leadership not to tolerate the posting in the next election of any candidate who had supported it.[79]

The conflict was reactivated in the wake of the Twelfth ECCI Plenum, when it became still clearer that organisational rivalries were fuelling the policy debate. In Berlin in October and November 1932 there was a round of attacks from the Party on the RFB, which, Party faithfuls complained, was 'getting completely out of line'. They received a characteristic answer from one RFB leader in Pankow:

In the past months the Party had cut off the fighting organizations completely and characterised them as 'Neumann-Formations'. The members of the '*Einheit*' [illegal RFB] were put out, and it was correct that just at present they weren't directly following the instructions of the Party. He was doing his best to keep the members under control, but if they didn't turn out for demonstrations there was nothing he could do about it. After all, the fighting formations were not created to go on public promenades.[80]

The Party pointedly refused to call out the RFB to help in the Berlin transport strike at the beginning of November.[81] By the end of the month, a new wave of 'organisational measures', combined with the agitational successes of that strike and the Communist gains in the Reichstag elections the same week, had effectively silenced opposition.[82]

In the course of the campaign of enforcement, the Party theoreticians and publicists developed their own stereotype of the 'terrorists': They came out of the elements most recently recruited to the Party, the young and 'parts of the unemployed'. They were therefore unschooled, subject to theoretical 'confusion' and easily swayed by 'antique, hackneyed "arguments" such as "intimidating the enemy" and "stirring up the masses"'. They were also peculiarly liable to react emotionally to SA violence, with feelings of 'despair and revenge'. All of this became particularly volatile in combination with a false understanding of the revolutionary perspective – either expectations of an immediately impending insurrection or, paradoxically, a belief that the Nazis should be allowed, or helped, to seize power as the necessary prelude to a proletarian uprising, or some unformulated combination of the two.[83]

This is not the place to discuss in detail the character and motivations of individual KPD terrorists. In fact, the biographies of Communist street-fighters suggest that the relationship between occupation and employment, age, organisational experience and political attitudes was rather more complicated than the Party leadership recognised.[84] But it is clear even at this level of policy analysis that if they had conformed to this stereotype, their errors of theory and practice would have been to a large extent implicit in the Party line itself and the terms in which it was articulated.

More important, examination of the ways in which policy was formed and publicly presented has something to tell us about the relationship between *different* levels of perception, articulation and motivation in party politics. The language of theoretical analysis took on new meanings when the Party had to apply it in practice to the demands and pressures of the German situation, and the discussion of tactical violence in general became in turn more focussed, its practice more extreme. Similarly, the gap that opened up between leadership and rank and file over the question of individual terror in the fight against the SA reflected not so much simple differences of opinion as divergent understandings of what that fight was about. The membership, on the whole, was not so much thinking incorrect thoughts as speaking a different language from that of the leadership – a third language, as it were, distinct from both the official discourse of Party analysis and the rhetoric through which Communist propaganda aimed to move the masses to action. Although the words were often the same – 'terror', 'fascism', 'organising the revolution' – the meaning individual members drew from the prescriptions of the leadership, like the way they perceived the uses of violence, was determined by their position in the struggles to which the Party directed them. The events that presented themselves to the theoreticians as problems for analysis and to the tacticians as agitational opportunities appeared to the membership most immediately as real threats and tasks demanding practical solutions. There certainly existed within the illegal organisations of the KPD a hard core of old-guard revolutionaries, who saw their actions in the light of proto-revolutionary terror. But for many Communists, by late 1931 the *wehrhafter Kampf* had become the fight against a direct menace to life and limb in which the stakes were raised with every new confrontation. The problem was the SA, the solution, its removal with the simplest, most effective, and most familiar means available. When the rank and file called for 'individual terror', it was because its functions had long since gone beyond the terroristic.

These reflections may not only help us to understand the KPD as a party caught between its analysis and its constituency, but also serve to remind us that the study of 'collective violence' is a study of politics. As such it raises in particularly vivid terms the familiar problem of locating the levels of experience and interpretation at which action is actually generated, a problem too easily obscured by the focus on violent actions themselves as objects and organising principles of research. The German Communists never developed an analysis or an argument adequate to deal with the several different kinds of action and expectation that coexisted within the Party and fed into the phenomenon of 'individual terror'. Historians might reasonably be expected to do better, if we could be at least as self-conscious about what it is we are trying to accomplish.

NOTES

1. See 'The International Situation and the Tasks of the Communist International' (Theses of the Sixth Comintern Congress), as reprinted in J. Degras (ed.), *The Communist International 1919–1943. Documents. Volume II: 1923–1928* (London, 1960) p. 459ff.; *Protokoll. X. Plenum des Exekutivkomitees der Kommunistischen Internationale* (Hamburg/Berlin, 1929) p. 50.
2. *Protokoll. X. Plenum*, p. 73.
3. 'Aus der Rede des Genossen Gussew . . . ', *Kommunistische Internationale* [KI] XI (1930) H. 9/10, p. 539f; R. Gerber, 'Über die jüngste Entwicklung der Bedingungen des Kampfes gegen die faschistische Diktatur in Deutschland', KI XI (1930) H. 8, p. 426.
4. 'Aufruf für die Bildung der revolutionären Einheitsfront in den

Wirtschaftskämpfen', in *Dokumente und Materialien zur Geschichte der deutschen Arbeiterbewegung. Band VIII. Januar 1924–Oktober 1929* (Berlin, 1975) Nr. 260. Cf. Institut für Marxismus-Leninismus beim ZK der SED, *Geschichte der deutschen Arbeiterbewegung*, IV (Berlin, 1966) p. 178f.

5. See *inter alia: Waffen für den Klassenkampf: Beschlüsse des XII. Parteitages der KPD* (Berlin, 1929) p. 27.

6. M. Jablonski, 'Die dritte Periode und der politische Massenstreik', KI X (1929), H. 45, p. 1685; cf. W. Florin, 'Revolutionäre Streikstrategie', *Die Internationale* XIII (1930) p. 520ff.

7. Degras, p. 522.

8. ZK der KPD, *Zwei Jahre Arbeit und Kampf* (Berlin, 1929) p. 400; 'Abteilung IA, Berlin, den 2. Mai 1929', Geheimes Staatsarchiv preussischer Kulturbesitz (GehStA) 219/45, p. 8ff.; *Dokumente und Materialien*, Nr. 274; *Waffen*, p. 24. Cf. K. G. P. Schuster, *Der Rote Frontkämpferbund 1924–1929* (Düsseldorf, 1975) p. 212ff.

9. Jablonski, 'Die dritte Periode . . . ', p. 1686.

10. [A. Bewer], *Brennende Fragen der boschewistischen Partei* (Metz, 1930) p. 2.

11. Cf. H. Hannover and E. Hannover-Drück, *Politische Justiz 1918–1933* (Frankfurt/M., 1966).

12. [Bewer], 21.

13. Ibid., 2f.; Jablonski, 'Die dritte Periode . . . ', p. 1686; *Waffen*, p. 34; A. Martynow, 'Die Illegale und legale revolutionäre Arbeit der kommunistischen Parteien im Lichte der russischen Erfahrung von 1904 bis 1914', KI X (1929) H. 22/23, p. 1269ff.

14. Martynow, 'Die illegale und legale . . . ', p. 1276.

15. *Protokoll. X. Plenum*, p. 45f.

16. *Internationale Press-Korrespondenz* [*Inprekorr*] X, Nr 24 (11 March 1930) p. 574.

17. 'Die Lehren der Berliner Maikämpfe und die nächsten Aufgaben der KPD, Resolution der Sitzung der erweiterten Berlin-Brandenburger Bezirks-Leitung der KPD', *Inprekorr* IX, Nr 42 (14 May 1929).

18. 'Bemerkenswerte Parolen und Agitationsmethoden der KPD und ihrer Hilfs- und Nebenorganisationen', Staatsarchiv Bremen (StABr) 4,65/IV.13.i.

19. International Institute for Social History, Amsterdam (IISG), Nachlass Grzesinski, Nr 1393; M. Buber-Neumann, *Von Potsdam nach Moskau* (Stuttgart, 1958) p. 251.

20. 'Die Lehren der Berliner Maikämpfe . . . '

21. Hermann Remmele referred at the Twelfth ECCI Plenum in 1932 to the prevalence of 'the mistaken view that unarmed demonstrations can no longer be carried out at the present time': *Inprekorr* XIII, Nr 13 (27 January 1933) 453.

22. R. Schlesinger, *Erinnerungen aus einer Zeit grosser Kämpfe. Bd. I: Wohin geht Deutschland? 1901–1933* (MS 1964?), p. 577; 'Denkschrift über Kampfvorbereitung und Kampfgrundsätze radikaler Organisationen', Bundesarchiv Koblenz (BAK) R134/58, p. 37ff.

23. *Inprekorr* IX, Nr 78 (19 August 1929) p. 1800.

24. See e.g. 'A. Langer', *Der Weg zum Sieg. Die Kunst des bewaffneten Aufstandes* (n.p., [1931]), p. 48. Cf. *Waffen*, p. 25. On the provenance and authorship of *Der Weg zum Sieg*, see Erich Wollenberg's introduction to the reprint of (A. Neuberg), *Der bewaffnete Aufstand*, (originally published 1928, reprint Frankfurt/M, 1971).

25. See G. Jasper, 'Zur innerpolitischen Lage in Deutschland im Herbst 1929', *Vierteljahrshefte für Zeitgeschichte* VIII (1960) p. 286; H. T. Burden, *The Nuremberg Party Rallies 1923–1939* (London, 1967) p. 49ff.; D. Orlow, *The History of the Nazi Party* (London, 1969) p. 170; *Die Rote Fahne* [RF] 6 August 1929.

26. See *Zwei Jahre Arbeit*, p. 476ff.; *Protokoll der Verhandlungen des 12. Parteitags der Kommunistischen Partei Deutschlands* (Berlin, 1929) pp. 377f., 467f., 484, 498; *Waffen*, pp. 16f., 89. Cf. R. Renner, 'Das Ergebnis der Landtagswahlen in Sachsen', *Internationale* XII (1929) p. 344ff; 'Resolution des Zentralkomitees zu den Sachsenwahlen und ihren Lehren', ibid., p. 351f.

27. Jasper, 282ff. Cf. J. K. von Engelbrechten and H. Volz, *Wir wandern durch das nationalsozialistische Berlin* (München, 1937) pp. 169, 185f., 224; J. K. von Engelbrechten, *Eine braune Armee entsteht. Die Geschichte der Berlin-Brandenburger SA* (Berlin/München, 1937) pp. 102f.; RF 25 August, 12 September, 26 September 1929 (for evidence of the SA's resurgence in Berlin).

28. RF 29 August 1929.

29. Cf. F. Rück, 'Verstärkte Aktivität der deutschen Nationalsozialisten', *Inprekorr* IX, Nr 74 (13 August 1929); RF 6 August 1929; 'Rundschreiben Nr 32 [of the Central Committee]', 24 August 1929, BAK R45IV/24.

30. W. Hirsch, 'Faschismus und Hitlerpartei', *Internationale* XV (1932), 43.

31. 'Die Braune Pest', RF 28 May 1930.

32. *Inprekorr* XI, Nr 49 (29 May 1931) 1161.

33. F. Fischer, 'Das Eindringen des Faschismus in die Reihen der Jugend in Deutschland', KI XI (1930), H. 38/39, p. 2073; H. Rau, 'Die KPD vor der Eroberung der Mehrheit der Arbeiterklasse', KI XI (1930), H. 37, p. 1995; Thälmann touched on this theme even as he rebuked the Communist Youth for fostering tendencies towards individual terror: 'Die Bedeutung des XII. Plenums . . . für den KJVD . . . ', in E. Thälmann, *Reden und Aufsätze 1930–1933* (Cologne, 1975), I, p. 375. Cf. also H. Jäger, 'Die NSDAP: VI, Der Nationalsozialismus und die Jugend', *Inprekorr* XII, Nr 47 (7 June 1932) p. 1478.

34. E. Thälmann, 'Volksrevolution über Deutschland' (Pamphlet, Berlin, 1931) reprinted in *Reden und Aufsätze*, I, pp. 90, 105. Cf. RF 24 January 1931.

35. See O. Ihlau, *Die Roten Kämpfer* (Meisenheim/Glan, 1969) pp. 40, 48; K. Rohe, *Das Reichsbanner Schwarz-Rot-Gold* (Düsseldorf, 1966), pp. 321f.; RF 22 October, 22 and 23 November 1930; Thälmann, 'Volksrevolution', p. 96.

36. Thälmann, 'Volksrevolution', p. 107.

37. 'Entschliessung der Berliner Bezirksleitung über die theoretischen und praktischen Aufgaben der Parteiorganisation', RF 10 January 1932. Cf. W. Florin, 'Fragen unserer Einheitsfrontpolitik', *Internationale* XV (1932) p. 341.

38. RF 13 November 1931, reprinted in Institut für Marxismus-Leninismus beim ZK der SED, *Geschichte der deutschen Arbeiterbewegung*, IV (Berlin, 1966) Nr 82.

39. 'Für revolutionären Massenkampf gegen individuellen Terror', RF 13 November 1931.

40. See *inter alia*, the Polbüro Resolution of 4 June 1930 on the fight against fascism, RF 15 June 1930 (reprinted in part in *Geschichte der deutschen Arbeiterbewegung* IV, Nr 66); Instructions of the Bezirksleitung Zentrum (Berlin) to the Staffelleitungen of the Kampfbund gegen den Faschismus, 11 September 1931, reprinted in Mitteilungen des Landeskriminalpolizeiamts Berlin, Nr 20 (15 October 1931) StABr 4,65/11.H.4.a.32.

41. Thus in the light of the results of the September 1930 Reichstag elections, the Central Committee conceded that in the 'main struggle between KPD and National Socialists, [the struggle] for hegemony over the labouring, non-proletarian strata', the NSDAP was still ahead: Rundschreiben Nr 12 des ZK der KPD, 18 September 1930, StABr 4, 65/II.A.12.a. Cf. T. Neubauer, 'Die Arbeit unter den kleinbürgerlichen Mittelschichten', KI XII (1931) H. 10, p. 460; S. Erkner, 'Die NSDAP und die Klassen', *Internationale* XIV (1931) p. 331f. On the impenetrability of the KPD's 'Kerntruppe', see RF 17 November 1931; W. H. 'Zur politischen Lage in Deutschland', *Inprekorr* XI, Nr 106 (6 November 1931) p. 2358; Hirsch, 'Faschismus und Hitlerpartei', p. 41.

42. See e.g. RF 27 May and 7 June 1930, 19 May 1932; H. Eberlein, 'Die Faschisten und die Betriebsrätewahlen', KI XII (1931) H. 31/32, p. 1426; *Inprekorr* XIII, Nr 17 (7 February 1933) 570. Cf. Hirsch, 'Faschismus und Hitlerpartei', p. 40; H. Jäger, 'Die NSDAP: V, Die soziale Zusammensetzung', *Inprekorr* XII, Nr 6 (3 June 1932) p. 1431.

43. 'Lehrbrief Nr 2, Faschismus und Sozialfaschismus', BAK R134/62, p. 95f.

44. The slogan had first been used in 1924, following the clash between Communists and Stahlhelm demonstrators in Halle which had provided the occasion for the founding of the RFB. Heinz Neumann resurrected it for use in the *wehrhafter Kampf*. It first reappeared in RF on 28 August 1929, and was the theme of a lead article on 5 November 1929: RF 15 May 1924, 28 August, 26 September, 19 October, 5 November, 31 December 1929. Cf. M. Buber-Neumann, *Kriegsschauplätze der Weltrevolution* (Stuttgart, 1967) pp. 269f.

45. See e.g. A. Norden, 'Das Bombenattentat auf den Reichstag', *Inprekorr* IX, Nr 84 (3 September 1929), for whom the fight against fascism is equivalent to giving 'bloody heads'; Gerber, 'Über die jüngste Entwicklung . . . ', p. 432f. The line also reflected the programmatic statements of Comintern analysts that new emphasis had to be placed on 'immediate, physical self-defence' as such: L. Alfred, 'Zur Frage des proletarischen Selbstschutzes', KI X (1929) H. 44, p. 1642. Cf. Buber-Neumann, *Von Potsdam nach Moskau*, p. 277f.

46. S. Heymann, 'Massenkampf gegen den Faschismus', *Internationale* XIII (1930) p. 536; R. Renner, 'Die Sachsenwahlen und ihre Lehren', *Internationale* XIII (1930) p. 404ff.

47. 'Über die Aufgaben der KPD. Resolution des ZK der KPD, bestätigt vom Erweiterten Präsidium des EKKI', *Inprekorr* X, Nr 36 (25 April 1930) p. 824f; RF 25 March 1930.

48. Mitteilungen des LKPA Berlin, Nr 12 (15 June 1930) StABr 4,65/IV.13.i.

49. Polbüro Resolution of 4 June 1930 (see n. 40).

50. 'Verschärfung der wirtschaftlichen und politischen Krise', *Internationale* XIII (1930) 673ff.; Mitteilungen des LKPA Berlin, Nr 19 (1 October 1930) StABr 4, 65/II.A.12.a; 'Das Ergebnis der Reichstagswahlen und die Aufgaben der Partei (Resolution des Polbüros des ZK)', StABr 4,65/II.A.12.a; L. Alfred, 'Für Klarheit in der Frage des proletarischen Selbstschutzes', KI XI (1930) H. 37, p. 2009.

51. E. Thälmann, 'Die KPD nach den Reichstagswahlen', in *Reden und Aufsätze*, I, p. 34.

52. Cf. E. Thälmann, 'Die KPD im Vormarsch', in *Reden und Aufsätze*, I, p. 24ff.; 'Wir führen das Volk zum Sieg über die faschistische Diktatur', ibid., p. 40ff.

53. Thälmann, 'Volksrevolution', pp. 79, 86, 115.

54. 'Mord über Deutschland: Erklärung des ZK der KPD . . . ', RF 18 March 1931.

55. E. Thälmann, 'Einige Fehler in unserer theoretischen und praktischen Arbeit und der Weg zu ihrer Überwindung' (December 1931) in *Reden und Aufsätze*, I, p. 295ff; T. Weingartner, *Stalin und der Aufstieg Hitlers* (Berlin, 1970) pp. 53ff. Cf. D. S. Manuilski, *Die kommunistischen Parteien und die Krise des Kapitalismus* (Hamburg; 1931) pp. 114ff. and *passim; Inprekorr* XI, Nr 38 (24 April 1931), p. 946ff., Nr 49 (29 May 1931) p. 48ff.

56. Cf. Landesarchiv Berlin 58/52, Sonderheft (fragments of the indictment in the Bülow-Platz killings); *Geschichte der deutschen Arbeiterbewegung* IV, 308; H. Wehner, *1933–45. Untergrundnotizen. Von KP zur SPD* (n.p., n.d. [pirated edition of hectograph manuscript of 1946]) p. 6; Buber-Neumann, *Kriegsschauplätze*, p. 311ff. and *Von Potsdam nach Moskau*, p. 257ff., for varying accounts of why and by whom the killings were ordered. For membership reactions: IISG, Nachlass Grzesinski, Nr 1385, 1386, 1391, 1677, 1678.

57. Reichsministerium des Inneren [RMI], IA 2130/15.7, Berlin 25.6.31., Geheim!;

Nachrichtensammelstelle im RMI, IAN 2160/1.10.a, Berlin 1.10.31; Vortrag über die kommunistische Bewegung, gehalten auf der Nachrichtenkonferenz vom 14.12.1931, von RR W. von Lengriesser: all StABr 4,65/II.A.12.a. Cf. Weingartner, 95. In June, the leadership of the Party's defence groups remarked reprovingly, 'Our comrades often talk about the imminent revolution; you often hear: It's starting this autumn!' and at the end of the year members of the illegal RFB were told that they were approaching 'great struggles': 'Only a short time remains to us until then': Kampfbund gegen den Faschismus, Bezirksleitung Ruhrgebiet, 9.6.31, StABr 4, 65/II.H.4.a.32; 'Rundschrieben Nr 1 zur politischen Lage und den nächsten Aufgaben', StABr 4, 65/VI.1000.44.d.1. On this period, see also E. Rosenhaft, *Between 'Individual Terror' and 'Mass Terror': The German Communists and 'Paramilitary' Violence 1929–1933* (Ph.D. Dissertation, University of Cambridge, 1979) Chapter 5.

58. *Reichsgesetzblatt*, 1931, I, Nr 67; W. H. 'Zur politischen Lage in Deutschland', p. 2357ff.; Thälmann, 'Einige Fehler', p. 298. Cf. *Geschichte der deutschen Arbeiterbewegung* IV, p. 304ff.

59. The Social Democratic leader Breitscheid responded to the KPD's anti-terror resolution of November 1931 with the declaration that a serious barrier between the two parties had been removed. See *Schulthess' Geschichtskalender* (1931) p. 216; Rohe, p. 392f.; RF 17 and 20 November 1931; P. Langner, 'Ein Betrugsmanöver Breitscheids', *Inprekorr* XI, Nr 109 (17 November 1931) p. 2473.

60. RF 20, 21, 23 October 1931; Thälmann, 'Einige Fehler', p. 320. Cf. Ministerialrat Dr. Guyet, 'Die kommunistischen Bestrebungen auf Bildung von Einheitsorganisationen mit Sozialdemokraten' (Report to Nachrichtenkonferenz 14.12.31) StABr 4,65/II.A.12.a.

61. IISG, Nachlass Grzesinski, Nr 1386.

62. Cf. W. Insarow, 'Schlagt die Waffe der Provokation aus den Händen der Bourgeoisie', *Inprekorr* XI, Nr 118 (18 December 1931). The police were quick to label the Resolution a politically-motivated 'declaration of legality', comparable to previous cases where the Party had re-emphasised its rejection of terror at times when the safety of its organisations was threatened. Aspects of the context in which the Resolution was issued bear this out: on 25 September, Ulbricht had declared before the Reichsgerichtshof that the only uprising on the KPD's agenda was 'the uprising of SPD workers . . . against their traitorous leaders', and the issuance of the Resolution anticipated by just a week a conference at which the interior ministers of the Länder were scheduled to discuss the means of suppressing political violence: Nachrichtensammelstelle im RMI, IAN 2160 d.6/a/27.11; Mitteilungen des LKPA Berlin, Nr 23 (1 December 1931) both StABr 4,65/II.A.12.b.18; W. Ulbricht, *Zur Geschichte der deutschen Arbeiterbewegung* I (Berlin, 1953) pp. 548f.; 'Niederschrift über die Konferenz der Innenminister der Länder . . . ' BAK R43I/2701a, 258–60. For insiders' views, cf. G. Regler, *Das Ohr des Malchus* (Köln/Berlin, 1958) p. 185; M. Reese, *Lebenserinnerungen* (MS 1953) p. 16.

63. 'Rundschreiben des ZK der KPD, 8.12.31', Landeshauptarchiv Koblenz 403/16776, pp. 681–733. Cf. Thälmann, 'Einige Fehler', p. 315ff.; E. Thälmann, 'Der revolutionäre Ausweg und die KPD' in *Reden und Aufsätze*, I, p. 447f., and the police report of the speech to the Central Committee on which this text was based: Mitteilungen des LKPA Berlin, Nr 8 (15 April 1932) StABr 4,65/IV.13.i.

64. K. Wrobel, 'Zum Kampf Wilhelm Piecks gegen imperialistischen Terror und Faschismus 1929–1932', *Zeitschrift für Geschichtswissenschaft* XXIII (1975) p. 1437. Cf. *Die Brüsseler Konferenz der KPD* (Frankfurt/M, 1975) p. 81; *Geschichte der deutschen Arbeiterbewegung* IV, p. 325f.

65. 'An alle Unterbezirks – und Bezirksleitungen des Kampfbundes gegen den Faschismus', StABr 4,65/II.H.4.a.32.
66. Mitteilungen des LKPA Berlin, Nr 13 (1 July 1930) StABr 4,65/II.A.12.a.
67. Weingartner, pp. 59ff., 101ff.; H. Weber, *Die Wandlung des deutschen Kommunismus* (Frankfurt/M, 1969) II, p. 233ff.; *Geschichte der deutschen Arbeiterbewegung. Biographisches Lexikon* (Berlin, 1970) pp. 345f.; E. Thälmann, 'Schlusswort auf dem XII. Plenum des EKKI', in *Reden und Aufsätze*, II, p. 271ff.; Resolution der Parteikonferenz der KPD über das XII. Plenum des EKKI und die Aufgaben der KPD, in *Reden und Aufsätze*, II, p. 462f.; *Inprekorr* XIII, Nr 11 (26 January 1933) p. 373.
68. For varying views on Neumann's tactical position, which generally concur on his 'adventurist' and 'irresponsible' attitudes, see Buber-Neumann, *Von Potsdam nach Moskau*, pp. 258, 288f.; Schlesinger, pp. 460, 580ff.; Reese, p. 16ff.; G. Schwarz, *Völker, höret die Zentrale* (Berlin, [1933]) p. 215; P. Merker, *Deutschland, Sein oder Nichtsein? Bd. I: Von Weimar zu Hitler* (Mexico City, 1944) p. 256; Wehner, p. 10f.
Cf also Weingartner, 230ff. On rank-and-file attitudes and Neumann's popularity: IISG, Nachlass Grzesinski, Nr 1678; BAK R45IV/5 and 27.
69. Cf. 'IAdII¹, 15.11.32', BAK R58/390, p. 182f.; *Inprekorr* XII, Nr 99 (22 November 1932) p. 3184; Thälmann, 'Die Bedeutung des XII. Plenums . . . für den KJVD', p. 384ff, esp. 390. Cf. also Weber, II, pp. 59, 117, 121, 200, 237, 257, 348; *Geschichte der deutschen Arbeiterbewegung. Biographisches Lexikon*, pp. 133, 378.
70. *Inprekorr* XIII, Nr 17 (7 February 1933) p. 570; 'IAdII¹, Berlin den 26.11.31', (Report of meeting of UBL Nordost), GehStA 219/20, p. 154f.; IISG, Nachlass Grzesinski, Nr 1390.
71. IISG, Nachlass Grzesinski, Nr 1388, 1388a, 1389; cf. RF 17 and 18 November 1931.
72. IISG, Nachlass Grzesinski, Nr 1389; Thälmann, 'Der revolutionäre Ausweg', p. 433; 'Berlin, den 12.12.31' (Report on meeting of UB Nordwest), GehStA 219/20, p. 197.
73. IISG, Nachlass Grzesinski, Nr 1390.
74. 'IAdII¹' (n. 70), 155; IISG, Nachlass Grzesinski, Nr 1392.
75. IISG, Nachlass Grzesinski, Nr 1391.
76. KJVD Gruppe Nordkap (UB Nord) to Central Committee, 19 November 1931, BAK R45IV/27.
77. IISG, Nachlass Grzesinski, Nr 1388a; Thälmann, 'Die Bedeutung des XII. Plenums . . . für den KJVD', p. 375; A. Hiller, 'Der KJVD im Kampf um die Gewinnung der Mehrheit der Arbeiterjugend', *Internationale* XV (1932) p. 83; E. Paffrath, 'Das ist die Rote Jungfront, die sich nicht verbieten lässt . . . ', *Militärgeschichte* XI (1972) p. 80ff.
78. IISG, Nachlass Grzesinski, Nr 1389, 1390, 1391; Regler, p. 185; 'Die Lage in der KPD', StABr 4, 65/II.A.12.a; 'IAdII¹, 24.12.31' (Report on UBL Conference, Nordost), BAK R58/390, p. 44.
79. Mitteilungen des LKPA Berlin, Nr 1 (1 January 1932) StABr 4, 65/VI.1000.44.d; cf. IISG, Nachlass Grzesinski, Nr 1391; Schuster, p. 234f.
80. 'IAdII¹, 28.11.32', GehStA 219/33, p. 76; cf. 'IAdII¹, 31.10.32', BAK R58/390, p. 146; 'IAdII¹, 15.11.32' (n. 69); 'Bericht über den am 14.11.32 . . . stattgefundenen UB Parteitag des UB Prenzlauer Berg', GehStA 219/9, p. 132ff; Wehner, p. 8.
81. 'IAdII¹, 15.11.32' (n. 69).
82. 'IAdII¹, 18.11.32', BAK R58/390, p. 194; 'Bericht einer Vertrauensperson . . . '

BAK R58/390, 295ff.; *Inprekorr* XII, Nr 98 (22 November 1932) p. 3158; 'Aus der Resolution des Bezirksparteitages der KPD Berlin . . . ' in H. Karl and E. Kücklich (eds), *Die Antifaschistische Aktion* (Berlin, 1965) Nr 87.

83. See e.g. RF 13 November 1931, 27 March 1932; Hiller, 'Der KJVD im Kampf', p. 83; 'Nach drei Wahlen', *Internationale* XV (1932) p. 222; D. S. Manuilski, *Die kommunistischen Parteien und die Krise des Kapitalismus* (Hamburg/Berlin, 1931) p. 87; *Inprekorr* XIII, Nr 13 (27 January 1933), p. 453; Thälmann, 'Einige Fehler', p. 297; E. Thälmann, 'Die neue Etappe in der Bolschewisierung der KPD', in *Reden und Aufsätze*, II, p. 229; Thälmann, 'Schlusswort', p. 252.

84. See Rosenhaft, *Between 'Individual Terror' and 'Mass Terror'*, Chapters 6 and 7.

21 Approaches to Political Violence: the Stormtroopers, 1925–33

Peter H. Merkl

The current wave of literature on political violence and terror makes it advisable to attempt at least a preliminary mapping out of approaches and perspectives in the study of political violence[1] before we plunge into the historical subject at hand. There appear to be at least five orientations, not to mention mixtures of them, that make up the universe of current and recent studies of political violence:

First of all, there is a large category of moralising literature; much but not all of it journalistic. Its general thrust goes toward showing what horrible things certain people have been doing to other human beings and to society. Frequently this literature of popular books and articles[2] also suggests how to counteract terror and violence or, at least, how to remove its social causes and reestablish a sense of equity and justice.[3] A subspecies of this moralising literature are works that call upon the 'oppressed' – by whatever definition, nationality, religion, social class – to work up the righteous anger to challenge and overthrow their oppressors, most likely by political violence of some sort.[4]

A second school uses the violent act itself, individual or collective, as the unit of analysis. Much of the quantitative analysis of wars and international conflicts fits this description and there have also been attempts to link international with internal conflicts.[5] A prominent recent example of this quantitative approach to domestic political violence can be found in the research of Charles, Louise, and Richard Tilly on the changing nature of violence in the century from 1830 to 1930. The Tillys counted the annual incidence of violent collective actions of a certain severity, that is involving specified numbers of participants and casualties, in France, Germany, and Italy and developed a theory of collective violence on this basis, namely that modernisation appeared to be accompanied by fundamental changes in the extent, duration, and intensity of domestic violent conflicts.[6] Other recent examples have tabulated different kinds of revolutionary violence and ranked various nations accordingly.[7] At an individual or incident level, the work of

367

Gerhard Botz on political violence in Austria, 1918–34, is exemplary in its emphasis on the violent act, frequently measured by the number of dead and seriously injured. Less detailed but similar accounts have been made of assassinations and of terrorist actions of various sorts.[8]

The third and perhaps most popular school has been oriented toward the study of the settings of political violence both in terms of its causes and its effects. A huge historical literature has explored the genesis of political violence and revolution in particular settings. Historically oriented socio- logists and political scientists have sought to draw generalised conclusions from many cases, beginning with Aristotle's *Politics*. The causes suggested have been such conditions as inequality, relative deprivation or arrested economic growth, nationalism or separatism, social tensions or class struggle, the perceived impossibility of reform, the delegitimisation of regimes, or a sense of *anomie*. Frequently, such a general cause had already been enshrined in a national or universal revolutionary ideology.[9] Interestingly, there has been very little comparative analysis of the effects of political violence, aside from single-case studies.[10] Such fascinating questions as whether political violence polarises a system, mobilises target populations, or delegitimises regimes, or just generates more violence still await authoritative generalisation.

There is, to say the least, great plausibility to political violence playing an ongoing role in the process of unfolding revolutions, particularly in escalating conflict and heightening revolutionary consciousness from one stage to the next. The effect of violence on the violent and those they represent, as well as on their victims and target populations, and the linkage between violent individuals and revolutionary organisations that socialise them and supply them with ideological justifications again is an underresearched subject,[11] at least in a comparative manner. All of these organisation- and process- oriented questions could form a body of literature on political violence.

The fifth category of political violence literature, finally, focusses on the violent individuals and how they became violent. There has always been some speculation as to the motives that might be driving individuals into violent behavior,[12] but relatively little empirical theorising and even less empirical research. Most of the empirical theory has been derived from psychology which has traditionally handled theories of individual aggression, frustration- aggression, value conflict, and even alienation, not to mention childhood maladjustments that might lead to aggressiveness.[13] One of the more notable recent interpretations has been that of Frederick J. Hacker who places particular emphasis on the relationship of the terrorist 'crusader' to an organisational setting, a sense of belonging, anticipated repression, and a yearning for communal identity.[14] Hacker's theorising covers the same methodological ground – psychological and social-psychological – as this writer's work on the early Nazis. There are also illuminating glimpses of the terrorist as an artist and solid analyses of the socio-economic backgrounds of politically violent persons.[15] Finally, the study of violent individuals can also focus on establishment violence of police or military which should be a part of military or law enforcement sociology.

I

To this quintuple division of current approaches we need to add a second list of categories of political violence in order to locate our subject properly:

It is a truism that there can be and have been many generically different kinds of political violence. The brief period of the Weimar Republic alone saw at least four basically different varieties of it, of which only a small part is accounted for by the rising NSDAP:

(1)   There were the civil-war-like clashes of opposing Independent Socialist (USPD) and other leftwing revolutionary armies and of the Freecorps and *Einwohnerwehren* in the years 1918–21, even though there never occurred a real revolution.

(2)   Individual terrorists and assassins such as those of Organisation Consul (OC) or the *Feme* on the right, and some romantic bands of outlaws on the left.

(3)   Violent nationalistic groups active in border and anti-separatist struggles in the East and under the French occupation, especially in the occupied Rhineland 1923/24, including bombing and sabotage squads.

(4)   Large paramilitary organizations whose street violence was generally ancillary to their propaganda function, even though it may sometimes have appeared to be a purpose in itself. This group includes most of the marching organisations such as the *Stahlhelm* veterans, the Communist Red Front, *Reichsbanner* republican guard, the Young German Order (*Jungdo*) and political youth organisations, and the Nazi stormtroopers (SA) who also drew many of their recruits from all of these categories and organisations.[16]

This paper will only deal with stormtrooper violence.

There was, of course, also a noticeable range from the notorious street and meeting-hall brawlers of the Red Front and the SA to the less frequent involvement of *Stahlhelm* and *Jungdo* in street violence. The official account of violent disruptions of political assemblies in the state of Prussia in 1930, for example, clearly shows that most disruptions were caused by Communists or stormtroopers. All casualty lists of the streetfighting of the years 1929–33 likewise were dominated almost exclusively by Communist and stormtrooper casualties.[17] Furthermore, the nature of the political violence of some organisations changed considerably over the fourteen short years of the Weimar Republic under the influence of various situations, restraints, and opportunities. In this fashion, for example, the extreme left went through several phases of organization for 'workers' defence' and quasi-military revolutionary violence before it arrived at the phase described under (4). The

Young German Order grew from an active Freecorps into a rather nonviolent if demonstrative youth organisation. And important parts of *Stahlhelm* likewise came from varyingly violent backgrounds to their non-violent posture of the pre-depression years, after which, in 1929/33, they struck a rather militant, but more political pose.

The post-1924 stormtroopers, by comparison, maintained greater continuity in their dedication to ostentatious violence, although even they had undergone a certain evolution in their views toward violence in the early 1920s. At first they had understood their function as that of a guard at rallies and demonstrations of their party and its speakers. The SA was born quite naturally with the first meeting-hall brawl at the Munich *Hofbräuhaus* on 24 February 1920, when the speaker, Adolf Hitler, found that his audience had been packed with leftwing opponents. As he reported, there was heckling, violent clashes, and finally, 'a handful of war comrades and other adherents' fought off the disrupters.[18] According to one account, armed veterans and bullies attacked the interlopers with sticks, rubber truncheons, horse whips, and pistol shots.

With their growing numbers and established uniforms, the SA took on more weight of its own as an instrument of massive demonstrations beginning with a 1922 rally protesting the Law for the Protection of the Republic. This trend finally culminated in the monster rallies and such gigantic SA demonstrations as the Braunschweig rally of 1931 when 100,000 stormtroopers were assembled for the sole purpose of marching them all day long in formation past Adolf Hitler.[19]

The specifically stormtrooper style of violence was also born in 1922 when the Munich SA, probably following the example of the Italian *squadristi*, began to make forays into Bavarian towns like Coburg and Landshut for propagandistic purposes and to 'break the red terror' there. In the case of Coburg, Hitler had been invited to a German Day, a patriotic observance of various nationalistic groups, and he brought with him eight hundreds of uninvited stormtroopers with flags and a band on a special train. The SA proceeded to 'conquer the town' from its socialist 'masters of the streets'. The characteristic procedure however, was hardly one of conquest or even temporary control, nor did it go to the length of *squadristi* assaults on socialist and trade-union buildings or leaders. Instead, the stormtroopers usually staged a march or two in uniformed formation through town and put in a similar appearance at a rally in a prominent place. Their arrival and presence in these socialist-dominated towns was evidently meant more as a 'showing of the flag' in a potentially hostile environment than as a confrontation between two paramilitary formations. Violent encounters usually ensued only as the marching stormtroopers would draw hecklers or whenever individual stormtroopers in taverns or on the streets would get into brawls with hostile individuals or small groups. What the stormtroopers regarded as a 'victory' was usually merely the silencing or ejecting of small numbers of vocal opponents in a small space, such as a meeting-hall, a tavern, or a piece of a street or square that had become a battleground. It is not important here to determine which side may have instigated or started the physical violence or whether the stormtroopers were more brutal than their opponents,[20] in other words, the questions that seem to preoccupy most people. What matters is the small scale and episodic nature of political violence in these early raids whose main function was clearly propagandistic.

II

There was an obvious gap between what Hitler wanted the SA to be in the early years and what Captain Roehm and his army friends made of it. Hitler's conception appears to have been as a partisan instrument suitable for propaganda and for terror, for spreading the faith as well as for 'the conquest of the streets'. The propaganda function implied strong ideological convictions, a proselytising fervor, a knowledge of effective propaganda techniques, and the sheer impact of uniformed marchers of the faith on the public. This crusade also required the determined use of force to protect the party's speakers and meetings, to disrupt rival speakers and meetings, and on occasion to engage in full-scale battles with paramilitary organisations of the left. Members of the SA were supposed to be the most active party members but not really separate as an autonomous, military organisation. With their windbreaks, ski-style caps, swastika armbands, and canes, the stormtroopers soon proceeded to show their mettle as Hitler's political soldiers and fighters of the faith.

But the circumstances and the heavy-handed sponsorship of the army instead made the SA into a *Reichswehr* reserve trained by the *Reichswehr*, organised with artillery and even cavalry units along *Reichswehr* lines, and tied to other quasi-military organisations in the *Kampfbund*. Early in 1923, Hermann Goering was called in to take command away from the army officers and a special bodyguard for Hitler was formed which came from different sources than the *Reichswehr* elements, chiefly workers and craftsmen. But it was too late. Hitler was unable to disentangle himself sufficiently from the military-nationalist junta in Bavaria during that turbulent year to make more than a token effort to seize power by himself: the abortive beerhall putsch.[21]

When the time came to reestablish the stormtrooper organisation, following an interval of prison and abortive reorganisation of the SA (*Frontbann*) by Roehm, Hitler had his opportunity to ensure that the SA would be his and his alone. He obviously wanted to avoid both the pre-1924 model of an autonomous quasimilitary *Wehrverband* or army reserve and a clandestine organisation of political terrorists. As he wrote in a letter to Roehm's replacement, Pfeffer von Salomon in 1926:[22]

What we need are not a hundred or two hundred daring conspirators but hundreds and hundreds of thousands of fanatical fighters for our faith . . . to work with gigantic mass demonstrations . . . conquering the streets. We have to make Marxism understand that National Socialism is going to be the next master of the streets, just as it is going to be the master of the German state some day.

His conception of the function of the SA had reverted back to the partisan propaganda and protection squads of the years before the military element won the upper hand in the SA, and also before autonomous, ill-considered actions of the SA were capable of getting him and the whole party outlawed again. His Basic Guidelines for the Reestablishment of the NSDAP of February 26 1925 specifically barred 'armed or quasimilitary formations' or conspiratorial groups such as *Organisation Consul, Wiking* (Ehrhardt), or the Freecorps and veterans groups from which the new SA could expect to draw many recruits.

Every stormtrooper would have to join the NSDAP and could not belong to any rival organisation at the same time. The SA was to be tightly controlled by the party leadership, but not on a local or regional level. As organised by the former Freecorps leader and Westphalian Nazi *Gauleiter* Captain Franz Pfeffer von Salomon in 1926, it became a nationwide, uniformly organised partisan army whose lower units were subordinated exclusively to the central leadership of SA and party. Pfeffer also received command over the Hitler Youth (HJ), the SS, and the Nazi student organisation. He created a rather flexible organisation which combined tactical independence with central control and encouraged the local leaders to recruit as many further members as possible. His organisational hierarchy of *Schar, Trupp, Sturm, Standarte*, and *Gausturm* turned out to be an excellent vehicle for the rapid expansion of the SA in the years 1930/33. By this time also, the brown shirts had been introduced, according to one source, from leftover uniform shirts of the East African colonial troops. *Sturm* numbers, buttons, and insignia were given these 'political soldiers' and they were instructed to appear only in closed formation. With every annual NSDAP rally, furthermore, the larger units were given quasi-regimental flags (*Standarten*) which were to be displayed on special occasions.

What was the purpose of this partisan army of 'political soldiers', the overthrow of the government? Ostensibly, it was the 'conquest of the streets' from the moderate and extreme left. During the half century of the struggle of the labor movement in Germany, street demonstrations in working-class areas had become a symbol of strength and dignity, a reinforcement of working-class solidarity as well as of defiance of outside authority. With the 'revolution' of 1918 and the establishment of the republic, this 'control of the streets' took on even greater symbolic significance for the organised working classes. In the hands of Socialist or Communist militants, the control of the streets on occasion implied also political violence, disruption of the meetings of opponents, or 'individual terror', that is, acts of terrorism by and against individuals. To the angry First World War veteran, Freecorps member, *Stahlhelmer*, or *Einwohnerwehr* vigilante, instances where the revolutionary host had actually taken control called for well-organised military action to regain control by force. To Hitler and the stormtroopers on the other hand, the object was a symbolic 'struggle against Marxism', not a struggle for control over specific strongpoints. He simply pretended that the 'Marxists' had taken over Germany. By grappling with the Communists and, less often, the *Reichsbanner*, the SA and SS could achieve tremendous propaganda victories in the eyes of the German bourgeoisie and the conservative right and, at the same time, attract an endless stream of new recruits for the movement: 'The first task of propaganda', according to Hitler's *Mein Kampf*, 'is the recruitment of bodies for the future organisation; the first task of organisation is to get people to carry on the propaganda'. But then he went on to add, 'The second task of propaganda is the undermining of the status quo and its infiltration with a new doctrine, while the second task of organisation must be the struggle for power in order to realise the doctrine completely'.

The symbolic conquest of the streets had already been rehearsed in the first years of the movement, at the first SA demonstration at a patriotic rally in Munich in 1922, and again in Coburg and in other Bavarian towns. In the 'struggle for Berlin' after 1926, the method was refined to perfection, when the new *Gauleiter* Josef Goebbels decided to take his SA directly into the 'reddest' parts of the city in order to provoke bloody confrontations with Communist antagonists and then to exhibit the injuries and casualties of his SA stalwarts to the public. Every time, the conquest was meant not so much as a gaining of control but as a bold and sanguinary, head-on confrontation, although in meeting-hall battles control for the duration of the meeting was, of course, important. In the streets, however, or at the rival group's hangout or meeting, a bold appearance and perhaps a quick confrontation was quite sufficient for propaganda purposes. Big city streets were not viewed as the military or the police might view them, as an object of physical control, but rather as a staging area for heroic happenings in which the bold stormtroopers had to put in an impressive appearance – no more than that. Thus a bogus enemy, the aggressive, brawling Communists or Socialists, was substituted for the real object, the conquest of state authority. This bogus enemy could easily be coaxed into physical confrontations with which the Nazis could impress and win over liberal and conservative, bourgeois supporters to their cause. If enough new recruits and voters could be found to support the NSDAP in national elections, the brown phalanx could take over the whole state.

III

The sought-out confrontations and the eager response by Communist militants soon created a strange sub-culture of political violence in Berlin which spread throughout the public life of the city and increasingly to the provinces as well. It was here that the individual propensities of violent men merged with the organised intent of large paramilitary party armies amidst a politically volatile and not very clear situation. The political alignments and consequences were unclear not only because neither the bourgeois right nor the republican defenders of the state – and not even the utterly misguided Communists – fully realised the significance of the Nazi menace,[23] until it was too late. They were unclear to the immediate participants also because of the curious shell-game of fighting the bogus enemy.

It strains our credulity today and certainly contradicts any notion of the rational purpose of political violence – for example that violence is merely extreme passion in pursuit of a goal or an enemy – but the SA clearly (and sometimes deliberately) appears to have been confused about the identity of its enemy. There is a large SA literature, written by participants in the violence of the early thirties,[24] in which a seething hatred for the police and the state of Weimar surfaces every now and then amid luxuriant details of battles with the bogus enemy in the streets and meeting-halls of Berlin and other places. The battles with Communists and, occasionally, the *Iron Front* are laced with tales of brutality and sadism meted out to the antagonists, horrible descriptions of their deeds and moral character, and accounts of internal comradeship and solidarity in the SA. Many of the generalised motives we mentioned earlier are there: cries of injustice, a sense of deprivation, frustration, especially arrested upward mobility or the fright of social demotion, a hatred of the well-born and well educated, and the anticipation of persecution and violence which goes to rationalise the SA-man's own violence. But the aggressive hostility is always focussed on the 'Marxist terror' that allegedly had to be broken by violence, namely by attacking the Communists who, in fact, were neither in power nor any less the object of police measures than the stormtroopers themselves. Occasionally, the real enemy is mentioned:[25]

The combined attack of government, the parties, their power and press would succeed in smothering the movement if it were not for the SA—This SA, however, is untiring and ever-present. It breaches and breaks the ring of lies, carrying leaflets from house to house, gluing up posters, and writing its election slogans in large letters in many a dangerous night. . . . It is the target of the enemy's hatred, There isn't a night in which SA men don't lie in the streets as victims of the Communist terror . . .

Occasionally, also, a statement slips out that, if they were not armed, policemen too could be hunted down and beaten up. But the SA, of course, prudently refrained from seeking any confrontation with the police even though they often bore grudges, and on occasion singled out Berlin police officials for verbal attacks. More typically, they strike heroic poses and switch enemies at their convenience:[26]

SA men never give in. They answer the enemy in kind. They put up terror against terror. When the KPD assaults a comrade, the SA smash the tavern where the murderous mob is known to be. And when the police arrest them by the hundreds during a propaganda campaign and drag them off to the *Alexanderplatz* [Berlin police headquarters], they smash up the hall in which they are locked up. They smash the benches, throw the telephones through the breaking windows, and tear out the water-line so that the upset police have to call the fire brigade for help.

The reader is left to wonder what strange personalities are lurking under the thin veneer of stormtrooper manliness.[27]

Another important feature of the subculture of political violence in Berlin was the establishment of bases where the stormtroopers of a particular *Sturm* could hang out, drink and find shelter from individual harrassment. By 1928, the first SA *Sturmlokale*, about 20 of them, had appeared in Berlin, 'fortresses in the battle zone . . . offering peace and security from the enemy . . . rest from the strenuous service . . . centres of SA life because of the regular *Sturm* and *Trupp* evenings there . . . Here the men experience what they almost always lack at home, a warm hearth, a helping hand . . . comradeship'.[28] The Communists also had their well-known hangouts and it soon became part of the sport to choose a *Sturmlokal* location as close as possible to that of the bogus enemy, preferably next door. In the same fashion, any Communist demonstration would call for a stormtrooper counterdemonstration the same day and, if the police had not objected, in the same street. Such occasions invariably led to the desired confrontations regardless of police strategies of separating the marching throngs. Somewhere along the route or after the demonstrations in taverns, back alleys, or on the trains, they would always find each other and engage in combat or pursuit. Such street battles, along with the violence accompanying election campaigns and a long string of massive meeting-hall battles, marked the long march of the stormtroopers through the Weimar Rupublic.

Needless to emphasise, all this violence produced a rapidly spiraling number of dead and injured, especially in Berlin. By 1929 there was also a new kind of confrontation, initiated by Communists who were evidently bent on real conquest of sorts. Three times in one week, they tried to storm the Treptow *Sturmlokal* of the SA, the second time allegedly with 180 men of the elite Liebknecht Hundreds and under police protection. The third time, the RFB completely destroyed the SA hangout. Soon, the SA began similar raids on KPD hangouts and continued to seek confrontations with the 'reds' wherever they could be found and provoked. In one month, from mid-September to mid-October of 1929, the Berlin SA had forty seriously injured comrades and its second casualty.[29]

The pace of the 'conquest of Berlin' accelerated dizzily with the onset of mass unemployment and the first Nazi landslide in the elections of September

1930. Physical clashes with the Communists, the *Reichsbanner* and the Berlin police now occurred continually and at times under macabre circumstances, as at Horst Wessel's funeral when the Communists attacked the procession and allegedly tried to seize the coffin as well. There were official attempts at harrassment and suppression, in particular the continual police searches for weapons, occasional mass arrests, decrees suppressing Goebbels' hatesheet *Der Angriff* for periods of time, and the so-called 'shirts-and-pants war' conducted by the government. A short time before the 1930 elections, brown shirts were outlawed and the SA had to switch to white shirts which in time had to be replaced with ordinary street clothes. The police in the meantime had to supply institutional clothing to the violators and take them home so that the latter could be collected. The change to white did not affect stormtroopers' activities too much although there were fears that the complete suppression of the SA would follow since the RFB had been outlawed too. Taking away the white shirts and all other identifying marks too, on the other hand, tended to confuse the stormtroopers and to bring combat down from massive quasi-military combat to the small group level where they could still identify friend and foe.

The nature of the combat with the Communists also took on more characteristic forms underneath a thin veneer of major propagandistic actions, such as the massive demonstrations against the pacifistic movie 'All Quiet on the Western Front' or a mock debate between Goebbels and Walter Ulbricht at Friedrichshain which really served to kick off a gigantic meeting-hall battle that 300 policemen were unable to stop.[30] By 1931, the SA accounts of the physical clashes in Berlin subtly shifted emphasis to a mention of 'wrestling club fighters with brass knuckles', 'a selection of our best sluggers', innkeepers and *Müttchen* (motherly caretakers), or girlfriends who hid the stormtroopers' weapons at times of police searches under their skirts, gunshot battles, and incidents where a handful of gunslingers simply opened the door of a *Sturmlokal* of the enemy and fired away. Some SA fighters had underworld names like *Mollenkönig*, *Revolverschnauze*, U-boat, *Schiess-müller*, and *Gummibein*; some of the *Stürme* were called Robber *Sturm*, Murderer *Sturm*, or Dancing Guild. One of the most chilling accounts is that of a battle at Raddatz *Festsäle* where 90 SA sluggers locked in their opponents and beat them without mercy or escape:[31]

> Twenty-five of the best sluggers of the SA are in front of the stage, to the left a strong contingent and to the right, above the door, the rest of the SA. So the Communists are in the terrible grip of fists, and hit by beer steins, and legs of chairs which almost immediately turns them to flight. While in the middle of the hall, the reds are literally being knocked down in rows, there is a desperate struggle at both [locked] emergency exits . . . One Communist tries to crash through the window head first to open a free path for his comrades. But he did not count on the metal screen in front of the window.

He falls back and the window glass severs both his ears. The other windows are too narrow. Their heads hang out while their backs are being thrashed resoundingly. The entrance has been barricaded with . . . chairs and tables so the police can't get in either . . . The Neukoelln Communists had 45 wounded, including 8 seriously, and one of them died.

From the memoirs of the Berlin chief of police, Albert Grzesinski, a similar picture of the escalation of violence between the Nazis and the Communists emerges there, beginning especially in the fall of 1930: 'Ordinary brawls had given way to murderous attacks. Knives, blackjacks, and revolvers had replaced political argument. Terror was rampant. Carefully prepared alibis helped the terrorists on both sides to escape conviction.'[32]

For this purpose, both extremist parties apparently organised four-man squads of 'hit-men' who would operate in districts of the city where none of them was known. Grisly death threats were communicated to the victims, including police officers. Grzesinski estimated that there were about twenty such squads in operation, but none of them was ever caught. In response the Social Democratic chief of police, over republican protests, revived the old Prussian 'protective custody' from an old mid-nineteenth century statute which permitted arrests without a court warrant. He badgered the Prussian diet into passing a series of special emergency laws in March and October of 1931. During a terror wave in May of the same year, 29 persons were murdered – twelve Communists, six Nazis, one *Stahlhelmer*, two Social Democrats, four policemen, and four of unknown political allegiance – including nine by Nazi assailants and thirteen by Communists. The KPD finally disavowed the use of 'individual terror' by the end of that murderous year. Grzesinski also describes some of the SA and KPD hangouts including one SA tavern where police found two life-sized puppets with the features of himself and of the Prussian Minister of the Interior, Carl Severing, their heads punctured with bullet holes from target practice by the young toughs. Most of the stormtroopers arrested in Berlin were under twenty years of age, generally between 17 and 20. As the chief of police put it, they were 'no longer adherents of a political creed – just gangsters . . . well-schooled in the methods which were to find their culmination in concentration camps and prison dungeons of the Third Reich'.[33]

The Nazi efforts to memorialise their own casualties, however dubious in some details, substantially bear out the impression of large-scale political mayhem throughout the republic. One Nazi source even offers statistics on the number of policemen allegedly killed by the Communists between 1918 and 1933, namely 216, of whom the bulk died in 1919 (21), 1920 (105), 1921 (42), and 1923 (17). Another 1972 policemen are said to have been injured by Communists, this time also including large numbers injured in 1929 (145), 1930 (274), 1931 (332), and 1932 (304). The same source claims 387 dead and 43,000 injured Nazis, not counting those killed during the Nazi manhunts of

1933 when some of the victims were waiting for their Nazi captors gun in hand. The list of Nazi casualties suggests 30 for the years 1924–9, 17 in 1930, 42 in 1931, 84 in 1932, and 33 in 1933 (until April). Of the casualties since 1930, 96 were said to have been shot and 40 stabbed.[34] The sketchy data on the Nazi casualties also suggest that their social composition was far more proletarian (56.8 per cent skilled and unskilled workers) than the SA at large, not to mention the NSDAP.

IV

What manner of men were attracted by the activities and the milieu of the stormtrooper army is very difficult to guess, the many speculations we cited above notwithstanding. The smooth impression of united will and discipline that SA leader Pfeffer von Salomon prescribed in an order of 1926 is obviously misleading.

'The only way the SA addresses the public is in closed formation . . . one of the strongest forms of propaganda. The sight of a large number of . . . uniformed and disciplined men marching in step whose unconditional will to fight is clear to see, or to guess, will impress every German deeply and speak to his heart in a more convincing and moving way than any written or spoken logic ever can.

Calm bearing and matter-of-factness underscore the impression of power, the force of the marching columns and of the cause for which they are marching. The inner force of the cause makes Germans jump to conclusions about its righteousness . . . if whole groups of people in planned fashion risk body, soul, and livelihood for a cause, it simply *must* be great and true.'

The SA Chief added, 'This emotional proof of the truth is not enhanced but disturbed and deflected by simultaneous appeals to reason or by advertisement. There must be no cries of "down with" . . . or "long live" . . . or posters about issues of the day, vituperation, speeches, handbills or popular amusements accompanying the display.' This was obviously the way the organisation wanted not only the public to see its rag-tag army of unruly young adults but also the SA men to see themselves. Calm bearing and discipline probably did not come easy. But if the raw recruits – which most of them were – could be told how important it was, perhaps they could measure up to the image.

The carefully stage-managed partisan struggle of the stormtroopers was also a way of maintaining discipline and revolutionary spirit among the membership toward the day when the final struggle for power might arrive. The SA men had to exercise their fanaticism and the 'spontaneous' gestures and shouts of the big rallies just as the recruits of the Imperial Army had had to exercise their goose step and clicking of the heels. Much of it was just a channeling of the motor instincts of physically well-trained, athletic young men whose marching feet could hardly be restrained. But in addition to this army-like militarisation, there also had to be indoctrination in the political mysteries, 'the idea of the Hitler movement', about which the master himself was amazingly vague. Beyond a sketchy synthesis of nationalism and non-Marxist socialism, with relatively little anti-semitism, and due respect to the all-emcompassing people's solidarity (*Volksgemeinschaft*), the SA men only knew whatever their local leaders might tell them. The fulcrum of stormtrooper ideology seems to have been, in the manner of George Orwell's *1984*, on the one hand a craven Hitler cult – love Big Brother – and on the other hand, hatred for the chosen enemy, the Marxists. And to keep the pot boiling, and the extremist temper fed, a never-ending series of hectic campaigns and activities kept the members busy. 'The impetus of the young movement was immense', *Sturmfuehrer* Horst Wessel wrote in his diary. 'One rally followed the other, each one crazier and stormier than the one before. Red Front (RFB) tried to break us up dozens of times, always in vain. There were street demonstrations, press campaigns, propaganda tours through the province, all creating an atmosphere of activism and high tension which could only help the movement.'[36]

It is not easy to summarise an inquiry into anything as vast as the individual motivations of a rapidly growing army of revolutionaries of whatever faith or intent, even if one has written a book about it.[37] Perhaps the best way to begin is with the variable of age which at once describes important motivational features and separates the motives of the older stormtroopers from the bulk which was very young indeed. Since a large part of the relevant historical experiences of rebellious individuals is, obviously, determined by their date of birth, the history-related motivation of the postwar generation of stormtroopers (born 1902 or later) is likely to differ profoundly from that of the war (born 1895–1901) or prewar generations (born 1894 or earlier).

We shall use the Abel Collection[38] of 581 NSDAP members including 337 SA men as a rough guide for want of better statistics. The postwar generation amounted to two-thirds of the stormtroopers (SA and SS) of 1933 and three-fifths of its middle and lower echelon leaders, a significantly larger share than in the NSDAP at large. This is to say that only a twelfth of the stormtroopers were in the prewar army, a sixteenth were among the volunteers of 1914, and, in fact, only a good quarter were war veterans. The most pivotal event of the era, the *Fronterlebnis* and the great war in all its manifestations, can explain only a small part of the individual motivations of the stormtroopers. Almost the same is true of the experience of the defeat of 1918 and of the revolutionary and counter-revolutionary stirrings of the first postwar years, such as Freecorps service.[39]

If it was not the great patriotic trauma, then what can explain the motivation of most stormtroopers? Given their youthfulness, our attention needs to be focussed on the Weimar youth culture which was characterised by a veritable eruption of youth activity and organised life encompassing, for example in 1927, some five million members of registered youth groups. All this was a generational revolt against parents and societal authority figures and some of it took specifically political form. Young people aged 18–25 also act very differently from older ones in many respects, beginning with such things as unfocussed enthusiasms and not conforming to the social restraints and values of adult society. The young SA toughs epitomised the generational revolt in its most violent and destructive form, rebels even without a cause or, at least, without a clear idea of what they were for.

There have been frequent attempts to explain the political motivation of Nazis and their stormtroopers by looking at their occupations on record, often in a rather primitive manner.[40] But here too, the age factor in the midst of mass unemployment makes occupational identity doubtful. Many young stormtroopers were unemployed, worked in jobs below their level of training, or had never found their first job. Those that could be considered to have a recognisable occupational identity, furthermore, had not had it long enough to place much faith in this as a source of political motivation. Even among the older stormtroopers who might have been formed by the social categories of a more stable age, interrupted military or civil-service careers or the war often obliterate the traces of the social tensions of prewar society. Finally, occupational identity, even where it can be firmly established, is not terribly helpful in explaining such extreme and violent political behaviour.

It would appear that there is really no satisfactory shortcut to explaining violent motivation except psychology and social psychology (including organisational psychology). We need to know something about the personalities involved, their earlier socialisation by family, school environment, and peer group (including youth groups); their current attitudes toward politics, toward other political actors and public authority and towards the use of violence; their political experiences and ideology, if any; and about their interaction with their stormtrooper peers. Even if we choose not to plumb the Freudian depths of personal motivation with models of frustration and aggression,[41] we cannot avoid thinking about why some individuals become physically aggressive while others do not.

Political violence occurs when individuals of violent propensity meet up with organisations and situations that encourage them and channel their aggression against an antagonist. From the Abel Collection it is easy to show the record of previous violence in the form of conflict with parents, school, police, or employers, often a long police record with court convictions and jail sentences.[42] We can also demonstrate the escalation toward individual violence from demonstrations and the like under the influence of membership in the stormtrooper movement. But we also need to show how the violent propensity of the individual grows under the challenge of the counter-violence of police and of the enemy, including the imagined or anticipated violence or repression on a paranoid mind. These attitudes and relationships have to be inferred and interpolated when we attempt to explain the motives of a historical movement.[43] The best way of confirming likely causal relationships in this murky area would be to set up similar studies with control groups of politically violent persons today, or at least to find historical control groups that are similarly rich in data. This still remains to be done.

NOTES

1. The writer is indebted for this survey of pertinent literature to Diana E. Reynolds, research assistant at the University of California, Santa Barbara.
2. There is no need to document the abundant popular literature on terrorism.
3. See, for example, J. Bowyer Bell, *A Time for Terror: How Democratic Societies Respond to Revolutionary Violence* (New York 1978), who recommends the avoidance of tyranny, flexible accommodation of challengers, and a stress on law and justice rather than law and order. See also T. Honderich, *Political Violence* (Ithaca, N.Y., 1976).
4. Such literature, again, is legion, especially with regard to nationalistic causes. But see also B. Moore Jr., *Injustice: The Social Basis of Obedience and Revolt* (New York, 1978) who pleads that before 'politically effective moral outrage' can develop, the underdogs must shake off their sense of the inevitability of oppression.
5. Of the numerous general literature, R. J. Rummel's 'dimensionality of nations' project deserves special mention. See Rummel 'The Relationship Between National Attributes and Foreign Conflict Behavior', in J. D. Singer (ed.), *Quantitative International Politics* (New York, 1965) pp. 187–214 and the writings of I. Feyerabend, L. F. Richardson, and M. Haas.
6. See the Tillys, *The Rebellious Century, 1830–1930* (Cambridge, 1975); and Ch. Tilly and E. Shorter, *Strikes in France, 1830–1968* (New York, 1974).
7. See, for example, F. R. von der Mehden, *Comparative Political Violence* (Englewood Cliffs, N. J., 1973), who distinguishes, among primordial (cultural or religious), separatist, revolutionary, coup, and student/electoral violence; or the work on 'internal war' by Harry Eckstein and others.
8. See G. Botz, *Gewalt in der Politik* (Munich, 1976), esp. chapter four; M. Clark Havens, C. Leiden, and K. M. Schmitt, *The Politics of Assassination* (Englewood Cliffs, N.J., 1970), chapter three; and W. Laqueur, *Terrorism* (Boston, 1977), chapter three. Police statistics often supplies good data for this perspective on political violence.
9. Recent examples of this general literature aside from those already cited, are several of the essays in M. H. Livingston, (ed.), *International Terrorism in the Contemporary World* (Westport, Conn., 1978); Anthony Burton's introduction to his reader, *Revolutionary Violence: The Theories* (New York, 1978); much of the current literature on fascist movements; P. Wilkinson, *Terrorism and the Liberal State* (London, 1977); and A. Parry, *Terrorism: From Robespierre to Arafat* (New York, 1976). See also the classic summary in C. Leiden and K. M. Schmitt, *The Politics of Violence: Revolution in the Modern World* (Englewood Cliffs, N.J., 1968) chapters 2 and 3.
10. But see, for instance, S. Bialer (ed.), *Radicalism in the Contemporary Age* (Boulder, Col., 1977).

11. See P. Merkl, *Political Violence Under the Swastika: 581 Early Nazis* (Princeton, 1975) parts III–4, IV, and V; and *The Making of a Stormtrooper* (Princeton, 1980) chapters 4 and 5 where the organisational setting of the early Nazi party, and its relation to ideology and violent behavior are analysed. See also E. Bittner, 'Radicalism and the Organization of Radical Movements', *American Sociological Review* 28 (1963) pp. 928–40 and the literature on organisational sociology and psychology.

12. See, for example, the contributions by J. A. Dowling and A. Storr to Livingston, which have strong overtones of Freudian analysis; Moore, Wilkinson, Parry, and Honderich. Further recent explanations are D. I. Warren, *The Radical Center* (Southbend, Ind., 1976) and W. Eckhardt and Ch. Young, *Governments Under Fire* (New York, 1977).

13. See especially the cultural emphasis of A. Bandura, *Aggression: A Social Learning Analysis* (Englewood Cliffs, N.J., 1973); also S. J. Breiner, 'The Psycho-Social Aspects of Violence', *U.S.A. Today* (September 1978); or R. Restak, 'The Origins of Violence', *Saturday Review* (12 May 1979), as well as J. Margolin, 'Psychological Aspects in Terrorism', in Y. Alexander and S. M. Finger (eds), *Terrorism: Interdisciplinary Perspectives* (New York, 1977) pp. 270–82 and T. R. Gurr's classic *Why Men Rebel* (Princeton, 1970).

14. *Crusaders, Criminals, Crazies: Terror and Terrorism in our Time* (New York, 1976) esp. pp. 12–16, 40–41.

15. See, for example, Laqueur, chapter four, and Botz, as well as the contributions to St. U. Larsen and B. Hagtvet (eds), *Who Were the Fascists?* (Oslo, 1980).

16. See this writer's *The Making of a Stormtrooper*, chapter 2.

17. Ibid., Table 2 and the last pages of chapter 2.

18. A. Hitler, *Mein Kampf* (New York, 1939) p. 405. Later accounts speak of the November 1921 rally as the hour of birth of the SA when there were a mere '46 fighting off 800 enemies'. See also H. Bennecke, *Hitler und die SA* (Munich, 1962) pp. 23–9, where the heavy involvement of the early SA with the army is detailed.

19. The use of uniformed men in massive demonstrations and at rallies, of course, was no monopoly of the SA. It had long been used by the *Stahlhelm* and other veterans groups and, with less of a uniformed and military bearing, was not unknown in socialist demonstrations long before the founding of *Reichsbanner* and Iron Front. The presence of large numbers of veterans of World War I in all groups facilitated the appearance of such formations.

20. Newspaper and autobiographical accounts almost invariably give a very slanted picture, depending on the identification of the writer with one side or the other. Even police reports and court records rarely are able to answer the question of responsibility any better than any adult can who breaks up a fight between small boys.

21. On the role of the *Reichswehr* and the circumstances of the 1923 imbroglio, see esp. H. J. Gordon, Jr., *Hitler and the Beer Hall Putsch* (Princeton, 1972) chapters 5–7, 14, and 20.

22. Quoted by Bennecke, p. 238.

23. The right wing (DNVP and *Stahlhelm*) assumed it could use the NSDAP for its own conquest of the state. The republican parties (Center, DDP, and SPD) were more worried about the assault of the right wing and of the Communists than about the seemingly transitory Nazi threat. The Communists (KPD) had been instructed to fight the 'social fascists' of the SPD rather than the Nazis and, in the Berlin transport workers strike of late 1932 and on earlier occasions, even made common cause with the right-wing enemies against the republican government of Prussia and of Berlin.

24. See esp. the extensive collection of the Munich Institut für Zeitgeschichte.
25. F. Stelzner, *Schicksal SA* (Munich, 1936) pp. 54–5.
26. Ibid., p. 55.
27. Somehow one is reminded of Charles De Gaulle's characterisation of revolting students as 'le chie-en-lit'.
28. J. K. von Engelbrechten, *Eine braune Armee entsteht* (Munich, 1937) p. 85.
29. Ibid., pp. 82–4, 98–106.
30. There were 60 injured. Ibid., pp. 145–8.
31. Ibid., p. 188.
32. *Inside Germany* (New York, 1939) p. 130.
33. Ibid., pp. 131–4. The author's count of riots and casualties in Prussia for the period of 1 June to 20 July 1932, is 461 political riots with 82 killed and 400 seriously injured.
34. W. Decker, *Kreuze am Wege zur Freiheit* (Leipzig, 1935) pp. 96, 109–32.
35. SA *Befehl*, 3 Nov. 1926.
36. Quoted by W. Sauer in K. D. Bracher, Sauer, and G. Schulz, *Die nationalsozialistische Machtergreifung* (Cologne, 1960) pp. 843–4.
37. See Merkl, *The Making of a Stormtrooper*, chapters 3–5.
38. Described by T. Abel himself in *The Nazi Movement* (New York, 1965).
39. The experience of border struggles and, in particular, of the Franco-Belgian occupation of the Rhineland in 1923 seems more prominent among the Abel respondents, but this is due at least in part to the disproportionate representation of such cases in the collection.
40. The nature of German census statistics is a hindrance to meaningful occupational analysis. Furthermore, to be sound, an assessment of social class has always required a great deal more than merely the occupation of the respondent, namely occupation of father, income level, educational training etc.
41. One of the intriguing attributes of disproportionate numbers of violent stormtroopers in the Abel Collection turned out to be that they had at an early point lost their fathers, or older brothers frequently to a hero's death in the great war. The sons or younger brothers thereby were doomed to follow in their footsteps to the bitter end.
42. See esp. the sections on the early Nazis who later became enforcers of the terror of the Third *Reich* in both, *Political Violence Under the Swastika* and *The Making of a Stormtrooper*.
43. Drawing attitudes from autobiographical statements, as in the case of the Abel vitae, may not be the most satisfactory method, considering the prevalence of highly subjective perspectives in respondents and in the researcher. This weakness can be corrected if the analysis is sufficiently aware of the pitfalls and if a broad range of social science methods is employed to corroborate hypotheses.

22 Non-Legal Violence and Terrorism in Western Industrial Societies: An Historical Analysis

Wolfgang J. Mommsen

Since the early 1960s we have been able to observe a general revival of violence and individual terror as a means to achieve a wide range of political aims, not only in relatively backward and internally disrupted societies of the Third World, but also in the great industrial nations of the West, in the USA, Japan and Central Europe. This phenomenon requires a more comprehensive explanation than the currently fashionable explanatory models in terms of social psychology or ideology. Since the end of the Second World War it has been possible, particularly in those countries and regions within the sphere of influence of the USA and her Western allies, to re-establish relatively stable democratic societies. The remarkable economic recovery of the 1950s facilitated the creation of functioning parliamentary systems that were accepted by the broad mass of the population as an appropriate form of modern government, even if their democratic spirit was still somewhat meagerly developed. Such revolutionary trends of the Left as did exist soon lost their momentum, while the number of potential adherents of extremist political groups of the Right also diminished steadily.

In the political climate of the 1950s neither on the Left nor the Right were there any significant groups which regarded violence and terror as the appropriate methods for the realisation of their aims. Undoubtedly, the experience of the war and the memory of National Socialist crimes of violence played their part in making it appear generally unthinkable, even among extremist fringe groups, to assert political objectives by violent means and in more or less open conflict with the normative forces of the State. The use of open violence against property or persons, regardless of whether it might be employed by the State or opposition minorities, was generally considered to be taboo, even though the newly established political systems could not yet claim to rest on a very firm foundation of legitimacy.

In a certain sense this holds true for eastern Central Europe as well. Here, under the manifest influence of the USSR, monolithic governments developed which knew how to handle the instruments of institutional violence with such consummate perfection that recourse to counter-violence remained limited to isolated outbreaks, such as 1953 in Berlin or 1956 in Hungary. In the nations of eastern Central Europe a repressive governmental machinery guaranteed that no forms of violent protest or violent resistance emerged, comparable to those employed by the terrorist movements with emancipatory or repressive tendencies, which developed particularly in the Third World. On the whole, the first two decades after 1945 were thus all over Central Europe, albeit for different reasons, a period of remarkable absence of violence, at least from the viewpoint of the respective political systems.

Since then we have grown accustomed to regard as anachronistic phenomena the terrorism and recourse to violence adopted by fringe groups of society, which see no chance of achieving their objective of revolutionising society by methods that remain within the law, at least not in the advanced industrial nations of the West. It was widely believed that in a functioning democratic society, which can rightly claim to enjoy a large degree of consensus as to its legitimacy on the part of its citizens, this sort of thing could not really happen and, if at all, only as the residue of social or political conditions already over and done with. This assumption appeared to be all the more justified since, in a period of steadily increasing prosperity, traditional class differences had become increasingly evened out. On the other hand it appeared only too readily comprehensible that on the fringes of the Western world, where extreme social problems and more or less glaring class differences continued to exist, the phenomenon of terror and violent protest by minority groups should be the order of the day. The terror campaign of nationalists in South Tyrol, that sought to force the Italian government to grant autonomy to the German minority in Italy, appeared to be the great anomaly in the otherwise peaceful political landscape of Central and Western Europe, especially as the lesson that political conflicts and clashes between divergent interests could only be really solved by gradually hammering out a compromise based on consensus on all sides, finally appeared to have sunk in.

In many countries of the Third World, of course, even during that period, manifold forms of terrorism and violence existed, arising from a wide variety of nationalist, economic or ideological motives. In Palestine, the Zionist movement conducted a major terror campaign against the British occupation forces and also against their Arab rivals, until in 1948 the British finally wearied of playing the unwanted policeman and of keeping the Jewish-Arab conflict under control. In the countries of the Indian sub-continent terrorism was an equally widespread phenomenon. Yet the most spectacular and at the same time most significant forms of terrorist warfare were those which, based on the Maoist doctrine of the war of liberation of oppressed nations against imperialism, emerged in a number of South American countries after Fidel Castro's victory in Cuba.[1] In this connection, the guerilla war in Bolivia in particular soon became a symbol of a new type of emancipatory struggle throughout the world. It was fought, with substantial participation by Cuban underground fighters, against the established authoritarian order and its alleged patron, the USA. Che Guevara lent it the splendour of his name and the immensely persuasive power of a social revolutionary doctrine, which amounted to a quasi-religious faith in the eventual emancipation of the Latin American masses from the imperialist yoke by a violent guerilla war. In this context, Che Guevara represented almost ideal-typically the position of an extreme and *gesinnungsethischer* politician of the Left, and as such his influence reached far beyond South America; he became a charismatic figure for many Left intellectuals not only on that continent but throughout the Western world. He, more consistently than anyone else, argued that the ground for the revolutionary rise of the masses could only be prepared by 'armed struggle' to the last, including if need be the sacrifice of one's own life, and that everything, therefore, depended on the deed. This doctrine, of course, was to prove much more successful than the guerilla war that was fought on this basis in the Bolivian countryside.[2] Of all the leftwing movements in South America the *Movimiento de Liberación Nacional* (*MLN*), better known as the Uruguayan *Tupamaro* movement, was relatively the most successful. It was the first to implement urban guerilla tactics, developed particularly by Carlos Marighella, and it succeeded for a time in effectively controlling large parts of Uruguay and in building up a virtual alternative system to the existing military regime. In regions such as these, right-wing counter-violence was, of course, not slow to respond, although it remains debatable to what degree this operated at the behest of the established powers, as was claimed by the *Tupamaros*.

From a European perspective, the emergence of such terrorist movements and activities, which very soon were to turn to the kidnapping of diplomats as hostages and thus directly to involve the European nations in their conflicts, at first appeared to represent a peripheral phenomenon, arising out of those countries' relatively archaic social conditions and South America's long tradition of violent politics. The advanced industrial nations appeared to be confronted by this phenomenon only indirectly; in Europe everything was quiet, with the exception of a few fringe zones contending with ethnic-national dissensions.

This, however, was to change abruptly. Ever since the late sixties, a number of politically and economically advanced countries have, rather surprisingly, been afflicted by more or less widespread terrorist activities. These terrorists and their supporters emerged from fringe groups of society, at first usually of the extreme Left, although very soon right-wing groups of a more or less neo-fascist character adopted these methods of 'armed struggle' in their turn.[3]

Japan, proverbial as a country of great national loyalty and social discipline, became overnight the battlefield for very vehement and violent conflicts between *Rengo Sekigun* (*VRA*) and the forces of order. In the wake of the so-called 'student's revolution' in West Germany, an extra-parliamentary protest movement emerged which, although torn by bitter internal rivalries, began with 'limited infractions of the rules' (Habermas), in order to bring their grievances to effective notice; eventually some of its scattered remains sought recourse to terrorist politics. Their extreme culmination was reached when the *Rote Armee Fraktion* (*RAF*) began its machiavellistically calculated 'armed struggle' against the established system of the Federal Republic – a system they denounced as fascist.

Italy, at the same time, began to turn into the battlefield between the *brigate rosse* and their neo-fascist counterparts, with the authorities apparently being unable to control this development. France, too, after the events of the 'red' May of 1968, experienced a phase of violence, largely carried out by extremist groups on the Left, although this made comparatively less impact, since in the early sixties in the wake of De Gaulle's decolonisation of Algeria, France had already experienced a series of terrorist actions, whose authors were mainly of the extreme Right. Numerous European regions meanwhile saw a revival of older national-revolutionary movements, more or less terrorist in character, particularly in Northern Ireland, the Basque region and for a time even in Brittany.

All this came as a great surprise, since the societies thus affected could claim to possess relatively well functioning parliamentary systems and a high degree of consensus as to their legitimacy on the part of their citizens. This surprise, however, was partly the result of a certain degree of self-deception at the time on the part of people who had grown accustomed to regarding the conditions of the fifties and early sixties as normal and accepted them as a matter of course. What they were in fact witnessing was the revival of a far older phenomenon. In Europe, too, terrorism and political violence have a long tradition, which only a few European societies were spared. Nevertheless, in the period when the modern constitutional state came into being and the industrial system emerged, social and political conflicts tended to be fought more and more in juridical forms, thus putting a restraint on violence, at least on non-legal violence, in public life. The State was gradually able to assert its 'monopoly of coercion' (Max Weber) not only in law but *de facto* as well. And yet throughout the nineteenth century there always remained fringe groups which resorted to methods of non-legal violence or more or less open terror, in order to achieve their aims; in part this was due to their refusal to recognise the mechanisms of the newly established legal order, which often cut across older unwritten legal traditions and which operated mostly to the disadvantage of the lower strata of society. In historical perspective, these post-war decades have thus been a rather exceptional period which has now been followed by a new phase, where the violent settlement of political conflicts, especially on the part of fringe groups is, regrettably, no longer subject to the same taboos and controls as during the first two decades after the Second World War.

The reasons for this are manifold. Some can be pinpointed with relative ease. Paradoxically, it was the relative pacification of Europe in the course of the so-called policy of detente between the super-powers which allowed conditions to emerge in which marginal political movements with extremist objectives could have any kind of chance. In the fifties the secular dissent between the two world systems, between Soviet Communism on the one hand and Western liberal Capitalism on the other, overshadowed the internal frictions within European societies. Regional and ethnic conflicts took second place to world-wide problems; during the Cold War the great ideological differences were polarised into diametrically opposed tendencies, with no proper alternative between the two. Only the relative calm which entered international relations after the end of the Stalinist era seems to have made possible the universal revival of extremist tendencies of very diverse character in the western nations – and partially even in Eastern Europe. Secondly, the comparative success of economic reconstruction after 1945 created the preconditions for the rise of movements which could afford to have idealistic motivations and call into question the existing social and economic order, essentially in moral terms.

Yet this is hardly sufficient to provide an adequate explanation for the revival of terrorism and of non-legal violence on the part of fringe groups, which deliberately contravene the established system of law and consciously challenge the power of the State. It requires a longer-term perspective than the experts have so far employed; current analyses in terms of social psychology, moral philosophy and socio-Marxism on the whole do not get us very far – even though they may provide significant individual insights – for they approach the phenomenon of modern terrorism without regard to the historical dimension.

Ever since the Luddites' violent protests against the social consequences of the Industrial Revolution, or the demonstrative acts of violence of Italian 'social rebels' against modern legalistic forms of law concerning the ownership of land, which contravened old customs, or the violent demonstrations by parts of the working classes in Germany against their miserable living conditions on the eve of the 1848/49 Revolution, there have always been cases where underprivileged groups employed a more or less organised use of force. Where the classical national movements in Europe are concerned, we have long grown used to consider their fight against the old order as legalised by the very course of history, although from a formal point of view they also employed terrorist methods even then. Garibaldi is rightly considered to be Italy's national hero! Nor do we any longer deny recognition to the radicals of 1848 who inscribed the fight against Metternich's system on their banner and even, like Robert Blum, sacrificed their lives to this cause. Yet this also makes clear how difficult it is to actually distinguish between 'legitimate' and 'illegitimate' forms of violence against the established order, and consequently between those forms of violence that are to be approved of and those that are to be condemned. Irrespective of this, it becomes obvious that the ideological patterns, just as the strategies of extreme terrorist movements, be they of Left or Right, are much older than the movements that confront us today.

In ideal-typical terms, the terrorist movements known to us can be divided into two categories, each characterised by a fundamentally different pattern of ideological justification for taking recourse to violence. They appear in the most diverse historical contexts, yet a certain time sequence between them can nevertheless be observed. The older type of terrorist movement resorts to the pattern of the 'good old laws' and customs that need to be reinstated. Seen from this angle, recourse to violence against the existing system, its symbols, representatives and institutions is not only plainly necessary but virtually constitutes a duty. Arguments of this sort are to be found for instance in the agrarian protest movement *Captain Swing* and more particularly in the case of the Russian Social-Revolutionaries; the latter indeed frequently assumed that the tsar, if only the truth were made known to him, would himself approve of their violent actions against exploiting landowners and reinstate the old laws. The justification of spontaneous rather than organised acts of violence sprang from the conviction that the existing traditional order was both the only just and the only appropriate one, and that violent actions against its being subjected to arbitrary change were thus, if seen in such a light, legitimate. Such movements therefore favour 'measured' forms of violence and terror, as a method of demonstrating against unbearable conditions rather than achieving radical change. Consequently the idea of turning to terrorist means in order to bring about a revolutionary change of society, is usually absent. Moderation, or the use of violence according to the principle of the commensurateness of means, is thus not only possible, but indeed the rule. This not by accident historically older variant of justifying violence in political and social conflicts is still oriented towards a relatively static *Weltbild*.

In the case of the second, historically more recent, category of terrorist movements the reverse is true. These operate from within a utopian conception of the world and see the destruction of the existing system as a necessary precondition for the natural emergence of a new, more equitable order. For this reason we find them prepared for a constant acceleration in the use of violence until the goal, the annihilation of the existing order, is achieved. Correspondingly, they are deeply committed to an ideology that is quite one-sidedly directed at the moral condemnation of the present, while the future society that is to arise from the ruins of the old is only outlined in exceedingly vague terms. It would be vain to look for precise plans as to how the existing social order is to be supplanted by a new one, since they are so deeply convinced of its pernicious character that every means in the fight against it appears legitimate. Nor is anything much said about the shape of the new society that is to be created. As a rule there is a complete absence of concrete statements regarding its nature; rather it is defined negatively, in the main, as the anti-type of the existing order. The theoretical position such

movements occupy is often characterised by an extreme form of
actionism; violent acts carry their own justification within them, as it were,
since violence, given the rotten nature of the existing order, is bound to be
good.

It is in classical Anarchism that we find this fundamental ideological pattern
most clearly developed. It was within its ambit that the theory of modern
terrorism, as a strategy for social change, was first formulated, despite the fact
that mainstream Anarchism expressly rejected organised violence and
advocated a humanitarian pacifist order without domination of any sort.
Bakunin's great and lasting historical achievement probably lies in his
criticism of Marx' revolutionary theory. From the outset he attacked it where
it was most vulnerable, i.e. by arguing that any revolutionary movement
which expects to emancipate the masses through the dictatorship of a
proletarian ruling elite, even if this is conceived of as only temporary, must
inevitably reproduce the very patterns of repression it is setting out to
remove.[4] Bakunin's utopian counter-proposals for the liberation of society to
freedom, on the other hand, depended throughout on the doubtful assumption that all that was needed was to break the fetters of the existing order and
to emancipate the individuals, so that they would regain their original state of
humanity. The fashionable argument that it is the 'institutional violence' of
States and societies which first provokes the use of 'counter-violence' is
already implied in Bakunin's theory, since all evils of the existing order, such
as for instance criminality, are ascribed exclusively to its coercive nature. Thus
the question about the concrete chances for and the conditions of a new, more
equitable order is disregarded from the outset, thus *a priori* blocking that field
of pragmatic compromise between ultimate values and concrete possibilities
which Max Weber has circumscribed with the term 'the ethics of
responsibility'.

Although present-day terrorist groups and movements occupy a multi-
plicity of ideological positions and are not infrequently at daggers drawn with
each other, they nevertheless follow this underlying pattern in their ideological
justification of violent strategies. The ruthless fight against the prevailing
system, as they see it from their very different viewpoints, is considered
necessary, if only because that system is thoroughly evil and corrupt,
irrespective of what the concrete chances for the success of their actions may
be. And it is precisely this relative hopelessness of their fight, at least in the
short or medium term, which appears to justify radical methods of combat,
and finally even individual terror that lacks any precise objectives. Max Weber
once said of revolutionary Syndicalism that it is 'either a futile whim of
intellectual romantics and the financial sacrifice of incompetent undisciplined
workers, *or* a conviction of an intensity amounting to religious faith, which
exists quite legitimately, *even* where there never *is* a goal that is being
"achieved"', or ever could be achieved.[5] The same can also be applied to

terrorist movements, in the narrower sense, irrespective of their political persuasion. They all conform to a pattern of religiously held social convictions, which makes them largely immune to pragmatic considerations, though it must be added that these attitudes usually only develop in the course of their persecution by the State, and in the increasing social isolation that follows from this.

As a rule, terrorist movements do not aspire to political power for themselves; at most, they intend to act as pioneers for other forces close to them. Yet, the fact that they are tiny minorities, who, at best, can hope to awaken the masses of the population only after a long fight, involving many losses, is precisely what determines their methods of operation. They cannot hope to conquer the control mechanisms of the existing society, or the existing governmental machinery, in one blow or even in a long and tenacious struggle, but only by their violent actions to bring the State to the point of internal collapse. The main purpose of attempts against representative figures is to undermine the standing of the existing order; the effect such actions have simply as signals is important, not the disruption they cause to the processes of government. The upsetting of public order, irrespective of the degree to which this is desired or achieved, aims at undermining its legitimacy in the eyes of the broad mass of the population. A further consideration is the demoralisation of the adherents of the existing order by violent actions, especially officialdom and judiciary, to the point where the entire system is brought to the brink of collapse. Nechaev, already in his 'Catechism of a Revolutionary', dating from 1869, provided the classical formulation of this basic rule of terrorist strategy which, with certain variations, is common to most terrorist movements we know of.[6]

From this basic tenet, however, flow two further secondary variants, which are no longer fixed exclusively on the system that is being challenged, but aim instead at the recruitment of new followers and at mobilising the public in the revolutionaries' favour. The first has become known by the slogan 'propaganda by deed', advocated by those sections within the Anarchist movement which resorted to methods of terror and individual violence, as a rule in circumstances not of their own making. Its analogy is to be found in numerous comparable movements of our own time, as for instance in the *Rote Armee Fraktion*. The absoluteness reflected in this swing to more or less radical methods of violence, involving even the risk of the terrorists' own life, possesses for certain people or groups, who tend in any case to reject existing conditions, great suggestive appeal. It provides additional confirmation of the rightness of their particular cause; violence is thus able to attract sympathisers and induce them to join such groups.

More important, and related to it, is the circumstance that the use of violence, particularly in unstable, insecure societies can have a positive impact on public opinion. Quite often the public shows itself impressed by the fact that such groups or movements do not merely 'talk' but 'mean business'; the suggestive effect Nazi terror had upon important sections of the German middle class was due to just this.

Against these 'advantages' – in terrorist perspective – it must be considered, however, that recourse to violence, particularly if concentrated on methods of 'individual terror' of the relatively aimless kind, can easily become an end in itself; this in turn is tantamount to a progressive discrediting of such movements and their ideological aims, nebulous as these may be. This latter phenomenon can be observed particularly clearly in the case of the 'combat units' of the Russian Socialist-Revolutionary Party, which in the end got quite out of control, simply perpetuating themselves while no longer possessing any concrete political objectives.[7]

To the degree that the chances of such movements achieving their goals become less and the repressive machinery of the forces of order pushes them underground, the ruthlessness of their acts of terror tends to increase. Such acts also become more desperate and hence more incalculable until in the end terrorism loses its character as a means to effect whatever social change it aspires to and instead becomes merely the means to reaffirm the faith in the justification of its own cause. What tends to get lost at the same time is the capacity to calculate the use of violence rationally, that is, the capacity to assess the optimal chances of achieving the desired objectives by a 'measured' use of violence; this in turn usually results in operating methods becoming more and more brutalised.

Thus it is not surprising that terrorist groups – particularly if they employ methods of individual terror – usually develop quasi-religious behaviour patterns and, in their internal structure and ethics, often resemble extreme religious sects. One of the most striking traits of such terrorist movements is the enormously stringent cohesive force of their own 'moral' norms within their own closed circles. Already Bakunin's secret societies, designed as the mainstay of anarchist doctrine, had the task, amongst other things, of ensuring strict ideological control over group members. Under modern conditions, too, numerous instances of this phenomenon, the enormous moral cohesion of terrorist groups, spring to mind. Andreas Baader and Gudrun Ensslin, even from their prison cells, were able not only to issue detailed instructions to their followers but to induce fellow prisoners to commit suicide. The American heiress, Patricia Hearst, after some weeks' exposure to the tremendously suggestive power of a terrorist group's ideology, articulated in high moral terms, was turned, not altogether surprisingly, from a victim of a kidnapping into an accomplice of her captors.

This of course is also to be explained by the external circumstances in which such groups live. Persecution by the State increasingly forces them to change their previous lifestyle and to adopt a strictly clandestine mode of life, with less and less chance of maintaining any close contact with the world around them or indeed of communicating with others on matters of ideology. Michael

Baumann has described this process very vividly.[8] Initially, the members of extremist circles in Berlin and elsewhere drew support from the student 'scene'; but soon they found themselves obliged to live in strictly closed and isolated circles, where the individual gradually loses the possibility of forming independent opinions. For, within his circle he is subjected to the constant pressure of solidarity and exposed to increasing reciprocal affirmation of those extreme ideological positions which induced him to join a terrorist group. Under such circumstances, loyalty to the movement's basic principles is not only required for reasons of his own survival, but also constantly re-activated and intensified, owing to the form communication necessarily takes within groups that have become thus isolated. The power the group wields over the individual, once he has become a member, is extreme and by no means purely physical. In the perspective of this type of group or movement, participation in violent actions in the end becomes a moral obligation and also a condition of full recognition as a worthy member of the group.

The ideological patterns and the strategic ground rules described above and their effect on group psychology can be found in radical movements of quite disparate persuasions and under very different historical circumstances; they remain essentially the same, even if there are variations of degree. The willingness to resort to violence in order to achieve certain political or social objectives is not the prerogative of specific ideological positions; on the contrary, all it requires is a great degree of tension between the reality as they perceive it and the goals they aspire to. This willingness can thus be found on the fringes of political movements of very different ideological persuasions, and it is therefore quite inappropriate to ascribe terrorism and strategies of violence mainly to political ideologies of the Left. History shows how extraordinarily broad is the spectrum of movements which, even if only for a short time and often only as a fringe phenomenon, have resorted intermittently to strategies of violence. This is equally true if one confines the perspective only to the history of Europe since the end of the eighteenth century, as has been done here. Historic retrospection shows also that both tactical methods (if we disregard for the moment the effects of technological progress) and the patterns of ideological justification have structurally remained largely the same over a period of one and a half centuries, even if the content of ideological programmes may differ widely. One is tempted almost to speak of an interchangeability of political contents. This is indirectly confirmed by the remarkable affinity frequently to be observed between violent movements of the Right and Left, and between nationalist and communist movements.

Historically we can distinguish the following types of radical movement which for a time have regarded, or indeed still regard violence, individual terrorism and, if need be, systematic guerilla warfare as legitimate weapons in their fight against the established order:[9]

(1) *Social protest movements* which still operate within the framework of a

traditional social order and see violence mainly as a *bargaining* counter or as a means to re-establish 'the good old law', but do not aim at a forcible change of society as a whole. This includes principally the manifold forms of social protest which we encounter in the main during the first half of the nineteenth century, such as the Luddites and 'Captain Swing's' agrarian protest movement in England, the revolts of the 1830s and 1840s in Germany, the social rebels in the Italian Appenines and the numerous peasant protest movements in economically backward countries of Europe, notably in Russia, Spain and Italy.

(2) *National emancipation movements* which seek to realise their ideal of national or ethnic autonomy by all imaginable means and, if necessary and under particularly adverse political circumstances, even by methods of individual terror. A movement like the Decembrist one must be included in this category, and even more so the radical groups within radical Italian nationalism, such as the Carbonari and – almost a century later – D'Annunzio's Blackshirts. Garibaldi's subsequently heroically idealised role in the Italian people's struggle for freedom is situated on the fringes of these phenomena, largely because history was eventually to prove him right. In the case of Germany we recall Karl Ludwig Sand's assassination of Kotzebue, even though it was a rather isolated instance. As far as the movements of national emancipation in Central Europe were concerned, strategies of violence and individual terror were never adopted on a large scale; not so in the case of radical national-revolutionary movements in the Balkans, whose actions – notably the assassination of the heir to the Austrian throne, Franz Ferdinand, by the Serbian student Prinčip – indirectly contributed significantly to the outbreak of the First World War. The numerous nationalist movements which have sprung up again in our own time, such as the Basque *ETA* or, within certain limits, the *Provisional IRA*, are the heirs to this older form of extremist nationalism.

(3) *Terrorist movements or groups of anarchist persuasion*, which work towards the annihilation of the existing order and the establishment of a society free from all violence and without any oppressive governmental apparatus, but which nonetheless take recourse to individual terror, since it appears to be legitimised in their view as counter violence. As a rule, they are to be found on the fringes of Anarchism, which on the whole, as a proletarian labour movement of a specific type, contrary to customary opinion, cannot be directly associated with strategies of terrorism and violence. Historically the most significant instances of recourse to non-legal violence are to be found in the Russian Socialist-Revolutionary and later in the Spanish Anarchist movements; but in many other places during the latter part of the nineteenth century extreme groups advocating strategies of violence or at least 'propaganda by deed' surfaced from time to time in many regions, as for instance in France in the 1880s and 1890s. Even on the fringes of German Social Democracy, otherwise known for its dedication to legalism and

discipline, these kinds of aspirations did not disappear entirely, much to the irritation of a party leadership committed to an orthodox marxist strategy – not even after the expulsion of Johann Most and the so-called *Jungen* – although virtually no terrorist actions of any substance were undertaken.[10] The Russian Bolshevik movement in its early days also employed terrorist tactics; these however did not really form part of its doctrine but arose out of the particularly oppressive conditions under which it had to operate in tsarist Russia.

(4)   *Anarcho-Syndicalist groups* which, by carrying the doctrine of 'direct action' against the class enemy to the extreme, did not shrink, at least for a time, from violence against property, mainly in the form of sabotage, and in some instances not even from violence against individuals, such as unpopular factory owners. Recourse to violence, however, never played a central role in these movements, but was as a rule a secondary consequence of extremely acute conflict or strike situations.

(5)   *Movements of integral nationalism*, which employ violence against people or property, as well as sabotage and in the last resort individual terror against an alleged 'internal enemy', with the object of re-establishing authoritarian forms of rule. Their aims are social-conservative, not social-revolutionary. The most significant example of this was the radical nationalist mafia in the Weimar Republic, responsible for a great number of so-called *Feme* murders as well as other acts of violence against groups whose political views were anathema to them.

(6)   *Fascist movements*, which employ the method of systematic terror mainly against the institutions and members of the parties of the Left, in order to initiate a process of nationalist regeneration within their country and at the same time to obtain the greatest possible public response to their own ideological objectives. The best known of these were the *squadri d'azione* of Italian Fascism in the early 1920s. The same traits, comparatively less developed, although not lagging behind the Italian model in the brutality of their methods, we find in the special combat gangs established by National Socialism in the 1920s and early 1930s, with the object of forcibly eliminating or terrorising political adversaries, while being more or less openly contemptuous of the State's forces of law and order. These instances show up with particular clarity that the cult of violence against dissidents increasingly became a substitute for coherent political ideology.

(7)   As their active heirs must be regarded the *neo-fascist groupings* which have recently re-appeared on a broader front, particularly in Italy and West Germany and to a lesser degree elsewhere. Their aimless acts of indiscriminate violence point to their lack of any clearly defined ideological conception. Here as elsewhere, it may be said, of course, that the more nebulous the theoretical orientation of such groups or individual perpetrators, the more brutal their methods, since violence must evidently compensate for the lack of proper ideological legitimisation.

(8)   Lastly we have to consider the *more recent terrorist* movements of the *neo-marxist*, or rather *pseudo-marxist* kind, which have grown out of the abortive student revolts of the late sixties, particularly the *Rote Armee Fraktion* and its successor organisations in Germany, the *brigate rosse* in Italy and similar, for a while particularly militant, groupings in Japan. They see themselves as guardians of the socialist idea, in contrast to the congealed bureaucratic Socialism behind the Iron Curtain and to what is called the 'social Fascism' of democratic socialist parties in the West, defining themselves at the same time as fundamentally anti-imperialist. The *RAF*, in particular, regarded itself as the extended arm of the Third World's liberation movements and intended to strike a blow at imperialism in its metropolitan centres by demonstrative acts of violence against multinational companies and their political dogsbodies and, in the last analysis, even against the West German State. It was not by accident that the Vietnam war triggered off the rise of this type of movement.

In a certain sense such movements can be interpreted as a rebounding of terrorist tendencies from the periphery to the metropolitan centres. Carlos Marighella's *Handbook of Urban Guerilla Warfare*[11] exerted a significant influence on the *Rote Armee Fraktion* tactics. In their ideological perception of themselves, the *RAF* conducted a 'proxy' war which was initially directed mainly at US installations in Germany, as well as against large industrial companies. In the face of effective counter-measures on the part of the police forces, the *RAF* was drawn increasingly into directing its attacks against the authorities of the Federal Republic and the established order. The *brigate rosse*'s anti-imperialist thrust is comparatively less well developed since they operate in a relatively much more disrupted society, and one subject to great social tensions, in a country with underdevelopment at its own front door everywhere, particularly in the South.

All these movements regard themselves as the vanguard of the coming socialist revolution; but as such they must first destroy the barnacled social structures and the system of government by individual terror and guerilla methods modelled on Latin American urban guerillas, before the ardently desired process of solidarisation with the broad mass of the workers can come about, for allegedly the latter are at present unconsciously caught in a system of *Konsumterror* and adaptive socialisation, and thus in no condition to stand up for their own 'class interests'.

At the same time the ideological assaults on imperialism and neo-colonialism serve to make more credible their attack on their own bourgeois democratic societies, with their high living standards and comparatively stable structures. It allows them to level direct accusations at the capitalist bourgeoisie at home for the backward conditions in Third World countries, and thus to discredit the 'affluent society', insofar as it exists, as massively inequitable and thriving at the expense of others. If we leave to one side for a moment the anti-imperialist arguments in the neo-marxist movements' ideological arsenal, which in any case are an indifferent rehash of current afro-marxist theories on underdevelopment,[12] we see that their strategic methods and aims all conform to familiar historic patterns. The *RAF* 'urban guerillas' first quasi-official manifesto of 1971[13] was published at a time when its acts of terror had not yet reached their greatest degree of brutality. It combined the traditional strategic arguments which the terrorist wing of classical Anarchism put forward a century before with massive polemics against imperialism, as the form of social organisation allegedly responsible both for the moral paucity of metropolitan societies and for the misery at the periphery. Apart from that, the arguments nowhere go beyond the classical postulation of terrorist theory in its anarchist variety; virtually all the latter's basic tenets are taken up again, essentially unchanged, above all the absolute primacy of practice over theory. It is only by violent action, so the argument runs, that one can establish whether a society is ripe for revolution, and action alone determines the nature of the future society: 'Without putting it into practice, reading *Das Kapital* is nothing but middle-class study. Without putting them into practice, programmatic declarations are nothing but twaddle . . .'[14] Equally, we find the classical formula of 'propaganda by deed' in only slightly modified form. Only by armed struggle can agitation by the Left be 'made concrete'.[15] The primary object would have to be 'to destroy the apparatus of government at certain points, to put it partially out of action and thus to do away with the myth of the system's omnipresence and invulnerability',[16] a formulation that might almost be taken as a paraphrase of the relevant recommendations in Nechaev's 'Catechism of a Revolutionary' of 1869.

These postulates conform to a familiar pattern of argumentation which terrorist groups, be they left or right, had already developed in the nineteenth century. It cannot have been altogether accidental that Bakunin's works were among the first texts which the Berlin nucleus of what was to become the terrorist group *Bewegung 2. Juni* published in a pirated edition.[17] The only original element in the ideology of these neo-marxist groups is indeed their identification with the aims of Third World anti-imperialist liberation movements; this makes moral condemnation of the conditions in the democratic industrialised societies of the West that much easier and also strikes at a vulnerable point in the West's ideological armour.

It is true that this ideological orientation – which these groups regard as consistently anti-imperialist – has brought one significant consequence: it has facilitated international co-operation between terrorist groups of various countries. In the 1970s Yassir Arafat's *PLO* played an important role in this connection and established some sort of key position for itself within an informal kind of terrorist International, mainly as the result of providing various forms of assistance, especially in the training of terrorists. The *RAF*, in particular, for some time massively identified itself with the Palestinian cause and, as a by-product, become a prey to a new variant of anti-semitism, again with that myopia, when it comes to historical perspective, which terrorist movements are generally prone to. It is particularly ironic that, on this point, pseudo-marxist and neo-fascist movements touch, even though they are bitterly opposed to each other on every other issue.

The universal revival of those forms of political conflict which take recourse to non-legal methods of violence, even in situations which cannot by any means be called pre-revolutionary, naturally poses the question of how this development came about. It would seem natural to connect the emergence of this type of movement with structural deficiencies in a given society, with mass poverty or other social problems, or with uncommonly repressive political conditions. Currently we can observe a tendency to deny such a connection and to seek the causes of illegal violence, from 'limited infractions of the rules' of a purely demonstrative kind via individual terror to full-blown guerilla warfare, mainly in factors which are only indirectly determined by the established social order and not at all by any serious deficiencies it may have. Instead analyses in terms of individual psychology, focusing on disorders of the individual's personality structure, are particularly popular. There is also a tendency to explain such phenomena simply in terms of the ruthless propaganda of violence put about by a small group of irresponsible intellectuals; this, ever since Metternich's days, has been the commonest explanation of politically deviant behaviour. More significant, I think, are approaches that focus on the problem of deficiencies in bringing up the younger generation.[18] Apart from that we find a widespread tendency to explain terrorist movements in terms of particular political circumstances. Jillian Becker, for instance, has developed the interesting, albeit hardly tenable, thesis that the Baader-Meinhof movement as well as comparable ones in Italy and Japan basically constitute a residual form of a fascist political mentality.[19]

A retrospective view, such as has been sketched out here, demonstrates, however, that these arguments do not suffice to provide an adequate explanation of the phenomenon of unlawful violence. It would be less than thorough to leave out of account the objective historical factors that may have triggered off these movements in individual instances; only in situations of political and social conflict or in periods of change in the climate of thought do movements of this kind find the social breeding ground they need in order to operate with any degree of success. And the most effective method of fighting terrorism is still to deprive it of its sympathisers. None of the forms of terrorism or non-legal violence known to history, can be traced back immediately and exclusively to the fact that the political system that was being challenged was blatantly unjust or lacked legitimacy in the eyes of its citizens. Not even in the case of *Narodnaya Volya* and the Socialist Revolutionaries in tsarist Russia can this be said without qualification. After all, there have been societies and periods in history, when no, or hardly any, terrorist violence occurred, even though the conditions were such that it could have been expected. Conversely, such activities have existed, and still do, in societies which can claim a high degree of consensus as to their legitimacy on the part of their citizens and nevertheless – or perhaps because of it – have been challenged by terrorist groups. Irrespective of this, it is impossible to establish a direct correlation between social tensions of whatever sort and the emergence of terrorist violence, for as a rule terrorist groups are very small indeed and cannot be considered truly representative of those groups, strata or classes that consider themselves to be deprived of legitimate rights and therefore oppose the system, for all they may, and often do, claim this to be the case. One must concede, on the other hand, that in potentially revolutionary situations terrorist activities can indeed turn into revolutionary struggle, as has been shown most notably by events in Iran since 1979. Yet it seems to be characteristic that recourse to strategies of non-legal violence in effect only happens when the prospect of getting rid of an existing political system by revolution either does not exist at all, at least in the short term, or is extremely unlikely.

If we look back on the known, extremely disparate historical instances where strategies of non-legal violence were employed, we tend to find that recourse to violence against a particular political or economic system and its representatives was taken only rarely with the *a priori* expectation of being able to provide the spark that would ignite a revolutionary development, of the kind Sorel expected from his idealised vision of a violent general strike by 'producers' (i.e. workers and employees).[20] Violent action, be it against property or people, was as a rule intended much more as a signal whereby the rulers were to be recalled to reason, or the masses to be enlightened as to the regime's manifestly unjust character. In the older movements of social protest, in particular, limited violence was first and foremost a means to reinforce certain material demands made by the social groups concerned; in other cases it was a question of symbolically destroying all those things which appeared to be the emblem of unlawful exploitation, such as tax lists, lists of services to be rendered to landlords without pay, and the like, on occasion also the barns or the manor house of a hated landowner. Very often we encounter purely symbolic acts by individuals, devoid of any connection with an organised movement, and thus largely of a spontaneous nature, such as van der Lubbe's setting fire to the *Charlottenburg Schloss* and the *Reichstag* in February 1933.

In other historical examples terror very often did not get beyond the level of 'an eye for an eye', that is to say, fringe groups responding to the sentencing or execution of one of their colleagues by deliberate attempts on the lives of prominent politicians and more frequently officials, judges or the representatives of the forces of order who had been directly involved in the prosecution proceedings, as in the case of the Spanish *pistoleros* during and after the First World War.[21] The model character of spectacular actions of this sort is also an important consideration: very frequently spontaneous follow-up actions occurred, undertaken by individuals or groups; and as a rule acts of 'individual terror' occurred in series that came and went over periods of ten or fifteen years, only to flare up again suddenly. It was often only the counter-measures by the State which prompted movements to rationalise their own strategies of violence. If conditions were particularly repressive, or if the State employed excessively drastic methods and mishandled the situation, the movements' own combat methods were intensified, to the point even of building up formal terror units or an infra-structure, which allowed them to conduct a full-scale guerilla war. Only the Fascist *squadri d'azurre* and the Nazi combat gangs set out from the start to seek bloody confrontations with their opponents, but not surprisingly in both cases the cult of violence tended to operate as a substitute for a positive, coherent and forward-looking ideology.

On the whole we find that among movements which supported various forms of non-legal violence it was the activists who cared least about rationalising their own actions in the light of their objectives, and where they did so at all it was only in the vaguest forms. It would nevertheless be true to say that political movements which aim at a thorough reconstruction of society, based on fundamentalist principles, resort to violent methods if, and only if, normal 'legal' ways of promoting their objectives are blocked, or if the chances for an immediate revolutionary policy are slight, because the population at large is lethargic or the security forces overwhelming; and even then it will only be small groups at the fringes who are prepared to go that far. On the other hand, in such situations it is relatively easy to find individuals or groups, who assume for themselves the role of a revolutionary vanguard and by violent means seek to remove the obstacles to a revolutionary development, in particular those forces which allegedly account for the population's passive subordination to the established order. They hope thereby to pave the way for a revolutionary development by undermining the established system's power prestige, by demoralising its government apparatus, or by actively mobilising the masses by means of 'propaganda' not of words but 'deeds'. Such explicit rationalisation of a policy of non-legal violence, however, is to be found only rarely; as a rule extreme moral indignation and emotional attitudes dominate.

This is shown by the fact that terrorist movements in the course of their struggle with the government's forces of order – provided the latter are capable of making their measures of persecution sufficiently effective – very easily begin to lose sight of their own political objectives, because their attention is focused one-sidedly on the counter-measures by the authorities. Quite often a quasi-automatic process begins to set in, whereby violence breeds ever new violence which is less and less connected with the group's political objectives. Increasingly, violent actions serve the purpose of 'punishing' the forces of order, of pressing for the release of imprisoned colleagues, or even of acquiring the necessary financial means for the creation of a more effective 'revolutionary' infra-structure. Ever since the Bolshevik actions during the pre-1914 period, this has mainly taken the form of so-called 'expropriations', usually bank raids. In the course of this sort of development, violent action often becomes virtually an end in itself, a means of self-perpetuation. As a rule, this tends to discredit the movement politically and ideologically, as witness the case of the *Red Army Faction*; from 1971 onwards it has been engaged in a sort of private war with the authorities, with the primary objective of pressing for the release of *RAF*-members, while politically it has maneouvred itself into a totally defensive position.[22]

If we conclude by looking once again at the spectrum of contemporary terrorist movements in Europe against the backcloth of history, we observe clearly that only in a very few respects were they able to evolve genuinely new strategies or new ideological justifications, despite the fact that the development of modern weaponry has immensely increased the purely technical potential of terror. Characteristic of all of them is that they tend to think schematically in terms of black and white, condemning existing conditions without being able to offer a more or less rational substantiation of their ideas or even a sketchy outline of the alternatives they propagate. They all obey the primacy of action, very often banking, in the manner of Georges Sorel, on the creative effect of violence as such; consequently they do not even care about a comprehensive theoretical justification of their own actions. Rather they assume that violence will set signals which will effect change, even though they themselves cannot muster sufficient support from the population at large seriously to embark on a policy of revolutionary innovation.

The thesis propounded by the neo-marxist terrorist movements, that is, that the preconditions for a proletarian revolution must first be created by terrorist means since under prevailing conditions the workers will simply not show any enthusiasm for it, betrays not only extreme intellectual arrogance but ultimately reflects despair rather than faith and self-assurance. Besides, it ignores the real problems attaching to the emancipation of the working classes under the actual conditions of Western industrialised societies, and indeed Soviet society, in the same way as does orthodox marxist-leninist doctrine; instead it is oriented on yesterday's ideologies and theories. This is even more true in the case of those nationalist movements which seek to achieve their aims by individual terror or even formal guerilla warfare, as for instance the *Provisional IRA* or the Basque *ETA*. These hope to enforce a unified nation state, or national autonomy for an ethnic group, by blood and terror, just at the precise historical moment when the old European order of nation states has become largely a thing of the past. They carry on traditions that existed mostly in national-revolutionary movements in the Balkans and also in older conflicts in Ireland itself. Neo-fascist violence appears as even more of an anachronism, though it seems to be supported only by relatively isolated groups or even solitary individuals, but is no less bloody and irrational for all that, as the bombings of Bologna railway station in August and of the Munich *Oktoberfest* in September 1980 have shown. Such acts appear to reflect exacerbation and despair more than the confidence that the future might belong to them. The ideal of an autonomous, ethnically homogeneous, strong, authoritarian State under fascist leadership seems to be altogether anachronistic and to have no chance of implementation.

This is not to say, however, that it will be easy to keep such movements in check. On the contrary, a look back at a century and a half of strategies of non-legal violence resorted to in very different political contexts suggests that Western societies will have to live with this sort of phenomenon for a long time to come, just as more than once in the past, sporadically and in very different circumstances, they had to contend with the same problem.

NOTES

1. Cf F. R. Allemann, 'Terrorismus in Lateinamerika – Motive und Erscheinungsformen' in Manfred Funke (ed.), *Terrorismus: Untersuchungen zur Struktur und Strategie revolutionärer Gewaltpolitik* (Düsseldorf, 1977) p. 178ff.
2. Cf. J. Gerassi (ed.), *Vinceremos! The Speeches and Writings of Che Guevara* (New York, 1968) p. 126.
3. For a comprehensive, albeit purely factual, survey see L. A. Sobel (ed.), *Political Terrorism*, 2 vols. (Oxford, 1975, 1978).
4. Interestingly enough, this aspect has recently been taken up by Rudolf Bahro, who based on it an alternative theory for democratic Socialism.
5. Letter by Robert Michels of 12/5/1909, *Michels Papers*, Fondazione Luigi Einaudi, Turin.
6. Sergei Nechaev's Catechism is reprinted in W. Laqueur (ed.), *The Terrorism Reader: A Historical Anthology* (London, 1979). On page 71 it says: 'in the first instance all those must be annihilated who are especially harmful to the revolutionary organisation, and whose sudden and violent deaths will also inspire the greatest fear in the government and, by depriving it of its cleverest and most energetic figures, will shatter its strength.'
7. Cf. M. Hildermeier, 'Zur Sozialstruktur der Führungsgruppen und zur terroristischen Kampfmethode der Sozialrevolutionären Partei Russlands vor 1917', *Jahrbuch für die Geschichte Osteuropas*, 20 (1972), p. 545f.
8. Cf. M. ('Bommi') Baumann, *Wie alles anfing* (Frankfurt, 1977) esp. p. 97ff.
9. Cf. on this W. Laqueur, *Terrorismus* (Kronberg/Taunus, 1977) p. 131ff. We are indebted to Laqueur for some important ideas, but are bound to differ considerably with his views, in that we think it necessary to establish a much more highly differentiated pattern for the various forms of violence than the one on which he has based his very valuable study.
10. For more detailed evidence see A. R. Carlson, *Anarchism in Germany*, vol. 1, *The Early Movement* (Metuchen/N. J., 1972) p. 173ff.
11. *Minimanual do guerrilheiro urbano*, the English version: *Mini Manual of the Urban Guerrilla* (London, 1971).
12. A survey in W. J. Mommsen, *Imperialismustheorien* 2nd edn (Göttingen, 1974) p. 91f.
13. A. Schubert, *Stadtguerilla. Tupamaros in Uruguay – Rote Armee Fraktion in der BRD* (Wagenbach, 1971).
14. Ibid., p. 115.
15. Ibid., p. 117.
16. Ibid., p. 118.

17. *Wie alles anfing*, p. 34f.
18. Cf. Funke (ed.), *Terrorismus*, as well as id., *Ausgewählte Literatur zu den Konflikten zwischen Extremismus und Demokratie*, Beilage zu *Das Parlament* B 37/38 (16/9/1978); also the somewhat one-sided survey by H. Glaser, *Die Diskussion über den Terrorismus: Ein Dossier*, Beilage zu *Das Parlament*, B 25/78 (24/6/78); and the rather sloppy commentary by M. Weber, 'Die tausend Zungen der Theorie: Wissenschaftler erforschen die Ursachen des Terrorismus', *Die Zeit*, 41 (3/10/1980); the collection of essays K. E. Becker and H.-P. Schreiner (ed.), *Anti-Politik: Terrorismus: Gewalt-Gegengewalt* (Hannover, 1979) is a further example of the general perplexity on this issue; an example of both the usefulness and the limits of psychological analysis in F. Hacker, *Terror, Mythos, Realität, Analyse* (Vienna, 1973); for a theoretical analysis in terms of political science see P. Waldmann, *Strategien politischer Gewalt* (Stuttgart, 1979).
19. *Hitler's Children: The Story of the Baader-Meinhof Gang*, 2nd edn (London, 1978).
20. Georges Sorel, with his myth of violence, which in itself is supposed to possess a liberating capacity and is seen as the essential agent for the revitalisation of Western culture, provides the ideological link between the theories of violence of the Left, mainly anarchist in origin, and of Fascism. Sorel's influence on Mussolini is on record, and his admiration for Lenin, as a great and creative man of power is also well-known. But the afro-marxist theories of someone like Frantz Fanon, who holds that the peoples of the periphery can only regain their national self-confidence by armed revolt against their colonial rulers and through the repercussions that result from this for the psychology of erstwhile colonial populations, may also be regarded as a further development of Sorel's position. Sorel's distinction between 'force', which oppresses human beings and alienates them from their humane existence, and 'violence', which is seen as the liberation from all chains and the prelude to a revitalisation of society, already anticipates the dichotomic theory of the oppressive 'structural violence' of bourgeois-capitalist society and the liberating counter-violence of the terrorist movements' revolutionary avantgarde. Obviously this represents only one aspect of Sorel's work which, taken as a whole, can hardly be said to have paved the way for terrorist social philosophies. On this cf. the brilliant essay by I. Berlin, 'Georges Sorel', *The Times Literary Supplement*, III/644 (31/12/1971).
21. Cf. M. Bookchin, *The Spanish Anarchists: The Heroic Years 1868–1936* (New York, 1977) p. 186ff.
22. A systematic weighting of the *RAF*'s acts of violence since May 1971, such as produced by Funke (ed.) *Terrorismus*, p. 331, and for more recent times also in: *Die Zeit*, No. 41 (3/10/1980), clearly shows an increasing shift of their objectives in a purely defensive, exclusive direction. Whereas initially offensives of a markedly demonstrative nature predominated – e.g. attacks on the right-wing press, such as the Springer publishing group, or on American military installations – since May 1967 there has been an increasing shift – in a ratio of 20 : 1 – to 'expropriations', break-ins with the purpose of obtaining documents, the taking of hostages in order to press for the release of imprisoned colleagues, on occasion, as in Mogadiscio, without concern for 'uninvolved' citizens. As a result, the movement has progressively lost its moral credit, even among its sympathisers.

Index

UNIVERSITY of WOLVERHAMPTON